S0-BGS-886

# THE PROOF FROM PROPHECY

# SUPPLEMENTS TO
# NOVUM TESTAMENTUM

EDITORIAL STAFF

C. K. Barrett, Durham
A. F. J. Klijn, Groningen—J. Smit Sibinga, Amsterdam

*Editorial Secretary*: H. J. de Jonge, Leiden

VOLUME LVI

LEIDEN — E. J. BRILL — 1987

BR
1720
.58
S52
1987

# THE PROOF FROM PROPHECY

*A Study in Justin Martyr's Proof-Text Tradition:*
*Text-Type, Provenance, Theological Profile*

BY

OSKAR SKARSAUNE

LEIDEN — E. J. BRILL — 1987

WITHDRAWN 29336
Fresno Pacific College M. B. Seminary
Fresno, Calif. 93702

ISSN 0169-9732
ISBN 90 04 07468 6

*Copyright 1987 by E. J. Brill, Leiden, The Netherlands*

*All rights reserved. No part of this book may be reproduced or translated in any form, by print, photoprint, microfilm, microfiche or any other means without written permission from the publisher*

PRINTED IN THE NETHERLANDS BY E. J. BRILL

*To Karin*

# CONTENTS

Part Three:
The setting, profile, and provenance of Justin's exegetical material

# PREFACE

When I started my first scholarship in Patristic Studies in 1973, I was only able to indicate two main areas of interest: Christology, and the relationship between the Church and the Synagogue. My tutor, Professor Carl Fr. Wisløff, suggested that Justin Martyr's *Dialogue with Trypho* might be a good starting point for both themes. It proved to be more than a starting point - I got stuck with that writing.

In retrospect, I have been struck by the fact that the present study fills a still vacant gap in what may be called the Scandinavian contribution to Justinian studies. The Swede Ragnar Holte in 1958 published a seminal study on Justin's *Logos* concept in the two *Apologies*, thus covering central themes in Justin's apologetics ('Logos Spermatikos. Christianity and Ancient Philosophy according to St. Justin's Apologies', *StTh* 12(1958), pp. 109-68). A major Danish contribution came in 1966 when Niels Hyldahl published his massive and learned study on Justin's *Dialogue,* chapters 1-9 (*Philosophie und Christentum. Eine Interpretation der Einleitung zum Dialog Justins (Acta Theologica Danica* 9, Copenhagen)). Notable contributions were also offered by Torben Christensen ('Til spørgsmålet om kristendommens hellenisering', *Festskrift til N. H. Søe* (Copenhagen, 1965), pp. 11-32) and Leif Grane ('Sammenhængen i Justins Apologi. Ulærde betragtninger over enheden i Justins tænkning', *DTT* 34(1971), pp. 110-129). - It may now be time for a Norwegian contribution on a subject not covered by these studies: Justin Martyr as exegete of the Old Testament.

Not only is there a gap here in the Scandinavian research on Justin - I believe the same is true in Justinian research as a whole. I briefly indicated this in an article published in 1976('Trekk fra nyere Justin-forskning', *DTT* 39, pp. 231-257), in which I briefly mapped the present state of research. Some suggestions concerning the setting and course of the present study were also made in another article ('The Conversion of Justin Martyr', *StTh* 30(1976)pp. 53-73). My subsequent research has led me to some substantial modifications of ideas expressed on the last page of that article. Its basic theses concerning *Dial.* 1-9 I still cherish.

Most Prefaces contain an element of apology, if not to say excuse. I suppose my most urgent apologetic need concerns the fact that some parts of this study may prove rather laborious reading. Some readers would perhaps be well advised simply to read the conclusions of Part One, and start directly with Part Two. For my own part, I found the textual analyses in Part One indispensable as a foundation for the rest of the work. The reader motivated to share with me the labour of laying this foundation, is kindly requested to study the appended synopses carefully.

Doing Patristics in Norway is a rather lonely affair. I am all the more grateful to those who helped and encouraged me. Professor Carl Fr. Wisløff initiated the project and has shown his interest in it ever since. Professor Einar Molland, whose death in 1976 deprived Norwegian theology of its Patristic scholar *par exellence*, kindly read through my preparatory articles. Much did I profit from his wise and sympathetic criticism and advise. I am also grateful towards the late Professor Torben Christensen of Copenhagen, whose encouragement meant much to me in the initial stages of this project. Later, Professor Edvin Larsson kindly accepted for discussion in two of his doctoral seminars parts of my first draft of the present study. His perceptive and constructive advise has been of great significance throughout the writing of this book. Professor Hans Kvalbein took the trouble of reading the final draft in its entirety, and some substantial improvements in the third Part are due to his suggestions. Dr. Frederick Hale read through my manuscript correcting my English. Had it not been for him, the style of the present study would have been much worse. All remaining deficiencies are entirely my own responsibility. A special word of gratitude is due to Professor Helmut Koester of Harvard, who kindly provided for me a Xerox copy of his otherwise inaccessible *Habilitationsschrift. Cand. theol.* Reidar Hvalvik undertook the unselfish task of compiling the indices.

This study was submitted to the University of Oslo as a doctorate thesis in February 1981. The public disputation was held the 8th of May 1982, professors Torben Christensen and William H.C. Frend being the appointed opponents. I wish in this place to express my gratitude for their constructive criticism. During the final revision of my manuscript I have tried to profit from their insights . It is hoped that this has resulted in some substantial improvements .

Since the manuscript in its first version was finished in February 1981, much relevant literature has appeared. While this has not made major modifications of the argument necessary, I have tried to take notice of relevant points of view in the footnotes.

A final word of gratitude is due to those who took care of the financial aspects of this project. *Det teologiske Menighetsfakultet*, Oslo, granted me a three-year scholarship 1973-76; *Norges Almenvitenskapelige Forskningsråd* a two-year scholarship 1976-78, and has contributed substantially to cover the printing costs of the present book.

I feel very honoured to have this study published in the *Supplements to Novum Testamentum*, and I say my sincerest thanks to the editorial board for their acceptance of this book to be published in the series, and to Publishers E.J. Brill for their excellent editorial work.

In a category by itself I should place the gratefulness I feel towards my wife for her unfailing patience, encouragement, and interest shown throughout these years. My dedicating the book to her, is only a small token of gratitude.

Oslo January 1985
Oskar Skarsaune

# ABBREVIATIONS

The names of the canonical books of the Bible are abbreviated as in the Revised Standard Version. Titles of the tractates of the *Mishnah* and the *Talmuds* are abbreviated as in Danby's translation of the *Mishnah*. For the Qumran writings, Lohse's symbols are employed. Other abbreviated titles of books from antiquity are thought to be self-explanatory or are explained at their first occurrence. In the notes, short titles of modern books or articles are sometimes used for quick reference. They are indicated within brackets in the Bibliography, or are thought to be self-explanatory.

Text editions, translations and works of reference:

| | |
|---|---|
| *ANF* (I-X) | *The Ante-Nicene Fathers* (American reprint of the Edinburgh Edition, 10 vols., Grand Rapids, 1975-78) |
| *BP* (I etc.) | *Biblia Patristica. Index des citations et allusions bibliques dans la litterature patristique* (ed. A. Benoit *et al.,* Paris, 1975ff) |
| CCL | *Corpus Christianorum, Series Latina* (Turnhout editions). |
| GCS | Die griechischen christlichen Schriftsteller der ersten drei Jahrhunderte (Leipzig, later Berlin editions). |
| Ges.-Buhl | W. Gesenius, *Hebräisches und aramäisches Handwörterbuch* (17. ed. by F. Buhl, Berlin-Göttingen-Heidelberg, 1915). |
| Ginzberg (I-VII) | L. Ginzberg, *The Legends of the Jews* (7 vols., Philadelphia, 1909-38). |
| JSHRZ | Jüdische Schriften aus hellenistisch-römischer Zeit (ed. W. G. Kümmel *et al.,* Gütersloh, 1973ff) |
| *NT Apoc.* (I-II) | E. Hennecke and W. Schneemelcher, *New Testament Apocrypha* (2 vols., English translation ed. by R. McL. Wilson, 1973/75). |
| OEChT | Oxford Early Christian Texts (ed. H.Chadwick, Oxford). |
| *Parisinus* | Greek manuscript nr. 450 of the *Bibliotheque Nationale de Paris.* |
| PG | *Patrologiae cursus completus, Series Graeca* (ed. J. P. Migne, Paris, 1857-66) |
| PL | *Patrologiae cursus completus, Series Latina* (ed. J. P. Migne, Paris, 1844-55) |
| P.-W. | Pauly-Wissowa-Kroll, *Realenzyklopaedie der klassischen Altertumswissenschaft* (Stuttgart, 1894ff). |
| *RAC* | *Reallexikon für Antike und Christentum* (ed. Th. Klauser, Stuttgart, 1950ff). |
| SC | Sources Chrétiennes (Paris, 1943ff) |
| Str. Bill. | H. L. Strack and P. Billerbeck, *Kommentar zum Neuen Testament aus Talmud und Midrasch* (4 vols., München, 1922-28) |
| *ThDNT* | *Theological Dictionary of the New Testament* (9 vols., ed. by G. Kittel and G. Friedrich, engl. transl. by G. W. Bromiley, Grand Rapids, 1964-74). |

## Periodicals and Series:

| | |
|---|---|
| ASNU | *Acta Seminarii Neotestamentici Upsaliensis* |
| AThANT | Abhandlungen zur Theologie des Alten und Neuen Testaments |
| BBB | Bonner Biblische Beiträge |
| BFChTh | Beiträge zur Förderung Christlicher Theologie |
| BGBE | Beiträge zur Geschichte der biblischen Exegese |
| BHTh | Beiträge zur historischen Theologie |
| BZ | *Biblische Zeitschrift* |
| BZAW | *Zeitschrift für die alttestamentliche Wissenschaft*, Beiheft |
| BZNW | *Zeitschrift für die neutestamentliche Weissenschaft, und die Kunde der älteren Kirche*, Beiheft |
| CBQ | *Catholic Biblical Quarterly* |
| DTT | *Dansk teologisk tidsskrift* |
| ÉB | Études Bibliques |
| ÉHPhR | Études d'histoire et de philosophie religieuses |
| Eph. Lov. | *Ephemerides Theologicae Lovanienses* |
| FRLANT | Forschungen zur Religion und Literatur des Alten und Neuen Testaments |
| HThKNT | Herders theologischer Kommentar zum Neuen Testament |
| HTR | *Harvard Theological Review* |
| HUCA | *Hebrew Union College Annual* |
| JBL | *Journal of Biblical Literature* |
| JEH | *Journal of Ecclesiastical History* |
| JJS | *Journal of Jewish Studies* |
| JQR | *Jewish Quarterly Review* |
| JSJ | *Journal for the Study of Judaism* |
| JTS | *Journal of Theological Studies* |
| KEKNT | Kritisch-exegetischer Kommentar über das Neue Testament, begründet von H. A. W. Meyer |
| LOPG | Libraire Orientaliste Paul Geuthner |
| MGWJ | *Monatsschrift für Geschichte und Wissenschaft des Judentums* |
| Nov. Test. | *Novum Testamentum* |
| NTS | *New Testament Studies* |
| RB | *Revue Biblique* |
| RÉJ | *Revue des Études Juives* |
| RHPhR | *Revue d'histoire et de philosophie religieuses* |
| RSR | *Recherches de science religieuse* |
| SBL Diss. Ser. | Society of Biblical Literature, Dissertation Series |
| SBL Mon. Ser. | Society of Biblical Literature, Monograph Series |
| SEÅ | *Svensk Exegetisk Årsbok* |
| SJT | *Scottish Journal of Theology* |
| Skr. N. V. | Skrifter utgitt av Det Norske Vitenskapsakademi |
| SNTSt Mon. Ser. | Society for New Testament Studies, Monograph Series |
| StANT | Studien zum Alten und Neuen Testament |
| STL | *Studia Theologica Lundensia* |
| StTh | *Studia Theologica* |
| Suppl. NT | Supplements to *Novum Testamentum* |
| Suppl. VT | Supplements to *Vetus Testamentum* |
| ThLZ | *Theologische Literaturzeitung* |
| ThZ | *Theologische Zeitschrift* |
| TTK | *Tidsskrift for teologi og kirke* |
| TU | Texte und Untersuchungen zur Geschichte der altchristlichen Literatur |
| VC | *Vigiliae Christianae* |
| VT | *Vetus Testamentum* |
| WMANT | Wissenschaftliche Monographien zum Alten und Neuen Testament |
| WUNT | Wissenschaftliche Untersuchungen zum Neuen Testament |
| WZKM | *Wiener Zeitschrift für die Kunde des Morgenlandes* |
| ZKG | *Zeitschrift für Kirchengeschichte* |

*ZNW*              *Zeitschrift für die neutestamentliche Wissenschaft und die Kunde der*
                   *älteren Kirche*
*ZThK*             *Zeitschrift für Theologie und Kirche*
*ZWTh*             *Zeitschrift für wissenschaftliche Theologie*

## Other abbreviations:

all.               allusion
MS                 manuscript
MT                 Massoretic text
NT                 New Testament
OT                 Old Testament

# A NOTE ON REFERENCES AND QUOTATIONS IN THE TEXT

In order to reduce the amount of Notes to proportionate dimensions, most references to primary sources are included in the text. Biblical references are given according to the principle adopted in the *Biblia Patristica*; i.e. chapters and verses are counted as in the Hebrew Bible (Kittel's), even in cases where the LXX editions deviate. An «a» or «b» appended to a Biblical verse reference implies no more than that the relevant text is found in the first or latter half of the verse. For patristic writers, I have also followed the *Biblia Patristica* in cases of conflicting or double reference systems. For other writings from antiquity, the numbering of chapters and passages is in each case that of the edition or translation listed in the Bibliography.

As a rule, these systems allow more precise references than simple page references. The latter are therefore omitted, except for the *Babylonian Talmud* and the *Midrashim*. Here I give the page reference of the employed translation in addition to the tractate, chapter and passage reference used in that translation. For *Mishnah* and *Talmud* tractates, a prefixed M. indicates that the *Mishnah* is quoted; a prefixed p means the *Palestinian Talmud*.

Unless otherwise indicated, texts and translations quoted are always those listed in the Bibliography. In quotations from rabbinical literature, elucidating inserts (within brackets) provided by the translator are always retained. To these are added (also within brackets) the dates of identifiable rabbis (as given by Billerbeck in his German translations, or in the Rabbinical Index, Str. Bill. VI), and important elucidations given by the translator in his notes. In a few cases where relevant secondary literature has referred to rabbinical works inaccessible to me in translation I have adopted the given reference, always indicating my source for it.

In the notes appended to the synopses, the symbols indicating different MSS have been adopted as found in the employed text editions. These notes make no claim to completeness; they only comprise variants of special relevance for the comparison of the texts in the synopses.

When two or more Biblical texts are referred to in conjunction, joined by a / , this means that they have been combined into one text in the source referred to.

# INTRODUCTION

Students of patristic exegesis have sometimes felt inclined to quote Shakespeare: «Though this be madness, yet there is method in't.»

My first encounter with Justin's exegesis conveyed an attraction very much in that vein. It seemed so strange, so utterly foreign to all I had learnt to associate with the term exegesis. And yet there seemed to be method in it, or if not method, then at least sense. Perhaps one should invert Shakespeare's saying: Though Justin's exegesis may be without method, it is not madness. There is much sense in it, and - as I increasingly came to appreciate - much theology.

I was all the more puzzled to discover that Justin's exegesis did not seem to attract much interest among most students of his writings. «The Dialogue with Trypho, while by no means a neglected piece of writing, has not attracted so much attention nor provoked so much discussion as the Apologies. The reason for this comparative neglect is not hard to find. The piece is nearly as long as the four Gospels combined, and as a whole is so astonishingly dull that to a general theological reader it can by no means have the same attraction as the Apologies.» E.R. Goodenough wrote this in 1923[1], and in 1985 the situation is basically the same. Some monographs devoted to the *Dialogue* have appeared, but they are concerned with its philosophical part, chapters 1-9[2]. Only a single, slight volume has appeared

---

1. E. R. Goodenough, *The Theology of Justin Martyr. An Investigation into the Conceptions of Early Christian Literature and Its Hellenistic and Judaistic Influences* (Jena, 1923, (repr. Amsterdam, 1968), p. 87. Compare A. von Harnack's statement, 10 years before: «*Zieht man die endlosen Bibelcitate, die häufigen in hohem Grade ermüdenden Wiederholungen und die ganz ungebührlichen Weitschweifigkeiten ab, so schrumpft das Buch (der Dialog) sehr zusammen, und das, was es bietet, erscheint in dem ungeheuren Blätterwerk so versteckt, dass man begreift, dass die Zahl der Arbeiter nicht gross ist, welche hier nach den Früchten zu suchen Lust und Mut haben.*» «*Dennoch muss man eine nicht gerechtfertigte Vernachlässigung des Buches in der Neuzeit constatieren.*» (*Judentum und Judenchristentum in Justins Dialog mit Trypho* (TU 39:1, Leipzig, 1913, pp. 47-98), pp. 48f).

2. N. Hyldahl, *Philosophie und Christentum. Eine Interpretation der Einleitung zum Dialog Justins (Acta theologica danica* IX, Kopenhagen 1966); J. C. M. van Winden, *An Early Christian Philosopher. Justin Martyr's Dialogue with Trypho Chapters. One to Nine (Philosophia Patrum* I, Leiden 1971); R. Joly, *Christianisme et Philosophie. Études sur Justin et les Apologistes grecs du deuxième siècle* (Université Libre de Bruxelles, Faculté de Philosophie et Lettres, 52, Brussels 1973), pp. 9-74; cf. surveys in T. Christensen, 'Nyere undersøgelser over Justins Dialog med jøden Tryfon cap. 1-9' ('Recent studies of Justin's Dialogue with Trypho the Jew, chs. 1-9 (Danish)), *DTT* 39 (1976), pp. 153-165; and my article, 'Trekk fra nyere Justin-forskning' ('Aspects of recent research in Justin' (Norwegian)), *DTT* 39 (1976), pp. 231-257, esp. pp. 245-254.

which is devoted to Justin the exegete[3]. One wonders whether most students still feel the way Goodenough did about Justin's exegesis - «astonishingly dull».

But in other respects the situation has changed, and changed considerably. Scholars like L. Goppelt and C. H. Dodd have taught us to see the New Testament exegesis of the OT in a new perspective[4]. This exegesis is not as atomistic and capricious as often thought. In the patristic field one could name J. Daniélou as one of those who has made us see the meaning and sense of patristic exegesis[5]. The present study would hardly be conceivable without the impetus given by this renewed interest in early Christian interpretation of the Bible.

Fascinating as I found Justin's exegesis, there was soon added another attraction. As I tried to listen to what Justin was saying, I thought I began to hear other voices behind his. They were blurred, however, and I had great problems when I tried to sort them out. Very often it was also difficult to distinguish them from Justin's own. But in some cases I felt quite sure that I heard what they said, because it was different from what Justin was saying. In other words, I became increasingly occupied with an attempt to disentangle the traditional material embodied in Justin's exegesis. And this became the theme of the present study.

Justin, like every exegete, has had teachers. He is drawing on an exegetical tradition - perhaps on several distinct traditions. One can conceive of several channels of transmission. (1) Justin could have learnt much by reading. Regrettably, we are not in a position to map his library. But we can be sure he had read several NT writings, and certainly other Christian writings containing OT exegesis. (2) He may have picked up some exegesis simply by listening to the homily preached each sunday. (3) He may

---

3. W. A. Shotwell, *The Biblical Exegesis of Justin Martyr* (London, 1965). L. W. Barnard, *Justin Martyr. His Life and Thought* (Cambridge, 1967) and E. F. Osborn, *Justin Martyr* (BHTh, 47, Tübingen 1973) have relevant remarks on Justin's OT text and exegesis in their comprehensive treatments of Justin (Barnard, pp. 17-24; Osborn, pp. 87-119). Mention should also be made of the following articles: J. Gervais, 'L' argument apologetique des propheties messianiques selon saint Justin', *Revue de l'Université d'Ottawa* 13 (1943), pp. 129-46/193-208; H. P. Schneider, 'Some Reflections on the Dialogue of Justin Martyr with Trypho' *SJT* 15 (1962), pp. 164-75; D. E. Aune, 'Justin Martyr's Use of the Old Testament', *Bulletin of the Evangelical Theological Society* 9 (1966), pp. 179-97; W. H. C. Frend, 'The Old Testament in the Age of the Greek Apologists A.D. 130-180', *SJT* 26 (1973), pp. 129-150 (on Justin, pp. 139ff). An unpublished dissertation is I. Posnoff, *Les Prophètes dans la synthèse chrétienne de saint Justin* (Louvain, 1948).

4. L. Goppelt, *Typos. Die typologische Deutung des Alten Testament im Neuen* (BFChTh 2. Reihe, 43, Gütersloh, 1939 (repr. Darmstadt, 1969)); C. H. Dodd, *According to the Scriptures. The Sub-structure of New Testament Theology* (London 1965 (1st. ed. 1952)).

5. See esp. *Sacramentum Futuri: Études sur les origines de la typologie biblique* (Études de Théologie Historique, Paris 1950); *Théologie du Judéo-Christianisme* (Tournai 1958) - for the convenience of the English reader I henceforward refer to the English edition: *The Theology of Jewish Christianity.* (The Development of Christian Doctrine before the Council of Nicaea, Vol. I, London, 1964); *Études d'exégèse judéo-chrétienne (Les Testimonia),* (Théologie Historique, 5, Paris 1966).

have been instructed in some kind of «school». He himself tried to win new converts to Christianity and strengthen the faith of intelligent Christians by lecturing. He says in the Martyrdom: «Anyone who wished could come to my abode and I would impart to him the words of truth.»[6] From Justin's «school» issued Tatian and certainly others of less fame. Justin himself may once have been a pupil of a similar school. And to judge from his writings, a main occupation of the school was exposition of the OT[7]. (4) Justin indicates that the debate with Trypho was not his only debate with a Jew, *Dial.* 50:1. He may have picked up scraps of Jewish exegesis in his debates with Jews.

I am in this study not primarily concerned with the channels of transmission, although that subject could not be ignored. I have made some proposals about the literary sources behind Justin's exegesis. Some of them we possess. In that case one can learn a great deal by simple comparison of Justin and his source. It is, of course, more difficult when one suspects a source now lost. I still think one can make some likely proposals, and I have had to take a stand with respect to some suggestions made by other scholars.

About Justin's education in a school we know next to nothing. I believe there is a considerable a priori probability that Justin should be seen as transmitting an exegetical school tradition, but the direct evidence is scanty, even if one regards Justin's report about his meeting with the Old Man as a highly stylized portrait of one of his Old Testament tutors.[8]

The main concern of the present study, however, lies with the *contents* of the tradition transmitted to Justin. I have tried to determine the extent of this traditional material, and further to grasp its theological profile and provenance, as far as possible. By doing this, two complementary aims are achieved: One learns something about the history of exegesis prior to Justin and thus, indirectly, more about Justin himself.

The traditio-historical outlook of the present study serves to differentiate its method and results from two other monographs which by their titles would seem to cover the same ground:

W.A. Shotwell, *The Biblical Exegesis of Justin Martyr* (London, 1965), is mainly concerned with Justin's exegetical procedure. On the question of exegetical tradition Shotwell is satisfied to point out precedents to specific exegetical arguments in earlier Christian writers and in Jewish exegesis, but he has no treatment of different layers in Justin's own text.

P. Prigent, *Justin et l'Ancient Testament* (Paris, 1964), is a massive book by any standard. The title, as well as Prigent's previous study of Barnabas,[9]

---

6. *Martyrdom* § 3 (Musurillo pp. 44f).
7. See my article 'The Conversion of Justin Martyr', *StTh* 30 (1976, pp. 53-73), pp. 70f.
8. Cf. *ibid.*
9. P. Prigent, *Les Testimonia dans le Christianisme Primitif. L'Épître de Barnabé I-XVI et ses Sources* (EB, Paris, 1961).

would lead one to expect a study of paramount importance to our subject. In his previous study of Barnabas, Prigent did with Barnabas much the same as I propose to do with Justin. It was Prigent's intention to carry on this line of research in Justin, but as the subtitle of his book on Justin shows, he got stuck in another, purely literary problem: *L'argumentation scripturaire du traité de Justin contre toutes les hérésies comme source principale du Dialogue avec Tryphon et de la première Apologie.* Prigent's thesis is this: In the first *Apology* and the *Dialogue*, Justin is largely excerpting from his previous *Syntagma against all heresies.* Short, non-LXX quotations in *1.Apol.* and *Dial.*, and the exegesis attached to these texts, derive from the *Syntagma.* Apart from non-LXX quotations, Prigent takes condensed passages in the *Dialogue* as indications that the *Syntagma* is being used. He also tries to reconstruct more original quotation sequences behind the present sequences in *Apology* and *Dialogue.* The original sequence is often thought to be scattered in different parts of Justin's preserved writings. Doublettes within the *Dialogue* derive from the better organized *Syntagma.* Prigent then retraces these reconstructed units in Irenaeus and Tertullian (and some other later writers), and finds that the reconstructed units really do occur in these later writers. Prigent takes this to mean that Irenaeus and Tertullian depend on the *Syntagma*, not the *Apology* or the *Dialogue.*

Prigent thinks that Justin - like Barnabas - employed «*recueils de Testimonia*» when writing the *Syntagma*, but «*il ne serait pas prudent ni même sage d'essayer de dégager les sources d'un écrit qu'on ne connaît que de manière médiate.*»[10] The *Syntagma* thus blocked Prigent's original purpose, viz. an investigation of pre-Justinian «testimony sources».

At this preliminary stage, only some general remarks can be made about Prigent's thesis. (1) If Justin had access to pre-Justinian testimony sources when writing his *Syntagma*, it is difficult to see why he should not still have access to the same sources when writing the *Apology* and the *Dialogue.* As we shall see, the relationship between the *Apology* and the *Dialogue* does not favour the idea that Justin relied exclusively on his earlier writings when writing later ones. I believe one has to revert Prigent's scale of probability: The hypothesis that Justin used «testimony sources» when writing his exegetical works is less specific - therefore more likely - than the hypothesis that Justin in his later writings only had access to this material via the *Syntagma.* (2) It is true that Irenaeus and Tertullian sometimes repeat Justin's texts and arguments in a better organized form than Justin himself has acheived in his preserved writings. Prigent takes this to mean that Irenaeus and Tertullian excerpted their material from Justin's *Syntagma*, where the organization - *ex hypothesi* - was good. In this way Justin is made

---

10. *Justin*, p. 81 Cf. also his programmatic statement p. 13:«. . . *je me suis fixé comme règle de ne pas tenter la critique des sources d'un écrit perdu.*» The same point of view is repeated pp. 263; 279; 289.

responsible both for the good order in the later writers and for his own chaos in the preserved writings. I find this hard to believe. For one thing, I believe Prigent systematically underestimates Irenaeus' and Tertullian's ability to organize Justin's material better than Justin himself. And it is not evident that a well-ordered source should be a good explanation of the apparent chaos in the preserved writings of Justin. On purely a priori grounds, one would rather imagine a multiplicity of sources which the author was not able to organize into a fully connected whole - Irenaeus and Tertullian improving Justin's first attempt. (3) Whenever Prigent finds traces of a source, he tends to identify this as the *Syntagma*, although nothing in the material itself points to that source. Only in a few instances does he contemplate the possibility that another source might be used.[11] It seems that Prigent has here fallen prey to his own hypothesis.

Nevertheless Prigent's analysis is often helpful for the purpose of the present study, and my own work with Justin's text has often been carried out in a constant dialogue with Prigent's points of view. I can fully endorse R. M. Grant's judgement of Prigent's work: «Though he has not recovered a lost document, he has greatly advanced the study of existing ones.»[12]

Now, it would seem that Prigent's thesis, even if correct, would be of minor relevance for the present study, because it does not take us behind Justin. But here P. Nautin[13] has given Prigent's thesis a twist which totally changes the situation in that respect. Nautin largely accepts Prigent's source analysis but rejects his identification of the source. Instead, he proposes that Justin's, Irenaeus', and Tertullian's common source was Aristo of Pella's *Controversy between Jason and Papiscus.*

Insofar as Nautin builds on Prigent's premises, the above objections are of some relevance concerning Nautin's theory also. But Nautin advances some other arguments which are independent of Prigent's and merit serious consideration. I believe Nautin's proposal has much to be said for it, but it should be pursued independently of Prigent's delineation of the *Syntagma* source.

In my own work with the source-critical problem, I have tried to conduct an internal analysis of Justin' s text, relying more on relevant supporting evidence in earlier writers than on Irenaeus and Tertullian, because the dependence of the latter writers upon Justin' s preserved works is often precluding safe conclusions with regard to their possible use of Justin' s sources. In the present study, the evidence in Irenaeus and Tertullian therefore plays a far more modest role than in Prigent's work. Nevertheless, Prigent's analysis has always been provocative and stimulating, and I have

---

11. Cf. *Justin*, pp. 171; 285.
12. R. M. Grant, Review of Prigent, *Justin*, *JBL* 84 (1965, pp. 440-43), p. 443.
13. P. Nautin, (Annual report of studies, in) *École des Hautes Études, Annuaire 1967/68* (Paris), pp. 162-167.

felt an obligation not to disagree with it without argument. In order not to burden the main text unduly with this rather technical argument, I have gathered most of my discussion with Prigent in Appendix I. It does not amount to a full-scale refutation of Prigent's analysis , but I believe that the evidence adduced there is sufficient to justify the procedure adopted in the present work: More confidence is put in an internal analysis of Justin's text, paying more heed to the signals contained in his own text than on signals in the later writers.

While Prigent's study mainly takes us into the intricate literary problems concerned with Justin' s sources there are other studies which give more attention to the problem raised in the present work - the question of Justin's tradition. Two proposals have been made which are relevant for the following disussion.

(1) It has been claimed that Justin is the heir of a *Lukan* tradition.[14] «*Jeder Leser von Justins Schriften wird unmittelbar erkennen, dass der bei Lukas nichtentfaltete Schriftbeweis sich offen bei Justin darbietet.*»[15] But what is meant by Lukan tradition? Presumably one has something more in mind than the probability that Justin had *read* Luke-Acts and become influenced by what he read. Is there some kind of chain of tradition which directly connects Justin with Luke? To put it bluntly: Does a «Lukan tradition» mean that Justin's teachers were Luke's disciples? These questions have hardly been raised in previous research because one has no means of answering them as long as Justin and Luke are just put side by side and compared as to their proof-text dossier[16] and their points of view. But when we venture to look behind Justin's text and try to get a grasp of the traditional material he has incorporated into his writings , we shall be able to get a clearer idea of what exactly the relationship between Luke and Justin is.

(2) In his study on the *Theology of Jewish Christianity*, J.Daniélou has suggested that i.a. some of Justin's exegesis derives from Judaeo-Christian sources.[17] Stated in this general way, Daniélou's proposal has, of course, a

---

14. This was argued by F. Overbeck, 'Über das Verhältniss Justins des Märtyrers zur Apostelge-schichte', *ZWTh* 15 (1878), pp.305-49; later taken up by J.C. O'Neill, *The Theology of Acts in its historical setting* (London, 1961), esp. pp. 10-53; and most recently argued by N. Hyldahl, *op. cit,* (note 2), pp. 261-72.

15. Hyldahl, p. 269.

16. A useful juxtapposition of Luke and Justin with regard to their proof-texts is provided by W.S. Kurz, *The Function of Christological Proof from Prophecy for Luke and Justin* (Yale Dissertation, 1976, available on microfilm.) He compares Luke and Justin on pp. 155-244/250-55. Briefly summarized, Kurz reaches the following conclusions: There is a great amount of parrallelism between Luke and Justin concerning the formal structure of their argument from prophecy. But there are important differences in theology and proof-text dossier. Luke lacks the pre-existence idea so prominent in Justin, and has a much more positive evaluation of the OT and Jewish Christians than Justin. Kurz does not pose the problem whether traditions discernible in Justin might be closer to Luke than Justin himself.

17. *Theology,* p. 53; and cf. the Index for references to Justin's material throughout the discussion of Judaeo-Christian *theologumena.*

very great degree of a priori probability - whatever one may think of Daniélou's attempt to construct a «theology of Jewish Chrisianity».[18] But there is in Daniélou's study no attempt to analyse and evaluate the whole of Justin's exegetical tradition with regard to its provenance and theological profile.[19] So this remains as a challenge.

Let me add some words on the *modus procedendi* of the present study. The method most in agreement with much work in the fields of tradition history and redactional criticism would be to conduct a contiuous analysis along all of Justin's exegetical exposition. Paying heed to stylistic differences and conflicting ideas within his text, one could then come out with more or less well-founded theories concerning traditions employed by Justin.[20] The problem with this approach is partly that it would require an enormous amount of pages. And I believe that in working with Justin's exegetical traditions, one may with profit adopt a simpler and more direct approach. For one thing, we have a not negligible amount of controlling evidence in texts earlier than Justin, which allows us a direct or indirect access to parts of the tradition on which he is drawing. And perhaps more important: We have in Justin's own works direct access to the core of his exegetical traditions — viz. the OT quotations themselves. If it can be proved that Justin's non-LXX OT quotations (1) are not taken from Biblical manuscripts, and (2) are not made by Justin himself, then the quotations themselves must be viewed as deposits of tradition, and searching for the theological concerns of that or those traditions, we should begin to look at the text of the OT quotations, then examine the context to see if the quotations were accompanied by some kind of exposition and comment when they reached Justin.

This is the approach adopted in this book, and it explains the function of Part I within the greater context. In this first Part, I claim to show two things.

---

18. On the problem of defining «Jewish Christianity», cf. the Introductory remarks to Part III below; p. 246f.

19. In his sequel volume, *Gospel Message and Hellenistic Culture. A History of Early Christian Doctrine before the Council of Nicaea* II (London-Philadelphia, 1973), Daniélou has a masterly summary of Justin's OT exegesis, pp. 200-220; but the traditio-historical problem is here only casually hinted at.

20. This is the procedure advocated by H. Stegemann in an extensive review of P. Prigent's book on *Barnabas* (cf. note 9), ZKG 73 (1962, pp. 142-153), p. 145: «*Eine Untersuchung der von Barn. aufgenommen Traditionen kann also sachgemäss nur so vorgehen, dass zunächst einmal der ganze «Brief» formal analysiert wird, man dann Gedankangang und Terminologie des Autors ermittelt und vorgegebene Traditionen isoliert. Erst in einem zweiten Arbeitsgang können diese Traditionen auf formale, in einem dritten auf inhaltliche Eigenarten, ihre Herkunft usw. hin befragt werden.*» I do not question the appropriateness of this method as such, but I think one shall have to show more methodological flexibility, adapted to the specific nature of the source in question. In Justin and Barnabas we have to do with *exegetical* traditions, and this allows a rather direct access to the focal points of the tradition: the OT quotations. I would also question the fruitfulness of a rigid separation of formal and *inhaltliche* criteria. But with this reservation, Parts II and III of the present study would roughly correspond to the second and third *Arbeitsgang* required by Stegemann.

(1) Justin's short, non- LXX quotations are not «free» quotations from memory, nor are they made *ad hoc* by Justin himself, modifying the standard LXX text. Nor are they taken from deviant Biblical manuscripts. They are taken from written, Christian sources (cf., though, the caution below), and in these sources we find the main sources of exegetical argument in Justin. (2) The long LXX quotations in Justin' s text are not secondary amplifications by later scribes , but are Justin's own excerpts from the Biblical manuscripts to which he had access. This indirectly confirms that Justin's short non-LXX quotations were taken from other sources than his Biblical manuscripts. I thus endorse one of Nautin's arguments against Prigent's *Syntagma* hypothesis: «*Il arrive plusieurs fois que Justin cite le même passage de l'Écriture de deux manières différentes selon qu'il l'emprunte à sa source ou qu'il le tire de son exemplaire de l'Écriture: preuve que l'auteur de la source ne s'était pas servi de la Bible de Justin.*»[21] Nautin here rightly points to the high relevance of those OT texts which are quoted in two versions in Justin. I shall begin by studying these cases, and within this group prominent position is given to those doubly rendered texts on which Justin himself comments. After tackling these textual problems, I move on to test my results on those cases where Justin's handling of his sources can be checked, since we possess the sources. At the same time, this serves as a preliminary study of Justin's relation to his known Christian predecessors.

After thus evaluating Justin's OT quotations as source material for his exegetical tradition, I move on in Part II to try to group the quotations in connected series of OT testimonies. The point of departure is the present disposition of the material in the *Apology* and the *Dialogue*, but I try to discern whether the material employed was differently organized prior to its inclusion in Justin's work. Let me emphasize that the term «source» in this context is meant to have a very wide application. If the transmission channel for some of Justin's material was a «school» tradition, the boundaries between written and oral sources may in some cases be floating. Written tracts may have served as basis for oral exposition.

In Part III I proceed to the traditio-historical analysis proper. The units of tradition delineated in Part II are taken as a point of departure, and in characterizing the theological tendencies of Justin's material I also draw on the textual analyses in Part I.

The authenticity of the three main works is taken for granted. P. Prigent has argued that also the preserved fragments of a tract *De Resurrectione* attributed to Justin should be regarded as genuine.[22] I find Prigent's arguments

---

21. Nautin, *op. cit.,* p. 164
22. *Justin,* pp. 36-64. For text editions of the fragments, cf. the Bibliography.

impressive,[23] but the issue is of minor importance for the present study, because the preserved fragments contain only sparse references to the Old Testament. The subject is briefly touched upon in Appendix I, nr. 1. I regard the *Martyrdom* as essentially authentic.[24] I also presuppose the current datings of Justin's works: *1. Apology* 150-155 AD;[25] *Dialogue* ca 160 AD.[26] My manual edition of the text has been Goodspeed's, but Archambault, Pautigny, and (in a few cases) Otto have also been consulted. Unless otherwise indicated, the Greek text of Justin is quoted as found in the *Parisinus*, also in cases where Goodspeed emends.[27]

What could be the relevance of a study conducted along these lines? For one thing, I think that what one learns in this way is worth knowing in itself. But there is a wider setting in which this kind of study gains some significance. «*Noch immer geht die methodische Rekonstruktion urchristlicher Geschichte im Blick auf den Übergang zur alten Kirche vom Eindruck des gleichsam shockartigen, eines zugleich materialen Umschlags, einer tiefgreifenden Umwälzung aus.*» This statement by H. Paulsen[28] is of course a sweeping generalization, but one can hardly deny its essential truth, at least as far as Protestant scholars are concerned. It is not my intention here or elsewhere to make an equally sweeping counterstatement about there being an essential continuity between the Christianity of the New Testament and that of the second century. The obvious thing to say is, of course, that there are continuities as well as discontinuities. This statement is bound to be true and is, therefore, a platitude. The interesting question to ask is where the continuities and discontinuities are found, and how and why they came about.

The present study contains no full-scale evaluation of this problem, but may provide some partial answers within a field which is marked by relatively rich and continuous source material - viz. the exegetical tradition. On a priori grounds one would perhaps here expect a great amount of continuity. It has been all the more surprising for me to find how complex and delicate the balance between continuity and break in fact is, precisely

---

23. Like Osborn, *op. cit.*, p. 13. For a contrary judgement, see R. Joly, *Christianisme et Philosophie. Études sur Justin et les Apologistes grecs du deuxième siècle* (Université Libre de Bruxelles, Faculté de Philosophie et Lettres 52, Brussels, 1973), pp. 128-130.

24. Cf. Bardenhewer, *Geschichte* I, p. 210; and esp. H. Musurillo, *Acts*, Introd. pp. XVII-XX.

25. Cf. e.g. Bardenhewer, *Geschichte* I, pp. 222f; Goodenough, *Theology*, pp. 80f; A. Ehrhardt, 'Justin Martyr's Two Apologies', *JEH* 4 (1953, pp, 1-12), pp. 8-12; Osborn, *op. cit.*, p. 8.

26. Cf. e.g. Bardenhewer, p. 230; Barnard, *Justin*, pp. 23f; Osborn, p. 8. It is irrelevant to my purpose to discuss the complex literary problems concerning the relationship between the first and second *Apology*, and the date of the second.

27. This remark does not apply in cases where Goodspeed emends faulty orthography or sheer «misprints» in the *Parisinus*.

28. H. Paulsen, 'Das Kerygma Petri und die urchristliche Apologetik', *ZKG* 88 (1977, pp. 1-37), p. 1.

within the exegetical field. I believe we have here a sensitive barometer indicating important shifts within the «mainstream» theology of the Early Church, a barometer which has not yet been read with sufficient care.

If I am right in this, an investigation of Justin's exegetical material may also be of help in determining Justin's general theological background. How is Justin's exegesis related to his apologetics? Is he a traditionalist in his exegesis and an innovator in his apologetics? Or do both elements of his theology derive from the same sources? And how deeply are they integrated? Two of the classic studies on Justin take quite opposite views on the matter. M. von Engelhardt[29] believed that Justin in his apologetics was an innovator, combining his inherited Greek philosophy in a rather mechanical way with his new faith - to the profit of neither. E. R. Goodenough, on the other hand, saw in Justin an heir of Hellenistic Judaism, borrowing both his apologetics and his exegesis from Jewish precursors, first and foremost Philo. Indirectly, the present study will take a stand in that debate, although the focus of interest is only on the exegetical tradition. The study will thus make a partial and indirect contribution to the very complex problems related to the «Hellenization» and/or «Judaization» of early Christianity.

---

29. M. von Engelhardt, *Das Christenthum Justins des Märtyrers. Eine Untersuchung über die Anfänge der katholischen Glaubenslehre* (Erlangen, 1878).

## JUSTIN'S SELF-UNDERSTANDING AS AN EXEGETE

A basic premiss for the present study is the conviction that Justin in his exegesis is handing on a received tradition. He may have modified it and added to it - but the basic groundwork of his exegesis is something he has received from his predecessors. It may be useful as a prelude to the following analyses to point out that this premiss corresponds to Justin's understanding of himself as an exegete. Justin presents his OT exegesis as something received.[1]

In order to substantiate this statement, it may be useful to take a closer look at the idea of exegetical tradition in Justin. According to his own understanding, Justin is handing on the *apostolic* exposition of the Scriptures, and this apostolic exegesis of the OT ultimately derives from Christ's own instruction of the apostles after his resurrection.

Before Christ's resurrection the meaning of the OT was hidden. «For if Christ was covertly preached by the prophets as about to be liable to suffering, and afterwards to be Lord of all, yet he could not be so understood by any, until he himself persuaded the apostles that these things were plainly (!) proclaimed in the Scriptures» (*Dial.* 76:6). When Christ rose from the dead, he appeared to the apostles «and taught them to consult the prophecies, in which it was predicted that all these things would happen,» and the apostles «received the power which he sent them .... and went out into every race of men, (and) they taught these things and were known as apostles» (*1. Apol.* 50:12). The same idea is expressed in somewhat different terms in *Dial.* 53:5: «For, after he was crucified, his disciples that were with him were scattered, until he rose from the dead, and persuaded them that it was thus prophecied concerning him that he should suffer. And when they were thus persuaded they went out even into all the world and taught these things.» In the two last passages we have also the idea that the expounding of the Scriptures is an essential part of the apostolic kerygma. All later exegesis in the Church depends on this basic apostolic instruction. In *1.Apol.* 49:5 Justin says about the apostolic preaching that the apostles «handed over the prophecies» to their Gentile audience : τὰς προφητείας παρέδωκαν. Because all later Christians have been taught the meaning of the Scriptures by the apostles, Justin can claim that Christians have their understanding of the OT directly from Christ. The structure of the Scriptural proof (A) corresponds to the structure (B) of what Christ said about the meaning of the Scriptures:

---

1. Cf. on this theme esp. D. E. Aune, 'Justin Martyr's Use of the Old Testament', *Bulletin of the Evangelical Theological Society* 9 (1966, pp. 179-97), pp. 179-182.

«He revealed . . . to us all that we have understood from
  (A) the Scriptures by his grace, having come to know him as
      First-born of God and before all created things, and son of the
      patriarchs, since he became incarnate by the Virgin who was of their
      race, and he endured becoming a man without form and honour,
      and liable to suffering.
  (B) Wherefore he said in his speeches . . . that
      The Son of Man must suffer many things and be rejected by the
      Pharisees and Scribes, and be crucified, and rise on the third day»
      (*Dial.* 100:2f).

In other words: When Justin expounds the OT, he does so as a pupil of
the apostles; he is carrying on the OT exegesis they learnt from Christ. I
think this throws light on a disputed term in Justin, namely «the grace to
understand», ἡ χάρις τοῦ νοῆσαι (τὰς γραφὰς).    N.Pycke[2] has tried to
understand this *«connaissance de grace»* as a supernatural knowledge
endowed by grace, and beyond the reach of human reason.[3] He has been
sharply contradicted by R.Joly,[4] who underlines the entirely rational contents of this knowledge: It is capable of compelling rational proof! According to Joly, the grace to understand is closely related to the Scriptural
proof.[5] I think this is a correct observation, and Joly is certainly right in his
basic criticism of Pycke. But then, what is «the grace to understand»? Joly
says: the typological method of interpretation. This is too vague and
general. The texts already quoted, especially *Dial.* 100:2, where the «grace»
is explicitly mentioned, should enable us to give a more precise answer:
The «grace to understand» simply is *the apostolic proof from the Scriptures*,
taught by Christ to the apostles and transmitted to all Christians. Without
this instruction the Scriptures are unintelligible - this is the valid point made
by Pycke. Justin can talk about the «grace to understand» and the apostolic
instruction in exactly the same terms: (1) Without «the grace to understand»
one cannot understand the Scriptures, *Dial.* 92:1; 119:1; (2) before Christ
revealed the meaning of the prophecies, they could not be understood,
*Dial.* 76:6.

This also makes clear the role of rational argument: Once the hidden
meaning of the Scriptures has been brought to light by Christ and the
apostles, it shows itself to be rational and convincing, and every denial of its
validity and cogency is due either to hatred of the truth (σκληροκαρδία,
*Dial.* 44: 1; 53:2; 68: 1; 95:4) or cowardice, *Dial.* 36:9; 44:1; 112:5. There is
thus no contradiction between the rationality of the Scriptural proof and the

2. N. Pycke, 'Connaissance rationelle et connaissance de grace chez saint Justin', *Eph. Lov.* 37
   (Louvain/Gembloux, 1961), pp. 52-85.
3. Cf. also Aune, p. 182:«He (Justin) stands as a counterpart of the Old Testament prophet and is
   able to perceive the true intent of their writings by means of charismatic illumination.» See
   further *idem,* pp. 186f.
4. R. Joly, *Christianisme et Philosophie,* pp. 104-113.
5. *Ibid,* pp. 108-111.

necessity of «the grace to understand».[6] This grace is identical with the apostolic exposition of the Scriptures, and Justin can therefore speak about it as something to be imparted to others by way of exposition and teaching: «This grace alone was given me of God, that I might understand his Scriptures, and of this grace I pray all of you to become partakers . . . », i.e. by following my exposition, *Dial.* 58:1, cf. also *Dial.* 78:10.

The main point I want to stress at this juncture, is Justin's idea that his OT exegesis is something received, a tradition which for him derives from the highest authority. Whether and in what sense his OT exegetical tradition (s) may be called »apostolic« is another question. In the present study I am satisfied to ask what provenance and what theological profile can be ascribed to these traditions. Those questions, of course, touch upon Justin's idea of apostolic origin, but only indirectly and in a more modest, historical way of posing the problem. The basic question concerning Justin's theological idea of apostolic origin may not be whether it is true or false as a historical statement, but in what sense it may be seen to correspond to a fundamental continuity of tradition within the development of Scriptural exegesis in the earliest Church.

---

6. L. Goppelt seems to imply such a contradiction:·*Justin weiss, dass sein Schriftverständnis letzlich Gnade ist, und sucht dennoch den Gegner logisch zu überführen! . . . Justin erwartet von rationaler Argumentation, was nur Verkündigung vermag.* « (*Christentum und Judentum im ersten und zweiten Jahrhundert. Ein Aufriss der Urgeschichte der Kirche* (BFChTh 2. Reihe 55, Gutersloh, 1954), p. 292. The same point of view is taken by P.J. Donahue in an unpublished dissertation (available on microfilm), *Jewisch-Christian Controversy in the Second Century: A Study in the Dialogue of Justin Martyr* (Yale, 1973), pp. 194f/211ff. ·The *Dialogue* is fundamentally conceived, despite occasional lapses, not as a logically convincing demonstration of the truth of Christian philosophy, but as a proclamation of the word.· (*Ibid*, p. 213). The modern reader may perceive this alternative, but hardly Justin. Aune, *art. cit.*, connects the »grace to understand« with Justin's conception that the charisma of prophecy has passed over from the Jews to the Church (Aune, pp. 181f/186f). As far as I can see, Justin never makes this connexion.

PART ONE:

# JUSTIN'S OLD TESTAMENT QUOTATIONS AND THEIR SOURCES

## CHAPTER ONE

# A BRIEF SURVEY OF PREVIOUS RESEARCH

The natural point of departure is K. A. Credner's monograph on OT quotations in Matthew and Justin (1838).[1] In this book a landmark is reached within this field of research. It is irrelevant to my purpose to relate the wider theoretical framework within which Credner conducted his textual studies in Justin. His significance in our context lies in the painstaking collations he made of Justin's entire quotation material, comparing it with the wealth of variant readings recorded in Holmes' and Parson's edition of the LXX. Such a complete collation of all Justin's OT quotations has not been made since, a fact which makes Credner's monograph a still valuable mine of information.[2]

Credner noted as a general characteristic of Justin's LXX quotations their hebraizing features,[3] and this lead him to reject the theory that the long LXX quotations in Justin were due to scribes «correcting» Justin's quotations to conform with the standard LXX text of their time. As additional support for his rejection of this proposal, Credner observed that Justin's own exegetical comments often prove that he read the relevant Biblical text exactly as it now reads in the *Parisinus*. He surmised that the hebraizing readings - a few

---

1. K. A. Credner, *Beiträge zur Einleitung in die biblischen Schriften*, 2. Band: *Das alttestament-liche Urevangelium* (Halle, 1838). Credner, pp. 312f, points to F. A. Stroth as an important precursor ('Beitrage zur Kritik uber die LXX Dolmetscher, aus Justin dem Märtyrer und anderen Kirchenvätern', *Repertorium für biblische und morgenländische Literatur* 2 (1778), pp. 66ff; 3, pp. 213ff; 5, p. 124).

2. It should be noted that Credner mainly took Justin's long LXX texts serious as witnesses to an early version of the LXX. He pays little attention to the short, non-LXX, often combined quotations in Justin. He takes these to be free quotations from memory.

   A little computation may be of interest here. If we except Justin's many Genesis quotations (on which, see below, pp. 454-56), the following statistics emerge (approximate figures):

   | Quotations comprising | | |
   |---|---|---|
   | 1 verse or part of verse: | 95 |
   | 2 verses: | 55 |
   | 3 verses: | 12 |
   | 4 verses: | 6 |
   | 5 verses: | 12 |
   | more than 5 verses: | 37 |

   This would suggest that there are two categories of quotations in Justin: The «normal» short quotation comprises one or two verses, the «normal» long quotation 5 verses or more.

3. According to Credner, *loc. cit.*, Stroth had already many valid observations: He observed that Justin's quotations often contained hebraizing readings, som of which could not be derived from Aquila, Symmachus, or Theodotion. He further noticed that Justin's text of the Twelve Prophets differed most from the LXX, while on the other hand his Isaiah and Psalms quotations were most in agreement with the LXX.

of which were influenced by the Targums - were due to an early revision of
the LXX carried out by Jewish Christians familiar with the Hebrew OT, and
affecting mainly the Messianic prooftexts. The short, very aberrant, and
often combined quotations in Justin, Credner most often explained as free
quotations from memory.[4]

In 1850, A. Hilgenfeld[5] launched the opposite point of view: The short,
non-LXX quotations in Justin derive from written sources and are authentic,
while later scribes have been at work in the long LXX quotations.[6] The latter
proposal was taken up by W. Bousset in 1891.[7] He meant to be able to
demonstrate that Justin's text of the Prophets - especially Isaiah - exhibited
distinctive readings peculiar to Lucian's recension. E. Hatch also supported
the correction theory, basing himself on inconsistencies between text and
comment in Justin.[8] A. Rahlfs in 1906 came to a conclusion similar to that of
Bousset concerning Justin's quotations from the Psalms.[9] It looked as if the
correction theory was inevitable, and the discussion seemed settled: Justin's long quotations are corrected from post-Lucianic LXX MSS; his authentic readings survive in the shorter quotations which escaped the correcting
activity of the scribes.[10]

It was not until 1953 that a new impetus was brought to bear on the
question. It came from an unexpected quarter - the Cave of Horror in the
Judaean Desert! That year D. Barthélemy published his epochmaking article
'Redécouverte d'un chaînon manquant de l'historie de la Septante',[11] which

---

4. This had also been argued by K. G. Semisch, *Die apostolischen Denkwürdigkeiten des
   Märtyrers Justinus* (Hamburg, 1848).
5. A. Hilgenfeld, 'Die alttestamentlichen Citate Justin's in ihrer Bedeutung für die Untersuchung
   über seine Evangelien', *Theologische Jahrbücher* 9 (1850), pp. 385-439/567-578.
6. This point of view had been put forward as early as in 1554 by J. Perion. He observed the
   agreement between Justin's Psalms quotations and the standard LXX text, and surmised that
   this was due to later copyists who knew the Psalter by heart. On Perion, cf. Hilgenfeld, p. 398,
   n. 2, and J. Smit Sibinga, *The Old Testament Text of Justin Martyr. I: The Pentateuch* (Leiden,
   1963), p. 14. Another proponent of the «correction theory» was J. G. Eichhorn in his
   *Einleitung in das Alte Testament* (1780/83). Eichhorn thought that Justin's LXX quotations
   had been corrected according to the Hexaplaric recension of the LXX. Hilgenfeld, on the
   other hand, bases his proposal on discrepancies between the LXX text of Justin's long
   quotations and his own comments and exegesis. «*Im allgemeinen .. strebten die Abschreiber ..
   danach, die justinischen Citate dem text. rec. conform zu machen.*» (p. 426). Concerning the
   short, deviant quotations in Justin, Hilgenfeld argues that they are not due to Justin's faulty
   memory, but derive from written sources.
7. W. Bousset, *Die Evangeliencitate Justins des Märtyrers in ihrem Wert für die Evangelienkritik von neuem untersucht* (Göttingen, 1891), pp. 18-32.
8. E. Hatch, *Essays in Biblical Greek* (Oxford, 1889), pp. 186-202/209-214.
9. A. Rahlfs, *Der Text des Septuaginta-Psalters* (Septuaginta-Studien, 2. Heft, Göttingen, 1907
   repr. Göttingen1965), pp. 203-207.
10. See e.g. the opinion expressed by P. Katz, 'Das Problem des Urtextes der Septuaginta', *ThZ* 5
    (1949), pp. 1-24, esp. 15-17.
11. In *RB* 60 (1953), pp. 18-29. Later reprinted in *Qumran and the History of the Biblical Text*, ed.
    by F. M. Cross and Sh. Talmon (Cambridge (Mass.)/London, 1975), pp. 127-139. Compare
    also the somewhat fuller treatment of Justin's material in *idem, Les Devanciers d'Aquila.
    Première publication intégrale du texte des fragments du Dodécapropheton* (Suppl. VT 10,
    Leiden, 1963), pp. 203-212.

contained a preliminary report of the readings in a Greek *dodekapropheton* scroll found in 1952. In this article, Barthélemy compared the text of this scroll - which he deems to be from the end of the first century AD - with Justin's long Micha quotation in *Dial.* 109:2f. His conclusion can hardly be disputed: Justin is quoting from the same recension of the LXX as is represented by the new *Dodekapropheton* scroll. One thus suddenly had early evidence confirming the authenticity of one of Justin's long quotations.[12] And the peculiar, hebraizing readings found throughout Justin's quotations from the Twelve Prophets observed long ago by Stroth - had found their natural explanation: Justin's *Dodekapropheton* text represents a Jewish, hebraizing recension of the LXX (called R or καιγε by Barthélemy).

But there was also another re-evaluation on its way in the camp of the LXX experts.[13] It affected the accepted views on the Lucianic recension. Scholars had long observed the presence of «Lucianic» readings in texts which were pre-Lucianic by as much as centuries. Various explanations had been offered, but the weight of the evidence is heavy, and gradually there has come about a re-evaluation of the whole problem.[14] The idea of some sort of proto-Lucianic recension of high antiquity has gained wide acceptance,[15] and some are even ready to drop «Lucian» entirely, deeming many

---

12. P. Katz recognized the importance of this. Concerning some of Justin's long quotations, he wrote in 1957:«It was .. plausible to consider these quotations as due to late sporadic revision similar to that observed in the inferior Philonic evidence (referring to his article from 1949 (note 10)). A fresh discovery, however, seems to open up a different vista»(referring to Barthélemy's 1953 article). P. Katz, 'Justin's Old Testament Quotations and the Greek Dodekapropheton Scroll', *Studia Patristica I* (TU 63, Berlin, 1957), pp. 343-53, quotation p. 345.

13. Useful surveys of recent developments in LXX research: H.M. Orlinsky, 'On the Present State of Proto-Septuagint Studies', *Journal of the American Oriental Society* 61 (1941), pp. 81-91 (repr. in *Studies in the Septuagint: Origins, Recensions, and Interpretations* (Library of Biblical Studies), ed. S. Jellicoe (New York, 1974), pp. 78-109); P. Katz 'Septuagintal Studies in the Mid-Century. Their Links with the Past and their Present Tendencies', *The Background of the New Testament and its Eschatology. In Honour of C. H. Dodd* (ed. by W. D. Davies and D. Daube, Cambridge, 1956), pp. 176-208; R. Hanhart, 'Fragen um die Entstehung der LXX', *VT* 12 (1962), pp. 139-163; J. W. Wevers, 'Proto-Septuagint Studies', *The Seed of Wisdom, Essays in Honour of J. T. Meek* (ed. W. S. Mc Cullough, Toronto, 1964 (repr. in S. Jellicoe (ed.), *Studies in the Septuagint,* pp. 128-157); G. Howard, 'The Septuagint: A Review of Recent Studies', *Restoration Quarterly* 13 (1970), pp. 154-64; S. Jellicoe, 'Septuagint Studies in the Current Century', *JBL* 88 (1969), pp. 191-199; *idem,* 'Prolegomenon', in *idem, Studies in the Septuagint,* pp. XIII- LXI.

14. Cf. esp. B. M. Metzger, 'The Lucianic Recension of the Greek Bible', in *idem, Chapters in the History of the New Testament Textual Criticism* (Leiden, 1963), pp. 1-41 (repr. in S. Jellicoe (ed.), *Studies in the Septuagint,* pp. 270-291).

15. Apart from the literature listed in the preceeding notes, cf. esp. F. M. Cross, 'The History of the Biblical Text in the Light of the Discoveries in the Judaean Desert', *HTR* 57 (1964, pp. 281-99), pp. 292-297. According to Cross, the Proto-Lucianic recension should be placed in the second or first century B.C., thus ante-dating Barthélemy's *kaige* recension. On the other hand, G. Howard has argued that Proto-Lucian should be identified with the *kaige* recension, 'Lucianic Readings in a Greek Twelve Prophets Scroll from the Judaean Desert', *JQR* (N.S.) 62 (1971/72). pp. 51-60.

Lucianic readings to be quite simply the readings of the old LXX.[16] There is at present also an increasingly felt difficulty in establishing what should be called «Lucianic» readings or MSS.[17]

It is obvious that this calls for a fresh re-examination of the master argument for the correction theory concerning Justin, viz. his allegedly Lucianic readings.

The new signals from the LXX experts have not gone without response from students of Justin. Already in 1956 H.Koester[18] made a fresh evaluation of Justin's «Lucianic», «hexaplaric» and other hebraizing readings in some of the Prophets and reached a conclusion updating Credner's point of view: Even the long citations from Isaiah exhibit such a peculiar combination of «Lucianic», «hexaplaric», and hebraizing readings not found in these recensions that they cannot easily be explained by later scribal »correction«. J.Smit Sibinga conducted a fresh collation of Justin's entire quotation material from the Pentateuch[19] and found much ancient material in Justin's texts irrespective of the length of the quotations. P.Prigent[20] in his frequent remarks on Justin's OT quotations also voices the same opinion: No systematic or thorough correction by later scribes has taken place.

A new consensus is apparently beginning to emerge, renewing the position of Credner, but with one important qualification: Justin's version of the LXX is not a Christian, but a Jewish revision - at least his text of the Twelve Prophets, and possibly also in other books.

But there remain several questions. If Justin's long LXX quotations stem from his own pen, what about the short, non-LXX quotations? Recent developments in proto-LXX studies have made the picture of LXX origins more complex than the classic theory proposed by P. de Lagarde but have not supported the radical alternative proposed by P.Kahle and A.Sperber.[21] According to the last mentioned scholars, one has to reckon with a plurality of rival Greek »Targums« prior to the establishment of a normative Greek text by the Church in the third and fourth centuries. To speak of »LXX« and »non-LXX« text, e.g. in Justin, would thus be an anachronism. Most LXX

16. E. Tov, 'Lucian and Proto-Lucian: toward a new Solution of the Problem', *RB* 79 (1972), pp. 101-113.
17. Cf. i.a. A.Pietersma, 'Proto-Lucian and the Greek Psalter', *VT* 28 (1978), pp. 66-82.
18. H. Koester, *Septuaginta und Synoptischer Erzählungsstoff im Schriftbeweis Justins des Märtyrers* (Habilitationsschrift, Heidelberg, 1956), pp. 1-50.
19. J. Smit Sibinga, *The Old Testament Text of Justin Martyr. I: The Pentateuch* (Leiden, 1963).
20. Prigent, *Justin, passim.*
21. Select titles: P. Kahle, 'Untersuchungen zur Geschichte des Pentateuchtextes', *Theologische Studien und Kritiken* 88 (Gotha, 1915), pp. 399-439; *idem,* 'Die Septuaginta: Prinzipielle Erwägungen', *Festschrift Otto Eissfeldt zum 60. Geburtstag* (ed. J. Fück, Halle, 1947), pp. 161-80; *idem,* 'Problems of the Septuagint', *Studia Patristica* I (TU, Berlin; 1957), pp. 328-338; A. Sperber, 'The New Testament and the Septuagint Translation of the Old Testament', *Tarbiz* 6 (1934), pp. 1-29; *idem,* 'New Testament and Septuagint', *JBL* 59 (1940), pp. 193-293; *idem,* 'How to edit the Septuagint', *H. A. Wolfson Jubilee Volume* (Jerusalem, 1965), pp. 751-73.

scholars have rejected this view and believe that the recent discoveries of early Jewish Greek texts rather support the Lagardean position, although with some substantial modifications.[22] The concept «LXX text» has become more complex and nuanced, but it has not been dissolved. In some respects it has gained more precise contours.

When, in the following, I speak about non-LXX texts in Justin, I mean texts containing readings not found in any known recension of the LXX.

As I stated earlier, Credner regarded these quotations in Justin to have been made freely from memory. This opinion has also been voiced recently by eminent authorities.[23] As we shall see, however, there are at least some cases where this theory can be proved wrong. Here the old theory about the »Testimony Book« offers itself as an alternativeve.[24] Did Justin take his non-LXX quotations from some sort of anthology? E.Hatch[25] suggested the existence of such »manuals«; R.Harris developed the theory to its classic formulation.[26] In Harris' version it has been subjected to cogent criticism by N.J.Hommes,[27] but the idea of »testimony collections« has received new support since the discovery of such collections at Qumran.[28] R.A.Kraft and

---

22. Cf. the review articles listed in note 13. «The *kaige* Recension is of decisive bearing on the debate over Septuagint origins. It brings a qualified victory to the Lagarde school, despite Paul Kahle's protestations to the contrary» (F. M. Cross, *art. cit.*, p. 283). Kahle defended his position in the article 'Die im August 1952 entdeckte Lederrolle mit dem griechischen Text der kleinen Propheten und das Problem der Septuaginta', *ThlZ* 79 (1954), cols. 81-94.

23. E.g. Wevers, *art. cit.*, pp. 152f. It seems Hilgenfeld's cogent criticism of this expedient explanation has been largely ignored.

24. Useful surveys of the development of the theory and the ensuing discussion in K. Stendahl, *The School of St. Matthew and its Use of the Old Testament* (ASNU XX, Lund, 1969 (2nd ed.)), pp. 207-217; G. T. Armstrong, *Die Genesis in der Alten Kirche. Die drei Kirchenväter* (BGBH 4, Tübingen, 1962), pp. 3-6; P. Prigent, *Les Testimonia*, pp. 16-28; and esp. J-P. Audet, 'L'Hypothèse des testimonia: remarques autour d'un livre récent'(viz. Prigent's *Les Testimonia*), *RB* 70 (1963), pp. 381-405.

25. E. Hatch, *op. cit.*, pp. 203f.

26. J. R. Harris, *Testimonies* I & II (Cambridge, 1916 & 1920). Harris' observations were carried further in D. Plooij, *Studies in the Testimony Book* (Verhandelingen der koninklijke Akademie van Wetenschappen te Amsterdam. Afdeeling letterkunde Nieuwe Reeks, Deel XXXII No 2, Amsterdam, 1932).

27. N. J. Hommes, *Het Testimoniaboek. Studiën over O.T. citaten in het N. T. en bij de Patres, met chritische beschouwingen over de theorieën van J. Rendel Harris en D. Plooy* (Amsterdam, 1935). One should note that Hommes does not reject the idea of «testimony collections»; he only criticizes the concept of a fixed «testimony book». Compare also the balanced position of O. Michel, *Paulus und seine Bibel* (BFChTh 2. Reihe 18, Gütersloh, 1929 (repr. Darmstadt, 1972), pp. 37-54: While rejecting the idea that Paul depends on testimony collections, Michel recognizes the plausibility of such material for a later period:«*Erst auf frühchristlichem Boden begegnen derartige Sammlungen, zuerst nachweisbar bei Melito von Sardes und Cyprian. Wahrscheinlich ist aber ihre Entstehungszeit viel früher zu legen, vielleicht setzt sie schon der Barnabasbrief voraus*»(p. 52).

28. 4 Q test is a collection of eschatological prophecies: Deut 5:28/f/18:18f; Num 24:15-17; Deut 33:8-11 (probably referring to the end-time prophet and the Messiahs of Israel and Aaron). These texts are put together with no comment. At the end, Josh 6:16 is quoted and interpreted. (The text was first published by J. M. Allegro, 'Further Messianic References in Qumran Literature. Document IV', *JBL* 75 (1956), pp.182-187). «The fragment ... appears to be about complete, ... it is clearly not part of a scroll» (Allegro, *ibid*, p. 182). «... nachlässige

P.Prigent have tried to reconstruct such sources behind Barnabas.[29] Prigent
also thinks Justin used such collections, but refrains from further research
because the *Syntagma* comes in between the preserved writings and the

und ortographisch merkwürdige Schrift. Kein offizielles Dokument, sondern privat?» (J.
Maier, *Die Texte vom Totem Meer. II: Anmerkungen* (München/Basel, 1960), p. 165). It is
perhaps too much said when Allegro comments: «There can be little doubt that we have in
this document a group of *testimonia* of the type long ago proposed by Burkitt, Rendel Harris,
and others to have existed in the early Church» (*ibid.*, p. 186). 4 Q flor are fragments of a scroll
of eschatological midrashim.   Sam 7:10-14 is interpreted i.a. in the light of Ex 15:17f and Am
9:11; Ps 1:1 is interpreted with reference to Is 8:11 and Ezek 37:23; the concluding text is Ps
2:1f. (The text was first published by J.M. Allegro, 'Fragments of a Qumran Scroll of
Eschatological Midrashim', *JBL* 77 (1958), pp. 350-54). As will be apparent in the following
study, this document is perhaps more relevant as an analogy to material used by the early
Fathers than 4 Q test.

29. R. A. Kraft, *The Epistle of Barnabas, its Quotations and their Sources* (Harvard Dissertation on
microfilm, 1961); P. Prigent, *Les Testimonia.* An important predecessor is H. Windisch in his
commentary on Barnabas (*Handbuch zum Neuen Testament, Ergänzungsband* III
(Tübingen, 1920), pp. 299-413).
Prigent's study has provoked two important contributions to the discussion of method
concerning the hypothesis of «testimony collections»: J.-P. Audet, 'L' Hypothèse des testimonia: remarques autour d'un livre récent, *RB* 70 (1963), pp. 381-405, and H. Stegemann's
review in *ZKG* 73 (1962), pp. 142-153. They both take issue with the five criteria listed by
Prigent (p. 28) as indicating the use of testimony collections: (1) composite citations; (2)
false attributions; (3) textual variants (shared by authors who do not depend on each other);
(4) citation sequences recurring in independent authors; (5) «*lorsqu'un auteur... invoque
une série des citations dans un but qui n'est manifestement pas celui qui a présidé au
groupement des textes, nous pouvons raisonnablement affirmer qu'il utilise une collection
de Testimonia.*» Stegemann (p. 144) objects against this that while these criteria may indicate
the use of a source, none of them are sufficient to prove that the source in question is a
«testimony collection» as envisaged by Prigent and others (cf. the same criticism in Audet, pp.
394ff). Composite quotations may derive from oral tradition or from written sources other
than testimony collections (Stegemann, *ibid.*; Audet, pp. 394.404). False attributions may be
due to memory failure in the author or his source (Stegemann, *ibid.*). Deviant readings may
stem from «vulgar» Biblical MSS circulating among the Christians (Audet, pp. 394f). It is
difficult to prove that an author is independent of another (Audet, pp. 393f).
On *a priori* reasons, I am inclined to grant all of these critical comments on Prigent's criteria.
Let me nevertheless add the following remark: When Audet suggests «vulgar» Biblical MSS as
an explanation of clearly non-LXX quotations, he appeals to an entity much more conjectural
than the supposed «testimony collections». There *is* evidence - Jewish and Christian - for OT
anthologies of various kinds, but there is no evidence whatever which can prove that Biblical
MSS were circulating with the extreme degree of non-LXX text required to explain the
evidence in Barnabas and Justin. And the almost total non-appearance of these «testimony»
readings in the LXX manuscript tradition tells strongly against this idea. Apart from this, I am
willing to grant that Prigent's list of criteria does not tell very much about the *nature* of the
hypothetical sources. I tend to agree with Stegemann's point of view: One should start the
examination of the material with an openness for several kinds of source material, and try to
observe whether the formal characteristics of the material points in any specific direction.
«*Oft wird man nur einige Möglichkeiten ausschliessen können und mehrere gleichberechtigt
neben einander offenlassen müssen. Manchmal werden Paralleluberlieferungen in anderen Schriften präzisierende Schlüsse zulassen.*» (p. 153 - cf. also a similar point of view in
Audet, pp. 404f). In accordance with this, I use the term «testimony source» in a very wide
meaning: *source of OT quotations other than a Biblical MS*, implying no prejudice deriving
from the traditional concept of «testimony collections». One final remark on criteria: I miss in
Prigent's list the following indication that a «testimony source» is being used: lack of
awareness of the Biblical context for a quotation. In writers having an atomistic approach to
Scripture this is no safe indication, but in Justin there is a conscious effort to place Biblical
texts in their proper contexts (cf. below, *passim.*).

testimony sources. P.Nautin tends to derive Justin's non-LXX quotations from the *Controversy between Jason and Papiscus.*[30]

One can thus safely state that while a consensus is beginning to emerge concerning Justin's long LXX quotations, views still differ widely as to the origin of his non-LXX quotations.

It is surprising to see how often scholars neglect Justin's own remarks on the textual problems in their treatment of Justin's OT text.[31] A comprehensive theory explaining Justin's texts *as well as his own remarks about them* is still lacking.

In the following re-examination of the material, I shall try to establish such a theory. The texts are treated in three turns. First I examine the texts on which Justin himself comments. Next follow the remaining texts which are rendered in two versions, one LXX and one non-LXX, since these instances are especially instructive. The theory propounded so far is then tested on cases where we can observe Justin working with known sources, i.e. OT quotations in Christian writers before him. In the first two sections the texts are treated in their OT order; in the last section I follow the order of the respective writings.

For comparison, I sometimes include in the synopsis texts from Irenaeus and Tertullian. The pertinent comment is given in Appendix I.

---

30. Cf. above, p. 5;8
31. Notable exceptions are Barthélemy and Koester in their above quoted works.

## CHAPTER TWO

A SELECTIVE ANALYSIS OF JUSTIN'S QUOTATION MATERIAL

*1. Textual variants on which Justin himself comments.*

(a) Gen 49:10f (cf. synopsis next page).

Before we turn to the evidence in Justin, a few words on the variants in the LXX MSS may be necessary (the table appended in the apparatus is adapted from E.Hatch who based it on the collations in Holmes and Parson).[1] Among the variants tabulated, only 1 and 2 seem to be primitive. (Nr. 3 can be explained as an attempt to adjust 2 to 1: It is graphically close to 2, but the meaning is that of 1. Variant 4 assimilates 3 further to 1, and 5 is an obvious conflation of 1 and 3).[2] The two primitive variants are alternative renderings of the Hebrew שילה read as שלו = אשר לו.[3] Variant 2 understands שילה the same way as does *Targum Onqelos:* «until the Messiah comes, whose is the kingdom».[4] However, the best MSS attestation lies with variant 1, and J.Wevers in the Göttingen LXX, like other LXX editors, is certainly right when he adopts this reading as the original LXX. How the other variant entered the MSS tradition is a question to which we shall return.

In Justin also two variants are original, on his own showing. In *Dial.* 120:4 he has an interesting discussion of the textual problem. He says that the Jews read ἕως ἂν ἔλθη τὰ ἀποκείμενα αὐτῷ, while the true «LXX»[5] reading is ἕως ἂν ἔλθη ᾧ ἀπόκειται.[6] If we then turn to *Dial.* 52:2, we find that Justin quotes the whole of Gen 49:8-12 in a text which is almost

---

1. Hatch, *Essays*, p. 168. Cf. also the table in Credner, *Urevangelium*, p. 52.
2. This explanation of the textual variants is already given by Credner, p. 53. Hatch, p. 169, obscures the picture and resorts to unnecessary conjecture.
3. Cf. Credner, p. 52 and Koester, *Schriftbeweis*, p. 36. Concerning the rendering of Gen. 49:10 in the LXX, cf. esp. L. Monsengwo-Pasinya, 'Deux textes messianiques de la Septante: Gen 49:10 et Ez 21,32', *Biblica* 61 (1980, pp. 357-376), pp. 364-367.
4. I quote the Targum according to the translation in M. Aberbach/B. Grossfeld, *Targum Onqelos on Genesis 49* (SBL Aramaic Studies 1, Massoula, 1976), p. 12.
5. Here and in the following discussions of textual questions in Justin, I use «LXX» as equivalent with 'claimed by Justin to be the translation of the Seventy', while LXX (without quotations marks) is used to denote the text of the LXX deemed to be original by modern scholars.
6. One notes with interest Eusebius' report on the text of Symmachus: «οὐ περιαιρεθήσεται» φησίν «ἐξουσία ἀπὸ' Ἰούδα» . . . «ἕως ἂν ἔλθη» φησίν «ᾧ ἀπόκειται» καὶ αὐτὸν ἔσεσθαι τῶν ἐθνῶν προσδοκίαν. (*Dem. Ev.* VIII:1:34, GCS 23, pp. 357f).

SYNOPSIS

| Gen 49:10f LXX ~ Dial. 52:2 | 1. Apol. 32:1 = 54:5 | Irenaeus, Dem. 57 (Cf. Appendix I, nr. 12) |
|---|---|---|
| οὐκ ἐκλείψει ἄρχων ἐξ Ἰούδα<br>καὶ ἡγούμενος ἐκ τῶν μηρῶν αὐτοῦ<br>ἕως ἂν ἔλθῃ ⎤ = Dial.<br>τὰ ἀποκείμενα αὐτῷᵃ ⎦ 120:3<br>καὶ αὐτὸςᵇ προσδοκία ἐθνῶν<br>δεσμεύων πρὸς ἄμπελον τὸν πῶλον αὐτοῦ<br>καὶ τῇ ἕλικι τὸν πῶλον τῆς ὄνου αὐτοῦ<br>πλυνεῖ ἐν οἴνῳ τὴν στολὴν αὐτοῦ ⎤ = Dial.<br>καὶ ἐν αἵματι σταφυλῆς ⎦ 54:1<br>τὴν περιβολὴν αὐτοῦ | οὐκ ἐκλείψει ἄρχων ἐξ Ἰούδα<br>οὐδὲ ἡγούμενος ἐκ τῶν μηρῶν αὐτοῦ<br>ἕως ἂν ἔλθῃ<br>ᾧ ἀπόκειταιᵇ ⎤ = Dial.<br>καὶ αὐτὸς ἔσται προσδοκία ἐθνῶν ⎦ 120:3 5<br>δεσμεύων πρὸς ἄμπελον τὸν πῶλον αὐτοῦ<br>πλύνων τὴν στολὴν αὐτοῦ ⎤ = 1. Apol.<br>ἐν αἵματι σταφυλῆς· ⎦ 32:7<br><br>= 1. Apol.<br>32:5<br><br>a) 1. Apol. 54:5: καὶ<br>b) So Dial. 120:3f (2x) and 1. Apol. 54:5 marg. 1. Apol. 32:1 and 54:5: ὁ ἀπόκειται<br>c) So 1. Apol. 32:5; 32:7; 54:5. 1. Apol. 32:1 inverts: πλύνων ἐν αἵματι σταφυλῆς τὴν στολὴν αὐτοῦ | There shall not lack a ruler from Judah<br>nor a leader from his loins<br>till He come<br>for whom it lies in store<br>and He shall be the expectation of the nations<br><br>washing His robe in wine<br>and his garment in the blood of the grape |
| a) Dial. 52:2 marg.: ὁ ἀπόκειται<br>b) Dial. 52:2 and 120:3: + ἔσται<br>(cf. Smit Sibinga, pp. 34—36)<br><br>Reading a) in the LXX MSS tradition (adapted from Hatch, Essays, p. 168):<br>1) τὰ ἀποκείμενα αὐτῷ: AB(D)FM, 16 cursives.<br>2) ᾧ ἀπόκειται: Mᵐᵃʳᵍ, 14 cursives.<br>3) ὁ ἀπόκειται: 6 cursives.<br>4) ὃ ἀπόκειται αὐτῷ: 3 cursives.<br>5) τὸ ἀποκείμενον αὐτῷ: 1 cursive | | |

identical with the LXX,[7] and containing the «Jewish» reading in vs. 10.(The margin reading in the *Parisinus* is certainly not original, cf. below). In *Dial.* 120:3, introducing the discussion referred to above, he again quotes vs. 10 in the same good LXX text.[8] It seems that for Justin this LXX text is «Jewish»!

Turning next to *1.Apol.* 32:1 and 54:5, we find vss. 10f quoted in a markedly different text. Beginning again in vs. 10, we can confidently state that it was this version of the text which contained the reading ᾧ ἀπόκειται, although some later scribe «corrected» to ἀπόκειται, in both cases. The proof of this is Justin's paraphrase of the text in *1.Apol.* 32:2: ἕως ἂν ἔλθῃ ᾧ ἀπόκειται τὸ βασίλειον. This paraphrase equals the interpretation of *Targum Onqelos,* and requires ᾧ in the Biblical text.[9] There is even a feature of the *Parisinus* itself which confirms the authencity of this reading. In copying Justin's paraphrase in *1.Apol.* 32:2, the scribe here also first wrote ὅ but recognized the absurdity of this and corrected to ᾧ. This probably shows that this scribe was accustomed to variant 3 in the LXX MSS tradition and - perhaps unconsciously - introduced this reading into the quotations in *1.Apol.* 32:1 and 54:5. In *Dial.* 52:2 he is content to note his familiar reading in the margin.

After these text-critical preliminaries, let us examine Justin's two versions a little more closely. There can be no doubt that the reading ᾧ ἀπόκειται makes Gen 49:10 more suited as a Christological testimony. The difference is well brought out by Smit Sibinga: «The phrase ᾧ ἀπόκειται is an ellipsis, implying the coming of a messianic ruler, the last one, it seems, from the house of Judah. ᾧ denotes this person. In τὰ ἀποκείμενα αὐτῷ, on the other hand, αὐτῷ denotes Judah. The expression eliminates the expectation of a person distinct from the tribe, and whatever is in store is due to 'Judah'.»[10] Compare Justin's remark in *Dial.* 120:3: «And that this was said not of Judah, but of the Christ, is plain.»

We thus arrive at the following conclusion: Justin in his long quotation (*Dial.* 52:2) follows a good LXX text. This text he characterizes as «Jewish». In the short quotations in the *Apology,* on the other hand, we find a deviant text, a non-LXX text, which Justin claims to be the reading of 'the Seventy'.

Let us proceed to an analysis of the variants in vs. 11. Apart from the fact that the text in *1.Apol.* 32/54 is somewhat telescoped, the important reading is this: «Washing his *robe* (στολή) in the *blood of the grape*». In the LXX text this is not so - here the robe (στολή) is washed in *wine,* while the

---

7. See the detailed collations in Credner, pp. 50-55; Smit Sibinga, pp. 34-36/75-81.
8. The emendations by Archambault and Goodspeed are quite misplaced, as Smit Sibinga has well schown, pp. 76f, also Koester, *Schriftbeweis,* p. 35, n. 2.
9. This is argued by Smit Sibinga, p, 76. The parallel in *Targum Onqelos* was pointed out by Credner, p. 54. A further proof is the recurrence of the reading ᾧ in Iren. *Dem,* 57 (see synopsis). I suspect Irenaeus partly copied his text from *1.Apol,* 32, see further below, Appendix I, nr.12. Cf. also Koester, *Schriftbeweis,* pp 35f, n. 3.
10. Smit Sibinga, p, 77.

περιβολή is washed in the blood of the grape.[11] Justin's exegesis of the passage presupposes the non-LXX text: The 'blood of the grape' is Christ's blood, and the στολή is the Church, *1.Apol.* 32:7-9. In *Dial.* 54:1f one can easily see how familiar Justin was with the non-LXX text: He first quotes vs. 11 according to the LXX text (which he has just quoted in *Dial.* 52), but then he interprets the text in a way which once again presupposes the non-LXX variant reading![12] (Christ washes his στολή, i.e. his own believers, in his own αἷμα). The same familiarity with the deviant text is brought out also in two allusions later in the Dialogue: αἵματι σταφυλῆς ... τὴν στολὴν αὐτοῦ πλύνειν (*Dial.* 63:2); πλύνειν αὐτὸν τὴν στολὴν αὐτοῦ ἐν αἵματι σταφυλῆς (*Dial.*76:2).

Let me add to this a further observation. In *1.Apol.* 32 and 54, where the non-LXX text is quoted, Justin seems to have no knowledge of the context of the passage. The prophecy is introduced in both cases as a saying by Moses. This indicates that Justin knows that the passage is taken from Genesis but that he probably did not have the Genesis context before him.[13]

This changes when we turn to *Dial.* 52. Here Justin quotes the complete LXX text and correctly states that the prophecy is spoken by the patriarch Jacob.[14] At this point I should like to adduce a statement made by R.A. Kraft in another context. Commenting on the quite laborious procedure necessary to verify a quotation from a Biblical scroll, Kraft says: "A priori, then, we might expect that someone who went to all the trouble of culling his OT quotations directly from an OT MS (1) would tend to give extensive quotations, and (2) often would show an awareness of the exact source from which the quotation comes. Our texts of Philo, J(ustin) M(artyr), and Theophilus of Antioch, for example, frequently exhibit such a firsthand knowledge of the Greek Scriptures . . ."[15]

I believe these are reasonable proposals, and I suggest the following explanation for the textual evidence in Justin: In *Apol.* 32/54 Justin is not

---

11. Credner, p. 54, seems to have overlooked this. Smit Sibinga has recorded all the relevant textual data, pp., 77-81. But no one seems to have noticed the decisive point in Justin's exegesis - resulting from the deviant text - : he has the στολή washed *in the "blood of the grape"*.
12. This seems to have been overlooked even by Koester, in his otherwise instructive and detailed treatment of the *Apology* and *Dialogue* parallels concerning Gen 49:11, *Schriftbeweis.* pp. 37f.
13. Harris observed this, and used it as an argument for his Testimony Book theory, *Testimonies* I, pp, 13f/90f. Harris argues that this ascription to Moses is not a casual carelessness, because Justin first solemnly introduces Moses as the first among the prophets, *I.Apol.* 32:1, and then goes on to repeat in 32:2: "... as was predicted by the divine and holy prophetic Spirit through Moses . . ." The same solemn ascription to Moses also recurs in *1.Apol.* 54:5.8. Cf. also Koester, p. 37.
14. The attribution to Jacob recurs in *Dial.* 52:4 and 53:4. In *Dial.* 54:1 it seems that Justin is trying to "save" his earlier reference to Moses in *1.Apol.* by the following precision: "... that which was *related* (ἀνιστορημένον) by Moses and *prophesied* by the patriarch Jacob . . ." In *Dial.* 63:2 and 76:2, he has apparently forgotten his better insight, and falls back to a simple reference to Moses, alluding to the non-LXX text of *1.Apol.* 32.
15. Kraft, *Epistle,* pp. 72f.

quoting from a Genesis MS, but from another source of some kind. For brevity's sake I shall call this a »testimony source«, for the present leaving the nature of this source open. This would mean that the deviant text in vs. 11 never stood in a Greek Genesis MS, and that would explain the complete absence of this variant text in the LXX MSS tradition. In Justin's day there were probably no LXX MSS reading ᾧ ἀπόκειται in vs. 10,[16] either. This reading seems to have originated within the Christian testimony tradition, probably introduced by a Christian familiar with the Targumic tradition, and making the Greek text more appropriate as a Christological testimony.[17] This reading became so authoritative within the Church[18] that Christian scribes later ventured to introduce it into some of the LXX MSS.

Now, let me emphasize again that Justin apparently regarded his nonLXX quotations as representing the true LXX; while he says that the (real) LXX text is »Jewish«. It must also be stressed that the »Jewish« text is identical with the text in the long quotation — i.e. Justin seems to regard the text of his Genesis MS as »Jewish«. Let us at this stage simply note this.

(b) Deut 32:8.

In *Dial.* 131:1 Justin quotes Deut 32:7b-9, apparently from a Deut MS, since the text shows *verbatim* agreement with the LXX except for one variant in vs. 8. Here the LXX reads ἔστησεν ὅρια ἐθνῶν κατὰ ἀριθμὸν ἀγγέλων θεοῦ , while Justin's text has . . . κατὰ ἀριθμοὺς υἱῶν' Ἰσραήλ.[19] This accords better with the Hebrew: למספר בני ישראל
In this case Justin has a correct text-critical remark. He says that ἀγγέλων θεοῦ is the reading of the Seventy, but adds that he has quoted the »Jewish« version to satisfy his Jewish interlocutor. No theological point is involved, and one suspects that the real reason why Justin here quotes the text in this form, is that he so read the text in his Deut MS. There is a concentration of long Deut quotations in *Dial.* 119-131, all taken from Deut 31f, and all with rather good LXX text. This strengthens the assumption that Justin is working directly with a Deut MS in this part of the *Dialogue*, and the reading in

---

16. This is also surmised by J. P. Smith in his comment on *Dem.* 57 (p. 192, n. 255).
17. Of special interest is the reading in the *Pseudo-Clementine Homilies*, ἕως ἂν ἔλθη οὗ ἔστιν (*Hom.* III:49:1, GCS 42, p. 75). Credner (pp. 53f) reasonably suggests that this text is due to direct contact with the targumic tradition. The reading of *Targum Onqelos* is also directly echoed among the Syrian fathers in their quotations of Gen 49:10: »till he comes to whom the kingdom belongs« (Ephrem, Aphrahat, Isaac of Antioch, *Acts of Judas Thomas*, etc., cf. R. Murray, *Symbols of Church and Kingdom, A Study in Early Syriac Tradition* (Cambridge, 1975), pp. 282-84).
18. There is solid witness to this reading among the Fathers: Irenaeus, Hippolytus, Novatian, Origen, Eusebius, Cyril of Jerusalem, Chrysostom, Ambrose, Jerome, Cyril of Alexandria, Theodoret (enumeration according to Smit Sibinga, List, p. X. and Hatch, *Essays,* p. 169).
19. I have rendered the LXX text according to the great majority of LXX MSS, like Rahlfs. Wevers in the Göttingen ed. adopts Justin's hebraizing reading as the original LXX. (αριθμους is probably a scribal corruption of αριθμον. cf. Smit Sibinga, p. 99.)

Deut 32:8 may suggest that it contained some readings due to a revision based on the Hebrew text.[20]

But from which source did Justin get his knowledge about the other, the LXX reading? It is relevant to note that *1.Clem.* 29:2 quotes Deut 32:8f in a context not unlike Justin's - and *1.Clem.* has the LXX reading. There is, in fact, a direct indication that *1.Clem.* is Justin's «testimony source» here. In *1.Clem.* 29 the Deut 32:8f quotation is followed by a composite quotation beginning with the phrase Ἰδού, κύριος λαμβάνει ἑαυτῷ ἔθνος ἐκ μέσου ἐθνῶν . . . . Justin seems to echo this phrase in *Dial.* 130:3, preparing his quotation of Deut 32:7-9: ἐκ πάντων δὲ τῶν γενῶν γένος ἑαυτῷ λαβὼν τὸ ὑμέτερον . . . To conclude: It may seem once again that Justin brands the text of his Biblical MS as «Jewish» while taking the text of his testimony source to be the true LXX. And in this case he happens to be right.

(c) Is 3:10 ; Is 5:20, etc.

| Is 3 : 9b. 10 a LXX = *Dial.* 17 : 2 = *Dial.* 133 : 2 | *Dial.* 136 : 2 | *Dial.* 137 : 3 |
|---|---|---|
| οὐαὶ τῇ ψυχῇ αὐτῶν | οὐαὶ τῇ ψυχῇ αὐτῶν λέγει κύριος | οὐαὶ αὐτοῖς |
| διότι βεβούλευνται | διὸ βεβούλευνται | ὅτι βεβούλευνται |
| βουλὴν πονηρὰν | βουλὴν πονηρὰν | βουλὴν πονηρὰν |
| καθ᾽ ἑαυτῶν | καθ᾽ ἑαυτῶν | καθ᾽ ἑαυτῶν |
| εἰπόντες | εἰπόντες | εἰπόντες |
| δήσωμεν τὸν | ἄρωμεν τὸν | ἄρωμεν τὸν |
| δίκαιον . . . | δίκαιον . . . | δίκαιον . . . |

In *Dial.* 17:2 Justin quotes Is 3:9b-11 in perfect agreement with the LXX. He either excerpted the text from an Isaiah MS, or a later scribe did so.

A closer study of the second occurrence of the text - in *Dial.* 133 and 136f - makes one opt for the first alternative. In *Dial.* 133:2 Justin quotes the whole of Is 3:9b-15, and again the text is good LXX with only minor variants,[21] a few of them perhaps old LXX readings, because they are closer to the Hebrew than the text preserved in the LXX MSS.[22] Turning to *Dial.* 137, we find that Justin quotes a phrase from this LXX Isaiah text and says that this is the reading of the «Jewish» text *he has quoted earlier in the*

---

20. The reading υἱῶν Ἰσραήλ is reported to have been the reading of Aquila and Theodotion, while Aquila is also credited with the reading υἱοὺς Ἰσραήλ, together with Symmachus (cf. Smit Sibinga, *ibid.*). Justin's reading may well be a case of recensional activity prior to these. Origen is reported to have found this reading in several LXX MSS, and to regard this reading as the original text, cf. Credner, p. 69. It may be worth noticing that Justin also has a hebraizing text to Deut 32:15 in *Dial.* 20:1. Smit Sibinga speculates that Justin's text may be due to a recension similar to the *kaige* text of the Twelve Prophets, p. 144. Cf also Koester, p. 35.

21. Cf. detailed collations in Credner, pp. 159/190-192.

22. Vs. 12: LXX ποδῶν, Justin ὁδῶν = MT; vs. 14: Justin's text omits a μετὰ which is without foundation in the MT.

*Dialogue.* One here has an almost perfect proof that the text in *Dial.* 17 and *Dial.* 133 stems from Justin's own pen.[23] And one observes once more that Justin seems to brand the text of his Biblical MS as «Jewish».

The text which Justin claims represents the true LXX is found in two slightly different versions in *Dial.* 136:2 and 137:3.(See the synopsis.) The decisive feature , according to Justin, is the reading ἄρωμεν instead of δήσωμεν, *Dial.* 137:3. In fact, Justin takes Is 3:10 to be a testimony on the slaying of Christ, and this presupposes the non-LXX reading ἄρωμεν.[24] This reading is not found in any LXX Isaiah MS[25] - it probably never occurred in an Isaiah MS, for there are indications that Justin took it from a testimony source.[26] Looking at the adjoining quotations in Justin, we find that he three times seems to follow the same sequence of texts:

| 1. Apol. 48:5 - 49:7 | Dial. 16:5 - 17:2 | Dial.133.2-5 |
|---|---|---|
| Is 57:1f | Is 57:1-4 | |
| (Is 65:1-3) | Is 52:5 | |
| | Is 3:9-11 | Is 3:9-15 |
| Is 5:20 | Is 5:18-20 | Is 5:18-25 |

Two facts deserve notice. (1) The Is 5:20 text in *1.Apol.* 49:7 is definitely non-LXX (very telescoped), which can be taken as a further indication that a testimony source is being used. (2) Influence from Is 57:1 can explain the ἄρωμεν reading in Is 3:10, because Is 57:1 twice contains this verb, and also in other respects is very close to Is 3:10 (ὁ δίκαιος ἀπώλετο . . . ἄνδρες δίκαιοι αἴρονται . . . ἦρται ὁ δίκαιος . . .). This influence from Is 57:1 strenghtens the assumption that these two texts were joined in Justin's testimony source, because in his own writings Is 57:1 and the ἄρωμεν version of Is 3:10 never occur together.

How familiar Justin was with the idea contained in these two testimonies is shown in a casual allusion in *Dial.* 119:3: καὶ μετὰ τὸ ἀναιρεθῆναι τὸν δίκαιον ἐκεῖνον . . . It is impossible to determine which of the texts Justin had in mind here; possibly he is referring to both.

---

23. Koester, p. 33, asks whether *Dial.* 17 or *Dial.* 133 is envisaged in Justin's backreference in *Dial.*137. Why not both?

24. Koester is probably right in suggesting that this reading is of Christian origin: «. . . *eine Steigerung gegenüber* δήσωμεν . . . *und zwar eine Steigerung, die offenbar die Deutung auf den Tod Jesu im Auge hat.*» (p. 34). I am not convinced by Hommes' attempt to derive the reading from Aristobulos, *Testimoniaboek,* p. 188.

25. It may be relevant to quote a remark by Hatch here, because of its relevance for my subsequent discussion concerning Justin's Bible manuscripts: «The fact that there are no variants in the MSS of the LXX (viz. concerning the reading δήσωμεν) is important in its bearing upon the tradition of the LXX text: it confirms the view that we owe that text to Jewish rather than to Christian scribes.» *(Essays,* p. 197).

26. Cf. Ziegler's remark in his Introduction to the Göttingen LXX Isaiah:«*Die von Justin für echt gehaltene Lesart* ἄρωμεν *wird von keiner Hs. gestützt. Vielleicht entstammt sie einem biblischen Florilegium oder «Testimonienbuch».»* (p. 20).

To conclude: Justin once more discredits the LXX text of his Isaiah MS as «Jewish», insisting that a non-LXX reading found in his testimony source is the true «LXX».

## (d) Is 7:14 (see synopsis next page).

It is obvious that Justin's quotation of Is 7:14 in *1.Apol.* 33:1 has Mt 1:23 as its direct or indirect source.[27] There are indications in the context which indicate that we should reckon with an intermediary source between Mt and Justin (cf. below, p. 144f). This intermediary source may account for the deviations from Matthew's text: To avoid any misunderstanding that the Messiah's actual name should be Emmanuel, the Greek transcription of this name has been dropped, and the translated name is introduced with the somewhat circumstantial: ἐροῦσιν ἐπὶ τῷ ὀνόματι αὐτοῦ. This is the only quotation of Is 7:14 in the *Apology*. Let us see what happens to this text in the *Dialogue*. In *Dial.* 43:5f Justin has a long LXX text, Is 7:10-17, with Is 8:4 interpolated in the middle of vs. 16; followed by this comment:«. . . you and your teachers dare to say that there is not said in the prophecy . . .'Ιδοὺ ἡ παρθένος ἐν γαστρὶ ἕξει,[28] but 'Ιδοὺ ἡ νεᾶνις ἐν γαστρὶ λήψεται καὶ τέξεται υἱόν . . .» One notices that the text which Justin asserts is the true »LXX« is identical with the Matthean text in *1.Apol.* 33:1, not the LXX text he has just been quoting, (and which reads λήψεται, not ἕξει). That is: The true LXX is for Justin once more the text of his testimony source.

However, in this case the »Jewish« text is not represented by the long LXX quotations in *Dial.* 43 and 66, because these texts do not contain the decisive »Jewish« reading νεᾶνις (although they do contain the »Jewish« reading λήψεται instead of ἕξει), and they contain an interpolation (Is 8:4) in Is 7:16 which probably was made by a Christian.[29] One hesitates to believe that this interpolation was present in an Isaiah scroll.

Justin seems to be totally unaware that there is an interpolation in his text, and builds his entire argument in *Dial.* 77f precisely on the interpolated verse![30] I am thus inclined to believe that Justin's two Isaiah quotations

---

27. Cf. Th. Zahn, *Geschichte des Neutestamentlichen Kanons,* 1:2 (Erlangen/Leipzig, 1889), pp. 486f.
28. The Matthean reading ἕξει has intruded into part of the LXX MSS tradition, but is hardly the original LXX reading, despite Ziegler's judgement in the Göttingen edition. Cf. Zahn, *loc. cit.*; Koester, *Schriftbeweis,* pp. 40f. There is much to be said for Credner's argument: »*Die Lesart* ἕξει *für* λήψεται, . . . *verdankt . . . ihre Entstehung, aller Wahrscheinlichkeit nach, dem Bemühen der Christen, jede Vorstellung von einer Empfängniss nach menschlicher Weise zu entfernen. Denn das* ἐν γαστρὶ λαμβάνειν, *sobald man es urgirt, erinnert mehr an den durch menschliche Zeugung hervorgerufenen Anfang der Schwangerschaft, als das weitere und unbestimmtere* ἐν γαστρὶ ἔχειν.« (p. 198).
29. The interpolation looks as if it was made with a view to the argument in *Dial.* 77f, cf. below.
30. Hilgenfeld, p. 406, and Koester, p. 42, both argue that Justin was completely unaware of any interpolation in his text when writing the *Dialogue.*

## IS 7:14 — SYNOPSIS

| Mt 1:23 | 1. Apol. 33:1 | Is 7:14 LXX = Dial. 43:5 = Dial. 66:2 |
|---|---|---|
| ᾽Ιδοὺ ἡ παρθένος ἕξει<br>ἐν γαστρὶ ἕξει<br>καὶ τέξεται υἱόν<br>καὶ καλέσουσιν<br>τὸ ὄνομα αὐτοῦ<br>᾽Εμμανουήλ<br>ὅ ἐστιν μεθερμηνευόμενον<br>Μεθ᾽ ἡμῶν ὁ θεός | ᾽Ιδοὺ ἡ παρθένος ⎤ = 1. Apol. 33:4<br>ἐν γαστρὶ ἕξει      ⎦ = Dial. 43:8<br>καὶ τέξεται υἱόν<br>καὶ ἐροῦσιν<br>ἐπὶ τῷ ὀνόματι αὐτοῦ<br><br>Μεθ᾽ ἡμῶν ὁ θεός | ᾽Ιδοὺ ἡ παρθένος<br>ἐν γαστρὶ λήψεται[a] ⎤ = Dial. 67:1<br>καὶ τέξεται υἱόν       ⎦<br>καὶ καλέσεται[b]      ⎤ = Dial. 68:6;<br>τὸ ὄνομα αὐτοῦ       ⎦ 71:3; 84:1<br>᾽Εμμανουήλ |
| "Jewish" text:<br>Dial. 43:8 = 67:1:<br>᾽Ιδοὺ ἡ νεᾶνις         ⎤<br>ἐν γαστρὶ λήψεται[a] ⎥ = Dial. 71:3; 84:3<br>καὶ τέξεται υἱόν        ⎦<br><br>a) Dial. 84:3: ἕξει | | a) So Lucianic MSS and Justin in the above passages. LXX^{SA-Q} (= Ziegler): ἕξει.<br>b) So Dial. 43:5. Dial. 66:2 man. prim.: καλέσει = LXX^{S.811.46}; corr.: καλέσουσιν = LXX^{26-106.130.534}. LXX^{A.B-V}; α; σ; θ (= Ziegler): καλέσεις (= MT). |

in *Dial.* 43 and 66 are taken from a Christian source which also contained an argument similar to the one in *Dial.* 77f.

In this case we shall therefore have to reckon with three versions of the same text in Justin: Is 7:14 = Mt 1:23 (in *1.Apol.* 33:1 and *Dial.* 43:8); a Christian interpolated version of Is 7:10-17 ( in *Dial.* 43/66); and a »Jewish« version of Is 7:14 reading νεᾶνις. Justin's Jewish version of Is 7:14 agrees with Aquila, Symmachus, and Theodotion in this reading. Did Justin already know of Aquila's version, or is he a witness to a revised text prior to Aquila?[31] Did the »Jewish« Isaiah scroll from which he quotes elsewhere in the *Dialogue* read νεᾶνις in Is 7:14?

The special feature about Is 7:14 in Justin is that in this case - and in this case only - he refuses to argue from the text recognized by the Jews. »For you recognize all those (texts) that I have brought forward to you, save that you made a contradiction about the text:'Behold, the virgin shall be with child . . .'«(*Dial.* 71:3).

To conclude: Although Is 7:14 has its peculiar problems in Justin (two Christian sources, one Jewish), we have found confirmation for our thesis concerning Justin and his »testimony sources«: Justin claims the text from Mt. 1:23 - probably transmitted through an intermediary source - as the true »LXX«.

(e) Ps 82:6f.

| Ps 82:6f LXX = *Dial.* 124:2 (»Jewish«) | *Dial.* 124:3 (»LXX«) |
|---|---|
| vs. 6 ἐγὼ εἶπα θεοί ἐστε<br>καὶ υἱοὶ ὑψίστου πάντες<br>vs. 7 ὑμεῖς δὲ<br>ὡς ἄνθρωπος[a] ἀποθνήσκετε<br>καὶ ὡς εἷς τῶν ἀρχόντων πίπτετε | ἰδοὺ δὴ<br>ὡς ἄνθρωποι ἀποθνήσκετε<br>καὶ ὡς εἷς τῶν ἀρχόντων πίπτετε |
| a) = LXX[R] and emended text in<br>   *Dial.* 124:2. LXX and MS reading<br>   in *Dial.* 124:2: ἄνθρωποι | |

In *Dial.* 124:2 Justin says that he will quote Ps 82 »as you yourselves interpret it«, i.e. in its »Jewish« version. There follows a text which in the *Parisinus* is almost perfect LXX.[32] The problem is that Justin then goes on to quote vs. 7 as 'the Seventy' translated it - the implication obviously being that their version was different from the »Jewish« text just quoted.[33] The only

---

31. Credner denies Justin's aquaintance with Aquila, p. 198, Koester likewise, p. 40.
32. Vs. 2: Justin omits διάψαλμα; vs, 3: Justin reads ὀρφανῷ and πτωχῷ for LXX ὀρφανὸν and πτωχόν, but here LXX R agrees with Justin. This is of considerable interest, cf. below.
33. In this case the comment by Credner is rather misleading. Credner thinks the entire issue has to do with the superscription of the Psalm, pp. 125-26. Hilgenfeld, pp. 389f, rightly rejected this proposal.

difference in the present text is that *Dial.* 124:3 reads ἰδοὺ δὴ instead of ὑμεῖς δὲ in *Dial.* 124:2. This cannot be the difference envisaged by Justin. His comments in *Dial.* 124:3 suggest that the difference in readings concerns the ἄνθρωποι of the LXX text.[34]

Justin's «Jewish» version of the Psalm exhibits agreement with the LXX R version of the Psalm in vs. 3, and this text probably contains the reading in vs. 7 which Justin originally copied in *Dial.* 124:2: ὡς ἄνθρωπος. This reading gives excellent meaning to Justin's discussion in *Dial.* 124:3[35]

This granted, I propose the following explanation for Justin's remarks: In *Dial.* 124:2 Justin is quoting Ps 82 from a Psalms MS containing some LXX R readings; in *Dial.* 124:3 he quotes from a testimony source, insisting in his usual way that this is the true text of 'the Seventy' - and being right concerning ἄνθρωποι, because his testimony source happened to have the most usual LXX reading.

(f) Ps 96.

Justin's complaint that the Jews have removed the words ἀπὸ τοῦ ξύλου from the text of Ps 96 (LXX: Ps 95), is perhaps his most wellknown text-critical remark.[36] But it seems that since Hatch no-one has made a thorough investigation of the textual evidence concerning Ps 96 in Justin.[37]

Let us first take a look at the quotation in *1.Apol.* 41:1-4. As one can easily glean from the synopsis (next page), this text is really much closer to 1 Chron 16:23-31 than to Ps 96, especially when Justin's text is compared with the readings in the uncials BS and the cursive 93 (= Brooke-McLean: e₂). In fact, the text in *1.Apol.* 41:1-4 looks like a carefully composed harmony between the two LXX texts, with 1 Chron 16 as the basic text.[38] In

---

34. Cf. Rahlfs, *Septuaginta-Psalter*, p. 205.

35. This emendation is accepted by most editors and translators of Justin's text (not Falls), and A. Rahlfs takes it for granted in his later article 'Über Theodotion-Lesarten im Neuen Testament und Aquila-Lesarten bei Justin', *ZNW* 20 (1921, pp. 182-199), p. 196. Cf. also H. B. Swete, *An Introduction to the Old Testament in Greek* (revised by R. R. Ottley, Cambridge, 1914), p. 423; Koester, *Schriftbeweis*, p. 44; Prigent, *Justin*, p. 299. Swete remarks that Justin throughout his Psalms quotations shows affinities with the MSS group ART, *op. cit.* p. 422.

36. Among the more important treatments of this textual problem in Justin, one may note: Credner, pp. 128f; Hilgenfeld, pp. 400-404; Hatch, pp. 192-96; Bousset, *Evangeliencitate*, p. 19; Rahlfs, *Septuaginta-Psalter*, pp. 205f; Harris, *Testimonies* I, pp. 11f; Hommes, pp. 91-98; P. Beskow, *Rex Gloriae. The Kingship of Christ in the Early Church* (Stockholm/Göteborg/Uppsala, 1962), pp. 99f; Daniélou, *Etudes*, pp. 55-61/72f; Prigent, *Les Testimonia*, pp. 113f; *idem, Justin*, pp. 173-180/184-187/193f.

37. Cf., however, Koester's many valuable observations, *Schriftbeweis*, pp. 42f.

38. That 1 Chron 16 is the basic text, has been overlooked by many commentators, who simply refer to the text in *1.Apol.* 41 as «Ps 96», e.g. Credner, pp. 127f («frei nach dem Gedächtniss»); Bousset, p. 19; Swete, *op. cit.* pp. 423f; Hommes, p. 96. But already Hilgenfeld pointed out that Justin's text is closer to 1 Chron 16 (with full synopsis pp. 401f); the same insight recurs in Hatch, pp. 193-196; Rahlfs, *Septuaginta-Psalter*, p. 205; Smit Sibinga, p. 26; n. 1; Koester, p. 43, n. 3; cf. also the references given in Goodspeed and the BP 1.

tab27

| 1 Chron 16 (LXX Rahlfs) | 1. Apol. 41:1–4 | Dial. 73:3–4 = Ps 96 (LXX Rahlfs) |
|---|---|---|
| 23. ᾄσατε τῷ κυρίῳ πᾶσα ἡ γῆ | ᾄσατε τῷ κυρίῳ πᾶσα ἡ γῆ | 1b. ᾄσατε τῷ κυρίῳ ᾆσμα καινόν<br>ᾄσατε τῷ κυρίῳ πᾶσα ἡ γῆ<br>2. ᾄσατε τῷ κυρίῳ |
| ἀναγγείλατε<br>ἐξ ἡμέρας εἰς ἡμέραν<br>σωτηρίαν αὐτοῦ | καὶ ἀναγγείλατε<br>ἡμέρας ἐξ ἡμέρας<br>τὸ σωτήριον αὐτοῦ | καὶ[a] εὐλογήσατε τὸ ὄνομα αὐτοῦ<br>εὐαγγελίζεσθε<br>ἡμέραν ἐξ ἡμέρας<br>τὸ σωτήριον αὐτοῦ<br>3. ἀναγγείλατε ἐν τοῖς ἔθνεσιν<br>τὴν δόξαν αὐτοῦ<br>ἐν πᾶσι τοῖς λαοῖς<br>τὰ θαυμάσια αὐτοῦ. |
| 25. ὅτι μέγας κύριος<br>καὶ αἰνετὸς σφόδρα<br>φοβερός ἐστιν ἐπὶ πάντας τοὺς θεούς<br>26. ὅτι πάντες οἱ θεοὶ<br>τῶν ἐθνῶν<br>εἴδωλα[a]<br>καὶ ὁ θεὸς ἡμῶν<br>οὐρανοὺς[b] ἐποίησεν | ὅτι μέγας κύριος<br>καὶ αἰνετὸς σφόδρα<br>φοβερός ἐστιν ὑπὲρ πάντας τοὺς θεούς<br>ὅτι πάντες οἱ θεοὶ<br>τῶν ἐθνῶν<br>εἴδωλα δαιμονίων εἰσίν<br>ὁ δὲ θεὸς<br>τοὺς οὐρανοὺς ἐποίησε | 4. ὅτι μέγας κύριος<br>καὶ αἰνετὸς σφόδρα<br>φοβερός ἐστιν ὑπὲρ[b] πάντας τοὺς θεούς<br>5. ὅτι πάντες οἱ θεοὶ<br>τῶν ἐθνῶν<br>δαιμόνια<br>ὁ δὲ κύριος<br>τοὺς οὐρανοὺς ἐποίησεν |
| 27. δόξα καὶ ἔπαινος<br>κατὰ πρόσωπον αὐτοῦ<br>ἰσχὺς καὶ καύχημα<br>ἐν τόπῳ[c] αὐτοῦ | δόξα καὶ αἶνος<br>κατὰ πρόσωπον αὐτοῦ<br>ἰσχὺς καὶ καύχημα<br>ἐν τόπῳ ἁγιάσματος αὐτοῦ | 6. ἐξομολόγησις καὶ ὡραιότης<br>ἐνώπιον αὐτοῦ<br>ἁγιωσύνη καὶ μεγαλοπρέπεια<br>ἐν τῷ ἁγιάσματι αὐτοῦ |
| 28. δότε τῷ κυρίῳ<br>πατριαὶ[d] τῶν ἐθνῶν<br>δότε τῷ κυρίῳ<br>δόξαν καὶ ἰσχύν | δότε τῷ κυρίῳ<br>τῷ πατρὶ τῶν αἰώνων | 7. ἐνέγκατε τῷ κυρίῳ<br>αἱ πατριαὶ τῶν ἐθνῶν<br>ἐνέγκατε τῷ κυρίῳ<br>δόξαν καὶ τιμήν |
| δόξαν | δόξαν | |

| | | |
|---|---|---|
| 29. δότε τῷ κυρίῳ<br>δόξαν ὀνόματος αυτοῦ ]^(c)<br>λάβετε δῶρα<br>καὶ ἐνέγκατε^(f)<br>κατὰ πρόσωπον αὐτοῦ<br>καὶ προσκυνήσατε τῷ κυρίῳ<br>ἐν αὐλαῖς ἁγίαις αὐτοῦ<br>φοβηθήτω<br>30. ἀπὸ προσώπου αὐτοῦ πᾶσα ἡ γῆ<br>κατορθωθήτω^(g) ἡ γῆ<br>καὶ μὴ σαλευθήτω<br>31. εὐφρανθήτω ὁ οὐρανός<br>καὶ ἀγαλλιάσθω ἡ γῆ<br>καὶ εἰπάτωσαν<br>ἐν τοῖς ἔθνεσιν<br>κύριος^(h) βασιλεύων | λάβετε χάριν<br>καὶ εἰσέλθετε<br>κατὰ πρόσωπον αὐτοῦ<br>καὶ προσκυνήσατε<br>ἐν αὐλαῖς ἁγίαις αὐτοῦ<br>φοβηθήτω<br>ἀπὸ προσώπου αὐτοῦ πᾶσα ἡ γῆ<br>καὶ κατορθωθήτω<br>καὶ μὴ σαλευθήτω<br>εὐφρανθήτωσαν<br><br>ἐν τοῖς ἔθνεσιν<br>ὁ κύριος ἐβασίλευσεν<br>ἀπὸ τοῦ ξύλου | 8. ἐνέγκατε τῷ κυρίῳ<br>δόξαν ἐν^(a) ὀνόματι αὐτοῦ<br>ἄρετε^(d) θυσίας<br>καὶ εἰσπορεύεσθε<br>εἰς τὰς αὐλὰς αὐτοῦ<br>9. προσκυνήσατε τῷ κυρίῳ<br>ἐν αὐλῇ ἁγίᾳ αὐτοῦ<br>σαλευθήτω<br>ἀπὸ προσώπου αὐτοῦ πᾶσα ἡ γῆ<br>10. εἴπατε<br>ἐν τοῖς ἔθνεσιν<br>ὁ κύριος ἐβασίλευσε |
| a) Some cursives: δαιμόνια<br>b) Some cursives: τοὺς οὐρανούς<br>c) Two cursives: τῷ ἁγιάσματι<br>   Other cursives: τόπῳ ἁγίῳ<br>d) BS: πατρί<br>e) Om. BS<br>f) One cursive: εἰσέλθατε<br>g) Pr. καὶ S*<br>h) Some cursives: ὁ κύριος | | a) Om. LXX<br>b) Thus L Th^P. Rahlfs LXX: ἐπί<br>c) Om. LXX<br>d) LXX: ἄρατε |

several cases, readings from Ps 96 have been substituted for readings in 1 Chron 16, and in two cases one finds combined readings: In *1.Apol.* 41:1 εἴδωλα from 1 Chron 16:26 and δαιμόνια from Ps 96:5 are combined into εἴδωλα δαιμονίων,[39] and in *1.Apol.* 41:2 there is a similar combination of τόπῳ and ἁγιάσματι into τόπω ἁγιάσματος.[40] The final addition of ἀπὸ τοῦ ξύλου[41] sufficiently proves that the conflated text is due to a Christian. There may be other indications too. In 1 Chron 16:29LXX we read: λάβετε δῶρα καὶ ἐνέγκατε κατὰ πρόσωπου αὐτοῦ . . . The sacrificial meaning of this is clear, and is even more stressed in the Ps 96LXX parallel: ἄρετε θυσίας καὶ εἰσπορεύεσθε εἰς τὰς αὐλὰς αὐτοῦ (vs. 8). In Justin's text there are neither δῶρα nor θυσίας. The text has been thouroughly spiritualized in a way reminiscent of Heb 4:16. Justin: λάβετε χάριν . . ., Heb: προσερχώ-μεθα . . . τῷ θρόνῳ τῆς χάριτος ἵνα λάβομεν ἔλεος καὶ χάριν εὔρωμεν . . .[42]

Did Justin compose this conflated text himself? I think one can exclude this possibility, because Justin seems to have no knowledge of the fact that 1 Chron 16 is the main source of the text.[43] In 1 Chron 16 the Psalm is sung by *Asaph* and his kinsmen, while Justin introduces the text as a *prophecy by David*. Besides, he does not accuse the Jews of having omitted the words ἀπὸ τοῦ ξύλου from 1 Chron 16, but from Ps 96 (95), *Dial.* 73:1! The one composing the conflated text is almost certainly the one responsible for the insertion of the targumizing addition ἀπὸ τοῦ ξύλου. In other words, if Justin himself composed the text, he could not have claimed *bona fide* that this text is the authentic LXX of Ps 96. But one has every reason to think that Justin claimed this *bona fide*.[44]

---

39. Some cursives in 1 Chron 16 read δαιμόνια (from Ps 96:5!), but none have Justin's combined reading. Cf. Hatch, p. 194.

40. Again some cursives in 1 Chron 16 show signs of contamination from Ps 96, but none have Justin's peculiar combination, cf. Hatch, *ibid.*

41. «No existing Greek MS of the Psalter is known to contain the words except cod. 156 ( . . . ), which gives them in the suspicious form ἀπὸ τῷ ξύλῳ. *A ligno* is found in the Sahidic and in the Latin of R and in some other O. L. texts. Cf. the hymn *Vexilla regis . . . regnavit a ligno Deus.*» (Swete, p. 424). There have been various attempts to explain this addition as arising from textual corruption. One has thought that the word ξύλον is an intrusion from vs. 12: τότε ἀγαλλιάσονται πάντα τὰ ξύλα τοῦ δρυμοῦ, or that there was a corruption of vs. 10 in the Hebrew text: יהוה מלך אף תכון being read as יהוה מלך על העץ (thus Beskow, *op. cit.*, p. 99, n. 4). Apart from the fact that these proposals are far from convincing in themselves, they probably start from a false premiss. We do not have to do with a casual corruption of a text, but with *deliberate* Christian «targumizing».

42. Hommes, p. 96, also regards the reading τῷ πατρὶ τῶν αἰώνων in Justin's text as a Christian modification. This may well be the case, but cf. the reading of MSS BS in 1 Chron 16:28.

43. Justin does not seem to be familiar with the books of Chronicles (or Ezra - Nehemiah). Apart from the text treated here, the BP I lists only an allusion in *Dial.* 127:3, but the reference may as well be to the parallel text in I Kings 8:11. On the other hand, Justin's quotation of 1 Chron 17:13f in *Dial.* 118:2 is incorrectly given as 2 Sam 7:14-16 in the BP I. But this text is partly non-LXX and may stem from a testimony source, cf. below. There is thus no quotation in Justin which can prove a familiarity with the books of Chronicles.

44. The fact that *Barn.* 8:5 seems to know the addition to Ps 96:10 (cf. Prigent, *Les Testimonia*, pp. 113f), proves that the addition is definitely pre-Justinian, but still Justin could be responsible for the conflated text in *1.Apol.* 41:1-4.

Let us turn to the evidence in *Dial.* 73. Justin here quotes Ps 96 in a pretty good LXX text (cf. apparatus in the synopsis), without the Christian addition in vs. 10. Since Otto's edition of Justin's text, almost all editors, translators and commentators have found fault with this and have proposed to insert ἀπὸ τοῦ ξύλου in vs. 10[45]. But this is hardly warranted. We have seen that Justin, to gratify his Jewish interlocutor, can give long LXX quotations with readings he himself considers to be wrong («Jewish»). And - NB! - so far we have never seen him introduce his own «LXX» readings into otherwise pure LXX texts. Hence there is no reason why he should have done this in *Dial.* 73:3f. He has made himself sufficiently clear about the true reading of vs. 10 in the context. Besides - from which source does Justin derive his knowledge that the Jews have deleted the Christian addition from their MSS? The simplest answer is: from the very Psalms MS Justin is excerpting in *Dial.* 73.

Consequently, there is no need for an emendation of the received text in *Dial.* 73:3f;[46] and I propose the following theory to explain both the textual evidence and Justin's text-critical remarks: In *1.Apol.* 41:1-4 Justin quotes a conflated and interpolated text based on 1 Chron 16 (main text) and Ps 96. He takes this text from some kind of testimony source, and believes it to be the authentic «LXX» of one of David's Psalms. In *Dial.* 73:1-4 he has had access to a Psalms MS and quotes the text from it. He observes that it is the 96th (95th) Psalm and that the words ἀπὸ τοῦ ξύλου are missing. His conclusion is that the Jews have deleted these words from the Psalms MSS.

Let me add some remarks on Ps 96:5. As we have seen, the conflated text in *1.Apol.* 41 here reads: οἱ θεοὶ τῶν ἐθνῶν εἴδωλα δαιμονίων εἰσίν, while the Ps 96LXX and *Dial.* 73:3f have δαιμόνια only. It is interesting to notice that in all allusions to this verse prior to *Dial.* 73:3f Justin seems to presuppose the conflated text: οἱ θεοὶ τῶν ἐθνῶν, νομιζόμενοι θεοί, εἴδωλα δαιμονίων εἰσίν (*Dial.* 55:2); ἐκεῖνα γὰρ εἴδωλά ἐστι δαιμονίων (*Dial.* 73:2). But after the septuagintal quotation in *Dial.* 73:3f, the allusions also become septuagintal, *Dial.* 79:4 and 83:4. It seems Justin has noticed the LXX reading in vs. 5 and adjusted his own terminology accordingly.

The point to be emphasized at this junction is once again that Justin indirectly brands the LXX text he is quoting in *Dial.* 73:3f as Jewish, i.e. as a

---

45. Cf. the remarks of Rahlfs, *Septuaginta-Psalter*, p. 205, n. 2. Otto introduced the words ἀπὸ τοῦ ξύλου into his text because he meant they were crucial to Justin's argument. Cf. his remark in the text-critical note *ad loc.* (p. 263): «Mirum cur haec verba, quae exciderunt culpa librariorum, in edd. non adiiciantur.» Otto is followed by Archambault and Goodspeed in their editions, and by Haeuser, Williams, and Falls in their translations.

46. In this I agree with Credner, pp. 128f, and Koester, p. 43: «*Der Widerspruch zwischen der von J. selbst als LA der Siebzig bezeichneten Textform und dem Text des Lemmazitates ist hier kein anderer als in der bisher besprochenen Fällen* (viz. Is 3:10; Deut 32:8; Gen 49:10; Is 7:14). *Auch dieses Lemma-Zitat ist unter diejenigen Zitaten des Dial. zu rechnen, die eine Überarbeitung nach jüdischen LXX-HSS durch Just. selbst erfahren haben.*» Cf. also note 5, *ibid.*

Synopsis on *Dial.* 72 (cf. Appendix I, nr. 55)

| Ps. Ezra, *Dial.* 72:1 | Lactantius, *Instit.* IV:18 | *Adu. Marc.* IV:40:3 |
|---|---|---|
| καὶ εἶπεν Ἐσδρας τῷ λαῷ<br>τοῦτο τὸ πάσχα ὁ σωτὴρ ἡμῶν καὶ ἡ καταφυγὴ ἡμῶν<br>καὶ ἐὰν διανοηθῆτε καὶ ἀναβῇ ὑμῶν ἐπὶ τὴν καρδίαν<br>ὅτι μέλλομεν αὐτὸν ταπεινοῦν ἐν σημείῳ<br>καὶ μετὰ ταῦτα ἐλπίσομεν ἐπ᾽ αὐτόν<br>οὐ μὴ ἐρημωθῇ ὁ τόπος οὗτος εἰς τὸν ἅπαντα χρόνον<br>λέγει ὁ θεὸς τῶν δυνάμεων<br>ἂν δὲ μὴ πιστεύσητε αὐτῷ μηδὲ εἰσακούσητε τοῦ κηρύγματος αὐτοῦ<br>ἔσεσθε ἐπίχαρμα τοῖς ἔθνεσι | et dixit Esdras ad populum:<br>hoc pascha Salvator noster est et refugium nostrum<br>cogitate et ascendat in cor vestrum<br>quoniam habemus humiliare eum in signo<br>et post haec sperabimus in eum<br>ne deseratur hic locus in aeternum tempus<br>dicit Dominus Deus virtutum<br>si non credideritis ei neque exaudieritis annuntiationem eius<br>eritis derisio in gentibus | aduersus me cogitauerunt<br>cogitatum dicentes<br>uenite coiciamus lignum<br>in panem eius<br><br>*Adu. Marc.*<br>III:19:3 |

| Jer 11:19, *Dial.* 72:2 | Jer 11:19 LXX | Tert. *Adv. Jud.* 10:12 | *Adu. Marc.* IV:40:3 |
|---|---|---|---|
| ἐγὼ ὡς ἀρνίον (ἄκακον)^1<br>φερόμενον τοῦ θύεσθαι<br>ἐπ᾽ ἐμὲ ἐλογίζοντο<br>λογισμόν λέγοντες<br>δεῦτε ἐμβάλωμεν ξύλον<br>εἰς τὸν ἄρτον αὐτοῦ<br>καὶ ἐκτρίψωμεν αὐτὸν<br>ἐκ γῆς ζώντων<br>καὶ τὸ ὄνομα αὐτοῦ<br>οὐ μὴ μνησθῇ οὐκέτι | ἐγὼ δὲ^a ὡς ἀρνίον ἄκακον<br>ἀγόμενον τοῦ θύεσθαι οὐκ ἔγνων<br>ἐπ᾽ ἐμὲ ἐλογίσαντο<br>λογισμόν πονηρόν^b λέγοντες<br>δεῦτε καὶ ἐμβάλωμεν ξύλον<br>εἰς τὸν ἄρτον αὐτοῦ<br>καὶ ἐκτρίψωμεν αὐτὸν<br>ἀπὸ^d γῆς ζώντων<br>καὶ ὄνομα αὐτοῦ<br>οὐ μὴ μνησθῇ οὐκέτι | venite mittamus<br>in panem eius lignum<br>et conteramus eum<br>a terra uiuorum<br>et nomen illius<br>non memorabitur amplius | |
| a) Lacking in *Dial.* 72:2 (lemma), but present in allusion *Dial.* 72:3. Scribal error? | a) Om. several MSS.<br>b) Om. several MSS.<br>c) Om. Lucianic MSS.<br>d) MS V: ἐκ. | | |

| Ps. Jer, *Dial.* 72:4 | Iren. *Adv. Haer.* III:20:4 | IV:22:1 | *Dem.* 78 |
|---|---|---|---|
| ἐμνήσθη δὲ κύριος | et commemoratus est Dominus | recommemoratus est Dominus | And the Lord, the Holy One of Israel |
| ὁ θεὸς ἀπὸ Ἰσραὴλ | Sanctus Israel | Sanctus Israel | bethought Him |
| τῶν νεκρῶν αὐτοῦ | mortuorum suorum | mortuorum suorum | of His dead, |
| τῶν κεκοιμημένων | qui dormierant | qui praedormierunt | who in the past had slept |
| εἰς γῆν χώματος | in terra sepultionis | in terra defossionis | in the dust of the earth |
| καὶ κατέβη | et descendit | et descendit | and went down |
| πρὸς αὐτοὺς | ad eos | ad eos | unto them |
| εὐαγγελίσασθαι | evangelizare | uti evangelizaret | to bring the good news |
| αὐτοῖς | | eis | |
| τὸ σωτήριον αὐτοῦ | salutem quae est ab eo | salutare suum | of salvation, |
| | uti salvaret eos | ad salvandum eos | to deliver them |

recensed text, while for Justin the authentic «LXX» evidently is the conflated text in *1.Apol.* 41.

(g) Ps.Ezra; Jer 11:19; Ps. Jer. (Cf synopsis on pp. 40f).

In *Dial.* 71:2 Justin complains that the Jews have removed certain passages from the «LXX». In *Dial.* 72:1-4 he goes on to enumerate three such deleted passages (the words ἀπὸ τοῦ ξύλου in Ps 96:10 are added as a fourth example in *Dial.* 73:1-4). Several scholars have observed that the list in *Dial.* 72 does not seem to be an *ad hoc* composition by Justin, because the texts have a marked inner thematic unity,[47] and the list includes a text which should not belong there. Let us take a closer look at the texts.

In the Ps. Ezra quotation the main catchword is πάσχα. The phrase τοῦτο τὸ πάσχα ὁ σωτὴρ ἡμῶν is reminiscent of 1 Cor 5:7: τὸ πάσχα ἡμῶν ἐτύθη Χριστός. This motif perhaps recurs in the Jeremiah quotation, where Christ the paschal lamb may be envisaged: ἐγὼ ὡς ἀρνίον [ἄκακον] φερόμενον τοῦ θύεσθαι . . .[48] Christ the paschal lamb is also referred to in the following allusion to Is 53:7: ὡς πρόβατον ἐπὶ σφαγὴν ἀγόμενος. (cf. below, pp. 301—303).

We thus have a sequence of texts concerning Christ the paschal lamb.[49] Only the first of these should belong to a list of deleted passages. Justin partly recognizes this. He avoids an inclusion of Is 53:7 in the list, and betrays uncertainty about Jer 11:19: it «is still written in some copies of those that are in the synagogue of the Jews, for they cut these words out only a short while ago.» One can hardly escape the impression that Justin has a feeling that he is on feeble ground when he includes Jer 11:19 in his list. Prigent's remark seems justified: Justin is in *Dial.* 72 quoting from a *groupement de prophéties destinées à annoncer la passion. Son intention présente le conduit à limiter son choix aux textes qui ne figurent pas dans le canon juif, mais il se laisse entraîner à retenir également* Jér 11,19, *et s'efforce de justifier la présence de ce texte.*[50] It would seem that this hypothesis also covers the Ps.Jer quotation: The *descensus* motif is a natural sequel to the passion testimonies.

To conclude: Justin is in *Dial.* 72 drawing on a testimony source, assuming as usual that its texts represent the true «LXX», and blaming the Jews for the fact that he has not been able to find them all in his Greek OT.

---

47. Harris, *Testimonies* I, p. 12; Daniélou, *Theology*, pp. 101f; Prigent, *Justin* pp. 174-176.
48. On Justin's text, cf. F. C. Burkitt, 'Justin Martyr and Jeremiah XI 19', *JTS* 33 (1932), pp. 371-73; C. Wolff, *Jeremia im Frühjudentum und Urchristentum* (TU 118, Berlin, 1976), pp. 180-84.
49. Harris, *Testimonies* I, p. 12, and Prigent, *Justin*, p. 174, give as the theme of *Dial.* 72: cross and passion (including also Ps 96:10). I believe the paschal lamb motif ought to be stressed. It is significant that Cyprian in *Test.* 11:15 has the sequence: Is 53:7.9.12; Jer 11:18f; Ex 12:3.5ff, all introduced by the heading *Quod ipse dictus sit ovis et agnus . . .* Ex 12 has here taken the place of the spurious Ezra quotation in Justin. Cf. Prigent, *Justin*, pp. 177/192f.
50. *Justin*, p. 175. The alternative explanations offered by Hommes, p. 97, are less convincing.

*Conclusions and suggestions.*

( 1 ) We have seen repeatedly that two versions of the same text both are original in Justin. He comments on the two versions himself. In these cases, at least, the existence of one LXX and one non-LXX text cannot be explained by «correction» carried out by later copyists.

(2) The deviant, non-LXX·quotations are not free quotations from memory, since Justin insists that the aberrant texts represent the authentic Septuagint. It is unthinkable that Justin should venture to evaluate the accuracy of Biblical MSS on the basis of his fallible memory. Besides, some of the non-LXX texts are quite long and carefully composed, and are quoted with considerable stability. Behind them must lie written sources. This does not exclude that Justin can sometimes quote fragments of these texts -or short texts - from memory. The significant point is that the variant readings in these texts did not originate in Justin's defective memory.

(3) We have seen reasons to think that the sources for the aberrant texts were not Biblical MSS.

(4) The readings which Justin brands as «non-LXX», «Jewish», seem to be those found in the Biblical MSS from which he himself copies his long LXX quotations, chiefly in the *Dialogue*. This point has hardly been sufficiently stressed in previous research.[51]

(5) Justin's remarks about «LXX» and «non-LXX» texts do not stem from true information about the LXX text. Three times he is partly right, but more often he is entirely wrong. This does not mean that there is no principle guiding his remarks. On the contrary, we have meant to discern a consistent principle: What Justin calls «LXX» text is the text of his testimony source(s), while the «Jewish» text is the text of his Biblical MSS.

How can all this be explained? Let me first pick up the suggestion that Justin's «Jewish» readings are those of his own Biblical MSS or, to put it more cautiously, the Biblical MSS to which he had access. This idea can be supported by two kinds of argument, the one drawn from our general knowledge about the production of OT MSS in Justin's day, the second from peculiarities in Justin's long Biblical quotations.

There is every reason to believe that at Justin's time the production of OT MSS in Christian circles was in its infancy.[52] The earliest LXX MSS which can be ascribed to Christian scribes (codex format!) stem from about the

---

51. It may be said, though, to be implied in Barthélemy's and Koester's studies, cf. esp. Koester, pp. 47-50.
52. See esp. the authoritative accounts of C. H. Roberts: 'The Christian Book and the Greek Papyri', *JTS* 50 (1949), pp. 155-168, and 'Books in the Graeco-Roman World and in the New Testament', *The Cambridge History of the Bible, I: From the Beginnings to Jerome* (ed. by P. R. Ackroyd/C. F. Evans, Cambridge, 1970), pp. 48-66. Cf. also N. A. Dahl, 'Bibelutgaver i oldkirken' ('Bible editions in the Early Church' (Norwegian)), *Kirkens arv og kirkens fremtid.* (J. Smemo Jubilee Volume) (Oslo, 1968), pp. 133-151.

middle of the second century.[53] It is significant that they do not derive from
professional scribes, but from «fluent writers who, used to writing, tried
hard for the most part to write in bookhands, but betray the documentary
styles with which they were familiar . . . This confirms what in any case
might have been guessed, that the earliest (Christian) manuscripts were the
product not of the book trade (i.e. professional scribes) but of communi-
ties whose members included businessmen and minor officials well used
to writing .»[54] Only in the latter part of the second century one finds
evidence pointing to the existence of Christian *scriptoria.*[55]

It is thus no surprise that when Justin set out to procure for himself Greek
Biblical MSS, he would get copies deriving from Jewish scribes. This, of
course, would also be the case if Justin culled some of his quotations by
visiting a synagogue and looking into its exemplar of the relevant LXX book
- or if he borrowed an exemplar from a Jewish friend. What matters here is
that on purely a priori grounds there is nothing surprising in the fact that
Justin should regard the text of the Biblical MSS as «Jewish», since in all
probability he would only, or usually, have access to MSS written by Jewish
scribes.[56]

When we turn to the texts themselves, we find ample confirmation for
this surmise. Barthélemy has convincingly shown that Justin's text of the
Twelve Prophets really is a Jewish text, a recension of the LXX carried out by
Jews striving to adjust the Greek Bible to the emerging normative Hebrew
text.[57] The fact that Justin happened to procure for himself an exemplar of
the Minor Prophets representing this text is a strong indication that Jews
were Justin's normal source for Biblical manuscripts.[58] As we have seen,
Justin's «Jewish» version of the LXX has traces of adjustment to the Hebrew
text even outside the Minor Prophets. (Smit Sibinga's study shows archaic,

---

53. So Roberts, *artt. citt.* Single exemplars of OT codexes copied by Christians may have existed
    at an earlier date, cf. «the Yale Genesis Fragment» from ca 80 AD, which probably stems from a
    Christian OT codex (see Dahl, *art. cit.*, p. 142, with reference p. 151).
54. Roberts, 'Books', pp. 62f.
55. *Ibid.*, p. 65.
56. Koester is probably right in referring to *1 Apol.* 31:5 as a direct confirmation that Justin's Bible
    MSS were Jewish: «. . . the books remain in the hands of the Egyptians down to the present;
    the Jews everywhere have them too.» (Koester, p. 49).
57. Cf. his above quoted works. «There is no reason to doubt that this Greek text was an early
    Jewish attempt to revise the standard Septuagint into conformity with a Proto-Massoretic
    Hebrew text, just as Aquila represents a sequent attempt to revise this revision in the
    direction of the official Rabbinic or Massoretic text which had been established by his day.
    We see, then, a series of attempts to bring the Greek Bible into conformity with a *changing*
    Hebrew textual tradition.» (F. M. Cross, 'The History of the Biblical Text in the Light of the
    Discoveries in the Judaean Desert', *HTR* 57 (1964, pp. 281-99), p. 283).
58. Cf. Barthélemy, 'Redécouverte', p. 130: *Justin cite un texte juif réel . . . De là nous pouvons
    inférer que les autres citations de Justin, et elles sont aussi amples que variées, représentent
    très vraisemblablement, dans ce qu'elles ont d'original, une recension rabbinique de la
    Septante qui avait cours entre 70 et 135.»* Cf. also *ibid*, p. 128.

sometimes hebraizing readings in much of Justin's Pentateuch material).
One can perhaps venture the suggestion that there may be valuable material in Justin's LXX quotations as yet unexploited in the study of early
recensions of the LXX.

It is now time to stress that Justin's complaints about Jewish alterations of
the LXX text may betray a certain knowledge about recensional activity
among the Jews. His general mistrust of the Biblical MSS from which he
draws some of his long quotations is more easily understood if Justin had
some knowledge about hebraizing recensions (καιγε, possibly also
Aquila) and suspected his own Biblical MSS to represent a recensed text.[59]
His *Dodekapropheton* text shows that this suspicion was in some cases
well-founded, although Justin in most cases was wrong about the original
LXX.

It remains to be asked why Justin so consequently should give preference to the text of the testimony source(s) when it differed from the text of
the Biblical MSS, and why he should feel so confident that the testimony
source(s) preserved the text of «the Seventy». What I have proposed above,
may be part of the explanation: The testimony sources derived from
Christian theologians, while the Biblical MSS derived from Jews. Justin
would naturally give preference to the Christian sources.[60]

But there may be another factor involved as well, which relates to Justin's
knowledge and use of Ps.Aristeas' legend about LXX origins. Justin relates
this legend in *1.Apol.* 31:2-5, and alludes to it very often when he speaks
about the Seventy and their translation.[61] The relevant point to stress here is
the function of *1.Apol.* 31:2-5 in the context. One can perhaps say that Justin
uses the Aristeas legend as an introduction to and commendation of the
Scriptural quotations he is going to give. The whole of *1.Apol.* 31 has this
commendatory character: The prophets were divinely inspired (31:1);
their oracles were uttered in successive generations from the uttermost
antiquity (31:8); their words were faithfully written down and were preserved by the Jewish kings (31:1); the translation into Greek was not a private,
unreliable enterprise, but one carried out officially by Jewish elders at the
request of Ptolemy, king of Egypt (31:2-4); the Greek version has been kept
faithfully by the Egyptians and by every Jew (NB!) throughout the world to
this day (31:5).

Thus the Gentile reader of the *Apology* is assured that the Greek oracles
he is about to read faithfully preserve the words of Hebrew prophets of high
antiquity, whose words are shown by their fulfilment to be true. I suspect

---

59. Cf. Barthélemy, Redécouverte; pp. 127f; *Devanciers*, pp. 203f.
60. Cf. Koester, *Schriftbeweis*, p. 48: «Die Voraussetzung für J.s Aussagen ist die, dass ihm alles,
    was die christliche Tradition bot, als richtiger Text der Septuaginta galt.»
61. *Dial.* 68:7; 71:1; 84:3; 120:4; 124:3; 131:1; 137:3.

that when Justin himself met the Aristeas legend,[62] it was precisely in the same setting and function as it has in *1.Apol.* 31: as an introductory, commendatory story introducing the Scriptural proof. Or, to put it a little more precise: The Aristeas legend about LXX origins - as Justin met it - had its setting *as an introduction to the Scriptural quotations in the testimony source(s)*. In this capacity the Aristeas story served to commend the Greek OT as such, not any particular version of it over against other versions.(One should especially note that the Jews here figure as *faithful transmitters* of the Greek OT text). In short, the setting of the story was *missionary* - as it is in *1.Apol.* 31 - not text-critical.

But when Justin detected discrepancies between the text of his testimony source(s) - presented to him as the text of the Seventy - and the text of the Bible MSS, the Aristeas legend took on a new significance for him. He now used it as a text-critical argument in favour of the texts which had for him been associated with the legend.

I think the theory which has here been delineated not only explains the textual evidence in Justin, but also his own remarks about the textual problems.

It will now be tested on the remaining cases of texts that were transmitted in two versions.

---

62. A comparison of Justin's version with the two main Jewish versions known to have existed prior to Justin - i.e. Ps. Aristeas (and Josephus' excerpts from it in *Ant.* XII :12-118) versus Philo's shorter account in *De Vit. Mos.* II:25-44 tends to show that Philo can be excluded as Justin's source. Justin's introductory phrase («When Ptolemy, king of Egypt, was founding a library, and set out to gather the writings of all mankind . . .») has no equivalent in Philo's version. For Philo the whole enterprise, right from the beginning, concerns the Torah only - due to Ptolemy's «ardent affection for our laws», and the fact that «some people, thinking it a shame that the laws should be found in one half only of the human race, the barbarians, and denied altogether to the Greeks, took steps to have them translated.» Justin's version rather resembles Ps. Arist. 9:«When Demetrius of Phalerum was put in charge of the king's library he was assigned large sums of money with a view to *collecting*, if possible, *all the books in the world* . . .» (In Ps. Aristeas it is a question of expanding the king's library, not founding it as in Justin). When Justin speaks of a double embassy to «Herod» - first for the Hebrew books and then for the translators - this has no equivalent in Ps. Arist. or Philo, although one might say with M. Hadas that «the twofold embassy .. is a natural expansion of Aristeas.» (Cf. his Introduction to his ed. of Ps. Aristeas; quotation p. 74). Justin's mention of *Herod* would seem to be a grave chronological error, which tells against careful reading of Aristeas. But one cannot exclude scribal error. (Or perhaps the suggestion of P. R. Weis may be right: Justin had knowledge of the Samaritan tradition according to which Herod was the name of Ptolemy's lieutenant in Palestine, cf. Weis' article 'Some Samaritanisms of Justin Martyr', *JTS* 45 (1944, pp. 199-205), p. 205. W. Schmid originally assumed textual corruption ('Die Textüberlieferung der Apologie des Justin', *ZNW* 40 (1941, pp. 87-137), pp. 121f),but later changed his mind and accepted Weis' proposal ('Ein rätselhafter Anachronismus bei Justinus Martyr', *Historisches Jahrbuch* 77 (1957/58), pp. 358-361). One should note, however, that written sources for this Samaritan tradition are from the 14th century. I wonder whether Weis' material may itself be somewhat anachronistic). The most significant deviation from both Jewish versions is of course the feature that Justin speaks of a translation of the *prophets*, while Ps. Arist. and Philo speak about the Law (only). Probably Justin's preface to the legend in *1.Apol.* 31:1 (the preservation of the prophets' words in Hebrew by the Judaean kings) was also part of the legend as he received it. All this combine to give support to Hadas' surmise:«Justin is either using a «memory» version of Aristeas supplemented by *cicerone* details, or the whole is from a cicerone who used a «memory» version.» (p. 75).

## 2. *Other texts transmitted in two versions.*

(a) Ex 3:2ff (see synopsis next page).

Justin has two major treatments of the theophany in the thorn-bush, one in *1.Apol.* 62:3 - 63:17, and the other in *Dial.* 59f (alluded to in *Dial.* 127:4). On closer inspection, some striking differences claim our attention.

The three texts in *1.Apol.* 63 show remarkable accordance with each other against the LXX, and may point to a written source[63] which combined phrases from Ex 3:2-6.10 and Ex 3:14f. Probably the identical texts in *1.Apol.* 63:11 and 63:17 reproduce this harmonistic source more exactly than the first quotation in *1.Apol.*63:6.[64] The decisive peculiarity of this source is that it makes it quite unambiguous that it is the angel of God who speaks to Moses and presents himself as the God of Abraham. In the LXX there is first an epiphany of the Angel of the Lord (vs. 2), after which, in vs. 6, *the Lord* speaks to Moses and presents himself as the God of Abraham.

This textual difference is reflected in Justin's treatments of the passage in *1.Apol.* 63 and *Dial.* 59f. In *1.Apol.* 63 he says that the Jews in their stupidity say that the Unnamable God himself, the Father, spoke to Moses, 63:1.11.14. The mistake of the Jews is thus that they identify the speaking ἄγγελος with God the Father,[65] while it is obvious that the Angel should be identified with the Son, who is called both ἄγγελος and ἀπόστολος because he is sent to bring messages from the Father (63:5.10.14).

In *Dial.* 59f Justin's argument is more complicated. He first quotes the full LXX text of Ex 2:23 - 3:16.[66] He then repeats his interpretation from *1.Apol.* 63: The Angel, speaking to Moses, being God (θεὸς ὤν), signified to Moses that he was the God of Abraham.

---

63. Cf. Smit Sibinga, p. 82: »These words are part of a testimony, condensed from Ex 3:2-6 evidently for polemical purposes.« Cf. also his remarks on pp. 37f.

64. Cf. P. Katz, Ἐν πυρὶ φλογός, *ZNW* 46 (1955, pp. 133-38), pp. 136f.

65. Smit Sibinga thinks something must be wrong with the text in *1.Apol.* 63. »'All the Jews' are said to interpret ἄγγελος (του) θεου as meaning God the Father, which apparently is absurd.« (p. 8lf). True, but that is exactly what Justin says about the Jewish interpretation: absurd. I can see no reason to mistrust the received text - on the contrary, cf. below.

66. Here the whole of Ex 2:24 - 3:15 is omitted with the formula καὶ τὰ λοιπὰ μέχρι τοῦ. All the decisive verses which play a role in Justin's argument are thus omitted. This can hardly be due to Justin, who states his own principle of selective quoting in *Dial.* 56:18: ». . . it does not seem to me necessary to write the same words again, when (1) *all of them have been written already,* but (2) only those *by means of which I made my proof* for Trypho and his companions.« The omission in *Dial.* 59:2 is unjustified in both respects. Moreover, the text which Justin in *Dial.* 56:18 says he has quoted already *in its entirety,* viz. Gen 18:1 -19:28(*Dial.* 56:2), is also radically abbreviated, with the same formula: καὶ τὰ λοιπὰ μέχρι τοῦ. Here the lazy scribe has betrayed himself beyond any doubt. Cf. B. Kominiak, *The Theophanies of the Old Testament in the Writings of St. Justin* (The Catholic University of America, Studies in Sacred Theology, 2nd Ser. 14, Washington, 1948), pp. 48f; Katz, *art. cit.* p. 137: »achtloser Schreibfaulheit«.

Ex 3 — SYNOPSIS

| 1. Apol. 63:7 | 1. Apol. 63:11 = 63:17 | Dial. 60:4 = Ex 3:2—4 LXX | Ex 3 LXX | Ex 3 LXX |
|---|---|---|---|---|
| καὶ ἐλάλησε Μωυσεῖ ἄγγελος θεοῦ | καὶ ἐλάλησεν ἄγγελος τοῦ θεοῦ τῷ Μωυσεῖ | ὤφθη δὲ αὐτῷ ἄγγελος κυρίου | vs.4 ἐκάλεσεν αὐτὸν κύριος | |
| ἐν φλογὶ πυρὸς ἐκ τῆς βάτου καὶ εἶπεν ἐγώ εἰμι ὁ ὤν | ἐν πυρὶ φλογὸς ἐν βάτῳ καὶ εἶπεν ἐγώ εἰμι ὁ ὤν | ἐν πυρὶ φλογὸς[a] ἐκ βάτου[b] | ἐκ τοῦ βάτου... vs.6 καὶ εἶπεν αὐτῷ ἐγώ εἰμι ὁ θεὸς τοῦ πατρός σου | vs.14 καὶ εἶπεν ὁ θεὸς πρὸς Μ. ἐγώ εἰμι ὁ ὤν... vs.15 κύριος ὁ θεὸς τῶν πατέρων ὑμῶν |
| θεὸς Ἀβραάμ θεὸς Ἰσαάκ θεὸς Ἰακώβ ὁ θεὸς τῶν πατέρων σου κάτελθε εἰς Αἴγυπτον καὶ ἐξάγαγε τὸν λαὸν μου | ὁ θεὸς Ἀβραάμ καὶ ὁ θεὸς Ἰσαάκ καὶ ὁ θεὸς Ἰακώβ καὶ ὁ θεὸς τῶν πατέρων σου | | θεὸς Ἀβραάμ καὶ θεὸς Ἰσαάκ καὶ θεὸς Ἰακώβ | θεὸς Ἀβραάμ καὶ θεὸς Ἰσαάκ καὶ θεὸς Ἰακώβ... |
| | | | vs.10 καὶ νῦν δεῦρο ἀποστείλω σε πρὸς Φαραω βασιλέα Αἰγύπτου καὶ ἐξάξεις τὸν λαόν μου τοὺς υἱοὺς Ἰσραηλ... | |

*1. Apol. 63:17*

*1. Apol. 63:11*

καὶ ὁρᾷ ὅτι ὁ βάτος καίεται πυρὶ ὁ δὲ βάτος οὐ κατεκαίετο
ὁ δὲ Μωυσῆς εἶπε[c] Παρελθὼν ὄψομαι τὸ ὅραμα τοῦτο τὸ μέγα[d]
ὅτι[e] οὐ κατακαίεται ὁ βάτος.
ὡς δ᾽ εἶδε κύριος ὅτι προσάγει ἰδεῖν
ἐκάλεσεν αὐτὸν κύριος ἐκ τῆς[f] βάτου...

a) = LXX B. LXX *rel.*: φλογὶ πυρός
b) LXX: τοῦ βάτου
c) LXX: εἶπεν δὲ Μωυσῆς
d) LXX: τὸ ὅραμα τὸ μέγα τοῦτο
e) = LXX B. LXX *rel.*: τί ὅτι
f) LXX: τοῦ

It will be seen that this exegesis again agrees perfectly with the deviant version of the text given in *1.Apol.* 63. But the identification of the Angel with the speaking Lord is not unambiguously warranted by the LXX text just quoted, and Justin therefore puts the following objection into Trypho's mouth: «We do not understand this from the words that have been brought before us, but that he who was seen in a flame of fire was an Angel, and he who conversed with Moses was God, so that both an Angel and God, two together, were in that vision.» Notice that this Jewish exegesis is different from the one related by Justin in *1.Apol.* 63. There the Jewish fault was to identify the Angel with the Father. Here Trypho is careful to deny this identification![67]

Justin in his first counter-argument hypothetically admits his opponent's thesis, and argues that even if the talking God was not the appearing Angel, he was still not the Father, because (1) he presents himself as the God of Abraham etc., and it has already been proved that the God who appeared to Abraham and the other patriarchs was not the Father, and (2) «no person whatever, even though he be of slight intelligence, will dare to say that the Maker and Father of the universe left all that is above heaven, and appeared on a little section of earth» (*Dial.* 60:2). Justin thus has to bolster his exegesis with a philosophical premise to make it stand up against the LXX text.

His second move is to withdraw the consent to his opponent's thesis and reaffirm the identity of the angel in vs. 2 with the speaker in vss. 4ff. The argument is that we find the same sliding from Angel of the Lord to God in other patriarch stories, and there the identity of Angel and God cannot be doubted. *Dial.* 60:5.

One gets the impression that Justin in *Dial.* 59f is adjusting an earlier exegesis, based on a non-LXX text, to match the full LXX text.[68] Notice that the Jewish exegesis also changes with the text. It seems that Justin in *Dial.* 59f — with his fuller acquaintance with the LXX — has become aware that the Jewish counter-argument to his own exegesis would run somewhat different from what he assumed in *1.Apol.* 63.

One final observation on *1.Apol.* 63: There is a striking duplication within this chapter. In 63:2-10 we find the quotation sequence Is 1:3; Mt 11:27; Mt 10:40; Ex 3:2ff. In 63:11-16 much the same sequence recurs: Ex 3:2ff; Is 1:3b; Mt 11:27. And the parallel is not confined to this: much the same argument and terminology recur in both passages. One has to assume that

---

67. Kominiak, *op. cit.*, in his otherwise very exact and perceptive analysis of Justin's argument on the thorn-bush theophany (pp. 48-58), seems to have overlooked the difference between the Jewish position in *1.Apol.* 63 and *Dial.* 59f, see esp. pp. 49/55-58.

68. I take this as a further indication that Justin's argument was originally not based on the LXX text.

Justin is twice using the same source,[69] and perhaps this source accounts for all the quotations in *1.Apol.* 63. There are other indications that Justin in *1.Apol.* 62f did not have the full Exodus text before him. In *1.Apol.* 62:3 he says that Moses pastured the sheep of his *maternal uncle* (actually, his father-in-law). And he has a very free quotation of Ex 3:5.[70] So, when he says in *1.Apol.* 63:9 — after the first non-LXX quotation of Ex 3:2ff — «Those who wish to can learn what followed from this (viz. by consulting the writings of Moses, *1.Apol.* 62:4), for it is not possible to put down everything in these (pages)», Justin may elegantly be camouflaging his own time-saving procedure: To give larger and more exact quotations might probably have caused him some extra work!

To conclude: In the *Apology* Justin is working with a testimony source, in the *Dialogue* he is working directly with the Exodus LXX. His exegesis is modified accordingly — this time Justin has not found it worthwile to discredit the LXX text.

It is hardly necessary to add that this proves beyond doubt that the LXX text in the *Dialogue* does not stem from a later copyist.

## (b) Num 24:17/Is 11:1/Is 51:5.

| Num 24:17b LXX | *Dial.* 106:4 | *1. Apol.* 32:12 |
|---|---|---|
| ἀνατελεῖ ἄστρον ἐξ Ἰακωβ καὶ ἀναστήσεται ἄνθρωπος ἐξ Ἰσραηλ | ἀνατελεῖ ἄστρον ἐξ Ἰακὼβ καὶ ἡγούμενος ἐξ Ἰσραήλ | ἀνατελεῖ ἄστρον ἐξ Ἰακώβ |
| Is 11:1 LXX | *Dial.* 87:2 | |
| καὶ ἐξελεύσεται ῥάβδος ἐκ τῆς ῥίζης Ιεσσαι καὶ ἄνθος ἐκ τῆς ῥίζης ἀναβήσεται | καὶ ἐξελεύσεται ῥάβδος ἐκ τῆς ῥίζης Ιεσσαι καὶ ἄνθος ἀναβήσεται ἐκ τῆς ῥίζης Ἰεσσαί (vss. 2.3b = LXX) | καὶ ἄνθος ἀναβήσεται ἀπὸ τῆς ῥίζης Ἰεσσαί |
| Is 11:10 LXX | Is 51:5 LXX = *Dial.* 11:3 | |
| . . . ἐπ' αὐτῷ ἔθνη ἐλπιοῦσι . . . | . . . καὶ εἰς τὸν βραχίονά μου ἔθνη ἐλπιοῦσι . . . | καὶ ἐπὶ τὸν βραχίονα αὐτοῦ[71] ἔθνη ἐλπιοῦσιν |

---

69. In this I agree with Prigent, *Justin* p. 122.
70. Cf. Smit Sibinga, pp. 36f.
71. The Qumran Is⁴ scroll reads the 3rd person in Is 51:5b - possibly due to a Messianic interpretation of the verse: «My salvation has gone forth, and *his* arm will rule the peoples; in *him* the coastland trusts, and for *his* arm ( ‏יזרועו‎ ) they wait.» Cf. R. N. Longenecker, *The Christology of Early Jewish Christianity* (Studies in Biblical Theology, 2nd Ser. 17, London, 1970), pp. 99f.

The combined quotation in *1.Apol.* 32:12 has been one of the favourite examples adduced by proponents of the Testimony Book hypothesis,[72] and even a critic like Hommes admits that the existence of a testimony source yields the most satisfactory explanation of Justin's attribution of the whole text to Isaiah: The source probably contained a catena of texts, and Justin took the reference «Isaiah» - perhaps occurring after the two Isaiah texts - to cover more than was intended in the source.[73] In any case it is evident that Justin regarded this combined quotation as a single text, cf. his comments in *1.Apol.* 32:13f.

The quotation is very skilfully composed. Most commentators have failed to recognize the third component, viz. Is 51:5. Instead they give Is 11:10 as the reference.[74] In fact, Is 11:10 seems to have been the link within Is 11 which called the somewhat parallel text Is 51:5 (cf. synopsis) to the mind of the composer of the text:

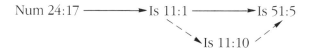

One hesitates in attributing such «concordantic» mastery of the Biblical text to Justin.

Turning to *Dial.* 106:4, we find another quotation of Num 24:17b, this time a fuller text, but again non-LXX. The variant reading ἡγούμενος (for LXX ἄνθρωπος, MT שבט ), is probably original in Justin, because Irenaeus has the same text: *orietur stella ex Iacob et surget dux in Israel (Adv.Haer.* III:9:2).[75] «A star shall rise out of Jacob, and a leader shall spring up from Israel» (*Dem.* 58). It is not impossible that Irenaeus copied his text from *Dial.* 106:4. (Cf. App.I, nr. 16). In any case, he confirms Justin's reading. (Several commentators have plausibly suspected an influence from Gen 49:10: οὐκ ἐκλείψει . . . ἡγούμενος . . .).[76] There seems to be no

72. Cf. esp. Harris, *Testimonies* I, pp. 10f/89; P. Beskow, *Rex Gloriae,* pp. 93f; P. Prigent, 'Quelques testimonia messianiques. Leurs histoire littéraire de Qoumrân aux Pères de l'église', *ThZ* 15 (1959), pp. 419-430, on Num 24:17 etc, pp. 426-428. Other important treatments of Justin's testimony include: Hommes, *Testimoniaboek,* pp. 107-114; J. Daniélou, 'L'étoile de Jacob et la mission chrétienne à Damas', VC 11 (1957, pp. 121-138), esp. pp. 124-127; *idem, Theology,* pp. 216-219; Smit Sibinga, pp. 49f/139.

73. This was proposed by Harris, I, p. 11, accepted by Hommes, p. 109. For a somewhat different explanation, cf. Prigent, 'Testimonia messianiques', p. 427, n. 20.

74. Pautigny and Goodspeed in their editions; the BP I; Rauschen in his translation; Prigent, 'Testimonia messianiques', p. 427. Smit Sibinga, p. 50, n. 2, recognizes an «influence» from Is 51:5. The correct reference is given by Hardy in his translation. Daniélou, *Gospel Message,* p. 212, refers to Is 42:4 - rather misleading.

75. A. Rousseau is certainly right in employing ἡγούμενος for *dux* in his Greek retroversion *ad loc.*

76. Cf. Smit Sibinga, p. 139. Hilgenfeld, 'Citate', adduces evidence from the Syriac Bible which corresponds to Justin's non-LXX reading, pp. 397f.

awareness of the Numeri context in *Dial.* 106:4: Justin attributes the prophecy to Moses, not Balaam. Hence, there is some probability in the assumption of a testimony source here also.

But there is a complicating factor. If Justin is quoting his source exactly both in *1.Apol.* 32 and *Dial.* 106, the source can hardly be the same in both cases. The inclusion of the second stichos of Num 24:17 would destroy the nice parallelism between the two stichoi from Num 24:17 and Is 11:1. So it was hardly ever present in the text quoted in *1.Apol.* 32:12. Are we straining the evidence when we conclude the possible existence of two testimony sources? We shall have to return to this suggestion on a broader basis below (p. 223, n. 85).

Turning to *Dial.* 87:2, we find Is 11:1-3 quoted in a pretty good LXX text. The only significant variants are in vs. 1, where Justin's text is somewhat smoother in its parallelism than the LXX (see synopsis). A look at the synopsis is sufficient to suggest the possibility that Justin in his rendering of vs. 1 is influenced from the «testimony» version in *1.Apol.* 32:12 - perhaps unconsciously. Apart from this, it seems likely that Justin is copying his Isaiah MS in *Dial.* 87:2.

The last element of the composite text, Is 51:5, is also encountered within a good LXX text in the *Dialogue*: *Dial.* 11:3 quotes Is 51:4f as a testimony on the new Law.

## (c) Deut 32:22 etc.[77]

| Deut 32:22a LXX<br>= *Dial.* 119:2 | *1. Apol.* 60:9 | 2 Kings 1:10 LXX<br>= 2 Kings 1:12 LXX |
|---|---|---|
| ὅτι πῦρ ἐκκέκαυται<br>ἐκ τοῦ θυμοῦ μου<br>καὶ[a] καυθήσεται<br>ἕως ᾅδου κάτω[b] | καταβήσεται<br>ἀείζωον πῦρ<br><br>καὶ καταφάγεται<br>μέχρι τῆς ἀβύσσου κάτω | καταβήσεται<br>πῦρ<br>ἐκ τοῦ οὐρανοῦ<br>καὶ καταφάγεται<br>σε . . . |
| a) = LXX codd. 54;59.<br>　　 LXX *rel.* om. καὶ<br>b) 　*Dial.* 119:2 om. κάτω | | Similar phrases occur<br>in. 2 Chron 7:1 and<br>2 Macc 2:10. Cf.<br>Smit Sibinga, p. 100. |

In *1.Apol.* 59f Justin seems to be following a tractate on borrowings from Moses in the philosophers, especially Plato. He quotes Gen 1:1-3 ( *1.Apol.* 59:2-4), relates Num 21:6-9 (the brazen serpent) with some *haggadic* embellishments (60:2-5), and finally quotes the text given above. This creates a nice tripartite sequence: Creation - Cross - Conflagration.

---

77. On this text in Justin, see esp. Smit Sibinga, pp.99f.

The text in *1.Apol.* 60:9 is introduced as a prophecy by Moses, which indeed is required by the context. But the text is much closer to 2 Kings 1:10 par. (see synopsis) than to the only relevant saying of Moses, Deut 32:22. Justin was familiar with some of the narratives in 2 Kings, but he has no formal quotations, and there is reason to doubt that he had the «concordantic» mastery of the Biblical text necessary to compose the harmonistic text in *1.Apol.* 60:9. Besides, the Plato quotations in *1.Apol.* 60 are also harmonistic.[78] And in *1.Apol.* 59:6 Justin says that «we know» (οἴδαμεν - he is handing on something received) that Moses spoke about Ἔρεβος before the poets. Probably this is a reference to the Hebrew ערב of Gen .1:4ff. If so, Justin was certainly not the one to detect this «correspondence». All this combine, I think, to give plausibility to Smit Sibinga's verdict: «It is unlikely that it (viz. the quotation in *1.Apol.* 60:9) ever occurred in a Bible text … it is more likely that Justin took it from the source which also provided him with the 'citations' from Plato in A 60.»[79] If this is right, it proves that we should not think of Justin's testimony sources as mere OT anthologies. In this case we have reason to suspect a tractate of some kind, which included Plato quotations as well.

Turning to *Dial.* 119:2 we find a LXX text of Deut 32:16-23.[80] But in this case it seems we should not look upon this long quotation as an expansion of the testimony text in the *Apology*, because a look at the context in *Dial.* 119 suggests that vs. 22 was not the text which prompted the quotation of vss. 16-23 in *Dial.* 119:2. One would rather seek the relevant »nucleus« in vs. 21b:»And I will make them jealous with a non-nation, with a nation that understandeth not will I make them angry.« If this is a correct assumption, there is every reason to think that Paul was Justin's guide to the Deut text in *Dial.* 119:2. Paul quotes Deut 32:21b in Rom 10:19,[81] and as we are going to see, Justin draws much quotation material from Rom 9-11. So it is rather Paul's testimony which has been expanded in *Dial.* 119:2.

(d) Is 1:7f/Jer 50:3b (see synopsis next page).

As one can easily glean from our synopsis, Justin in his allusions to Is 1:7f in *Dial.* 16:2; 52:4 and 108:2 has abandoned the non-LXX, combined testimony in *1.Apol.* 47:5, and is now alluding to the LXX text. On the general parallelism between *1.Apol.* 47-49; *Dial.* 16f and *Dial.* 108, see above, p. 31, and below, pp. 160f/182.

---

78. See C. Andresen, 'Justin und der mittlere Platonismus', *ZNW* 44 (1952/53, pp. 157-95), p. 189:»*Irrigerweise wird in den Textausgaben von Krüger und Goodspeed nur auf Tim. 36 B/C verwiesen. In Wirklichkeit hat Justin das Platonzitat aus Tim.36 B und 34 A/B kombiniert.*« The quotation of Plato, *Epist.* II 312 E in *1.Apol.* 60:9 is also somewhat free, cf. Hardy's note *ad loc.*

79. Smit Sibinga, p. 100.

80. There are only a few minor variants and one omission caused by oversight, cf. the detailed collations and comments in Credner, pp. 70-72 and Smit Sibinga, pp. 99/ 144f.

81. Substituting ὑμᾶς for LXX αὐτούς.

Is 1:7f/Jer 50:3b — SYNOPSIS

| Is 1:7f LXX | 1. Apol. 47:5 | Dial. 16:2 | Dial. 52:4 | Dial. 108:3 |
|---|---|---|---|---|
| vs. 7<br>ἡ γῆ ὑμῶν ἔρημος<br>αἱ πόλεις ὑμῶν<br>πυρίκαυστοι<br>τὴν χώραν ὑμῶν<br>ἐνώπιον ὑμῶν<br>ἀλλότριοι<br>κατεσθίουσιν αὐτὴν<br>καὶ ἠρήμωται<br>κατεστραμμένη<br>ὑπὸ λαῶν ἀλλοτρίων<br>vs. 8<br>ἐγκαταλειφθήσεται·<br>ἡ θυγάτηρ Σιων<br>ὡς σκηνὴ<br>ἐν ἀμπελῶνι<br>καὶ ὡς<br>ὀπωροφυλάκιον<br>ἐν σικυηράτῳ... | ἡ γῆ αὐτῶν ἔρημος<br><br>ἔμπροσθεν αὐτῶν<br>οἱ ἐχθροὶ αὐτῶν<br>αὐτὴν φάγονται | αἱ χῶραι ὑμῶν ἔρημοι<br>καὶ αἱ πόλεις<br>πυρίκαυστοι<br>καὶ τοὺς καρποὺς<br>ἐνώπιον ὑμῶν<br>κατεσθίουσιν ἀλλότριοι | ἡ γῆ ὑμῶν ἠρημώθη<br><br><br><br><br><br>καὶ ὡς<br>ὀπωροφυλάκιον<br>καταλέλειπται | ὑμῶν τῆς πόλεως<br>καὶ τῆς γῆς<br>ἐρημωθείσης.... |
| Jer 50:3b LXX<br>καὶ οὐκ ἔσται<br>ὁ κατοικῶν ἐν αὐτῇ<br>ἀπὸ ἀνθρώπου<br>καὶ ἕως κτήνους | καὶ οὐκ ἔσται<br>ἐξ αὐτῶν<br>ὁ κατοικῶν ἐν αὐτῇ | καὶ μηδεὶς<br>ἐξ ὑμῶν<br>ἐπιβαίνῃ<br>εἰς τὴν Ἰερουσαλὴμ | | |

(e) Is 1:11-15/Is 58:6f (see synopsis next page).

Justin quotes Is 1:11-15 in *1.Apol.* 37:5-8 in a very modified form. I have indicated in the margin of the synopsis that the many replacements within the text, and the addition of Is 58:6f at the end of it, serve to give the text a well-ordered structure. One can also observe how the composer of the text created telescoped sayings by combining different parts of the text according to the principle A + A'B = AB, or similar procedures. (We saw a similar procedure at work in the composition of Num 24:17/Is 11:1/Is 51:5 above).

A special nicety is involved in the combination of Is 1:11ff and Is 58:6f. Among the things condemned in Is 1:11ff is the μεγάλη ἡμέρα νηστείας (non-LXX text) - probably meant to refer to the Day of Atonement (cf. *Dial.* 40:4f; 46:2; 111:1; and see below, p. 179). νηστεία is also the central theme in Is 58:3ff.

Especially vss. 5f are worth quoting (LXX text): οὐ ταύτην τὴν νηστείαν ἐξελεξάμην καὶ ἡμέραν ταπεινοῦν ἄνθρωπον τὴν ψυχὴν αὐτοῦ οὐδ᾽ ἂν κάμψῃς ὥς κρίκον τὸν τράχηλόν σου καὶ σάκκον καὶ σποδὸν ὑποστρώσῃ οὐδ οὕτως καλέσετε νηστείαν δεκτήν οὐχὶ τοιαύτην νηστείαν ἐγὼ ἐξελεξάμην λέγει κύριος ἀλλὰ ... It is with this ἀλλὰ our composer begins his free quotation of Is 58 in *1.Apol.* 37 - the preceeding condemnation of the Jewish fast he thought sufficiently covered by the somewhat parallel saying in Is 1:13.

The well thought-out and careful composition of the text in *1.Apol.* 37 does not indicate a loose quotation from memory.[82] The preceeding quotation (Is 66:1) has the same anti-cultic content, so perhaps Justin is quoting from a source with anti-cultic testimonies.[83]

There is no other quotation of Is 1:11ff in Justin's writings,[84] but Is 58:6f recurs as a long LXX excerpt (Is 58:1-11) in *Dial.* 15:1-6. This text is LXX throughout,[85] with a few hebraizing readings.[86] It probably stems from Justin's «Jewish» Isaiah scroll - some possible later corruptions excepted. As we saw above, Justin is quoting from the Jewish Isaiah in *Dial.* 16f, and the long Isaiah quotations in *Dial.* 13-15 confirm that Justin had an Isaiah MS

82. As posited by Credner, p. 187.
83. So also Prigent, *Justin,* p. 250.
84. Two allusions may be noted: to vs. 13 in *Dial.* 13:1 (σεμιδάλεως προσφοραῖς); and to vs. 15 in *Dial.* 27:2 (πλήρεις τὰς χεῖρας αἵματος - the sequence of words here is closer to the deviant text in *1.Apol.* 37:5-8 than to the LXX text).
85. See the detailed collation in Credner pp. 170f and his comments pp. 226-228. Cf. also Bousset, *Evangeliencitate,* pp. 26f.
86. Vs. 4:᾽ Ἰδοὺ for LXX Εἰ; vs. 5: νηστείαν καὶ ἡμέραν δεκτὴν for LXX νηστείαν δεκτὴν; vs. 11: πηγὴ ὕδατος for LXX πηγή. In the two latter cases Justin accords with some LXX cursives. Bousset, *Evangeliencitate,* pp. 26f, takes these variants among the «Lucianic» readings which prove that the text of the Parisinus on this point is not original. But we now know that hebraizing, recensed texts existed prior to Lucian, and that the Lucianic text contains many old readings. (Cf. above).

before him when writing *Dial.* 13-17.[87] As I shall point out below (pp. 168f), there are good reasons to think that the anti-cultic source behind *1.Apol.* 37 is employed once more in *Dial.* 13-15. It thus seems we are right in regarding *Dial.* 15 as a widely expanded version of the Is 58:6f component in the combined testimony in *1.Apol.* 37. Justin's familiarity with this non-LXX version of the text is demonstrated in his passing allusion in *Dial.* 40:4.

| | *1. Apol.* 37:5—8 | | Is 1 LXX | |
|---|---|---|---|---|
| **Negative** Festivals | τὰς νουμηνίας ὑμῶν<br>καὶ τὰ σάββατα<br>μισεῖ ἡ ψυχή μου<br>καὶ μεγάλην ἡμέραν<br>νηστείας καὶ ἀργίαν<br>οὐκ ἀνέχομαι | vs. 13b | τὰς νουμηνίας ὑμῶν<br>καὶ τὰ σάββατα<br><br>καὶ ἡμέραν μεγάλην<br>οὐκ ἀνέχομαι<br>νηστείαν καὶ ἀργίαν | vs. 14a καὶ τὰς νουμ. υ.<br>καὶ τὰς ἑορτὰς ὑμῶν<br>μισεῖ ἡ ψυχή μου |
| Temple | οὐδ᾽ ἂν ἔρχησθε<br>ὀφθῆναί μοι<br>εἰσακούσομαι ὑμῶν<br>πλήρεις αἵματος<br>αἱ χεῖρες ὑμῶν | vs. 12a | οὐδ᾽ ἂν ἔρχησθε<br>ὀφθῆναί μοι . . . | vs. 15b καὶ ἐὰν πληθύνητε<br>τὴν δέησιν, οὐκ<br>εἰσακούσομαι ὑμῶν<br>αἱ γὰρ χεῖρες ὑμῶν<br>αἵματος πλήρεις |
| Sacrifices | κἂν φέρητε σεμίδαλιν<br>θυμίαμα<br>βδέλυγμά μοί ἐστι<br>στέαρ ἀρνῶν<br>καὶ αἷμα ταύρων<br>οὐ βούλομαι<br>τίς γὰρ ἐξεζήτησε<br>ταῦτα<br>ἐκ τῶν χειρῶν ὑμῶν | vs. 13a<br><br><br>vs. 11b<br><br>vs. 12b | ἐὰν φέρητε σεμίδαλιν μάταιον<br>θυμίαμα<br>βδέλυγμά μοί ἐστι<br>. . καὶ στέαρ ἀρνῶν<br>καὶ αἷμα ταύρων καὶ τράγων<br>οὐ βούλομαι<br>τίς γὰρ ἐξεζήτησε<br>ταῦτα<br>ἐκ τῶν χειρῶν ὑμῶν | |

| | | *Dial.* 15:4f = Is 58:6f LXX | |
|---|---|---|---|
| **Positive** | ἀλλὰ διάλυε<br>πάντα σύνδεσμον<br>ἀδικίας<br>διάσπα<br>στραγγαλιὰς βιαίων<br>συναλλαγμάτων<br>ἄστεγον καὶ γυμνὸν<br>σκέπε<br>διάθρυπτε πεινῶντι<br>τὸν ἄρτον σου | vs. 6 . . ἀλλὰ λῦε<br>πάντα σύνδεσμον<br>ἀδικίας<br>διάλυε<br>στραγγαλιὰς βιαίων<br>συναλλαγμάτων<br>vs. 7 διάθρυπτε πεινῶντι<br>τὸν ἄρτον σου<br>καὶ πτωχοὺς ἀστέγους<br>εἰσάγαγε[a] εἰς τὸν οἶκόν σου<br>ἐὰν ἴδης γυμνόν περίβαλε . . . | . . καὶ<br>πᾶσαν συγγραφὴν<br>ἄδικον<br>διάσπα |

*Dial.* 40:4
διασπῶντες στραγγαλιὰς βιαίων συναλλαγμάτων

a) So Justin and several LXX MSS. Ziegler:
εισαγε

---

87. As a matter of fact, the long quotations in *Dial.* 13-16 are from the same part of Isaiah: Is 52-58; and are quoted in an approximate Biblical sequence: Is 52:10-54:6; 55:3-13; 58:1-11; 57:1-4.

To conclude: In the cases studied so far, we have repeatedly observed that non-LXX texts which seem to be taken from testimony sources in the *Apology,* recur as longer, LXX quotations in the *Dialogue.*

## (f) Is 29:13f

| Mt 15:8f = Mk 7:6f | *Dial.* 27:4 | Is 29:13f LXX = *Dial.* 78:11 |
|---|---|---|
| "ὁ λαὸς οὗτος" τοῖς χείλεσίν με τιμᾷ ἡ δὲ καρδία αὐτῶν πόρρω ἀπέχει[b] ἀπ' ἐμοῦ μάτην δὲ σέβονται με διδάσκοντες διδασκαλίας ἐντάλματα ἀνθρώπων _| [*1. Clem.* 15:2][*2. Clem.* 3:5] _ [= *Dial.* 140:2 =] | τοῖς χείλεσιν αὐτὸν μόνον τιμῶντες τῇ δὲ καρδία πόρρω αὐτοῦ ὄντες ἰδίας διδασκαλίας ... διδάσκοντες | ἐγγίζει μοι ὁ λαὸς οὗτος τοῖς χείλεσιν αὐτῶν τιμῶσι με ἡ δὲ καρδία αὐτῶν πόρρω ἀπέχει ἀπ' ἐμοῦ μάτην δὲ σέβονταί με ἐντάλματα ἀνθρώπων καὶ διδασκαλίας διδάσκοντες[a] ... |
| a—a) Mk = *1. Clem:* οὗτος ὁ λαὸς b) *1. Clem.* = *2. Clem.:* ἄπεστιν | | (a) So *Dial.* 78:11. LXX transp. διδάσκοντες before ἐντάλματα |
| 1 Cor 1:19 | Is 29:14 LXX = *Dial.* 32:5 = *Dial.* 123:4 | |
| ἀπολῶ τὴν σοφίαν τῶν σοφῶν καὶ τὴν σύνεσιν τῶν συνετῶν ἀθετήσω | διὰ τοῦτο ἰδοὺ προσθήσω τοῦ μεταθεῖναι[a] τὸν λαὸν τοῦτον[b] καὶ μεταθήσω αὐτοὺς καὶ ἀπολῶ[c] τὴν σοφίαν τῶν σοφῶν καὶ τὴν σύνεσιν τῶν συνετῶν[d] κρύψω[e] | διὰ τοῦτο ἰδοὺ ἐγώ[b] προσθήσω τοῦ μεταθεῖναι[a] τὸν λαὸν τοῦτον καὶ μεταθήσω αὐτοὺς καὶ ἀπολῶ τὴν σοφίαν τῶν σοφῶν αὐτῶν τὴν δὲ σύνεσιν τῶν συνετῶν ἀθετήσω |
| | a) *Dial.* 123:4: μεταθῆναι b) *Dial.* 123:4: + λέγει κύριος c) *Dial.* 32:5: ἀφελῶ d) *Dial.* 32:5: + αὐτῶν e) *Dial.* 32:5 mg: ἀθετήσω | a) So *Dial.* 78:11 corr., from μεταθῆναι b) = several LXX MSS |

Concerning Is 29:13 in Justin, the following points should be made: The allusion in *Dial.* 140:2 presupposes Matthew's ( = Mark's) version of the text. One can suggest the same for the allusive quotation in *Dial.* 27:4, but the indications here are minimal. The allusions in *Dial.* 39:5 and 80:4 are too short or free to warrant any conclusion. It seems obvious that Justin in *Dial.* 78:11 is copying his Isaiah MS, i.e. he has looked the text of his «testimony source» (in this case Matthew) up in the relevant LXX book.

Concerning the two separate quotations of Is 29:14 in *Dial.* 32:5 and 123:4, one may speculate whether Paul's somewhat shorter quotation of Is

29:14b in 1 Cor 1:19 was Justin's guide to this verse. The evidence is hardly such as to warrant any safe conclusion. In any case it seems patent that Justin in both cases is copying the text from his Isaiah MS. His reading κρύψω in *Dial.* 32:5 and 123:4 agrees with the LXX against Paul. In *Dial.* 32:5 the Pauline ἀθετήσω is noted in the margin; this makes the same reading in *Dial.* 78:11 suspect as a scribal correction.[88] The various minor variants between the three *Dialogue* quotations of Is 29:14 are probably due to careless copying by later scribes. (Probably the non-LXX reading ἀφελῶ is original). The simplest assumption is thus that Justin in each case is copying from his Isaiah MS.


(g) Is 35:5f (synopsis next page).

My comments on this text can be summary, because there is a very extensive discussion of it in Prigent, *Justin,* pp. 165-69. I think Prigent's analysis for the most part is convincing.

Justin's text in *1.Apol.* 48:2 is a conflation of material from Is 35:6; Mt 11:5; and Is 26:19 (the reading ἀναστήσονται). The combined text produces a prophecy which announces (1) *healings* (Is 35:6/Mt 11:5) and (2) *raising of the dead* (Mt 11:5/Is 26:19). Justin has several allusions to this combination:

ᾧ δὲ λέγομεν    (1) χωλοὺς καὶ παραλυτικοὺς ... ὑγιεῖς πεποιηκέναι
                αὐτὸν
        καὶ (2) νεκροὺς ἀνεγεῖραι ... *(1. Apol.* 22:6)
προφητευθέντα (1) θεραπεύσειν αὐτὸν πᾶσαν νόσον
        καὶ (2) νεκροὺς ἀνεγερεῖν ... *(1. Apol.* 54:10)
... ὅταν δὲ τὸν Ἀσκληπιὸν νεκροὺς ἀνεγείραντα καὶ τὰ ἄλλα πάθη θεραπεύσαντα παραφέρῃ, οὐχὶ τὰς περὶ Χριστοῦ ὁμοίως προφητείας μεμιμῆσθαι ... *(Dial.* 69:3).


Especially the last allusion is interesting, because in *Dial.* 69 Justin has substituted the non-LXX text of *1.Apol.* 48 by a long LXX excerpt of Is 35:1-7. In the LXX text there is no mention of the raising of the dead. The comments after the quotation prove that the long LXX text is due to Justin himself. He is here excerpting his Isaiah MS.[89] It is all the more interesting that Justin in the context before and after the quotation seems to have the deviant text of *1.Apol.* 48 in mind also. Once again one can thus observe Justin's great familiarity with the text-form found in his testimony source.

---

88. In this I agree with Bousset, *Evangeliencitate,* p. 42.
89. Collation and comments on the text in Credner pp. 163f/208.

| Mt 11:5 (par. Lk 7:22) | 1. Apol. 48:2 | Is 35 LXX (= Dial. 69:5) | Iren. Adv. Haer. IV:33:11 |
|---|---|---|---|
| | τῇ παρουσίᾳ αὐτοῦ ἁλεῖται χωλὸς ὡς ἔλαφος καὶ τρανὴ ἔσται γλῶσσα μογιλάλων | vs.6: τότε ἁλεῖται ὡς ἔλαφος ὁ χωλός καὶ τρανὴ ἔσται γλῶσσα μογιλάλων... | adventu ejus quemadmodum cerbus claudus saliet et plana erit lingua mutorum |
| τυφλοὶ ἀναβλέπουσιν | τυφλοὶ ἀναβλέψουσι | vs.5: τότε ἀνοιχθήσονται ὀφθαλμοὶ τυφλῶν | et aperientur oculi caecorum |
| καὶ χωλοὶ περιπατοῦσιν | | καὶ ὦτα κωφῶν ἀκούσονται. | et aures surdorum audiunt |
| λεπροὶ καθαρίζονται | καὶ λεπροὶ καθαρισθήσονται | | et manus resolutae et genua debilia ⎤ = Is 35:3 |
| καὶ κωφοὶ ἀκούουσιν | | Is 26:19 | firmabuntur |
| καὶ νεκροὶ ἐγείρονται | καὶ νεκροὶ ἀναστήσονται | ἀναστήσονται οἱ νεκροί καὶ ἐγερθήσονται | et resurgent |
| καὶ πτωχοὶ εὐαγγελίζονται | καὶ περιπατήσουσιν | οἱ ἐν τοῖς μνημείοις... | qui in monumentis sunt mortui |
| | | Mt 8:17 αὐτὸς τὰς ἀσθενείας ἡμῶν ἔλαβεν καὶ τὰς νόσους ἐβάστασεν | et ipse infirmitates nostras accipiet et langores portabit |
| | | a) Dial. 69:5 om. ὁ | On Irenaeus' text, cf. Appendix I, nr. 29. |

(h) Is 42:1-4 (synopsis next page).

Justin quotes this text twice, with a different text in each case. The text in *Dial.* 123:8 is mixed. It is LXX in vs. 1a and vss. 3b-4, while it goes with Mt 12:18b-20a in vss. 1b-3a.[90] The LXX text in vs. 1a is certainly original, because only this text contains the terms 'Jacob' and 'Israel', and it is to explain that Christ is called both Jacob and Israel that Justin quotes the text at all, *Dial.* 123: 8f.[91] If a corrector has been at work in this text, he should rather be held responsible for the introduction of the Matthean peculiarities[92] - i.e. he has made a LXX text non-LXX. This is not the role commonly ascribed to the supposed corrector.

We have seen elsewhere that some of Justin's «testimony» texts have incorporated phrases from Matthew (and we shall see more examples later). I therefore tend to believe that the text in *Dial.* 123 in its present form is taken from a testimony source, although this cannot be proven conclusively.[93]

The text in *Dial.* 135:2 is LXX throughout, but with several variants which betray contamination from Mt 12:18-21. The remarkable reading in vs. 3b, ἕως οὗ νῖκος ἐξοίσει κρίσιν, looks like a shortening conflation of LXX and Mt 12:20b. (It should be noted that at this point the text in *Dial.* 123:8 is purely LXX). The several contaminations of the text must stem from a scribe who had Mt 12:18-21 fresh in his mind while he was copying the LXX. It could be Justin himself[94] (there is a cluster of long Isaiah quotations in *Dial.* 133-135).

To conclude: Justin may be working with a testimony source in *Dial.* 123:8,[95] turning directly to the Isaiah LXX in *Dial.* 135:2 — the Matthean contaminations stemming from Justin or a later scribe.

---

90. Apart from some minor variants between Mt and Justin, there is one markedly septuagintal element in Justin's parallel text: In vs. 1b he reads with the LXX ἐξοίσει for Mt's ἀπαγγελεῖ. This may be a contamination from the LXX text in the course of scribal transmission. But the contamination could also stem from Justin or even his source. ἐξοίσει recurs in vs. 3b in a similar context - this perhaps influenced the reading in vs. 1b, and may have done so at a very early stage of the text's transmission.

91. This is well observed by Hilgenfeld, p. 571.

92. This is the position of Bousset, *Evangeliencitate,* pp. 39f.

93. Hilgenfeld, loc. cit., surmises a common source behind Mt and Justin. On *a priori* reasons, I should think an intermediary source is far more likely.

94. Bousset, pp. 39f, thinks that Justin faithfully copied his LXX, while the Matthean elements were introduced by a later scribe. Bousset apparently finds it incredible that Justin should have done what, according to Bousset, a later scribe did. Why? Prigent says that the text in *Dial.* 135 has been corrected according to the LXX (p. 298). I tend to agree, and would not exclude the possibility that the corrector is Justin himself.

95. There are indications of this in the context also, but to this we shall return in due course. Cf. Prigent, *Justin,* p. 298.

## Is 42:1-4

| *Dial.* 135:2 = Is 42:1—4 LXX | *Dial.* 123:8 | Mt 12:18—21 |
|---|---|---|
| 1. Ἰακὼβ ὁ παῖς μου<br>ἀντιλήψομαι αὐτοῦ<br>καὶ[a]Ἰσραὴλ ὁ ἐκλεκτός μου<br>προσδέξεται[b] αὐτὸν<br>ἡ ψυχή μου<br>δέδωκα[c] τὸ πνεῦμα μου<br>ἐπ' αὐτόν<br>καὶ[d] κρίσιν τοῖς ἔθνεσιν<br>ἐξοίσει | Ἰακὼβ ὁ παῖς μου<br>ἀντιλήψομαι αὐτοῦ<br>Ἰσραὴλ ἐκλεκτοῦ μου<br><br><br>θήσω τὸ πνεῦμά μου<br>ἐπ' αὐτόν<br>καὶ κρίσιν τοῖς ἔθνεσιν<br>ἐξοίσει<br>οὐκ ἐρίσει | Ἰδοὺ ὁ παῖς μου<br>ὃν ᾑρέτισα<br>ὁ ἀγαπητός μου<br>εἰς ὃν εὐδόκησεν<br>ἡ ψυχή μου<br>θήσω τὸ πνεῦμά μου<br>ἐπ' αὐτόν<br>καὶ κρίσιν τοῖς ἔθνεσιν<br>ἀπαγγελεῖ<br>οὐκ ἐρίσει |
| 2. οὐ κεκράξεται[e]<br>οὐδὲ ἀκουσθήσεται<br>ἔξω<br>ἡ φωνὴ αὐτοῦ<br>3. κάλαμον τεθραυσμένον[f]<br>οὐ συντρίψει<br>καὶ λίνον[g] τυφόμενον[h]<br>οὐ σβέσει<br>[i]ἕως οὗ νῖκος[i]<br>ἐξοίσει κρίσιν<br>4. ἀναλήψει[j]<br>καὶ οὐ θραυσθήσεται<br>ἕως ἂν θῇ<br>ἐπὶ τῆς γῆς κρίσιν<br>καὶ ἐπὶ τῷ ὀνόματι αὐτοῦ<br>ἐλπιοῦσιν ἔθνη[k] | οὔτε κράξει<br>οὔτε ἀκούσεταί τις<br>ἐν ταῖς πλατείαις<br>τὴν φωνὴν αὐτοῦ<br>κάλαμον συντετριμμένον<br>οὐ κατεάξει<br>καὶ λίνον τυφόμενον<br>οὐ μὴ σβέσει<br>ἀλλὰ εἰς ἀλήθειαν<br>ἐξοίσει κρίσιν<br>ἀναλήψει<br>καὶ οὐ μὴ θραυσθήσεται<br>ἕως ἂν θῇ<br>ἐπὶ τῆς γῆς κρίσιν<br>καὶ ἐπὶ τῷ ὀνόματι αὐτοῦ<br>ἐλπιοῦσιν ἔθνη | οὐδὲ κραυγάσει<br>οὐδὲ ἀκούσει τις<br>ἐν ταῖς πλατείαις<br>τὴν φωνὴν αὐτοῦ<br>κάλαμον συντετριμμένον<br>οὐ κατεάξει<br>καὶ λίνον τυφόμενον<br>οὐ σβέσει<br>ἕως ἂν ἐκβάλῃ εἰς νῖκος<br>τὴν κρίσιν<br><br><br><br><br>καὶ τῷ ὀνόματι αὐτοῦ<br>ἔθνη ἐλπιοῦσιν |

a) LXX om. καὶ
b) LXX: προσεδέξατο
c) LXX: ἔδωκα, but LXX 87; 97; 228 = *Dial.* 135:2
d) LXX om. καὶ, but present in Bo.
e) LXX add.: οὐδὲ ἀνήδει.
f) So LXX 93; 410; 958. Most LXX MSS (= Ziegler) : τεθλασμένον.
g) Dial. 135:2 *man. prim.:* λίθον, *corr.:* λίνον.
h) LXX: καπνιζόμενον
i-i) LXX: ἀλλὰ εἰς ἀλήθειαν = *Dial.* 123:8.
j) = LXX 88; 407. Most LXX MSS (= Ziegler): ἀναλάμψει
k) LXX transp. = MT.

(i) Is 42: 6f

| Dial. 26:2 = Dial. 65:4<br>= Is 42:6f LXX<br>= Barn. 14:7 | Dial. 122:3 |
| --- | --- |
| ἐγὼ κύριος ὁ θεὸς<sup>a</sup> | ἐγὼ κύριος |
| ἐκάλεσά σε δικαιοσύνη | ἐκάλεσά σε τῇ δικαιοσύνῃ |
| καὶ κρατήσω τῆς χειρός σου | καὶ κρατήσω τῆς χειρός σου |
| καὶ ἐνισχύσω<sup>b</sup>σε | καὶ ἰσχύσω σε |
| καὶ<sup>c</sup> ἔδωκά σε | καὶ θήσω σε |
| εἰς διαθήκην γένους | εἰς διαθήκην γένους |
| εἰς φῶς ἐθνῶν | εἰς φῶς ἐθνῶν |
| ἀνοῖξαι ὀφθαλμοὺς τυφλῶν | ἀνοῖξαι ὀφθαλμοὺς τυφλῶν |
| ἐξαγαγεῖν<sup>d</sup> ἐκ δεσμῶν | ἐξαγαγεῖν ἐκ δεσμῶν |
| δεδεμένους<sup>e</sup> | πεπεδημένους |
| καὶ ἐξ οἴκου φυλακῆς | |
| καθημένους ἐν σκότει | |

a) *Barn.* + σου
b) *Dial.* 26:2 = *Dial.* 65:4 = *Barn.* 14:7: ἰσχύσω
c) = MT and several LXX MSS. Ziegler om.
d) *Barn.* 14:7 prefixes καὶ
e) *Dial.* 26:2 = *Dial.* 65:4 = *Barn.* 14:7: πεπεδημένους

The LXX text in *Dial.* 26:2 may be copied from the LXX text in *Barn.* 14:7 (same excerpt). Some of *Barnabas'* variants are not shared by Justin, however. And in *Dial.* 65:4 the same LXX text of Is 42:6-7 occurs within a longer LXX excerpt: Is 42:5-13. This makes it almost certain that Justin in *Dial.* 26 also is copying his Isaiah MS, and that the peculiar reading πεπεδημένους may have been contained in it, if this is not a contamination from the partly non-LXX text in *Dial.* 122:3. In the latter case I suspect a testimony source, because the quotation is preceeded by a citation of Is 49:6 (*Dial.* 121:4, non-LXX), and the reading θήσω σε in Is 42:6 can be explained as contamination from Is 49:6: τέθεικα σε. This contamination is more easily explained if the two texts occured together in a testimony source.

It thus seems we shall have to posit a testimony source parallel to *Barnabas*.

(j) Is 53:12

Justin has several quotations from and allusions to verses or phrases from Is. 53, but there is only one instance where one has reason to suspect a non-LXX text as his source. In *1.Apol.* 50:3-11 Justin quotes Is 52:13 -- 53:8 in a LXX text. But this text is prefixed by a non-LXX version of Is 53:12 in *1.Apol.* 50:2. It is treated as if it were an integral part of the following text. There is a striking affinity with Lk 22:37. In *1.Apol.* 51:5 Is 53:12 recurs in a LXX text (within the longer LXX excerpt Is 53:8-12 in *1.Apol.* 51:1-5).

| 1. Apol. 51:5 = Is 53:12 LXX | 1. Apol. 50:2 | Lk 22:37 |
|---|---|---|
| διὰ τοῦτο αὐτὸς κληρονομήσει πολλοὺς καὶ τῶν ἰσχυρῶν μεριεῖ σκῦλα ἀνθ ὧν παρεδόθη εἰς θάνατον ἡ ψυχὴ αὐτοῦ καὶ ἐν τοῖς ἀνόμοις ἐλογίσθη καὶ αὐτὸς ἁμαρτίας πολλῶν ἀνήνεγκε καὶ διὰ τὰς ἀνομίας αὐτῶν αὐτὸςᵃ παρεδόθη | ἀνθ ὧν παρέδωκαν εἰς θάνατον τὴν ψθχὴν αὐτοῦ καὶ μετὰ τῶν ἀνόμων ἐλογίσθη αὐτὸς ἁμαρτίας πολλῶν εἴληφε καὶ τοῖς ἀνόμοις ἐξιλάσεται | καὶ μετὰ ἀνόμων ἐλογίσθη |

a) Om. Ziegler.

Justin's deviant version of Is 53:12 reveals itself as a Christian reworking of the LXX text by more than one token. First, there is the parallel to Lk 22:37, which hardly is accidental. Probably Luke's version was worked into the new text. Secondly, the passive construction of the LXX; «His soul was delivered . . .», is changed to the active: «They delivered his soul». «They» is probably to be taken as a reference to the Jews. The introduction of ἐξιλάσκειν - in itself a perfect rendering of MT יפגיע [96] - serves to emphasize the idea of expiatory suffering.

I suspect we have to do with a Christian version of Is 53:12 which Justin found in a testimony source, [97] and which he prefixed to the long quotation as a fitting summary of the whole Isaiah chapter. [98]

## (k) Is 55:3-5

Justin cites this text twice, in Dial. 12:1 (non-LXX) and Dial. 14:4-7 (as part of the long LXX text Is 55:3-13).

---

96. This is pointed out by Katz, 'Justin's Old Testament quotations and the Greek Dodekaprop-heton Scroll', Studia Patristica I (TU 63, Berlin 1957, pp. 343-53), p. 348.

97. ἐξιλάσκειν is a hapax leg. in Justin - it did not belong to his vocabulary and is thus hardly his own modification of the text, cf. also the recourse to the Hebrew text.

98. Cf. Hilgenfeld's remark, p. 433: «Fast möchte man glauben, er habe anfangs nur diesen Vers anführen wollen, sodann sich aber entschlossen, den ganzen Abschnitt vollständig und genauer abzuschreiben.»

| *Dial.* 14:4 = Is 55:3—5 LXX | *Dial.* 12:1 |
|---|---|
| vs. 3 . . . εἰσακούσετέ[a] μου<br>καὶ ζήσεται[b] ἡ ψυχὴ ὑμῶν<br>καὶ διαθήσομαι ὑμῖν<br>διαθήκην αἰώνιον<br>τὰ ὅσια τοῦ[c] Δαυεὶδ<br>τὰ πιστά<br>vs. 4 ἰδοῦ μαρτύριον[d] αὐτὸν<br>ἔθνεσι δέσωκα[d]<br>ἄρχοντα καὶ προστάσσοντα<br>ἔθνεσιν<br>vs. 5 ἔθνη ἃ οὐκ οἴδασί[e] σε<br>ἐπικαλέσονταί σε<br>καὶ λαοί οἳ οὐκ<br>ἐπίστανταί σε<br>ἐπὶ σὲ καταφεύξονται<br>ἕνεκεν τοῦ θεοῦ σου . . . | ἀκούσατέ[a] μου τοὺς λόγους<br>καὶ ζήσεται ἡ ψυχὴ ὑμῶν<br>καὶ διαθήσομαι ὑμῖν<br>διαθήκην αἰώνιον<br>τὰ ὅσια Δαυεὶδ<br>τὰ πιστά<br>ἰδοῦ μάρτυρα[b] αὐτὸν<br>ἔθνεσι δέδωκα<br><br><br>ἔθνη ἃ οὐκ οἴδασί σε<br>ἐπικαλέσονταί σε<br>λαοί οἳ οὐκ<br>ἐπίστανταί σε<br>καταφεύξονται ἐπὶ σέ<br>ἕνεκεν τοῦ θεοῦ σου . . . |
| a) = S* and others. Ziegler:<br>   ἐπακούσατέ.<br>b) LXX + ἐν ἀγαθοῖς, but under<br>   *obelus* in several MSS, and<br>   om. V = MT.<br>c) Om. LXX.<br>d—d) = S. Ziegler: ἐν ἔθνεσι<br>   δέδωκα αὐτόν. The om. of ἐν goes with MT<br>e) = S and several other MSS.<br>   Ziegler: ἤδεισάν. | a) = LXX MS 62<br>b) = Aquila and Symmachus. |

As one can see from the apparatus appended to the synopsis, both texts exhibit some hebraizing features, mostly so the text in *Dial.* 12. The difference between the texts may be due to careless copying, so I shall not insist on the existence of a testimony source in this case. Yet the coincidence with Aquila and Symmachus in the reading μάρτυρα in *Dial.* 12:1 is striking. And the hebraizing features in both texts gain importance when we observe that in *Dial.* 14:5-7 the rest of the long Isaiah quotation is good LXX text. I think there is much to be said for Prigent's comment: The text in *Dial.* 12:1 derives from a source other than an Isaiah scroll, «*quant à la seconde* (i.e. *Dial.* 14), *il la copie assurément dans un exemplaire grec d'Isaie. Il faut insister, ici il est parfaitement clair qu'il faut exclure l'intervention d'un scribe correcteur, dont le zéle se serait éveillé subitement entre les chapitres 12 et 14 du Dialogue! C'est evidemment Justin lui-même qui intervient pour retoucher et ajouter à un développement qui est pour lui un donné.*»[99] I should like like to add: Some of the hebraisms in vss. 3-5 in *Dial.* 14 - that is: the part of the text overlapping the text in *Dial.* 12 - may well be Justin's own unconscious contaminations from the «testimony» text in *Dial.* 12.

---

99. *Justin,* p. 240.

(1) Is 65:1-3 etc. (synopsis next page).

The quite complex textual evidence displayed in the synopsis is not easily explained. Credner feels sure that Justin is copying his Isaiah MS in *Dial.* 24:4, and aptly supports this surmise by the observation that there is a cluster of long Isaiah quotations in *Dial.* 24-27.[100] Credner further regards the quotations in the *Apology* as free quotations from memory. But he is so impressed by the differences between the texts there and in the *Dial.*, that he concludes that *«Justin den Text seinem Gedächtniss nach einer anderen Handschrift eingeprägt hatte, als die bei der Abfassung des Dialogs benutzte war.»*[101] This is a possible explanation, but in this case one should also reckon with the possibility of casual scribal corrections of one of the two long texts (*1.Apol.* 49:2-4 and *Dial.* 24:4) - or perhaps in both. The only allusion to the text, *Dial.* 119:4 - which should be exempt from the suspicion of scribal correction - goes with *Dial.* 24:4 in the reading ἐπεκαλέσαντο (majority of LXX MSS: ἐκάλεσαν), but with *1.Apol.* 49:2-4 in the readings ἐπερωτῶσιν; τῷ ἔθνει; τὸ ὄνομά μου. So perhaps we should not think of any systematic correction of either of the two long texts - both may preserve Justinian readings, and both may contain casual scribal modifications, perhaps most so in *Dial.* 24.

Let us take a closer look at the text in *1.Apol.* 49:2-4. A most striking non-LXX feature of this text is the omission of the words ὅλην τὴν ἡμέραν. Decidedly non-LXX is also the phrase ἐπὶ τοὺς πορευομένους ἐν ὁδῷ οὐ καλῇ. There can be no doubt about the authenticity of these textual features, because they occur twice more, in *1.Apol.* 38:1 (quoting Is 65:2 only) and in the combined quotation in *1.Apol.* 35:3f (Is 65:2/Is 58:2b). If the text in *1.Apol.* 49:2-4 was «doctored» by a later scribe, at least vs. 2 seems to have been left intact - the one verse most in need of doctoring! So the whole text was probably not doctored much. How shall we explain these non-LXX readings in vs. 2? A glance at the synopsis is sufficient to suggest that the text in *1.Apol.* 49 is a mixed one: Outside vs. 2 it generally goes with the LXX, but in vs. 2 it follows the «testimony» text of *1.Apol.* 35:3f and *1.Apol.* 38:1 (also *Dial.* 114:2).

I suggest the following over-all explanation: In *1.Apol.* 35:3f Justin is quoting a modified and combined Isaiah text from a testimony source. He repeats part of the same text in *1.Apol.* 38:1 and *Dial.* 114:2. In *1.Apol.* 49:2-4 he has looked up the text in an Isaiah MS. He keeps the testimony version of vs. 2, but expands the quotation with LXX text in vss. 1 and 3. In *Dial.* 24 he has abandoned the testimony source altogether and quotes directly from an

---

100. Credner p. 234. He also correctly notes that again all the quotations are from the same part of Isaiah. The sequence is: Is 65:1-3; 63:15-64:12; Is 42:6f; Is 62:10-63:6; 58:13f.
101. *Ibid.*

| Dial. 24:4 = Is 65:1—3a LXX | 1. Apol. 49:2—4 | Dial. 119:4 | Rom 10:20f |
|---|---|---|---|
| 1. ἐμφανὴς (γαρ) ἐγενήθην^a) τοῖς ἐμὲ μὴ ζητοῦσιν^b) εὑρέθην τοῖς ἐμὲ μὴ ἐπερωτῶσι^b εἶπα^c) ἰδού εἰμι ἔθνεσιν^d) οἳ οὐκ ἐπεκαλέσαντό^e) μου τὸ ὄνομα^f) <br>    = Dial. 97:2 | ἐμφανὴς ἐγενήθην τοῖς ἐμὲ μὴ ἐπερωτῶσιν εὑρέθη τοῖς ἐμὲ μὴ ζητοῦσι εἶπον ἰδού εἰμι ἔθνη οἳ οὐκ ἐκάλεσαν τὸ ὄνομά μου ἐξεπέτασα τὰς χεῖράς μου | ἐμφανὴς ἐγενήθη τοῖς μὴ ἐπερωτῶσιν αὐτόν <br><br> ἰδοὺ θεός εἰμι φησὶ τῷ ἔθνει οἳ οὐκ ἐπεκαλέσαντο τὸ ὄνομά μου <br> 1. Apol. 35:3f | εὑρέθην (ἐν) τοῖς ἐμὲ μὴ ζητοῦσιν ἐμφανὴς ἐγενόμην τοῖς ἐμὲ μὴ ἐπερωτῶσιν |
| 2. ἐξεπέτασα τὰς χεῖράς μου^g) ^h)ὅλην τὴν ἡμέραν^h) ἐπὶ λαὸν ἀπειθοῦντα καὶ ἀντιλέγοντα ^j)τοῖς πορευομένοις ὁδῷ οὐ καλῇ^j) ἀλλὰ ὀπίσω τῶν ἁμαρτιῶν αὐτῶν 3. λαὸς^k)ὁ παροξύνων με ἐναντίον μου.... | ἐπὶ λαὸν ἀπειθοῦντα καὶ ἀντιλέγοντα ἐπὶ τοὺς πορευομένους ὁδῷ οὐ καλῇ ἀλλ' ὀπίσω τῶν ἁμαρτιῶν αὐτῶν ὁ λαὸς ὁ παροξύνων με ἐναντίον μου | ἐγὼ ἐξεπέτασα τὰς χεῖράς μου ἐπὶ λαὸν ἀπειθοῦντα καὶ ἀντιλέγοντα ἐπὶ τοὺς πορευομένους ἐν ὁδῷ οὐ καλῇ αἰτοῦσί με νῦν κρίσιν καὶ ἐγγίζειν θεῷ τολμῶσιν <br>   = 1. Apol. 38:1 <br>   = Dial 114:2 | ὅλην τὴν ἡμέραν ἐξεπέτασα τὰς χεῖράς μου πρὸς λαὸν ἀπειθοῦντα καὶ ἀντιλέγοντα <br> Dial. 15:3 = Is 58:2bLXX <br> αἰτοῦσί με νῦν κρίσιν δικαίαν καὶ ἐγγίζειν θεῷ ἐπιθυμοῦσι |

a) = S' and other MSS. Ziegler: ἐγενόμην

b)-b) ζητοῦσιν and ἐπερωτῶσιν are transposed by several LXX MSS = MT

c) S and others: εἶπον

d) LXX: τῷ ἔθνει

e) = MSS 377,564,565. LXX: ἐκάλεσαν

f) Some LXX MSS (= Ziegler): τὸ ὄνομά μου

g) Dial. 97:2: μου τὰς χεῖρας

h)-h) Om. Dial. 97:2.

i) = Lucianic MSS. Ziegler: πρός

j)-j) = S, Hexaplaric and Lucianic MSS. Ziegler:
   οἳ οὐκ ἐπορεύθησαν ὁδῷ ἀληθινῇ. Dial. 97:2 reads
   πονηρευομένους — an obvious corruption.

k) LXX: ὁ λαὸς οὗτος. Om. οὗτος 407 = MT.

Isaiah MS - not necessarily the same as in *1.Apol.* 49. The genuineness of the text in *Dial.* 24:4 is supported by the partial doublet in *Dial.* 97:2.

This is the picture which somehow emerges, I think, even if one allows for a certain measure of scribal interference.

(m) Is 65:22.

| MT | *Dial.* 81:3 | Is 65:22LXX = *Dial.* 81:2 |
|---|---|---|
| כִּי כִימֵי<br>הָעֵץ<br>יְמֵי<br>עַמִּי | κατὰ γὰρ τὰς ἡμέρας<br>τοῦ ξύλου<br>αἱ ἡμέραι<br>τοῦ λαοῦ μου ἔσονται... | .. κατὰ γὰρ τὰς<sup>a</sup> ἡμέρας<br>τοῦ ξύλου τῆς ζωῆς<br>αἱ ἡμέραι<br>τοῦ λαοῦ μου ἔσονται...<br>a) *Dial.* 81:2: τῆς -<br>scribal error? |

In *Dial.* 81:1f Justin has a long LXX excerpt of Is 65:17-25. The testimony nucleus is to be found in vs. 22, as his subsequent remarks show. Now, while the LXX excerpt reads κατὰ γὰρ τὰς ἡμέρας τοῦ ξύλου *τῆς ζωῆς* αἱ ἡμέραι τοῦ λαοῦ μου . . ., Justin in his subsequent repetition of this phrase omits τῆς ζωῆς, *Dial.* 81:3. One would assume that this was a deliberate omission, since for him the «tree» in Is 65:22 is not the tree of life, but the tree of knowledge. But then it deserves notice that Justin's reading in *Dial.* 81:3 agrees perfectly with the MT. And how could Justin ever have arrived at his exegesis if the LXX text was his point of departure?

One should therefore consider the possibility that Justin's reading in *Dial.* 81:3 preserves the text of his testimony source, which had recourse to the Hebrew text, and - unlike the LXX - took the tree to be the tree *of knowledge.* Justin is dependent on this in his own exegesis, although he uses the LXX text in *Dial.* 81:1f.[102] Justin's remark in *Dial.* 81:3 (τὸ οὖν εἰρημένον ἐν τοῖς λόγιος τούτοις, ἔφην κατὰ τὰς ἡμέρας . . .) proves that he himself had a long quotation in *Dial.* 81:1f, and although some amount of scribal interference cannot be excluded, the analogy in similar cases points to an essential authencity of the long text. Justin may not have noticed that the LXX text excluded his exegesis, or he may have chosen to ignore it. In any case, he sticks to the «testimony» text in his exegesis.

(n) Is 66:24; Ezek 14:14/20 etc.; Is 1:9.[103] (synopsis next page).

We start our examination of this cluster of testimonies with a closer look at *Dial.* 140:3. According to his own introduction *Dial.* 140:2, Justin is here going to enumerate Scriptural testimonies proving that the merits of the fathers - or membership in a certain people - are of no avail when it comes

---

102. As far as I am aware, no-one has so far noticed this discrepancy between the text of the long LXX excerpt and Justin's exegesis in *Dial.* 81 - not even Prigent, who argues that Justin in *Dial.* 81 depends on the *Syntagma (Justin*, pp. 22-24).

103. On this cluster of testimonies, cf. esp. Prigent, *Justin* pp. 311-318.

| Is 1:9 LXX = Rom. 9:29 | Dial. 140:3 = 1. Apol. 53:7 |
|---|---|
| καὶᵃ εἰ μὴ κύριος σαβαωθ ἐγκατέλιπεν ἡμίν σπέρμα ὡς Σοδομα ἂν ἐγενήθημεν καὶ ὡς Γομορρα ἂν ὡμοιώθημεν | καὶᵃ εἰ μὴ κύριος σαβαωθᵇ ἐγκατέλιπεν ἡμῖν σπέρμα ὡς Σοδομα ἂνᶜ καὶ Γομορρα ἐγενήθημεν |
| a) Om. Rom. 9:29 | a) Om. 1. Apol. 53:7<br>b) Om. 1. Apol. 53:7<br>c) 1. Apol. 53:7 reads ἂν after Γομορρα |

| Ezek 14:20 | Dial. 140:3 | Dial. 45:3 | 2. Clem. 6:8 |
|---|---|---|---|
| καὶ Νωε καὶ Δανιηλ καὶ Ιωβ ἐν μέσῳ αὐτῆς, ζῶ ἐγώ, λέγει κύριος, ἐὰν υἱοὶ ἢ θυγατέρες ὑπολειφθῶσιν ... | κἂνᵈ Νωε καὶ Ιακωβ̅ καὶ Δανιηλ <br><br> ἐξαιτήσωνται υἱούςᵇ ἢ θυγατέρας | κἂν Νωε καὶ Δανιηλ καὶ Ιακωβ <br><br> ἐξαιτήσωνται υἱοὺς καὶ θυγατέρας | ἐὰν ἀναστῇ Νῶε καὶ Ιωβ καὶ Δανιήλ |
| Ezek 14:18 | | | |
| ... οὐ μὴ ῥύσωνται υἱοὺς οὐδὲ θυγατέρας ... | οὐ μὴ δοθῇᶜ αὐτοῖς̅ | οὐ δοθήσεται αὐτοῖς | οὐ ῥύσονται τὰ τέκνα αὐτῶν ἐν τῇ αἰχμαλωσία |
| Dt 24:16 | | | |
| οὐκ ἀποθανοῦνται πατέρες ὑπὲρ τέκνων καὶ υἱοὶ οὐκ ἀποθανοῦνται ὑπὲρ πατέρων ἕκαστος ἐν τῇ ἑαυτοῦ ἁμαρτίᾳ ἀποθανεῖται | ἀλλ οὔτε πατὴρ ὑπὲρ υἱοῦ οὔτε υἱὸς ὑπὲρ πατρός· ἀλλ ἕκαστος τῇ ἁμαρτία αὐτοῦ ἀπολεῖται | ἀλλ ἕκαστος τῇ | |
| Ezek 14:14 | | | |
| ... αὐτοὶ ἐν τῇ δικαιοσύνῃ αὐτῶν σωθήσονται ... | καὶ ἕκαστος τῇ ἑαυτοῦ δικαιοπραξία σωθήσεται | αὐτοῦ δικαιοσύνη ... σωθήσεται | |

= Dial. 44:2

a) Dial. 44:2: ἐὰν
b) Dial. 44:2 prom. ἢ
c) Dial. 44:2: δοθήσεται

| Dial. 44:3 = Is 66:24 LXX | Dial. 140:3 |
|---|---|
| καὶ ἐξελεύσονται καὶ ὄψονται τὰ κῶλα ᵃτῶν παραβεβηκότων ἀνθρώπωνᵃ ὁ γὰρᵇ σκώληξ αὐτῶν οὐ τελευτήσει καὶ τὸ πῦρ αὐτῶν οὐ σβεσθήσεται καὶ ἔσονται εἰς ὅρασιν πάσῃ σαρκί | ὄψονται τὰ κῶλα τῶν παραβεβηκότων ὁ σκώληξ αὐτῶν οὐ παύσεταιᵃ καὶ τὸ πῦρ αὐτῶν οὐ σβεσθήσεται καὶ ἔσονται εἰς ὅρασιν πάσῃ σαρκί |
| a-a) LXX: τῶν ἀνθρώπων τῶν παραβεβηκότων ἐν εμοί<br>b) 2. Clem. om. γὰρ | a) 1. Apol. 52:8: παυθήσεται |

= 2. Clem. 7:6
= 17:5

= 1. Apol. 52:8

= Dial. 44:2

to the question of salvation. Then three texts follow, introduced as «Isaiah», «Ezekiel», «and again Isaiah». None of the three texts agree with the LXX. Especially the Ezekiel quotation is very deviant, and besides composite. Obviously this text does not derive from an Ezekiel MS.

This points to a testimony source, and two other passages in Justin, *1.Apol.* 52f and *Dial.* 44f, seem to depend on the same source. The most conspicuous variants in the quotations in *Dial.* 140:3 recur in these other passages. *Dial.* 44f is especially interesting. In *Dial.* 44:2 Ezek 14:20/18 is quoted in the same non-LXX text which recurs in *Dial.* 140:3, but without the added components from Dt 24:16 and Ezek 14:14. However, in his repetitive paraphrase of the text in *Dial.* 45:3, Justin obviously alludes to the *whole* non-LXX text, a text not yet quoted, but given in full 95 chapters later! This proves beyond doubt that Justin had access to the source behind *Dial.* 140:3 already when he wrote *Dial.* 44f.[104]

The only text in this cluster which seems to have been looked up in a LXX scroll and quoted accordingly, is Is 66:23f in *Dial.* 44:3. Justin's familiarity with the deviant testimony version (reading παύσεται/παυθή-σεται for LXX τελευτήσει) is shown in his passing allusion in *Dial.* 130:2: τὰ κῶλα τῶν παραβεβηκότων ὑπὸ σκώληκος καὶ ἀπαύστου πυρὸς δια-βιβρώσκεσθαι μέλλειν . . .

It is relevant to note that Ezek 14:14/20 (non-LXX, but different from Justin's) and Is 66:24b (essentially LXX) occur close to each other in *2.Clem.* 6f (6:8 and 7:6 respectively, no OT quotation in between). *2.Clem.* is hardly Justin's direct source (different text-types), but some kind of common tradition seems probable.

(o) Jer 2:13/Is 16:1/Jer 3:8 (synopsis next page).

This combined quotation is a favourite example in all discussions on «testimonia».[105] The close parallel in *Barn.* 11:2f points to some kind of common tradition. A comparison of the two texts reveals the following points:

(1) Both authors treat the text as one single quotation, attributed to «the prophet» (Barnabas) or «Jeremiah» (*Dial.* 114:5).

(2) Both writers have the same combination of Jer 2:13 and Is 16:1(f).

(3) Justin cannot have Barnabas as his direct source, because he deviates from the LXX when Barnabas agrees, and vice versa.

Justin must have had a source other than Barnabas, but representing a similar tradition.[106]

---

104. So also Prigent, p. 315.
105. See i.a. Hatch, *Essays*, pp. 204/208f; O. Michel, *Paulus und seine Bibel* (BFChTh 2.Reihe 18, Gütersloh, 1929) pp. 37-39; R. A. Kraft, 'Barnabas' Isaiah Text and the «Testimony Book» Hypothesis', *JBL* 79 (1960, pp. 336-350), pp. 346-348; *idem, Epistle*, pp. 222-226; Prigent, *Les Testimonia*, pp. 91-93.
106. Cf. esp. Kraft, 'Isaiah text' pp. 347f; C. Wolff, *Jeremia im Frühjudentum und Urchristentum* (TU 118, Berlin, 1976), pp. 184f.

Let me add that Justin besides this testimony source also seems to have had direct access to the Jeremiah LXX. His passing allusion in *Dial.* 14:1 has a LXX reading not found in the combined quotation: τὸ ὕδωρ τῆς ζωῆς.

| *Dial.* 114:5 | *Barn.* 11:2f | Jer 2:12 f LXX |
|---|---|---|
| | Ἔκστηθι οὐρανέ<br>καὶ ἐπὶ τούτῳ<br>πλεῖον φριξάτο ἡ γῆ | Ἐξέστη ὁ οὐρανὸς [σφόδρα]<br>ἐπὶ τούτῳ<br>καὶ ἔφριξεν ἐπὶ πλεῖον[a]<br>λέγει κύριος |
| οὐαὶ ὑμῖν | ὅτι δύο καὶ πονηρὰ<br>ἐποίησεν ὁ λαὸς οὗτος | ὅτι δύο καὶ πονηρὰ<br>ἐποίησεν ὁ λαός μου |
| ὅτι ἐγκατελίπετε[a]<br>πηγὴν ζῶσαν<br>καὶ ὠρύξατε ἑαυτοῖς<br>λάκκους<br>συντετριμμένους<br>οἳ οὐ δυνήσονται<br>συνέχειν ὕδωρ | ἐμὲ ἐγκατέλιπον<br>πηγὴν ὕδατος ζῶσαν[a]<br>καὶ ἑαυτοῖς ὤρυξαν<br>βόθρον θανάτου | ἐμὲ ἐγκατέλιπον<br>πηγὴν ὕδατος ζωῆς[b]<br>καὶ ὤρυξαν ἑαυτοῖς<br>λάκκους<br>συντετριμμένους<br>οἳ οὐ δυνήσονται<br>ὕδωρ συνέχειν |
| | | Is 16:1f LXX |
| μὴ ἔρημον ᾖ<br>οὗ ἐστι<br>τὸ ὄρος Σιών | μὴ πέτρα ἔρημός<br>ἐστιν<br>τὸ ὄρος τὸ ἅγιόν μου<br>Σινᾶ<br>ἔσεσθε γὰρ ὡς<br>πετεινοῦ νοσσοὶ<br>ἀνιπτάμενοι<br>νοσσιᾶς ἀφῃρημένοι | ... μὴ πέτρα ἔρημός<br>ἐστι<br>τὸ ὄρος Σιων<br>ἔσῃ γὰρ ὡς<br>πετεινοῦ<br>ἀνιπταμένου<br>νεοσσὸς ἀφῇρημένος ... |
| | | Jer 3:8 LXX |
| ὅτι Ἰερουσαλὴμ<br>βιβλίον ἀποστασίου<br>ἔδωκα ἔμπροσθεν ὑμῶν | | ... καὶ ἐξαπέστειλα αὐτὴν<br>καὶ ἔδωκα αὐτῇ<br>βιβλίον ἀποστασίου ... |
| a) *Dial.* 19:2 adds<br>αὐτὸν, due to<br>context. | a) So H. S reads<br>πηγὴν ζωῆς, G reads<br>πηγὴν ζῶσαν. | a) Several MSS add<br>or prefixe ἡ γῆ<br>b) Several MSS: ζῶντος |

(To the left of the first column, running vertically: = *Dial.* 19:2)

(p) Jer 4:3f; Jer 9:24f; Deut 10:16 (synopsis next page).

Before we turn to the passages in Justin, a few words on the textual evidence in Barnabas are in place. In the Greek witnesses, *Barn.* 9:5 contains a sequence of three texts: Jer 4:3f; Dt 10:16; Jer 9:25, while the Latin version has the middle quotation closer to Jer 4:4 (Symmachus) or Is 1:16.

It is difficult to say which version represents the original. Kraft opts for the Latin as the *lectio difficilior*.[107] On the other hand, the evidence in Justin and the analogy with Jer 2:13 etc. lend weight to the Greek version. In any case,

---

107. Kraft, *Epistle,* p. 186, n. 10; and in his *SC* edition of the text. K. Lake and Funk/Bihlmeyer in their editions follow the Greek text - correctly, I believe.

| Barn. 9:5 (Funk/Bihlmeyer) | Dial. 15:7–16:1 | Dial. 28:2f | Jer 4 LXX |
|---|---|---|---|
| τάδε λέγει κύριος<br>ὁ θεὸς ὑμῶν<br>... | | | vs.3 ... τάδε λέγει κύριος<br>τοῖς ἀνδράσιν Ιουδα<br>καὶ τοῖς κατοικοῦσιν<br>Ιερουσαλημ |
| μὴ σπείρητε<br>ἐπ᾽ ἀκάνθαις<br>περιτμήθητε<br>τῷ κυρίῳ ὑμῶν<br>... | | νεώσατε ἑαυτοῖς νεώματα<br>καὶ μὴ σπείρετε<br>ἐπ᾽ ἀκάνθαις<br>περιτέμνετε<br>τῷ κυρίῳ | νεώσατε ἑαυτοῖς νεώματα<br>καὶ μὴ σπείρητε<br>ἐπ᾽ ἀκάνθαις[a]<br>vs.4 περιτμήθητε<br>τῷ θεῷ ὑμῶν |
| τὴν ἀκροβυστίαν<br>τῆς καρδίας ὑμῶν ... | περιτέμεσθε οὖν<br>τὴν ἀκροβυστίαν<br>τῆς καρδίας ὑμῶν ... | καὶ περιτέμνεσθε<br>τὴν ἀκροβυστίαν<br>τῆς καρδίας ὑμῶν | καὶ περιέλεσθε[b]<br>τὴν ἀκροβυστίαν<br>τῆς καρδίας ὑμῶν ... |
| | | | Deut 10:16 LXX |
| περιτμήθητε[a]<br>τὴν σκληροκαρδίαν ὑμῶν<br>καὶ τὸν τράχηλον ὑμῶν<br>οὐ σκληρυνεῖτε[a] | περιτμήθητε<br>τὴν σκληροκαρδίαν ὑμῶν<br>καὶ τὸν τράχηλον<br>οὐ σκληρυνεῖτε ἔτι ... | | καὶ περιτεμεῖσθε.<br>τὴν σκληροκαρδίαν ὑμῶν<br>καὶ τὸν τράχηλον ὑμῶν<br>οὐ σκληρυνεῖτε ἔτι |
| | + Deut 10:17 in a loose<br>LXX text | | Jer 9 LXX |
| ...<br>ἰδοὺ<br>λέγει κύριος | | Jer 9:24.25a = LXX except for<br>two omissions<br>... | vs.24 ἰδοὺ ἡμέραι ἔρχονται<br>λέγει κύριος ... |
| πάντα τὰ ἔθνη<br>ἀπερίτμητα ἀκροβυστίᾳ<br>ὁ δὲ λαὸς οὗτος<br>ἀπερίτμητος καρδίᾳ | 1. Apol. 53:11<br>Ισραηλ<br>ἀπερίτμητος τὴν καρδίαν<br>τὰ δὲ ἔθνη<br>τὴν ἀκροβυστίαν | ὅτι πάντα τὰ ἔθνη<br>ἀπερίτμητα<br>καὶ πᾶς οἶκος Ισραηλ<br>ἀπερίτμητος καρδίας αὐτῶν | vs.25 ...ὅτι πάντα τὰ ἔθνη<br>ἀπερίτμητα σαρκί<br>καὶ πᾶς οἶκος Ισραηλ<br>ἀπερίτμητοι καρδίας αὐτῶν |
| a-a) So, with minor variants, S; H; and G.<br>Kraft conj. from the Latin: καὶ περιτμήθητε τὴν πονηρίαν<br>ἀπὸ τῆς καρδίας ὑμῶν ~ Jer 4:4 Symmachus. | | | a) Sᶜ: ἀκάνθας<br>b) Several minuscules: περιτέμνεσθε (=MT):<br>c) Some Lucianic MSS (=MT):<br>omit. σαρκί |

Jer 4:4 and Dt 10:16 are so close to each other that they were almost bound
to become confused, combined, and interchanged in the course of testimony tradition and transmission.

Turning to Justin, let us first take a look at the non-LXX version of Jer
9:25b in *1.Apol.* 53:11.[108] This text has a neat antithetic parallelism: Israel is
uncircumcised in the heart, while the Gentiles are uncircumcised in their
ἀκροβυστία. The last word is not present in the LXX to Jer 9:25. Exactly the
same antithetic parallelism is found in *Barn* 9:5, only inverted. One is led to
think of a common textual tradition.

In *Dial.* 15:7 we have an allusion to Jer 4:4. This is immediately followed
in *Dial.* 16:1 by a formal quotation of Dt 10:16f (basically LXX). Maybe we
have here traces of a source similar to *Barn.* 9:5, Greek version.

In *Dial.* 28:2f we find two LXX quotations, Jer 4:3b.4 and Jer 9:24f. It
seems Justin is again working with a source similar to *Barn.*9:5, but looking
the texts up in a LXX Jeremiah scroll. So we are probably etitled to suspect a
common source behind *1.Apol.* 53:11; *Dial.* 15f, and *Dial.* 28, its actual text
being preserved only in *1.Apol.* 53:11.

(q) Jer 31:31f

| Jer 31 LXX; Heb 8:7—8; *Dial.* 11:3 | *Ker. Pt.* fragm. 5 | *Dial.* 67:9 |
|---|---|---|
| 31. ἰδοὺ ἡμέραι ἔρχονται φησὶ[a] κύριος καὶ [b]διαθήσομαι τῷ οἴκῳ Ισραηλ καὶ τῷ οἴκῳ Ιουδα[b] διαθήκην καινήν | ἰδοὺ<br><br>διατίθεμαι<br>ὑμῖν<br><br>καινήν διαθήκην | καὶ ὅτι . . .<br><br><br><br><br>καινὴν διαθήκην διαθήσεσθαι |
| 32. οὐ[c] [d]κατὰ τὴν διαθήκην[d] ἣν διεθέμην[e] τοῖς πατράσιν αὐτῶν ἐν ἡμέρᾳ [f]ἐπιλαβομένου μου[f] τῆς χειρὸς αὐτῶν ἐξαγαγεῖν αὐτοὺς ἐκ γῆς[g] Αἰγύπτου . . . | οὐχ<br>ὡς διεθέμην<br>τοῖς πατράσιν ὑμῶν<br>ἐν ὄρει Χωρήβ | . . . παρὰ<br>τὴν<br><br>ἐν ὄρει Χωρήβ |

a) Heb 8 = *Dial.* 11:3 = several LXX MSS: λέγει.
b-b) Heb 8: καὶ συντελέσω ἐπὶ τὸν οἴκον ᾽Ισραὴλ καὶ ἐπὶ τὸν οἴκον ᾽Ιούδα.
c) *Dial.* 11:3: οὐχ.
d-d) *Dial.* 11:3 om.
e) Heb 8: ἐποίησα.
f-f) *Dial.* 11:3: ἢ ἐπελαβόμην.
g) *Dial.* 11:3: τῆς = LXX V.

Justin's excerpt from Jer 31 is not the same as in Hebrews, and his text
agrees with the LXX where Heb 8 deviates, and vice versa. (The reading
λέγει instead of φησί in Heb 8:7 and *Dial.* 11:3 is hardly significant,

---

108. Justin quotes the text as «Isaiah».

because this seems to be an old reading within the LXX MSS tradition). There is thus hardly any dependence upon Hebrews on the level of text-type.

This makes a comparison with the deviant version of Jer 31:31f preserved in a fragment of the *Kerygma Petrou* all the more interesting. It is difficult to avoid the impression that Justin in his allusion to Jer 31:31f in *Dial.* 67:9, presupposes exactly the version found in the *Kerygma*. Turning to his comment on Jer 31:31f in *Dial.* 11:2, one is again inclined to hear an echo of the text preserved in the *Kerygma*: ὁ γὰρ ἐν Χωρὴβ παλαιὸς ἤδη νόμος καὶ ὑμῶν μόνων.[109] It seems that Justin's own word for the mountain of the Law was not Horeb, but Sinai, *Dial.* 127:3. (Horeb is only found in the two allusions to Jer 31:31f.) I am therefore inclined to believe that Justin was familiar with the version of Jer 31:31f preserved in the *Kerygma*. The LXX text (basically) quoted in *Dial.* 11:3 is probably an amplification of this non-LXX testimony.

But there are also traces of influence from the context in Hebrews. The following parallel is hardly accidental:

| Heb 8:13 | *Dial.* 11:2 |
|---|---|
| ἐν τῷ λέγειν καινὴν πεπαλαίωκεν τὴν πρώτην | νόμος δὲ κατὰ νόμου τεθεὶς τὸν πρὸ αὐτοῦ ἔπαυσε καὶ διαθήκη μετέπειτα γενομένη τὴν προτέραν ὁμοίως ἔστησεν... |

An influence from Hebrews may also be recognised in *Dial.* 67:9: ἡ δὲ παλαιὰ διαθήκη ... *μετὰ φόβου καὶ τρόμου* διετάγη τοῖς πατράσιν ὑμων ..., cf. Heb 12:21: *ἔκφοβός* εἰμι καὶ *ἔντρομος*. There is no τρόμος in the LXX of Ex 20:18-20.

We shall thus have to conclude that behind *Dial.* 11:2f and *Dial.* 67:9 we recognise both the *Kerygma Petrou* (non-LXX text) and Hebrews (exegesis).

(r) Zech 2:15

| Zech 2:15 LXX | *Dial.* 119:3 | *Dial.* 115:1 |
|---|---|---|
| καὶ καταφεύξονται ἔθνη πολλὰ ἐπὶ τὸν κύριον ἐν τῇ ἡμέρᾳ ἐκείνῃ καὶ ἔσονται αὐτῷ εἰς λαὸν καὶ κατασκηνώσουσιν ἐν μέσῳ σου ..... | καὶ καταφεύξονται ἔθνη πολλὰ ἐπὶ τὸν κύριον ἐν ἐκείνῃ τῇ ἡμέρᾳ εἰς λαόν καὶ κατασκηνώσουσιν ἐν μέσω τῆς γῆς πάσης | καὶ προστεθήσονται ἔθνη πολλὰ πρὸς κύριον ἐν τῇ ἡμέρᾳ ἐκείνῃ καὶ ἔσονταί μοι εἰς λαόν καὶ κατασκηνώσω ἐν μέσω σου ..... |

---

109. This last parallel is observed by Prigent, *Justin*, p. 237. (Prigent writes *Kerygmata Petrou*, but the *Kerygma Petrou* is meant).

In *Dial.* 119:2f Justin quotes several texts concerned about God's new people: Deut 32:16-23 (testimony nucleus vs. 21, see above p. 53); Zech 2:15; Is 62:12; Is 65:1. We have already seen reasons to believe that some testimony source is at play behind the first and last of these quotations. Is 62:12 is a free quotation of the LXX text. Turning to Zech 2:15, one first notices the vague introductory formula, . . . ὡς ἔφασαν οἱ προφῆται. Next one observes two variant readings in the text: omission of καὶ ἔσονται αὐτῷ, and τῆς πάσης instead of σου. The first may be a scribal error, but the second is hardly accidental. When the text was isolated from its context -presumably in the testimony source[110] - the σου lost its reference. It was replaced by the universalistic phrase ἐν μέσῳ τῆς γῆς πάσης. Notice that this testimony version of the text clearly is based on the common LXX text.

Turning to *Dial.* 115:1, we find an extensive quotation of Zech 2:14 - 3:2, but this text neither agrees with *Dial.* 119:3 nor with the LXX. Barthélemy is probably right in recognizing this text as part of the καιγε recension of the Twelve Prophets. This means that the long text found in *Dial.* 115 is the text Justin found in his exemplar of the Twelve Prophets.[111]

If Justin had noticed the textual variants, he would probably have insisted that the testimony version in *Dial.* 119:3 was the true «LXX», while the text in *Dial.* 115:1f was «Jewish». And he would not have been entirely wrong.

(s) Zech 9:9 (see synopsis next page)

Let us first take a look at the text in *1.Apol.* 35:11. Justin says that this is a prophecy foretelling that Jesus would enter Jerusalem on the foal of an ass, recalling Mt 21:1-11 par. Justin's quotation is close to Mt 21:5 from ἰδοὺ onwards ( omission of δίκαιος καὶ σώζων αὐτός; and reading υἱὸν ὑποζυγίου). The reading ἐπὶ πῶλον ὄνον in Justin may be an attempt to eliminate the apparent implication in Matthew's text that Jesus rode on two beasts.[112]It thus looks as if from ἰδοὺ onwards Matthew's quotation is the direct or indirect source behind *1.Apol.* 35:11.[113] But Matthew's introductory phrase

---

110. Cf. the verdict of Barthélemy, *Devanciers,* p. 211: «. . . *sans doute empruntée à un recueil de Testimonia* . . .» Prigent also argues that a source is at play in *Dial.* 119:3f, *Justin,* pp. 289f.

111. Barthélemy, *loc. cit.* I have indicated the hebraizing features in the part of the text which is included in the synopsis. A full list is given by Barthélemy, *ibid.*

112. I believe this is a simpler explanation than the one offered by Bousset, *Evangeliencitate,* pp. 34f ( followed by Prigent, *Justin.* p.284), viz. that Justin's LXX text has been assimilated to the Western version of Mt 21:5 by a later scribe. However, one has to admit that the remarkable reading ἐπὶ πῶλον ὄνον υἱὸν ὑποζυγίου may be due to scribal corruption of the text. Instead of amending (like Otto): ἐπὶ ὄνον καὶ πῶλον υἱὸν ὑποζυγίου (=Mt 21:5 - so also Pautigny's ed., and Prigent, p.283, without comment), one could contemplate the much simpler emendation ἐπὶ πῶλον ὄνου, υἱὸν ὑποζυγίου. This would accord with Justin's introduction to the quotation: . . . καθεσθησόμενος ἐπὶ πῶλον ὄνου . . . My explanation of the modification *vis-a-vis* Matthew's text would still hold good.

113. So also Massaux, p. 497, who believes, however, that Justin began to quote the LXX, but was reminded of Mt 21:5, and finished his quotation with this text. Cf., however, the criticism in Prigent, *Justin,* p. 283.

| John 12:15 | Mt 21:5 | 1. Apol. 35:11 | Zech 9:9 LXX | Dial. 53:3 (καιγε?) |
|---|---|---|---|---|
| μὴ φοβοῦ θυγάτηρ Σιών [cf. MT Zeph 3:16: אל תיראי ציון ] ἰδοὺ ὁ βασιλεύς σου ἔρχεται | εἴπατε τῇ θυγατρὶ Σιών   ἰδοὺ ὁ βασιλεύς σου ἔρχεται σοι | χαῖρε σφόδρα θύγατερ Σιών κήρυσσε θύγατερ Ἰερουσαλήμ ἰδοὺ ὁ βασιλεύς σου ἔρχεται σοι | = Zeph 3:14LXX χαῖρε σφόδρα[a] θύγατερ Σιών κήρυσσε θύγατερ Ιερουσαλημ ἰδοὺ ὁ βασιλεύς σου ἔρχεται σοι δίκαιος καὶ σῴζων αὐτός | χαῖρε σφόδρα θύγατερ Σιών ἀλάλαξον[a] κήρυσσε θύγατερ Ἰερουσαλήμ ἰδοὺ ἕξει[b] σοι δίκαιος καὶ σῴζων αὐτός |
| καθήμενος ἐπὶ πῶλον ὄνου | πραῢς καὶ ἐπιβεβηκὼς ἐπὶ ὄνον καὶ ἐπὶ πῶλον υἱὸν ὑποζυγίου | πρᾶος ἐπιβεβηκὼς ἐπὶ πῶλον ὄνον ὑποζυγίου | πραῢς καὶ ἐπιβεβηκὼς ἐπὶ ὑποζύγιον καὶ πῶλον νέον | καὶ πραῢς καὶ πτωχός[c] ἐπιβεβηκὼς ἐπὶ ὑποζύγιον καὶ πῶλον ὄνου[d] |
| = Is 62:11LXX | | | a) So several cursives in Zeph 3:14. Ziegler om. | a) Cf. MT הריעי  b) Cf. MT יבא  c) Doublet for MT עני  d) Cf. MT בן אתנות |

has been substituted by a longer introduction, which occurs in identical words in Zech 9:9 LXX and Zeph 3:14 LXX. And Justin quotes the whole text as Zephaniah. One can here make many suggestions as to how this reference arose,[114] especially when one has in mind that John in Jn 12:15 prefixes his quotation of Zech 9:9 with a phrase reminiscent of Zeph 3:16 (MT). Perhaps we shall have to reckon with a source between Mt 21:5 and *1.Apol.* 35:11,[115] where the close parallels in Zeph 3:14ff and Zech 9:9 were combined. In any case, the reference to Zephaniah probably has more to it than Justin's faulty memory.

Turning to *Dial.* 53:2f, we find first a paraphrase of Matthew's story of the ass and its foal.[116] Justin then goes on to quote the whole of Zech 9:9 with correct reference. The text exhibits signs of a recension on the basis of the Hebrew text, and is deemed καιγε by Barthélemy.[117]

We have here another example that Justin in the Dialogue does not directly quote the text of his testimony source, but looks up the text in a Biblical MS and quotes it accordingly.

(t) Zech 12:10-12 etc.

In *1.Apol.* 52:10 Justin says he is going to quote a prophecy by Zechariah. The text in fact turns out to be a nicely constructed poem with phrases reminiscent of different prophetic passages. P. Prigent has recognized three strophes in the text.[118] Following Prigent we can break down the text in the following way:

|   | | |
|---|---|---|
| 1 | Ἐντελοῦμαι τοῖς τέσσαρσιν ἀνέμοις<br>συνάξαι τὰ ἐσκορπισμένα τέκνα<br>ἐντελοῦμαι τῷ βορρᾷ φέρειν<br>καὶ τῷ νότῳ μὴ προσκόπτειν | —————— cf. Zech 2:10<br>(and Is 11:12)<br>—————— cf. Is 43:5f |
| 2 | καὶ τότε ἐν Ἰερουσαλὴμ κοπετὸς μέγας<br>οὐ κοπετὸς στομάτων ἢ χειλέων<br>ἀλλὰ κοπετὸς καρδίας<br>καὶ οὐ μὴ σχίσωσιν αὐτῶν τὰ ἱμάτια<br>ἀλλὰ τὰς διανοίας<br>κόψονται φυλὴ πρὸς φυλήν | —————— cf. Zech 12:11<br>—————— cf. Joel 2:12f<br>and Is 29:13<br>—————— cf. Zech 12:12 |

---

114. Cf. Prigent, *Justin,* pp. 284f.

115. So also J. P. Smith *Demonstration,* p. 198, n. 280; Prigent, *Justin,* pp. 283f.

116. Only Matthew has two beasts. Justin's ἐπικαθίσας recalls Matthew's ἐπεκάθισεν, Mt 21:7. A shorter narrative is found in *1.Apol.* 32:6. There are som striking non-synoptic agreements between the two versions in Justin, *1.Apol.* 32:5f and *Dial.* 53:2f. I shall return more fully to this in Part II below. Here it is sufficient to point out the great probability that this non-synoptic Gospel narrative was part of Justin's source for the deviant Zech 9:9 quotation. Cf. pp. 140ff and Koester, *Schriftbeweis,* p. 92.

117. *Devanciers,* p. 211.

118. *Justin,* p. 316.

καὶ τότε ὄψονται εἰς ὃν ἐξεκέντησαν ———————— cf. Zech 12:10
καὶ ἐροῦσι
τί κύριε ἐπλάνησας ἡμᾶς⌉ ———————————— cf. Is 63:17
3 ἀπὸ τῆς ὁδοῦ σου ⌋
ἡ δόξα ἣν εὐλόγησαν οἱ πατέρες ἡμῶν⌉
ἐγενήθην ἡμῖν εἰς ὄνειδος           ⌋ ——————— cf. Is 64:10

This well-constructed text is hardly a loose quotation from memory.[119] Let us take a closer look at some details. Strophe 2 has as its basic theme the κοπετός motif from Zech 12:11f - well-known from the New Testament: Mt 24:30; Rev 1:7. But whereas in both of the NT passages the ones who beat their breasts are πᾶσαι αἱ φυλαὶ τῆς γῆς, in Justin's text they are clearly the Jews. And further, the κοπετός motif has been interpreted by the addition of Joel 2:12f: A *real* repentance of heart and mind is going to take place.

We find the same structure in strophe 3. Here also the basic text (Zech 12:10) is well-known from the NT: They shall look at the one whom they pierced, ἐξεκέντησαν, John 19:37; Rev. 1:7. But again the meaning of this is qualified by added texts ( Is 63:17 and 64:10),which testifies to a *sincere* repentance on the part of Israel.

The first strophe also has a NT foundation: Mt 24:31 par. Mk 13:27, a synoptic passage which alludes to Zech 2:10 and Deut 30:4. In Justin's text, this basic OT reference has again been enriched by added allusions. Let us briefly tabulate the most important NT parallels:

| 1. Apol. 52:10—12 | Mt 24:30f | Rev 1:7 |
|---|---|---|
| 1) *Synagein* motif<br>Zech 2:10<br>Is 43:5f | 3) *Synagein* motif<br>Zech 2:10/Dt 30:4 | |
| 2) *Kopetos* motif<br>Zech 12:11f<br>Joel 2:12f | 1) *Kopetos* motif<br>Zech 12:11ff | 2) *Kopetos* motif<br>Zech 12:11f |
| 3) *Opsontai* motif<br>Zech 12:10<br><br>Is 63:17/64:10 | 2) Epiphany of the<br>Son of man<br>Dan 7:13f | 1) *Opsontai* motif<br>Dan 7:13/Zech 12:10 |

On the textual level, one notes that Justin's text, like John 19:37 and Rev 1:7, reads ἐξεκέντησαν in Zech 12:10 - against LXX κατωρχήσαντο.[120] (In all his allusions to this verse, Justin sticks to the non-LXX reading: *Dial.* 14:8; 32:2; 64:7; 118:1). Direct influence from the Johannine texts is

119. Cf. Prigent, *ibid.,* against the verdict of Rahlfs, 'Aquila-Lesarten', p. 192.
120. That is, the non-Lucianic LXX MSS. The Lucianic MSS follow Theodotion: (εἰς) ὃν ἐξεκέντησαν. This is a perfect rendering of the MT, while the LXX has misread דקרו as רקדו

possible, but also dependence on an «Ur-Theodotion» version of the LXX. One should not exclude a direct recourse to the Hebrew text, because this is indicated at the end of Justin's text. Here Justin, like Symmachus, reads εἰς ὄνειδος, which is a misreading לחרפה of the MT לחרבה = LXX συνέπεσεν.[121]

To conclude, the combined text in *1.Apol.* 52:10-12 seems to be composed by someone familiar with NT parousia testimonies, being able to enrich them from other relevant OT passages, and probably having access to the Hebrew text. The author is very concerned about Israel, and seems to take a much more positive view of Israel's eschatological *metanoia* than Justin himself.[122]

Of the components in *1.Apol.* 52:10-12, Justin only quotes Is 63:17 and Is 64:10 elsewhere. Both times the quotations occur within long LXX excerpts, and none of the peculiar readings in *1.Apol.* 52:12 are retained: *Dial.* 25:2-5 quotes Is 63:15 -64:12; *1.Apol.* 47:2f quotes Is 64:9-11.[123] One has reason to doubt that *1.Apol.* 52:12 was Justin's «guide» to these texts. He had hardly identified the two Isaiah components in the combined text.

In this instance, therefore, we do not have a real case of deliberate substitution of «testimony» text by LXX text. The double rendering is probably accidental.

There is, however, another passage which shows that Justin in all probability had looked up Zech 12:10-12 in a Biblical MS when writing the *Dialogue*. In *Dial.* 32:2 he alludes to Zech 12:10-12 in the following way: «. . . a second (advent) when ye will recognize Him whom ye pierced (ἐπιγνώσεσθε εἰς ὃν ἐξεκεντήσατε) and all your tribes will lament, tribe over against tribe, *the women alone and the men alone.* . . .» The underlined words correspond to nothing in *1Apol.* 52:10-12, but give the essence of Zech 12:12. We have seen elsewhere that Justin's MS of the Twelve Prophets probably represented the καιγε recension of the LXX. This same recension is probably paraphrased here.[124] The peculiar reading ἐπιγνώσεσθε (LXX : ἐπιβλέψονται, *1.Apol* 52:12: ὄψονται) - which recurs in the allusions *Dial.* 14:8; 64:7 - may be a translation variant of Hebrew נבט *hif.*, cf. Num 12:8; 23:21; Is 38:11; Ps 119:8.[125] The reading thus may have been present in the καιγε version of Zech 12:10.[126]

---

121. Cf. Katz, 'OT quotations', p. 348.
122. Cf. Prigent, *Justin,* p. 316.
123. Detailed collations of the texts in Credner, pp. 231-33.
124. So also Berthélemy, *Devanciers,* p. 211. He points to the translation of לבד by κατ' ἰδίαν against LXX: καθ᾽ ἑαυτὴν (or ἑαυτάς).
125. Ges.-Buhl translates in these references : «wahrnehmen».
126. Prigent, *Justin,* p. 80, argues that the reading ἐπιγνώσεσθε was the reading found in Zech 12:10-12 as quoted in the *Syntagma.* If so, the Syntagma was not Justin's source for *1. Apol.* 52:10-12!

(u) Ps 22:8b, 9a

| Mt 27:39 (= Mk 15:29) | 1. Apol. 38:6 | Dial. 101:3 |
|---|---|---|
| οἱ δὲ παραπορευόμενοι ἐβλασφήμουν αὐτὸν | | πάντες οἱ θεωροῦντές με ἐξεμυκτήρισάν με |
| κινοῦντες τὰς κεφαλὰς αὐτῶν καὶ λέγοντες ... | ἐλάλησαν ἐν χείλεσιν ἐκίνησαν κεφαλὴν λέγοντες | ἐλάλησαν<sup>a</sup> ἐν χείλεσιν ἐκίνησαν κεφαλήν |
| Mt 27:43 (Mt only) | | |
| πέποιθεν ἐπὶ τὸν θεόν ῥυσάσθω νῦν | ῥυσάσθω ἑαυτόν | ἤλπισεν ἐπὶ κύριον ῥυσάσθω αὐτόν <sup>b</sup>σωσάτω αὐτόν<sup>b</sup> |
| εἰ θέλει αὐτὸν | | ὅτι θέλει αὐτόν |
| | «fulfilment report» 1. Apol. 38:8 | ... οἱ γὰρ θεωροῦντες |
| Mt 27:40 (= Mk 15:30) | σταυρωθέντος γὰρ αὐτοῦ | αὐτὸν ἐσταυρωμένον τὰς κεφαλὰς ... ἐκίνουν |
| | ἐξέστρεφον τὰ χείλη | καὶ τὰ χείλη διέστρεφον |
| σῶσον σεαυτόν <sup>a</sup>εἰ υἱὸς εἰ τοῦ θεοῦ<sup>a</sup> [καὶ] κατάβηθι ἀπὸ τοῦ σταυροῦ | καὶ ἐκίνουν τὰς κεφαλὰς λέγοντες ὁ νεκροὺς ἀνεγείρας ῥυσάσθω ἑαυτόν | καὶ τοῖς μυξωτῆρσιν ... ... υἱὸν θεοῦ ἑαυτὸν ἔλεγε καταβὰς περιπατείτω σωσάτω αὐτὸν ὁ θεός |
| a-a) Mt only | | a) Dial. 101:3 pref. καὶ b-b) Om. Dial. 101:3, but present in Dial. 98:3: scribal error. |

In *1.Apol.* 38:6-8 we find a tightly composed passage with two main elements: a shortened, partly non-LXX version of Ps 22:8f, and a short narrative reporting the fulfilment of the prophecy contained in the Psalm verses. Psalm text and narrative are mutually adapted to each other, and H. Koester is probably right when he argues that neither was created *ad hoc* by Justin, but both elements were taken from the same source.[127] We shall have to return to this suggestion more fully below. Here we just notice that the narrative contains a phrase not contained in the Psalm or the synoptic Gospels: ἐξέστρεφον τὰ χείλη.

Turning to the parallel in *Dial.* 101:3, we find a double modification. First, the Psalm quotation is amplified and quoted according to the LXX. Secondly, the corresponding narrative is also somewhat changed. The narrative in *1.Apol.*38:8 is basically retained ( note especially the phrase καὶ

---

127. Koester, *Schriftbeweis,* pp. 64-67.

τὰ χείλη διέστρεφον), but new features are added: τοῖς μυξωτῆρσιν . . .
διαρρινοῦντες, echoing the LXX of Ps 22:8a, but cf. also the same allusion
in Luke (23:35: ἐξεμυκτήριζον δὲ καὶ οἱ ἄρχοντες). Further, the words of
the mockerers are now a free version of Mt 27:40b.

In short, while Justin is still drawing on the source employed in *1.Apol.*
38:6-8, he has also turned to the primary sources: LXX and Matthew,[128] and
possibly Luke.

(v) Ps 22:17.19/Ps 3:6 (synopsis next page).

We start with *1.Apol.* 38:4f. Here the combined quotation from Pss 22 and
3 is introduced as a single quotation within a catena of quotations. The
whole sequence (*1.Apol.* 38:1-6) runs: Is 65:2; Is 50:6-8; Ps 22:19/17/Ps 3:6;
Ps 22:8f.

Is 65:2 is a non-LXX testimony text treated above (p. 65). Is 50:6-8 is
approximately LXX; Ps 22:8f is non-LXX (telescoped). We take as a working
hypothesis that Justin is employing a testimony source, and turn to *Dial.*
97:1-3. Here we find the following sequence: Ps 3:5f; Is 65:2; Is 57:2; Is 53:9;
Ps 22:17-19. The two Psalm texts have here been looked up in the LXX, as
shown also by the precise introduction to Ps 22:17-19: «And again David . . .
in the twenty-first Psalm . . .» Is 65:2 is given in the same LXX text which
Justin used in the longer quotation in *Dial.* 24 (see synopsis and discussion
above, pp. 65—67). Is 57:2 is LXX, Is 53:9 somewhat telescoped LXX.

It thus seems that Justin in *Dial.* 97:1-3 is working with the same source as
in *1.Apol.* 38[129] but correcting the texts to agree with the LXX. It is a certainty
that he had a Psalms MS before him when writing *Dial.* 97: In *Dial.* 98 he
quotes the whole of Ps 22:1-24 (LXX text).

Turning to *1.Apol.* 35:3-5, we find probably a third instance where the
same source is used. Here the sequence is: Is65:2/58:2; Ps 22:17/19. In Ps
22, vss. 17 and 19 are quoted in the right order, but apart from this the
non-LXX text is very close to *1.Apol.* 38.

The existence of a common source behind these three passages in Justin
is suggested also by a comparison with two passages in Barnabas.

In *Barn.* 5:13f we find the quotation sequence: Ps 119:120a/Ps 22:17a; Is
50:6f. Barnabas' texts are non-LXX, but are also different from Justin's.[130]
Some kind of common tradition (or intermediary source) between *Barn.*
5:13f and Justin (esp. *1.Apol.* 38) must be supposed. In *Barn.* 6:6 we have a
combined quotation, consisting of phrases from Ps 22:17; Ps 118:12, and Ps
22:19. Obviously Barnabas in these two passages is drawing on sources
which combined shortened versions of Ps 22, vss. 17 and 19, with other

---

128. Cf. Koester, *ibid.*
129. So also Prigent, *Justin,* pp. 204f.
130. Detailed analysis in Prigent, *Les Testimonia,* pp. 166-68; Kraft, *Epistle,* pp. 142-147.

| 1. Apol. 38:4 | Ps 22 LXX = Dial. 97:3 | 1. Apol. 35:5 | Barn. 6:6 |
|---|---|---|---|
| αὐτοὶ ἔβαλον κλῆρον ἐπὶ τὸν ἱματισμόν μου | vs. 17 ... συναγωγὴ πονερευομένων περιέσχον με ὤρυξάν[a] | αὐτοὶ ὤρυξάν μου πόδας καὶ χεῖρας | περιέσχον με συναγωγὴ πονερευομένων ἐκύκλωσάν με ⎤ ὡσεὶ μέλισσαι κηρίον ⎦ = Ps 118:12a |
| καὶ ὤρυξάν μου πόδας καὶ χεῖρας | χεῖράς μου καὶ πόδας[b] vs. 19 (= Jn 19:24) διεμερίσαντο τὰ ἱμάτιά μου ἑαυτοῖς καὶ ἐπὶ τὸν ἱματισμόν μου ἔβαλον κλῆρον | καὶ ἔβαλον κλῆρον ἐπὶ τὸν ἱματισμόν μου | καὶ ἐπὶ τὸν ἱματισμόν μου ἔβαλον κλῆρον |
| | Ps 3 LXX = Dial. 97:1 | 1. Clem. 26:2 | |
| ἐγὼ δὲ ἐκοιμήθην καὶ ὕπνωσα καὶ ἀνέστην ὅτι κύριος ἀντελάβετό μου | vs. 6 ἐγὼ ἐκοιμήθην καὶ ὕπνωσα ἐξηγέρθην ὅτι κύριος ἀντιλήμψεταί[c] μου | ἐκοιμήθην καὶ ὕπνωσα ἐξηγέρθην ὅτι σὺ μετ' ἐμοῦ εἶ | |
| | a) In Dial. 97:3 the quotation begins here b) Dial. 97:3 adds μου = Lucianic MSS and others c) S and Dial. 97:1: ἀντελάβετό | | |

related Psalms texts, in a way similar to, but not identical with the source recognizable in Justin.

A final observation: The quotation of Ps 3:6/23:4 in *1.Clem.* 26:2 shows that Ps 3:6 was a resurrection testimony prior to Justin, although here the resurrection of the believer is at stake. As one can see from the synopsis, there is no direct dependence on the part of Justin.

(w) Ps 19:6.

In *1.Apol.* 54:9 Justin says: «When they (i.e. the demons ) learned that it was said, as has been quoted, in the ancient prophecies:᾽ Ἰσχυρός ὡς γίγας δραμεῖν ὁδόν, they said that Hercules was ἰσχυρός and had traveled over the whole earth.» The reference to an earlier quotation must be to *1.Apol.* 40:1-4, where we find Ps 19:3-6 quoted in full. But there the text of Ps 19:6, in accordance with the LXX, reads ἀγαλλιάσεται ὡς γίγας δραμεῖν ὁδόν.The ἰσχυρός, on which so much emphasis is laid in *1.Apol.* 54:9, is lacking.

In *Dial.* 69:3 we have a perfect parallel to *1.Apol.* 54:9, and again the ἰσχυρός is emphasized. But in the previous quotation of Ps 19:2-7 in *Dial.* 64:8 the word is missing. However, the long LXX text is presumably Justin's own, because in the introduction to the quotation he alludes to Ps 19:7 LXX: ὅτι ἀπ᾽ ἄκρων τῶν οὐρανῶν προέρχεσθαι ἔμελλεν καὶ πάλιν εἰς τοὺς αὐτοὺς τόπους ἀνιέναι . . ., *Dial.* 64:7. In *1.Apol.* 40:1-4 it also seems that the LXX text is original, because the following long quotation of Ps 1f in *1.Apol.* 40:8-19 indicates that Justin had his Psalms MS before him when writing this part of the *Apology.*[131]

To conclude: Justin was very familiar with a testimony version of Ps 19:6 with the non-LXX addition ἰσχυρός , but in his two long quotations he has looked the text up in his Psalms MS.

(x) Ps 24:7f (synopsis next page).

The non-LXX version of this text quoted in *1.Apol.* 51:7 is clearly adapted to the Christological reference the text has in Justin: It is an ascension testimony. The «gates» are the gates of heaven.

In *Dial.*36:3-4 Justin has turned to a Psalms MS and quotes a LXX text with none of the peculiarities of the «testimony» version. He includes one LXX term in his exegesis: ἄρχοντες . But even in *Dial.* 36:5, i.e. the comment following the LXX quotation, characteristic sayings of the text in *1.Apol.* 51:7 break through (see synopsis). The same is true in *Dial.* 85:4. Even in

---

131. In attributing the long LXX quotations to Justin, I agree with Credner, pp. 113-115; Koester, *Schriftbeweis,* pp. 45f, - against Bousset, *Evangeliencitate,* p. 19. Prigent seems ambiguous, *Justin,* pp. 108, n.1.

| Ps 24:7f LXX = Dial. 36:4 | 1. Apol. 51:7 | Dial. 36:5 | Dial. 85:4 |
|---|---|---|---|
| vs. 7<br>ἄρατε πύλας,<br>οἱ ἄρχοντες ὑμῶν　 = Dial. 85:1<br>καὶ ἐπάρθητε　 = Dial. 127:5<br>πύλαι αἰώνιοι<br>[a]καὶ εἰσελεύσεται[a]<br>ὁ βασιλεὺς τῆς δόξης<br>vs. 8<br>τίς ἐστιν οὗτος<br>ὁ βασιλεὺς τῆς δόξης<br>κύριος κραταιὸς καὶ δυνατός<br>[b]κύριος δυνατός[b] ἐν πολέμῳ | ἄρατε πύλας οὐρανῶν<br><br>ἀνοίχθητε<br><br>ἵνα εἰσέλθη<br>ὁ βασιλεὺς τῆς δόξης<br><br>τίς ἐστιν οὗτος<br>ὁ βασιλεὺς τῆς δόξης<br>κύριος κραταιὸς<br>καὶ κύριος δυνατός | ... κελεύονται οἱ ἐν τοῖς<br>οὐρανοῖς ...<br>ἄρχοντες<br>ἀνοῖξαι<br>τὰς πύλας τῶν οὐρανῶν<br>ἵνα εἰσέλθη<br>οὗτος, ὅς ἐστι βασιλεὺς<br>τῆς δόξης | ἐπᾶραι τὰς πύλας<br><br>ἵνα εἰσέλθη<br>οὗτος ὁ ἐκ νεκρῶν ἀναστὰς<br>κύριος τῶν δυνάμεων ... |

a-a) Dial. 85:1:
ἵνα εἰσέλθη
b-b) Om. by Dial. 36:4

the LXX quotation in *Dial.* 85:1 a «testimony» reading has intruded (ἵνα εἰσέλθῃ). E. Hatch remarks that this particular reading is a better rendering of the Hebrew text than is the LXX text.[132] Perhaps the one responsible for the «testimony» version had access to the Hebrew text.

(y) Ps 72:5/17(synopsis next page).

Justin quotes the whole of Ps 72 in *Dial.* 34:3-6 and vss 1-5 and 17b-19 in *Dial* 64:6. The text is LXX with some «Lucianic» features (some of them indicated in the apparatus of the synopsis).[133]

When we turn to *Dial.* 121:1f we meet an entirely different version of vs. 17.[134] The text is condensed, and instead of the LXX text πρὸ τοῦ ἡλίου διαμενεῖ we read: ὑπέρ τὸν ἥλιον ἀνατελεῖ. In this way the text is assimilated to other testimonies containing the catchword ἀνατέλλειν/ ἀνατολή (see synopsis). One should note especially the close parallelism between the combined testimony (Num 24/17/Is 11:1/51:5) in *1.Apol.* 32:12 and the deviant version of Ps 72:17 in *Dial.* 121:1. The significance of this is corroborated by the observation that in both contexts the *anatellein* testimonies are preceded by Gen 49:10(f) in the same non-LXX version. One suspects that the source behind *1. Apol.* 32 is once more being employed in *Dial.* 120f. This source may also account for the second *Anatellein* testimony in *Dial.* 121, viz. Zech 6:12. It is not called for by the present context in the *Dialogue*, and may have been added for no better reason than the fact that Justin found it in his source. We thus get the following parallelism:

| *1.Apol.* 32 | *Dial.* 120:2-121:2 |
|---|---|
| Gen 49:10f non-LXX | Gen 49:10 non-LXX, with comments on the textual problem (not necessary in the context) |
| Num 24:17 etc.: *anatellein* motif, Gentiles putting their hope in the Messiah | Ps 72:17 (non-LXX) and Zech 6:12: *anatellein* motif, Gentiles receiving blessing through the Messiah. |

The allusions to Ps 72:5 in *Dial.* 45:4 and 76:7 combine this verse with Ps 110:3.[135] Perhaps this reflects a combined «testimony» version of the two Psalm verses, but no such text is quoted in Justin. (Cf. below, 235). That Ps 72:5/17 played a role in testimony material prior to Justin is suggested by joint allusion to these verses in *2.Clem.* 14:1.

---

132. *Essays,* p. 191.
133. Full collation in Credner, pp. 123-25.
134. Cf. comments in Hommes, *Testimoniaboek,* pp. 67ff.
135. On this combination, cf. Prigent, *Justin,* pp. 92-94.

| Ps 72 LXX | Dial. 121:1 | Dial. 76:7 | 1. Apol. 32:12 |
|---|---|---|---|
| vs. 5: καὶ συμπαραμενεῖ τῷ ἡλίῳ καὶ πρὸ τῆς σελήνης γενεᾶς[a] γενεῶν | | καὶ Δαυεὶδ δὲ πρὸ ἡλίου καὶ σελήνης ἐκ γαστρὸς γεννηθήσεσθαι αὐτόν....   cf. Ps 110:3 | ἀνατελεῖ ἄστρον.... |
| vs. 17: ἔσται[b] τὸ ὄνομα αὐτοῦ εὐλογημένον εἰς τοὺς αἰῶνας πρὸ τοῦ ἡλίου διαμενεῖ [c]τὸ ὄνομα αὐτοῦ[c] καὶ εὐλογηθήσονται[d] ἐν αὐτῷ πᾶσαι αἱ φυλαὶ τῆς γῆς πάντα τὰ ἔθνη μακαριοῦσιν αὐτόν. | τὸ ὄνομα αὐτοῦ εἰς τὸν αἰῶνα ὑπὲρ τὸν ἥλιον ἀνατελεῖ καὶ ἐνευλογηθήσονται ἐν αὐτῷ πάντα τὰ ἔθνη | *Dial. 121:2* ὑπὲρ τὸν ἥλιον ἀνατελεῖ τὸ ὄνομα αὐτοῦ | καὶ ἐπὶ τὸν βραχίονα αὐτοῦ ἔθνη ἐλπιοῦσιν |

= *Dial.* 64:6

= *Dial.* 34:3

= *Dial.* 64:6

= *Dial.* 34:6

a) *Dial.* 34:3: εἰς γενεὰς = La^G
b) *Dial.* 34:6: ἔσται = Lucianic texts
c-c) Add. *Dial.* 34:6mg.
d) *Dial.* 34:6 = 64:6: ἐνευλ.. = Lucianic MSS.

(z) Ps 110 (synopsis next page).

It seems that Ps 110 is represented in two text-types in Justin, one Septuagintal represented by the long quotations in *1.Apol.* 45:2-4; *Dial.* 32:6; *Dial.* 63:6; and the other non-LXX contained in the long quotation in *Dial.* 83:2 and the shorter quotations in *Dial.* 56:14; 83:1.4; 127:5.[136]

Most of the variants are irrelevant to our purpose. The significant diffe-rences occur in vs. 2. It must be said at once that the textual evidence is rather confusing. Justin comments on Ps 110:2 in *1.Apol.* 45:5 and *Dial.* 83:3f. Let us compare the comments with the texts. In *1.Apol.* 45:5 the ῥάβδος δυνάμεως is identified as the mighty word which the apostles preached ἀπὸ᾽ Ἰερουσαλήμ. This confirms the reading ἐξ ᾽Ιερουσαλήμ in the text. It is in harmony with the comment on Is 2 : 3f ( ᾽εκ γὰρ Σιὼν ἐξελεύσεται νόμος καὶ λόγος κυρίου ἐξ ᾽Ιερουσαλήμ) in *1.Apol.* 39:3 : ἀπὸ γὰρ᾽ Ἰερουσαλὴμ ἄνδρες δεκαδύο τὸν ἀριθμὸν ἐξῆλθον εἰς τὸν κόσμον . . . So far everything is clear: The ῥάβδος δυνάμεως being sent out from Jerusalem is the apostolic kerygma.

But who is the sender of the ῥάβδος? In the LXX text it is no doubt God = κύριος. (The reference in σοι is to the Messiah). But Justin hardly under-stood the verse in this way. As we shall see, for him the sender of the ῥάβδος is not God but Christ. It is therefore perhaps not accidental that Justin drops κύριος in his repetition of vs. 2 in *1.Apol.* 45:5 (᾽Ράβδος δυνάμεως ἐξαποσ-τελεῖ σοι ἐξ ᾽Ιερουσαλήμ), and he probably takes the σοι as a reference to the recipient of the kerygma, i.e. the believer, cf. the ἡμεῖς in the last clause in *1.Apol.* 45:5. Are we justified in suspecting a non-LXX «testimony» version of Ps 110:2 behind the long LXX excerpt in *1.Apol.* 45? (Cf. below, p. 231)

Turning to *Dial.* 83:3f, we find that Justin is quite emphatic in his identification of Christ as the sender of the ῥάβδος: «Who does not know that he (i.e. Hezekiah) did not send the sceptre of power *into* (εἰς) Jerusalem, and did not rule in the midst of his enemies? For was it not God who turned his enemies away while he wept and moaned? But our Jesus has sent forth into (εἰς) Jerusalem the sceptre of power, namely, the call of repentance to all the nations over which the demons used to rule . . .»

It is obvious that Justin takes the subject of the verbs ἐξαποστελεῖ and κατακυριεύσει to be Christ. This accords with his exegesis in *1.Apol.* 45.

But in *Dial.* 83 the ῥάβδος ( = the call to the Gentiles ) is sent *into* Jerusalem, or ἐπὶ ᾽Ιερουσαλήμ in the text of the Psalm. There can be no doubt that this reading in the Psalm text is original, because without it one can see no reason why Justin should introduce this idea of a sending *into*

---

136. This stability in the rendering of both versions tells against Credner's view that *Dial.* 83:2 is a free quotation from memory, pp. 131f. Cf. also the textual analysis of Koester, *Schriftbeweis,* pp. 46f.

| *Dial.* 32:6 = Ps 110:1—4LXX | *Dial.* 83:2 | |
|---|---|---|
| vs. 1<br>Εἶπεν ὁ κύριος τῷ κυρίῳ μου<br>κάθου ἐκ δεξιῶν μου<br>ἕως ἂν θῶ τοὺς ἐχθρούς σου<br>ὑποπόδιον τῶν ποδῶν σου | Λέγει κύριος[a] τῷ κυρίῳ μου<br>κάθου ἐκ δεξιῶν μου<br>ἕως ἂν θῶ τοὺς ἐχθρούς σου<br>ὑποπόδιον τῶν ποδῶν σου | = *Dial.* 56:14<br>= *Dial.* 83:1<br>= *Dial.* 127:5 |
| vs. 2<br>ῥάβδον δυνάμεως<br>ἐξαποστελεῖ σοι[a] κύριος<br>ἐκ Σιών[b]<br>καὶ κατακυρίευε ἐν μέσῳ<br>τῶν ἐχθρῶν σου    = *1. Apol.* 45:2—4 | ῥάβδον δυνάμεως<br>ἐξαποστελεῖ<br>ἐπὶ Ἰερουσαλήμ<br>καὶ κατακυριεύσει ἐν μέσῳ<br>τῶν ἐχθρῶν σου | *1. Apol.* 45:5<br>ῥάβδον δυνάμεως<br>ἐξαποστελεῖ σοι<br>ἐξ Ἰερουσαλήμ |
| vs. 3<br>μετὰ σοῦ ἡ ἀρχὴ<br>ἐν ἡμέρᾳ τῆς δυνάμεός σου<br>ἐν ταῖς λαμπρότησι<br>τῶν ἁγίων σου[c]<br>ἐκ γαστρὸς πρὸ ἑωσφόρου<br>ἐγέννησά σε    = *Dial.* 63:3 | ἐν λαμπρότητι<br>τῶν ἁγίων<br>πρὸ ἑωσφόρου<br>ἐγέννησά σε | *Dial.* 83:4<br>ἐν τῇ λαμπρότητι<br>τῶν ἁγίων<br>ἐκ γαστρὸς πρὸ ἑωσφόρου<br>ἐγέννησά σε |
| vs. 4<br>ὤμοσε κύριος<br>καὶ οὐ μεταμεληθήσεται    = *Dial.* 33:1<br>Σὺ[d] ἱερεὺς εἰς τὸν αἰῶνα<br>κατὰ τὴν τάξιν Μελχισεδέκ    = *Dial.* 33:2 | vs. 4 identical with<br>*Dial.* 32:6 | |

a) = Luclanic group. Rahlfs: σου ἐξαποστελεῖ  
b) *1. Apol.* 45:3:[b] Ἰερουσαλήμ  
c) = Luclanic group. Rahlfs om. σου  
d) = Luclanic group. Rahlfs: Σὺ εἶ

a) *Dial.* 56:14: ὁ κύριος

Jerusalem at all.[137] The opposite direction of the sending in *1.Apol* 45(text and comment) is much more natural.

One gets the impression that Justin in *Dial* 83 is trying to adjust his exegesis of Ps 110:2 (as found in *1.Apol* 45) to a version of the text which originally had another purpose. One can perhaps find an indication of this original intent in Justin's comments on Hezekiah. «Who is not aware that he was not the redeemer of Jerusalem? And who does not know that he did not send the sceptre of power into Jerusalem, and did not rule midst of his enemies?» This idea about the Psalm's Messiah *redeeming Jerusalem* with his mighty ῥάβδος, seems rather unrelated to the idea of the apostolic mission *out from* Jerusalem (=*1.Apol* 45), and may very well reflect the original idea behind the deviant version of Ps 110:1-4 in *Dial* 83. Perhaps we have before us a «testimony» version reflecting Judaeo-Christian concern about Jerusalem (after 135 AD? ), and expressing the same eschatological orientation towards Jerusalem as we find e.g. in *Dial* 80f and related texts (see further pp. 401ff).

One last remark on the deviant text of Ps 110:1-4 in *Dial* 83:2. This text lacks the first stichos of vs.3. It is perhaps more than a coincidence that Justin never *quotes* (separately) or comments or alludes to this stichos. Probably the source in which Justin found the text of Ps 110:1-4 was important to his whole treatment of the Psalm.

To conclude: Behind the present LXX text of Ps 110 in *1.Apol* 45 we have seen reasons to suspect a deviant «testimony» version of Ps 110:2 ( perhaps simply lacking the σοι of the LXX text). In *Dial* 83 we encounter another testimony version with another orientation. Justin tries to synthesize two exegetical ideas in his comments on this text.

(zz) Dan 7:13 (synopsis next page).

My comments on this text can be brief, because I have little to add to what has been said by D.Barthélemy and P.Prigent.[138] Let me briefly state the facts.

In *1.Apol* 51:9 we find a non-LXX and non-«θ»text which looks like a conflation of Dan 7:13 and Mt 25:31. It is introduced as «Jeremiah». One of the distinctive features of the text is the reading ἐπάνω τῶν νεφελῶν. Compare with this the allusions in *Dial* 14:8: ... τὴν δευτέραν αὐτοῦ παρουσίαν, ὅτε ἐν δόξῃ καὶ ἐπάνω τῶν νεφελῶν παρέσται ..., and *Dial* 120.4: ... καὶ προσδοκᾶται πάλιν παρέσεσθαι ἐπάνω τῶν νεφελῶν. Even more striking is the correspondence between the deviant text in *1.Apol*

---

137. Smit Sibinga thinks that the Psalm text (ἐπὶ) as well as Justin's comments on the text (reading εἰς 'Ιερουσαλὴμ) have been subjected to scribal «corrections», p. 55. He finds the text as it stands «clearly impossible». I should prefer to say: difficult, but not impossible - and certainly more improbable as a later scribal modification than as Justin's own reading. (Smit Sibinga's proposal that the ἐπὶ arose from a misreading of ΠΙΠΙ (= יהוה ) is sheer conjecture).

138. Barthélemy, 'Redécouverte', p. 136; P. Prigent, *Justin,* pp. 78f.

| Mt 25:31 | 1. Apol. 51:9 | Dial. 31:1 | Dial. 31:3 cf. Dan 7:13 "θ" and LXX |
|---|---|---|---|
| ὅταν δὲ ἔλθῃ<br>ὁ υἱὸς τοῦ ἀνθρώπου<br>ἐν τῇ δόξῃ αὐτοῦ | ἰδοὺ<br>ὡς υἱὸς ἀνθρώπου<br>ἔρχεται<br>ἐπάνω τῶν νεφελῶν<br>τοῦ οὐρανοῦ | ὡς υἱὸς γὰρ ἀνθρώπου<br><br>ἐπάνω νεφελῶν ἐλεύσεται<br>... | ... καὶ ἰδοὺ<br><br>μετά[a] τῶν νεφελῶν τοῦ οὐρανοῦ<br>ὡς υἱὸς ἀνθρώπου [b]ἐρχόμενος[b]... |
| καὶ πάντες<br>οἱ ἄγγελοι<br>μετ' αὐτοῦ... | καὶ<br>οἱ ἄγγελοι αὐτοῦ<br>σὺν αὐτῷ | ... ἀγγέλων<br>σὺν αὐτῷ... | |

a) LXX: ἐπὶ
b-b) θ: ἐρχόμενος ἦν; LXX: ἤρχετο.

51:9 and Justin's introduction to the quotation of Dan 7:9-28 in *Dial.* 31:1 (see synopsis).

This shows how deeply engraved in Justin's memory the «testimony» text was, because no *angels* appear in the Daniel text which follows the introduction, and it reads μιδεασ τεστιμονν ιν τεετά τῶν νεφελῶν.

As is well known, this long Daniel text has readings which agree both with LXX and «Theodotion».[139] It is almost certainly original in Justin, because he begins his comment after the quotation with the words «When I ceased», which indicates a long quotation. As Prigent remarks: *«Le texte de la citation offre en Dial. 31 plus de quarante accords importants avec les LXX contre Théodotion et une quinzaine d'accords avec Théodotion contre les LXX. Cet éclectisme n'est évidemment pas le fruit d'une correction ultérieure, c'est bien le texte que Justin a lu et recopié».*[140]

However, is it certain that Justin's text is «eclectic»? Barthélemy has made the proposal that Justin's Daniel text represents the καιγε recension which «Theodotion» later revised.[141]

If so, one can speculate that if Justin had made any comments on the textual discrepancies in Dan 7:13, he would in his usual way have insisted that the text of *1.Apol.* 51:9 was the true «LXX», while the text in *Dial.* 31 was a «Jewish» revision of the text. And - again - in the latter respect he might very well have been right.

*Conclusions.*

(1) The evidence surveyed in this chapter confirms our hypothesis in ch. 1 above: Justin has two sources for his OT quotations, viz. «testimony sources» and LXX MSS. The text of the testimony sources tends to be non-LXX, and as a rule Justin's exegesis presupposes these non-LXX texts. This means that they had great authority for him and that they should be seen as part of an exegetical tradition.

(2) Justin often neglects discrepancies between his inherited exegesis and the LXX text he quotes. But sometimes he tries to adjust his interpretation to the LXX text. This proves that the LXX texts are not secondary corrections by later scribes.

---

139. A useful synopsis is given by Swete, *Introduction,* pp. 421-22; comments pp. 422f. I prefer to write «Theodotion» and «θ» with quotation marks, because it is far from certain that the «Theodotion» text in Daniel has anything to do with Theodotion's translation. Cf. esp. A. Schmitt, *Stammt der sogenannte «θ» - Text bei Daniel wirklich von Theodotion?*(Nachrichten der Akademie der Wissenschaften in Göttingen aus dem Jahre 1966, Philologisch-Historische Klasse 8 (pp. 279-392), Göttingen 1966).

140. *Justin,* p. 78.

141. See Barthélemy, 'Redécouverte', p. 136: *«Si nous supposons.. que Justin témoigne ici encore pur notre recension, nous ne manquerons pas d'être frappés par le fait que Théodotion ne manifeste, ici du moins, aucune connaissance directe de la LXX non-recensée, mais semble avoir pris pour base notre texte.»* Prigent, *Justin,* p. 78, seems to be unaware of Bartélemy's proposal.

(3) The testimony sources seem to have contained «targumizing» texts as well as composite quotations created with great care. They should not be easily dismissed as free quotations from memory. Sometimes they betray direct recourse to the Hebrew text. As far as the Greek evidence goes, they seem to have the «standard» LXX as their point of departure, while on the other hand Justin's long LXX quotations may show signs of recensional activity even outside the Twelve Prophets.

There is thus some substance to Justin's insistence that his testimony texts represent the LXX, while his long LXX excerpts represent a Jewish, recensed text.

(4) So far we have left the precise nature of the «testimony sources» an open question. But we have seen indications that one should not think of mere quotation anthologies. They seem to have contained interpretation and arguments attached to the texts, and they seem to have included quotations from sources other than the OT (in one instance Plato, more often the NT).

(5) It is evident that Justin has a more than casual acquaintance with these testimony sources. Their textform in OT quotations is deeply engraved on his mind - witness his frequent allusions. He often interprets a LXX text as if the «testimony» text had been read. This may point to some kind of «school tradition» as the milieu which furnished Justin with the testimony sources, or some of them. In any case, it is evident that the text of these sources had great authority for Justin and that his exegesis has been decisively shaped by them.

Let me add a final note on the deviations contained in Justin's non-LXX text. I believe J. Daniélou and R. le Deaut right to stress that the «interpolated» and «modified» Biblical quotations should not be seen as wilful forgeries of the Bible text, but as an expression of genuine concern for the deeper meaning of the sacred text.[142] Paraphrase and interpolation of elucidating comment are not foreign methods to the Jewish Targums - but the Targumists conceived of themselves as interpreters and transmitters of the text's meaning, not as interpolators. Daniélou is probably right when he takes the very modified «testimony» quotations in the NT and the earliest Fathers as direct witnesses of Judaeo-Christian work with the Biblical text, applying the Jewish method of targumizing: «the method itself derives from a Judaistic environment to which Hellenistic literary methods were com-

---

142. J. Daniélou, *Theology*, pp. 88-97; idem, *Études*, p. 7; R. le Deaut, 'Un phénomene spontané de l'hermeneutique juive ancienne: le «targumisme»', *Biblica* 52 (1971), pp. 505-25; idem, 'La tradition juive ancienne et l'exégèse chretienne primitive', *RHPbR* 51 (1971), pp. 31-50, esp. pp. 43-50.

pletely foreign.»[143] We may thus have here a first indication about the provenance of Justin's testimony tradition.

### 3. Justin and earlier Christian writers.

It may seem illogical to reserve the treatment of known sources until after the analysis of unknown sources. My justification for doing so is partly the fact that any analysis of the relationship between, say, Justin and Matthew soon would have become entangled in the question of intermediary sources between the two writers. We would thus have had to treat the «testimony source» problem in any case, and partly on less instructive material.

Besides, the present arrangement now allows us to test the assumptions advanced in the previous section: Does Justin's treatment of the sources known to us confirm our ideas about his relation to his unknown sources?

The following survey is limited to the question of OT quotations; it is not intended as a full-scale assessment of the literary relations between Justin and his various precursors. But even this limited aspect may cast light on how Justin the exegete employed these sources, and which writers were of special significance for him.

### (a) Paul[144]

#### (α) Romans

Apart from *Barnabas, 1.Clement,* and Matthew, there is no other Christian writing - prior to Justin - with which he has so many quotations in

---

143. *Theology,* p. 89 Cf. also his statement in *Études,* p. 7: «*En fait, nous nous trouvons ici en présence d'une méthode exégétique qui relève du milieu juif où est apparu le christianisme. Le texte de l'Écriture n'avait pas encore le caractère fixé qu'il a reçu plus tard. Les targumim, en traduisant la Bible de l'hébreu en araméen, y apportaient des précisions. La traduction des Septante présentait des libertés analogues. . . . Un des aspects de l'enseignement chrétien primitif était une exégèse de l'Ancien Testament à la manière des rabbis. En ajoutant des mots qui rendaient plus précise l'application des textes au Christ, les judéo-chrétiens n'avaient pas le sentiment de fausser l'Écriture. Ils estimaient au contraire en être les exégètes authentiques, dans la mesure où le Christ était bien celui dont parlait l'Écriture. . . . Ainsi ces citations sont un vestige précieux de la littérature judéo-chrétienne. Elles attestent que les judéo-chrétiens se considéraient comme les Juifs fidèles à qui appartenait l'Ancien Testament.*»An indirect confirmation that this may be right is the fact that Justin himself no longer has this self-conscious attitude *vis-a-vis* the very text of the OT.

144. Generally on the relation between Paul and Justin, see i.a. A. Thoma, 'Justins literarisches Verhältnis zu Paulus und zum Johannisevangelium', *ZWTh* 18 (1875), pp. 383-412/490-565 (on Paul, pp. 383-412); M. von Engelhardt, *Christenthum,* pp. 353-374; Bousset, *Evangeliencitate,* pp. 40/121-123; E. Aleith, *Paulusverständnis in der Alten Kirche* (BZNW 18, Berlin, 1937), pp. 34-39; E. Massaux, *Influence de l'Évangile de saint Matthieu sur la littérature chrétienne avant saint Irénée* (Universitas catholica Lovaniensis Dissertationes, Ser. II, 42, Louvain/Gembloux, 1950), pp. 508f/562-69; Shotwell, *Exegesis,* pp. 50-55; A. Lindemann, *Paulus im ältesten Christentum* (BHTh 58, Tübingen, 1979), pp. 353-367. Cf. also Th. Zahn, *Geschichte des Neutestamentlichen Kanons* I:2 (Erlangen/Leipzig, 1889), pp. 563-575.

common as Romans. Of a sum total of 49 explicit and implicit OT quotations in Romans, Justin has parallels to 14(29%). I will therefore go in some detail here and use Romans as a test case: How does Justin use this source? How exact are his renderings of OT texts in Romans?

The method employed has been to check every OT quotation in Romans against its occurrence or non-occurrence in Justin. In deciding what should be seen as quotation rather than allusion in Romans, I have preferred the judgements of the 25th ed. of Nestle over against the 26th (Aland) edition. The following table summarizes the evidence . My conclusions are indicated briefly in the table. The most important cases are studied synoptically in a seperate section (below, pp. 114 - 129)'The table contains cross-references to this section, or to discussions elsewhere.

| Romans | Paul | Justin |
|---|---|---|
| 1:17 | Hab 2:4 | --- |
| 2:24 | Is 52:5b non-LXX | *Dial.* 17:2: Is 52:5b LXX, but with one devitation common with Paul. Influence from Romans? (Cf. synoptic study 1). |
| 3:4 | Ps 51:4 | --- |
| 3:10—18 | Ps 14:1—3/Ps 5:9/ Ps 140:3/Ps 10:7/ Is 59:7f/Ps 36:1 | *Dial.* 27:3: essentially = Rom 3:12—17, but with some minor omissions and replacements. Not introduced as a formal quotation. Dependent on Romans. |
| 3:20 | Ps 143:2 | --- |
| 4:3, cf. 4:9 | Gen 15:6 | *Dial.* 11:5: all. to Rom 4:10f. *Dial.* 23:4: all. to Gen 15:6, which also all. to Paul's exegesis in Rom 4:10f. *Dial.* 92:3: Gen 15:6 = Rom 4:3 against LXX, and all. to Paul's exegesis. *Dial.* 119:5f: all. Gen 15:6. In all cases: Direct dependence upon Romans (Cf. synoptic study 2). |
| 4:7f | Ps 32:1f (LXX) | *Dial.* 141:2: Ps 32:2, somewhat telescoped. The last stichos of vs. 2 omitted, as in Romans. Probably dependent upon Paul. (Cf. synoptic study 3) |
| 4:17 | Gen 17:5 | *Dial.* 11:5; 119:4: allusions, dependent upon Romans. |
| 4:18 | Gen 15:5 | --- |
| 7:7 | Ex 20:17 | --- |

| 8:36 | Ps 44:22 | --- |
|---|---|---|
| 9:7 | Gen 21:12 | --- |
| 9:9 | Gen 18:10.14 | --- |
| 9:12 | Gen 25:23 | --- |
| 9:13 | Mal 1:2f | --- |
| 9:15 | Ex 33:19 | --- |
| 9:17 | Ex 9:16 | --- |
| 9:20 | Is 29:16 | --- |
| 9:21 | Jer 18:6 | --- |
| 9:25f | Hos 2:25/2:1 | Cf. *Dial.* 19:5: Hos 1:9. Argument possibly dependent upon Romans. (Cf. synoptic study 4). |
| 9:27f | Is 10:22f | --- |
| 9:29 | Is 1:9 (LXX) | *1. Apol.* 53:7 and *Dial.* 140:3: Is 1:9 telescoped. *Dial.* 32:2 and 55:3: all. Possibly dependent upon Romans. (Cf. synoptic study 5). |
| 9:33 cf. 10:11 | Is 28:16/8:14 | --- |
| 10:5 | Lev 18:5 | --- |
| 10:6—8 | Deut 30:12—14 | --- |
| 10:13 | Joel 3:5 | --- |
| 10:15 | Is 52:7 | --- |
| 10:16 | Is 53:1 | *Dial.* 42:2: Is 53:1f; *Dial.* 114:2: Is 53:1 (the same excerpt as in Rom 10:16). In both cases: Direct dependence upon Romans (Cf. synoptic study 6) |
| 10:18 | Ps 19:5 | *Dial.* 42:1: Ps 19:5 (the same excerpt as in Rom 10:18). Direct dependence upon Romans (Cf. synoptic study 6). |
| 10:19 | Deut 32:21 | *Dial.* 119:2: Deut 32:16—23. Paul's quotation probably the testimony nucleus behind Justin's long excerpt. (Cf. above p. 53). |
| 10:20f | Is 65:1f | *1. Apol.* 49:2—4 and *Dial.* 24:4: Is 65: 1—3, not dependent upon Romans, cf. above, pp. 65 - 67 *Dial.* 119:4: Allusive quotation of Is 65:1 - probably from memory. Perhaps inspired from Romans. (Cf. synoptic study 7). |

| 11:2 | Ps 94:14 | --- |
|------|----------|-----|
| 11:3f | 1 Kings 19:10.14.18 (non-LXX) | *Dial.* 39:1 = Rom 11:3f, copied almost *verbatim*. |
| 11:8 | Deut 29:3/Is 29:10 | --- |
| 11:9f | Ps 69:23f/Ps 35:8 | --- |
| 11:26f | Is 59:20f/Jer 31:33f/ Is 27:9 | --- |
| 11:34f | Is 40:13/Job 15:8 | --- |
| 12:17 | Prov 3:4 | --- |
| 12:19 | Deut 32:35 | --- |
| 12:20 | Prov 25:21f | --- |
| 13:9 | Ex 20:13—15.17 Lev 19:18 | --- |
| 14:11 | Is 49:18/Is 45:23 | *1. Apol.* 52:5f: Ezek 37:7f/Is 45:23 No dependence upon Romans, cf. below, 436 |
| 15:3 | Ps 69:10 | --- |
| 15:3 | Ps 18:50 | --- |
| 15:10 | Deut 32:43 (one stichos) | *Dial.* 130:1: Deut 32:43 (the whole LXX verse); *Dial.* 130:4: = Rom 15:10. In both cases direct recourse to Romans (Cf. synoptic study 8). |
| 15:11 | Ps 117:1 | --- |
| 15:12 | Is 11:10 | --- |
| 15:21 | Is 52:15 | *Dial.* 118:4: Is 52:15—53:1. An expanded LXX version of Paul's quotation. |

One observation immediately leaps to the eye when one surveys this table: Justin's quotations are not evenly distributed among Paul's. Justin has to a great extent taken over Paul's quotations *in blocks*. (He has 5 of the 8 texts in Rom 2-4; 5 texts out of 6 in Rom 10:16-11:4).

Let me add that the same holds true the other way round. The quotations in common with Romans are not evenly distributed in the *Dialogue*, but are concentrated in two blocks:

| *1. Apol.* 49:2—4 | Rom | 10:20f | |
| " 53:7: | 9:29 | | |

| *Dial.* 11:5: | Rom | 4:3.17 | |
| " 17:2: | " | 2:24 | |
| " 19:5: | " | 9:25f? | |
| " 23:4: ┐ | " | 4:3—10 | |
| " 24:4: | " | 10:20f | |
| " 27:3: | " | 3:10—18f | |
| " 32:2: | " | 9:27—29/11:5 | First block |
| " 39:1: | " | 11:3f | |
| " 42:1f: | " | 10:16—18 | |
| " 44:1: | " | 9:7 | |
| " 46:6: | " | 11:3 | |
| " 47:5: | " | 2:4 | |
| " 55:3: | " | 9:29 | |
| " 92:3: ◄ | " | 4:3ff | |
| " 114:2: | " | 10:16 | |
| " 118:4: | " | 15:21 | |
| " 119:2: | " | 10:19 | Second block |
| " 119:4: | " | 4:17 | |
| " 119:5f: | " | 4:3ff | |
| " 130:1.4: | " | 15:10 | |
| " 140:3: | " | 9:29 | |
| " 141:2: | " | 4:7f | |

This observation strengthens the impression gained by a detailed examination of each case of common quotations: Justin seems in most cases to be directly drawing on Romans when he has OT quotations in common with Romans. This conclusion may be further corroborated by the following consideration. Justin did not have at his disposal a convenient Nestle or Aland edition of Romans in which OT quotations were written in bold script and references given in the margin. He would quite simply have difficulties in recognizing all quotations in Romans, especially the implicit quotations which are not marked as such by any formula. Let us try a little computation.

Of the approximately 50 quotations in Romans, 13 are not clearly marked as such.[145] Justin has only one of these (which makes 8%),viz. Ps 19:5 in *Dial.* 42:1. We have seen above that Justin was very familiar with this Psalm. 23 quotations are marked out by the formula καθὼς γέγραπται or similar expressions.[146] Justin has 6 of these (which makes 26%), two from Is 52, two

---

145. Rom 9:7: Gen 21:12; 9:9: Gen 18:10/14; 9:12: Gen 25:23; 9:20: Is 29:16; 9:21: Jer 18:6; 10:6-8: Deut 30:12-14; 10:13:Joel 3:5; 10:18: *Ps 19:5;* 11:2: Ps 94:14; 11:34f: Is 40:13/Job 15:8; 12:17: Prov 3:4; 12:20: Prov 25:21f; 13:9: Ex 20:13-15.17, Lev 19:18

146. Rom 1:17: Hab 2:4; 2:24: *Is 52:5b;* 3:4 Ps 51:4; 3:10-18: *Ps 14:1-3 etc;* 3:20: Ps 143:2; 4:3: *Gen 15:6;* 4:17: *Gen17:5;* 4:18: Gen 15:5; 7:7: Ex 20:17; 8:36: Ps 44:22; 9:13: Mal 1:2f; 9:17: Ex 9:16; 9:33: Is 28:16/Is 8:14; 10:15: Is 52:7; 11:8: Deut 29:3/Is 29:10; 11:26f: Is 59:20f etc; 12:19: Deut 32:35; 14:11: Is 49:18/ 45:23; 15:3: Ps 69:10; 15:9: Ps 18:50; 15:10: *Deut 32:43;* 15:11: Ps 117:1;15:21: *Is 52:15.*

from Gen 15-17, one from the Psalms and one from Deut 32 - all of them texts with which Justin elsewhere shows familiarity. (He has identified Rom 2:24 as Isaiah, *Dial* 17:2 - but maybe he is here dependent on an intermediary source, cf.p.114 ;Rom 3: 10ff has in *Dial* 27:3 the general introduction βοᾶ; in *Dial.* 23:4 (Gen 15:6) he echoes Paul's reference in Rom 4:3: ἡ γραφή; in *Dial.* 130:1 he has identified the speaker in Rom 15:10 as Moses; and the quotation in Rom 15:21 is identified as Isaiah in *Dial.* 118:4).

In the remaining 13 quotations Paul gives a reference to a book or person. Of these, Justin has 7 (which makes 54%).[147] In other words: There is a significantly increased frequency of common quotations in those cases in which Paul clearly introduces his quotations as such. This, I believe, proves that Justin's recourse to the quotation material in Romans is direct - and not via an intermediary source or tradition - also in most cases in which an atomistic comparison of the two writers yield no safe conclusion.

Apart from this rather technical reason for Justin's selection of quotation material in Romans, one may add that Justin's theological outlook should also be taken into consideration. Some of Paul's theological positions are ignored or not shared by Justin, and it is only natural that the corresponding OT material should not be used by him.

Considering Justin's anti-Jewish polemics, we should on a priori grounds expect a concentration on chs. 2-4 and 9-11 in Romans, and this partly coincides with the evidence. Taking a closer look at Justin's omissions, we notice that in Rom 2-4 he has omitted the texts which Paul has adduced to prove that every man is a sinner, Ps 51:4 and Ps 143:2. Ps 14:1-3 etc. in Rom 3:10-18 is turned into an anti-Jewish text by Justin.

In Rom 9 he has none of the quotations concerned with divine election and/or predestination, Rom 9:6-24. He starts his borrowings with the catena in Rom 9:25ff. The omission of Rom 9:33 - 10:15 is not so easily explained, nor would it be surprising to find the quotations of Rom 11:8-11 in Justin.

On the other hand, Paul's positive sayings about future redemption for Israel in Rom 11:26ff have found no echo in Justin's theology in general, so it is not surprising that the corresponding OT texts should be missing in Justin.

Now, I do not want to create the impression that Justin had any intention of using every OT quotation in Romans, and that therefore every omission needs an explanation. One can rather say that the striking fact about Justin's relation to Romans is the considerable number of OT texts he shares with Paul, and further that so many omissions can be accounted for. This indicates that Justin found Romans a very valuable source of prooftexts and argument which he probably exploited to the best of his ability and insight,

---

147. Rom 4:7f: *Ps 32:1f;* 9:15: Ex 33:19; 9:25f: Hos 2:25/Hos 2:1; 9:27f: Is 10:22f; 9:29: *Is 1:9;* 10:5: Lev 18:5; 10:16: *Is 53:1;* 10:19: *Deut 32:21;* 10:20f: *Is 65:1f;* 11:3: *1 Kings 19:10.14;* 11:4: *1 Kings 19:18;* 11:9f: Ps 69:23f/35:8; 15:12: Is 11:10.

and as far as it suited his own polemical purposes. As we shall see, one can hardly say the same about any other NT writing - except perhaps Galatians - and this seems to me a significant observation.

Concerning Justins's way of handling Romans as a «testimony source», the following observation can be made: Justin uses the OT texts in Romans much the same way as we posited above concerning his use of the hypothetical testimony sources.

(1) He can take over non-LXX quotations in Paul, and in such cases he copies Paul faithfully. He is even very close to his source in allusive, informal quotations.

(2) But he can also look Paul's quotation up in the relevant OT book, especially when he is very familiar with that particular book (Isaiah, Psalms, Deut 32). In these cases he will normally extend the quotation beyond the excerpt found in Paul.

A final remark: When reading through the passages where the Pauline texts occur, one is struck by the fact that they rarely are pivotal texts in Justin's argument. They are rather additional supporting material. That is: The Pauline material seems to have been added to an already existing, largely non-Pauline groundwork of testimonies. I am here content merely to indicate this. We shall have to pursue this point further at a later stage in our inquiry.

For the rest of the Pauline epistles, full surveys of all quotation material have been judged unneccesary. I only include brief notices on the relevant parallels between the two authors.

(β) 1 Corinthians

| 1 Cor | OT quotation | Justin |
|---|---|---|
| 1:19 | Is 29:14b | *Dial.* 78:11: Is 29:13f LXX. *Dial.* 32:5; 123:4: Is 29:14, the whole verse, LXX. Context in Justin different from Paul's, probably no direct dependence. Cf. above, pp. 57f. |
| 10:7 | Ex 32:6 LXX | *Dial.* 20:1: Ex 32:6 non-LXX; Deut 32:15. A similar combination in *1. Clem.* 3:1. Justin probably dependent upon a testimony source parallel to *1. Clem.* (Cf. synoptic study 9). |
| 10:26 | Ps 24:1 | *Dial.* 36:3—4: Ps 24 LXX. Test. nucleus in vss. 7f — no dep. upon Paul. |

To conclude: There is no certain borowing from 1 Cor in Justin.[148]

### (γ) 2 Corinthians

The only common quotation is Is 49:8 in 2 Cor 6:2 and *Dial.* 122:5. Paul has a short excerpt; Justin has the whole verse and stresses a part of the verse that is not included in Paul. The contexts are so different as to render it quite unlikely that there is any dependence on Paul in *Dial.* 122.

### (δ) Galatians

Of Paul's 11 quotations (three of which are common with Romans: 143:2; Gen 15:6; Hab 2:4), Justin has parallels to three:

| Gal | OT quotation | Justin |
|-----|--------------|--------|
| 3:10 | Deut 27:26 non-LXX | *Dial.* 95:1: Deut 27:26. The same non-LXX text as in Paul, directly copied from him. (Cf. synoptic study 10). |
| 3:13 | Deut 21:23b non-LXX | *Dial.* 96:1: Deut 21:23b. The same non-LXX text as in Paul, directly copied from him. (Cf. synoptic study 10). |
| 4:27 | Is 54:1LXX | *1. Apol.* 53:5: Is 54:1LXX. Direct dependence upon Galatians probable, but also possible echoes of *2. Clem.* 2:3. (Cf. synoptic study 11). |

No doubt Justin had Galatians 3 before his eyes when writing *Dial.* 95f, and in this instance the Pauline material occurs at a pivotal point in Justin's argument. This calls for further analysis of this passage in Part II (below, pp. 216ff).

---

148. Let me underline that this conclusion, here as elsewhere, only is meant to apply to OT quotations. A. Thoma, *art. cit.,* suggests that 1 Cor 10:4 is echoed in *Dial.* 114:4: Christ is the καλὴ πέτρα ... ποτιζοῦσα τοὺς βουλομένους ... πιεῖν (p. 398). This may well be the case, but one can hardly state this with certainty.

(ε) Ephesians

Justin seems to have taken his quotations of Ps 68:19 from Eph 4:8:

| Ps 68:19 LXX | Eph 4:8 = *Dial.* 39:4 = *Dial.* 87:6 |
|---|---|
| ἀνέβης εἰς ὕψος<br>ᾐχμαλώτευσας αἰχμαλωσίαν<br>ἔλαβες δόματα<br>ἐν ἀνθρώπῳ . . . | ἀναβὰς[a] εἰς ὕψος<br>ᾐχμαλώτευσεν αἰχμαλωσίαν<br>ἔδωκεν δόματα<br>τοῖς ἀνθρώποις[b] |
|  | a) *Dial.* 39:4 = 87:6: ἀνέβη<br>b) *Dial.* 87:6: υἱοῖς τῶν ἀνθρώπων |

I can see no reason to avoid the simplest theory: Justin depends on Paul.[149] It deserves notice that Justin is dependent on Paul also elsewhere in *Dial.* 39.

Summary conclusion on Justin and Paul:

Within the *corpus Paulinum*, Justin seems to have made special use of Romans and Galatians - and almost only in the *Dialogue*.

Justin's handling of his Pauline sources exemplifies the procedures we posited for his handling of other, hypothetical testimony sources. His quotations are as a rule exact, but he can sometimes substitute them for longer LXX excerpts.

(b) Matthew (and Mark)[150]

Let me first point out that Mathew is Justin's main source for synoptic material in general.[151] Here we are concerned about OT quotations only, but it holds true to say that a close examination of OT material in Mark and Matthew tends to prove that Justin takes all the Marcan material via Matthew ( only a few possible exceptions, see below). The Marcan material shall therefore be included in this paragraph, as we go through the Matthean OT quotations to find their parallels in Justin.

I first present the evidence in a table. (F = fulfilment quotation).[152]

---

149. Bousset, *Evangeliencitate*, p. 121, n. 1, posits a common source, but without any argument. Credner, to whose discussion Bousset refers, argues convincingly for direct dependence (Credner, pp. 119f). So also Prigent, *Justin*, p. 114.

150. For a general review of common quotation material in Matthew and Justin, cf. Hilgenfeld, 'Citate', pp. 567-578.

151. Cf. the detailed demonstration of this in E. Massaux, *Influence*, pp. 466-505/510-555.

152. I.e. a quotation introduced by a «fulfilment formula». I find it irrelevant to list here the quite extensive literature concerning Matthew's OT quotations. Three recent studies are: K. Stendahl, *The School of St. Matthew and its Use of the Old Testament* (ASNU XX, 2nd ed., Lund, 1969); R.H. Gundry, *The Use of the Old Testament in St. Matthew's Gospel* (Suppl.NT 18, Leiden, 1967); W. Rothfuchs, *Die Erfüllungszitate des Matthäus-Evangeliums. Eine biblisch-theologische Untersuchung* (BWANT 5. Folge 8, Stuttgart, 1969).

| Mt | Justin |
|---|---|
| 1:23: Is 7:14 F | *1. Apol.* 33:4: non-LXX version indirectly dependent on Mt 1:23. See comment pp. 32 - 34 |
| 2:6: Mic 5:1 F | *1. Apol.* 34:1 and *Dial.* 78:1: non-LXX text taken directly from Mt 2:6. (Cf. synoptic study 12). |
| 2:15: Hos 11:1 F | --- |
| 2:18: Jer 31:15 F | *Dial.* 78:8: non-LXX quotation taken from Mt 2:18. (Cf. synoptic study 13). |
| 2:23: Is 11:1? F | --- |
| 3:3: Is 40:3 | *Dial.* 50:3—5: Is 39:8 — 40:17 LXX. Inspired by Mt 3:3 or Lk 3:4—6 (= Is 40:3—5) |
| 4:4: Deut 8:3<br>4:6: Ps 91:11f<br>4:7: Deut 6:16<br>4:10: Deut 6:13 | ---<br>---<br>--- — — — [Temptation story]<br>*Dial.* 125:4 = Mt 4:10. On *Dial.* 103:6, cf. p. 222f. |
| 4:14—16: Is 8:23-9:1 F | --- |
| 8:17: Is 53:4 F | Long LXX quotations of Is 53 in *1. Apol.* 50 f and *Dial.* 13, but in different context and with different purpose. No separate quotation of Is 53:4. |
| 9:13: Hos 6:6 | --- |
| 10:35f: Mic 7:6 | --- |
| 11:5: Is 35:5f etc. | *1. Apol.* 48:2: Testimony version combined from Mt 11:5 (par. Lk 7:22) and Is 35:6f/Is 26:19. From a testimony source dependent on Matthew. *Dial.* 69:5: Is 35:1—7 LXX. See discussion above, pp. 58f. |
| 11:10: Ex 23:20/Mal 3:1 | *Dial.* 75:1f: Ex 23:20f, but in an entirely different setting. Hardly dependent on Mt. Cf. pp. 419f. |
| 11:23: Is 14:13.15 | --- |
| 12:18—21: Is 42:1—4 | *Dial.* 123:8: Is 42:1—4, LXX text with contaminations from Mt 12:18—21. *Dial.* 135:2: Is 42:1—4 LXX with fewer Matthean readings. Cf. above, pp. 60f. |
| 12:40f: Jon 1:17 etc. | *Dial.* 107f: Exposition of Jonah incident, close to Mt 12:39ff, but with additional LXX material. (Cf. synoptic study 14). |
| 13:14f: Is 6:9f F | *Dial.* 12:2 and 33:1: allusions presupposing a deviant «testimony» version, unlike the LXX text in Mt 13:14f. (Cf. synoptic study 15). |
| 13:35: Ps 78:2 F | --- |
| 15:8f: Is 29:13 | *Dial.* 27:4; 39:5; 80:4: all., no conclusion possible as to text-type. *Dial.* 140:2: all. presupposing the text of Mt 15:8f. *Dial.* 78:11: Is 29:13f LXX (some deviations). Cf discussion above, pp. 57f. |

| 19:4: Gen 1:27<br>19:5: Gen 2:24<br>19:7: Deut 24:1 | ─── ⎤<br>─── ⎥ ─ ─ ─ ─ [Discussion on divorce]<br>───⎦ |
|---|---|
| 21:5: Is 62:11/<br>Zech 9:9 F | *1. Apol.* 35:11: Testimony version partly dependent on Mt 21:5.<br>*Dial.* 53:3: Zech 9:9 καιγε? Cf. above, pp. 74 - 76. |
| 21:13: Is 56:7/Jer 7:11 | *Dial.* 17:3: conflated text from Mk 11:17/Mt 21:13/<br>Lk 19:46. (Cf. synoptic study 16). |

| 21:16: Ps 8:3 | --- |
|---|---|
| 21:33: Is 5:1f | --- |
| 21:42: Ps 118:22f | Possible all. in *Dial.* 126:1, but more likely to Is 28:16. |
| 22:24: Deut 25:5/<br>Gen 38:8 | --- |
| 22:32: Ex 3:6 | *1. Apol.* 63:17 dependent on Mt 22:31f, but the text of<br>Ex 3:6 different, see discussion above pp. 47 - 50. |
| 22:37: Deut 6:5<br>22:39: Lev 19:18 | ---<br>--- |
| 22:44: Ps 110:1 | *1. Apol.* 45:2—4; *Dial.* 32:6; *Dial.* 83:2: long quotations of Ps 110.<br>*Dial.* 56:14; 83:1; 127:5: Ps 110:1. No trace of Matthew's non-LXX<br>reading ὑποκάτω (= Mk 12:36). See discussion pp. 86 - 88. |
| 23:38: Jer 12:7 etc. | --- |
| 23:39: Ps 118:26 | --- |
| 24:15: Dan 9:27 etc. | --- |
| 24:29: Is 13:10 etc. | --- |
| 24:30f: Zech 12: 10—12<br>/Dan 7:13 | *1. Apol.* 52:10—12: composite quotation of Zech 12:10—12<br>with elements reminiscent of Mt.<br>No direct dependence, cf. above, pp. 76 - 78. |
| 26:31: Zech 13:7 | *Dial.* 53:6: Zech 13:7 καιγε? (not like Mt 26:31).<br>*Dial.* 53:5: all. Justin probably directed to this text by Matthew.<br>(Cf. synoptic study 17). |
| 26:64: Dan 7:13/<br>Ps 110:1 | Ps 110:1 never referred to the parousia in Justin.<br>But cf. the sequence Dan 7/Ps 110 in *Dial.* 31f. |
| 27:9f: Zech 11:12f<br>Jer 32:6—9 F | --- |
| 27:34: Ps 69:22 | --- |
| 27:35: Ps 22:19 | *1. Apol.* 35:5; 38:4: Combined quotation Ps 22:19/17/Ps 3:6.<br>*Dial.* 97:3: Ps 22:17—19 LXX. Paraphrases of Mt 27:35 in<br>*1. Apol.* 35:7 and *Dial.* 97:3. Justin dependent upon a testimony<br>source in the *Apology,* having besides direct recourse to Matthew<br>in the *Dialogue,* cf. above, pp. 80 - 82. |
| 27:39: Ps 22:8b ⎤<br>27:43: Ps 22:9 ⎦ | *1. Apol.* 38:6: Ps 22:8b. 9a non-LXX, possibly influenced from<br>Mt 27:39—43. Testimony source. *Dial.* 101:3: Ps 22:8b. 9a LXX,<br>references to Mt 27:39—43. Direct dependence, cf. above, pp.79f. |

| 27:46: Ps 22:2a | *Dial.* 99:1: Ps 22:2 quoted according to the LXX, interpreted as in Mt 27:46 (par. Mk 15:34). (Cf. synoptic study 18). |
| 27:48: Ps 69:22 | --- |

Let us begin with a few comments on statistics. Of approximately 65 quotations and allusions in Mt, Justin has parallels to 22 (34%), but there is direct dependence in no more than 14 cases (22%). There is thus a slightly less use of Matthew's OT material than is the case with Romans. However, this is hardly significant, since much OT material in Jesus' discussions with the Pharisees on *halakic* questions would be irrelevant to Justin. And many allusions in Matthew would be even more difficult to detect than in Romans. One can therefore conclude that Matthew was an important source of OT texts to Justin.

It must be noted, however, that only five of Matthew's 11 formal fulfilment quotations recur in Justin. This shows that Justin's series of proof-texts relating to the Gospel story is no simple excerpt from Matthew, although Matthew is a major source for Gospel material.

### (c) Luke[153]

Some of Luke's OT material is common with Matthew, and has been discussed already. I add here a list of Luke's peculiar OT quotations and their ocurrence in Justin.

| Lk | Justin |
|---|---|
| 3:22(Western text): Ps 2:7 | *Dial.* 88:8: Ps 2:7 = the words said by the voice from heaven at Jesus' baptism, as in Lk 3:22 (Western text). *Dial.* 103:6 Ps 2:7, the same text as in *Dial.* 88:8. *Dial.* 122:6: Ps 2:7f; Justin's point is in vs. 8. Probably no direct dependence. |
| 4:18f: Is 61:1f | *Dial.* 12:2: Perhaps all. to Is 61:1 (so the BP I), but rather to Mt 11:5 par. |
| 22:37: Is 53:12 | *1.Apol.* 50:2: Is 53:12non-LXX, related to Lk 22:37. See discussion above, pp. 62f. |
| 23:35: Ps 22:8a | *Dial.* 101:3: Ps 22:8f, corresponding Gospel narrative, possibly influenced from Lk 23:35. See above pp. 79f. |
| 23:46: Ps 31:6 | *Dial.* 105:5: Ps 31:6= Lk 23:46 (non-LXX). Probably direct dependence. |

153. On the relationship between Luke and Justin, see below, pp. 250f, with notes. A study especially devoted to the common stock of OT prooftexts is W.S. Kurz, *The Function of Christological Proof from Prophecy for Luke and Justin* (Yale Dissertation on microfilm, 1976). Cf. also Massaux, pp. 505-507/556-560.

I refrain from extensive synopses and comments here. Justin has nowhere a programmatic quotation of Is 61:1f corresponding to Luke's. But
apart from this, Justin seems to have been observant of one or two of the
quotations peculiar to Luke. On the special problems concerned with Ps
2:7, see further discussion below, pp. 199, n. 53, and p. 223.

## (d) Acts

The proximity between Acts and Justin has often been observed among
scholars.[154] It is all the more striking to find that Justin has framed his own
Scriptural proof almost totally independent of the argument from Scripture
found in the apostolic speeches in Acts. The following table displays the
evidence.(Stephen's numerous non-formal quotations and paraphrases in
Acts 7 have not been included.)

| Acts | Justin |
|------|--------|
| 1:20: Ps 69:26<br>     Ps 109:8 | ---<br>--- |
| 2:17—21: Joel 3:1—5 | *Dial.* 87:6: Joel 3:1f, some features common with LXX against Acts, some readings common with Acts against LXX. Telescoped text. Intermediary testimony source between Acts and Justin? (Cf. synoptic study 19). |
| 2:25—28: Ps 16:8—11 | --- |
| 2:30: Ps 132:11 | *Dial.* 68:5: Paraphrase of 2. Sam. 7:12ff, possibly influenced by Ps 132:11. Hardly any direct dependence. |
| 2:34f: Ps 110:1 | See discussion above, pp. 86 - 88.<br>Justin's understanding of Ps 110:1 similar to Luke's,<br>but probably transmitted to him via intermediary source. |
| 3:22f: Dt 18:15.18/<br>     Lev 23:29 | --- |
| 3:25: Gen 22:18 | --- |
| 4:11: Ps 118:22 | --- |
| 4:25f: Ps 2:1f | *1. Apol.* 40:11—19: Ps 2:1—12. Exegesis of Ps 2:1f reminiscent of Acts 4:27. Some influence.<br>(Cf. synoptic study 20). |
| 7:42f: Am 5:25—27 | *Dial.* 22:2—5: Am 5:18 — 6:7 καιγε text, but with LXX contaminations. Maybe Acts 7:42f was Justin's guide to this text.<br>(Cf. synoptic study 21). |
| 7:49: Is 66:1f<br>(LXX with some<br>variants) | *1. Apol.* 37:3f = *Dial.* 22:11: Is 66:1 non-LXX, different from Acts. Probably a testimony source other than Acts.<br>(Cf. synoptic study 22). |

154. Cf. the Introduction (above, p.6); and below, pp. 250f.

| | |
|---|---|
| 8:32f: Is 53:7b.8a LXX | *1. Apol.* 50:3—11: Is 52:13—53:8; continued in *1. Apol.* 51:2—5: Is 53:8—12. Text divided in the middle of the Acts excerpt from Is 53:8a. *Dial.* 13:2—9: Is 52:10 — 54:6. *Dial.* 72:3; 89:3; 90:1; 111:3: allusions to Is 53:7b. *Dial.* 114:2: Is 53:7b. No sure indication of dependence. (Cf. synoptic study 23). |
| 10:36 (cf. 13:26): Ps 107:20 | --- |
| 10:38: Is 61:6 | --- |
| 10:39: Deut 21:22 | See on Gal 3:13. |
| 13:33: Ps 2:7 | See on Lk 3:22. |
| 13:34: Is 55:3 | *Dial.* 12:1: Is 55:3—5 testimony source? See above pp. 63f. *Dial.* 14:4—7: Is 55:3—13 LXX. Context different in Justin. Probably no dependence. |
| 13:35: Ps 16:10 | --- |
| 13:41: Hab 1:5 | --- |
| 13:47: Is 49:6b LXX | *Dial.* 121:4: Is 49:6, larger excerpt than in Acts, some non-LXX readings. Perhaps a testimony source other than Acts, cf. below, p. 348f. |
| 15:16f: Am 9:11f | --- |
| 28:26—28: Is 6:9f (LXX) | *Dial.* 12:2 and 33:1: allusions pointing to a testimony source, non-LXX text. (Cf. synoptic study 15). |

Evaluating this list, it may be relevant to point out that some of the crucial proof-texts in Acts are missing in Justin: Ps 16:8-11 (Acts 2:25-28, partly repeated 13:35); Deut 18:15 etc. (Acts 3:22f); Am 9:11f (Acts 15:16f). One does not gain the impression that Acts was a main source of proof-texts to Justin. His direct borrowings are remarkably few, and some of his parallel material may be due to intermediary sources.

(e) John[155]

In the following table some of the more important quotations in John not found in Justin are also included.

155. General surveys of the relationship between John and Justin: A. Thoma, 'Justin's literarisches Verhältnis zu Paulus and zum Johannisevangelium', *ZWTh* 18 (1875), pp. 383-412/490-565 (the latter part concerns John); W. Bousset, *Evangeliencitate*, Anhang I, pp. 115-121; J. N. Sanders, *The Fourth Gospel in the Early Church. Its Origin & Influence on Christian Theology up to Irenaeus* (Cambridge, 1943), pp. 20-32; J. S. Romanides, 'Justin Martyr and the Fourth Gospel', *The Greek Orthodox Theological Review* 4 (1958/59), pp. 115-34; F.-M. Braun, *Jean le Théologien et son Évangile dans l'église ancienne* (EB, Paris, 1959), pp. 135-144; J. M. Davey, 'Justin Martyr and the Fourth Gospel', *Scripture* 17 (1965), pp. 117-22; Massaux, *Influence*, pp. 507f/560-62.

| John | Justin |
|------|--------|
| 1:23: Is 40:3 | *Dial.* 50:3—5: Is 39:8 — 40:17. See on Mt 3:3 |
| 6:31: Ps 78:24/Ex 16:4 | *Dial.* 57:2: all. to Ps 78:25. Testimony source other than John. |
| 6:45: Is 54:13 | --- |
| 7:42: 2 Sam 7:12 and Mic 5:1 | *Dial.* 68:5: paraphrase 2 Sam 7:12—16<br>*1. Apol.* 34:1 = *Dial.* 78:1: Mic 5:1 from Mt 2:6.<br>See synoptic study 12. No dependence upon John. |
| 10:34: Ps 82:6 | *Dial.* 124:8: non-LXX testimony: Ps 82:7. |
| 12:13: Ps 118:25f | --- |
| 12:15: Zeph 3:16 (MT)/<br>Zech 9:9 | *1. Apol.* 35:11: non-LXX Zech 9:9, but<br>closer to Mt 21:5. See above, pp. 74 - 76. |
| 12:38: Is 53:1 | See on Rom 10:16, synoptic study 6. John has one more *stichos* than Paul. In *Dial.* 114:2 Justin has the same excerpt as Paul, not John. Justin depends on Paul rather than John. |
| 12:40: Is 6:10 | *Dial.* 12:2 and 33:1: allusions to Is 6:10 non-LXX text, partly deriving from John 12:40. Probably intermediary source. (Cf. synoptic study 15). |
| 13:18: Ps 41:10<br>15:25: Ps 69:5 | ---<br>--- |
| 19:24: Ps 22:19 | See above, pp. 80 - 82. No dependence. |
| 19:36: Ex 12:10 etc. | --- |
| 19:37: Zech 12:10 | See above, pp. 76 - 78. No direct dependence. |

It seems that in no single case can a direct borrowing from John in Justin be demonstrated. But there are no doubt points of contact between John's OT material and Justin's testimony sources.

## (f) 1 Peter

| 1 Pet | Justin |
|-------|--------|
| 1:16: Lev 19:2 etc. | --- |
| 1:24f: Is 40:6—8 | *Dial.* 50:3f: Is 40:1—17, no dependence on 1 Pet; see above, on Mt 3:3. |
| 2:3: Ps 34:8 | --- |
| 2:6—8: Is 28:16; Ps 118:22; Is 8:14 | *Dial.* 114:4 and 126:1: all. to Is 28:16. Impossible to specify a source. (Cf. synoptic study 24). |
| 2:9: Is 43:20/Ex 19:6/ Is 61:6 | --- |
| 2:10: Hos 2:25 | See above on Rom 9:25. (Synoptic study 4). Justin probably dependent on Paul. |

| | |
|---|---|
| 2:22: Is 53:9<br>2:24: Is 53:4/12<br>2:24: Is 53:5<br>2:25: Is 53:6 | See discussion in synoptic study 23. Little overlapping between 1 Pet and Justin in their short quotations and allusions. |
| 3:10   12: Ps 34:12—16 | --- |
| 3:14f: Is 8:12f | --- |
| 4:18: Prov 11:31 | --- |
| 5:5: Prov 3:34 | --- |

No direct borrowing on the part of Justin is capable of proof. Some contact with regard to Is 53 cannot be excluded.

## (g) Hebrews[156]

Of a sum total of ca. 40 OT quotations in Hebrews, Justin har parallels to 12. They come as follows:

| Hebrews | Justin |
|---|---|
| 1:5; 5:5: Ps 2:7 | Cf. on Lk 3:22. No dependence upon Hebrews. |
| 1:5: 2 Sam 7:14 (par.<br>1 Chron 17:13) | *Dial.* 118:2: 1 Chron 17:13f non-LXX.<br>No dependence upon Hebrews. |
| 1:6: Deut 32:43 | *Dial.* 130:1: Deut 32:43; *Dial.* 130:4 = Rom 15:10. Justin depends on Paul rather than Hebrews. (Cf. synoptic study 8). |
| 1:8f: Ps 45:7f | *Dial.* 56:14: Ps 45:7f — the same excerpt as in Hebrews, but deviations from LXX text against Hebrews.<br>*Dial.* 63:4: Ps 45:7—13 LXX — begins with the same words as the excerpt in Hebrews. Some contact cannot be ruled out. (Cf. synoptic study 25). |
| 1:13: Ps 110:1 | No indication that Hebrews is specifically used for any of Justin's many allusions to and short quotations of this verse. |
| 2:12: Ps 22:23 (one non-<br>LXX reading) | *Dial.* 106:1f: Ps 22:23 LXX with comment. No sign of direct contact with Hebrews. (Cf. synoptic study 26). |
| 3:2.5: Num 12:7 (all.) | *Dial.* 46:3; 56:1; 79:4; 130:1: allusions. If Justin has a specific source for his allusions, it is *1. Clem.* 43:1 rather than Hebrews. (Cf. synoptic study 27). |
| 5:6; 7:1ff: Ps 110:4;<br>Gen 14:18—20 | *Dial.* 19:4: joint paraphrase of Ps 110:4 and Gen 14:18—20, obviously dependent upon Hebrews. *Dial.* 33:2: all. to Gen 14:18—20, same remark. (Cf. synoptic study 28). |
| 8:7—12; 10:16f:<br>Jer 31:31ff | *Dial.* 11:3: Jer 31:31f. Some devitations from the LXX in both writers, but no common deviation. The context in Hebrews possibly echoed in *Dial.* 11:2. (Cf. above, pp. 72f). |

---

156. For a general survey of the relationship between Hebrews and Justin, see Zahn, *Kanon* I:2, pp. 577-79.

| 11:5: Gen 5:24 | *Dial.* 19:3: paraphrase of Gen 5:24 possibly influenced from Hebrews. (Cf. synoptic study 29). |
| 11:18: Gen 21:12 | *Dial.* 56:7: Gen 21:9—12. Entirely different context and purpose, no influence. |

General conclusions: Although Justin has copied none of his formal OT quotations directly from Hebrews, it is practically certain that he knew this writing and made use of it. This can only be said of the *Dialogue*, however.

### (h) *1.Clement* [157]

*1. Clement* quotes frequently from the OT.[158] Of ca 86 quotations,[159] Justin has parallels to 21 (24%). In most of these cases, however, there seems to be no direct dependence, at least not with regard to the text-type of the quotations. The following chart tabulates the parallels.

| *1. Clement* | Justin |
| --- | --- |
| 3:1: Ex 32:6/ Deut 32:15 | *Dial.* 20: Ex 32:6; Deut 32:15. Not directly dependent on *1. Clem.*, but related testimony source. (Cf. synoptic study 9). |
| 8:2: Ezek 33:11 | *1. Apol.* 15:8: Allusion to Ezek 33:11(?); two non-LXX words common with *1. Clem.* The agreement may be accidental, cf. the context in Justin (synoptic study 30). |
| 8:4: Is 1:16—20 (a few non-LXX readings) | *1. Apol.* 44:3—5 (par. *1. Apol.* 61:7—8): Is 1:16—20, but with different non-LXX readings. Common tradition, but no direct dependence. (Cf. below, p. 230) |
| 10:6: Gen 15:5f | *Dial.* 11:5; 23:4; 92:3; 119:5f: quotations and allusions to Gen 15:6, but dependent on Rom 4. See above on Rom 4:3 (synoptic study 2). |
| 12:2—7: Josh 2:3—5. 9—14. 18f | *Dial.* 111:4: Rahab's scarlet cord. Reminiscent of *1. Clem.*, but with additional details from the LXX narrative. (Cf. synoptic study 31). |
| 15:2: Is 29:13 | *Dial.* 24:4: allusion exceeding *1. Clem.'s* excerpt. See above, pp. 57f. |
| 16:3—14: Is 53:1—12 | See below, pp. 125. No dependence in Justin. |
| 16:15: Ps 22:7—9 (LXX) | *1. Apol.* 38:6: Ps 22:8b. 9a non-LXX. *Dial.* 101:3: Ps 22:8f LXX. Probably no influence from *1. Clem.* See above, p. 79f. |

157. Generally on *1. Clement* and Justin, see M. von Engelhardt, *Christenthum*, pp. 394-401.
158. See full survey in D.A. Hagner, *The Use of the Old and New Testament in Clement of Rome* (Suppl. NT 34, Leiden, 1973), pp. 21-132.
159. The counting is based upon Hagner's list, *op. cit.*, p. 351.

| 17:5<br>43:1 } all. to Num 12:7 | *Dial.* 46:3; 56:1; 79:4; 130:1: allusions to Num 12:7.<br>*Dial.* 56:1 close to *1. Clem.* 43:1. See above on Heb 3:2.5.<br>(Cf. synoptic study 27). |
|---|---|
| 26:2: Ps 3:6/Ps 23:4 | *1. Apol.* 38:4: Ps 22:19/17/Ps 3:6 non-LXX.<br>*Dial.* 97:1: Ps 3:5f LXX. No direct dependence on *1. Clem.*,<br>but related testimony source. See above, pp. 80 - 82 |
| 27:7: Ps 19:2—4 | *1. Apol.* 40:3—6: Ps 19:3—6. Deviates from the LXX where<br>*1. Clem.* agrees, and vice versa. Different excerpt, no depen-<br>dence. *Dial.* 64:8: Ps 19:2—7; where overlapping with *1. Apol.*<br>40:1—4: same text. |
| 29:2: Deut 32:8f LXX | *Dial.* 131:1: Quotation of Deut 32:7b—9 with a non-LXX<br>reading. Justin says, however, that the LXX = *1. Clem.* reading<br>is the true «LXX». *1. Clem.* may thus be Justin's «testimony source»<br>in this case, cf. discussion above, pp. 29f. |
| 32:2: Gen 15:5/<br>Gen 22:17/Gen 26:4 | *Dial.* 119:6 — 120:2: all. Gen 15:6; all. Deut 32:20; quot. *Gen*<br>*26:4;* quot. Gen 28:14; all. Gen 49:10; all. *Gen 22:17.* Not the<br>same phrases as in *1. Clem.* Some related testimony tradition? |
| 33:5: Gen 1:26f non-LXX | *Dial.* 62:1: Gen 1:26f LXX. Justin's<br>argument is related to *Barn.* 5:5; 6:12, not to *1. Clem.* |
| 34:3: Is 40:10/Is 62:11/<br>Prov 24:12 | *Dial.* 50:3—5: Is 39:8—0:17 LXX. *Dial.* 26:3—4: Is 62:10—63:6.<br>The testimony nucleuses behind these long LXX excerpts are<br>other than *1. Clem.* 34:3. No dependence. |
| 35:7—12: Ps 50:16—23 | *Dial.* 22:7: Ps 50:1—23. No common deviations from the LXX.<br>Justin's point lies in vss. 8—15: no dependence.<br>But cf. on *1. Clem.* 52:3 |
| 36:4: Ps 2:7f | *Dial.* 88:8; 103:6: Ps 2:7 from Lk 3:22 (Western text).<br>See discussion pp. 199/223.<br>*Dial.* 122:6: Ps 2:7f, the same excerpt as in *1. Clem.* 36:4. Both<br>writers: LXX text. Dependence not impossible, but Justin's<br>point is different from Clement's |
| 36:5: Ps 110:1 | The same remark as to Heb. 1:13. |
| 50:6: Ps 32:1f | *Dial.* 141:2: Ps 32:2, probably from Rom 4:7f.<br>(Cf. synoptic study 3). |
| 52:3: Ps 50:14f/<br>Ps 51:19a | *Dial.* 22:7—10: Ps 50:1—23 LXX. Not impossible that<br>*1. Clem.* 52:3 was Justin's guide to this text. |
| 54:3: Ps 24:1 | *Dial.* 36:3—4: Ps 24:1—10. The testimony nucleus is in vss. 7ff.<br>No dependence on *1. Clem.* |

General conclusion: It may be that in one instance *1. Clem.* is Justin's source for a «testimony» reading (Deut 32:8); and in three or four cases was Justin's guide to relevant OT material. Considering the great bulk of OT quotations in *1.Clem.* this may seem little, but one has to keep in mind that the setting and purpose of *1.Clem.* is very different from Justin's writings. A striking feature is the relatively great number of cases in which Justin seems not directly dependent upon *1.Clem.*, but on a testimony source embodying a closely related tradition.

(i) *2. Clement*[160]

| 2. Clem. | Justin |
|---|---|
| 2:1: Is 54:1 | *1. Apol.* 53:5: Is 54:1, text = LXX = Gal 4:27 = *2. Clem.* 2:1. Exegesis related to *2. Clem.* See above on Gal 4:27 (Synoptic study 11). |
| 3:5: Is 29:13 | *Dial.* 78:11: Is 29:13f. *Dial.* 140:2: Is 29:13b = Mt 15:9. See above, pp. 57f. |
| 6:7: all. to Jer 6:16 | *Dial.* 123:3: all. to Jer 6:16, but to different words. |
| 6:8: Ezek 14:14/20 | *Dial.* 44:2; 45:3; 140:3: Ezek 14:14/20, but no direct dependence. See above, pp. 67 - 69 |
| 7:6; 17:5: Is 66:24 | *1. Apol.* 52:8; *Dial.* 140:3: Is 66:24, but no direct dependence. See above, pp. 67 - 69 |
| 13:2.4: Is 52:5 | *Dial.* 17.2. Is 52:5. A testimony version related to *2. Clem.* may be hidden behind Justin's LXX text. (Cf. synoptic study 1). |
| 14:1: Possible all. to Ps 72: 5/17 | *Dial.* 76:7: joint allusion to Ps 72:5/17/ Ps 110:3. Related tradition, but no direct dependence. |
| 14:1: Jer 7:11 | *Dial.* 27:3: Conflated quotation of the synoptic rendering of Jer 7:11. No influence from the non-LXX text in *2. Clem.* |

One cannot with certainty claim direct literary dependence upon *2. Clement* in Justin. But the stock of common OT material is considerable.

(j) *Barnabas*[161]

Barnabas is the Christian writing before Justin with which he shares the greatest amount of OT material. If we leave out here the typologies in *Barn.* 7f; 12:2-9 (they shall be treated below in Part III), and further omit the numerous quotations in the allegorization of the dietary laws in ch. 10 (to which Justin has no parallels), there remain in *Barnabas* ca. 64 formal quotations. Justin has parallels to 34 of these (53%). The common quotations are briefly analyzed in the following chart, and the most significant cases receive some comment.

---

160. Generally on the relation between *2.Clement* and Justin, see M. von Engelhardt, *Christenthum*, p. 401-410.
161. General surveys of the relationship between *Barnabas* and Justin: M. von Engelhardt, pp. 375-94; W. A. Shotwell, *Exegesis*, pp. 65f; E. F. Osborn, *Justin Martyr*, pp. 160f.

| *Barn.* | Justin |
|---|---|
| 2:5: Is 1:11—13 \ 15:8: Is 1:13 } (~ LXX) | *1. Apol.* 37:5—8: Is 1:11—15 non-LXX. Test. source, see above pp. 55f. |
| 2:7—8: Jer 7:22f/Zech 8:17/Zech 7:10 | *Dial.* 22:6: Jer 7:21f/Jer 31:32. Deviating from the LXX *and* from Barn. No direct dependence, but related testimony source. |
| 3:1—5: Is 58:4—10, some deviations from LXX | *1. Apol.* 37:8: Is 58:6f (combined with Is 1:11—15), non-LXX, no common deviations with *Barn.* *Dial.* 15:1—6: Is 58:1—11, several agreements with LXX against Barn. Probably exerpted from an Isaiah MS. See above, pp.55f. |
| 4:4: Dan 7:24 non-LXX and non-»θ« 4:5: Dan 7:7f (same remark) | *Dial.* 31:2—7: Dan 7:9—28 καιγε? Copied from a Dan MS, point lies in vss. 13f. No dependence on *Barn.* |
| 4:11: Is 5:21 LXX, two variants | *Dial.* 133:4f: Is 5:18—25. In vs. 21 one variant common with *Barnabas,* but this is shared with several LXX MSS. Justin's text certainly copied from Isaiah MS, see above, pp. 30f. Testimony nucleus: vs. 20. No dependence. |
| 5:2: Is 53:5/7 (~ LXX), baptismal context | *Dial.* 13: Is 52:10 — 54:6 LXX. Baptismal context. See further below, pp. 178f. On Justin's numerous allusions to Is 53:5.7, see synoptic study 23. — Dependence on Barnabas possible. |
| 5:5: Gen 1:26 \ non- 6:12: Gen 1:26.28 } LXX | *Dial.* 62:1: Gen 1:26—28 LXX. Justin's point anticipated in *Barn.* See further below, p. 389 |
| 5:12: Zech 13:7 | *Dial.* 53:6: Zech 13:7 καιγε? Probably inspired from Mt 26:31 (see on this text). No dependence on *Barnabas'* deviant text. |
| 5:13: Ps 22:21/ Ps 119:120/Ps 22:17 | *1. Apol.* 35:5.7.8; 38:4f: Ps 22:17/19 non-LXX, but no common features with *Barnabas'* combined quotation. Different testimony source, see above, p. 80f. |
| 5:14: Is 50:6/7 (telescoped, non-LXX) | *1. Apol.* 38:2f: 50:6—8a~LXX, one common deviation with *Barn.* from the LXX. Influence from *Barn.* possible, but not necessary. (Cf. synoptic study 32). |
| 6:2-4: Is 28:16 \ Is 50:7 \ Ps 118:22.24. } | The »Stone« { *Dial.* 114:4; 126:1: all. to Is 28:16. Impossible to specify a source. (Cf. synoptic study 24). |
| 6:6: Ps 22:17b/ Ps 118:12a/Ps 22:19b | *1. Apol.* 35:5.7f; 38:4f: Ps 22:17/19. Testimony source other than *Barn.,* but related tradition. See above, pp.?? |
| 6:7: Is 3:10 LXX | *Dial.* 133:2: Is 3:9—15 \ *Dial.* 17:2: Is 3:9—11 } = LXX *Dial.* 136:2: Is 3:9f / *Dial.* 137:3: Justin claims that the non-LXX reading ἄρωμεν is the true »LXX«. *Barn.* not his testimony source. Cf. above, pp. 80f. |
| 6:16: Ps 22:23 non-LXX | *Dial.* 106:2: Ps 22:23—24 LXX, point not unlike *Barnabas'.* (Cf. synoptic study 26). |
| 9:1: Ps 18:45a | *Dial.* 28:6: Ps 18:44b.45a LXX. Perhaps inspired from *Barn.* 9:1 or a parallel testimony source. (Cf. synoptic study 33). |

| | |
|---|---|
| 9:1: Is 33:13/Jer 4:4 non-LXX | *Dial.* 70:2f: Is 33:13—19~LXX. Justin's point lies in vs. 16: no dependence on *Barn.* 9. Jer 4:4: see below on *Barn.* 9:5 |
| 9:3: Is 40:3 non-LXX | *Dial.* 50:3—5: Is 39:9—40:17 LXX. Justin probably depends on Mt 3:3 or Lk 3:4—6, see above on Mt 3:3. |
| 9:5: Jer 4:3—4 non-LXX | *Dial.* 28:2: Jer 4:3f non-LXX, but other deviations than in *Barnabas.* Cf. above, pp. 70 - 72. |
| 9:5: Deut 10:16 (MSS S and H) *or:* Jer 4:4b (MSS L) | *Dial.* 16:1: Deut 10:16f LXX. Related testimony source, cf. above, pp. 70 - 72. |
| 9:5: Jer 9:24f non-LXX | *1. Apol.* 53:11: Jer 9:25 non-LXX, but other deviations than in *Barnabas. Dial.* 28:3: Jer 9:24f LXX. See above, pp. 70 - 72. |
| 10:10: Ps 1:1 non-LXX 11:6: Ps 1:3—6 LXX | *1. Apol.* 40:8—19: Ps 1f LXX. On possible testimony nuclei behind this, cf. p. 159f. |
| 11:2f: Jer 2:12f/ Is 16:1f non-LXX | *Dial.* 114:5: Jer 2:13/Is 16:1/Jer 3:8 non-LXX. Other deviations than in *Barnabas:* related testimony source. Cf. above, pp. 69f. |
| 11:4f: Is 45:2f/Is 33:16f non-LXX | *Dial.* 70:2f: Is 33:13—19 ~ LXX. *Barnabas* takes Is 33:16f as a testimony referring to the baptized; for Justin it is a testimony on Jesus being born in a cave. It seems that Justin exploits this text independently of *Barnabas.* |
| 12:5: Is 65:2 non-LXX, close to Rom 10:21 | *1. Apol.* 35:3f: Is 65:2/Is 58:2b non-LXX, other deviations, probably no influence from *Barnabas. 1. Apol.* 38:1; *Dial.* 114:2: excerpts from the text in *1. Apol.* 35. *1. Apol.* 49:2—4; *Dial.* 24:4: Is 65:1—3 ~ LXX. *Dial.* 97:2: Is 65:2 from the text of *Dial.* 24. Cf. above, pp. 65 - 67. |
| 12:10: Ps 110:1 | The same remark as on Heb. 1:13. |
| 13:7: Gen 17:5 | *Dial.* 11:5; 119:4: allusions dependent on Rom 4:17. |
| 14:7: Is 42:6—7 | *Dial.* 122:3: Is 42:6.7a non-LXX. *Dial.* 26:2; 65:4: Is 42:6f LXX. All three texts sharing one non-LXX reading with *Barnabas,* but Justin rather dependent upon a parallel testimony source, cf. above, p. 62. |
| 14:8: Is 49:6b.7a non-LXX | *Dial.* 121:4: Is 49:6 ~ LXX, other deviations, different excerpt: no direct dependence on *Barnabas.* |
| 15:1: Ex 20:8/Ps 24:4 | Cf. *Dial.* 12:3. No direct dependence, but related tradition. |
| 15:4: Ps 90:4 cf. 2 Pet 3:8 | *Dial.* 81:3: Ps 90:4. All three versions of Ps 90:4 are non-LXX, and also different from each other. Justin probably depends on a source other than *Barn.* or 2 Pet. |
| 16:2: Is 40:12/Is 66:1 LXX | *1. Apol.* 37:3; *Dial.* 22:11: Is 66:1 non-LXX. No direct dependence on Barnabas, see on Acts 7:49. (Cf. synoptic study 22). |

General remarks:

As far as one can trust the evidence in the *Parisinus,* Justin has never copied an OT quotation from *Barnabas*.[162] Beyond this statement, our conclusions at this stage can only be provisional. We shall have to return to a final assessment of the relation between Justin and *Barnabas* when we have finished our traditio-historical analysis in Part III.

So far, I do not want to exclude the possibility that *Barnabas* in some cases is Justin's guide to OT texts, and even in a few cases furnishes him with exegetical argument. But the striking fact is the great majority of cases where not *Barnabas,* but some kind of parallel source, accounts for the parallels between the two writers. This makes me inclined to believe that this may be the explanation also in those cases where no strict proof is possible.[163]

---

162. This general conclusion substantiates Kraft's estimates concerning the Isaiah variant readings in *Barnabas:* ·Barnabas is more often in agreement with Irenaeus (about 67% of the time), than with the others (i.e. Justin, Tertullian, Clement of Alexandria, Cyprian, and Ps.Gregory) and is most frequently in disagreement with Justin (about 60%) and Ps. Gregory (about 67%).· (R.A. Kraft, 'Barnabas' Isaiah Text and the ·Testimony Book· Hypothesis', *JBL* 79 (1960, pp. 336-350), p. 348, n. 91.)

163. M. von Engelhardt is quite unambiguous in his conclusion: Justin has not used Barnabas (*Christenthum,* p. 375).

# Detailed synoptic studies of the most important parallels

(1) Is 52:5b

| LXX | | Rom 2:24 | Dial. 17:2 |
|---|---|---|---|
| δὶ ὑμᾶς<br>διὰ παντὸς<br>τὸ ὄνομά μου<br>βλασφημεῖται<br>ἐν[a] τοῖς ἔθνεσι | = 2. Cl.<br>13:2 | τὸ γὰρ ὄνομα τοῦ θεοῦ<br>δὶ ὑμᾶς βλασφημεῖται<br>ἐν τοῖς ἔθνεσιν | δὶ ὑμᾶς<br>τὸ ὄνομά μου<br>βλασφημεῖται<br>ἐν τοῖς ἔθνεσι |

a) *2. Clem.* add. πᾶσιν

Justin has the same excerpt from Is 52:5 as Paul, and like him omits the διὰ παντὸς. But in other respects he follows the LXX, and we have seen reasons above (pp. 30f) to suspect a testimony source behind *Dial.* 17. In this respect, Prigent[164] has made a valuable observation: In *2.Clem.* 13:2 the Isaiah text is quoted twice; the second, non-LXX version reads: οὐαὶ δὶ ὃν βλασφημεῖται τὸ ὄνομά μου (this is close to the version of Is 52:5b found in Ign. *Trall.* 8 and Polyc. *Philad.* 10). Now, οὐαὶ is the introductory word in Is 3:9 and Is 5:20. Prigent may therefore be right in concluding that Is 52:5b was also part of the source behind *Dial.* 17. If so, all three texts have been looked up in the LXX, and Justin's text may also have been influenced by Rom 2:24.

Direct influence from *2. Clem.* 13:2 LXX text is unlikely, see synopsis.

(2) Gen 15:6

| LXX | Rom 4:3 = Dial. 92:3 | | Gal 3:6 |
|---|---|---|---|
| καὶ ἐπίστευσεν<br>Αβραμ τῷ θεῷ<br>καὶ ἐλογίσθη<br>αὐτῷ<br>εἰς δικαιοσύνην | ἐπίστευσεν δὲ<br>Αβραὰμ τῷ θεῷ<br>καὶ ἐλογίσθη<br>αὐτῷ<br>εἰς δικαιοσύνην | = 1. Clem.<br>10:6 | καθὼς Ἀβραὰμ<br>ἐπίστευσεν τῷ θεῷ<br>καὶ ἐλογίσθη<br>αὐτῷ<br>εἰς δικαιοσύνην |

The complete textual agreement between Rom 4:3 and *Dial.* 92:3 is a first indication that Romans is Justin's source. Allusions to Paul's exegesis confirm this: «For not even to Abraham was witness borne by God that he was righteous because of his circumcision, but because of his faith», *Dial.* 92:3, cf. Rom 4:9f. The same closeness to Rom 4 is displayed in *Dial.* 23:4:

---

164. *Justin*, pp. 233f.

| Rom 4 | *Dial.* 23:4 |
|---|---|
| vs. 10 πῶς οὖν ἐλογίσθη; | καὶ γὰρ αὐτὸς ὁ Ἀβραὰμ |
| ἐν περιτομῇ ὄντι | ἐν ἀκροβυστίᾳ ὢν |
| ἢ ἐν ἀκροβυστίᾳ; | |
| vs. 11 ... σφραγῖδα | |
| τῆς δικαιοσύνης | διὰ τὴν πίστιν ἣν ἐπίστευσε τῷ θεῷ |
| τῆς πίστεως ... | ἐδικαιώθη καὶ εὐλογήθη |
| vs. 3 τί γὰρ ἡ γραφὴ | ὡς ἡ γραφὴ σημαίνει |
| λέγει ... [Gen 15:6] | |
| vs. 11 καὶ σημεῖον ἔλαβεν | τὴν δὲ περιτομὴν |
| περιτομῆς ... | εἰς σημεῖον ... ἔλαβεν ...[165] |

To conclude: Justin depends on Paul for his quotation of Gen 15:6 in *Dial.*92:3 and he reproduces the text of his source very exactly.

*1.Clem.* 10:6 has a quotation of Gen 15:5f (non-LXX = Rom 4:3) but the exegesis is different from Paul's, and Justin has no echo of *1.Clem.* at this point.

(3)Ps 32:1f

| Rom 4:7f = Ps 32:1f LXX = *1. Clem.* 50:6 | *Dial.* 141:2 |
|---|---|
| μακάριοι ὧν | |
| ἀφέθησαν αἱ ἀνομίαι | |
| καὶ ὧν ἐπεκαλύφθησαν | |
| αἱ ἁμαρτίαι | |
| | |
| μακάριος ἀνὴρ | μακάριος |
| οὖ[a] οὐ μὴ λογίσηται | ᾧ οὐ μὴ λογίσεται |
| κύριος ἁμαρτίαν | κύριος ἁμαρτίαν |
| [b]οὐδέ ἐστιν | |
| ἐν τῷ στόματι αὐτοῦ δόλος[b] | |
| | |
| a) Lucianic MSS ᾧ | |
| b-b) Om. Rom. 4:7f | |

The omission of ἀνὴρ in Justin's text is probably deliberate, because he uses the text as a proof that both *angels* and men have the opportunity for repentance and forgiveness of sins, *Dial.* 141:2. Since Paul's text agrees with the LXX, one cannot say for certain whether Justin is quoting from Rom 4:8 or a Psalms MS. (The Lucianic reading ᾧ is present in some witnesses to Rom 4:8 also). The shortness of this quotation in Justin perhaps votes for Romans as the source. In any case one suspects that Paul was Justin's guide to this text. Romans is a more likely candidate than *1. Clem.* 50:6, because Paul's and Justin's excerpt from the Psalm end with the same words.

(4)Hos 2:25 etc.

Justin has no quotation of Paul's text, but in *Dial.* 19:5 he alludes to Hos 1:9, the verse preceeding Hos 2:1 (contained in Paul's quotation). He also names Hosea as the Biblical source. Perhaps he was guided to this text by Paul's quotation (introduced in Rom 9:25: ὡς καὶ ἐν τῷ Ὡσηὲ λέγει). Paul applies the re-naming of «Not-my-people» to «My people» to the Gentiles. Justin interprets Hos 1:9 in a similar, complementary vein: The Jews, «The people», become the «Not-people».

---

165. Cf. A. Thoma, *art. cit.*: «Hier ist besonders merkwürdig, wie Justin das σημεῖον *des Paulus* . . heraushebt und betont . . . » (p. 396, with synopsis).

(5) Is 1:9

We have seen above that in *1. Apol.* 53:7 and *Dial.* 140:3 we shall probably have to reckon with an intermediary source between Romans and Justin (see pp. 67 - 69).

However, in both of his allusions to this text, *Dial.* 32:2 and *Dial.* 55:3, the non-LXX words εἰς σωτηρίαν occur. They recall the phrase τὸ ὑπόλειμμα σωθήσεται of Rom 9:27 (= Is 10:22), immediately preceeding Paul's LXX quotation of Is 1:9. It is thus not impossible that Justin was aware of Paul's use of Is 1:9 in Romans.

(6) Is 53:1

| Is 53:1 LXX = Jn 12:38: |  |
|---|---|
| κύριε, τίς ἐπίστευσε τῇ ἀκοῇ ἡμῶν | = Rom 10:16 = *Dial.* 114:2 |
| καὶ ὁ βραχίων κυρίου τίνι ἀπεκαλύφθη | |

The fact that Justin has the same excerpt as Paul in *Dial.* 114:2 is a strong indication that Paul was his source (rather than John). Justin's quotation is preceeded by a citation of Is 65:2. This text is also quoted in the context in Romans, 10:21. Turning to *Dial.* 42:1f, we find a passage where dependence upon Rom 10:16-18 is a certainty:

| Rom 10:16-18 | *Dial.* 42:1f |
|---|---|
| *Ἡσαΐς* γὰρ λέγει, κύριε, τίς... | ... καὶ ὁ Δαυεὶδ λέγει |
| | Εἰς πᾶσαν τὴν γῆν... ⎤ = Ps 19·5a |
| | ... τὰ ῥήματα αὐτῶν. ⎦ = Rom 10:18 |
| ἄρα ἡ πίστις ἐξ ἀκοῆς, | Καὶ ὁ *Ἡσαΐας*... ὅτι οὐχὶ *τῇ ἀκοῇ* |
| ἡ δὲ ἀκοὴ *διὰ ῥήματος Χριστοῦ*... | αὐτῶν [sc. τῶν ἀποστόλων] πιστεύουσιν |
| Εἰς πᾶσαν τὴν γῆν... ⎤ = Ps 19:5a | ἀλλὰ *τῇ αὐτοῦ* τοῦ πέμψαντος αὐτοὺς |
| ... τὰ ῥήματα αὐτῶν. ⎦ | [sc. τοῦ Χριστοῦ] *δυνάμει*... |
| | Κύριε, τίς... [Is 53:1.2a LXX]. |

In *Dial.* 42:1f we have an instructive example of the two ways in which Justin can handle a «testimony source»: Ps 19:5a he takes over *verbatim*, while he looks Is 53:1a up in his Isaiah MS and quotes an expanded version of Paul's testimony.[166] We have seen before that Justin in such cases sometimes tries to interpret new features of the text, introduced with the expanded LXX text. In *Dial.* 42:3 he adds an interesting exegesis of Is 53:2a - the element not present in Romans. But this new exegesis - probably Justin's own - echoes other Pauline passages, e.g. 1.Cor 12:12.

(7) Is 65:1

I have already argued (above p. 53) that Deut 32:21 in Rom 10:19 is the hidden testimony nucleus behind the long LXX quotation of Deut 32:16-23 in *Dial.* 119:2. In Romans, Deut 32:21 is followed by Is 65:1f; in *Dial.* 119:3f the Deut text is followed by Zech 2:15; Is 62:12; *Is 65:1*. One may reasonably suggest that Rom 10:20f suggested the quotation of Is 65:1 in *Dial.* 119. But the text quoted is not that of Paul, it is rather a mixture of the two LXX texts in *1.Apol.* 49:2 and *Dial.* 24:4. (See synopsis and discussion above, pp. 65-67). It seems that in *Dial.* 119:4 we have a genuine quotation from memory, suggested by the quotation sequence in Romans.

---

166. That Justin has an Isaiah MS before his eyes, is also indicated by the phrase concluding the quotation: καὶ τὰ ἐξῆς τῆς προφητείας προλελεγμένα.

(8) Deut 32:43

| Deut 32:43 LXX = *Dial.* 130:1 | Rom 15:10 | Heb 1:6 |
|---|---|---|
| εὐφράνθητε οὐρανοὶ ἅμα αὐτῷ καὶ προσκυνησάτωσαν αὐτῷ πάντες ἄγγελοι[a] θεοῦ [καὶ τὰ ἑξῆς τοῦ λόγου ἐπέφερον ταῦτα] εὐφράνθητε ἔθνη μετὰ τοῦ λαοῦ αὐτοῦ καὶ ἐνισχυσάτωσαν αὐτῷ πάντες ἄγγελοι θεοῦ... | | αὐτῷ καὶ προσκυνησάτωσαν πάντες ἄγγελοι θεοῦ |
| | εὐφράνθητε ἔθνη μετὰ τοῦ λαοῦ αὐτοῦ ⎤ = *Dial.* 130:4 | |
| a) = several LXX MSS and Ode 2:34. Wevers: υἱοί. | | |

That Romans 15:10 is the testimony nucleus behind the LXX excerpt of the whole of Deut 32:43 in *Dial.* 130:1 is made likely by the short quotation in *Dial.* 130:4. This coincides perfectly with Rom 15:10.

Did Justin also depend on Heb 1:6? The reading ἄγγελοι θεοῦ (for LXX υἱοὶ θεοῦ) could be said to indicate this. However, one cannot exclude the possibility that both the author of Hebrews and Justin had Deut MSS which contained the reading ἄγγελοι,[167] cf. part of the LXX MSS tradition and Ode 2.[168] This question probably must remain *sub judice*.

(9) Ex 32:6

| 1 Cor 10:7 | LXX | *Dial.* 20:1 | *1.Clem.* 3:1 |
|---|---|---|---|
| | Ex 32:6 | | |
| ἐκάθισεν ὁ λαὸς φαγεῖν καὶ πεῖν καὶ ἀνέστησαν παίζειν | ... καὶ ἐκάθισεν ὁ λαὸς φαγεῖν καὶ πιεῖν καὶ ἀνέστησαν παίζειν | ὁ λαὸς ἔφαγε καὶ ἔπιεν καὶ ἀνέστη τοῦ παίζειν | ἔφαγεν καὶ ἔπιεν |
| | Deut 32:15 | καὶ πάλιν | |
| | καὶ ἔφαγεν ᾽Ιακὼβ καὶ ἐνεπλήσθη | ἔφαγεν ᾽Ιακὼβ καὶ ἐνεπλήσθη καὶ ἐλιπάνθη[a] | καὶ ἐπλατύνθη καὶ ἐπαχύνθη |
| | καὶ ἀπελάκτισεν ὁ ἠγαπημένος ἐλιπάνθη ἐπαχύνθη ἐπλατύνθη καὶ ἐγκατέλιπεν θεὸν τὸν ποιήσαντα αὐτόν ... | καὶ ἀπελάκτισεν ὁ ἠγαπημένος ἐλιπάνθη ἐπαχύνθη ⎤ ἐπλατύνθη⎦ καὶ ἐγκατέλιπε θεὸν τὸν ποιήσαντα αὐτόν a) = MT | καὶ ἀπελάκτισεν ὁ ἠγαπημένος |

---

167. Cf. esp. Smit Sibinga, pp. 145f. See also A. Thoma, *art. cit.,* pp. 404f.
168. Cf. K. J. Thomas, 'The Old Testament Citations in Hebrews', *NTS* 11 (1964/65, pp. 303-25), p. 304.

Again Justin differs from Paul's (LXX) text. One could reasonably call Justin's quotation of Ex 32:6 in *Dial* 20:1 a free quotation from memory, if it were not for the evidence in *1.Clem* 3. Here we find a combined quotation, joining the same texts Justin has joined in *Dial.* 20, and reading ἔφαγε(ν) καὶ ἔπιεν in Ex 32:6 like Justin. So one suspects that Justin in *Dial.* 20:1 is drawing on a testimony source[169] similar to the one employed in *1.Clem.3.* Perhaps he identified the second component as belonging to Deut 32 - the chapter with which he elsewhere shows familiarity. The Deut 32:15 quotation may thus have been looked up in the LXX.[170] Cf. the introduction: ὡς καὶ Μωυσῆς φησιν.

It is far from certain that 1 Cor 10:7 was Justin's guide to Ex 32:6 in *Dial* 20:1. A source similar to the one behind *1.Clem.* is more likely.

(10) Deut 21:23b and Deut 27:26[171]

| LXX | Gal 3 | *Dial.* 95:1f |
|---|---|---|
| | vs. 10 | |
| | ὅσοι γὰρ ἐξ ἔργων *νόμου* | καὶ γὰρ πᾶν γένος ἀνθρ. |
| Deut 27:26 | εἰσὶν *ὑπὸ κατάραν* εἰσὶν | εὑρεθήσεται *ὑπὸ κατάραν* |
| | γέγραπται γὰρ ὅτι | ὃν κατὰ *τὸν νόμον* Μωυσέως |
| ἐπικατάρατος | ἐπικατάρατος | ἐπικατάρατος . . . |
| πᾶς ἄνθρωπος | πᾶς | πᾶς |
| ὅστις οὐκ ἐμμενεῖ | ὃς οὐκ ἐμμένει | ὃς οὐκ ἐμμένει |
| ἐν πᾶσιν τοῖς λόγοις | πᾶσιν τοῖς γεγραμμένοις | ἐν τοῖς γεγραμμένοις |
| τοῦ νόμου τούτου | ἐν τῷ βιβλίῳ τοῦ νόμου | ἐν τῷ βιβλίῳ τοῦ νόμου |
| ποιῆσαι αὐτούς . . . | τοῦ ποιῆσαι αὐτά | τοῦ ποιῆσαι αὐτά |
| | vs. 11 | |
| | ὅτι δὲ ἐν νόμῳ *οὐδεὶς* | καὶ *οὐδείς* . . . πάντα |
| | δικαιοῦται . . . δῆλον . . . | ἐποίησεν . . . |
| | | εἰ δὲ οἱ *ὑπὸ τὸν νόμον* |
| | | *τοῦτον ὑπὸ κατάραν* |
| | | φαίνονται εἶναι . . . |
| | vs. 13 | |
| | Χριστὸς ἡμᾶς ἐξηγόρασεν | εἰ οὖν καὶ τὸν ἑαυτοῦ |
| | ἐκ τῆς κατάρας τοῦ νόμου | Χριστὸν *ὑπὲρ* τῶν ἐκ |
| | γενόμενος | παντὸς γένους ἀνθρώπων |
| | | ὁ πατὴρ τῶν ὅλων |
| | *ὑπὲρ* ἡμῶν *κατάρα* | τὰς πάντων *κατάρας* |
| | ὅτι γέγραπται | ἀναδέξασθαι ἐβουλήθη . . . |
| Deut 21:23b | | *Dial.* 96:1 |
| ὅτι κεκατηραμένος | ἐπικατάρατος | ἐπικατάρατος |
| ὑπὸ θεοῦ | | |
| πᾶς κρεμάμενος | πᾶς ὁ κρεμάμενος | πᾶς ὁ κρεμάμενος |
| ἐπὶ ξύλου . . . | ἐπὶ ξύλου | ἐπὶ ξύλου |

---

169. This is also suggested by Smit Sibinga, p. 138; and Prigent agrees, *Justin,* p. 257.
170. That is, a LXX revised after the MT - cf. Smit Sibinga's remark: «This specific revision of the LXX on the basis of a Hebrew text is known only from Justin's citation. It seems likely that we deal with an exact parallel of xXII gr . . . » (i.e. Barthélemy's *kaige* recension of the Twelve Prophets), p. 144.
171. Cf. esp. the extensive discussions of this text in Justin in Smit Sibinga, pp. 94-99/140f, and Th. Stylianopoulos, *Mosaic Law,* pp. 103-108.

No doubt Justin had Gal 3 before his eyes when writing *Dial.* 95f.[172]

(11) Is 54:1

On the level of text-type, one can hardly conclude anything concerning the internal relationships between the three relevant occurrences of this text - Gal 4:27; *2.Clem.* 2:1; *1.Apol.* 53:5 - because they agree exactly with each other and with the standard LXX text. Paul may be the common source for *2.Clem.* and Justin. It should be noticed, however, that Justin's exegesis of the text is very close to the one in *2.Clem.*, and partly non-Pauline:

| *2.Clem.* 2:3 | *1.Apol.* 53:5f |
|---|---|
| ... ἔρημος ἐδόκει εἶναι ἀπὸ τοῦ θεοῦ ὁ λαὸς ἡμῶν νυνὶ δὲ *πιστεύσαντες* *πλείονες* ἐγενόμεθα τῶν δοκούντων ἔχειν θεόν | ... ἔρημα ... ἦν πάντα τὰ ἔθνη ἀληθινοῦ θεοῦ ... *πλείονες* οἱ ἀπὸ τῶν ἐθνῶν *πιστεύοντες* τῶν ἀπὸ Ἰουδαίων καὶ Σαμαρέων ... |

This is hardly sufficient to prove direct dependence upon *2.Clem.*, but some kind of common tradition is strongly suggested. It seems probable that Galatians was not Justin's only source for this testimony.

(12) Mic 5:1

| Mt 2:6 = *1.Apol.* 34:1 = *Dial.* 78:1 | Mic 5:1 LXX |
|---|---|
| καὶ σύ Βηθλεεμ γῆ Ἰούδα οὐδαμῶς ἐλαχίστη εἶ ἐν τοῖς ἡγεμόσιν Ἰούδα ἐκ σοῦ γὰρ ἐξελεύσεται ἡγούμενος ὅστις ποιμανεῖ τὸν λαὸν μου ᵃτὸν Ἰσραήλᵃ | καὶ σύ Βεθλεεμ οἶκος τοῦ Εφραθα ὀλιγοστὸς εἶ τοῦ εἶναι ἐν χιλιάσιν Ιουδα ἐκ σοῦ μοι ἐξελεύσεται τοῦ εἶναι εἰς ἄρχοντα ἐν τῷ Ισραηλ ... |
| a-a) Om. *Dial.* 78:1 and *1. Apol.* 34:1 | |

In this case there can be no doubt: Justin copies his text from Mt 2:6 both in *1. Apol.* 34:1 and *Dial.* 78:1.[173] In the latter case the direct recourse to Mt 2 is evident also in the context. Justin's only modification is to drop the final τὸν Ἰσραήλ. This is certainly intentional: For Justin God's people is the (mostly Gentile) Church, not Israel. The absence of these words proves that the exact rendering of Mt 2:6 in Justin's text stems from himself, not a later scribe.[174]

---

172. The omission of πᾶσιν in the quotation of Deut 27:26 in *Dial.* 95 may be a scribal error, because Justin immediately seems to allude to it: οὐδεὶς . . πάντα ἐποίησεν. Smit Sibinga - on feeble grounds (text emendation) - tends to posit an intermediary (or common) source between (or behind) Paul and Justin, *loc. cit.* Cf. the detailed - and to my mind convincing -criticism in Stylianopoulos, *loc. cit.*

173. Cf. Hilgenfeld, 'Citate', pp. 568f; Massaux, *Influence*, pp. 496/524f.

174. In this I agree with Barthélemy, *Devanciers*, p. 207, - against Bousset, *Evangeliencitate*, p. 37.

(13) Jer 31:15

| Mt 2:18 = Dial. 78:8 | Jer 31:15 LXX |
|---|---|
| φωνὴ ἐν ᾽Ραμὰ ἠκούσθη<br>κλαυθμὸς καὶ ὀδυρμὸς πολύς<br>᾽Ραχὴλ κλαίουσα τὰ τέκνα αὐτῆς<br>καὶ οὐκ ἤθελεν[a] παρακληθῆναι<br><br>ὅτι οὐκ εἰσίν | ... φωνὴ ἐν Ραμα ἠκούσθη<br>θρήνου καὶ κλαυθμοῦ καὶ ὀδυρμοῦ<br>Ραχηλ ἀποκλαιομένη<br>οὐκ ἤθελε παύσασθαι<br>ἐπὶ τοῖς υἱοῖς αὐτῆς<br>ὅτι οὐκ εἰσιν |
| a) Dial. 78:8: ἤθελε | |

Again Justin copies this text from Mt 2, as the context in Dial. 78 amply shows.[175]

(14) The sign of Jonah

For Justin, the sign of Jonah has two aspects: (1) Jonah's «resurrection» from the fish on the third day, and (2) the repentance and conversion of the Ninevites, Dial. 107. The only evangelist who has both aspects (explicit), is Matthew in 12:38—41. This corresponds to the fact that Justin in Dial. 107:1 quotes Jesus' saying about the sign of Jonah in a form close to Mt 12:39 (= Mt 16:4).[176] Justin is therefore probably referring to Matthew when he writes in Dial. 107:1: γέγραπται ἐν τοῖς ἀπομνημονεύμασιν ὅτι ... However, Justin's verb συζητοῦντες has its equivalent only in Mk 8:11: συζητεῖν. This may be accidental, if Justin is not using some harmonistic source.[177]

Apart from this, it is obvious that Justin in Dial. 107 has turned from Mt 12:38-41 to the complete book of Jonah, probably in a καιγε recension.[178]

(15) Is 6:10

| Is 6:10 LXX = Acts 28:27<br>= Mt 13:15 | John 12:40 | Dial. 12:2 |
|---|---|---|
| ἐπαχύνθη γὰρ ἡ καρδία — —<br>τοῦ λαοῦ τούτου καὶ<br>τοῖς ὠσὶν[a] βαρέως ἤκουσαν<br>καὶ τοὺς ὀφθαλμοὺς αὐτῶν<br>ἐκάμμυσαν<br><br>μήποτε ἴδωσιν<br>τοῖς ὀφθαλμοῖς<br>καὶ τοῖς ὠσὶν ἀκούσωσιν<br>καὶ τῇ καρδίᾳ συνῶσιν<br>καὶ ἐπιστρέψωσιν<br>καὶ ἰάσομαι αὐτούς | — — — — — — — — — —<br>τετύφλωκεν αὐτῶν<br>τοὺς ὀφθαλμοὺς<br>καὶ ἐπώρωσεν αὐτῶν<br>τὴν καρδίαν<br>ἵνα μὴ ἴδωσιν<br>τοῖς ὀφθαλμοῖς<br><br>καὶ νοήσωσιν τῇ καρδίᾳ<br>καὶ στραφῶσιν<br>καὶ ἰάσομαι αὐτούς | ἔτι γὰρ<br>τὰ ὦτα ὑμῶν πέφρακται<br>οἱ ὀφθαλμοὶ ὑμῶν<br>πεπήρωνται καὶ<br>πεπάχυται ἡ καρδία |
| a) LXX + αὐτῶν | Dial. 33:1: τὰ δὲ ὦτα ὑμῶν πέφρακται<br>καὶ αἱ καρδίαι πεπώρωνται. | |

---

175. Cf. esp. Massaux, pp. 527f.
176. Dial. 107:1, like Mt 16:4, omits the final τοῦ προφήτου of Mt 12:39. See detailed synopsis and comment in A. J. Bellinzoni, The Sayings of Jesus in the Writings of Justin Martyr (Suppl. NT 17, Leiden, 1967), p. 121. Cf. also Massaux. pp. 539f.
177. Cf. Bellinzoni, loc. cit.
178. Cf. Barthélemy, Devanciers, pp. 207/209f.

The two allusions in Justin exhibit common non-LXX readings which suggest an underlying non-LXX version of the text. This text seem to have had readings both from the LXX (= Acts 28 and Mt 13) and John's version. The verb φράσσω occurs in no known Greek version of Is 6:10, but is used elsewhere in the LXX in a verse with similar terminology, Prov 21:13: ὅς φράσσει τὰ ὦτα τοῦ μὴ ἐπακοῦσαι ἀσθενοῦς . . .

(16) Is 56:7/Jer 7:11 = Mt 21:13

This text is analyzed in detail by Bellinzoni.[179] Justin's text (*Dial.*17:3) shows agreement with the synoptics against the LXX. It is introduced as a saying of Jesus, not as an OT text, and is followed by another Jesus logion (Mt 23:23 etc). Between the two logia there is a paraphrase of Mt 21:12.

Justin has no consciousness of quoting an OT prophecy in this case: he adds an apology for breaking his principle of only quoting the OT (*Dial.* 18:1)

(17) Zech 13:7

| *Barn.* 5:12 | Mt 26:31 | Zech 13:7 LXX | *Dial.* 53:6 καιγε |
|---|---|---|---|
| | | ῥομφαία ἐξεγέρθητι ἐπὶ τοὺς ποιμένας μου καὶ ἐπ᾽ ἄνδρα πολίτην αὐτοῦ λέγει κύρος παντοκράτωρ | ῥομφαία ἐξεγέρθητι ἐπὶ τὸν ποιμένα[a] μου καὶ ἐπ᾽ ἄνδρα τοῦ λαοῦ μου[b] λέγει κύριος τῶν δυνάμεων[c] |
| ὅταν πατάξωσιν τὸν ποιμένα αὐτῶν τότε ἀπολεῖται τὰ πρόβατα τῆς ποίμνης | πατάξω τὸν ποιμένα καὶ διασκορπισθήσονται τὰ πρόβατα τῆς ποίμνης | πατάξατε τοὺς ποιμένας καὶ ἐκσπάσατε τὰ πρόβατα καὶ ἐπάξω τὴν χεῖρά μου . . . | πάταξον[d] τὸν ποιμένα[e] καὶ διασκορπισθήσονται[f] τὰ πρόβατα αὐτοῦ |
| | | | a) = MT  b) MT: עמיתי . *Dial.* 53:6 = Symmachus  c) MT: צבאות  d) MT: הך  e) MT: את הרעה  f) MT: ותפוצין |

In *Dial.* 53:2-4 Justin is paraphrasing Mt 21:1-11, and quotes Matthew's testimony (Zech 9:9) in an expanded καιγε text. In *Dial.* 53:5f he goes on to paraphrase Mt 26:30f (and cf. Mt 26:56), and again he seems to have looked Matthew's testimony up in a καιγε scroll of the Twelve Prophets.[180]

---

179. *Op. cit.,* pp. 111f. Cf. also Massaux, pp. 510-512.
180. Cf. Barthélemy, *Devanciers,* pp. 211f.

(18) Ps 22:2

| Dial. 99:1 | Ps 22:2a LXX | Mt 27:46 |
|---|---|---|
| ὁ θεός, ὁ θεός μου <br> πρόσχες μοι <br> ἵνα τί <br> ἐγκατέλιπές με | ὁ θεὸς ὁ θεός μου <br> πρόσχες μοι <br> ἵνα τί <br> ἐγκατέλιπές με | ηλι ηλι <br><br> λεμα <br> σαβαχθανι |
| | Mk 15:34 | |
| ... σταυρωθεὶς γὰρ <br> εἶπεν <br> ὁ θεός ὁ θεός <br> ἵνα τί <br> ἐγκατέλιπές με | ὅ ἐστιν <br> μεθερμηνευόμενον <br> ὁ θεός μου ὁ θεός μου <br> εἰς τί <br> ἐγκατέλιπές με | τοῦτ᾽ ἔστιν <br><br> θεέ μου θεέ μου <br> ἱνατί <br> με ἐγκατέλιπες |

It is difficult in this case to assert with certainty that Mt rather than Mk was Justin's source. In quoting Ps 22:2a, Justin has his Psalms MS before him (Ps 22:2-24 just quoted in *Dial.* 98). In rendering Jesus' actual words on the cross, his text is a mixture of Mt, Mk and Ps 22:2 LXX.[181] It seems we have another example of a Gospel narrative being stylized so has to fit an OT prediction perfectly.

(19) Joel 3:1-5

| Joel 3:1—2 LXX | Acts 2:17f | Dial. 87:6 |
|---|---|---|
| καὶ ἔσται μετὰ ταῦτα <br><br><br> ἐκχεῶ ἀπὸ τοῦ πνεύματός <br> μου ἐπὶ πᾶσαν σάρκα <br> καὶ προφητεύσουσιν <br> οἱ υἱοὶ ὑμῶν καὶ <br> αἱ θυγατέρες ὑμῶν <br> καὶ οἱ πρεσβύτεροι ὑμῶν <br> ἐνύπνια ἐνυπνιασθήσονται <br> καὶ οἱ νεανίσκοι ὑμῶν <br> ὁράσεις ὄψονται <br><br> καὶ ἐπὶ τοὺς δούλους <br><br> καὶ ἐπὶ τὰς δούλας <br><br> ἐν ταῖς ἡμέραις ἐκείναις <br> ἐκχεῶ ἀπὸ <br> τοῦ πνεύματός μου | καὶ ἔσται ἐν ταῖς <br> ἐσχάταις ἡμέραις, <br> λέγει ὁ θεός <br> ἐκχεῶ ἀπὸ τοῦ πνεύματός <br> μου ἐπὶ πᾶσαν σάρκα <br> καὶ προφητεύσουσιν <br> οἱ υἱοὶ ὑμῶν καὶ <br> αἱ θυγατέρες ὑμῶν <br> καὶ οἱ νεανίσκοι ὑμῶν <br> ὁράσεις ὄψονται <br> καὶ οἱ πρεσβύτεροι ὑμῶν <br> ἐνυπνίοις <br> ἐνυπνιασθήσονται <br> καί γε ἐπὶ τοὺς δούλους <br> μου <br> καὶ ἐπὶ τὰς δούλας <br> μου <br> ἐν ταῖς ἡμέραις ἐκείναις <br> ἐκχεῶ ἀπὸ <br> τοῦ πνεύματός μου <br> καὶ προφητεύσουσιν | καὶ ἔσται μετὰ ταῦτα <br><br><br> ἐκχεῶ τὸ πνεῶμά[a] <br> μου ἐπὶ πᾶσαν σάρκα <br><br><br><br><br><br><br><br><br><br> καὶ ἐπὶ τοὺς δούλους <br> μου[b] <br> καὶ ἐπὶ τὰς δούλας <br> μου[b] <br><br><br><br> καὶ προφητεύσουσι |
| | | a) = α′ σ′ MT <br> b)> MT |

The strange feature about this text is that it combines Joel 3:1a καιγε (?)[182] with Joel 3:2 = Acts 2:18. I do not know how to explain this. Is the mixed text due to Justin himself? If he had

---

181. Bellinzoni, *Sayings*, has failed to include Ps 22:2 LXX in his analysis, pp. 119f.
182. Barthélemy calls the reading τὸ πνεῦμα (instead of LXX ἀπὸ τοῦ πνεύματος) «un élément recensionell», *Devanciers*, p. 208.

taken the care to look up the text in his exemplar of the Twelve Prophets, and besides had Peter's introduction in Acts 2:16 before his eyes (τοῦτό ἐστιν τὸ εἰρημένον διὰ τοῦ προφήτου 'Ιωήλ), why should he be content with the vague introduction καὶ πάλιν ἐν ἑτέρα προφητεία εἴρηται? This rather sounds like the introductory formula before a ·testimony· text. Perhaps the first part of the text is not really taken from a καιγε version of the Twelve Prophets, but composed by someone who had direct access to the Hebrew text. The text might be the work of someone condensing the Acts testimony into a much shorter and tighter text, concentrating on the gift of prophecy. In any case, I find it most likely that the Joel testimony in Acts 2 was transmitted to Justin via an intermediary source.[183]

(20) Ps 2:1f

This quotation in Acts is not part of a Scriptural argument, but is included in a prayer. Nevertheless, Justin seems to echo phrases of this prayer in his own comments on the Psalm:

| Acts 4:27f | 1.Apol. 40:6 |
|---|---|
| 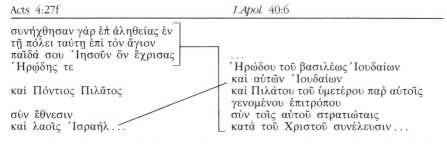 | |
| συνήχθησαν γὰρ ἐπ᾽ ἀληθείας ἐν τῇ πόλει ταύτῃ ἐπὶ τὸν ἅγιον παῖδά σου 'Ιησοῦν ὃν ἔχρισας 'Ηρώδης τε | ... 'Ηρώδου τοῦ βασιλέως 'Ιουδαίων καὶ αὐτῶν 'Ιουδαίων |
| καὶ Πόντιος Πιλᾶτος | καὶ Πιλάτου τοῦ ὑμετέρου παρ᾽ αὐτοῖς γενομένου ἐπιτρόπου |
| σὺν ἔθνεσιν καὶ λαοῖς 'Ισραήλ... | σὺν τοῖς αὐτοῦ στρατιώταις κατὰ τοῦ Χριστοῦ συνέλευσιν... |

Justin's words in 1.Apol. 40:6 are clearly a comment on just that part of the Psalm which is quoted in Acts 4.(Note the final line: κατὰ τοῦ κυρίου καὶ *κατὰ τοῦ Χριστοῦ* αὐτοῦ.) There is thus no need to posit any intermediary source in this case.

(21) Am 5:25-27

| Am 5:25—27 LXX | Acts 7:42f | Dial. 22:3f |
|---|---|---|
| μὴ σφάγια καὶ θυσίας προσηνέγκατέ μοι τεσσαράκοντα ἔτη[a] | μὴ σφάγια καὶ θυσίας προσηνέγκατέ μοι ἔτη τεσσαράκοντα ἐν τῇ ἐρήμῳ | ... μὴ σφάγια καὶ θυσίας προσηνέκατέ μοι ἐν τῇ ἐρήμῳ |
| οἶκος Ισραηλ[b] | οἶκος 'Ισραήλ | οἶκος 'Ισραήλ λέγει κύριος |
| καὶ ἀνελάβετε τὴν σκηνὴν τοῦ Μολοχ καὶ τὸ ἄστρον τοῦ θεοῦ ὑμῶν Ραιφαν τοὺς τύπους αὐτῶν οὓς ἐποιήσατε ἑαυτοῖς καὶ μετοικιῶ ὑμᾶς ἐπέκεινα Δαμασκοῦ λέγει κύριος... | καὶ ἀνελάβετε τὴν σκηνὴν τοῦ Μολὸχ καὶ τὸ ἄστρον τοῦ θεοῦ [ὑμῶν]· Ραιφάν τοὺς τύπους οὓς ἐποιήσατε προσκυνεῖν αὐτοῖς καὶ μετοικιῶ ὑμᾶς ἐπέκεινα Βαβυλῶνος | καὶ ἀνελάβετε τὴν σκηνὴν τοῦ Μολὸχ καὶ τὸ ἄστρον τοῦ θεοῦ ὑμῶν 'Ραφάν τοὺς τύπους οὓς ἐποιήσατε ἑαυτοῖς καὶ μετοικιῶ ὑμᾶς ἐπέκεινα Δαμασκοῦ λέγει κύριος... |
| a) The words ἐν τῇ ἐρήμῳ (=MT) are found in different positions in A; B; V; Q; Lucianic group *et al.* Omitted by Ziegler. b)+ λέγει κύριος A; Q, *et al.* | | |

---

183. Prigent also excludes direct dependence upon Acts 2:17f, *Justin*, p. 114.

It is obvious that Justin has a *Dodekapropheton* MS at his disposal in *Dial.* 22:2-5. Barthélemy finds the text to represent the καιγε version, but with some LXX influence, probably due to later scribes (and especially in the part of the quotation shared by Acts 7:42f).[184] At the end of the quotation in Acts there are two markedly non-LXX readings: προσκυνεῖν αὐτοῖς and ἐπέκεινα βαβυλῶνος. Justin's text follows the LXX on both points, so he does not seem significantly influenced from Acts 7:42f on the textual level. But possibly Acts 7 was instrumental in pointing out this important text to him. It is worthwhile to note that in Acts 7 Am 5:25-27 is followed by Is 66:1 (Acts 7:49f). In *Dial.* 22, Am 5:18 -- 6:7 is followed by Jer 7:21f (non-LXX); Ps 50:1-23; and *Is 66:1* (*Dial.* 22:11).

(22) Is 66:1f

| Is 66 LXX | Acts 7:49f | *1.Apol.* 37:3 = *Dial* 22:11 |
|---|---|---|
| ... ὁ οὐρανός μοι θρόνος ἡ δὲ γῆ ὑποπόδιον τῶν ποδῶν μου ποῖον οἶκον οἰκοδομήσετέ μοι[a] <br> ἢ ποῖος[b] τόπος τῆς καταπαύσεώς μου πάντα γὰρ ταῦτα ἐποίησεν ἡ χείρ μου... <br><br> = *Barn.* 16:2 | ὁ οὐρανός μοι θρόνος ἡ δὲ γῆ ὑποπόδιον τῶν ποδῶν μου ποῖον οἶκον οἰκοδομήσετέ μοι λέγει κύριος ἢ τίς τόπος τῆς καταπαύσεώς μου οὐχὶ ἡ χείρ μου ἐποίησεν ταῦτα πάντα | ποῖον μοι[a] οἶκον οἰκοδομήσετε[b] λέγει κύριος ὁ οὐρανός μοι θρόνος καὶ ἡ γῆ ὑποπόδιον τῶν ποδῶν μου |
| a) + λέγει κύριος Luc. MSS et al. b) *Barn.* 16:2: τίς | | a) Om. *Dial.* 22:11 <br> b) *Dial.* 22:11: ᾠκοδομήσατέ μοι; *1. Apol.* 37:3 οἰκοδομήσεται |

Perhaps we have in *1.Apol.* 37:3 and *Dial.* 22:11 another text condensed from a quotation in Acts. The two ocurrences in Justin point to a written source other than Acts, but very probably Stephen's polemical use of Is 66:1f in Acts 7:49f lies behind this testimony source.

Barnabas testifies to the existence of such testimony versions of the text. He quotes Is 40:12/Is 66:1 as one text. But he was not Justin's direct source.

(23) Is 53

This is not the place to enter into a full-scale discussion of Justin's sources for his use of Is 53 and various phrases from this chapter. *1.Apol.* 50f and *Dial.* 13 prove that he was at least sometimes working directly with the Isaiah LXX. It may be idle to speculate on which particular quotation of or allusion to Is 53 in the NT was of special importance to him. I have already hinted that the quotation of Is 53:4 in Mt 8:17 hardly played any role in Justin. The various possible allusions to Is 53 in the Gospel passion narratives[185] probably were too subtle to be seized on by him. Turning to 1 Peter, we find allusions to Is 53:4.5.6.9.12 in 1 Pet 2:22-25, but only two of these allusions recur in Justin:

---

184. Barthélemy, *Devanciers,* pp. 208f. recognizes only two recensional readings in Am 5:18-27, while there are several in Am 6:1-7. He explains this by assuming scribal corrections in Am 5:18-27. Prigent, on the other hand, assumes that Am 5:18-27 is taken from Justin's *Syntagma,* while Am 6:1-7 is added (by Justin) from a *kaige* MS (*Justin,* pp. 260f). The parallel in Acts 7:42f may suggest that Prigent is right in supposing a testimony source behind the first part of the quotation, and this may have had a LXX text, or a LXX basis for its text.

185. Mt 27:12 (silence of Jesus), allusion to Is 53:7? Mt 27:38 (Jesus crucified among criminals), probable allusion to Is 53:12, made explicit in Lk 22:37 (cf. above, pp. 62f); Mt 27:60 (Jesus buried in Joseph's tomb) - allusion to Is 53:9?

(1) 1 Pet 2:22 ἁμαρτίαν οὐκ ἐποίησεν οὐδὲ εὑρέθη δόλος ἐν τῷ στόματι αὐτοῦ (Is 53:9), cf. *Dial.* 102:7: ἀνομίαν (=LXX) γὰρ οὐκ ἐποίησεν οὐδὲ δόλον τῷ στόματι.

(2) 1 Pet 2:24 οὗ τῷ μώλωπι ἰάθητε (Is 53:5), cf. *Dial.* 17:1: δι' οὗ τῶν μωλώπων ἴασις γίνεται; *Dial.* 32:2: τῷ μώλωπι αὐτοῦ ἡμεῖς ἰάθημεν; *Dial.* 43:3: τῷ μώλωπι αὐτοῦ ἰαθῶμεν; *Dial.* 95:3: τῷ μώλωπι αὐτοῦ ἴασις γένηται; *Dial.* 137:1: αὐτοῦ τοὺς μώλωπας οἷς ἰαθῆναι πᾶσι δυνατόν ὡς καὶ ἡμεῖς ἰάθημεν. One cannot exclude here a dependence on 1 Pet, but the parallels may be accidental. The long formal quotation of Is 53:7b.8a in Acts 8:32 would be easy to locate for Justin. But he has nowhere the same excerpt, although he often alludes to the phrase with which the Isaiah quotation in Acts 8 begins: ὡς πρόβατον ἐπὶ σφαγὴν ἤχθη, cf. *Dial.*. 32:2 = 90:1: ὡς πρόβατον ἀχθήσεσθαι; *Dial.* 72:3 ὡς πρόβατον ἐπὶ σφαγὴν ἀγόμενος; *Dial.* 89:3: ὡς πρόβατον ἐπὶ σφαγὴν ἀχθήσεται; *Dial.* 111:3: αὐτὸς ὡς πρόβατον ἐπὶ σφαγὴν ἤχθη; *Dial.* 114:2: αὐτὸς ὡς πρόβατον ἐπὶ σφαγὴν ἤχθη, καὶ ὡς ἀμνὸς ἐναντίον τοῦ κείραντος. It is perhaps relevant to note the constant use of ἐπὶ (= LXX and Acts 8:32) in these allusions, because Justin's long Isaiah text in *Dial.* 13 reads εἰς. However, the long quotation in *1.Apol.* 50 reads ἐπὶ, so one cannot exclude scribal error in one of the two cases.

Justin's allusions to Is 53:8 (*Dial.* 32:2; 43:3; 63:2; 68:4; 76:2; 89:3) partly refer to the last portion of the verse (not included in the Acts 8 quotation) - *Dial.* 43:3 and 89:3 - and partly have a context utterly foreign to Acts (viz. virgin birth of Jesus, *Dial.* 32:2; 43:3; 68:4; 76:2; 89:3). So the most one can say, is that Acts 8:32f may be echoed in Justin's allusions to Is 53:7b.

One must also reckon with the continued use of Is 53 in the testimony tradition after the NT writers. *1.Clem.* 16:3-14 quotes the whole of Is 53:1-12 (mainly LXX).[186] On the level of text-type, however, there is no interdependence between *1.Clem.* and Justin. Barnabas quotes phrases from Is 53:5/7 in *Barn.* 5:2 - in a context quite similar to *Dial.* 13. But again there is no complete correspondence between Justin's excerpts from and allusions to Is 53:5.7 and Barnabas' excerpt. Cf. the following table:

| *Barn.* 5:2 | Justin |
|---|---|
| ἐτραυματίσθη διὰ τὰς ἀνομίας ἡμῶν καὶ μεμαλάκισται διὰ τὰς ἁμαρτίας ἡμῶν | --- |
| τῷ μώλωπι αὐτοῦ ἡμεῖς ἰάθημεν | *Dial.* 17:1; 32:2; 43:3; 95:3; 137:1. |
| ὡς πρόβατον ἐπὶ σφαγὴν ἤχθη⌉ | *Dial.* 32:2; 72:3; 89:3; 111:3. |
| καὶ ὡς ἀμνὸς ἄφωνος ἐναντίον τοῦ κείραντος αὐτόν ⌋ | *Dial.* 114:2 |

As one can easily observe, Barnabas may be an alternative source for some of the allusions studied above.

(24) Is 28:16 *et al.* The «Stone» testimonies

| Is 28:16 LXX = *Barn.* 6:2 | 1 Pet 2:6 |
|---|---|
| ἰδοὺ ἐγὼ[a] ἐμβαλῶ εἰς τὰ θεμέλια Σιων λίθον πολυτελῆ ἐκλεκτὸν ἀκρογωνιαῖον ἔντιμον ... | ἰδοὺ τίθημι⌉ ἐν Σιὼν ⌋ = Rom 9:33 λίθον ἐκλεκτὸν ἀκρογωνιαῖον ἔντιμον ... |
| a) Om. *Barn.* 6:2 | *Dial.* 114:4: ... τοῦ ἀκρογωνιαίου λίθου .. *Dial.* 126:1: λίθος ἀκρογωνιαῖος ... |

---

186. Detailed collation in D. A. Hagner, *The Use of the Old and New Testament in Clement of Rome* (Suppl. NT 34, Leiden, 1973), pp. 49-51.

The whole complex of «Stone» testimonies is frequently used already in the NT: Ps 118:22 (Mt 21:42 par. Mk 12:10f; Lk 20:17; Acts 4:11); Is 8:14/28:16 (Rom 9:33; 1 Pet 2:6-8). Barnabas carries the tradition on in 6:2: Is 28:16 and Ps 118:22. It is almost surprising that Justin should have made so little of these proof-texts. It is impossible to know what particular source led Justin on to his allusions in *Dial.* 114:4 and 126:1.

### (25) Ps 45:7f

In *Dial.* 56:14 Justin quotes the same excerpt from Ps 45 as does the author of Hebrews in 1:8f. Justin quotes a LXX text where Hebrews deviates, and one should not exclude the possibility of an intermediary source, cf. below, p. 209.

Justin's long excerpt in *Dial.* 63:4 (Ps 45:7-13) also begins with the same words as that in Heb 1:8f. Some sort of contact with Hebrews cannot be excluded.

Justin extracts two Christological points from this longer text: (1) The Messiah is called and is God, vss 7f; and (2) he is προσκυνητός, vs.13a (*Dial.* 63:5; 68:3.9; *Dial.* 38:1; 126:1). The motif of the *proskynesis* is not included in the Hebrews quotation of Ps 45, but in Heb 1:6, preceeding the Ps 45 quotation, we read: καὶ προσκυνησάτωσαν αὐτῷ πάντες ἄγγελοι θεοῦ (= Deut 32:43, cf. above p. 117) This may explain why Justin concentrated on exactly this motif in his treatment of the full LXX text of Ps 45. His added comment on vss.11-13a in *Dial.* 63:5 is a typical example of Justin's independent exegesis of LXX material not included in his testimony source.

### (26) Ps. 22:23

| Heb 2:12 | Ps 22:23f LXX = *Dial.* 106:2 (= *Dial.* 98:5) | *Barn.* 6:16 |
|---|---|---|
| ἀπαγγελῶ τὸ ὄνομά σου τοῖς ἀδελφοῖς μου ἐν μέσῳ ἐκκλησίας ὑμνήσω σε | διηγήσομαι τὸ ὄνομά σου τοῖς ἀδελφοῖς μου ἐν μέσῳ ἐκκλησίας ὑμνήσω σε οἱ φοβούμενοι κύριον . . . . | ἐξομολογήσομαι σοι ἐν ἐκκλησίᾳ ἀδελφῶν μου καὶ ψαλῶ σοι ἀναμέσον ἐκκλησίας ἁγίων |

In *Dial.* 106:1f Justin, as part of his continuous exegesis of Ps 22, also comments on the opening phrase of Ps 22:23. His context and exegesis is different from that of Hebrews, and he also has no echo of the non-LXX reading ἀπαγγελῶ. There is thus probably no dependence here. On the level of text-type, one can certainly say the same about *Barn.* 6:16. But here the idea is closer to Justin's.

### (27) Num 12:7

Justin has several allusions to Moses «the faithful servant»: πιστός θεράπων: *Dial.* 46:3; 79:4; 130:1. ὁ *μακάριος καὶ πιστός* θεράπων θεοῦ: *Dial.* 56:1.

In Hebrews and *1. Clement* we find similar designations of Moses: πιστὸν ὄντα . . . ὡς καὶ Μωϋσῆς ἐν ὅλῳ τῷ οἴκῳ αὐτοῦ: Heb 3:2. Μωϋσῆς . . πιστὸς ἐν ὅλῳ τῷ οἴκῳ αὐτοῦ ὡς θεράπων: Heb 3:5. Μωϋσῆς πιστὸς ἐν ὅλῳ τῷ οἴκῳ αὐτοῦ: *1.Clem.* 17:5. ὁ *μακάριος πιστὸς* θεράπων ἐν ὅλῳ τῷ οἴκῳ Μωϋσῆς: *1.Clem.* 43:1.

There need be no literary dependence between Justin and these two writers. «Moses the faithful servant» may well have been a current honorary designation.[187] Yet the parallel between *1.Clem.* 43:1 and *Dial.* 56:1 is striking.

---

187. Cf. O. Michel, *comm.* to Hebrews, p. 84.

(28)Ps 110:4; Gen 14:18-20

| Heb | Dial. 19:4 | Dial. 33:2 |
|---|---|---|
| 7:1<br>οὗτος γὰρ ὁ Μελχισέδεκ<br>... ἱερεὺς τοῦ θεοῦ<br>τοῦ ὑψίστου . . .‾ ‾ ‾ ‾¬<br>7:2                                 ¦<br>ᾧ καὶ δεκάτην          ¦<br>ἀπὸ πάντων ἐμέρισεν ¦<br>⸗᾽Αβραάμ                    ↓ | ἀπερίτμητος ἦν<br>ὁ ἱερεὺς<br>τοῦ ὑψίστου<br>Μελχισεδέκ<br>ᾧ καὶ δεκάτας<br>προσφορὰς ἔδωκεν<br>᾽Αβραάμ . . . | . . . ὃν τρόπον ὁ Μελχισεδὲκ<br>ἱερεὺς<br>ὑψίστου . . . καὶ τὸν<br>ἐν περιτομῇ<br><br>προσενέγκαντα<br>᾽Αβραὰμ |
| καὶ εὐλογήσας αὐτόν | καὶ εὐλόγησεν αὐτόν | εὐλόγησεν . . . |
| 7:11<br>. . . κατὰ τὴν τάξιν<br>Μελχισέδεκ<br>ἕτερον ἀνίστασθαι ἱερέα | οὗ κατὰ τὴν τάξιν<br>τὸν αἰώνιον ἱερέα<br>ὁ θεός καταστήσειν . . . | |

Hebrews is the only known writing prior to Justin which makes Ps 110:4 a major Christological testimony. One cannot reasonably doubt that Justin depends on Hebrews for his own treatment of this text.

However, Justin's treatment is somewhat different from the one given in Hebrews. While the point in Hebrews is that the Levitic priesthood - through Abraham - offered tithes to Melchizedek, thereby recognizing his superior position (this superior position also being effected in Melchizedek's blessing of Abraham), Justin turns the emphasis into an uncircumcised-versus-circumcised polemic: The uncircumcised Melchizedek, representing all uncircumcised believers, blessed the circumcised Abraham. One wonders whether this twist of the idea from Hebrews is Justin's own invention. ( It involves a *prima facie* chronological error: In Gen 14, Abraham is not yet circumcised.[188] Now, while Justin's wording in *Dial.* 33:2 seems to imply this error, in *Dial.* 19:4 he formulates with greater care: « Abraham was the first to receive the circumcision that is after the flesh, and was blessed by Melchizedek». *Dial.* 33:2 may be a condensed expression of the same thought, and one should therefore not rashly suppose a mistake here.) In *Dial.* 19:2-5 circumcision is Justin's theme throughout, so one is probably entitled to conclude that the added motive in the material from Hebrews is Justin's own modification of his source.

(29)Gen 5:24

In *Dial.* 19:3 Justin has a paraphrase of Gen 5:24, similar to the one in Heb 11:5. But both writers reproduce the LXX terminology; the similarity may therefore not be significant. In both authors, however, the mention of Enoch is preceeded by a paraphrase of Gen 4:4 on Abel. The fact that Hebrews very likely is used as a source in *Dial.* 19:4 makes me inclined to believe that Hebrews may have influenced *Dial.* 19:3 also.

(30) Ezek 33:11

| Ezek 33:11 LXX | 1. Clem. 8:2 | 1. Apol. 15:8 |
|---|---|---|
| ζῶ ἐγώ λέγει κύριος<br>οὐ βούλομαι<br>τὸν θάνατον<br>τοῦ ἀσεβοῦς<br>ὡς τὸ ἀποστρέψαι<br>τὸν ἀσεβῆ ἀπὸ τῆς ὁδοῦ<br>αὐτοῦ καὶ ζῆν αὐτόν | ζῶ γὰρ ἐγώ λέγει κύριος<br>οὐ βούλομαι<br>τὸν θάνατον<br>τοῦ ἁμαρτωλοῦ<br>ὡς τὴν μετάνοιαν | θέλει γὰρ<br>ὁ πατὴρ ὁ οὐράνιος<br>τὴν μετάνοιαν<br>τοῦ ἁμαρτωλοῦ<br>ἢ τὴν κόλασιν αὐτοῦ |

188. So A. L. Williams, Introduction, p. XXXIV, and his note *ad Dial.* 32:2 (p. 65).

Justin's paraphrase in *1.Apol.* 15:8 shares the non-LXX words ἁμαρτωλός and μετάνοια with *1.Clem.* The significance of this is difficult to evaluate, because immediately preceeding Justin's paraphrase both words occur in a Jesus logion: οὐκ ἦλθον καλέσαι δικαίους ἀλλὰ ἁμαρτωλοὺς εἰς μετάνοιαν. Indeed, the whole context in *1.Apol.* 15:7f is replete with terminology derived from the Jesus logion, and one does not feel certain that Justin's comment on it in 15:8 entails any reference to Ezek 33:11 at all. A dependence on *1.Clem.* 8 is thus far from certain.

(31) Josh 2:3-5.9-14.18f

In Clement's long paraphrase of Josh 2, only the last part has an equivalent in Justin:

| Josh 2:18 LXX | *1.Clem.* 12:7f | *Dial.* 111:4 |
|---|---|---|
| ... καὶ θήσεις τὸ σημεῖον τὸ σπαρτίον τὸ κόκκινον τοῦτο ἐκδήσεις εἰς τὴν θυρίδα δἰ ἧς κατεβίβασας... | καὶ προσέθεντο αὐτῇ δοῦναι σημεῖον ὅπως ἐκκρεμάσῃ ἐκ τοῦ οἴκου αὐτῆς κόκκινον | καὶ γὰρ τὸ σύμβολον τοῦ κοκκίνου *σπαρτίου* οὗ ἔδωκαν ἐν ᾿Ιεριχῶ οἱ ἀπὸ ᾿Ιησοῦ τοῦ Ναυῆ πεμφθέντες κατάσκοποι ῾Ραὰβ τῇ πόρνῃ, εἰπόντες προσ*δῆσαι* αὐτὸ |
| Josh 2:15 LXX | | *τῇ θυρίδι δἰ ἧς αὐτοὺς ἐχάλασεν* |
| καὶ κατεχάλασεν αὐτοὺς διὰ τῆς θυρίδος | | ὅπως λάθωσι τοὺς πολεμίους |
| | πρόδηλον ποιοῦντες ὅτι διὰ τοῦ αἵματος τοῦ κυρίου λύτρωσις ἔσται πᾶσιν τοῖς πιστεύουσιν καὶ ἐλπίζουσιν ἐπὶ τὸν θεόν | ὁμοίως τὸ σύμβολον τοῦ αἵματος τοῦ Χριστοῦ ἐδήλου δἰ οὗ οἱ πάλαι πόρνοι καὶ ἄδικοι ἐκ πάντων τῶν ἐθνῶν σώζονται ἄφεσιν ἁμαρτιῶν λαβόντες ... |

It seems probable that Justin depends on *1.Clem.*[189] or a very similar source for his Rahab typology, but it is also obvious that *1.Clem.* was not his only source: He adds LXX details not found in *1.Clem.* (cursivated in the synopsis).

---

189. So also D. E. Aune, 'Justin Martyr's Use of the Old Testament', *Bulletin of the Evangelical Theological Society* 9 (1966) (pp. 179-97), p. 197.

(32) Is 50:6-8

| Is 50:6-8a LXX = *1.Apol.* 38:2f | *Barn.* 5:14 |
|---|---|
| | ἰδού |
| τὸν νῶτόν μου δέδωκα[a] | τέθεικά μου τὸν νῶτον |
| εἰς μαστίγας | εἰς μάστιγας |
| [b]τὰς δὲ[b] σιαγόνας μου | καὶ τὰς σιαγόνας |
| εἰς ῥαπίσματα | εἰς ῥαπίσματα |
| τὸ δὲ πρόσωπόν μου | τὸ δὲ πρόσωπόν μου |
| οὐκ ἀπέστρεψα ἀπὸ αἰσχύνης | |
| ἐμπτυσμάτων | |
| καὶ κύριος βοηθός μου ἐγενήθη[d] | |
| διὰ τοῦτο οὐκ ἐνετράπην | |
| ἀλλὰ ἔθηκα | ἔθηκα |
| τὸ πρόσωπόν μου | |
| ὡς στερεὰν πέτραν | ὡς στερεὰν πέτραν |
| καὶ ἔγνων ὅτι οὐ μὴ αἰσχυνθῶ | |
| ὅτι ἐγγίζει ὁ δικαιώσας με... | |

a) *1.Apol* 38: τέθεικα
b-b) *1. Apol.* . 38: καὶ τας = LXX 736; Sa; Syp. *et al. patres*
c) *1.Apol.* 38: ὁ κύριος
d) *1.Apol.*38: ἐγένετο = LXX 91; 534

Justin's text could be characterized as a LXX excerpt with one contamination from *Barn.* 5:14: τέθεικα instead of LXX ἔδωκα. However, the context in *1 Apol.* 38 shows that a testimony source other than *Barn.* is being employed in the rest of the chapter. The non-LXX reading may therefore stem from this source, if it was not present in Justin's Isaiah MS. Influence from *Barn.* is thus uncertain.

(33) Ps 18:45

| Ps 18 LXX = *Dial.* 28:6 | *Barn.* 9:1 |
|---|---|
| 44. λαός ὃν οὐκ ἔγνων ἐδούλευσέ μοι | |
| 45. εἰς ἀκοὴν ὠτίου ὑπήκουσέ μου[a] | εἰς ἀκοὴν ὠτίου ὑπήκουσάν[a] μου |
| a) = LXX U; R; A; Lucianic MSS. Rahlfs: μοι | a) = LXX S; Sy (=MT) |

In *Dial.* 28:2f we have surmised (above, p. 72) the adaption of a testimony source parallel to *Barnabas.* The added quotations in *Dial.* 28:5f (Mal. 1:10-12 and Ps 18:44f) seem to be prompted by the same source. If Justin had taken the care to look *Barnabas'* quotation up in a Psalms MS, we should have expected a more extensive quotation and some exegetical comment in *Dial.* 28:6.

General conclusions:

(1) It seems our surmises about Justin's handling of his «testimony sources» can be substantiated in most of the cases where we can observe Justin working with a known source. He normally quotes exactly. He can also look non-LXX quotations up in the relevant Biblical MS and excerpt the LXX text — normally making a larger excerpt than the one contained in his source.

(2) We have also had several occasions to observe that while Justin shares a considerable amount of quotations with his Christian precursors, the text-type of his quotations often do not stem directly from these sources, but from some intermediary or common source. This is especially striking with regard to *1.* and *2. Clement* and *Barnabas,* but it also seems to be the case with John and Acts. It seems to be true about all these writers that Justin made little if any use of them as direct sources for OT texts, but the amount of shared references is remarkably high, especially with regard to *Barnabas.* This clearly points to testimony sources besides these known writings.

(3) Justin's relation to Matthew is more complex. There is much Matthean material in OT texts which are not quoted directly from Matthew. In other words, Justin's unknown testimony sources had digested a considerable amount of Matthean OT quotations and allusions.

But besides, Justin sometimes has direct access to Matthew and quotes OT texts directly from him. In most cases, these quotations stand out as supplementary testimonies grafted on to a groundwork of texts not taken directly from Matthew. (The direct borrowings are most frequent in the *Dialogue*; in the *Apology* Mic 5:1 in *1.Apol.* 34:1 may be the only instance). And one notices that Justin by no means has made a complete use of Matthew's distinctive fulfilment quotations.

(4) The writer to whom Justin can be seen to have the most direct relation is Paul. Only a few of Paul's OT quotations seem to have reached Justin via intermediary sources — for the most part Justin is quoting directly from Paul, mostly Romans and Galatians. He focuses on Paul's texts concerning Jews and Gentiles; in one instance he makes use of Paul's argument concerning the cross of Christ (Gal 3:13, *Dial.* 95f). But again one observes that the Pauline testimonies often seem grafted on to a groundwork of testimonies which are not Pauline. We shall have opportunity in Part III to a fuller examination of this relationship.

(5) One final word on Luke. Since Luke in recent research has been given prominent position among Justin's predecessors, it may be of relevance to point out that on the level of OT proof-texts the picture is rather ambiguous. There are some marked Lukan elements in Justin's testimony material —not directly taken from Luke. There are also some echoes of the speeches in Acts — especially Stephen's. But here again the theory of intermediary sources can hardly be avoided. And some of the most distinctive features in

Luke's OT proof are conspicuously lacking in Justin, e.g. the use of Is 61:1f as a testimony on Jesus' anointing with the Spirit, and Ps 16:8-11 as a central resurrection testimony. Deut 18:15ff and Am 9:11f are also lacking in Justin.

One can perhaps conclude from this that Justin's OT proof-text sources were not as markedly Lukan as Justin himself has often been deemed to be. On the level of proof-texts, one rather gets the impression that Matthean, Lukan, and Johannine elements have been combined in an independent way, by a tradition having its own profile.

These suggestions are provisional. We shall be able to make more definite statements when we have delineated the «groundwork» of Justin's proof-text tradition in Part II.

PART TWO:

TESTIMONY CLUSTERS AND THE DISPOSITION OF
*1.APOL.* 31ff AND *DIAL.* 11-141

## CHAPTER ONE

A BRIEF SKETCH OF PREVIOUS RESEARCH

A feature that has struck most commentators reading Justin's exegetical expositions is his remarkably bad organization of the material. One often searches in vain for a coherent line of argument, because Justin allows himself to follow all kinds of digressions, and sometimes seems to follow rather far-fetched associations.[1]

Of course this represents a challenge to the modern scholar who finds it fascinating to search for the hidden order behind the apparent chaos. Several attempts have been made in that respect. K.Hubik,[2] following suggestions by Wehofer,[3] tried to delineate a disposition for the *Apology* and the *Dialogue* according to the rules of rhetoric in antiquity. His analysis was later deemed «unglaublich künstlich» by Bousset,[4] and is indeed rather artificial in several particulars. Hubik failed to pay attention to the inherent disposition and connexions of the exegetical material employed by Justin.

The first to make a more careful investigation of the inherent structure of the Scriptural proof were A. von Ungern-Sternberg[5] and W.Bousset.[6] Concerning the *Apology*, both scholars point to *1.Apol.* 31:7 as a dispositional sketch, which is carried out in *1.Apol.* 32-35/48-53; chs. 36-47 standing out as a great insertion.

Von Ungern-Sternberg recognizes that some of the testimonies in this insertion have as their theme the preaching of the Gospel to all nations - a

---

1. Two representative statements: «*Justin, à n'en pas douter, ne sait pas composer. Peut-être a-t-il esquissé un plan avant d'écrire, mais sa pensée est toujours prête à suivre toutes les idées qui se présentent, et il les suit en effet dans des digressions parfois trés enchevétrées.*» (Archambault, Introduction, p. LXXXVII). «Were he writing today, he would be one of those scholars who place one line of text at the head of the page and cover the rest with lumpy footnotes.» (H. Chadwick, 'Justin Martyr's Defence of Christianity', *Bulletin of the John Rylands Library* 47 (1965, pp. 275-297), p. 278.

2. K. Hubik, *Die Apologien des hl. Justinus des Philosophen und Märtyrers. Literarhistorische Untersuchungen* (Theologische Studien der Leo Gesellschaft 19, Wien, 1912).

3. Th. M. Wehofer, *Die Apologie Justins des Philosophen und Märtyrers in literaturhistorischer Beziehung zum erstenmal untersucht* (Römische Quartalschrift, Suppl. Heft 6, Roma, 1897). Wehofer's argument is briefly summarized and criticized by Bardenhewer, *Geschichte* I, pp. 220f.

4. Bousset, *Schulbetrieb*, p. 283, n. 1.

5. A. Freiherr von Ungern-Sternberg, *Der traditionelle alttestamentliche Schriftbeweis «de Christo» und «de Evangelio» in der Alten Kirche bis zur Zeit Eusebs von Caesarea* (Halle a. S., 1913).

6. W. Bousset, *Jüdisch-Christlicher Schulbetrieb in Alexandria und Rom. Literarische Untersuchungen zu Philo und Clemens von Alexandria, Justin und Irenaeus* (FRLANT, Neue Folge, 6, Göttingen 1915), pp. 282-308.

thematic unity not called for by their present function within Justin's context. Justin has to do with *"einem ihm bereits gegebenen und von ihm nicht bewältigten Traditionsstoff. . . . Wenn wir von der Darstellung Justins in cc.32ff seine schriftstellerischen Eigentümlichkeiten in Abrechnung bringen, so gewinnen wir erst den originalen und weit strafferen Zusammenhang, durch welchen der S(chrift) B(eweis) sich auszeichnete. . ."*[7] Concerning the *Dialogue*, von Ungern Sternberg proceeds with a more summary analysis of *Dial.* 11-30 (Jewish ceremonial practices); *Dial.*. 31-117 (»Schriftbeweis *de Christo*«); and *Dial.* 118-141 (Gospel preached to all nations). In the Christological section (31-117) von Ungern-Sternberg recognizes the same basic pattern as in *1.Apol.* 32-35/ 48-53; the additions and elaborations are mainly due to the different and more demanding addressees of the *Dialogue*.

Bousset conducted his analysis independently of von Ungern-Sternberg but often agrees with him. However, Bousset takes the idea of an employed tradition a step further. He tries to reconstruct smaller, well-organized units behind Justin's presentation, and surmises that these units correspond to »Schriftbeweistraktate« which Justin employed when writing the *Apology* and the *Dialogue*. It is not relevant here to give a detailed report of Bousset's analysis - we shall often have opportunity to return to it in the following analysis. In the judgement of the present writer, Bousset's observations are often trenchant, and his analysis as a whole is hardly surpassed by any later writer.[8] Special mention should be made, however, of H. Koester's form-critical analysis of certain sections of Justin's *Apology* and *Dialogue*. Koester takes over Bousset's concept of Scriptural proof tractates, and tries to discern their formal structure. His observations are relevant also in the present study.[9]

A recent attempt to find a coherent scheme on the level of OT quotations is F. M.-M. Sagnard's article on Justin's *Dialogue*.[10] While Sagnard pays careful attention to the structure of the quotation material, he pays insufficient attention to inherent tensions and different layers of the Scripture

---

7. Von Ungern-Sternberg, *op. cit.,* pp. 12f.
8. N. J. Hommes, *Testimoniaboek*, endorses Bousset's point of view. A. Nussbaumer, *Das Ursymbolum nach der Epideixis des hl. Irenaus und dem Dialog Justin's des Märtyrers mit Trypho* (Forschungen zur Christlichen Literatur- und Dogmengeschichte 14:2, Paderborn, 1921) is an attempt to discern a »creed« pattern as the organizing principle in Justin and Irenaeus. The study is marred by a very conjectural and artificial reconstruction of sources behind Irenaeus' *Epideixis*. Nussbaumer tries to fit the whole of Justin's *Dialogue* into the pattern he has extracted from one of the sources in the *Epideixis*. Here again his analysis is rather artificial, and seems to have been largely ignored by other scholars. The main flaw in Nussbaumer's analysis of Justin is his failure to treat Justin's material on its own terms. But the idea of a »creed« pattern deserves notice.
9. H. Koester, *Septuaginta und Synoptischer Erzählungsstoff im Schriftbeweis Justins des Märtyrers* (Habilitationsschrift, Heidelberg, 1956).
10. F. M.-M. Sagnard, 'Y a-t-il un plan du »Dialogue avec Tryphon«?', *Melanges Joseph de Ghellinck, I: Antiquité* (Gembloux, 1951), pp. 171-182.

exposition and therefore often misses important points already made by Bousset. He also unduly neglects the dispositional remarks made by Justin himself. His study therefore remains an unsatisfactory torso.

An approach from a different and apparently opposite angle has been made in two recent works on the early Christian dialogues as a literary genre by M.Hoffmann and B.R.Voss.[11] These scholars are occupied only with the present text of the *Dialogue*, and Hoffmann makes the interesting proposal that some of the disorderly digressions in the *Dialogue* are intentional — they serve to characterize Trypho as one with whom it is difficult to argue because he always diverts the line of argument. I think one shall have to keep this dimension of the *Dialogue* in mind when analyzing its structure. But of course this point of view is of little help in the *Apology.*[12]

The most recent large-scale treatment of the subject is Prigent's monograph on Justin and the OT. His analysis again probes behind Justin's present disposition in search for the organization of the *Syntagma.* Prigent in some details is able to refine Bousset's analysis, but at the same time he is less able to explain the disorderly arrangement of Justin's preserved writings. If the disposition of the *Syntagma* was good, as Prigent seems to think, why should it have worsened so much in the *Apology* and the *Dialogue?*

My purpose in the following analysis is to grasp the intricate interplay between an inherent structure of the quotation material employed, and Justin's own shaping of the material. This presupposes that Justin employed source material which had a certain structure and that this structure not always coincides with the plan he imposed upon the material. I think this presupposition is well established by von Ungern-Sternberg's, Bousset's and Prigent's analyses, and it will be further substantiated in the analysis below.

I believe it is essential for such an analysis to start from the surface structure of Justin's exposition. The scholars most concerned to probe behind the surface level of Justin's text, have sometimes overlooked important clues given by Justin himself in what we may term his »dispositional remarks«, i.e. statements by himself or Trypho concerning the progress of the debate.[13] I shall try to pay due attention to this.

---

11. M. Hoffmann, *Der Dialog bei den christlichen Schriftstellern der ersten vier Jahrhunderte* (TU 96, Berlin, 1966); pp. 10-28; B. R. Voss, *Der Dialog in der frühchristlichen Literatur (Studia et test. antiqua* IX, München, 1970), pp. 26-39.

12. A detailed analysis of the disposition of *1.Apol.* 1-22 is given in U. Hüntemann, 'Zur Kompositionstechnik Justins. Analyse seiner ersten Apologie', *Theologie und Glaube, Zeitschrift f. d. katholische Klerus* 25 (1933), pp. 410-428. For *1.Apol.* 23ff Hüntemann's analysis is very summary and of little help to our purpose.

13. To my mind, this is the main flaw of Sagnard's article, cf. note 10.

For *a priori* reasons, one would expect to find Justin's exegetical »gro-undwork« tradition in its most »pure« form in the *Apology*. As we have seen, Justin seems to add elements from i.a. Matthew and Paul in the *Dialogue*.

I shall therefore start my analysis with the *Apology*, tracing related mate-rial in the *Dialogue*, and finally turn to the Christological section of the *Dialogue* which exhibits a different profile compared with the Christologi-cal section of the *Apology*.

CHAPTER TWO.

*1.Apol.* 31ff

In *1.Apol.* 31:7 Justin has an anticipatory summary of what he is going to prove in the Scriptural exposition:

»We find it predicted in the books of the prophets that Jesus our Christ would

(1) come,

(2) born of a virgin,

(3) grown to manhood,

(4) healing every sickness and every disease and raising the dead,

(5) hated and unacknowledged and crucified, dying,

(6) and rising again and ascending into heaven,

       both really being and being called Son of God.

       [We find it also that]

(7) men sent by him would proclaim these things to every race of mankind,

(8) and that men of the Gentiles especially would believe in him.«

As observed by Bousset, von Ungern-Sternberg and others, this disposition can be said to be carried out in chapters 32-35 and 48-53 of the *Apology*.[1] We find the following elements:

(1) The coming of the Messiah: *1.Apol.* 32(Gen 49:10f; Num 24:17/ Is 11:1/Is 51:5).

(2) The virgin birth of the Messiah: *1.Apol.* 33(f) (Is 7:14; Mic 5:1).

(3) The hidden growing up of the Messiah: *1.Apol.* 35:1f (Is 9:5a).

(4) The healings of the Messiah: *1.Apol.* 48:1-3(Is 35:5f etc.).

(5) The passion of the Messiah: *1.Apol.* 50f (Is 52:13—53:12).

(6) The ascension of the Messiah: *1.Apol.* 51:7(Ps 24:7ff).

       The glorious return of the Messiah: *1.Apol.* 51:8f

       (Dan 7:13).

       The resurrection of all men: *1.Apol.* 52 (Ezek 37:7f;

       Is 66:24; Zech 12:10-12).

(8) Gentiles believing rather than Jews: *1.Apol.* 53 (Is 54:1; Is 1:9; Jer 9:25).

---

1. K. Hubik, *op. cit.,* enumerates *1.Apol.* 32-35; 45; 47-53 as the passages in which the disposition is carried out (pp. 131f). Bousset, *Schulbetrieb,* pp. 300-303, recognizes Justin's disposition in *1.Apol* 32-35; 48-53: »Der Traktat zum Weissagungsbeweis«; von Ungern-Sternberg likewise, pp. 8f. H. Koester, *Schriftbeweis,* enumerates *1.Apol.* 32-35:1a.10f; 48; 50-53 (p. 62)

Element 7 in Justin's disposition is missing, but it is hinted at in *1.Apol.* 50:12, and is treated extensively within the "great insertion",[2] *1.Apol.* 36-47. As we shall see below, the correspondences marked out in the above tables also require some other modifications, but for the present we shall take these tables as our starting point. Let us take a closer look on this sequence of testimonies in the *Apology*, in each case examining the parallels in the *Dialogue.* For convenience, I shall refer to this sequence of testimonies as the «creed» sequence, having in mind the creed-1ike appearance of the passages in which Justin summarizes his Scriptural proof.[3]

### 1. The "creed" sequence: 1.Apol. 31-35.48.50-53 and parallels in the Dialogue.

(a) The coming of the Messiah: *1.Apol.* 32 and parallels.

(α) The final King of Judah; Gen 49:10f: *1.Apol.* 32 and *Dial.* 52.54

In the *Apology,* the treatment of the testimonies on the Jesus story begins with an extensive comment on Gen 49:10f in *1.Apol.* 32:1-11. This exposition runs strikingly parallel to the one in *Dial.* 52-54. (see synopsis next page). This parallel calls for several comments. First, one notices a rather stable scheme of exposition: (A) The relevant scriptural phrase is quoted, introduced by τὸ δὲ (εἰρημένον) . . . Next (B), there follows a short exegesis of the exact meaning of the Scriptural phrase, introduced by the words σημαίνει or μηνύει or equivalents. Finally (C), a short historical narrative is appended, in which the historical fulfilment of the prophecy is pointed out. Let us call the elements of this ABC-pattern «prophecy», «exposition», and «fulfilment report».[4]

Next, one notices that the expositions and fulfilment reports run strikingly parallel. Especially striking are the non-synoptic words and phrases common to the fulfilment reports (in the synpsis:2C, italicized words).[5]

---

2. Cf. Bousset, *op. cit.,* p. 300: «ein grosser Excurs»; cf. also von Ungern-Sternberg, pp. 12f (quoted above).

3. Cf. e.g. *Dial.* 39:7; 63:1. It is relevant to notice that in Irenaeus' famous summary of the Christian faith (*Adv.Haer.* I:10:1), the Christological «creed» reporting Christ's career is placed in the *third* «article» as a summary of *what the Spirit foretold through the prophets!* There is thus a valid insight in Nussbaumer's study (cf. p. 136, note 8); his error is that he let the «creed» cover too much material in Justin's writings.

4. I have framed this designation as an equivalent to Koester's term «Bericht der Erfüllung», *Schriftbeweis,* pp. 64/66.

5. One should note also the constant use of τὰ Ἱεροσόλυμα in these fulfilment reports. This is not Justin's usual name of Jerusalem. Most often he says᾿Ιερουσαλήμ (*1.Apol.* 39:3; 45:5; 47:4; 49:5; *Dial.* 17:1; 22:11; 34:7; 51:2; 80:1.5; 81:4; 83:3f; 85:7; 99:2; 109:1; 110:2; 113:5; 117:2; 127:3; 138:3), or (with the article) ἡ᾿Ιερουσαλήμ (*Dial.* 16:2; 40:2; 83:1; 92:2; 123:6; 138:1). Ἱεροσόλυμα without the article occurs more rarely (*1.Apol.* 34:2; *Dial.* 40:5; 77:4; 88:6 - in the last case: entry into Jerusalem!): τὰ Ἱεροσόλυμα occurs in the three passages concerned with the entry into Jerusalem, and besides only in two cases: *Dial.* 36:3; 40:4. (In this list all occurrences within Scriptural quotations are excluded).

## Gen 49:10f - synopsis

| 1. Apol. 32/35 | Dial. 52—54 |
|---|---|
| Gen 49:10—11 non-LXX | Gen 49:8—12 LXX |
| Exegesis of Gen 49:10: Roman occupation means end to ruler and King in Judaea, accordingly the Messiah must now have come | Exegesis of Gen 49:10: Prophetic succession — the prophets always anointing the kings — breaking off with John the Baptist, accordingly the Messiah must have come |
| Gen 49:11 — detailed exegesis:<br>(1) A: τὸ δὲ *αὐτὸς ἔσται προσδοκία ἐθνῶν*...<br> B: μηνυτικὸν ἦν... that men of every nation will look forward to his coming again<br> C: as you can clearly see... for men of every race are looking (προσδοκῶσι) for him who was crucified in Judaea | Gen 49:11 — detailed exegesis:<br>A: τὸ δὲ... *καὶ αὐτὸς ἔσται προσδοκία ἐθνῶν*...<br> B: συμβολικῶς δύο παρουσίας αὐτοῦ ἐσήμανε, and also that the Gentiles should belive in him<br> C: which... you can see for yourselves. For we look forward (προσδοκῶμεν) to his coming again |
| (2) A: τὸ δὲ *δεσμέυων πρὸς ἄμπελον τὸν πῶλον*...<br> B: σύμβολον δηλωτικὸν ἦν τῶν γενησομένων τῷ Χριστῷ... | A: καὶ τὸ *δεσμεύων*...<br><br> B: καὶ τῶν ἔργων... γενομένων ὑπ αὐτοῦ... προδήλωσις ἦν<br><br> C: (1) πῶλος = believing Gentiles |
| C: πῶλος γάρ τις ὄνου εἱστήκει<br><br>*ἔν τινι εἰσόδῳ* κώμης πρὸς ἄμπελον δεδεμένος<br><br>ὃν *ἐκέλευσεν*<br><br>ἀγαγεῖν *αὐτῷ*... τοὺς γνωρίμους αὐτοῦ... ἐκάθισε καὶ εἰσελήύθεν εἰς τὰ Ἱεροσόλυμα... | (2) καὶ ὄνον δέ τινα... σὺν πώλῳ αὐτῆς προσδεδεμένην<br>*ἔν τινι εἰσόδῳ* κώμης<br><br>Βεθσφαγῆς λεγομένης ... *ἐκέλευσε* τοὺς μαθητὰς αὐτοῦ ἀγαγεῖν *αὐτῷ*<br><br>καὶ ἐπικαθίσας ἐπεισελήλυθεν εἰς τὰ Ἱεροσόλυμα... |
| *1. Apol. 35:10f:*<br>καθεσθησόμενος ἐπὶ πῶλον ὄνου καὶ εἰσελευσόμενος εἰς τὰ Ἱεροσόλυμα...<br>Zech 9:9 non-LXX | Zech 9:9 καιγε |
| | (3) ὄνον ὑποζύγιον = Jews, πῶλος = Gentiles |
| (3) | Zech 13:7 καιγε, input from Mt 26:31 |

| (4) A:<br>B/C:<br><br><br><br>B: | τὸ γὰρ *πλύνων τὴν στολήν*. . .<br>was predictive of the passion which he was to suffer, cleansing by his blood those who belive on him.<br>Men who believe on him called a στολή by the divine Spirit. The Logos, Seed of God, dwells in them. | A:<br>B/C:<br><br>B: | καὶ τὸ. . *πλυνεῖ ἐν οἴνῳ τὴν στολήν*. .<br>signified that he would wash in his blood those who believed him.<br><br>The Holy Spirit calls those who receive remission of sins through Christ his στολή. Christ dwells among them in power. |
|---|---|---|---|
| (5) A:<br>B:<br><br><br>(C:<br><br><br>B: | τὸ δὲ . . . *αἶμα τῆς σταφυλῆς*. . .<br>a sign that he would have blood ἀλλ' οὐκ ἐξ ἀνθρωπείου σπέρματος ἀλλ' ἐκ θείας δυνάμεως<br>How he was made flesh and became man we shall describe below)<br>As the blood of the grape was not made by man, but by God, so Christ's blood should not come from human seed, but from God's power | A:<br>B:<br><br><br><br><br>B: | τὸ δὲ *αἶμα τῆς σταφυλῆς*. . .<br>signifies that Christ have blood οὐκ ἐξ ἀνθρώπου σπέρματος ἀλλ' ἐκ τῆς τοῦ θεοῦ δυνάμεως<br><br><br>For just as it was not man, but God that begat the blood of the vine, so also he signified beforehand that the blood of Christ would not be of human generation, but of God's power |

The significance of this might be regarded negligible if the *Dialogue* passage were regarded as directly dependent upon the *Apology* passage. But such is hardly the case. One observation points clearly to the conclusion that Justin in the *Dialogue* has direct recourse to the source behind *1.Apol.* 32: In *1.Apol.* 32,5f, while commenting on Gen 49:11 («Binding his foal to the vine and washing his robe in the blood of the grape»), Justin has the following fulfilment report: «For an ass's foal was standing at the entrance of a village, bound to a vine . . . when it was brought he mounted and sat on it and entered into Jerusalem.» One would expect here a quotation of the corroborating prophecy Zech 9:9. And one do in fact find this text quoted - only a little delayed and out-of-context in *1.Apol.* 35:10f. We have analysed this quotation above  (pp. 74 - 76)  and found it to derive from a testimony source.  One observes that the fulfilment report in *1.Apol* 32:6 is partly repeated  in 35:10,  thus creating an inelegant repetition. Everything goes to show that Justin has split up something that belonged together in his source: The exposition of Gen 49:11 and the quotation of Zech 9:9. And in the *Dialogue* we find exactly this connexion we have surmised in the source behind the *Apology* (see synopsis). One can add that a reason for the delay in *1.Apol.* 35 is not difficult to find: Justin is writing for readers unfamiliar with the Jesus story, and he would not introduce a testimony referring to the Passion before that theme had been introduced (in *1.Apol.* 35:3ff). In the *Dialogue* he was under no similar restraints, and could produce the sequence of his source uninhibited.

Taking as a working hypothesis that Justin in *1.Apol.* 32/35 and *Dial.*
52-54 is using a source containing OT prophecies, expositions and fullfil-
ment reports, it is easy to recognize the different procedure in the *Apology*
and the *Dialogue*. In the *Apology*, Justin reproduces the source rather
faithfully, only re-arranging the material by not quoting Zech 9:9 in its
proper place. In the *Dialogue*, three things have changed: The OT prophecies are no longer quoted in the modified, non-LXX versions present in the
source, but are quoted in full directly from Biblical MSS. (Nevertheless an
exegesis presupposing the non-LXX text is retained, cf. above p. 27f.). (2)
The exposition is much more elaborate. This is especially evident in the
exegesis of Gen 49:10. In *1.Apol.* 32 Justin was satisfied to report the
fulfilment of Gen 49:10 in very simple terms:«You can enquire precisely
and learn up to whose time the Jews had their own ruler and king . . . after
his (Christ's) apearance you (Romans) began to rule over the Jews and
gained control of their whole land» (*1.Apol.* 32:2f). In *Dial.* 52 Justin is
aware that this is too simple. The Jewish kingdom ceased in Israel before
Jesus appeared: The Jews can rightly point out that Herod was not a Jew,
*Dial.* 52:3. This makes the rather complicated argument in the whole of
*Dial.* 49-52 necessary. We shall return to it in some detail below (pp. 195f.).
(3) The fulfilment report is enriched with details taken directly from
Matthew, even an OT prophecy contained in Matthew is reproduced, Zech
13:7, but like the other OT prophecies it is not quoted directly from the
testimony source (in this case Matthew), but from Justin's Dodekapropheton scroll (καιγε text, cf. above, synoptic study 17).

In other words: In the *Dialogue* Justin is much more independent in his
handling of his source. He has turned to the primary sources behind the
testimony source, that is, he has turned to the LXX and Matthew.

(β) The rising star; Num 24:17/Is 11:1/51:5; Ps 72:17; Zech 6:12: *1.Apol.*
32 and *Dial.* 121.

In *1.Apol.* 32 the testimony following upon Gen 49: 10f is a combined
text with three components, viz, Num 24: 17/Is 11:1/51:5 (*1.Apol.* 32: 12, cf.
the textual analysis above, pp. 50 - 52). The text is composed so as to run
strikingly parallel to Gen 49:10:

| Gen  49:10 | Num  24:17 etc. |
|---|---|
| The coming Messiah | The rising Star from Jacob |
| of Judah | and the flower from Jesse, |
| αὐτὸς ἔσται προσδοκία | ἐπὶ τὸν βραχίονα αὐτοῦ |
| ἐθνῶν | ἔθνη ἐλπιοῦσιν |

Justin himself is aware of the similarity of the two texts : καὶ 'Ησαίας δὲ,
ἄλλος προφήτης, τὰ αὐτὰ δι' ἄλλων ῥήσεων προφητεύων οὕτως
εἶπεν . . .

(*1.Apol.* 32:12). A short fulfilment report - presupposing the combination of Num 24: 17 with Is 11:1 — follows in *1.Apol.* 32:13f.

This suggests that the text was composed as a counterpart to Gen 49: 10, and that Justin has his two OT quotations in *1.Apol.* 32 from the same source.

Turning to *Dial.* 121, we come across a second testimony, Ps 72: 17, which seems textually modified so as to match Gen 49: 10 and Num 24: 17 etc. (cf. textual analysis and synopsis above, p. 85) :

| *1.Apol.* 32:12 | *Dial.* 121:1 | Ps 72:17LXX |
|---|---|---|
| | τὸ ὄνομα αὐτοῦ... | ... πρὸ τοῦ ἡλίου |
| ἀνατελεῖ ἄστρον | ὑπὲρ τὸν ἥλιον *ἀνατελεῖ* | διαμενεῖ |
| ἐξ 'Ιακώβ... | | τὸ ὄνομα αὐτοῦ... |
| καὶ ἐπὶ | καὶ ἐνευλογηθήσονται | |
| τὸν βραχίονα αὐτοῦ | ἐν αὐτῷ | |
| ἔθνη ἐλπιοῦσιν | πάντα τὰ ἔθνη | |

As one can see, the decisive catchword ἀνατελεῖ in *Dial.* 121:1 is only present in Justin's deviant version of Ps 72:17, not in the LXX. This is hardly accidental. Further, in *Dial.* 121:2 is added Zech 6:12: καὶ πάλιν Ἀνατολὴ ὄνομα αὐτοῦ. To this is further added an allusion to Zech 12:10-12. None of these texts, or the extensive comment attached to Ps 72:17 in *Dial.* 121:2, are called for by the theme treated in *Dial.* 120f (which is the line of election within Israel). I take this as an indication that a source with another orientation is being used, and notices that in *Dial.* 120: 3 Gen 49: 10 is quoted - with comment on the difference of reading between the «Jewish» (really LXX) text and Justin's «testimony» text in *Dial.* 120 : 4f. This comment — and the whole treatment of the textual question — is not called for by the present context in *Dial.* 120f, and does indeed indicate that Justin in *Dial.* 120f is using a source with a different purpose compared with Justin's own. Nothing goes against the assumption that it was the same source as the one used in *1.Apol.* 32. The fact that no other OT quotation intervenes between Gen 49: 10 («testimony» version, *Dial.* 120: 4) and Ps 72: 17 («testimony» version, *Dial.* 121:1) , points in the same direction.

I thus take as a preliminary conclusion that Gen 49: 10f; Num 24 : 17 etc.; Ps 72 : 17; and Zech 6: 12 belonged together in a testimony source which is being used in *1.Apol.* 32; *Dial.* 52-54; and *Dial.* 120f. This source seems to have been patterned on an ABC- scheme : (A) Prophecy - (B) Exposition -(C) Fulfilment report.

(b) The birth of the Messiah; Is 7:14: *1.Apol.* 33 and *Dial.* 84.

*1. Apol.* 33 contains an elaborate explanation of Is 7: 14. Again it is possible to trace vestiges of the scheme present in *1.Apol.* 32 :[6]

*Prophecy:* τὸ οὖν 'Ιδοὺ ἡ παρθένος ... *Exposition:* σημαίνει οὐ συνουσιασθεῖσαν τὴν παρθένον συλλαβεῖν ... *Fulfilment report:* καὶ ὁ ἀποσταλεὶς δὲ πρὸς αὐτὴν τὴν παρθένον ... ἄγγελος θεοῦ

| | |
|---|---|
| εὐηγγελίσατο αὐτὴν εἰπών ἰδοὺ συλλήψῃ ἐν γαστρὶ ⌉ cf.<br>ἐκ πνεύματος ἁγίου ⌏ Lk 1:31<br>καὶ τέξῃ υἱόν ⌋<br>καὶ υἱὸς ὑψίστου κληθήσεται<br>καὶ καλέσεις τὸ ὄνομα αὐτοῦ 'Ιησοῦν<br>αὐτὸς γὰρ σώσει τὸν λαὸν αὐτοῦ ἀπὸ τῶν ἁμαρτιῶν αὐτῶν. | *Protevangelium Iakobi* 11:3:<br>«... a power of the Lord shall overshadow you; wherefore also that holy thing which is born of you<br>*shall be called the Son of the Highest.* ⌉ = Lk<br>*And you shall call this name*⌉ 1:32<br>*Jesus;*<br>*for he shall save his people* ⌏ = Mt 1:24<br>*from their sins.* ⌋ |

One notices that the fulfilment report is stylized so as to match the prophecy perfectly. That Justin did not entirely formulate it *ad hoc* is demonstrated by the close parallel in the *Protevangelium Iakobi*, where much the same combination of Matthean and Lukan elements occurs. Probably all three elements (Prophecy - Exposition - Fulfilment report) were present in Justin's source. And - as pointed out by Koester[7] - it seems the same source is employed once more in *Dial.* 84:

| *1. Apol.* 33:4 | *Dial.* 84:3 |
|---|---|
| | ὑμεῖς δὲ ... παραγράφειν τὰς ἐξηγήσεις ...<br>τολμᾶτε, λέγοντες μὴ ἔχειν τὴν γραφὴν<br>ὡς ἐκεῖνοι ἐξηγήσαντο, ἀλλ' |
| τὸ οὖν ἰδοὺ ἡ παρθένος<br>ἐν γαστρὶ ἕξει | ἰδού, φησίν, ἡ νεᾶνις<br>ἐν γαστρὶ ἕξει,<br>ὡς μεγάλων πραγμάτων |
| σημαίνει<br>οὐ συνουσιασθεῖσαν<br>τὴν παρθένον<br>συλλαβεῖν | σημαινομένων<br>εἰ γυνὴ ἀπὸ συνουσίας<br>τίκτειν ἔμελλεν. |

This parallel makes it easier to recognize the material Justin has added to his source in *1.Apol.* 33f: a consideration on the necessity of foreannouncement in 33:2f; and a comment on the identity of the Logos with the Spirit overshadowing Mary in 33:6.9; further a comment on the meaning of the name Jesus in 33:7f. In *1.Apol.* 34 Justin has added the Micah prophecy from Mt 2:6. I suspect this is Justin's own addition to a preexisting scheme, because the text seems copied directly from Mt 2:6 (see above, synoptic study 12).

---

6. Cf. Koester, *op. cit.,* pp. 67 f.
7. *Op. cit.,* pp. 39-42.

(c) The hiddenness of the Messiah; Is 9:5a: *1.Apol* 35:1f.[8]

For Justin, the proof for the fact that Jesus should be hidden until he grew to manhood is found in the immediate transition from παιδίον to νεανίσκος (NB: LXX: υἱός) in Justin's non-LXX version of Is 9:5a.[9] Once again we observe the close interrelation between non-LXX text and exegesis.

Strictly speaking, the fulfilment report is lacking here, but is given implicitly in the introduction to the quotation: ὅπερ καὶ γέγονεν ... After the quotation Justin feels compelled to explain an expression in Is 9:5a which somehow sidetracks his argument: οὗ ἡ ἀρχὴ ἐπὶ τῶν ὤμων. (The exposition is introduced with the usual formula: μηνυτικὸν (ην)). This is a prediction of the cross, Justin explains, and immediately he adds Is 65:2/58:2 and Ps 22:17/19. According to the disposition in *1:Apol* 31:7 Justin is here running ahead of his scheme, because he has not yet treated the healings of Jesus.[10] Maybe he is also running a little ahead of his source, because there is evidence in the *Dialogue* which indicates that the theme of the hiddenness of the Messiah had as its necessary counterpart the idea that the Messiah is revealed as such by *being anointed by Elijah, Dial.* 8:4; 49:1. But an extensive analysis of this theme at the present stage would take us too far into the *Dialogue,* and I presently just indicate that in Justin's source the idea of Jesus' anointing as Messiah - that is, his baptism at the hand of John (=«Elijah») — may have been complementary to the Is 9:5 testimony in *1.Apol* 35:lf. (Cf. the analysis below, pp.195 - 198).

(d) The passion of the Messiah; Is 65:2/58:2; Ps 22:17/19 etc.: *1.Apol* 35; 38; and *Dial* 97.

In *1.Apol* 35:3-9 we find another example of the familiar pattern from *1.Apol* 32: (A) Non-LXX prophecy, (B) exposition, and (C) fulfilment report. In my analysis of the non-LXX texts above (pp. 80 - 82), I pointed out *1.Apol* 38 and *Dial* 97 as close parallels, in which the same source is used. In addition to the synopses given on pp. 66;81, I add here a brief synoptic juxtapposition of non-LXX texts and fulfilment reports in *1.Apol* 35:

---

8. Cf. esp. Prigent, *Justin,* pp. 279-285.
9. This is Bousset's interpretation of the meaning of Justin's quotation (*Schulbetrieb,* p. 300, n. 2) - very likely correct.
10. Is this an indication that the healings originally were not included in the source Justin is following in *1.Apol* 35? On this suggestion, see further below, pp. 148-50

| Prophecy | Fulfilment report |
|---|---|
| ἐξεπέτασα τὰς χεῖράς μου... | ᾿Ιησοῦς δὲ Χριστὸς ἐξετάθη τὰς χεῖρας |
| αἰτοῦσί με νῦν κρίσιν... | αὐτὸν ἐκάθισαν ἐπὶ βήματος καὶ εἶπον κρῖνον ἡμῖν. (Cf. *Gospel of Peter* 7: ... καὶ ἐκάθισαν αὐτὸν ἐπὶ καθέδραν κρίσεως λέγοντες δικαίως κρῖνε βασιλεῦ τοῦ ᾿Ισραήλ.) |
| ὤρυξάν μου χεῖρας καὶ πόδας | ἐξήγησις τῶν ἐν τῷ σταυρῷ παγέντων ἐν ταῖς χερσὶ καὶ τοῖς ποσὶν αὐτοῦ ἥλων ἦν. (Cf. *Gospel of Peter* 21: καὶ τότε ἀπέσπασαν τοὺς ἥλους ἀπὸ τῶν χειρῶν τοῦ κυρίου ...) |
| ἔβαλον κλῆρον ἐπὶ τὸν ἱματισμόν μου... | μετὰ τὸ σταυρῶσαι αὐτὸν ἔβαλον κλῆρον ἐπὶ τὸν ἱματισμὸν αὐτοῦ, καὶ ἐμερίσαντο ἑαυτοῖς οἱ σταυρώσαντες αὐτόν. |

The parallels to two of the fulfilment reports in the *Gospel of Peter* point to some kind of common tradition;[11] Justin is not creating freely. Koester is probably right when he argues that the fulfilment reports were included in the source from which Justin has taken the non-LXX OT quotations.[12]

To conclude: In *1.Apol.* 32-35 Justin has been following his «testimony source» quite closely, only delaying the Zech 9:9 quotation. According to the disposition in *1.Apol.* 31:7, he has also deferred the healing testimony (*1.Apol.* 48:1-3). But was this text contained in the source behind *1.Apol.* 32-35? Let us note that in his other summaries of the Jesus story Justin does not include the healings of Jesus (*1.Apol.* 21:1; 42:4; 46:5; *Dial.* 63:1; 85:2; 126:1; 132:1).This may indicate that the answer to the above question is no, and in that case Justin is more faithful to his source in *1.Apol.* 35 than his disposition in *1.Apol.* 31:7 will make us believe. We shall have to test this assumption in the next section, pp. 48 - 50.

Before we turn to the healing testimony, however, we shall have to consider briefly the reason for the great insertion which breaks off the Jesus story, *1.Apol.* 36ff. Justin himself motivates this from hermeneutical reasons: It is necessary to say some words on the modes of speech used in the prophecies. But why precisely at the present stage in the exposition? Justin has told his readers (*1.Apol.* 31:7) that the prophets foretold everything

---

11. Cf. the detailed analysis in Prigent, *Justin*, pp. 281f.
12. Koester, *Schriftbeweis*, pp. 94f. Cf. also Prigent, *Justin*: «On peut assurément parler ici de *Testimonia*, mais je ne pense pas que le mot ni la realité qu'il recouvre rendent parfaitement compte des caractères du document supposé. En effet il ne peut s'agir d'une list des citations nues.» (pp. 282f).

about Jesus. He would naturally expect his readers to think that a prophecy is a saying in which the prophet speaks *about* the Messiah, - and in *future* tense. Gen 49:10f; Is 7:14; Mic 5:1 - they all do that. The problems start with Is 9:5. Here there is no prophet speaking, but an unspecified «we», and they speak in *aorist,* they do not prophesy! Is 65:2; Ps 22:17/19, the same: spoken in *aorist* - and who is the speaker?

Exactly these two questions are treated in the insertion *1.Apol.* 36ff: Who speaks, and what tenses are used in prophecy? The insertion is thus not out of place, but the modern reader will certainly feel it is far too extensive. The really interesting question concerning this hermeneutical excursus is of course which material Justin uses to exemplify his hermeneutical teachings. To this we shall return in due course.

(e) The healings of the Messiah; Is 35:5f: *1.Apol.* 48:1-3.

We first notice that this passage seems a little out of context. In the preceeding passage, ch. 47, Justin has been treating the devastation of Judaea. He then abruptly introduces the new theme: «How it was prophesied that our Christ would heal all diseases and raise the dead, hear what was spoken . . .» After text and comment, he immediately goes on to speak of the persecution of Christ and Christians. As we shall see below, this belongs together with the theme in ch. 47. And in *1.Apol.* 49:1 we find a remark which shows that Justin has not yet finished his hermeneutical excursus: «These words are spoken as in the character of the Christ himself . . .» It thus seems that *1.Apol.* 48:1-3 is an insertion into a pre-existing framework. We must therefore seek the context to which the healing testimony originally belonged. This is no doubt found in two or three passages in the *Apology* and the *Dialogue* concerned with the demonic imitation of the Gospel story found in Greek mythology. The Greek poets have, so to speak, framed pseudo-creeds.[13]

«They say that Dionysius

was born son of Zeus by his intercourse with Semele . . .

and, after being torn in pieces

and having died,

rose again

and has ascended into heaven.» *(Dial.* 69:2).

«They say that Hercules

was strong (ἰσχυρόν) and travelled round the whole earth,

---

13. Already M. von Engelhardt observed this: «. . . *man gewinnt den Eindruck, als habe Justin nicht von sich aus diese Auswahl getroffen. Es scheint, als habe man die einzelnen Sätze des Symbolums regelmässig zu gewissen Stücken der griechischen Mythologie in Beziehung gesetzt.»* (*Christenthum,* p. 290, n. ***).

and that he was born to Zeus of Alcmena,
and died,
and has ascended into heaven . . .» *(Dial.* 69:3).

To better bring out the parallels, we tabulate two of the relevant passages (allusions in parenthesis):[14]

| *1. Apol.* 54 | *Dial.* 69f | |
| --- | --- | --- |
| Gen 49:10f<br><br>(Is 53)<br>(Ps 24:7) | Gen 49:10f<br>(Is 7:14)<br>(Is 53)<br>(Ps 24:7) | Dionysius |
| Gen 49:10f<br>Ps 24:7 | | Bellerophon |
| Is 7:14 | | Perseus |
| Ps 19:6 | Ps 19:6<br>(Is 7:14)<br>(Is 53)<br>(Ps 24:7) | Hercules |
| Is 35:5 etc.<br>(testimony version) | (Is 35:5f etc.<br>test. version)<br>Is 35:1—7 LXX | Asclepius |
| | Dan 2:34<br>Is 33:16 | Mithra |
| | Is 7:14 | Perseus |

Cf.also two passages in *1.Apol.* 21f:

«In saying that the Word, who is the first offspring of God, was born for us without sexual union, as Jesus Christ our Teacher, and that he was crucified and died and after rising again ascended into heaven, we introduce nothing new beyond (what you say of) those whom you call sons of Zeus. You know how many sons of Zeus the writers whom you honor speak of - Hermes, the hermeneutic Word and teacher of all; Asclepius, who was also a healer and after being struck by lightning ascended into heaven - as did Dionysius who was torn in pieces; Heracles, . . . and Bellerophon who, though of human origin, rode on the divine horse Pegasus» (*1.Apol.* 21:1f).

«When we say, as before, that he was begotten by God as the Word of God in a unique manner beyond ordinary birth, this should be no strange thing for you who speak of Hermes as announcing word from God. If someone objects that he was crucified, this is in common with the sons of Zeus, as

---

14. Prigent, *Justin,* pp. 160-171, in a detailed analysis of these passages, argues that *Dial.* 69f is not directly dependent upon *1.Apol.* 54, but on a common source (cf. also Bousset, *Schulbetrieb,* p. 288). I find his argument on this point persuasive.

you call them, who suffered . . . If we declare that he was born of a virgin, you should consider this something in common with Perseus. When we say that he healed the lame, the paralytic, and those born blind, and raised the dead, we seem to be talking about things like those said to have been done by Asclepius» (*1.Apol.* 22:2-6).

The most relevant point to note in our context is the occurrence of the two testimonies Is 35:5f and Ps 19:6. We have studied both texts above (pp. 58;82). They are adapted to fit exactly the function they have in this context: The myth about Hercules imitates a prophecy about Christ: ἰσχυρὸς ὡς γίγας . . . (Ps 19:6 with addition of non-LXX word ἰσχυρὸς), cf. *1.Apol.* 54:9: τὸν Ἡρακλέα *ἰσχυρὸν* καὶ ἐκπερινοστήσαντα τὴν πᾶσαν γῆν ἔφασαν; *Dial.* 69:3: τὸν Ἡρακλέα *ἰσχυρὸν* καὶ περινοστήσαντα πᾶσαν τὴν γῆν . . . The crucial cathword is a word only found in Justin's deviant text.

Is 35:5f etc. has also been modified to fit this function: Christ should heal the sick *and raise the dead* - this was imitated in the Asclepius myth.

Ps 19:6 is only quoted in *1.Apol.* 54 and *Dial.* 69 (there is a casual allusion in *Dial.* 76:7 based on the use made of Ps 19 in *Dial.* 30 (see below, pp. 174 -177) and *Dial.*64:8); the contaminated version of Is 35:5f is only alluded to in *1.Apol.* 22:6; 54:10; *Dial.* 69:3 - i.e. in the passages where I have posited use of the hypothetical source.

For the sake of convenience I shall label this source «the tract on Greek mythology»,[15] implying no prejudice with regard to Prigent's theory that this tract was part of the *Syntagma,* or Nautin's proposal that it was part of Quadratus' *Apology.*[16]

This tract must have had a somewhat other orientation than the source employed by Justin in *1.Apol.* 32-35. It was not concerned with a prophecy -fulfilment scheme, but with correspondences between OT texts and Greek mythology. It exhibits a tendency to group the material along a «creed» sequence not unlike the one in *1:Apol.* 32-35/50f, but with partly different testimonies.[17] I suggest that *1.Apol.* 48:1-3 is an insertion from this source.

---

15. Following Bousset, *Schulbetrieb,* p. 288.

16. Prigent, *Justin,* pp. 158-171 (but cf. his wise reservation: «*On comprendra que personnelle-ment je suis tenté de l'identifier avec le Syntagma. Toutefois je reconnaîs volontiers ne pas en avoir administré la preuve et me déclare satisfait si l'on m'accorde l'existence d'une source utilisée par Justin dans les passages en question.*» (p. 171)); P. Nautin, 'Genese 1,1-2, de Justin à Origène', *In Principio. Interprétations des premiers versets de la Genèse* (Études Augustiniennes, Paris, 1973, pp. 61-94), p. 67. The only preserved fragment of Quadratus' *Apology* (*apud* Eus. *E. H.* IV:3:2) concerns those who were *healed* or *raised from the dead* by Christ. This would agree with Justin's modified version of Is 35:5f/Mt 11:5 in *1.Apol.* 48. Nautin's proposal is attractive, but the evidence is scanty indeed, and hardly allows for even probable surmises.

17. One could object that Gen 49:10f, as quoted in *1.Apol.* 54:5, is identical with the text of *1.Apol.* 32:1. However, looking at the context in *1.Apol.* 54, one observes that only vs. 11 is envisaged, likewise in *Dial.* 69. The text, in other words, is not so perfectly adapted to the present context as it is in *1.Apol.* 32. I therefore suspect that the quotation in *1.Apol.* 54 is copied from *1.Apol.* 32.

(f) The passion of the Messiah; Is 53: *1.Apol.* 50:1 - 51:6.

Isaiah 53 is the first text within the «creed» sequence which Justin quotes extensively from the LXX. This serves to underscore the importance accorded to this testimony by Justin. At the same time it makes an assessment of his source in this instance especially difficult. If a source is at play - and the presence of the non-LXX version of Is 53:12 clearly indicates this - it seems for the most part to be «buried» beneath the long LXX excerpt. It deserves notice, however, that in *Barn.* 5:2 Is 53:5/7 is an important testimony on Christ's suffering, and that Justin has frequent allusions to precisely these verses when speaking about the suffering of Christ (Cf. synoptic study 23 above, with references). For Justin, Is 53:7 is a testimony on Christ the paschal lamb, and *Dial.* 13; 40:1-3; 72, and 111:3f are especially important passages in the *Dialogue*. I shall have to pursue this theme more fully in my analysis of the *Dialogue* below (pp. 168f). At this stage it is sufficient to point out that the frequent parallelism between Barnabas and Justin in their Christological testimonies makes one inclined to believe that Is 53:5 and 53:7 may lurk in the background as traditional testimony nucleuses behind the long LXX excerpt.

(g) Ascension of the Messiah; Ps 24:7f : *1.Apol.* 51: 6f and parallels.

In *1.Apol.* 51:6-9 one gets the impression that Justin is in a hurry to bring his Christological proof to an end. The exposition of the ascension testimony, Ps 24:7f (on the text, cf. above, p. 81), is therefore very summary and betrays little of the common ABC-pattern discerned in the previous paragraphs. It may be recognized, however, in the treatment of Ps 24:7f in *Dial.* 36:

*Exposition*: . . . they who were appointed by God rulers in the heavens are bid open the gates of heavens, that this very One who is King of glory may enter in, and may go up and sit on the right hand of the Father, until He has set His enemies as His footstool, as has been made plain by the other Psalm (110:1).

*Fulfilment report*: For when the rulers in heaven saw Him with his form without form, and without honour and glory (Is 53:2), they did not recognize Him, and were enquiring: Who is this King of Glory . . . (*Dial.* 36:5f).

One notices that in *Dial.* 36:3-4 Justin quotes the full LXX text of Ps 24. But his Exposition and Fulfilment report concern only Ps 24:7f, and presuppose the non-LXX testimony text quoted in *1.Apol.* 51:7. This makes one inclined to believe that the treatment of Ps 24 in *Dial.* 36:5f derives from the same source as the quotation in *1.Apol.* 51:7.

One should also notice the presence of allusions to Is 53 and Ps 110:1 in *Dial.* 36. In the *Apology's* sequence, Is 53 is the testimony quoted prior to Ps 24:7f, and one may find indications in the *Apology* and elsewhere in the *Dialogue* that Ps 110:1 did follow Ps 24:7f in Justin's source:(1)If we look

closer at the two introductions to Is 52:13 - 53:8a and Is 53:8b-12 in *1.Apol.*
50:1 and 51:1 respectively, we find that they not only announce the texts
from Is 53, but also Dan 7:13 and Ps 110:1f: «How, being made man for us,
he endured suffering and dishonor (Is 53), and will come again with glory
(Dan 7:13)[18] — hear the prophecies..» ( *1.Apol.* 50:1). «In order to testify to
us that he who suffered these things is of ineffable origin and *reigns over his
enemies,* the prophetic Spirit spoke thus..»( *1.Apol.* 51:1). The nearest reference of the italicized words is certainly Is 53:12, but the formulation
βασιλεύει τῶν ἐχθρῶν also echoes Ps 110:2: κατακυρίευε ἐν μέσῳ τῶν
ἐχθρῶν σου. (2) Returning to the *Dialogue,* we make the following observations: (a) *Dial.* 31-36 contains the sequence Dan 7; Ps 110; Ps 72; Ps 24,
i.e. the sequence postulated behind *1.Apol.* 51:6-9, but in reversed order
with Ps 72 added. (b) We have noticed already that in *Dial.* 36:5 Ps24:7f is
connected explicity with Ps 110:1. (c) Exactly the same combination, but
this time in the form of formal quotations, is found in *Dial.* 127:5. (d) The
exposition of Is 7:14 in *Dial.* 84 is surrounded by an exposition of Ps 110:1-4
in *Dial.* 83 and Ps 24:7f in *Dial.* 85:1-6. (e) When we finally consider the
close connection between Dan 7:13 and Ps 110:1 in the NT (Mt 26:64 par.),
it seems a reasonable surmise that Ps 110:1 belonged to the sequence of
texts which Justin is following in *1.Apol.* 50f. Then why did he not quote it?
The answer may be simple: He had quoted it already in *1.Apol.* 45:1-4. The
introductory comment in 45:1 echoes the sequence Ps 24:7f/Ps 110:1:
«Now hear how it was said through David the prophet, that God the Father
of all would take up Christ into heaven after rising him from the dead, and
then wait to smite his enemies . . .»

I conclude that Ps 110:1 (or 110:1f) probably belonged to the sequence
of texts in Justin's source behind *1.Apol.* 32-35/50f.

(h) The return of the Messiah; Dan 7:13: *1.Apol.* 51:8f.

Justin's treatment of this text is as summary as in the preceeding case. But
here we should clearly not look for the familiar pattern of Exposition and
Fulfilment report, for here Justin's «creed» sequence has passed into that
part of Christ's career which is still future. Justin comments on this in *1.Apol.*
52:1-3, introducing the theme of the two parousias. We shall return to this in
a moment.

Let me here just remark that the source behind *1.Apol.* 51:8f seems to be
employed once more in *Dial.* 31. Here Justin has allusions and comments
to Dan 7:13 which presuppose the non-LXX text quoted in the *Apology,* not
the καιγε text quoted in the *Dialogue* (cf. above, pp. 88-90).

---

18. We have here *en miniature* the scheme of the two parousias, treated separately below. I
therefore believe one is entitled to hear a refere

(i) The resurrection and the judgement; Ezek 37:7f/Is 45:23; Is 66:24: *1.Apol.* 52: 3-9 and parallels.

After some remarks about the relationship between prophecies already fulfilled and prophecies yet to be fulfilled *(1.Apol.* 52:1f), and a brief introduction of the idea of the two parousias in *1.Apol.* 52:3 (cf. below, pp. 154 - 156), Justin adds two testimonies on the resurrection of the dead (Ezek 37:7f/Is 45:23) and the judgement (Is 66:24). It seems that in the «creed» sequence Justin is here following, the idea of Christ's coming as the triumphant Son of Man (Dan 7:13) is closely associated with the idea that he is coming to *judge* the living *and the dead.* One should compare the relevant phrase in the Old Roman creed, and similar phrases in the creed-like summaries of the kerygma in earlier writers, especially 2 Tim 4:1 in which the ideas of epiphany and kingdom (Dan 7:13f), and of judging the living and the dead, are immediately joined, cf. also Acts 10:42; 1 Pet 4:5; Polycarp *ad Phil.* 2:1 (in a creed-like sequence).

I have surmised above (pp. 67 - 69) that the source at play in *1.Apol.* 52:3-9 also underlies *Dial.* 44f and *Dial.* 140:3f. The parallels in the *Dialogue* suggest that the quotation of Is 1:9 in *1.Apol.* 53:7 may derive from the same source which is used in *1.Apol.* 52:3-9 (cf. synopsis of texts p. 68):

| *Dial.* 44f | *Dial.* 140:3 | *1.Apol.* 52f |
|---|---|---|
| | Is 1:9 non-LXX | Ezek 37:7f etc. non-LXX |
| Ezek 14:20/18 non-LXX | Ezek 14:20/18/Deut 24:16/ Ezek 14:14 non-LXX | |
| Is 66:23f LXX | Is 66:24 non-LXX | Is 66:24 non-LXX |
| Allusion: Ezek 14/20/18/ | | - - |
| Deut 24:16/Ezek 14:14 | | Is 1:9 non-LXX |

Let us take a closer look at another parallel to this sequence, viz. *2. Clem.* 6f. In these chapters, the author of *2. Clem.* is concerned with baptismal parainesis centered around the following idea: If we do not keep *the seal of baptism* undefiled, we shall not be saved *in the resurrection.* As Scriptural testimonies, Ezek 14:20/18 (strongly non-LXX) and Is 66:24 are quoted. In the Ezek quotation, the idea of resurrection is interpolated into the Scriptural quotation itself (the underlined words correspond to nothing in the LXX): ἐὰν <u>ἀναστῆ</u> Νῶε καὶ Ἰὼβ καὶ Δανιήλ, οὐ ῥύσονται τὰ τέκνα αὐτῶν <u>ἐν τῆ αἰχμαλωσία</u>. This accords admirably with the emphasis on resurrection in Justin's passages. In the discussion of Ezek 14:14etc. in *Dial.* 44f, a phrase recurs twice apropos that text: Will they (i.e. the Jews believing in Christ) be saved *in the resurrection of the dead?* (ἐν τῆ τῶν νεκρῶν ἀναστάσει), *Dial.* 45:2; 45:4. Nothing in Ezek 14 or Justin's argument in *Dial.* 44f would require this emphasis on the idea of resurrection. We notice as a further parallel between our two writers that the idea of *baptism* is present in Justin also:

| 2.Clem. 6:8f | Dial. 44:2-4 |
|---|---|
| Ezek 14:20/18 | Ezek 14:20/18 |
| | Is 66:23f |
| «But if even such righteous men . . . | «You must . . . take pains to recognize |
| with what confidence shall we enter | the way by which remission of your sins |
| into the royal palace of God, if we keep | shall come to you and the hope of the |
| not our baptism pure and undefiled?» | inheritance of the good things that have |
| 2.Clem. 7:6 | been announced . . . you should recognize |
| «For of those who have not kept the | this Christ, and, washing yourselves in |
| seal of baptism he says: | the laver . . . for the remission of sins, |
| Is 66:24.» | live without sin henceforth.» |

There is an unmistakable ring of baptismal catechesis in these passages, which is no surprise in a «creed» sequence of testimonies: The Messiah is coming to judge the living and the dead - so be baptized and live without sin henceforth in order to be saved!

I conclude that the resurrection testimonies in *1.Apol.* 52:3ff belong to the same source - or at least to the same tradition - as the one employed in the previous context. (For a suggestion that Justin may have employed the same material in his treatise *On the Resurrection*, cf. Appendix I, nr. 1 ).

(j) The recognition of the Messiah; Zech 12:10-12 etc.: *1.Apol.* 52:10-12

The components of the composite quotation contained in this passage have been analyzed above. The basic text no doubt is Zech 12:10-12. In a sense, one can recognize in this text the *telos* of the whole testimony sequence leading up to it.

The most obvious parallel in the *Dialogue* is *Dial.* 32:1-3. Following the treatment of Dan 7 in *Dial.* 31, Justin here adds extensive allusions to Is 53, Zech 12:10-12, Ps 24:7f, Ps 110:1 and the two parousias theme. A further parallel is found in *Dial.* 14:8. In the following paragraph, these passages are set within their proper context.

(k) The two parousias: *1.Apol.* 52:1-3

«The prophets foretold two comings of Christ - one, which has already happened, as that of a dishonored and passible man, and the second, when . . . he will come from heaven in glory with his angelic host . . .» *(1.Apol.* 52:3). This important theme seems to be intimately connected with the testimonies in *1.Apol.* 32-35/50-52. In the above statement, we recognize the allusions to Is 53:2 and Dan 7:13 (non-LXX version of *1.Apol.* 51:1). Reviewing other passages on the theme of the two comings in the *Dialogue,* we find a remarkably constant terminology, and a constant group of Biblical references:

| Dial. | First coming | Second coming |
|---|---|---|
| 14:8 | ἄτιμος<br>ἀειδὴς } (Is 53:2f)<br>θνητός | ἐν δόξῃ (Dan 7:14)<br>ἐπάνω τῶν νεφελῶν.. (Dan 7:13<br>καὶ ὄψεται... ⌉ test.)<br>εἰς ὃν ἐξεκέντησαν ⌋ (Zech 12:10) |
| 31:1 | τοῦ πάθους αὐτοῦ<br>οἰκονομίᾳ | τῇ ἐνδόξῳ... παρουσίᾳ,<br>ὡς υἱὸς γὰρ ἀνθρώπου ἐπάνω<br>νεφελῶν ἐλεύσεται...<br>ἀγγέλων σὺν αὐτῷ<br>ἀφικνουμένων (Dan 7:13 test.) |
| 32:2 | τὸ εἶδος αὐτοῦ } (Is 53:3)<br>ἄδοξον<br>(several all. to Is 53)<br>δύο παρουσίας...<br>μίαν μὲν ἐν ᾗ<br>ἐξεκεντήθη ὑφ᾽ ὑμῶν | <br><br><br><br>δευτέραν δὲ ὅτε }<br>ἐπιγνώσεσθε εἰς ὃν (Zech 12:<br>ἐξεκεντήσατε } 10—12) |
| 34:2 | παθητὸς γενόμενος<br>πρῶτον | καὶ πάλιν<br>παραγινόμενος<br>μετὰ δόξης καὶ (Dan 7:13f)<br>αἰώνιον τὴν βασιλείαν.. |
| 36:1 | παθητὸς Χριστὸς | ἔνδοξος.. ἐλευσόμενος<br>καὶ κριτὴς πάντων... (Dan 7:13f)<br>καὶ αἰώνιος βασιλεὺς |
| 49:2 | παθητός<br>καὶ ἄτιμος καὶ ἀειδὴς (Is 53:3) | ἔνδοξος καὶ<br>κριτὴς ἁπάντων ἐλεύσεται |
| 49:7 | ὁ Χριστὸς τῇ πρώῃ παρουσίᾳ<br>ἄδοξος ἐφάνη | |
| 52:1 | Ad Gen 49:8—12:<br>διὰ ᾽Ιακὼβ.. προεφητεύθη ὅτι<br>δύο τοῦ Χριστοῦ παρουσίαι<br>ἔσονται, καὶ ὅτι ἐν τῇ<br>πρώτῃ παθητὸς ἔσται | πάλιν παραγενησόμενον |
| 52:4 | Gen 49:10: καὶ αὐτὸς<br>ἔσται προσδοκία ἐθνῶν<br>συμβολικῶς δύο παρουσίας<br>αὐτοῦ ἐσήμανε | |
| 110:2 | παθητὸς<br>καὶ ἄδοξος καὶ ἄτιμος (Is 53:3)<br>καὶ σταυρούμενος | μετὰ δόξης<br>ἀπὸ τῶν οὐρανῶν παρέσται |
| 120:4 | | καὶ προσδοκᾶται πάλιν<br>παρέσεσθαι ἐπάνω τῶν νεφελῶν |
| 121:3 | ἐν τῇ<br>ἀτίμῳ καὶ ἀειδεῖ (Is 53:3)<br>καὶ ἐξουθενημένῃ<br>πρώτῃ παρουσίᾳ αὐτοῦ | ἐν τῇ ἐνδόξῳ αὐτοῦ<br>παρουσίᾳ |

There can be no doubt that we have to do with a stereotyped scheme attached to the «creed» sequence of testimonies. One notices different emphases, however, in the *Apology* and the *Dialogue*.

In the *Apology*, the idea is the following: Since the prophecies covering the first coming of Christ can be shown to have been fulfilled in great detail, we may safely conclude that those prophecies which predict His glorious second coming will also be fulfilled. The thrust of the argument is directed towards Gentile readers; the purpose of the argument is to convince them that Christ's return is imminent, and that all men must repent in order to be justified when Christ comes to judge the living and the dead. In the *Dialogue*. the emphasis is a different one. Here the two parousias scheme is used as a main answer to Jewish complaints about Jesus not fulfilling the triumphant messianism of the Old Testament. (Clearly seen e.g.in *Dial.* 31:1; 32:1f). It is, so to speak, a hermeneutical key to OT messianic prophecies, exemplified in the quotation sequence to which it seems closely related. Justin only once employs the two parousias scheme outside this context, viz. in his treatment of the two goats, *Dial.* 40:4. In this case none of the usual terminology or Scriptural references appear.

One final remark on the testimony sequence in *1.Apol.* 32-35/50-52: These texts not only prove point by point the prophetic prediction of the Jesus story. Some of them are made to cover several aspects of the history of Jesus, and the texts are often expounded with the help of others within the sequence. Gen 49:10f not only announces the coming of the Messiah - also his supernatural birth (αἷμα σταφυλῆς); his passion (washing his «robe» in his blood); even his second coming («he shall be the expectation of the Gentiles») is foretold in this single text. Is 53 not only announces the passion of the Messiah; it also tells of his supernatural birth (vs. 8b: who shall declare his origin?); his triumph after death (vs. 12); even his glorified return is predicted in Is 52:13-15. Is 53 is made the clue to Ps 24:7f: The reason why the heavenly princes did not recognize the King of Glory was that he came from his passion ἀειδῆ καὶ ἄτιμον τὸ εἶδος καὶ ἄδοξον, *Dial.* 36:6. Zech 12:10-12 comprises both parousias: The one in which Messiah the should be pierced, and the second in which he will be recognized by the Jews, *Dial.* 32:2.

In *Dial.* 76:1 Justin is even able to find a prophecy on the virgin birth in the ὡς of Dan 7:13: ὡς υἱὸς ἀνθρώπου.

I think these observations substantiate the assumption that in *1.Apol.* 32-35/50-52 we have a closely knit unit of testimonies which very likely are excerpted from a single source - a source containing OT prooftexts and short narratives («fulfilment reports») and very likely applying the herme-neutical scheme of the two parousias.

(1) Gentiles more believing than Jews: *1.Apol.* 53

Justin begins this chapter by stating that the Scriptural proof is now finished. He goes on to summarize some of the main contentions in the preceeding chapters. This confirms our impression that Justin in ch. 52 has followed his source to the end and now looks back on a fulfilled task.

In *1.Apol.* 53:5-12 he goes on, however, to add three testimonies (Is 54:1; Is 1:9; Jer 9:25) concerned with point 8 in the disposition in *1.Apol.* 31:7 (see above,139): Gentiles believing rather than Jews. We have seen already, from the parallel passages in *Dial.* 44f and *Dial.* 140, that Is 1:9 probably belonged to the same testimony cluster as Ezek 37:7f and Is 66:24. The evidence in *2.Clem.* even suggested that Is 54:1 *may* have been part of the same material. If so, Justin in *1.Apol.* 53:5-9 is adding more testimonies from the source which he employed in 52:3-9.

The final testimony in *1.Apol.* 53 is Jer 9:25. We have seen above that this text recurs in the section *Dial.* 15:7 -16:1, and that *Dial.* 16:2 - 17:2 is closely related to *1.Apol.* 49. I suggest that *1.Apol.* 53:10-12 is a delayed completion of the material used in *1.Apol.* 49.(See further below, pp. 160 - 162.)

## 2. *The great insertion. 1.Apol. 36-49*

As we have seen, Justin regards these chapters as a necessary hermeneutical excursus. The disposition is given in *1.Apol.* 36:1f: Examples will be given in which (A) the prophecy is a (formal) prediction; (B) the Father is speaking; (C) the Son; (D) the people responding to one of them. This classification contains two kinds of criteria which may cross each other: the tense of the prophetic saying (A), and the speaking subject (BCD). The disposition is carried out in the sequence BCADC: Utterances by the Father, *1.Apol.* 37; utterances by the Son, *1.Apol.* 38; future and past tense in the prophecies, *1.Apol.* 39-45 (with two excurses: *1.Apol.* 43f on the compatibility of divine foreknowledge and human freedom of choice; and *1.Apol.* 46 on the responsibility of those living before Christ); utterances by the people, *1.Apol.* 47; a prophecy in which the Son speaks, *1.Apol.* 49:1-4.

Even a superficial reading of these chapters of the *Apology* is sufficient to observe that many of the texts adduced are inappropriate as examples of the principles they are said to exemplify. A closer analysis confirms that the texts are not grouped together *ad hoc* but seem to derive from testimony clusters which are composed for other purposes. Especially from *1.Apol.* 40 onwards it is evident that the theme inherent in the material used breaks through Justin's announced purpose. I shall now turn to an analysis of the structures that can be discerned in the testimony material.

(a) Anti-cultic testimonies: *1.Apol.* 37

As examples of utterances by the Father, Justin quotes Is 1:3f;Is 66:1; Is 1:11-15/Is 58:6f. The two last quotations are markedly non-LXX (see above, pp.124 and 55f),and have a common theme: they are anti-cultic texts. It deserves to be noticed that strictly speaking none of them are prophecies (not even according to Justin's strictures in *1.Apol.* 36). The first text is LXX, and anti-Jewish rather than anti-cultic. A tempting piece of speculation is this: To find examples of prophecies spoken by the Father, Justin turned to the prophetic book with which he was most familiar: Isaiah. The very first saying here, Is 1:2-4, is spoken by God,[19] and Justin excerpted a part of this text - with which he happened to be familiar: *1.Apol.* 63:2.12. In Is 1:5-9 there is no «I» in the text, and in 1:9 apparently the prophet is speaking. The next passage in which the «I» of God reappears is Is 1:11ff. Coming to this text, Justin realized that it was contained in an anti-cultic source with which he was very familiar. He turned to this source and there also found the Is 66:1 quotation. Both texts were thus quoted from this source.

I offer this more as a suggestion of how *1.Apol.* 37 might have been composed than as a theory of what actually happened. In any case it seems clear that the last two texts are not grouped together at random. They derive from a testimony source with an easily recognized purpose.

(b) The passion and crucifixion of the Messiah: *1.Apol.* 38

We have seen already that *1.Apol.* 38 employs the source behind *1.Apol.* 35 once more (see above, pp. 80-82). What is of special relevance in this context is to observe that the last quotation, Ps 22:8f, is not an example fit for Justin's purpose (no «I» speaking), and that a fulfilment report has been taken over with the text - a report not called for from hermeneutical reasons. Thus *1.Apol.* 38 completes our picture of the source behind this chapter and ch. 35:
Is 65:2/Is 58:2 - fulfilment report
Ps 22:19/17/Ps 3:6 -fulfilment report
Ps 22:8f - fulfilment report
Whether Is 50:6-8a (= LXX) was also part of this source is hard to say with certainty. The parallel in *Barn.* 5:13 - 6:6 suggests a positive answer.

All the prophecies in *1.Apol.* 38 are in the past tense. Justin does not comment directly on this but goes on to devote the next chapters to the question of the tense used in prophecies.

(c) The law going out from Zion: *1.Apol.* 39-46[20]

If we leave out for the moment the two excurses (*1.Apol.* 43f and 46), the quotation sequence is this: Is 2:3f; Ps 19:3-6; Ps 1f; Ps 96/1 Chron 16; Ps

---

19. Justin probably took notice of the introduction to the oracle in Is 1:2: κύριος ἐλάλησεν.

110:1-3. Among these, Is 2:3f is a good example of prophecy in the future tense, cf. the introduction to this text: «When the prophetic Spirit speaks as prophesying things to come, he says: ... ( *1.Apol.* 39:1). But the two follo-wing texts are not suited as examples of this, and Justin is obviously aware of this: Ps 19 is introduced as an appendix to Is 2:3f, and Ps 1f as an appendix to Ps 19. Coming to Ps 96, this is followed by a rather vague remark: «Now when the prophetic Spirit speaks of things to come as if they had already happened, as is illustrated in that which has been quoted ...»( *1.Apol.* 42:1). The rest of *1.Apol.* 42 makes it plain that Ps 96 is in mind, especially the aorist ἐβασίλευσεν. But one can easily see that the Psalm as a whole is not a good example of prophecy in the past tense.

Ps 110:1-3 is introduced in a way which makes it look as if the hermeneu-tical discussion has now totally been lost sight of. The remarks following the text are also completely irrelevant as to the question of modes of prophecy.

All this combines to suggest that this series of texts was not created *ad hoc* by Justin, but existed prior to their present use and had another purpose. This original purpose is in fact easily recognizable, because Justin betrays it on several occasions: *Ad* Is 2:3f: «This has really happened: For a band of twelve men went forth from Jerusalem ... and by the power of God they testified to every race of mankind that they were sent by Christ to teach to all the word of God ...»( *1.Apol.* 39:2f). *Ad* Ps 19:3-6: «Hear now how predictions were made about those who were to proclaim his teaching and testify to his manifestation ...»( *1.Apol.* 40:1). *Ad* Ps 96: «But in our time Jesus Christ, who was crucified and died, rose again and, ascending into heaven, began to reign; and on account of what was proclaimed by the apostles in all nations as (coming) from him, there is joy for those who look forward to the incorruption which he promised» ( *1.Apol.* 42:4). *Ad* Ps 110:1-3: «The phrase, 'He will send forth the rod of power for you from Jerusalem', is a prediction of the mighty word which his apostles, going forth from Jerusa-lem, preached everywhere ...»( *1.Apol.* 45:5). In short, the idea embodied in these texts is *the apostolic mission,*[21] or, to put it differently: *The reign of the risen Christ through the apostolic kerygma.* The only text which does not seem immediately to fit this idea is Ps 1f. But behind this extraordinarily long excerpt one may reasonably suspect a submerged testimony in Ps 2:8f. In idea this text is close to Ps 110:2, and there is also a catchword connec-tion: ποιμανεῖς αὐτοὺς ἐν ῥάβδῳ σιδηρᾷ.[22]

Besides, Ps 1:3-6 functions as a testimony on baptism in *Barn* 11:6-11. Justin may have been familiar with the same application of the text, and

---

20. On this section, cf. Bousset, *Schulbetrieb,* pp. 300-302; Prigent, *Justin,* pp. 228-232. Bousset seems not to have recognized the basic thematic unity between the texts employed in *1.Apol.* 39ff. But cf. the instructive comments by von Ungern-Sternberg, pp. 11f.

21. So also von Ungern-Sternberg, *loc. cit.*

22. I suggest this more as a supplement than as an alternative to Prigent's hypothesis that the submerged testimony is to be sought in Ps 2:10ff, *Justin,* p. 230.

therefore included Ps 1 in his quotation. Baptism would not be a foreign element in a context treating the apostolic mission.

I shall comment further on this cluster of testimonies below in tracing its use in the *Dialogue*. Let me here just note that it is hardly by accident that Is 2:3f comes first in the series. This text - and its parallel in Mic 4 - is *the* testimony on the apostolic mission in Justin. The apostolic kerygma is the Law and Word of God going out from Zion/Jerusalem.

Let us now turn to the excursus in *1.Apol.* 43f. Justin here asserts that the phenomenon of prophetic foreknowledge in no way means that human choice and responsibility are annulled. On the contrary, «we have learned from the prophets . . . that penalties and punishments and good rewards are given according to the quality of each man's actions» ( *1.Apol.* 43:2). The corresponding testimonies are given in *1.Apol.* 44:1 (Deut 30:15/19) and 44:3f (Is 1:16-20). I shall suggest below (p. 369f) that these two testimonies derive from a source concerned with exhortations to accept baptism. That is, thematically these texts are quite close to the testimonies on the apostolic mission and may very well derive from the same source.

(d) The devastation of Judaea: *1.Apol.* 47-49

We have seen above that *1.Apol.* 48:1-3 very likely is an insertion into a connected sequence of texts and arguments.[23] This sequence can be summarized as follows: The Jews have been expelled from the destroyed Jerusalem (Is 64:9-11; Is 1:7/Jer 50:3 - *1.Apol.* 47) because they slew the Just One and persecute his followers (Is 57:1f - *1.Apol.* 48:4f); this strange behaviour of the Jews is also predicted in the prophecies (Is 65:1-3; Is 5:20 -*1.Apol.*49). I have argued above (pp. 30f) that *1.Apol.* 48:4 - 49:7 is parallel to *Dial.* 16:5 - 17:2 and *Dial.* 133:2-5. The parallelism between the first two passages extends beyond the common features pointed out above, however. Cf. the following table:

| *1.Apol.* 47-49 | *Dial.* 16f |
|---|---|
| Devastation of Judaea foretold: Is 64:9-11 | Devastation of Judaea a just punishment for the Jews |
| Jerusalem is laid waste: Is 1:7/Jer 50:3 | allusions to combined text |
| The Jews slew the Just one<br><br>ἅμα τοῖς ἐπ᾽ αὐτὸν ἐλπίζοθσιν | «For ye slew the Just One and his prophets before him καὶ νῦν τοὺς ἐλπίζοντας ἐπ᾽ αὐτὸν» |
| Is 57:1f | Is 57:1—4<br>Is 52:5 |
| Is 65:1—3<br>Is 5:20 | Is 3:9—11<br>Is 5:18—20 |

23. So also Prigent, *Justin*, p. 232.

In both passages the Hadrianic decree (after the Bar Kokhba uprising) is seen as a punishment for the killing of the Just One. The decree forbade Jews to appear within eyesight of Jerusalem. Justin makes us believe that in implementing the decree, the Romans made circumcision the identification mark excluding the Jews from Jerusalem. This may well be correct, and in that case the circumcision theme in *Dial*. 16 was probably integral to the source employed. In other words, *1.Apol*. 47-49 was not the source of *Dial*. 16f, but both passages are independent adaptions of a common source.

In *Dial*. 15:7 - 16.1 the theme of circumcision is introduced by three texts: Jer 4:4 (all.); Deut 10:16f; Lev 26:40f. As we have seen above, *Dial*. 28:2f has a largely parallel sequence: Jer 4:3f; Jer 9:24f. If we take it that these circumcision testimonies were part of the source employed in *Dial*. 16f, this corroborates our assumption above that the quotation of Jer 9:25 (non-LXX) in *1.Apol.* 53:11 is a delayed addition from the same source which underlies *1.Apol.* 47-49.

Did the quotation Is 65:1-3a - or part of it - also belong to this source? There are interesting parallels in two other passages in the *Dialogue*. First, in *Dial.* 119:3f: «After that Just One was slain (Is 57:1; Is 3:10) we sprouted up afresh as another people»; Zech 2:15; Is 62:12; *Is 65:1*. The same theme of the new people of Gentiles is present in *1. Apol.* 49: « . . . the peoples of the Gentiles who were not looking for him would worship him . . .» (49:1). I do not want to press this parallel, because in *Dial.* 119 the Is 65:1 quotation may well be inspired by Rom 10:20 (cf. above,synoptic study 7). The other parallel is perhaps more telling. In *Dial.* 24f we find the following elements: New law from Zion (Is 2:3); new people (Is 26:2f); free allusive composition with Is 2:3 as focal text; *Is 65:1-3*; Is 63:15 - 64:11 (Cf. *1.Apol.* 47:2f: Is 64:9-11. The longer excerpt in the *Dialogue* ends with the same words!) I take this as indicating that a common source is at play in *1.Apol.* 47-49 (53:10-12); *Dial.* 16f; *Dial.* 24f, and *Dial.* 119:3f, and - further - that this source may very well be the same as the one we recognised behind *1.Apol.* 39-46 (Is 2:3f being the main text). That this last assumption is not fortuite is shown by the fact that Justin in *1.Apol.* 49 once again alludes to the theme of the apostolic mission: ». . . men of the Gentiles, who had never even heard about Christ until his apostles who came forth from Jerusalem testified to the things about him and gave them the prophecies . . .« (*1.Apol.* 49:5).

Justin also joins *1.Apol.* 49 to the preceeding section, *1.Apol.* 39-46, by including Is 65:1-3 among the texts exemplifying the hermeneutical principles enumerated in *1.Apol.* 36:2: Is 65:1-3 is spoken ὡς ἀπὸ προσώπου αὐτοῦ τοῦ Χριστοῦ, *1.Apol.* 49:1.

We have so far established a reasonable probability for the hypothesis that the section chs. 39-49 (48:1-3 excluded) in the *Apology* forms a unity, the theme of which is (1) the apostolic mission out from Jerusalem (*1.Apol.* 39-46), and (2) the unbelief and punishment of the Jews (Hadrianic decree), the belief of the Gentiles (*1.Apol.* 47-49). It is obvious that these two themes correspond to elements 7 and 8 in the disposition in *1.Apol.* 31:7 (above, p. 139).

We thus arrive at the conclusion that within the great insertion *1.Apol.* 36-49, it is only the anti-cultic testimonies in ch. 37 which fall outside the material envisaged by Justin in *1.Apol.* 31:7. Thus, in the great insertion, Justin has accomplished two tasks: He has given an instruction in hermeneutics, and he has presented important Scriptural material on the suffering of the Messiah (*1.Apol.* 38); the apostolic mission (*1.Apol.* 39-46); the punishment of the Jews; and the Gentiles as a new people (*1.Apol.* 47-49), and the healings of the Messiah (*1.Apol.* 48,1-3).

One question remains: What is the relationship between *1.Apol.* 39-49 and the creed testimonies? In *1.Apol.* 31:7 they are treated as a unity. Does this reflect that the two blocks of material belonged together in Justin's testimony source? I am content here merely to state this question. We shall have to pursue the problem in our analysis of the *Dialogue* and return to it on a broader basis in our traditio-historical analysis in Part Three.

### 3. Remaining material: 1.Apol. 54-68

It is sufficient to our purpose to treat these chapters in a more summary manner. Most of the material has been treated already in Part One.

*1.Apol.* 54: Adaption of the tract on Greek mythology.

*1.Apol.* 55:5: Justin here has a curious quotation of Lam 4:20. In Irenaeus (*Dem.* 71; *Adv.Haer.*III:10:3) and Tertullian (*Adv.Marc.* III:6:7; V:11:12; *Adv.Prax.* 14:10), Lam 4:20 is used as a testimony for Spirit Christology: The Spirit of God's countenance is Christ. Justin has a different application: Man's nose is a type of the cross. The text of the testimony has been changed accordingly. Since this is the only occurrence in Justin, one can hardly say much about the provenance of this testimony.

*1.Apol.* 59f contains a little tract on Plato's borrowings from Moses. It has been analysed in some detail above, pp. 52f.

*1.Apol.* 61 repeats the baptismal testimony Is 1:16-20.

*1.Apol.* 62-64 contains an appendix on chs. 54-58 and 61: The demons not only imitated and distorted the prophecies concerning Christ, they even imitate Christian baptism, *1.Apol.* 62, and the sayings of Moses about creation (Gen 1:1), *1.Apol.* 64. Into this appendix has been inserted *1.Apol.* 63, an excursus on Jewish non-understanding of the Scriptures. The text used as example, Ex 3, has been treated in detail above, pp.47-50. The insertion is prepared in *1.Apol.* 62:2-4: The demons have not only imitated baptism (62:1), but even other cultic practises of the pagans betray that they are imitations of things said in the Scriptures, such as the taking off of shoes at the entrances of temples. This the demons took from Ex 3:5. This text is thus the connecting link between chs. 62 and 63. It is markedly non-LXX.

| *1. Apol.* | | *Dial.* 52—54 | *Dial.* 120f |
|---|---|---|---|
| | Gen 49:10f ◄─┐<br>Num 24:17/Is 11:1/51:5 ◄─ ─ ─ ─ ─ ─ ─ ─ ─ ─ ─ ► | Gen 49:8—12/Zech 9:9 | Gen 49:10<br>Ps 72:17<br>Zech 6:12 |
| | Is 7:14 │ | | |
| | Mic 5:1 from Mt 2:6 | | |
| 32—35: The<br>Jesus story | Is 9:5<br>Is 65:2/58:2 | *1. Apol.* 38<br>Is 65:2<br>Is 50:6—8 | *Dial.* 97<br>Ps 3:5f<br>Is 65:2 |
| | Ps 22:17/19 │<br>Zech 9:9 ◄─┘ | Ps 22:19/17/Ps 3:6 | Ps 22:17—19 |

| 37: Anti-cultic | Is 1:3f<br>Is 66:1<br>Is 1:11—15/Is 58:6f | | |

| | Is 2:3f<br>Ps 19:3—6 (Ps 19:5)<br>Ps 1f (Ps 2:8f?)<br>Ps 96/1 Chron 16 | | |
| 39—46: The New<br>Law = The<br>apostolic<br>kerygma | Deut 30:15/19 Exhortation to baptism<br>Is 1:16—20 | | |
| | Ps 110:1—3 (vs. 2) | | |

| | | *Dial.* 15—17/28 | *Dial.* 108/119 |
|---|---|---|---|
| | Is 64:9—11<br>Is 1:7/Jer 50:3 | Devastation of Judaea,<br>all. to Is 1:7/Jer 50:3 | Devastation,<br>all. to Is 1:7 |
| | Is 35:5f from the tract on Greek<br>mythology, cf. *1. Apol.* 54 and *Dial.* 69f | | |
| 47—49: The<br>slaying of the<br>Just and the<br>devastation of<br>Judaea | Is 57:1f<br>Is 65:1—3<br>Is 5:20 | Is 57:1—4 ...<br>Is 3:9—11<br>Is 5:18—20 | all. Is 57:2 ...<br>Is 65:1 |

| | Is 53<br>Ps 24:7f<br>(Ps 110:1)<br>Dan 7:13 | | |
| 50—52: The<br>Jesus story<br>continued | Ezek 37:7f/Is 45:23<br>Is 66:24 | On the resurrection of the dead and the<br>responsibility of the individual man,<br>cf. parallels in *Dial.* 44f and 140:3f | |
| | Zech 12:10—12 etc. | | |
| | Is 54:1   Is 1:9 | | |
| | Jer 9:25 | Jer 9:25f etc. | |

| 63: | The theophany in the thorn-bush     *Dial.* 56ff | | |

As testimonies on the non-understanding of the Jews, Justin adduces Is 1:3 and Mt 11:27 (quoted first in *1.Apol.* 63:2f, and then again in the doublet passage *1.Apol.* 63:11ff). We shall have to pursue the original intent of this at a later stage (cf. pp. 211ff).

The table on page 163 summarizes my analysis so far. In suggesting a connexion between the anti-cultic testimonies of *1.Apol.* 37 and the testimonies exhorting to baptism in *1.Apol.* 44, I anticipate a result of my subsequent analysis of parallel material in the *Dialgoue.*

## CHAPTER THREE

## THE DIALOGUE

### Introductory remarks: Dispositional elements and techniques in the *Dialogue*

Justin's *Dialogue* is a most ambitious work. Probably Justin regarded as deems the strength of his exposition precisely those features which a modern reader its weaknesses - the numerous excurses on all kinds of tangential themes. It seems Justin wanted to obtain a double effect with this excursus technique. First, he would impress the reader with his own ability to answer all possible questions and objections, however *malapropos* they might be. To make sure the reader did not miss this point, Justin once puts it in Trypho's mouth in plain words: «You seem to me to have passed through much controversy with many people about all the subjects under discussion, and therefore are ready to answer everything you are asked» (*Dial.* 50:1). Next, Justin wanted indirectly to characterize his Jewish interlocutor as «fond of strife and superficial» (φιλέριστος καὶ κενός), *Dial.* 64:2.[1] The reader's eventual irritation at the many digressions is to be blamed on Trypho. Justin, on the other hand, answers all questions with angelic patience: «Even though you act maliciously I will continue answering whatever argument you put forward and use in objection» *(ibid.)*. The reader may also feel the many repetitions tedious. But again - blame Trypho or his companions. Trypho sometimes retracts previously given consent and thus makes repetitions necessary, *Dial.* 67:7.11; 68:2.

Another device to justify repetitions is the two-day framework. On the second day some new listeners are present, who need repetitions of material presented on the first day. Two sections stand out: *Dial.* 92f on the law («. . . has already been shown by me in what I have said. But because of those who have come to-day I think it well to repeat it almost all again,» 92:5); *Dial.* 126-129 on the theophanies («. . . the succeeding statements from the books of Moses, . . . already explained by me, I again repeated», 126:5).

---

1. This is pointed out by Hoffmann, *Der Dialog*, p. 28: «*Die Einsichtslosigkeit der Juden macht literarisch das häufige Aufheben der Zugeständnisse Tryphons, die vielen törichten Fragen, die langatmigen Wiederholungen, kurz die ganze Uneinheilichkeit der Schrift notwendig. . . . Hieraus könnte geschlossen werden, dass die Unordnung und Planlosigkeit des Haupt-dialogs sowie seine dialogische Struktur nicht das Ergebnis einer literarischen Unfähigkeit Justins ist - dass er einen Dialog ja ganz anders schreiben kann, beweist er im Proömdialog (Dial. 1-8) -, sondern ein beabsichtigtes literarisches Ausdrucksmittel zur Charakterisierung der Juden.*» Essentially the same point of view was already expressed by Hubik, *op. cit.*, p. 32.

Even with these justifications, Justin seems to have had a feeling that he repeats some items so often that an apology is needed: «... even though I often repeat myself, I know I do not speak foolishly. For it is absurd to see the sun, and the moon, and the stars, ever taking the same course, and the same changes of hours; and also (to see) the mathematician, if asked how much twice two are, though he has often said four, not ceasing to say again that they are four, ... and then to find him who draws his discourses from the Scriptures of the prophets not citing always the same Scriptures, but considering that he himself can produce and say something better than Scripture» (*Dial.* 85:5).

No doubt Justin wanted his readers not only to follow his exposition, but also to remember the basic texts and arguments. Justin is very much *a teacher*, wanting his audience to learn by heart the main truths. And one can hardly deny that his procedure in the *Dialogue* in this respect is quite effective.

Turning to a more minute examination of Justin's dispositional procedure, one at once observes that several remarks, both by Justin and Trypho, are concerned with the progression of the debate and which themes should be discussed. These remarks deserve careful attention by anyone investigating the structure of the *Dialogue*.[2] I shall take as a working hypothesis that these remarks reflect Justin's conscious plan when writing the *Dialogue*, while text sequences which seem to betray other purposes, or which create unwarranted deviations in the disposition, may reflect use of sources with an inherent disposition (or purpose) different from Justin's.

Special attention must be paid to the sources we have meant to find behind the *Apology*. We have seen already examples of repeated use of the same sources in the *Dialogue*.

### 1. The new law and the new covenant: Dial. 11-47

Let us first take a look at the dispositional remarks within (or relevant to) this section.

In *Dial.* 8:3f Trypho states his objections to Christianity in the following way:
1) You have forsaken God and placed your hope on a man.
2) To be acceptable to God, you must keep his commandments: circumcision, sabbath etc.
3) «But Messiah, if indeed he has ever been and now exists anywhere, is unknown, and does not even know himself at all, nor has any power, until

---

2. This aspect is unduly neglected by Sagnard in his analysis, *art. cit.*, while Hubik on the other hand concentrates exclusively on these elements in the *Dialogue*, cf. esp. *op. cit.* pp. 9-11.

Elijah shall have come and anointed him, and shall have made him manifest to all . . .»

Point 3 here is answered by Justin in *Dial.* 48ff, and one can roughly say that points 1 and 2 are answered in *Dial.* 11-47.

In *Dial.* 10:3f Trypho specifies that the first matter to be discussed is Christian non-observance of the Law, especially the commandment of circumcision. «Have you not read: 'That soul shall be cut off from his people which shall not be circumcised on the eighth day'?»(*Dial.* 10:3).

Let us review the dispositional remarks within the section.

In *Dial.* 32:1 Trypho objects to Justin's quotation of Dan 7 about Christ:- But your Messiah was not glorious; he was crucified and died the death cursed by the Law (Deut 21:23). A preliminary answer is given in *Dial.* 32:2: Is 53 portrays the Messiah in his first coming as inglorious etc. But clearly Trypho's objection is a first pointer to the discussion on Deut 21:23 and the death on the cross in *Dial.* 89-96. We have here the first of many *anticipatory remarks.*

In *Dial.* 35:1 Trypho requests a digression on Christian heretics; the first clearly marked digression, and, as usual, caused by Trypho.

In *Dial.* 36:1 Justin begins to build up expectation of a proof that Jesus is the Messiah. Let us tabulate the remarks in chs. 36 - 48:1:

36:1 Trypho: Two parousias granted - «yet prove that this is he about whom all this was prophesied.» Justin: As you desire - in the suitable place.

39:7 Trypho: «Creed» pattern granted - «but prove to us that this Jesus is he.» Justin: In the suitable place. «But now I will pursue the connexion of the subjects on which I have begun to address you.»

42:4 Justin: Sufficient has been said about the law. «I pass on and address myself to the next subject»:

43:4 Justin: «I turn to speak about the mystery of his birth, for this now claims our attention.»(Is 7:10-17).

43:8 Justin: You say that Is 7:14 reads «young woman» and refers to Hezekiah; «I will try in this particular to make a short exposition of it against you.»

45:1f Trypho: I seem to interrupt the discussion, but let me ask: What about those who lived according to the law of Moses? Justin: Question granted, subject will be resumed later (46f: further questions in the same vein by Trypho).

48:1 Trypho: We have now heard your opinion on these subjects. Take up and finish your discourse where you left off. You assert that Christ pre-existed, was born man and suffered — now prove it.

*Dial.* 48ff

Trypho's request in *Dial.* 36:1 and 39:7 that it should be proved that Jesus is the Messiah, must mean that whatever is the function of *Dial.* 30-39, these chapters are not meant as parts of this proof.[3] According to Justin's dispositional remarks, they should be seen as part of the discussion *on the law*. The proof of Jesus' messiahship begins systematically in *Dial.* 48 (although anticipated in *Dial.* 43), and the first question treated - whether Jesus was anointed by Elijah - corresponds exactly to Trypho's objection against Jesus being the Messiah in *Dial.* 8:4. It is thus evident that we should visualize the transition from «law» theme to «Messiah» theme the following way:

| The new law | | | Jesus is the Messiah |
|---|---|---|---|
| *Dial.* 11:1 - 43:2 | 43:3-8 | 44-47 | 48ff |

After these preliminaries, let us turn to a detailed analysis of *Dial.* 11 - 43:2.

### (a) *Dial.* 11f

This passage forms a kind of prelude to the whole discussion, containing summary expression of ideas which are proved later. Three testimonies on the new law and covenant are quoted: Jer 31:31; Is 51:4f; Is 55:3-5. The three texts are perfectly adapted to their context, and one lacks only the main text on the new law, Is 2:3f. It comes later and very likely was part of this cluster of testimonies.[4]

### (b) *Dial.* 13-15

In *Dial.* 13:1 we meet a polemical juxtaposition of Jewish washing and Christian baptism. The Jewish lustrations are associated with «the blood-shedding of goats and sheep, or the ashes of an heifer and offerings of meal» - a mixture of Heb 9:13f and Is 1:13. Christian baptism, on the other hand, is associated with the blood of Christ; testimony: Is 52:10 -54:6.

The presence of an allusion to Is 1:13 first claims our attention. In *1.Apol.* 37:5-8 we met a deviant version of Is 1:11-15/Is 58:6f which contained polemics against New Moons, Sabbaths, Great Fast Day. Compare with this Trypho's enumeration of disputed points in *Dial.* 8:3: You should keep the sabbath, the feasts, and God's new moons. Compare further Justin in *Dial.* 12:3, i.e. immediately before the allusion to Is 1:13: «If any has not clean hands (Is 1:15b = *1.Apol.* 37:6: »Your hands are full of blood«), let him wash

---

3. This has been overlooked by numerous commentators who take *Dial.* 30ff as the opening of the Christological proof in the *Dialogue*, e.g. von Engelhardt, *Christenthum*, p. 222; Bousset, *Schulbetrieb*, p. 283; von Ungern-Sternberg p. 17; Sagnard, p. 176; to some extent Prigent, *Justin*, pp. 74ff.
4. Cf. esp. Prigent, *Justin*, pp. 236f.

(λουσάσθω, cf. Is 1:16a: λούσάσθε), then he is clean» (cf. Is 1:16a καθαροì γένεσθε).

It seems that Is 1:11-15.16 is in the background in *Dial* 8:3 and 12:3 -13:1. This encourages us to ask: Is there any trace of the second element in Justin's composite quotation, viz. Is 58:6f? It is obviously the testimony nucleus in *Dial* 15: «Learn to fast the true fast of God . . .» (Is 58:1-11). Between *Dial* 13:1 (Is 1:13) and *Dial* 15 (Is 58:6f) we find the following elements:

(1) Is 52:10 - 54:6
(2) Allusion to Jer 2:13
(3) Typological significance of unleavened bread
(4) Second, expanded LXX quotation of Is 55:3-13
(5) Short notice on the two parousias motif

Element 5 is an obvious addition, apparently coming too late and primarily referring to the quotation of Is 53.[5] Element 3 may seem surprising, but as we shall see below, there are good reasons to think that it was part of the material Justin is using in *Dial* 13-15. Element 4 is introduced as a repetition. Justin has just been quoting Is 52:10 - 54:6 from his Isaiah MS; he only had to read on some verses to find the text he had just quoted in *Dial* 12 (from a testimony source - see above, pp. 63f). So he adds a fuller LXX excerpt in *Dial* 14:4-7. We thus retain the elements 1-3 as parts of the original sequence. Jer 2:13 is a baptismal testimony already in Barnabas (see above, pp. 69f), and Is 53:5/7 also occur in a context with baptismal terminology in Barnabas (5:1f).[6]

We thus seem to encounter in *Dial* 12:3 - 15:6 an underlying sequence of testimonies running like this: Is 1:11-15/Is 58:6f; Is 1:16; Jer 2:13; unleavened bread; Is 53:5.7, containing polemics against Jewish lustration, contrasting blood of sacrifices with Christ's blood, and regarding Christian baptism as abrogating the whole sacrificial system. Whether this testimony sequence belonged to the same source as the new law and covenant testimonies, must so far remain an open question. (Cf. below, pp 172f).

### (c) *Dial* 16-19:2

We have already analysed part of this section above (*Dial* 15:7—17:2, see pp. 160 - 162), and have found that it reflects the situation after the Bar Kokhba uprising and the Hadrianic decree: Because the Jews slew the Just One and now persecute his believers (Is 57:1f; Is 3:9f; Is 5:20), their land and city is laid waste (Is 1:7 etc; Is 64:9-11), and they are by their circumcision excluded from Zion. I have shown above that *1.Apol* 47-49 (+ 53:10-12)

---

5. So also Prigent. *Justin*, p. 249.
6. On *Barn.* 5:1f, cf. below, p. 178. I am thus not convinced that the long Is 53 quotation is so secondary in the context as Bousset and Prigent will make us believe, *Schulbetrieb*, p. 298, n. 1; *Justin*, p. 247.

and *Dial.* 16f here draw on a common source, most fully exploited in *Dial.* 16f. The theme of circumcision is emphasized by three polemic testimonies (15:7 - 16:1): Jer 4:4; Deut 10:16f; Lev 26:40f. Justin even ventures to see circumcision as given by God *with a view to* the Hadrianic decree: Circumcision was given to the Jews so that they in the present time should be excluded from Jerusalem! One suspects that Justin here makes an inference not made in his source, but to this we shall have to return below. (Cf. pp. 295f.).

In *Dial.* 17:3-4 Justin adds some Gospel sayings against the Jews. This is in conflict with his principle of arguing only from the Scriptures recognized by the Jews, and Justin apologizes for this in *Dial.* 18:1. Were the Jesus *logia* present in his source?

In *Dial.* 18:2 is added another allusion to Is 1:16, and Justin then refers back to *Dial.* 8:3:

| *Dial.* 8:3 | *Dial.* 18:2 |
|---|---|
| Trypho: <br> First, be circumcised <br> then ... keep the Sabbath <br> and the Feasts <br> and God's New Moons. | For we should in fact be keeping <br> even this circumcision.. <br> and the sabbaths <br> and the feasts ... <br> if we did not know the reason why <br> it all was enjoined even on you, <br> namely, because of your trans- <br> gressions and σκληροκαρδία. |

The last sentence in *Dial.* 18:2 introduces a new theme, viz. the reason why God commanded the sacrificial cult. This is an anticipatory remark; the theme is developed in *Dial.* 19:5 - 22:11. But before coming to this exposition, Justin adds in *Dial.* 19:2 another polemic on Jewish lustration versus Christian baptism, this time expressly quoting Jer 2:13. Which means: In *Dial.* 18:2 - 19:2 Justin is back to the source employed in *Dial.* 12:3 - 15:6.

Did the intervening anti-circumcision testimonies also belong to the same source? If so, it would mean that the anti-cultic polemic in *1.Apol.* 37 derives from the same material as *1.Apol.* 47/49, i.e. that the entire material within the great insertion in *1.Apol.* 36—49 has the same provenance. The issue calls for further examination (Cf. below, pp. 173f/293ff).

(d) *Dial.* 19:3 - 23:5

*Dial.* 19:3f contains a new polemic of another kind against circumcision: The patriarchs until Abraham were uncircumcised, but nevertheless righteous. Circumcision is thus not necessary for rightousness. The sabbath also is included in this polemic: not one of the just men observed the sabbath until Moses.

This argument in *Dial.* 19:3f is carried on in *Dial.* 23 and 27:5 (cf. 28:4), and is partly repeated in *Dial.* 92f.[7] Let us briefly review the arguments:

(1) Adam created uncircumcised: 19:3.
(2) Patriarchs righteous without circumcision (or sabbath):19:3f; 23:1; 27:5; 92:2.
(3) Female sex cannot be circumcised, but can attain righteousness: 23:5.
(4) Sabbath prohibition overruled by other precepts: 27:5.
(5) Nature does not observe sabbath: 23:3.
(6) Egyptians, Moabites, and Edomites also circumcised, without profit: 28:4.
(7) Unless circumcision, sabbath, and other ritual commandments were given for a special reason (sinfulness of Israel), God must be said to have changed, which is absurd: 23:1f; 92:2.5.

*Dial.* 19:5f contains an argument which supplements and completes the above: God enjoined the ceremonial laws on Israel only to accomodate their predeliction for idolatry and apostasy - demonstrated in the incident of the golden calf, Ex 32. This argument is substantiated with suiting testimonies in *Dial.* 20-22 in the following order: Dietary laws, *Dial.* 20 (testimonies: Ex 32:6; Deut 32:15);[8] the sabbath, *Dial.* 21 (testimony: Ezek 20:19-26); sacrifices, *Dial.* 22:1-11 (testimonies: Am 5:18-6:7; Jer 7:21f; Ps 50:1-23); the temple, *Dial.* 22:11 (testimony: Is 66:1).

The first testimony on the dietary laws, Ex 32:6, is taken from the narrative of the golden calf episode. It is thus well adapted to the argument in *Dial.* 19:5f. But in the other testimonies there is no explicit statement that the making of the golden calf was the reason why the other regulations were imposed. The most one can say, is that Justin could take this to be implied in Am 5:25 and Jer 7:21f. On the other hand, the testimonies in *Dial.* 21f —sabbath; sacrifices; temple worship — accord admirably with the themes and the polemics in Is 1:11ff, quoted in *1.Apol.* 37:5-8. And Is 66:1 is common to the two passages, *1.Apol.* 37:3f and *Dial.* 22:11.

Let us take as a working hypothesis that the source underlying *1.Apol.* 37:3ff and *Dial.* 12:3 - 15:6 also is at play in *Dial.*21f, probably enriched with related material, especially Am 5:18ff which may have been suggested to Justin by Acts 7:42f (see above, synoptic study 21).

It seems that the source we reconstruct in this manner, comes quite close to a section of *Barnabas.* viz. 2:4 - 3:5. Here we find the following sequence: Is 1:11-13; Jer 7:22f/Zech 8:17; Ps 51:19; Is 58:4-10. We have often had occasion to observe that Justin's sources run largely parallel to material in *Barnabas* - we can thus probably take the present parallelism as a confirmation of our hypothesis.

---

7. Prigent, *Justin,* pp. 264-267, argues that *Dial.* 92f is a direct re-employment of the source behind *Dial.* 19/23 etc. His argument is persuasive.
8. With an excursus in *Dial.* 20:2-4 on Gen 9:3.

As we have seen, *Dial.* 23 links back to the arguments advanced in *Dial.* 19:3f and thus forms an inclusion with the beginning of the section analysed in this paragraph. Besides, Justin makes an inclusion with *Dial.* 10:3 by repeating Trypho's challenging text on circumcision, Gen 17:14, and explaining the meaning of it.

### (e) *Dial.* 24-29

*Dial.* 24 is a climax to the whole discussion so far. The theme of circumcision is again brought into focus, together with an allusion to Is 2:3 (and perhaps Jer 31:31): ἄλλη διαθήκη τὰ νῦν, καὶ ἄλλος ἐξῆλθεν ἐκ Σιὼν νόμος (24:1). In *Dial.* 24:2 some testimonies on the new people follow; these will be treated below. *Dial.* 24:3 forms an eloquent climax. Justin exhorts his listeners/readers to come to Jerusalem to see God's salvation. The whole paragraph is made up of Scriptural allusions and quotations,[9] with Is 2:3 furnishing the main catchwords and the dominant idea. The sequence is this: Ps 128:4f; Is 2:5b; Jer 3:17/Is 2:2-4; Is 65:1-3 (Is 65:1a separated from the rest of the quotation by βοᾷ διὰ 'Ησαίου —probably indicating that Is 65:1a is the original testimony).[10] The focal significance of Is 2:3 in this chapter brings it close to *1.Apol.* 39; the concluding testimony on the new people, Is 65:1a, reminds one of *1.Apol.* 49.

*Dial.* 25 is a polemic based on Is 63:18, for which the whole of Is 63:15 -64:11 is quoted. As we have seen above, there is reason to suspect that the original testimony behind the long LXX excerpt is Is 64:9-11, cf. *1.Apol.* 47. If so, we have another example that Justin can include new LXX material outside the traditional testimonies in his discussion in the *Dialogue.*[11]

In *Dial.* 26 we find quotations of Is 42:6f and Is 62:10 - 63:6. In *Barn.* 14:6f we find the sequence Is 62:12 (allusion: λυτρωσάμενον ἡμας . . . ἑτοιμά-σαι ἑαυτῷ λαὸν ἅγιον); Is 42:6f. This suggests that Is 62:12 is the testimony nucleus behind the long Is 62:10ff quotation in *Dial.* 26.[12] This is confirmed in *Dial.* 119:3: «But we are not only a people, but also a holy people, as we have already proved: καὶ καλέσουσιν αὐτὸν λαὸν ἅγιον, λελυτρωμένον ὑπὸ κυρίου» (= Is 62:12a. There is no prior quotation of Is 62:12 except within the long excerpt in *Dial.*26).

This theme of the new people can be said to be implicitly present in *1.Apol.* 47/49, and we thus arrive at the conclusion that *Dial.* 25f is largely parallel to those chapters in the *Apology.*

*Dial.* 27: Trypho objects to Justin's treatment of the sabbath that other prophecies expressly bid to keep the sabbath: Is 58:13f. P.Prigent[13] has

---

9. Cf. the analysis in Hatch, *Essays*, pp. 211f, and Prigent, *Justin*, pp. 267-269.
10. So Prigent, *Justin*, p. 269.
11. In this I disagree with Prigent, *ibid.*
12. Cf. Prigent, *Justin*, p. 270.
13. *Justin*, p. 241.

noted an allusion to this same prophecy in Justin's mouth in *Dial.* 12:3: »If any (among you is an) adulterer, let him repent, then he has kept τὰ τρυφερὰ καὶ ἀληθινὰ σάββατα τοῦ θεοῦ.» Cf. Is 58:13: τὰ σάββατα τρυφερά, ἅγια τοῦ θεοῦ σου.[14] Other parallels between the two passages can also be noted:

| *Dial.* 12:3 | *Dial.* 27:2 |
|---|---|
| εἴ τις ἐστὶν ἐν ὑμῖν ἐπίορκος ἢ κλέπτης · · · εἴ τις μοιχός μετανοησάτω . . . εἴ τις καθαρας οὐκ ἔχει χεῖρας . . . | · · · μήτε κοινωνοὶ κλεπτῶν . . . μετανοήσαντες . . . . . . πλήρεις τὰς χεῖρας αἵματος |

One suspects that some kind of common material underlies the two passages. This assumption is strengthened when one observes that *Dial.* 12:2 and *Dial.* 27:4 seem to draw on a common stock of anti-Jewish accusations.[15]

I am thus inclined to conclude that in *Dial.* 27 the source behind *Dial.* 12:2 - 15:6 and 21f - or at least related material - is once more being employed.

In *Dial.* 27:5 (and 28:4) Justin carries on the argument in *Dial.* 19:3f and *Dial.* 23, see above p. 171.

*Dial.* 28:2f contains testimonies exhorting to true, inward circumcision: Jer 4:3f and Jer 9:24f. We have compared this sequence with *Dial.* 15:7 - 16:1 and *Barn.* 9:4f above. Some kind of source, parallel to *Barnabas,* is at play. *Dial.* 28:5 adds to this Mal 1:10-12 and Ps 18:44f. Thematically these texts are concerned with the new people, and are thus close to *1.Apol.* 49; *Dial.* 16f and *Dial.* 24. The closeness to *Dial.* 16f suggests that they were contained in the same source from which the circumcision testimonies in *Dial.*28 were taken.[16]

*Dial.* 29 is summary in character.[17]

To conclude: In *Dial.* 11-29 Justin seems to follow a single source of tradition rather closely. Its dominant motif is the New Law idea, combined with a polemic concerning the ceremonial components of the Mosaic law, and substituting baptism for animal sacrifices. An important subsidiary motif is the anti-circumcision polemic which relates to the Hadrianic decree, and a corresponding New People concept.

---

14. This is the reading of *Dial.* 27:1 and some Lucianic LXX MSS. Ziegler: τῷ θεῷ.
15. This is analysed in great detail by Prigent, *Justin,* pp. 240f/243-245. Prigent compares the present passage with *Dial.* 20:4 and *Dial.* 123:3f.
16. This is essentially the conclusion which is also reached by Prigent, *Justin,* p. 277-79. One should notice the fact that Ps 18:45 in Barnabas occurs not far from the circumcision testimonies, *Barn.* 9.
17. Cf. Prigent's analysis, *Justin,* pp. 277-79.

*Dial.* 11-29 is thus a close parallel to *1.Apol.* 37/39-49, and seems to draw on the same source of tradition. Indirectly, this confirms my surmise that *1.Apol.* 39-49 is a thematic unity, and suggests that the anti-cultic testimonies in *1.Apol.* 37 derive from the same source.

(f) *Dial.* 30-39[18]

*Dial.* 30. Paragraph 1 of this chapter repeats the argument of *Dial.* 23:1f. Justin adds: The law of Moses cannot be called eternal, because it contains commandments of a provisional character. The adjective eternal can only be applied to the prophecy «coming after Moses». Paragraph 2: «And this, Gentlemen, has been said by the Psalm . . .» Justin has not quoted any Psalm in the immediately preceeding context, and in his next sentence («And that we who have been made wise by them ackowledge that they are sweater than honey..»), the «them» is without reference. (The first αὐτά of 30:2 cannot refer to τὰ τοιαῦτα διδάγματα in 30:1, because these are clearly not meant to be part of the eternal law, but only temporary accommodations to the sinfulness of the Jews.) There is no doubt, however, which Psalm Justin has in mind. Several allusions point to Ps 19:

| Ps 19 LXX | *Dial.* 30 (not in sequence) |
|---|---|
| 8. ὁ νόμος τοῦ κυρίου ἄμωμος ἐπιστρέφων ψυχάς | . . . τὸν λαὸν ὑμῶν . . . εἰς ἐπιστροφὴν καὶ μετάνοιαν τοῦ πνεύματος κέκληκε . . . |
| ἡ μαρτυρία κυρίου πιστή σοφιζουσα νήπια | . . . ἵνα μετὰ τὸ ἐπιστρέψαι πρὸς θεὸν . . . . . . οἱ σοφισθέντες . . . |
| 10. τὰ κρίματα κυρίου ἀληθινά 11. . . . καὶ γλυκύτερα ὑπὲρ μέλι καὶ κηρίον | . . . καὶ ὅτι γλυκύτερα ὑπὲρ μέλι καὶ κηρίον ὁμολογοῦμεν ἀυτά . . . |
| 14. καὶ ἀπὸ ἀλλοτρίων φεῖσαι τοῦ δούλου σου . . . τότε ἄμωμος ἔσομαι . . . | . . . ἵνα ἀπὸ τῶν ἀλλοτρίων . . . συντηρήσῃ ἡμᾶς . . . ἄμωμοι ὦμεν . . . |
| 15. κύριε, βοηθέ μου καὶ λυτρωτά μου. | . . . βοηθὸν γὰρ ἐκεῖνον καὶ λυτρωτὴν καλοῦμεν . . . |

This table i.a. makes it plain what the reference of «them» in *Dial.* 30:2 is, viz. τὰ κρίματα κυρίου, Ps 19:10. It also makes clear what Justin is referring to when he says that (not the law of Moses but) the prophecy coming after Moses is αἰώνιος. He is paraphrasing Ps 19:10: ὁ φόβος κυριου . . . διαμένων εἰς αἰῶνα αἰῶνος, - probably taking ὁ φόβος κυρίου as referring to obedience to Christ's law.

---

18. On this section, see esp. Bousset, *Schulbetrieb,* pp. 283-285; Sagnard, 'Plan du *Dialogue',* pp. 176-178; Prigent, *Justin,* pp. 74-116.

So why is a quotation of Ps 19 missing? Archambault[19] and Williams[20] suggest a lacuna in the text; Prigent thinks the quotation was present in Justin's source, but not in the text of the *Dialogue,* which abbreviates the source.[21]

Let us take a look at the last sentence in *Dial.* 30:1:

πολλοῖς γὰρ ἀνθρώποις ἄλογα καὶ οὐκ ἄξια θεοῦ τὰ τοιαῦτα διδάγματα ἔδοξεν εἶναι, μὴ λαβοῦσι χάριν τοῦ γνῶναι ὅτι
(1) τὸν λαὸν ὑμῶν πονηρευομένον καὶ ἐν νόσῳ ψυχικῇ ὑπάρχοντα εἰς ἐπιστροφὴν καὶ μετάνοιαν τοῦ πνεύματος κέκληκε,
(2) καὶ αἰώνιός ἐστι μετὰ τὸν Μωυσέως θάνατον προελθοῦσα ἡ προφητεία.

Of course the second (2) part of the sentence may still be governed by the ὅτι in the first part: «and that the prophecy . . .», but we would perhaps expect another ὅτι: καὶ ὅτι αἰώνιός . . .

Besides, phrase 1 is a good summary of what Justin can expect his readers to have the «grace to understand», since this sentence repeats the argument of *Dial.* 19:5f etc. The same cannot be said of phrase 2. «The prophecy published after the death of Moses» is a new concept. Exactly what is its reference? I believe the answer is Ps 19 itself. Ps 19 is a psalm - or a prophecy - by David, thus published after Moses, and Justin's point may be that the νόμος, μαρτυρία, δικαιώματα, ἐντολή etc. spoken of in Ps 19:8ff, and said to be *eternal,* should not be identified with the law of Moses, but with the *eternal components* of the law, identical with the *law of Christ.* This interpretation of «the prophecy» as a reference to Ps 19 itself is confirmed when we look at the last sentence in *Dial.* 30:2: «And it is clear to all that we who believe in Him even ask him that he will preserve us from the aliens (namely the evil and deceitful spirits), *as the words of the prophecy says. . .*» (ὁ λόγος τῆς προφητείας). Here «the prophecy» clearly refers to Ps 19:8ff.

I am therefore inclined to agree with Archambault and Williams that there is a lacuna in the text, and I tentatively locate it between phrases 1 and 2 of the last sentence in *Dial.* 30:1. The lacuna presumably contained a quotation of Ps 19:8ff or perhaps the whole Psalm. Phrase 2 of the last sentence in *Dial.* 30:1 is on this hypothesis part of the commentary following Ps 19, and the two first sentences of *Dial.* 30:2 receive their missing reference: «And this, Gentlemen, has been said by the Psalm (viz. Ps 19). And that we who have been made wise by them (viz. τὰ κρίματα κυρίου, Ps 19:10) acknowledge that they are sweeter than honey and the honeycomb (cf. Ps 19:11: γλυκύτερα ὑπὲρ μέλι καὶ κηρίον), is evident . . .»

We move on to ask what function Ps 19 has in the progress of argument in *Dial.* 30. Let me first point out an important feature about the new law/covenant idea in *Dial.* 11f and 24. The new law going out from Jerusalem is the apostolic kerygma. Through this kerygma Christ himself reigns. Justin can thus call Christ a lawgiver, νομοθέτης, *Dial.* 12:2; even ὁ καινὸς νομοθέτης, *Dial.* 14:3; 18:3 (certainly to distinguish him from Moses who is called lawgiver in *Dial.* 112:3 and 127:1). But he brings out the idea even better when he speaks about Christ being in his very person the new law and the new covenant, *Dial.* 11:2.4; 43:1.

*This means that Justin cannot finish his discussion on the law without bringing in Christ the New Law!*

Turning to Ps 19, we first notice that Ps 19:5 is a testimony to the apostolic mission in Rom 10:18, and as such underlies the long quotation of Ps 19:3-6

19. Archambault, note *ad loc.* (p. 131).
20. Williams, note *ad loc.* (p. 59).
21. *Justin,* pp. 75-78.

in *1.Apol.* 40:1f. Next, Ps 19:6 is a testimony to Christ ruling world-wide, *1.Apol.* 54:9; *Dial.* 69:3; 76:7. Both ideas for Justin come together in the idea of the *new law*, and now Justin only had to read on to vs. 8 to meet this very term: ὁ νόμος τοῦ κυρίου ἄμωμος . . . It is thus evident that Ps 19 was well suited to introduce the idea of Christ the new law. And as we shall see, this is the main idea in the whole of *Dial.* 30-39.[22]

In *1.Apol.* 45 we encountered Ps 110:1-3 as another testimony on the same motif: Christ rules over his enemies, the demons (vs. 1), through his mighty word going out from Jerusalem (vs. 2). This agrees perfectly with Justin's comment on Ps 19:14 in *Dial.* 32:2f, and points to the quotation of Ps 110:1-7 in *Dial.* 32:6.

The third main testimony on the apostolic mission/new law in *1.Apol.* 39ff is Ps 96/1 Chron 16: ὁ κύριος ἐβασίλευσεν ἀπὸ τοῦ ξύλου. Now, Justin is perfectly aware that his Jewish interlocutors do not recognize this testimony, *Dial.* 73:1; cf. *Dial.* 71:2: «. . . these passages, since I am aware that all who are of your nation deny them, I do not adduce in such enquiries as we are now making, but I . . . discuss those which are still aknowledged among you.»

I therefore suspect that Ps 99:1-9 in *Dial.* 37:3-4 is a substitute for Ps 96. Cf. the opening words in Ps 99: ὁ κύριος ἐβασίλευσεν. Reminiscent of Is 2:3 is Justin's version of Ps 99:2: κύριος ἐκ Σιὼν μέγας . . . ἐπὶ πάντας τοὺς λαοὺς (LXX : ἐν Σιων). Ps 99:5 is close to Ps 110:1: προσκυνεῖτε τῷ ὑποποδίῳ τῶν ποδῶν αὐτοῦ, and vs. 9 again recalls Is 2:3: καὶ προσκυνεῖτε εἰς ὄρος ἅγιον αὐτοῦ (Is 2:3: ἀναβῶμεν εἰς τὸ ὄρος κυρίου . . .). Ps 99 is thus an ideal substitute for Ps 96 within the new law sequence.

The remaining testimonies in *Dial.* 30-39 (viz. Dan 7:9-28; Ps 72; Ps 24; Ps 47:5-9; Ps 45; Ps 68:19) all emphasize *the universal reign of Christ.* It is not difficult to imagine how Justin selected these texts. Dan 7:13f and Ps 24:7f were related to Ps 110:1 in the «creed» sequence: Ps 24:7f ascension, Ps 110:1 reign, Dan 7:13f return of Christ. In *Dial.* 31f/36 Justin has just reversed the sequence. We have heard echoes of the source behind *1.Apol.* 51:6-9 in *Dial.* 31:1 already (see pp. 88 - 90), and we notice cursory remarks on the two parousias motive, *Dial.* 31:1; *Dial.* 32:2. In his exegesis of Ps

---

22. Prigent takes as the theme of *Dial.* 30-39 «l'ascension et le règne du ressuscité» (*Justin*, p. 77). This in itself is a valid description, but Prigent fails to observe the connexion with the idea of the apostolic mission, hence with *1.Apol.* 39ff and the «new law» concept. That is why he calls *Dial.* 30 «l'amorce de la section christologique», *ibid.* Cf. also Sagnard, p. 176: «une suite de textes messianiques, une première annonce et une prélude de l'Incarnation». No! Not a prelude to the incarnation, but a description of Christ's *present reign.* The function of *Dial.* 30-39 within the context is well observed by Donahue, *Controversy,* pp. 108f: «In his first effort to justify this failure (by Christians) to observe the law, Justin argues that a later covenant supersedes an earlier one. Christ has superseded the law, and thus the law is no longer valid . . . Justin introduces Christology to justify the Christian's failure to observe the law. At the point at which it first appears, the Christological argument is subsidiary to the discussion of the law.»

24:7ff (*Dial.* 36:5f), Justin again presupposes the testimony version of *1.Apol.* 51:7, and refers to Is 53, cf. *1.Apol.* 50f.

Ps 47:6-10 (*Dial.* 37:1) is not encountered in the «creed» sequence in *1.Apol.* Perhaps it is another substitute for Ps 96 (it immediately preceeds the other substitute, Ps 99 in *Dial.* 37:3f). Cf. vs. 9: ἐβασίλευσεν ὁ θεὸς ἐπὶ τὰ ἔθνη. Besides, Ps 47:6 is an excellent sequel to the ascension Psalm 24: ἀνέβη ὁ θεὸς ἐν ἀλαλαγμῷ.

Ps 45:8 is one of Justin's prooftexts for the fact that Scripture knows another God beside the Creator. In this capacity the text is quoted together with Ps 110:1 in *Dial.* 56:14. Ps 45:7 contains the idea of the Messiah's ῥάβδος, so important in Ps 110:2.

Ps 68:19 in *Dial.* 39:4 is a Pauline ascension testimony.

It is thus not difficult to see the sequence in *Dial.* 30-39 as a re-adaption and expansion of the material used in *1.Apol.* 39-45. But I think one can go one step further in source analysis and suggest that even another source, partly parallel to the «law» sequence in *1.Apol.* 39ff, is being adapted in *Dial.* 30-39. We shall encounter this source behind the Christological section of the *Dialogue*, and since an extensive analysis of the material would take us far into that section, I postpone this analysis for the present (see below, pp. 199ff).

(g) *Dial.* 40-42

In *Dial.* 39:7 Trypho demands a proof that Jesus is the Messiah. Justin answers (39:8): «It has already been proved, Gentlemen, for those who have ears ... But that you may not think that I am at a loss, and unable to draw up proofs for what you require, I will do so at a suitable place, as I promised. But now I will pursue the connexion of subjects on which I have begun to address you». There can thus hardly be any doubt that Justin intended *Dial.* 40-42 to be read as a continuation of the «law» theme. Nevertheless, these chapters stand clearly out from their context. They are concerned with a new aspect of the law, viz. the typological significance of certain OT precepts. In *Dial.* 43:1f Justin proceeds to a rapid repetition of earlier arguments contained in *Dial.* 19:3-20:4; *Dial.* 23 etc.(see pp. 170 -172), and then quite abruptly turns to a discussion on the virgin birth in 43:3ff. This theme is always in the *Dialogue* part of the proof that Jesus is the Messiah. Several of the texts in *Dial.* 30-39 are also quoted again for this purpose. Let me suggest that the other source behind *Dial.* 30-39 mentio-ned above, was a source concerned precisely with the Massiahship of Jesus and that Trypho's request in *Dial.* 39:7 really is a request that Justin should exploit this source, or this aspect of the source, more fully. *Dial.* 43:3-8 is thus a continuation of *Dial.* 30ff. If this surmise is correct, *Dial.* 40-42 on the level of Justin's disposition is a continuation of the «law» theme, but on the level of source analysis an insertion into connected material in *Dial.* 30-39 and 43.[23] We now turn to the internal structure of *Dial* 40-42. It is easy to recognize the outline of this passage:[24]

(1) Type on the passion: Paschal lamb, 40:1-3.
(2) The two parousias: The two goats on Atonement Day, 40:4f.
(3) The eucharist: Offering of fine flour, 41:1-3.
(4) Baptism: Circumcision on the 8th day, 41:4.
(5) Apostolic mission: 12 bells on the High Priest's robe, 42:1-3.

In *Dial.* 42:4 Justin indicates that this is but a selection from a much larger material: «And in fact all other things . . . which were appointed by Moses, I can enumerate and prove to be types, and figures, and announcements of those persons who were foreknown as about to believe in him, and similarly of those things which were to be done by Christ himself.« True, Justin may want to impress his readers, and one should not take a statement as this at face value, but certainly Justin is right in claiming that he had access to more typological exegesis than included in *Dial.* 40-42. We find ample proof of this in the rest of the *Dialogue*, and it is convenient to include some of this extraneous material in the following analysis. (Cf. especially *Dial.* 14:2f: unleavened bread; 111:1: two goats; 111:3f: paschal lamb).

We shall now try to discern which passages and texts elsewhere in the *Apology* and the *Dialogue* seem to be related to the material in *Dial.* 40-42.

*Paschal lamb*: In *Dial.* 40:1 Justin says that believers anoint their own houses, namely themselves, with Christ's blood. »For that form in which God formed Adam, became the house of the inbreathing that God gave.« We must return to this interesting passage in Part Three. Let me anticipate some conclusions: Justin is thinking of baptism as the event in which Christ's blood is applied to the believer, and is working with an Adam/baptizand typology (cf. *Barn.* 6:8-19).

In *Barn.* 5:1 Is 53:5/7 is introduced in a similar baptismal context: «. . . that we should be sanctified by the remission of sin, that is, by his sprinkled blood». We then turn to *Dial.* 111:3: «For Christ was the paschal lamb (τὸ πάσχα) who was sacrificed . . . as also Isaiah said: He was led as a lamb to slaughter (Is 53:7).» To complete our survey, let us include also *Dial.* 72: (1) Ps.Ezra: τοῦτο τὸ πάσχα ὁ σωτὴρ ἡμῶν καὶ ἡ καταφυγὴ ἡμῶν . . .; (2) Jer 11:19: ἐγὼ ὡς ἀρνίον φερόμενον τοῦ θύεσθαι . . . (3) Is 53:7: ὡς πρόβατον ἐπὶ σφαγὴν ἀγόμενος . . . If we take these texts together, the following picture emerges: Justin was familiar with a paschal lamb typology which included testimonies like Is 53:7; Jer 11:19, and Ps. Ezra as paschal lamb testimonies, and further associated the blood of Christ the paschal lamb with baptism.

---

23. Bousset has clearly seen the parenthetical character of *Dial.* 40-42, but fails to see the connexion between *Dial.* 30-39 and 43 *(Schulbetrieb,* p. 285).
24. Cf. Bousset, *Schulbetrieb,* p. 285; Sagnard, 'Plan du Dialogue', p. 178.

I think this throws light on *Dial.* 13f. As we noticed, Is 53 is here adduced as a testimony to baptism: Christ's blood - applied to the believer in baptism - cleanses from sin, not the blood of goats or sheep (αἷμα . . . προβάτων). The parallel in Heb 9:13f has no sheep, but instead ταύροι. One suspects here in the polemics against blood of *sheep* a polemic against the Jewish paschal lamb.

This paschal lamb motif underlying the quotation Is 52:10 - 54:6 in *Dial.* 13:2-9 explains why Justin in *Dial.* 14:1 again reverts to baptism and then in *Dial.* 14:2f goes on to typologize the *unleavened bread.* This is a quite natural sequel to a treatment of *the paschal lamb.*

To conclude: It seems that *Dial.* 13f; 40:1-3; 72; and 111:3f belong together and draw on a common source.[25]

*The two goats:* Let me first point out that Justin's term for Atonement Day is ἡ νηστεία, *the Fast, Dial.* 40:4f; 46:2 (here τὸ πρόβατον τοῦ πάσχα and ἡ νηστεία are again mentioned in conjunction); 111:1. This term is not used in the LXX of Lev 16 nor in any other passage concerned with the Day of Atonement (this is true also of the MT). Justin shares it, however, with *ho reads a deviant version of Lev 23:29:* Ὃς ἂν μὴ νηστεύσῃ τὴν νηστείαν, uanátQ e'joleureyulísetai *(Barn.* 7:3, cf. also 7:4). But one does not need to go outside Justin at all to find a possible source for this non-LXX term. In Justin's deviant version of Is 1:11-15 in *1.Apol.* 37 we read: καὶ μεγάλην ἡμέραν νηστείας καὶ ἀργίαν οὐκ ἀνέχομαι.(The corresponding LXX phrase reads: . . . καὶ ἡμέραν μεγάλην οὐκ ἀνέχομαι' νηστείαν καὶ ἀργίαν καὶ τὰς νουμηνίας ὑμῶν . . .) Whatever the reference of the LXX's «great day» is, there can be no doubt that «the great day of the fast» in *1.Apol.* 37:5 is the Day of Atonement.

We have seen already that Is 1:11ff is in the background in *Dial.* 12:3 -13:1. So we have probably here another link to this section of the *Dialogue.*

A confirmation of this comes in *Dial.* 40:5. After setting forth the typological significance of the two goats, Justin goes on: «For he (Christ) was an offering on behalf of all sinners who wish to repent, and fast with the fast which Isaiah reckons such, when they pluck asunder the knots of hard contracts . . .» We have seen above (p. 55f) that this allusion to Is 58:6 presupposes the non-LXX version of this text contained in the combined testimony in *1.Apol.* 37:8. We have here an obvious link to the source behind *1.Apol.* 37 and the related passages in the *Dialogue.*

*The offering of fine flour:* Justin is no doubt referring to Lev 14:10ff[26] (LXX: . . . λήψεται δύο ἀμνοὺς ἐνιαυσίους ἀμώμους καὶ πρόβατον ἐνιαύσιον ἄμωμον καὶ τρία δέκατα σεμιδάλεως εἰς θυσίαν . . .) But it may seem

---

25. Or - to put it more cautiously - related material.
26. This is even clearer in the related passage *Dial.* 112:4. Here Justin castigates the Jewish teachers for their useless discussions, i.a. διὰ τί σεμιδάλεως μέτρα τόσα καὶ ἐλαίου μέτρα τόσα ἐν ταῖς προσφοραῖς . . .

arbitrary to pick out the σεμίδαλις and attach such importance to it. It is mentioned explicitly only once in Lev 14:10ff, where it plays a minor role in the sacrificial act described. There is also in Lev 14:10ff no use of the technical term προσφορά used by Justin: ἡ τῆς σεμιδάλεως . . . προσφορά. It is otherwise when we turn to Is 1:13 as paraphrased in *Dial.* 13:1: σεμιδάλεως προσφοραῖς. We notice that these words are interpolated in a paraphrase of Heb 9:13f, and we have already observed one modification of the text of Hebrews made to match material in *Dial.* 40.

Once again it seems we are led to the source behind *1.Apol.* 37 and *Dial.* 13.

*Circumcision and the High Priest's robe*: We find no anti-circumcision polemic in *1. Apol.* 37. But in *1.Apol.* 47-49 such a polemic is present by implication (cf. *Dial.* 16f, and above pp. 160 - 162), and it is here coupled to the «Law out from Zion» theme (= apostolic mission) in *1.Apol.* 39-46. This corresponds to the same juxtaposition of circumcision polemic and «Law out from Zion» motif in *Dial.* 24:1: «This too I could therefore prove to you, . . . that the eight day (of circumcision) had a certain mystical meaning . . . But that I may not seem to digress to other subjects, I cry aloud: Understand that the blood of that circumcision is rendered useless, and we have believed the blood that bringeth salvation. Now have another Covenant and another Law gone forth from Zion . . .»

If we take it that Justin's temptation for «digression» in *Dial.* 24:1 derives from the employed source - which had more to say - this source might well be identical with the one behind *Dial.* 41:4. Further, the coupling of circumcision polemic and «Law out from Zion» idea is also present in *Dial.* 41f: In *Dial.* 42 there follows a typology on the apostles'mission, bolstered with Ps 19:5 as a direct prophecy, cf. *Dial.* 30 and the analysis *ad* loc.

To conclude: Although the typologies in *Dial.* 41:4 and 42:1 have no direct counterparts in *1.Apol.* 37, they seem related to material in *1.Apol.* 39-49 (and *Dial.* 24), and this - indirectly - may strenghten our impression that *1.Apol.* 37 and *1.Apol.* 39ff derive from the same source of tradition.


(h) *Dial.* 44-47

We have seen (pp. 67 - 69 and 153f) that *Dial.* 44f; *Dial.* 140:3 and probably *1.Apol.* 52:5-8/53:5-7 draw on a common source emphasizing that each man's salvation is dependent on his own choice, denying collective salvation for Israel. An additional observation can be made at this stage: In *Dial.* 44:4 there is a clear allusion to Is 1:16. As we have seen, for Justin this text is the classic exhortation to baptism, and in *1.Apol.* 44 occurs together with another testimony on each man's choice, Deut 30:15/19.

The thematic closeness and the common link with Is 1:16(ff) may be an indication that Deut 30:15/19; Ezek 14:14/20 etc.were part of the same source, which not only urged each man to a right decision, but also presented to him the eschatological horizon of his choice, Ezek 37:7f etc; Is

66:24; and warned the Jew against any hybris based on carnal descent, Ezek 14:14/20; Is 1:9.

In *Dial.* 45:4 there is a Christological passage, containing a joint allusion to Ps 110:3 and Ps 72:5, followed by a mention of the virgin birth. We shall have to return to this passage below ( cf. pp. 199ff).

Taken as a whole. *Dial.* 44-47 is a rather well-constructed unit marking the end of the discussion on the law: *Dial.* 44: exhortation, preparing *Dial.* 45: What about the law-obedient pious men in the OT? - and *Dial.* 46f: What about law-obedient Jewish Christians? (*Dial.* 46:3-7: a repetition of earlier arguments about the law).

The following table is meant to visualize the conclusions of our analysis (allusions within parenthesis):

| *Apology* | *Dialogue* |
|---|---|
| *1. Apol.* 37: Anticultic testimonies: *Is 1:11-15/58:6f; Is 66:1.* Sacrifices not acceptable. | *Dial.* 13-15: Christian baptism abrogates the sacrificial cult: *(Is 1:13-16):* Baptism makes pure, not sacrifices. Is 53:7: The cleansing power in baptism is Christ's blood. He is the true paschal lamb. True meaning of unleavened bread. Jer 2:13: Jewish washings versus Christian baptism. *Is 58:1-11:*True fasting |
| | *Dial.* 18-23: Is 1:16 ⎱ Wash with Christian baptism! Jer 2:13 ⎰ Cultic prescriptions an accomodation to Israel's *sklerokardia:* Ex 32:6; Deut 32:15; Ezek 20:19-26; Am 5:18 - 6:7; Jer 7:21f; Ps 50:1-23; *Is 66:1.* |
| | *Dial.* 27f: True sabbath: Is 58:13f True circumcision: Jer 4:3f etc. |
| | *Dial.* 40-42: Typology of the Law |

(Continued next page)

| |
|---|
| *1. Apol.* 39-45: Christ is the new Law, now going out from Zion: *Is 2:3f; Ps 19:3-6; Ps 1f; 1 Chron 16/Ps 96; Ps 110:1-3* |
| *1. Apol.* 47-49: The Jews slew the Just One, and are now excluded from their land and city: *Is 64:9-11; Is 1:7/Jer 50:3; Is 57:1f; Is 65:1-3; Is 5:20* |

| |
|---|
| *Dial.* 11f: Christ is the new Law now going out from Zion: Jer 31:31f; Is 51:4f; Is 55:3-5 |
| *Dial.* 24-26: Same theme: *Is 2:2-4* et al.; *Is 65:1-3;* Is 63:15 - *64:11;* Is 62:10 - 63:6 |
| *Dial.* 16f: The Jews slew the Just One; are now excluded from their land by their carnal circumcision: (Jer 4:4); Deut 10:16f; Lev 26:40f; *(Is 1:7/Jer 50:3);* Is *57:1-4;* Is 52:5; Is 3:9-11; *Is 5:18-20* |

*Dial.* 30-39: The risen Christ is the new Law:
Ps 19

Dan 7:9-28

*Ps 110:1-7*          Inserts from a source on Christology

Ps 72
Ps 24

Ps 47:6-10   *cf. Ps 96*
Ps 99:1-9

Ps 45

Ps 68:19 cf. Eph 4:8

*Dial.* 43: Is 7:10ff

| |
|---|
| *1. Apol.* 52:3-9: Imminence of resurrection and judgement |

| |
|---|
| *Dial.* 44-47: Who shall be saved in the resurrection? |

## *2. The new law and the new people, Dial. 108 - 141*

(a) *Dial.* 108-110.

This unit contains quotation and comments on Mic 4:1-7: The law going out from Zion = the apostolic *kerygma*. This is closely parallel to *1.Apol.* 39. But one can also find parallels to *1.Apol.* 47f: In *Dial.* 108:3 there is an allusion to Is 1:7; in *Dial.* 110:6 a quotation of Is 57:1. *Dial.* 108:1 - 109:1 forms an elegant transition from the Sign of Jonah theme (*Dial.* 107) to the theme of the apostolic mission: The repentance of the Ninevites prefigures that Gentiles rather than Jews should become believers. The joint occurence of material parallel to *1.Apol.* 39 and *1.Apol.* 47-49 is another indication that these sections in the *Apology* belong together.[27]

---

27. This parallel in the *Apology* is also a sufficient reason for letting this section of the *Dialogue* start with *Dial.* 108 - against Prigent, *Justin,* pp. 216ff.

(b) *Dial.* 111f.

This section repeats earlier material from *Dial.* 40:4; 90:4f; 40:1-3; 91:4. To this is added the typology of Rahab's cord, *Dial.* 111:4. The idea of Christ's propitiary passion and blood is prominent in most of the types mentioned in this section, and it thus prepares

(c) *Dial.* 113f.[28]

In *Dial.* 113:1-5 the changing of Joshua's name is used as a transition to a new theme: The second circumcision performed by Joshua is a type of Christian baptism, *Dial.* 113:6 - 114:5 (with an hermeneutical excursus in *Dial.* 114:1-3). This passage spells out what Justin hinted at in *Dial.* 12:3 («A second circumcision is now necessary . . .») and *Dial.* 24:2 (»Jesus Christ circumcises all them who will, with knives of stone . . .«)Notice the sequence in *Dial.* 24:1f: Is 2:3 — second circumcision; exactly parallel to *Dial.* 109f — *Dial.* 113:6 - 114:5. In *Dial.* 114:5 is added the combined text Jer 2:13/Is 16:1/Jer 3:8 analysed above, pp. 69f. Let us at this stage take a closer look at some details in the text. The two sayings added to Jer 2:13 (baptismal testimony, *Dial.* 14:1), read:
(1) Is there to be a desert where the mountain of Zion is? Is 16:1.
(2) For I have given Jerusalem a bill of divorce in your presence. Jer 3:8.

I suspect here a reference to the Hadrianic decree: The mountain of Zion is not going to be deserted ( the answer of the first question is shown to be »No« by the interrogative particle μὴ), although the Jewish inhabitants have been divorced from Jerusalem (Hadrianic decree). Implication: Uncircumcised Christians will inhabit Jerusalem instead of the Jews.

That this is not farfetched is shown by the prominence of the Jerusalem (or Holy Land) theme in the context: »Jesus Christ (will) turn the dispersion of the people, and will distribute the good land to each . . . For the one (Joshua) gave them the inheritance for a time . . . but the other (Jesus) will, after the holy resurrection, give us our possession for ever« (*Dial.* 113:3f). »This is he who is to shine in Jerusalem as an everlasting light. This is he who is always King of Salem and everlasting Priest of the Most High, according to the order of Melchizedek« (*Dial.* 113:5). One should also notice the close connection between the themes »second circumcision«, new people, invitation to Jerusalem, in *Dial.* 24.

As we have seen above (pp.160 - 162), *1.Apol.* 47-49 and *Dial.* 16f are two independent adaptions of a common source, the idea of which can be reconstructed as follows: Because of their rejection of the Just One, the Jews have been excluded from Jerusalem, and Jerusalem laid waste (Is 1:7/Jer 50:3; Is 64:9-11). The Hadrianic decree is here clearly envisaged. It excluded every circumcised person from Jerusalem.

---

28. Cf. Prigent, *Justin,* pp. 134-138.

The theme of *Dial.* 113f is generally very close to this: Circumcision excludes from Jerusalem/the land, »second circumcision« admits. And the combined testimony in *Dial.* 114:5 contains several catchword connections to the texts in *1.Apol.* 47:

| Is 64:9 | Is 16:1 |
|---|---|
| ἐγενήθη ἔρημος Σιων | μὴ ἔρημον . . . τὸ ὄρος Σιων |
| | Jer 3:8 |
| ὡς ἔρημος ἐγενήθη Ιερουσαλημ | Ἰερουσαλὴμ βιβλίον ἀποστασίου ἔδωκα |
| Is 1:7 | |
| ἡ γῆ αὐτῶν ἔρημος | |
| ἔμπροσθεν αὐτῶν . . . | ἔμπροσθεν ὑμῶν |

To conclude: *Dial.* 113f is closely related to *1.Apol.* 47; *Dial.* 16f; *Dial.* 24f, and may enrich our picture of the contents of the source behind those passages.[29]

For the sake of convenience, I include here a related passage coming later in this part of the *Dialogue*:

## (d) *Dial.* 133 - 139.

Let us start with *Dial.* 138, where Justin begins: «You know . . . that it is said of God in Isaiah with reference to Jerusalem: At the time of Noah's flood I saved thee.» The quotation is a very free rendering of Is 54:8f. It is true that Is 54:1ff is spoken «with reference to Jerusalem», but Jerusalem is not directly mentioned in the text (not in the whole of Is 54), and Justin's inexact quotation makes one doubt that he had the Isaiah text before his eyes. The Jerusalem reference may therefore have another explanation.

In *Dial.* 138:3 - after the exposition of the Noah typology - Justin goes on to say: God said this (viz. Is 54:8f) «to the people that obey him, for whom he also prepared beforehand a rest in Jerusalem.» Is it gratuitous to suppose that Justin in *Dial.* 138 is working with the same Jerusalem-oriented source which he used in *1.Apol.* 47-49; *Dial.* 16f; *Dial.* 24f? The reference to Jerusalem may stem from this source, not from the Isaiah context in Is 54. We notice that *Dial.*138 is related to *Dial.* 113f through the themes of baptism and Jerusalem/Holy Land.

The «land» theme is also prominent in the allegoric exegesis of Noah's curse and blessing in *Dial.* 139.

Turning to *Dial.* 133-137, we notice two facts: This section is clearly related to *Dial.* 138f, but also to *Dial.* 16f etc. Let us briefly list the contents:[30]

---

29. Prigent. *loc. cit.,* tries to establish connexions to *Dial.* 56.62 and *Dial.* 75f. Justin no doubt has allusions to those passages, but I doubt that these links were inherent in his source material. Cf. on *Dial.* 56-62 and *Dial.* 75 below.
30. For a detailed analysis of these chapters, I refer to Prigent, *Justin,* pp. 305-311, and Part III below.

133: Is 3:9-15; Is 5:18-25, Jews slaying Jesus and persecuting Christians, cf. *Dial.* 17:1f.

134: Jacob-Leah-Rachel typology: Jacob=Christ; Leah=Synagogue; Rachel=the (Gentile) Church. Anticipation of *Dial.* 139 in *Dial.* 134:4: «For since Noah gave to his two sons the seed of the third for bondage to them . . .»

135:1-3: Is 43:15; Is 42:1-4: Christ = Jacob/Israel.

135:4 - 136:2: Is 65:8.9-12; Is 2:5f: Christians shall inherit the holy mountain.

136:2f: Jews slew the Just One, Is 3:9f.

137:1f: Summary, Jews reviling Jesus.

137:3: Discussion of the text of Is 3:10.

Let us also notice that *Dial.* 140:1 contains a summary which takes Jacob and Noah typology together.

To conclude: The evidence seems to suggest that *Dial.* 133-139 is closely related to the source behind *1.Apol.* 47-49; *Dial.* 16f; *Dial.* 24-26 and possibly - *Dial.* 113f.

### (e) *Dial.* 115 - 119

*Dial.* 115f forms a connected commentary on Zech 3:1-7.[31] But only Zech 2:14 - 3:2 is quoted in the present text of the *Dialogue*.[32] By the name Joshua this unit is connected with the preceeding chapters. The theme of baptism/ remission of sins is also common with *Dial.* 113f. *Dial.* 115f may therefore derive from the same source, but the lack of parallels within Justin's writings makes a firm conclusion impossible.[33]

In *Dial.* 117 we find another quotation of Mal. 1:10-12, with extensive comments. By this quotation *Dial.* 117 is connected with *Dial.* 41:1-3 and *Dial.* 28:5. As we have seen above (p. 173), Mal 1:10-12 in *Dial.* 28:5 points to the source behind *1.Apol.* 47-49 and *Dial.* 24ff: Jews unbelieving, Gentiles believing and obedient. Prigent observes an allusion to Is 52:5 in *Dial.* 117:3 - this links our chapter to *Dial.* 17, i.e. the same source.[34] This may be seen as an additional argument for the assumption that the same source is being used in *Dial.* 113f, especially if *Dial.* 115f also derives from it.

*Dial.* 118. In 118:1 Justin repeats briefly the texts Zech 12:10-12; Ps 110:4 and Is 57:2, with back-references to earlier expositions. 118:2 contains two texts on Christ's reign in the new Jerusalem, 1 Chron 17:13f and Ezek 45:17-25. We shall have to inquire below whether there be any connexion between these testimonies and the millennial ideas in *Dial.* 80f (cf. p. 204f)

---

31. A late side-remark on *Dial.* 113:3 in *Dial.* 115:5f excepted.
32. Cf. Prigent's excellent analysis, *Justin*, pp. 143f. Prigent is probably right in supposing that in Justin's source Zech 3:1-7 was quoted.
33. Prigent is rather definite: «Il est clair que Justin utilise ici une source, assurément la même qu'aux chapitres 113-114.» (*Justin*, p. 144).
34. *Justin*, p. 286.

*Dial.* 118:3 contains allusions to Jer 31:31 and Is 55:3, and forms an inclusion with *Dial.* 8:4:

| *Dial.* 8:4 | *Dial.* 118:3 |
|---|---|
| Trypho: You have accepted a vain (ματαίαν) rumour... | Not in vain (μάτην) have we believed on him... |

*Dial.* 118:4 contains a testimony to the fact that the Gentiles would believe, the Jews not, Is 52:15 - 53:1. As we have seen, in *Dial.* 118:4 - 119:6 Justin apparently is using Rom 9:14ff as one of his sources. In Romans we find the sequence Is 53:1; Ps 19:6; Deut 32:21; Is 65:1.2, and this recurs in the present passage of the *Dialogue:* Is 52:15 - 53:1; Deut 32:16-23; ... Is 65:1 (cf. above, p. 116). But besides, *Dial.* 119:3f seems also to use again the source behind *1.Apol.* 47-49 and *Dial.* 24-26.[35]

To conclude: Repeating excurses excluded, it seems that Justin in *Dial.* 108 - 119 is following a single source quite closely. The least one can say, is that the material in this source is related to the source behind *1.Apol.* 39-49; *Dial.* 16f; *Dial.* 24-26, and there is nothing which excludes identity.

(f) *Dial.* 120f.[36]

In this passage we find an interesting argument concerning the blessing of Abraham: It is not conferred on all of Abraham's carnal descendants, but only through a narrow line of election leading up to Christ: Abraham → Isaac (Gen 26:4) → Jacob (Gen 28:14) → Judah (Gen 49:10) → Perez → Jesse → David. Coming to David, Justin states that the promise of blessing now no longer says «in his seed», but «in him», Ps 72:17 (deviant version).

I have argued above (p. 85) that the non-LXX versions of Gen 49:10 and Ps 72:17 employed here derive from the «creed» source behind *1.Apol.* 32ff, and that the modified texts were created to other purposes than the argument Justin is developing in *Dial.* 120f. Thus, while Justin's argument in *Dial.* 120f is strikingly Pauline (Gal 3:16), the quotation material has another provenance. This would suggest that Justin is working very creatively in *Dial.* 120f: using a nonPauline material to argue a Pauline point of view.

(g) *Dial.* 121:4 - 123:2.

This is a rather well-composed unit treating the following question: Do the oracles in Isaiah about salvation of Gentiles refer to Jewish proselytes or

---

35. We have seen above (p. 74 ) that a testimony source has furnished Justin with his text of Zech 2:15 in *Dial.* 119:3.
36. For once, Prigent's analysis, *Justin*, pp. 293f, is not very helpful.

Gentile Christians? The sequence of texts is this: Is 49:6; Is 42:16/43:10; Is 42:6f;[37] Jer 31:31 (all.); Is 2:3 (all.); Is 49:6; Ps 2:7f; Is 14:1.

The parallels to this section occur in *Dial* 11 and 24 (new covenant and new law) and in *Dial* 26 (Is 42:6f). The text Is 55:3-5 quoted in *Dial* 12:1 also has many catchwords in common with the testimonies in *Dial* 121:4 -123:2.

One is thus probably justified in joining this section to the «new law from Zion» testimonies in *Dial* 11:3 - 12:1; 24-26, and 109 - 119; i.e. in *Dial* 121:4 Justin is back to his source since *Dial* 108.

A confirmation that we are on the right track can be found in *Barn.* 14:6-9. Here we find a quotation sequence on the salvation of the Gentiles: Is 62:12; Is 42:6f; Is 49:6f; Is 61:1f. Is 62:12 is present behind the long LXX excerpt Is 62:10ff in *Dial* 26:3-4, immediately following Is 42:6f; and is quoted in *Dial* 119:3—a passage already seen to depend on the same source as in *Dial* 26. I therefore conclude that in *Dial* 121:4 - 123:2 Justin is using the same source as in *Dial* 108 -119.[38]

*Dial* 123:2-4 contains a cluster of anti-Jewish texts, a natural contrast motif: While the Gentiles believe, the Jews do not.


(h) *Dial* 123:5-9

This section comprises two elements. In 123:5f we find a series of testimonies proving that Christians are the new Israel, another Israel[39] (Jer 31:27; Is 19:24f; Ezek 36:12). A joint allusion to Jer 31:27 and Ezek 36:12 recurs in *Dial* 136:2. *Dial* 135:4 - 136:2 is devoted to an exegesis of Is 65:8-12, a fourth text which seems closely related to the testimonies in *Dial* 123:5f. The second element, *Dial* 123:7-9, contains a more indirect argument that Christians are Israel: Is 42:1-4 proves that Jesus is «Jacob» and «Israel», and Christians descend from Christ. Here also there is a parallel statement of the same argument in *Dial* 135. On closer inspection, one observes that the argument is most clearly stated in *Dial* 135, while in *Dial* 123:9 there is a strange flexion in the line of thought. Justin argues that Christ is Israel, but instead of drawing the conclusion that Christians derive their right to the name Israel from him, Justin says: Just as the Jewish nation derived their name Israel from Jacob, so Christians derive from Christ their right to be - sons of God! (The translations of Haeuser, Williams and Falls

---

37. On the text of this quotation, cf. above, p. 62. I there surmised on purely textual grounds that a testimony source is at play in *Dial* 122.

38. This is also Prigent's conclusion, *Justin*, p. 296.

39. Justin says in *Dial* 123:7 that he has already shown at great length that Christians are Israel. Cf. Prigent's remark: «*L'allégation est fausse, c'est la première fois dans le Dialogue que le titre d'Israël est revendiqué par les chrétiens. Cette erreur s'explique parfaitement si l'on admet que Justin se réfère au traité qu'il a déjà plusieurs fois utilisé.*» (*Justin*, p. 297).

are probably somewhat misleading on this point:«Therefore, as your people was called after that one Jacob, surnamed Israel, so we ... are ... both called and in reality are, Jacob and Israel and Juda and Joseph and David and true children of God» (Falls, the others similar). This overlooks the ὡς introducing the chain «Jacob etc.» Archambault is probably correct: «... *de même nous... comme Jacob..., nous sommes appelés et nous sommes véritables enfants de Dieu.*») Prigent may be right in seeing this flexion in the line of thought as a conscious preparation for *Dial.* 124.[40] Instead of saying explicitly that Christians are called Israel, Justin says that they are called sons of God, a theme not called for in the preceeding discussion. But even with this flexion, Justin has to strain the line of argument further in *Dial.* 124, because the text adduced here, Ps 82, does not prove that Christians are called sons of God (unless in a very indirect way). One could say on the contrary that Ps 82:6f tells of how men lost their intended status as sons of God. This is plain in Justin's commentary in *Dial.* 124:3f.

This somewhat awkward transition between *Dial.* 123 and 124 indicates that Justin here is changing sources.

### (i) *Dial.* 124f

Justin's text-critical remarks about Ps 82:7 suggest that the testimony nucleus is to be found in this verse, or perhaps vss 6f. If so, *Dial.* 124 and 125 can be seen to fit together in a nice thematic sequence: Christ conquers (*Dial.*125) where Adam (and Eve) failed (*Dial.* 124). *Dial.* 125 contains an etymology of the name Israel, this is probably the reason why the whole of *Dial.* 124f was included in Justin's exposition. I shall return below to the question which other passages in the Dialogue may be related to *Dial.* 124f (pp. 199f).

*Dial.* 126 - 129 is a repetition of the section on the theophanies within the Christological part of the *Dialogue*, and will be treated below. (pp. 206ff).

### (j) *Dial.* 130 - 133.

Justin begins this section by stating that he will quote some words not previously cited. The quotation which follows is Deut 32:43, a Pauline testimony (Rom 15:10). Exactly the stanza quoted by Paul is the decisive phrase within Justin's long quotation of the whole verse. Justin's contention is that the words «his people» («Rejoice, ye Gentiles, with his people») do not mean all the Jews, but only the patriarchs and prophets and others who were acceptable to God. It almost looks as if Justin is a little worried about a possible implication of the Pauline text. We saw that Justin used Romans in *Dial.* 118f, so he probably reverts to Romans here.

---

40. *Justin*, pp. 298f.

The next quotation, Deut 32:7-9 (*Dial.* 131:1), is subjected to a not very clear exposition in *Dial.* 130:3. On textual grounds, we have posited the use of a testimony source here, which may well be *1.Clem.* 29:2. In *1.Clem.* the Deut text is applied to Christians without further ado. Justin has apparently looked the text up in a Deut MS and has not found this application evident. The text speaks of the election of the Jews, and Justin is only able to retain the reference to Christians by a *qal wa homer* inference: When God could elect the unworthy and disbelieving Jews to become «Jacob» and «Israel», how much more so the believing Christians!

*Dial.* 131:2 - 132:3 contains no explicit quotation. It contrasts the unbelief of Israel during the desert wandering with the belief of Christians. The enumeration of miracles during the wilderness years of Israel contains some incidents treated earlier in the *Dialogue*,[41]follows Ps 78 to a great extent,[42] and contains one non-biblical haggadic embellishment: the clothes «of your young people grew along with them» (131:6). It concludes by contrasting God's favours with Israel's making of the golden calf (132:1). As Prigent points out, this same contrast motive is present elsewhere in the *Dialogue: Dial.* 20:4 and 73:6.[43] To this one may add *Dial.* 19:5: The Jews were «ungrateful» (ἀχάριστος) when they made the golden calf.

In *Dial.* 132:1-3 Justin adds some Joshua typology: sun standing still at the bidding of Joshua; heifers carrying «the tabernacle of witness» (sic!) to the farm of Oshea. Prigent may be right in thinking that another recourse to the source behind *Dial.* 113f is taking place.[44]

*Dial.* 133 - 140:1 has been treated above, pp. 184f.

(k) *Dial.* 140:2 - 141:4.

*Dial.* 140:2 stresses that the Jews should not prefer the tradition of their teachers to God's own commandments, Jer 2:13 and Is 29:13.

*Dial.* 140:3 adds that carnal descent from Abraham is of no avail when it comes to the question of salvation. The testimonies have been treated fully above, pp. 67 - 69/180f.

*Dial.* 141:1-4 emphasizes human (and angelic) free-will and the necessity of repentance. The passage is thus well fitted as a concluding exhortation.

To conclude: *Dial.* 108-141 draws heavily on the same kind of material as we found in *1.Apol.* 39-49 and *Dial.* 11-29. But Justin has made some insertions from other sources. The following table summarizes our results:

---

41. The brazen serpent, Moses' outstreched hands, Joshua defeating Amalek.
42. Cf. Prigent's analysis, p. 303.
43. *Justin*, p. 304.
44. *Justin*, pp. 304f.

| 108-110 | The devastation of Judea, the Law going out from Zion | |
|---|---|---|
| | | 111f Diverse repetitions |
| 113f | Joshua typology, new circumcision | |
| 115f | Joshua the High Priest | |
| 117 | The spiritual sacrifice of the new people | |
| 118 | Transition to the new people theme | |
| 119 | The new people | |
| | | 119-121 Pauline argument: Christians children of Abraham; Christ Abraham's seed |
| 121-123 | Isaiah's prophecies about the Servant refer to Christ | |
| | | 124 f Christ is «Israel», conquering where Adam was conquered |
| | | 126-129 Repetition about theophanies |
| | | 130: Pauline testimony reconsidered |
| | | 131 Deut 32:8f reconsidered |
| 132f | Unfaithful Israel | |
| 133 | Jews slew the Just One | |
| 134 | Jacob-Leah-Rachel typology | |
| 135 | Christ is «Jacob» and «Israel», Christians are the seed of Jacob | |
| 136f | Jews slew the Just One | |
| 138 | Christians inherit Jerusalem through baptism | |
| 139 | Christians inherit the Holy Land | |
| 140f | Concluding remarks: Repentance necessary for Jews also | |

### 3. The proof that Jesus is the Messiah: Dial. 48-107.

It may be convenient to start this analysis with a brief repetition of the material already found to derive from the sources behind *1.Apol.* 32ff. We meant to recognize the following re-adaptions of these sources:

*Dial.* 52-54:  from the »creed« sequence, on Gen 49:10f.

*Dial.* 69f:  from the tract on Greek mythology.

*Dial.* 72:  from the «creed» sequence or a closely related source: Christ the paschal lamb; the descent of Christ.

*Dial.* 73f:  cf. *1.Apol.* 41: Ps 96 - Christ the new Law.

*Dial.* 84:  from the «creed» sequence: Virgin birth, Is 7:14.

*Dial.* 97:  from the «creed» sequence: The passion of the Messiah.

This leaves us with a lot of new, added, material in *Dial.* 48-107. It will be our task to analyze this material, and try to grasp the ways in which Justin has combined it with the material from *1.Apol.* 32ff.

The main outlines in *Dial.* 48ff are easily recognized:

(1) Introductory remarks: Demonstration that Jesus is the Messiah is successful even if demonstration that he pre-existed as God should fail. *Dial.* 48.

(2) The precursor of the Messiah: Elijah/John the Baptist; Gen 49:10f, *Dial.* 49-54.

(3) The divine pre-existence of the Messiah, *Dial.* 55-62.

(4) The virgin birth of the Messiah, *Dial.* 63-86.

       → Appendix: How is divine pre-existence compatible with Is 11:2f? *Dial.* 87f.

(5) The passion and death of the Messiah. *Dial.* 89-106.

(6) The resurrection of the Messiah, *Dial.* 107.

This simple outline conceals, however, a complexity of subdivisions and excurses, especially within section (4). The dispositional remarks also constitute an intricate web, the structure of which is not easily tabulated on the limited space of book pages.

We start with *Dial.* 48-86. The following two analytic tables try to capture the intricate superstructure of dispositional elements and at the same time signalize main blocks of related material.

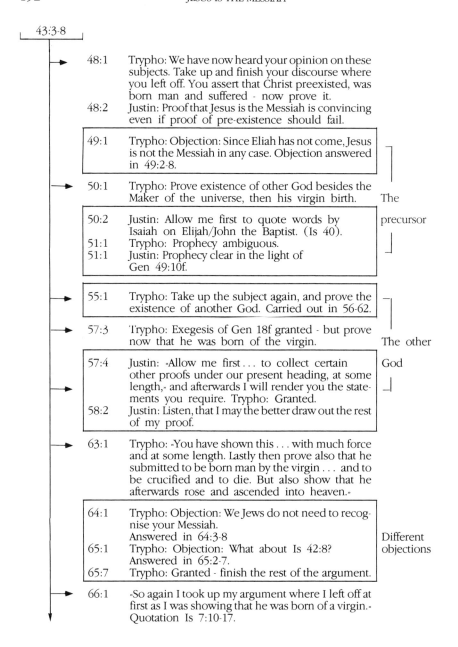

43:3-8

48:1    Trypho: We have now heard your opinion on these subjects. Take up and finish your discourse where you left off. You assert that Christ preexisted, was born man and suffered - now prove it.

48:2    Justin: Proof that Jesus is the Messiah is convincing even if proof of pre-existence should fail.

49:1    Trypho: Objection: Since Eliah has not come, Jesus is not the Messiah in any case. Objection answered in 49:2-8.

50:1    Trypho: Prove existence of other God besides the Maker of the universe, then his virgin birth.

50:2    Justin: Allow me first to quote words by Isaiah on Elijah/John the Baptist. (Is 40).

51:1    Trypho: Prophecy ambiguous.

51:1    Justin: Prophecy clear in the light of Gen 49:10f.

The precursor

55:1    Trypho: Take up the subject again, and prove the existence of another God. Carried out in 56-62.

57:3    Trypho: Exegesis of Gen 18f granted - but prove now that he was born of the virgin.

57:4    Justin: «Allow me first . . . to collect certain other proofs under our present heading, at some length,» and afterwards I will render you the statements you require. Trypho: Granted.

58:2    Justin: Listen, that I may the better draw out the rest of my proof.

The other God

63:1    Trypho: «You have shown this . . . with much force and at some length. Lastly then prove also that he submitted to be born man by the virgin . . . and to be crucified and to die. But also show that he afterwards rose and ascended into heaven.»

64:1    Trypho: Objection: We Jews do not need to recognise your Messiah. Answered in 64:3-8

65:1    Trypho: Objection: What about Is 42:8? Answered in 65:2-7.

65:7    Trypho: Granted - finish the rest of the argument.

Different objections

66:1    «So again I took up my argument where I left off at first as I was showing that he was born of a virgin.» Quotation Is 7:10-17.

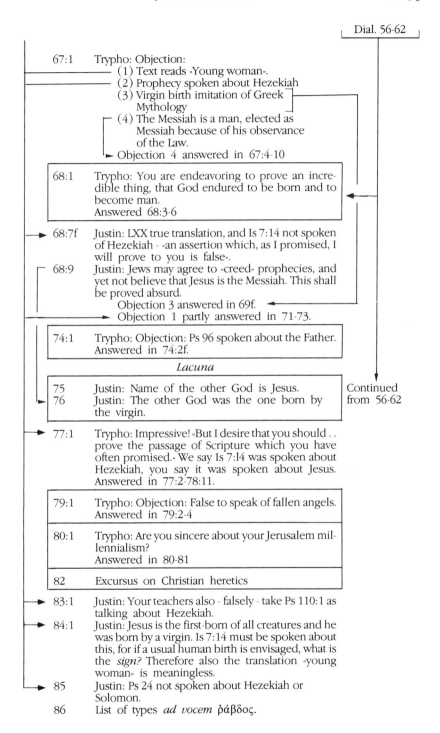

Dial. 56-62

67:1 Trypho: Objection:
(1) Text reads «Young woman».
(2) Prophecy spoken about Hezekiah
(3) Virgin birth imitation of Greek Mythology
(4) The Messiah is a man, elected as Messiah because of his observance of the Law.
Objection 4 answered in 67:4-10

68:1 Trypho: You are endeavoring to prove an incredible thing, that God endured to be born and to become man.
Answered 68:3-6

68:7f Justin: LXX true translation, and Is 7:14 not spoken of Hezekiah - «an assertion which, as I promised, I will prove to you is false».

68:9 Justin: Jews may agree to «creed» prophecies, and yet not believe that Jesus is the Messiah. This shall be proved absurd.
Objection 3 answered in 69f.
Objection 1 partly answered in 71-73.

74:1 Trypho: Objection: Ps 96 spoken about the Father.
Answered in 74:2f.

*Lacuna*

75 Justin: Name of the other God is Jesus.
76 Justin: The other God was the one born by the virgin.

Continued from 56-62

77:1 Trypho: Impressive! «But I desire that you should . . prove the passage of Scripture which you have often promised.» We say Is 7:14 was spoken about Hezekiah, you say it was spoken about Jesus.
Answered in 77:2-78:11.

79:1 Trypho: Objection: False to speak of fallen angels.
Answered in 79:2-4

80:1 Trypho: Are you sincere about your Jerusalem millennialism?
Answered in 80-81

82 Excursus on Christian heretics

83:1 Justin: Your teachers also - falsely - take Ps 110:1 as talking about Hezekiah.

84:1 Justin: Jesus is the first-born of all creatures and he was born by a virgin. Is 7:14 must be spoken about this, for if a usual human birth is envisaged, what is the *sign?* Therefore also the translation «young woman» is meaningless.

85 Justin: Ps 24 not spoken about Hezekiah or Solomon.

86 List of types *ad vocem* ῥάβδος.

As indicated in the tables, many excurses stand out as only loosely integrated into the mainline argument. Mostly, they are prompted by questions from Trypho. We notice the following:

*Dial* 64f: Two excurses on Jewish objections.

*Dial.* 67: Excursus on Jesus' observance of the Law.

*Dial.* 69f: Excursus on Greek mythology (insert from the tract on this subject, cf. above, pp. 148 - 150).

*Dial.* 71-74: Excursus on the LXX; and further excursus on Ps 96, provoked by Trypho (material from the same tradition as the one behind *1.Apol.* 32ff, cf. below, pp. 282ff).

*Dial.* 79: Excursus on demons.

*Dial.* 82: Excursus on Christian heretics.

*Dial.* 92f: Repetition of the argument on the Law in *Dial.* 19-23.

If we subtract this material, we are left with a rather complicated christological argument which we must now analyse in some detail.

(a) *Dial.* 48.

*Dial.* 48 is a kind of prelude to the discussion of the virgin birth and the divine pre-existence of Jesus. The proof that Jesus is the Messiah, says Justin, is compelling even if Trypho should not be convinced of Christ's divine pre-existence and his birth by the virgin. Some scholars have mistakenly concluded that these themes are of minor importance to Justin.[45] That is clearly not the case; on the contrary: It is easily shown that pre-existence and virgin birth are of the utmost importance to Justin (cf. below, 199ff). What Justin wants to say is rather this: Even a Christian with an adoptionist - i.e. defective - Christology, is able to produce a convincing case for Jesus' Messiahship. He wants Trypho to admit this, even if Trypho is not willing to follow Justin's argument for divine pre-existence and virgin birth.

Now, why did Justin pick out these two themes for this kind of comment? It seems he considered the proofs offered in *Dial.* 55f complicated and laborious - more so, perhaps, than the rest of the Christological proof. The exposition following in 55ff makes one believe that especially the idea of divine pre-existence is at stake. If so, it is tempting to read Justin's remarks in *Dial.* 48 as indications of his use of sources: In *Dial.* 49ff Justin is aware of using a more advanced and difficult Christological tradition than the one

---

45. E. R. Goodenough, *Theology*, unwarrantedly makes this inference: «. . . Justin's own belief in the Virgin Birth has not the ring of conviction which he manifests on other points . . . In both the First Apology ( *1.Apol.* 22:1) and the Dialogue ( *Dial.* 48:2f) he admits that the Virgin Birth is not an essential part of the Christian Faith, and says that the divine nature of Christ can be proved quite independently of the story of His birth.»(p. 239). Justin says no such thing. What he says in *Dial.* 48:2f is that the Messiahship of Jesus is demonstrable even if the proof of divine nature and virgin birth (the two cannot be separated for Justin) should not convince Trypho.

used in the *Apology* (in the *Apology* the idea of pre-existence is lacking!). We shall see whether this suggestion can be substantiated in the following analyses.

(b) *Dial.* 49-54/87f: John the Baptist, Gen 49:10f, and Is 11:2f.

Trypho begins by saying that he surely would prefer an adoptionist Christology (cf. *Dial.* 48), but he denies the possibility of proof that Jesus is the Messiah even on these terms, since Elijah has not yet come. Trypho apparently attaches great importance to this argument, because it is the first one he mentions - in *Dial.* 8:4: «But Messiah, if indeed he has ever been and now exists anywhere, is unknown, and does not even know himself at all nor has any power, *until Elijah shall have come and anointed him,* and shall have made him manifest to all.»

Justin's first rebuttal is to introduce the motive of the two parousias: Elijah shall certainly precede Christ - in his second advent! He even was Christ's precursor in the first parousia, but in a lowly fashion corresponding to the inglorious fashion of the first advent: John the Baptist was »Elijah« because the spirit of Elijah was conferred to him (*Dial.* 49:2-8).

Justin now uses one of his favourite techniques to underline the superabundance of proofs he is able to marshall: He lets Trypho declare himself satisfied before Justin has finished all he has to say on the subject (*Dial.* 50:1). *Dial.* 50:2-6 then quotes a vastly expanded version of the synoptic testimony on John, Is 40:3. *Dial.* 51 brings out the argumentative value of this quotation. The cry ἑτοιμάσατε τὰς ὁδοὺς κυρίου, are the words of a prophetic forerunner, more precisely, the last prophet. To drive home this point, Justin then in *Dial.* 52-54 combines the forerunner motive with his earlier treatment of Gen 49:10f in the *Apology.* There is, however, one important modification. In *1.Apol.* 32 Justin was satisfied to report the fulfilment of Gen 49:10 in very simple terms: «You can enquire precisely and learn up to whose time the Jews had their own ruler and king . . . after his (Christ's) appearance you (Romans) began to rule over the Jews and gained control of their whole land» (*1.Apol.* 32:2f). In *Dial.* 52 Justin is aware that this is too simple. The Jewish kingdom ceased in Israel before Jesus appeared. The Jews can rightly point out that Herod was not a Jew, *Dial.* 52:3.

Justin retorts that (1) the office of High Priest continued until the time of Jesus, and (2) the office of prophet likewise continued until Jesus. «There never ceased a prophet from among you who was κύριος and ἡγούμενος and ἄρχων of your people. For the spirit in the prophets *used to anoint and appoint even your kings.* One gets the impression that Justin is more satisfied with the second of these answers, partly because it allows him to bring in John the Baptist again, and thus link the exposition of Gen 49:10 to the Elijah theme. The sentence I underlined above is especially relevant:

The Jewish kings received their anointing from the spirit present in the prophets - Elijah's spirit was present in John.[46]

Everything here builds up to the conclusion that Jesus received his messianic anointing from John. That would be a perfect answer to Trypho's challenge in *Dial.* 8:3 and 49:1.[47]

But Justin never draws this conclusion. The elaborate exposition about Elijah's spirit being transferred to John (*Dial.* 49:3-8), and the Jewish kings being anointed by the spirit present in the prophets - runs out into nearly nothing in *Dial.* 52-54. There is no question of John anointing Jesus; on the contrary, what happens is that Jesus does something to John: He makes him stop prophesying and baptizing (*Dial.* 51:2; 52:3f)!

Let us take as a working hypothesis that Justin in *Dial.* 49-51 is employig a source which argued that Jesus received his messianic anointing from John = »Elijah«, and which conceived of the messianic anointing as an anointing with the Spirit. We now turn to test this surmise on the partly parallel section *Dial.* 87f.

Trypho here raises an objection on the basis of Is 11:2f: If the Messiah pre-exists as God, why should he need to be endowed with the gifts of the Spirit enumerated in Is 11:2f (*Dial.* 87:2)? One notices that Trypho does not directly mention the baptism of Jesus. This corresponds to the fact that Justin in *Dial.* 87:3—88:2 finishes his discussion on Is 11:2f without even once mentioning that Jesus was baptized by John! This is not accidental. Indirectly, Justin refuses to connect Is 11:2f with Jesus' baptism.[48] Nevertheless, Justin in *Dial.* 88:3-8 goes on to treat Jesus' baptism quite extensively, without any provocation from Trypho. Again one gets the impression that Justin is working with a source in which Is 11:2f and Jesus' baptism were joined,[49] and this would accord perfectly with the idea inherent in the material used in *Dial.* 49-51.

Now, let us take a closer look at Justin's exegesis of Is 11:2f. The decisive phrase is ἀναπαύσεται ἐπ' αὐτὸν πνεῦμα θεοῦ. One should expect an interpretation along the lines of John 1:32f (... καὶ ἔμεινεν ἐπ' αὐτὸν): the Spirit should find its lasting *rest* in Jesus, i.e. abide permanently on him. Traces of this exegesis are to be found in *Dial.* 87:5: «... those gifts ... when

---

46. P. Beskow surmises that the Jewish idea that the oil of anointing disappeared in Joshia's day is Justin's target, *Rex Gloriae*, p. 115.

47. E. Bammel, 'Die Täufertraditionen bei Justin', *Studia Patristica* 8 (TU 93, Berlin, 1966, pp. 53-61), speaks about »die Taufe als eine Salbung durch Elias - dies Herzstück der Argumentation gegen Tryphon...« (p. 58). True, that would be the final stroke in Justin's argument, but Bammel seems not to have noticed that Justin never pins down this »Herzstück«.

48. This is overlooked by some commentators who say that Justin takes Is 11:2f as a testimony on the baptism of Jesus - e.g. K. Schlütz, *Isaias 11:2 (die sieben Gaben des Hl. Geistes) in den ersten vier christlichen Jahrhunderten* (Alttestamentliche Abhandlungen 11:4, Münster im Westf., 1932), pp. 43-46; Beskow, *Rex Gloriae*, pp. 114f,

49. This is observed by D. A. Bertrand, *Le baptême de Jesus. Histoire de l'exégèse aux deux premiers siècles* (BGBE 14, Tübingen, 1973), p. 94, n. 1.

they had taken their rest in Christ (ἀνάπαυσιν λαβόντα), should... be given by the gracce of the power of that Spirit to them that believe on him...»

That is: Because the Spirit found permanent rest on Christ, he is now the spender of *charismata.* The same idea is also embodied in *Dial.* 39:2, where a list of Christian *charismata* is inspired by Is 11:2 (and 1 Cor 12:8-10).[50]

But this exegesis of ἀναπαύσεται is only hinted at by Justin. The main thrust of his argument in *Dial.* 87 goes in another direction: ἀνάπαυσιν ποιεῖσθαι means πέρας ποιεῖσθαι, *Dial.* 87:3. With Christ the *charismata* (among the Jews) should *cease.* ἀνεπαύσατο ... τοῦτ᾽ ἔστιν ἐπαύσατο, *Dial.* 87:5.

This is an exegesis assimilated to Justin's ideas about the relation between John and Jesus in *Dial.* 49-51: Just as Jesus made John cease prophesying and baptizing, so he puts an end to the distribution of the gifts of the Spirit among the Jews. One suspects that Justin here also diverts the intention of his source. Unless Is 11:2f and the baptism of Jesus were joined in Justin's source, it is difficult to understand why he should bring in Jesus' baptism (*Dial.* 88:3-8) at all.

In his treatment of Jesus' baptism, Justin has one concern: Nothing happened to Jesus - everything had a proclamatory significance only. Even the descent of the dove had only a proclamatory function: «We know that he did not come to the river (Jordan) as though He were in need ... of the Holy Spirit coming upon him in the form of a dove ...»(*Dial.* 88:4); «... the Holy Spirit fluttered down on him in the form of a dove, for men's sake ...» (*Dial.* 88:8).

Let me add a final observation: Justin is unusually laudatory in his answer to Trypho's question concerning Is 11:2f: «You have asked a most sensible and intelligent question; for indeed it does seem to be a puzzle» (*Dial.* 87:3). I take this to mean that Justin has put into the mouth of Trypho a difficulty Justin himself felt concerning the John = «Elijah» source with which he is working in *Dial.* 49-51 and *Dial.* 87f. The source in all probability understood the baptism of Jesus as a messianic anointing with the Spirit. Justin felt this too risky and open to adoptionist Christology. That is why he diverts the argument in *Dial.* 87f, and deprives the line of thought in *Dial.* 49ff of its final stroke.

Now, in which context in Justin's Christological material would the idea of Messianic anointing fit in? We notice once again Trypho's challenge in *Dial.* 8:4: «But Messiah, if indeed He has ever been and now exists anywhere, is unknown and does not even know Himself at all nor has any power,

---

50. Concerning Justin's list of charismata, cf. Schlütz, *op. cit,* pp. 41f; C. Oeyen, 'Die Lehre der göttlichen Kräfte bei Justin', *Studia Patristica* 11 (TU 108, Berlin, 1972), pp. 215-221; Prigent, *Justin,* pp. 112f.

until Elijah shall have come and anointed Him, and shall have made Him manifest to all.» Trypho here clearly hints at a distinct concept: the *hiddenness* of the Messiah previous to his *anointing* by Elijah. One is immediately reminded of *1.Apol.* 35:1:«How the Messiah after his birth was to live *hidden from other men* until he grew to manhood, . . . hear the predictions . . .» In the «creed» sequence in the *Apology* Is 11:2f would fit admirably as the testimony on Messianic anointing with the Spirit. The idea that Elijah and his prophetic successors used to anoint the kings, and that the final «Elijah» (John) anointed the final King (Jesus), seems perfectly adapted to the first testimony in the «creed» sequence: Gen 49:10 (the final King of Judah). Besides, the two parousias motif, connected with the «creed» sequence, seems integral also to the «Elijah» material in *Dial.* 49.

I conclude that there is a great probability that Justin's suppressed material on Messianic anointing (Is 11:2f in *Dial.* 49-51 and 87f) derives from the «creed» sequence employed in the *Apology*. In any case it is so close to the «creed» material in theological profile that I regard it as part of the same tradition.

But was Justin's suppression of the anointing concept just his own idea, or does he also employ another source with a different orientation? Let us take a closer look at Justin's account of Jesus' baptism. The narrative in *Dial.* 88:3.8 is clearly divided in two parts, each of which receives its proper comment:[51]

(1) «When Jesus came to the river Jordan . . .
    (a) when Jesus went down to the water,
       fire was even kindled in the Jordan,
    (b) and when he was rising up from the water,
       the Holy Spirit fluttered down upon him as it were a dove,
    as the Apostles of this our Christ himself has written.«
Comment:  Christ was not in need
       (a) of being baptized, nor
       (b) of receiving the Holy Spirit.
       But like his birth and crucifixion it was on
       behalf of men, who »from the time of Adam had
       fallen under death and the deceit of the serpent,
       each man acting ill by his own fault.«
(2) »When Jesus came to the Jordan, being supposed to be the son of
    Joseph the carpenter . . .
    (b´) the Holy Spirit fluttered down on him . . . as I said before,
    (c) and a voice came at the same time out of the heavens» —
       it had been predicted by David - «Thou art my Son, to-day
       have I begotten thee.»

---

51. This is not sufficiently noticed by Bammel, *art. cit.*, who tends to contrast the two parts of the narrative.

Comment: This means that Christ's »birth« began for men when he was
proclaimed to them.

Except for element a, Justin's narrative is a harmonization of the synoptic
accounts. There are some other non-synoptic details in the context, however, which may indicate a non-synoptic source besides the synoptic Gospels.[52] Be that as it may, what is important in our context, is to determine the
interpretation of Jesus' baptism inherent in Justin's narrative. I think one has
to emphasize the Son of God concept. Men believed that Jesus was the son
of Joseph, but the heavenly voice proclaimed him as God's son. In line with
this, *Dial.* 88:4f presents Christ as the second Adam, conquering where
Adam was conquered. It is relevant to emphasise that this narrative does not
seem adapted to the concept of Jesus' baptism as an anointing carried out
by John. John is not active at all in the baptism proper.[53] In other words: The
narrative is well chosen by Justin, and it hardly presupposes an application
of Is 11:2f to the baptism of Jesus. This strengthens the assumption that
Justin's narrative derives from a source which regards Christ as endowed
with his full *dynamis* from his birth, cf. *Dial.* 77f which will be examined in
some detail below.

Let us conclude. It seems that Justin in *Dial.* 87f is labouring with two
sources: one which conceived of Jesus' baptism as a Messianic anointing,
fulfilling Is 11:2f; and another which conceived of the event in different
categories, stressing Christ as the second Adam, fully endowed with his
dynamis *before* his baptism (*Dial.* 88:2). We shall see if we can trace more
material from this second source as we now turn to Justin's treatment of the
virgin birth.

(c) *Dial.* 63f; 66; 77-85 (par. 31-38/43): The virgin birth.

In *Dial.* 63:2f and 76:1-3.7 we encounter a cluster of short qutations and
allusions, all concentrating on the virgin birth. *Dial.* 43:3 and 45:4 have
traces of the same cluster.

| *Dial.* 43:3 | *Dial.* 63:2f | *Dial.* 76:1f.7 |
|---|---|---|
|  |  | Dan 7:13      *Dial.* 100:3f |
|  |  | Dan 2:34 |
| Is 53:8 | Is 53:8 | Is 53:8 |
|  | Gen 49:11 |  |
| *Dial.* 45:4 | Ps 110:3f | Ps 110:3 |
|  |  | Ps 72:5/17 |
| Ps 110:3 | (Ps 45:13) | Ps 45:13 |
| Ps 72:5 |  |  |

52. Cf. Bammel, *art. cit.*, and W. Bauer, *Leben Jesu*, pp. 134-139.

53. One could argue that the rendering of the heavenly voice according to Ps 2:7 is an expression
of adoptionist Christology. But this I doubt. The author of the narrative may have done no
more than recognizing the allusion to Ps 2:7 in the synoptic version of the voice, and then
»correcting« the text to agree perfectly with the OT text. One should note that in Justin the
heavenly voice is not rendered as part of the narrative, but as an OT predicition of what was
going to be said at Jesus' baptism.

The point Justin wanted to make by these testimonies is formulated with great uniformity: The Messiah should not be of human seed / not be of human origin. The position against which these texts are used by Justin is not difficult to discern. Cf. Trypho in *Dial.* 49:1: «All of us Jews expect that Christ will be man of human origin (ἄνθρωπος ἐξ ἀνθρώπων).... one must certainly acknowledge that he is man of human origin.» Trypho in *Dial.* 67:2: «You should rather say that this Jesus was man of human origin.» In *Dial.* 68:5 he puts against Is 53:8 a paraphrase of 2.Sam 7:12-16: «How then does the word say to David that of his loins (ἀπὸ τῆς ὀσφύος)[54] God will take to himself a son, and will establish the kingdom for him and will set him on the throne of his glory?» A human Messiah of David's seed, that is what Trypho presents as the Jewish expectation, an ἄνθρωπος ἐξ ἀνθρώπων.[55]

Intimately bound up with the idea that the Messiah is not an ἄνθρωπος ἐξ ἀνθρώπων, is the idea that he - therefore - has divine, superhuman power over Satan and demons. *Dial.* 45:4: «Now he was also before Morning Star and moon, and endured to be made flesh and be born by this Virgin who was of the race of David, in order that by this dispensation of God the serpent who did evil in the beginning, and the angels who became like it, might be destroyed...» *Dial.* 76:6: «'I give you authority to tread upon serpents and scorpions ... and on every form of the enemy's power.' So now we who believe on Jesus our Lord who was crucified under Pontius Pilate exorcise all the demons and evil spirits, and thus hold them subject to us.»

No doubt these texts and ideas are meant to substantiate the Christian interpretation of the textually disputed testimony Is 7:14. They testify the pre-existence (Ps 110:3; Ps 72:5/17) and non-human origin of the Messiah (Is 53:8; Dan 2:34; - are Gen 49:11 and Dan 7:13 Justin's own additions *ad hoc?*); further his being worthy of *proskynesis*, Ps 45:13.

This tendency to circumvent the textually problematic Is 7:14 is also present in the main treatment of Is 7:10ff in the *Dialogue*. The burden of proof hinges not on this verse, but on the interpolated verse Is 8:4. The connexion between Is 7:10ff and the cluster of testimonies we have been studying is further brought out by the fact that they serve as introductions to the two quotations of Is 7:10ff (*Dial.* 43:3ff: Is 53:8 ⟶ Is 7:10ff - followed by other texts from the cluster in *Dial.* 45:4. *Dial.* 76-78: The whole cluster ⟶ Is 7:10ff ⟶ main discussion of this text). If we take as a working

---

54. The LXX in 2 Sam 7:12 has ἐκ τῆς κοιλίας (=MT) while 2 Chron 6:9 reads ἐκ τῆς ὀσφύος. This last phrase is perhaps chosen in *Dial.* 68:5 to underline that the Messiah is *of David's seed.* Also in other respects the paraphrase has a slight adoptionist flavour: λήψεται ἑαυτῷ υἱὸν ...

55. Justin does not deny the davidic lineage of Jesus. He is even able - like other writers of the second century - to avoid a merely adoptionist davidic lineage through Joseph: the davidic lineage runs through Mary. Cf. W. Bauer, *Das Leben Jesu im Zeitalter der neutestamentlichen Apokryphen* (Tubingen, 1909), pp. 27ff.

hypothesis that this cluster of testimonies belonged to Is 7:10ff as auxiliary and corroborating testimonies, this would throw light on the connexion between *Dial.* 32-38 and *Dial.* 43. It is easily seen that the auxiliary virgin birth testimonies to a large extent coincide with the Psalms quoted in *Dial.* 32-38: Ps 110; Ps 72; Ps 45. We saw above that this section of the *Dialogue* (*Dial.* 30-39) was based on the new law testimonies in *1.Apol.* 39ff. But we also indicated (p. 177) that another source might be employed. It is now time to pursue that suggestion.

We find in *Dial.* 32-36 a Jesus-versus-Hezekiah (Ps 110. *Dial.* 32:1) and a Jesus-versus-Solomon polemic (*Dial.* 34:1f *ad* Ps 72; *Dial.* 36:2.6 *ad* Ps 24) which is not directly called for by the new law theme. A similar Jesus-versus-Hezekiah polemic is, however, basic to Justin's exposition of Is 7:10ff. If we take it that the same polemic was attached to the testimonies associated with Is 7:10ff also, this may explain the occurrence of this motive in *Dial.* 32-36.

If this is right, two sets of testimonies are hidden behind the long LXX excerpts in *Dial.* 30-39: the new law testimonies, and the virgin birth testimonies. This would explain the rather abrupt introduction of Is 7:10ff and the virgin birth theme in *Dial.* 43.

We now turn to the main section on Is 7:10ff, *Dial.* 63ff. Trypho demands proof for the virgin birth, *Dial.* 63:1, and Justin answers by enumerating some relevant texts, Is 53:8; Gen 49:11; Ps 110:3 (*Dial.* 63:2f).But then he seems to digress into a chain of quotations having no relevance: Ps 45:7-12; Ps 99:1-7; Ps 72:1-19 (vss. 6-16 omitted); Ps 19:2-7 (*Dial.* 63 - 64:8).In *Dial.* 65 there is a digression caused by Trypho, in *Dial.* 66 there follows a quotation of Is 7:10-17 (Is 8:4 interpolated in vs. 16, see above, p. 132), and after several digressions in *Dial.* 67-75, Justin is back to his theme in *Dial.* 76-78, explaining the meaning of Is 7:10ff (Is 8:4). As an introduction, Justin quotes some of the other virgin birth testimonies, Dan 7:13; Dan 2:34; Is 53:8; Gen 49:11, expands on the rule of Christ (quoting Is 9:5b), and alludes to Ps 72:5/17; Ps 110:3; Ps 19:6?; Ps 45:13 (*Dial.* 76). After two more digressions in *Dial.* 79 and 80-82, Justin finishes his discussion in *Dial.* 83-85: Ps 110:1 does not refer to Hezekiah; Is 7:14 is meaningless unless it predicts something wonderful; Ps 24 does not refer to Solomon, Hezekiah, or any other Jewish king.[56] (In *Dial.* 87 we find again the last testimony in the *Dial.* 30-39 sequence, Ps 68:19).

To summarize: In *Dial.* 63:3 - 64:8; 66; 77f; 83:1 - 85:4 Justin is re-using the material in *Dial.* 30-38.43. The whole sequence is triggered by the quotation of Ps 110:3 in *Dial.* 63:3, and prepares the discussion of Is 7:10ff

---

56. In *Dial.* 85:7-9 Justin adds a quotation of Is 66:5-11, purportedly to motivate his great patience in repeating Scriptural passages. His introduction, however, reveals that the text had another orientation: «. . . the mystery of the new birth» (of Christians). On this testimony, cf. Appendix I:E.

in *Dial.* 77f. The apparent deviation in the line of thought in *Dial.* 63:4ff is thus more apparent than real.

The quotation sequence in *Dial.* 30-39/43 is partly based on a source treating the virgin birth, in which a polemic against Jewish attribution of Is 7:14 etc. to Hezekiah played a great role. The testimonies in this source partly crop up in *Dial.* 63:2 and *Dial.* 76.

Now let us take a closer look at Justin's exposition of Is 7:10ff in *Dial.* 77f. The argument is summarized in the following table.

|  | *Dial.* 77f |
|---|---|
| 77:2f | Is 8:4 does not suit Hezekiah. |
| 77:4 | Short paraphrase of Mt 2:1-12, introducing the Magi theme. |
| 78:1f | A more extensive rendering of Mt 2:1-12, including fulfilment quotation Mic 5:1. |
| 78:3 | Paraphrase of Mt 1:18-20. |
| 78:4 | Paraphrase of Mt 1:24; Lk 2:1-5; Mt 2:13. |
| 78:5 | Allusions to Lk 2:6f; Mt 2:1-12, with mention of a cave as the place of Christ's birth, cf. *Protev. Jacobi* 18-21. |
| 78:6 | Prophetical testimony (Is 33:16, cf. *Dial.* 70:1-3) and demonic imitation of the cave. |
| 78:7f | Paraphrase of Mt 2:14-18 including quotation of the fulfilment citation Jer 31:15. |
| 78:9f | Application of Is 8:4 to the Magi story, Mt 2:1-12. |

It is obvious that Mt 2:1-12 is the nucleus around which the remaining material from Mt and Lk is arranged as auxiliary or merely embellishing evidence . Let us note that this use of Mt 2:1-12 may explain why Ps 45:13 was included in the testimony cluster studied above. Ps 45:13: καὶ προσκυνήσεις αὐτῷ, Mt 2:11:καὶ πεσόντες προσεκύνησαν αὐτῷ.

It is obvious that Justin here employs a source quite different from the rather unpolemical tract on the virgin birth in *1.Apol.* 33. There, Justin was content to quote Is 7:14 and report the fulfilment (Lk 1:31f/Mt 1:21). The treatment in the *Dialogue* works with other gospel material and is much more polemically developed. The main argument against application to Hezekiah is that Is 8:4 describes a super-human feat never accomplished by him. This prophecy announces a king who will set men free from demons *already while he is still a baby.* Cf. *Dial.* 88:2:«For even when He was born He held his power (δύναμιν τὴν αὐτοῦ).» Justin is here answering part of Trypho's challenge in *Dial.* 8:4: If the Messiah exists, he is unknown and has *no* δύναμις. It would seem that Justin's material in *Dial.* 77f perfectly matches the tendency of the narrative of Jesus' baptism in *Dial.* 88:3-8.

One is further reminded of the exposition in *Dial.* 76:6 (Christ's rule over demons), and the anti-Hezekiah and anti-Solomon polemics in *Dial.* 32-36 and 83:

(1) Ps 110 cannot be applied to Hezekiah, because the Psalm envisages an eternal priest (vs. 4), a divine role not fulfilled by Hezekiah, *Dial.* 33:1.

Ps 110:1f does not suit Hezekiah, for he did not rule in the midst of his enemies. Christ rules over his enemies, the demons. *Dial.* 83:1-4.

(2) Ps 72 cannot be applied to Solomon, for his reign was not universal and he was not lord over the demons, on the contrary, he was their slave. *Dial.* 34:7f.

(3) Ps 24 is not referring to Solomon (or Hezekiah, *Dial.* 85:2f), for he was not κύριος τῶν δυνάμεων, *Dial.* 36:5: 85:1-3.

The controversy is formulated in a general way in *Dial.* 68:8: «Whatever (your teachers think) they can drag into supposed agreement with human actions, this they say was not spoken of our Jesus Christ, but of him of whom they endeavour to explain it. Thus this passage also (Is 7:14) which we are now discussing, they have taught you is spoken of Hezekiah . . . »

To conclude: Justin's argument on the virgin birth in *Dial.* 77f derives from a source in which Jesus the Son of God, the second Adam, is contrasted with Hezekiah and Solomon. They were only human, while the Son of God is divine and has power over Satan and demons. This *dynamis* he had from the very beginning, even as a baby.

In this source, the textually disputed Is 7:14 is bolstered by a cluster of supporting testimonies, and passages like *Dial.* 32-36; 43; 63f; 66; 76; 83-85 seem to draw on the same source. Its theological outlook is clearly of the «recapitulation» type.

It may be convenient at this point to include an analysis of the apparently unmotivated insertion of the millienarian material in *Dial.* 80f.

(d) *Dial.* 80f and parallels: The millennium.

I think one can suggest a connexion between *Dial.* 83 and the excursus on the millennium in *Dial.* 80-81. As we have seen above, the deviant version of Ps 110 in *Dial.* 83 is perfectly adapted to the anti-Hezekiah polemics found in *Dial.* 83:3: Hezekiah was not the redeemer of Jerusalem. He did not rule over his enemies in Jerusalem. As the positive counterpart to this, *Dial.* 80f is perfect: *Christ* shall rule in Jerusalem together with his believers. *He* is the redeemer of Jerusalem!

Let me add an observation on *Dial.* 32f at this point. This passage is the first in which Jesus-versus-Hezekiah polemics occurs, called forth by a quotation of Ps 110:1-7 (LXX). The introduction to the quotation contains some seemingly irrelevant elements (underlined in the following quotation): « In order therefore that the subject under discussion may be clearer to you, I will say to you also other words which have been spoken by blessed David, from which you will see that Christ has been called even Lord by the Holy Spirit of prophecy and that the Father . . . was leading him up from the earth and seating him on his right hand, until he should make his enemies his footstool. *For this comes to pass from the time that our Lord Jesus Christ was taken up into heaven after his rising from the dead. For the times were nigh completion, and he that was to speak bold and blasphemous words against the Most High was already at the doors, who, Daniel declares, will hold dominion for a season, seasons and half a season»* (*Dial.* 32:3). To this Justin adds a polemic against Jewish exegesis of Dan 7:25: It is not right to interpret «a season» as a hundred years. Justin does not state what the right interpretation is, and ends hastily with an apology for the whole excursus on Dan 7:25: «And all these things which I said by way of digression do I say unto you, in order that . . . you may cease leading both yourselves and them that hear you astray». One gets the impression that Justin is here abbreviating a much richer source which contained polemic exegesis of Ps 110:1 in conjunction with Dan 7:25. The correct exegesis of Dan 7:25 according to Justin is probably the one found in Rev 11:2; 13:5. The Jewish exegesis destroys Christian *Naherwartung.* In Justin's source Ps 110:1 must have been set in an apocalyptic framework: Christ's enemies are made his footstool even through the last climax of opposition, cf. also *Dial.* 110:2: In the second parousia Christ «will come with glory from the heavens, when also the Man of apostasy, who also speaketh strange things against the Most High, will dare to do lawless deeds on earth against us Christians.»

This common link to apocalyptic motives in *Dial.* 32 and *Dial.* 80f may be a further indication that in the Jesus-versus-Hezekiah source employed in both places, apocalyptic millennialism played an important role in the discussion. Trypho's question in *Dial.* 80:1 - quoted above - seems to imply that the millennial kingdom in Jerusalem had been the final masterstroke in Justin's argument concerning Jesus versus Hezekiah. This cannot be said to be the case in the present text of the *Dialogue,* but may very well have been the case in Justin's source - and we do not know the exact contents of the lacuna in *Dial.* 74:3f. On this problem, see below, pp. 213 - 215.

But this anti-Hezekiah motiv is hardly the only link which connects *Dial.* 80f with the other «recapitulation» passages in the *Dialogue.* There is in *Dial.* 80f. a distinct «recapitulation» concept in Justin's exegetical argument on Is 65:17-25. It is only hinted at quite incidentally, and may have been more fully developed in the source containing the non-LXX reading upon which Justin builds his exegesis (cf. above, p. 67). The millennial exegesis of Is 65:22 is obtained by a combination of eschatology with the story of Adam's fall in Paradise. In the millennium, the *reversal of Adam's fall* reaches its fulfilment: The people of God enjoys a Paradisic «day», like Adams «day», but receiving life where Adam earned death.

Finally, the excursus on demonology in *Dial.* 79 is not unrelated to the dominant role played by the idea of Christ's rule over demons in the Jesus-versus-Hezekiah polemic. It may well derive from the same source, but the lack of parallels precludes safe conclusions.[57]

Are there other passages in the *Dialogue* which derive from this millennial tradition? *Dial.* 118:2 is a likely candidate. Justin here first renders the

---

57. I do not feel convinced by Prigent's argument for the unity of *Dial.* 79 and *Dial.* 80f, *Justin,* pp. 21-24.

Nathan prophecy in an interesting version: It is not taken from 2 Sam 7:14-16, but from the slightly different parallel in 1 Chron 17:13f.[58]

| 2 Sam 7 LXX | 1 Chron 17 LXX | *Dial.* 118:2 |
|---|---|---|
| vs. 14 ἐγὼ ἔσομαι αὐτῷ εἰς πατέρα καὶ αὐτὸς ἔσται μοι εἰς υἱόν καὶ ἐὰν ἔλθῃ ἡ ἀδικία αὐτοῦ καὶ ἐλέγξω αὐτὸν ἐν ῥάβδῳ ἀνδρῶν καὶ ἐν ἁφαῖς υἱῶν ἀνθρώπων vs. 15 τὸ δὲ ἔλεός μου οὐκ ἀποστήσω ἀπ᾽ αὐτοῦ καθὼς ἀπέστησα ἀφ᾽ ὧν ἀπέστησα ἐκ προσώπου μου vs. 16 καὶ πιστωθήσεται ὁ οἶκος αὐτοῦ καὶ ἡ βασιλεία αὐτοῦ ἕως αἰῶνος ... | vs. 13 ἐγὼ ἔσομαι αὐτῷ εἰς πατέρα καὶ αὐτὸς ἔσται μοι εἰς υἱόν καὶ τὸ ἔλεός μου οὐκ ἀποστήσω ἀπ᾽ αὐτοῦ ὡς ἀπέστησα ἀπὸ τῶν ὄντων ἔμπροσθέν σου vs. 14 καὶ πιστώσω αὐτὸν ἐν οἴκῳ μου καὶ ἐν βασιλείᾳ αὐτοῦ ἕως αἰῶνος. | ἐγὼ ἔσομαι αὐτῷ εἰς πατέρα καὶ αὐτὸς ἔσται μοι εἰς υἱόν καὶ τὸ ἔλεός μου οὐ μὴ ἀποστήσω ἀπ᾽ αὐτοῦ καθὼς ἐποίησα ἀπὸ τῶν ἔμπροσθεν αὐτοῦ καὶ στήσω αὐτὸν[a] ἐν τῷ οἴκῳ μου καὶ ἐν τῇ βασιλείᾳ αὐτοῦ ἕως αἰῶνος. |

a) = MT: והעמדתיהו

As is shown in the synopsis, Justin's version is closer to the Hebrew of 1 Chron 17 than the LXX text: Justin has correctly στήσω for והעמדתיהו , while the LXX seems influenced by the parallel in 2 Sam. This is an indication that we have to do with testimony material.

The relevant question in our context is which meaning Justin attached to the last phrase of the Nathan oracle: στήσω αὐτὸν ἐν τῷ οἴκῳ μου καὶ ἐν τῇ βασιλείᾳ αὐτοῦ. Justin at once comments on the «house» by referring to Ezekiel: «And Ezekiel says that the ruler (ὁ ἡγούμενος) in the house (ἐν τῷ οἴκῳ) is no other than this one (i.e. Christ). For he is the chosen Priest ...» Archambault and Goodspeed in their editions give Ezek 44:3 as the reference, this is taken over by the BP I. The Ezekiel passage reads: διότι ὁ ἡγούμενος, οὗτος καθήσεται ἐν αὐτῇ (sc. the gate of the new temple) τοῦ φαγεῖν ἄρτον ἐναντίον κυρίου. It seems the editors have fastened on the term ἡγούμενος as pointing to this passage in Ezekiel, but the text does not speak about the «ruler» fulfilling priestly functions in the «house», i.e. the temple. One need not seek far, however, to find a text which precisely ascribes such a function to the ruler, and which contains some other catchwords also found in Justin, viz. Ezek 45:17-25. The Messianic ἀφηγού

---

58. This is not observed by Archambault or Goodspeed in their editions of Justin' text - they give 2 Sam 7:14-16 as the reference. This is taken over by Haeuser, L. Williams, and Falls, and is also the reference given in the *BP* I.

μενος⁵⁹ is here portrayed as leading a sacrificial cult with θυσίαι and σπονδαί (vs. 17); in vs. 19 we find the catchwords αἷμα, οἶκος, and θυσιαστήριον. This corresponds perfectly to Justin's comment on the Ezekiel allusion: «And do not think that Isaiah or the other prophets say that when he appears again sacrifices (θυσίας) of blood (αἷμα) or of drink-offerings (σπονδαί) will be offered on the altar (θυσιαστήριον). They speak only of true and spiritual praises and thanksgivings.»

Justin is in *Dial.* 118:2 combining the last phrase of the Nathan oracle with the Ezekiel prophecy about the new Jerusalem, the new Temple, and the priestly functions of the Messiah in the new Temple,⁶⁰ esp. Ezek 45:17-25. To Justin's mind - or in the concept of his source - this explains what is meant by στήσω αὐτὸν ἐν τῷ οἴκῳ μου. But he has obviously felt a need to ward off a too literal understanding of the restoration of the Temple cult envisaged by Ezekiel.

Justin's concept of a rebuilt «house» of the Lord in Jerusalem, in which Christ is officiating as a High priest, has the ring of being a millennial concept, and his cautions rather strengthens than weakens this impression. I take as a working hypothesis that this material is somehow related to the millennarian tradition of *Dial.* 80f, and tentatively subsume it under the heading of the «recapitulation» source.

We have now finished the analysis of the material most intimately connected with Justin's treatment of the virgin birth, and go on to analyse the material on Christ's divine pre-existence.


(e) *Dial.* 55-62; 75: The divine pre-existence

Although the testimonies on the virgin birth clearly contain the idea of pre-existence (Ps 72:5/17; Ps 110:3), Justin never *argues* the pre-existence of Jesus from these texts. He has reserved this argument for the closely knit and self-contained exposition in *Dial.* 56-62 (par. 126-129 ). Since *Dial.* 128:1 also contains a repetition of *Dial.* 75, I shall include this latter chapter in the following analysis.

The argument in *Dial.* 56-62/75 can most briefly be delineated like this: There exists besides God the Father another God (*Dial.* 56-62), whose name is Jesus (*Dial.* 75). Obviously, Justin has regarded the occurrence of the very name of Jesus a great strength of this argument, cf. Trypho in *Dial.* 89:1: «. . . I acknowledge that the name Jesus has impressed me . . .»

---

59. Rendering MT   נשׂיא   . The LXX rendering of this Hebrew term varies: ἡγούμενος in Ezek 44:3; 45:7; ἀφηγούμενος in 12:10; 21:17.30; 22:6; 45:8.16f.22; 46:2.4.8.10.12.16-18; 48:21f; ἄρχων in 7:27; 19:1; 26:16; 27:21; 30:13; 32:29; 34:24; 37:25; 38:2f; 39:1.18.
60. The rabbis have polemic utterances against identifying the priest of the rebuilt Temple with the Messiah, cf. Klausner, *Messianic Idea*, p. 515.

Now, in itself this argument neither speaks of incarnation nor virgin birth. Trypho tries to exploit this, and Justin is therefore at pains to connect this argument with the virgin birth theme. In *Dial.* 75 he does this simply by taking the two themes together: «If then we know that that God (bearing the name Jesus) has been made manifest to Abraham ... how can we be at a loss, and not believe that according to the will of the Father of the universe he can also have been born man by a virgin - when we have, besides, so many passages of Scripture from which we may clearly understand that even this has taken place ...» The 'many passages of Scripture' here clearly refers to the virgin birth testimonies, but one cannot say that Justin really succeeds in proving that the one born by the virgin is identical with the second God called Jesus. The same weakness is implied in the sequence *Dial.* 56-62/63ff.

In *Dial.* 68, however, Justin has a more detailed argument. Trypho begins by saying that his previous objections to Justin are motivated by the fact that «you are endeavouring to prove an incredible and almost impossible thing, that God (i.e. the other God; argument in *Dial.* 56-62 being granted) endured to be born and to become man» (*Dial.* 68:1). Justin's first retort is not very persuasive: «Do you think that any one else is spoken of in the Scriptures as one to be worshipped (Ps 45:13) and as Lord (Ps 110:1) and God (Ps 45:7f), save he who made the universe, and save Christ, who was proved by so many Scriptures to have become man?» (*Dial.* 68:3). The implicit argument must be: Since the Messiah of the OT is said to be προσκυνητός, θεός etc., he cannot be another than the second God also found in the OT (*Dial.* 56-62).

Justin then brings in Is 53:8: The fact that the Messiah's generation should be without explanation, because of non-human origin, points to the secret of God becoming man, *Dial.* 68:4. Trypho objects that Nathan's oracle to David (quoted above, p. 200) speaks about a Messiah of David's loins, i.e. a Messiah of *known human origin, Dial.* 68:5. Justin answers: Nathan's oracle must be interpreted in the light of Is 7:14. «Isaiah explained exactly how that which was spoken in a mystery to David by God would happen» (*Dial.* 68:6). It is not unusual, adds Justin, that later prophets make plain obscure oracles by earlier prophets.

Justin in this way uses the «not of human seed» motive connected with the virgin birth testimonies to tie down the second God of *Dial.* 56-62 in incarnation and virgin birth. Besides, the very name Jesus is of course in itself a persuasive argument, cf. Trypho's admission in *Dial.* 89:1.

In this way the identity of the Messiah as Jesus is corroborated, and the theme of pre-existence and non-human origin receive an extensive foundation in *Dial.* 56-62.75.

We must now take a closer look at the section 56-62 (par. 126-129). It is immediately apparent that the section has two main subdivisions: *Dial.* 56-60 treats the theophanies to the patriarchs and Moses (with *Dial.* 62:5 as an added appendix), while *Dial.* 61f treats the idea of Christ as a mediator when the world was created (Prov 8:22ff and Gen 1:26).

The latter idea is obviously traditional, cf. Col 1:15ff; Heb 1:3; Barn. 5:5; 6;12. But the argument on the theophanies is not met with prior to Justin. Is it his own invention? Let me point out that on formal criteria *Dial.* 56-60 is quite singular in the whole *Dialogue.* In no other part of the *Dialogue* is the exegetical debate so much a real dialogue as in the main section on the theophanies. Trypho is very co-operative, poses only relevant questions, makes valuable summaries of previous argument, and declares himself satisfied with Justin's exposition. One gets the impression that Justin here has gained more freedom and independence in the handling of his exegetical argument than elsewhere in the *Dialogue.* This corresponds to the fact that he is obviously working directly with the Genesis and Exodus LXX, as his long LXX excerpts demonstrate.

This would indicate that the question of sources here is especially delicate. One should probably not so much look for literary sources as for traditional testimonies and arguments.

In order to do this, we should have to analyse in great detail the argument in *Dial.* 56ff, to find the pivotal points around which the whole argument hinges. I omit this analysis, however, because I have nothing to add to the excellent analysis carried out by B. Kominiak.[61] I find his reconstruction of Justin's line of thought convincing, and I am here content to reproduce Justin's argument by way of a short summary without much justifying argument:

(a) One of the three men appearing to Abraham at Mamre (Gen 18) was not an angel (as first claimed by Trypho), but God, as Gen 18:10 taken together with Gen 21:12 proves (Trypho concedes this). But this God was not identical with the Father (as claimed by Trypho), as Gen 19:24 proves.

(b) In the Jacob theophanies, the God appearing to Jacob cannot be God the Father, since the appearing God is also called Angel of God - that is, he carries out the Father's will and must be numerically distinct from the Father.

(c) In the thornbush theophany, the God who appeared to Moses was not the Father, since the appearing God calls himself the God of Abraham, Isaac, and Jacob, which means the God *who appeared* to Abraham etc., and it has already been proved that this God was not the Father. Besides, this God is identical with the appearing Angel of the Lord in the thornbush theophany, because the sliding from «Angel of the Lord» to «God» in Ex 3 has striking parallels in the Jacob theophanies. (The

---

61. B. Kominiak, *The Theophanies of the Old Testament in the Writings of St. Justin* (The Catholic University of America, Studies in Sacred Theology 2nd Ser. 14, Washington, 1948); cf. also Prigent, *Justin* pp. 117-138.

same kind of argument may be tacitly presupposed in the appendix on Joshua's theophany, *Dial.* 62:5: sliding from «Chief commander of the host of the Lord» to «Lord».).

To this summary I should like to add an element not treated by Kominiak. In my opinion it is highly relevant for Justin and provides his argument with its masterstroke:

(d) The *name* of the second God who appeared to Abraham etc. was not made known to them (Ex 6:3), but was made known to Moses as *Jesus*, Ex 23:20 (*Dial.* 75).

A glance through this summary is sufficient to suggest that the pivotal testimony around which the theophany argument ultimately hinges, is Gen 19:24 (cf. also Justin's own summary in *Dial.* 56:1). D.C. Trakatellis has aptly observed that in *Dial.* 56:12-15 Gen 19:24 is quoted together with Ps 110:1 and Ps 45:7f in a way which indicates their belonging together in a cluster of testimonies proving that Scripture knows two Gods or two Lords: Gen 19:24 two Lords; Ps 110:1 two Lords, Ps 45:7f two Gods.[62] These testimonies are only concerned with proving a duality of Gods or Lords in the OT; there is no question of the theophanies as such, as the two Psalms testimonies make plain.

If we take it that the «two Gods» testimonies are the traditional basis from which Justin works, we may be able to appreciate his originality and purpose with the theophany argument. Let me briefly recall two formal characteristics of *Dial.* 56-60: (1) Justin is here not arguing from isolated proof-texts; writes with full command of several chapters of the Genesis (Exodus) LXX, and argues his point by combining texts several chapters apart. (2) Trypho is very cooperative (esp. *Dial.* 60:3), and praises Justin's exegetical procedure:«We should not bear with your words if you did not

---

62. *Pre-Existence*, pp. 65f. Cf. also Beskow, *Rex Gloriae*, pp. 84f. Two additional observations can be made which confirm this. (1) In *Dial.* 34:2, immediately after the exposition of Ps 110:1.4, Justin says: «Christ is proclaimed as King and Priest and God and Lord and Angel and Man and Chief Captain and Stone . . .» In this sequence, King, Priest, God, and Lord are related to the texts quoted in the context: Ps 110:1.4; Ps 72:1; Ps 24:7; Ps 46:7ff; Ps 45:7f. But Angel and Man and Chief Captain do not belong to this series, they are titles derived from the theophany texts in *Dial.* 56ff. This juxtapposition of textual material in *Dial.* 32-38 and 56-62 can be explained on the assumption that some of the texts were traditional testimonies in both series: the one underlying *Dial.* 32ff and the one underlying *Dial.* 56ff, viz. Ps 110:1; Ps 45:7f. (2) Justin always quotes a LXX version of Gen 19:24. But it should be noted that this textform is not fully suited to prove Justin's point: The text does not say that the Lord (on earth) made fire and brimstone rain upon Sodom and Gomorrah from *the Lord in heaven*. In the LXX text the heaven is not connected with the Lord, but with the fire and the brimstone: θεῖον καὶ πῦρ παρὰ κυρίου ἐκ τοῦ οὐρανοῦ. In analogous cases we have often seen that Justin for his exegesis depends on a non-LXX text which is better adapted to his exegesis. Perhaps we have a trace of such a non-LXX «testimony» text in an allusion in *Dial.* 60:5: . . . ἐν τῇ κρίσει τῶν Σοδόμων κύριον παρὰ κυρίου τοῦ ἐν τοῖς οὐρανοῖς τὴν κρίσιν ἐπενηνοχέναι . . . I will not insist on this, because Justin might well paraphrase the text more in line with his exegesis in any case. Yet the analogies elsewhere make me inclined to believe that a «testimony» version of Gen 19:24 may linger in the background.

refer everything to the Scriptures. For you are anxious to draw your proofs from them . . .» (*Dial.* 56:16). Justin is said to carry out his argument «in a manner worthy of true piety» (*Dial.* 58:2). And the most surprising feature of all: Precisely on the topic of «another God», Trypho declares himself convinced by Justin's argument:«You have shown this, my friend, with much force and at considerable length . . .»(*Dial.* 63:1). There is, in fact, no other topic in the *Dialogue* concerning which Trypho declares himself so fully convinced by Justin's argument. This is of course quite unrealistic. In the entire *Dialogue* there is hardly any argument more offensive to a Jew than the argument concerning the Second God in *Dial.* 56-60.

All taken together, this calls for an explanation. And I think there is a setting in which all the striking features of *Dial.* 56-60 make excellent sense. Suppose *Dial.* 56-60 is primarily anti-Marcion. The following points could be made:

(1) Marcion complained that the allegorical exegesis current among ecclesiastical OT expounders was invalid. The Jews were right to interpret the OT Scriptures literally.[63] In *Dial.* 56-60 Justin tries to be painfully faithful to the exact wording of his texts. (While in other parts of the *Dialogue* a modern reader is offended by fanciful *eisegesis,* in *Dial.* 56 60 he would complain that Justin is over-literal!). Justin makes the Jew emphasize this: You keep close to the wording of Scripture - therefore I, as a Jew, am obliged to admit your conclusions.

(2) There are some anti-Marcion remarks not strictly called for by the present context. Trypho:«You are anxious to draw your proofs from them (the Scriptures), and you declare that *there is no God above the Maker of the universe*» (*Dial.* 56:18). Justin:»There both exists and is mentioned in Scripture a God and Lord other than, and less than, the Maker of the universe . . . above Whom there is no other God . . .« (*Dial.* 56:4, cf. also *Dial.* 56:11; 60:5). Justin stresses this anti-Marcion topic in contexts in which Trypho has made no accusation that Justin believes in another God above the Maker of the universe. It seems as if Justin is eager to make Trypho his theological and exegetical ally against an un-named opponent: Marcion!

(3) As I am going to argue in Part III (cf.below,p.412f), the point at issue in dialogues with the Jews at Justin's time was not the theophanies as such, but rather the question of a »Second God«. To this purpose, the isolated testimonies like Gen 19:24; Ps 110:1 etc., were fully sufficient. On the other hand, Marcion would not be very impressed to hear that the OT knew two Gods. But proving that the subject of the anthropomorphic theophanies was Jesus himself, and that Jesus so far from being unknown in the OT was the very God of Abraham, Isaac, and Jacob - that would be something

---

63. Cf. A. von Harnack, *Marcion,* pp. 62f and 84f (with references).

different. Having a Jew admit that the OT knows of a Second God, messenger of God the Father, bearing the name Jesus - that would be something to bring against Marcion and his disciples!

(4) I have emphasized that Justin in *Dial.* 56-60 is working directly with the full LXX text of the relevant Biblical passages, and that his argument depends on creative combination of verses chapters apart. This in itself is sufficient to indicate that Justin in *Dial.* 56-60 is making an original contribution to OT exegesis. He may have started from traditional testimony nucleuses, but he has developed an impressive exegetical argument transcending the simple »testimony« approach. He may be hinting at this in a remark by Trypho: »We have never yet heard any one making these enquiries, investigations, or proofs« (*Dial.* 56:16).

As I am going to argue in Part III, most of Justin's exegetical source material in its present form dates from the years immediately following the Bar Kockba revolt. Marcion is not yet in view. By the time Justin was writing his *Syntagma against Marcion,* anti-Marcion polemic would be a novelty; there would be need and room for fresh and creative argument. And if this new anti-Marcion polemic is reproduced once more in this part of the *Dialogue,* it would account for the vivid and constructive dialogue with Trypho Justin has succeeded in creating here.

Many traditional Christian proof-texts had by this time already been met with traditional Jewish counter-proofs, and Marcion may have exploited the latter ones in his polemic. In *Dial.* 56-60 Justin produces new arguments against which no Jewish answers were ready-made, and he has Trypho admit this. One can hardly escape the impression that Justin has an inventor's pride with regard to his argument in *Dial.* 56-60.

(5) The above observations receive a firm foundation when we investigate the only parallel to the theophany section within the *Apology,* viz. *1.Apol.* 63. As we have remarked above, Justin seems twice to recur to a source combining the following texts: Is 1:3; Mt 11:27; Ex 3:2ff. What could be the intent of this? Let us see what the texts say: Is 1:3: Israel does not know or understand God. Mt 11:27: Nobody knows the Father except the Son.[64] Ex 3:2ff: The angel said to Moses:'Ἐγώ εἰμι ὁ ὤν (interpolated from Ex 3:14), the God of Abraham, Isaac and Jacob. One is reminded of Jesus' debate with the Sadducees, Mk 12:18-27 par. Mt 22:23-33/Lk 20:27-40. In the Mk/Mt version, Jesus rebukes the Sadducees for not knowing the Scriptures nor the power of God, Mk 12:24/Mt 22:29. The quotation of Is 1:3 in Justin could well follow this up. The stress on God as the God of the

---

64. Cf. the detailed analysis of Justin's version of Mt 11:27 in Bellinzoni, *Sayings,* pp. 25-28. Cf. also Lebreton, *Histoire,* pp. 591-598, and Massaux, *Influence,* pp. 499f/533f. In Bellinzoni and Lebreton there are tables of later patristic parallels to Justin's version, which for the most part do not seem to depend directly on him. Some kind of non-canonical version of this saying thus seems to have existed.

resurrection may be present in the interpolation from Ex 3:14 in Ex 3:2ff:«I am the Being One».

Now, anti-Sadduceeic polemic was hardly relevant after 70 AD, and is hardly the polemic setting for the material in *1:Apol.* 63. But one can suggest another setting which would make sense of the polemic concerning resurrection and besides give further explanation for the peculiar combination of testimonies in Justin, viz. the anti-Marcion polemic.

Apart from a reaffirmation of the resurrection, it would be relevant to point out against Marcion that he was unwise in aligning himself with the Jews in their rejection of Christian exegesis of the OT, because the Jews do not know God (Is 1:3), only Jesus knew the God of the OT as his own Father, Mt 11:27.[65]

In fact, Justin alludes to the synoptic passage in *1.Apol.* 63:17, and has a curious saying which would be perfectly anti-Marcion: The patriarchs Abraham, Isaac and Jacob are «Christ's men». In *Dial.* 80:4 Justin says that some Christian heretics blaspheme the God of Abraham, Isaac and Jacob by saying there is no resurrection of the dead, cf. also *Dial.* 35:5. In *Dial.* 81:4 Justin once more reverts to the synoptic passage, this time in an essentially Lukan version.

I think this confirms the assumption that the original intent of Justin's source in *1.Apol.* 63 was anti-Marcion. Is Justin here excerpting his own anti-heretic Syntagma? In this case it would seem a likely hypothesis.[66]

I conclude that the section on the theophanies, *Dial.* 56-60, is one of Justin's own substantial contributions to the traditional argument employed elsewhere in the *Dialogue.* He has probably presented it for the first time in his anti-Marcion *Syntagma,* briefly recalling part of it quite incidentally in *1.Apol.* 63, and then coming back to the theme in a fresh way in the *Dialogue.*

Let us now return to the material in *Dial.* 61f, the other main component in the section on divine pre-existence. I have remarked already that this is traditional material. On the formal level one notices that in *Dial.* 61f the dialogue with Trypho breaks down, and Justin is back to his bad habit of uninterrupted monologue. The content, briefly summarized, is this: Christ is God's Wisdom in person, being mediator at the creation of the world (Prov 8:22ff) and of man (Gen 1:26). This idea accords with the main point in the «recapitulation» passages: Jesus is the Son of God who is superior to Hezekiah and Solomon and any other purely human king, because he partakes in the divine *dynamis* of God. His divine pre-existence is a main

---

65. In fact, Mt 11:27 par. Lk 10:22 is reported to have been one of Marcion's favourite testimonies, see Tertullian, *Adv.Marc.* IV:24f, and Harnack, *Marcion,* p. 90. Marcion took Jesus' saying to mean that the Father was not known prior to Christ's coming. By coupling this text with Is 1:3, Justin turns it against Marcion: The *Jews* did not know the Father because they did not know the Son.

66. I am thus inclined to grant Prigent's *Syntagma* hypothesis in this case, cf. *Justin,* pp. 122-126.

emphasis in the testimonies we ascribed to this source (Ps 110:3; Ps 72:17 LXX etc., cf. above, p. 199ff), and I conclude tentatively - and partly in order not to multiply sources unnecessarily - that the material in *Dial.* 61f derives from the «recapitulation» source.

(f) The lacuna in *Dial.* 74

We shall treat two questions: How much of Justin's argument is missing, and how can one reconstruct a train of thought bridging the lacuna?

Some scholars, like Th. Zahn[67] and A. L. Williams,[68] take as their clue empty cross-references behind the lacuna: *Dial.* 79:1.4; 80:2; 85:6; 105:4; 142:1. If these references refer to lost material in the lacuna, it must have been quite extensive. «The omission doubtless extends to some pages».[69] «. . . *ein nicht unbeträchtlicher Teil des Werkes*».[70]

Other scholars, like P. Prigent, try to reconstruct a connected train of thought bridging the lacuna. Prigent ends up with a minimum of lost text.[71]

I think the first of these procedures commends itself as the more objective. And it is hardly accidental that four out of the six faulty references after the lacuna (*Dial.* 79:1.4; 85:6; 105:4) are concerned with *angelology and demonology,* and that four of the references come in the chapters immediately following the lacuna. The sixth, *Dial.* 142:1, is strictly speaking no cross-reference at all, but presupposes an earlier mention of Justin's imminent departure. One can easily imagine remarks about this in the missing text. Whatever else it has contained, it must of necessity have comprised the narrative of the closing of the first day's discussion, and the opening of the second day, and in this context remarks on Justin's impending departure the second day would be no surprise.

The thematic closeness of the empty cross-references, and their distribution, is a strong argument that they really point to material in the lacuna. Now, if we take these as our clue, this does not exclude the attempt to discern the line of argument which originally bridged the transition from the first to the second day.[72]

In *Dial.* 74:2f, Justin seems to begin an extensive exposition of Ps 96. This Psalm contains two traditional testimonies, vs. 5 (the gods of the peoples are demons) and vs.10 (the Lord reigned (from the tree)). The first testimony would lead Justin on to his theory about the Gentile gods being

---

67. Th. Zahn, 'Studien', pp. 37-45.
68. Williams, Introduction, pp. XVII - XIX, and in his notes to *Dial.* 79:1.4; 80:2; 105:4. Cf. also Archambault, Introduction, pp. LXIX - LXXXI, and notes *ad locc*
69. Williams, p. XIX.
70. Zahn, p. 43. Harnack took the same view, *Judentum,* p. 47.
71. *Justin,* pp. 193f/324, n. 1. Bousset takes a similar view, *Schulbetrieb,* pp. 288f.
72. Prigent in his attempt to reconstruct a connected line of thought from *Dial.* 74;3 to 74:4, ignores the empty references behind the lacuna. The same can be said about Bousset, *loc. cit.*

fallen angels, *1.Apol* 5:1f; *2.Apol* 5:2-6. He hints at this in *Dial* 73:2 and refers to it casually - as something previously expunded? - in *Dial* 79:4 and 83:4. Angelology/demonology is exactly one of the themes of the empty cross-references behind the lacuna.

The second testimony (Ps 96:10) has for its theme Christ's rule as king. It is not surprising if this led Justin on to statements about Christ's millennial reign in Jerusalem, cf. the cross-references in *Dial* 80:1f.

We thus find that Ps 96 provides both themes found in the empty references behind the lacuna.

As a rule, cross-references in *Dial* 75ff refer to things said *on the first day*, and it seems reasonable to suppose that the remarks on angelology and millennialism concluded the discussion of the first day. Probably Justin ended on a triumphant note, cf. Trypho's remark in *Dial* 80:1:»..or did you concede aknowledgement of this (i.e. millennium in Jerusalem), *that you might appear to overcome us completely in our discussion?*« - i.e.(probably), our discussion yesterday.

There are no means of knowing how the discussion on the second day started, but obviously the name of Jesus must soon have come to the fore. Perhaps the controversy about Ps 96 being spoken of the Father or Christ prompted this theme. Justin would have ample opportunity to refer to the earlier discussion about the other God revealing himself to the patriarchs, and would then drive home the argument by proving that the name of this second God was Jesus. This would form an excellent prelude to *Dial* 75:1: «Now it was likewise declared by Moses in a mystery in the book of Exodus . . . that the name of this God, which he says was not made known to Abraham or to Jacob (cf.Ex 6:3 and *Dial* 56ff) was also Jesus.» The summing up in *Dial* 75:4 also points to a fresh repetition of *Dial* 56ff.

However this may be, our present text starts in the middle of a quotation from Deut 31 (viz. vss. 16-18). Taking a closer look at this chapter, we find that it contains important ideas well-known to Justin: (1) Joshua, not Moses, shall lead Israel into the land, Deut 31:2-8; cf. *Dial* 113:3: Joshua, not Moses, led the people into the land. (2) Joshua receives and distributes the inheritance: σὺ κατακληρονομήσεις αὐτὴν αὐτοῖς, Deut 31:7; cf. *Dial* 113:4 on Joshua: ἔδωκεν αὐτοῖς τὴν κληρονομίαν. This would suggest that the whole of Deut 31:2-18 was quoted in Justin's text. Turning to the repetition of this material in *Dial* 125ff, we find a confirmation of this: *Dial* 126:6 quotes Deut 31:2f - apparently without any justification in the context. The reconstructed text in *Dial* 74:4 explains why. It is thus reasonable to suppose that the Joshua/Jesus theme now prominent in *Dial* 75 really started in the part of the text now lost. Looking at *Dial* 75:2 and 113:1f it seems that Justin in these passages refer to the changing of Joshuas name as something well-known. In fact, no earlier exposition of this incident is to be found. Did such an exposition open the treatment of the Joshua theme on the second day? This would accord perfectly with *Dial* 75:1: The (second) God *too* had the name Jesus (ὅτι αὐτοῦ τὸ ὄνομα τοῦ θεοῦ καὶ ' Ιησοῦς ἦν . . .). This sentence seems to presuppose (1) an earlier mention of «this very God» (i.e. the God of the theophanies), and (2) an earlier mention of the name Jesus/Joshua.

A final remark on the lacuna: If one supposes that Justin's *Dialogue* was bound in two codices when the damage occurred[73] - each codex comprising one day's discussion - it is not surprising that the damage to the text of the *Dialogue* should affect the beginning and the middle part of Justin's text: The most exposed leafs are the first and last ones in each codex. Perhaps we are lucky to have the end of the *Dialogue* virtually unhurt.

### (g) *Dial.* 86: Types of the cross

This list seems originally to have been composed with ῥάβδος as the catchword. Three excurses interrupt the list: (1) *ad vocem* Jacob in 86:2, Justin appends a reference to Jacob's ladder. From this he goes on to the stone anointed by Jacob, and this triggers one more excursus (2) on Christ as stone, and one (3) on anointing (*Dial.* 86:3). In *Dial.* 86:4 the list of ῥάβδοι is continued, with some other «tree» testimonies added. Most of the «rod» passages are concerned with *rod and water.*

Moses dividing the sea with his rod

Moses bringing forth water from the rock with his rod

Moses casting his rod into the water at Marah

Jacob casting his rod into water-troughs

Jacob crossing the river with his rod

Elisha casting a rod into the river Jordan

One suspects a baptismal reference in these cases, and in the last passage (on Elisha) this is made explicit. I suggest that this list of baptismal ῥάβδος passages underlies *Dial.* 86.[74] Justin may have appended the list *ad vocem* ῥάβδος in Ps 110:2 in *Dial.* 83:2. As we have seen, *Dial.* 83 combines two expositions of Ps 110 — one «missionary» and one «millennial». The «rod» list behind *Dial.* 86 accords well with a missionary exegesis of Ps 110:2. It may also be related to other passages containing sacramental typology, esp. *Dial.* 40f and 113f. We shall have to return to this below (pp. 374ff).

### (h) *Dial.* 89-106: The passion and death of Jesus.

This section also shows great modifications when compared with the *Apology.* The main testimony on the passion in *1.Apol.* 50f, Is 53, is already quoted in *Dial.* 13, and Justin has refrained from another quotation in *Dial.*

---

73. In the *Sacra Parallela* there is a lemma said to be ἐκ τοῦ πρὸς Τρύφωνα β΄ λόγου - which may indicate that the *Dialogue* at that time traditionally was bound in two books, cf. Zahn, 'Studien', p.45.

74. In this I agree with J. Daniélou, *Theology,* p. 277; and disagree with Prigent, *Justin,* pp. 197f. Cf. the treatment of *Dial.* 86 in Part III.

89ff. There are some allusions to single verses, however *(Dial.* 89:3 alludes to Is 53:3.7.8.12; *Dial.* 90:1 alludes to Is 53:7; *Dial.* 95:3: Is 53:5; *Dial.* 97:2: Is 53:9; *Dial.* 100:2: Is 53:3; *Dial.* 102:7: Is 53:9).

The cluster of passion testimonies employed in *1.Apol.* 35.38 recurs in *Dial.* 97. This traditional material is surrounded by two great blocks: an extensive commentary on Deut 21:23 in *Dial.* 89-96, and a continuous commentary on Ps 22 in *Dial.* 98-106. We shall analyse each of these units a little closer.

### (α) *Dial.* 89-96:

An excursus immediately points itself out. In *Dial.* 92f Justin repeats the essence of his discussion on the law in *Dial.* 16ff. The excursus is called forth by Justin's argument concerning the brazen serpent, and is inserted into the section dealing with the serpent, *Dial.* 91:4 - 94:5. Moses broke his own prohibition against images - this raises the whole question about the true meaning of the law.

The section on the brazen serpent is in its turn incorporated into the treatment of Deut 21:23. This starts in *Dial.* 89:2 (challenge by Trypho), is carried on in 90:1 (new challenge by Trypho), and is completed in *Dial.* 95f. The catchword connecting these passages with the brazen serpent passage is κατάρα: The serpent was accursed, a crucified man is accursed (Deut 21:23). Broadly speaking, Justin has combined a Johannine motive with a Pauline argument.

In between this material there are two sections treating the battle against Amalek (*Dial.* 90:40f and 91:3) and Moses' prophecy about a Messiah from Joseph (*Dial.* 91:1-3). One is led to ask whether this combination of motives could be part of the tradiiton used by Justin. We first take notice of the parallels in the *Dialogue*:

(1) ┌ 90:1:        Deut 21:23
    ┌ 90:4f:       The battle of Amalek
    │ 91:1-3:      The Messiah of Joseph
    └▶91:3fin.     The battle of Amalek
      91:4
      94:1-5   }   The brazen serpent
    └▶95f:         Deut 21:23 interpreted
      97:1:        The battle of Amalek
(2) 111:1:         The battle of Amalek
    112:1f:        The brazen serpent
    112:2fin.      The battle of Amalek
(3) 131:4:         The brazen serpent
    131:4f:        The battle of Amalek

One observes from this how intertwined the two themes of «Amalek» and «brazen serpent» are. It is relevant to notice that the same combination occurs in rabbinic literature. «'And it came to pass, when Moses held up his hand', etc. (Ex 17:11). Now, could Moses' hands make Israel victorious or could his hands break Amalek? It merely means this: When Moses raised his hands towards heaven, the Israelites would look at him and believe in him who commanded Moses to do so; then God would perform for them miracles and mighty deeds. Similar to this:'And the Lord said unto Moses: Make thee a fiery serpent', etc. (Num 21:8). Now, could that serpent kill or make alive? It merely means this: When Moses did so, the Israelites would look at him and believe in him who commanded Moses to do so; then God would send them healing» (*Mekh.* Amalek I:119-127, pp.143f). (There is a close parallel in *M.R.Sh.* 3:8.)[75]

Justin's joining of these two narratives is thus not without rabbinic (Tannaitic) parallels.[76] One notices, on the other hand, that the Pauline argument in *Dial.* 95 is never repeated or alluded to in the later parallels (*Dial.* 111f and 131:4f) or elsewhere in the *Dialogue*. This suggests that it is Justin's own addition to a given tradition.

The proof that such a tradition existed, is found in *Barn.* 12:2-9. Here the two themes of brazen serpent and Amalek battle are interconnected in the following way:

12:2-4: Amalek battle
12:5-7: Brazen serpent
12:8f: Amalek battle

*Barnabas* has no trace of the Pauline argument in this context, - a further confirmation of our surmise above.

Was *Barnabas* Justin's source? I shall treat this question in some detail in Part III (below, p. 393ff). Here it is relevant to point to an element found in Justin but not in *Barnabas*: The quotation of Deut 33:13-17 and the comments on this text in *Dial.* 91:1-3. This unit seems closely knit to the «Amalek» theme, which preceedes and follows the treatment of Deut 33:17. Let us compare this with a rabbinic passage. In a midrash on Gen 32:6 (Jacob says: I have oxen, asses . . .) it is said: «Ox alludes to Joseph, as it says, 'His firstling bullock, majesty is his'(Deut 33:17) . . . Now the grandson of Joseph is destined to destroy Amalek, as it says, 'And Joshua discomfited Amalek and his people with the edge of the sword'(Ex 17:13).» (*Gen. Rab.* 75:12, pp. 698f). We meet here Joshua - a descendant of Joseph and an Ephraimite, Num 13:8 - in the role of the Messiah ben Ephraim, the warrior Messiah who defeats Amalek (= Rome). We shall return to this theme more fully below. Here it is sufficient to note the rabbinic combination of ideas: *Joshua* is the *son of Joseph* (Deut 33:17) who defeats Amalek.

---

75. Cf. the comments in Str. Bill. III, p. 192.
76. This was pointed out by T. W. Manson,'The Argument from Prophecy', *JTS* 46, (1945, pp. 129-36), pp. 131f.

It seems Justin is here drawing on rabbinic tradition not conveyed to him by *Barnabas.* The topics of the brazen serpent, the battle of Amalek, and the Messiah of Joseph, should all be seen as traditional deposits, and probably as belonging together already in Justin's source. But how is this material related to the Pauline argument of *Dial.* 95 concerning Deut 21:23?

If we take the term «curse» as our clue, the following passages are relevant:

(1) «Moses was the first to exhibit this apparent curse of him (i.e. Christ) by the typical acts he performed.»(*Dial.* 90:3). Here «apparent curse» is quite simply - based on Deut 21:23 - a circumscription for «death by crucifixion». But one should note the qualification «apparent» (δοκοῦσα).[77]

(2) «For the spirit of prophecy speaking by Moses did not teach us to believe on a serpent, since it declares that it was cursed in the beginning by God.» *(Dial.* 91:4). Justin here introduces the cursing of the serpent in Gen 3. He exploits this as an argument that the brazen serpent must be meant as a type: By choosing precisely the cursed serpent for a saving sign, Moses made it plain that the saving faith should not be directed towards the serpent, but towards him of whom the serpent was a type.

(3) The Jews curse «even them who prove that he who was crucified by you is the Christ. And, besides, you deem it right to prove that he has been crucified as an enemy of God and accursed, which is the result of your unreasonable opinion.»( *Dial.* 93:4). This passage seems to imply a denial of the idea that Deut 21:23 should be applied to Jesus. It thus corresponds to the qualification «apparent» in passage 1 above.

(4A) «Just as God commanded the sign to be given by the brazen serpent, and yet is guiltless, so even in the Law does a curse lie against men who are crucified. (B) Yet a curse does not lie any longer against the Christ of God, for by him he saves all them that have done deeds that deserve a curse.» (*Dial.* 94:5). Element A here seems to hint at an argument which is nowhere developed by Justin: Just as the Law (viz. the prohibition against images) was suspended when the type was made (cf. *Dial.* 94:1) - so the Law (viz. Deut 21:23) was suspended when the realization took place. I.e. Christ was not cursed, despite Deut 21:23. This may also be the reasoning underlying passage 1 and 3 above. I suggest that this reflects a fully developed argument in Justin's source, cf. below, p. 238.

Element B looks like a transition to the Pauline argument stated in *Dial.* 95:1f:

---

77. Cf. esp. the analysis of C.W. van Unnik, 'Der Fluch der Gekreuzigten. Deuteronomium 21,23 in der Deutung Justinus des Märtyrers', *Kerygma und Logos. Festschrift für Carl Andresen zum 70. Geburtstag* (Göttingen - Zürich, 1979, pp. 483-499), pp 489-491. Van Unnik is probably right to see the qualification «apparent» as indicating that the incident in question contains a *sign:* When the Law *appears* to curse Christ - which should be impossible - this is a pointer to a deeper meaning of the «curse». There is thus only an apparent, but no real application of Deut. 21:23 to Christ.

(5) «For every race of men will be found to be under a curse according to the Law of Moses. For 'cursed' it is said, 'is every one who remaineth not in all the things that are written in the book of the Law, to do them'(Deut 27:26). And no one ever did all exactly ... but some have kept the commands more, and some less, than others. But if they who are under the Law are plainly under a curse, because they have not kept everything, how much more will all the Gentiles plainly be under a curse, as serving idols, and corrupting boys, with all other abominations. If, therefore, the Father of the universe purposed that his own Christ should receive on himself the curse of all, on behalf of men of every race, knowing that he would raise him up after being crucified and dying, why do you speak of him who endured the suffering of these things in accordance with the purpose of the Father as though he was accursed, and do not rather lament for yourselves?«

If my surmises above are essentially correct, one has reason to think that Justin must have formulated the present passage with the greatest circumspection: He seems fully aware that according to Paul, Deut 21:23 after all has a valid reference to Christ. The apologetics concerned to refute this application (passages 1; 3 and 4A above), may have taken Deut 21:23 in a non-Pauline, more superficial meaning: »cursed« = finally rejected as Messiah. In that case one would naturally have to deny any application of Deut 21:23 to Jesus. Justin in *Dial.* 95 would not withdraw this denial of the idea that Christ - for his own part - was »cursed«, i.e. rejected as Messiah. At the same time he has grasped the Pauline idea in Gal 3:13: Christ vicariously suffered the curse resting on all men. This is clearly stated in *Dial.* 95:1f.[78] I think this sufficiently explains the careful »yes and no« balance concerning Deut 21:23 in *Dial.* 95:1f.[79]

---

78. Cf. A. Thoma, 'Justin's literarisches Verhältnis zu Paulus und zum Johannisevangelium ' *ZWTh* 18 (1875, pp. 383-412/490-565), pp. 401f. Stylianopoulos is wrong when he states: »Paul applies Dt 21:23 to Christ, but Justin does not. Justin accepts that Dt. 21:23 entails a curse on crucified men, but the case of God's Messiah is for him an exception (*Dial.* 94:5).« (*Mosaic Law*, p. 105, n. 68) This is correct for Justin's recapitulation source, not for Justin himself. Cf. also Stylianopoulos, p. 103, n. 64, and Smit Sibinga, p. 97. Van Unnik, *art. cit.,* is right to stress the importance of *Dial.* 95 within Justin's argument, pp. 492-494, 498. But van Unnik does not raise the question of conflicting traditions behind Justin's treatment of Deut 21:23, and therefore his assessment of Justin's relationship to Paul is marked by ambiguity and unwarranted conjectures about a common tradition behind both authors.
Shotwell, *Exegesis,* pp. 33f, takes *Dial.* 95:1 as one of his main examples of Hillel's rule *qal waḥomer* in Justin: If they who are under the law are plainly under a curse, because they have not kept everything, how much more will all the Gentiles plainly be under a curse ... No doubt this is a good example of the *qal waḥomer* principle. But one need go no further than the NT to find frequent use of this kind of reasoning. The example does not prove that Justin had learnt this kind of reasoning from the rabbis - besides, this is simple, straightforward logic which hardly calls for any specific »source«.
79. One should note in this connexion that Tertullian reports *(Adv.Marc.* I:11; III: 18; V:3) that Marcion argued from Deut 21:23 that Jesus was not the Demiurg's Messiah, cf. Harnack, *Marcion,* p. 112.

(6) In *Dial.* 95:4 - 96:2 another interpretation of Deut 21:23 is added: It may also be taken as a prophecy about the Jews cursing Jesus and Christians. This looks like an after-thought, added to give polemic sting to the whole discussion.

If the above interpretation and source analysis of Justin's text is correct, it proves that Justin gave priority to the Pauline argument concerning Deut 21:23, despite all its »dangers« in Justin's polemic context. The Pauline interpretation is directly and cogently stated. One notes the Pauline influence also in the description of Jews and Gentiles: The Jews are those »under the Law«, their piety is far better than the gross sins of Gentiles. This is quite another atmosphere than in the other sayings about Jews and Gentiles in Justin.

The non-Pauline argument that Deut 21:23 is not valid for Jesus, is on the other hand markedly suppressed, cf. esp. passage 4A above.[80]

It remains to be asked in what context we should situate the non-Pauline material used in *Dial.* 91 and 94. I think the following parallel is significant:

| *Dial.* 94:2 | *Dial.* 88:4 |
|---|---|
| He would destroy the power of the serpent, who caused the transgression to be made by Adam. | He did not endure being born and crucified as being in need… but it was all on behalf of the race of men, which from the time of Adam had fallen under the death and deceit of the serpent, each man acting ill by his own fault. |

One should further compare *Dial.* 76:6 and *Dial.* 78:9. The common denominator of these passages is the idea that Christ is the second Adam, conquering where Adam was conquered. In other words: These passages all contain the idea of »recapitulation«: Christ, in conquering the devil and the demons, shows himself to be the Son of God and head of a new humanity, freed by him from the hostile powers. This idea is deeply embedded in the anti-Hezekiah material in *Dial.* 77f; it also shines through in *Dial.* 88 and *Dial.* 91; 94. I take as a working hypothesis that the non-Pauline material on the brazen serpent in *Dial.* 91; 94 derives from the same source which was employed in *Dial.* 77f and 88 (and the relevant adjacent and parallel passages in *Dial.* 31-38; 43; 63f; 76).

(β) *Dial.* 98-106: Ps 22.

Apart from *Dial.* 56-60, this section is perhaps one of the most ambitious in the whole *Dialogue.* Justin is no longer satisfied with quoting isolated,

---

80. I thus reach a conclusion partly contradicting van Unnik's concluding remarks, *art.cit.* pp. 498f.

non-LXX testimonies from Ps 22. He goes on to quote the LXX text of the whole Psalm and to give a verse-by-verse commentary.[81]

The traditional testimonies no doubt were his clue. They told him to see Ps 22 as a text predicting details in the passion story. To some extent, Justin has succeeded in extending this point of view to the whole Psalm. The traditional testimonies, viz. vss. 2; 8f; 15 (? - prayer in Gethsemane. *Dial.* 103:7f. cf. below, Appendix I, nr. 2 ); 17-19, have been enriched by the following:

| | |
|---|---|
| 2b.3: | Prayer in Gethsemane, *Dial.* 99:2f. |
| 7: | Christ despised at his passion, *Dial.* 101:2. |
| 12-14: | Christ surrounded and without helper at his arrest. *Dial.* 103:1-4. |
| 16: | Christ silent before Pilate. *Dial.* 102:5, repeated 103:9. |
| 16b. 17a: | Death of Jesus. *Dial.* 104:1f. |
| 21: | Death on a cross, *Dial.* 105:2 (with excursus on the fate of souls after death, *Dial.* 105:4-6). |
| 21f: | Jesus' prayer in death, *Dial.* 105:3. |
| 23: | Christ resurrected, *Dial.* 106:1f. |

But Justin has not been able to carry through this constant reference to the passion story. Some verses are referred to Christ's humility without specific reference to the passion:

| | |
|---|---|
| 5f: | Jesus recognized the fathers as his fathers and set his hope on God alone, *Dial.* 101:1f. |
| 11b.12a: | Jesus puts his hope on God alone, not on his own wisdom etc., *Dial.* 102:6. |

One verse is referred to Christ's birth:

| | |
|---|---|
| 10b: | Christ was saved from Herod's murder of the children, *Dial.* 102:1f (with excursus on free will, 102:3f). |

The most interesting comments, however, are attached to vss. 4 (*Dial.* 100:1-6); 14b (*Dial.* 103:5f), and 23 (*Dial.* 106:3f). These passages are only superficially related to the Psalm verses or phrases which they purport to elucidate. On the other hand, they show clear inter-relations to each other and to other passages in the *Dialogue.*[82]

---

81. Bousset feels certain that the commentary on Psalm 22 existed prior to its incorporation in the *Dialogue, Sculbetrieb,* pp. 292f. One of his arguments is this: «*Es ist doch ein merkwürdiges Zusammentreffen, dass Justin nur in diesem Abschnitt des ganzen Dialogs und hier nun volle dreizehn Mal den bekannten Ausdruck* ἀπομνημονεύματα *für die synoptischen Evangelien gebraucht.*» True, Justin uses the same term in *1.Apol.* 66:3 and 67:3, but Bousset has a ready explanation: Justin used this term early in his career as a Christian writer (*1.Apol.* and commentary on Ps 22), but avoided it at a later stage (i.e. when writing the *Dialogue).* - I find it difficult to evaluate the force of this.

82. I am thus inclined to believe that they represent insertions from another source, and that they were not created *ad hoc* as a part of the Ps 22 commentary. This would represent a precision of Bousset's theory: Granted that the commentary on Ps 22 existed prior to its inclusion in the *Dialogue,* it did probably not comprise these «recapitulation» passages. They seem interpolated during the writing of the *Dialogue,* and may stem from another source which is also employed elsewhere in this section of the *Dialogue:* the «recapitulation» source. On this, see immediately below.

| *Dial.* 100 | *Dial.* 103/106 |
|---|---|
| Christ is called «Israel» and «Jacob», 100:1 | Christ gave his name «Israel» to Jacob, 106:3 |
| Mt 11:27 with comment,100:1f | |
| Passion prediction (+ comment on the term «Son of man»), 100:3 | Allusion to passion predictions, 106:1 |
| Peter confessed Christ as God's Son. He received a new name: Peter | Christ changed Peter's name, 106:3 |
| Christ is σοφία, ἡμέρα, ἀνατολή ⎯⎯⎯⎯⎯⎯⎯⎯⎯⎯▶ μάχαιρα, λίθος, ῥάβδος, Jacob and Israel, 100:4 | Num 24:17; Zech 6:12, 106:4 <br><br> Christ gave his name «Israel» to Jacob, 106:3 |
| «. . has become man by the Virgin, in order that by the same way in which disobedience caused by the serpent took its beginning, by this way it should also take its destruction», 100:4 Eve was deceived by the serpent and begat death, Mary was obedient and begat him «by means of whom God destroys both the serpent and those angels and men that became like it, but for them that repent of their evil deeds, and believe on him, does he work deliverance from death», 100:5f | The devil tempted Jesus after his baptism. «For as he led Adam astray, he thought that he could do some harm to him also», 103:6 |

At first sight, the passages *Dial.* 100 and *Dial.* 106 seem to lack any thematic coherence. But I think the organizing principle becomes transparent when we look at the NT material employed. There are in *Dial.* 100 and 106 obvious allusions to the Caesarea Philippi incident as told by Matthew. Taking this as our clue, we find in Mt 16:16-23 the following sequence:

(1) Peter's confession («Son of the living God»), vs. 16.

(2) Changing of Peter's name, vs. 18.

(3) Passion prediction, vs. 21.

(4) Jesus tempted by Peter = Satan, vss. 22f.

Elements 1-3 are easily recognized in *Dial.* 100 and 106:1-3. The fourth element calls for further comment.

There are some indications that Justin in *Dial.* 100 and *Dial.* 103:6 is following a source in which Mt 16:16-23 and the temptation story were joined together. In *Dial.* 103:6 Justin quotes a version of Jesus' rebuke of Satan, in which the first phrase reads: «Get behind me, Satanas». This is incorporated into the temptation story from Mt 16:23, i.e. from Jesus' rebuking of Peter. The phrase does not occur in the original text of either Mt 4:10 or Lk 4:8.[83]

---

83. Cf. synopsis and comments in Bellinzoni, *Sayings,* pp. 38f.

Other indications of a harmonistic source can also be found. In his rendering of the passion prediction in *Dial.* 100:3, Justin does not quote Mt 16:21 exactly, but a harmonized version which is closer to Lk 9:22. (The same version recurs in *Dial.* 51:2 and 76:7, which proves the existence of a written source.)[84] In *Dial.* 103:6 one can also detect traces of harmonization with Luke: The heavenly voice at Jesus' baptism is rendered according to Ps 2:7, i.e. the «western» reading in Lk 3:23, and the phrase καὶ ἀποκρίνασθαι αὐτῷ τὸν Χριστόν, *Dial.* 103:6, recalls Lk 4:8: καὶ ἀποκριθεὶς ὁ ᾽Ιησοῦς εἶπεν αὐτῷ.

The employment of a harmonistic source in which temptation story and Caesarea Philippi incident were put together, is thus a satisfactory explanation for the apparently chaotic combination of themes in *Dial.* 100, and further explains the links between *Dial.* 100; 103:6 and 106:1-3.

The common denominator in these passages is the idea of Jesus as God's Son, the second Adam. In the temptation story the Son of God is tested as a second Adam - the temptation follows after the heavenly voice has proclaimed: «Thou art my Son . . .», *Dial.* 103:6. At Caesarea Philippi Peter recognizes that Jesus is the Son of God, and immediately Jesus is again tested, by Peter = Satan. We here probably face early gospel exegesis which interpreted the Son of God concept in »recapitulation« terms: Christ proves himself to be the Son of God by conquering where Adam was conquered. (The Eve/Mary typology in *Dial.* 100:5f is an additional motif in accord with the basic idea.) The tradition we have delineated here must be related to the tradition behind *Dial.* 124f. In *Dial.* 125 we find the name »Israel« applied to Jesus and elucidated by means of the temptation story. In *Dial.* 124 we have a »recapitulation« passage related to *Dial.* 100:4-6. Taking the recapitulation motive as our clue, *Dial.* 45:4 and *Dial.* 76:3-7 are again called to mind. These passages connect the recapitulation theme with the virgin birth testimonies (cf. above, p. 199ff), and in *Dial.* 76:7 we encounter the same harmonistic version of Jesus' passion prediction as in *Dial.* 100:3. The connexion between recapitulation concept and virgin birth theme is also hinted at in *Dial.* 43:1 and *Dial.* 84:2.

It thus seems that the passages we have been surveying, are related to the »Jesus-versus-Hezekiah« or »recapitulation« source we delineated above. I shall take as a working hypotheses that they derive from this source. [85]

---

84. Cf. Bellinzoni, pp. 30-32. I find Bellinzoni's arguments for a harmonistic source persuasive.
85. In my analysis of Justin's quotations of Num 24.17 above, I tentatively suggested that the quotations in *1.Apol.* 32:12 and *Dial.* 106:4 derive from different sources. The present analysis confirms this.

(i) *Dial.* 107: The sign of Jonah

The resurrection of Jesus is already brought in apropos vs. 23 in Ps 22 (*Dial.* 106:1f). Justin now turns to the decisive Scriptural proof for the resurrection on the third day. For once, he quotes as his text a NT passage, Mt 16:4. However, this Jesus logion points to the book of Jonah as OT testimony on the resurrection, and we have seen already that Justin in *Dial.* 107 is working directly with the book of Jonah (καιγε version? cf. above, p. 120).      One gets the impression that/Justin here is working directly with the NT and the Greek OT.

The sign of Jonah leads over to the idea of the repentance among Gentiles and the unbelief of the Jews, *Dial.* 108ff.

With this, our analysis of the Christological section of the *Dialogue* is finished. The following table is an attempt to visualize our findings.

«Recapitulation»                                    Additions from other sources:
material:

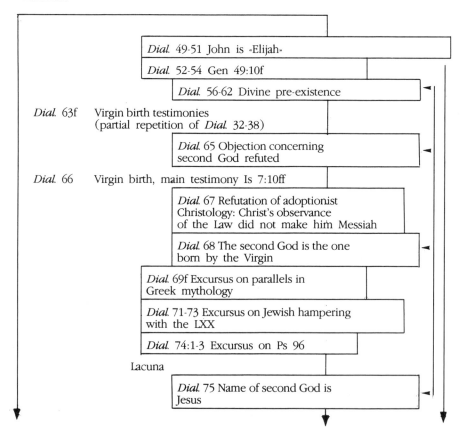

Dial. 49-51 John is «Elijah»

Dial. 52-54 Gen 49:10f

Dial. 56-62 Divine pre-existence

Dial. 63f    Virgin birth testimonies
(partial repetition of *Dial.* 32-38)

Dial. 65 Objection concerning second God refuted

Dial. 66    Virgin birth, main testimony Is 7:10ff

Dial. 67 Refutation of adoptionist Christology: Christ's observance of the Law did not make him Messiah

Dial. 68 The second God is the one born by the Virgin

Dial. 69f Excursus on parallels in Greek mythology

Dial. 71-73 Excursus on Jewish hampering with the LXX

Dial. 74:1-3 Excursus on Ps 96

Lacuna

Dial. 75 Name of second God is Jesus

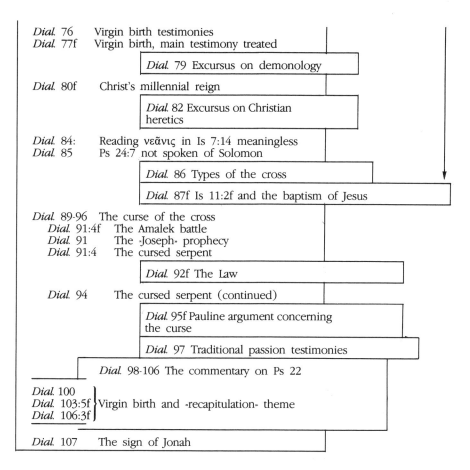

*Dial.* 76        Virgin birth testimonies
*Dial.* 77f       Virgin birth, main testimony treated

        *Dial.* 79 Excursus on demonology

*Dial.* 80f       Christ's millennial reign

        *Dial.* 82 Excursus on Christian
        heretics

*Dial.* 84:       Reading νεᾶνις in Is 7:14 meaningless
*Dial.* 85        Ps 24:7 not spoken of Solomon

        *Dial.* 86 Types of the cross

        *Dial.* 87f Is 11:2f and the baptism of Jesus

*Dial.* 89-96    The curse of the cross
    *Dial.* 91:4f    The Amalek battle
    *Dial.* 91        The ·Joseph· prophecy
    *Dial.* 91:4      The cursed serpent

        *Dial.* 92f The Law

*Dial.* 94        The cursed serpent (continued)

        *Dial.* 95f Pauline argument concerning
        the curse

        *Dial.* 97 Traditional passion testimonies

        *Dial.* 98-106 The commentary on Ps 22

*Dial.* 100
*Dial.* 103:5f ⎫ Virgin birth and ·recapitulation· theme
*Dial.* 106:3f ⎭

*Dial.* 107       The sign of Jonah

·Recapitulation· material outside *Dial.* 48-107:
    *Dial.* 31-38 and 43: parallel to *Dial.* 63f and 84f
    *Dial.* 118:2: Christ is eternal King and Priest in the House of the Lord
            in Jerusalem (millennial theme)
    *Dial.* 124f: Men loosing their status as sons of God, Christ re-conquering
it.

*Preliminary conclusions:*

It is time to summarize our findings so far, before we go on to make some conjectures as to the identity and nature of the posited sources. Taking the testimony material as our clue, we have meant to discern two main blocks of such material in Justin:

(A) The one, which I call the «kerygma source», is clearly evidenced in the *Apology,* containing

(a) a proof that Jesus is the Messiah. This is constructed within a simple prophecy - fulfilment scheme, containing (A) OT prophecy, (B) short exposition, and (C) fulfilment report (harmonistic Gospel account of «synoptic» type, sometimes including non-synoptic features related to known non-canonical Gospel material). A further characteristic is the employment of the two parousias pattern.

(b) a proof that the reign of the risen Christ through the apostles' kerygma was foretold in the Scriptures and is now a present reality. Converts are invited to join in the Messianic salvation in Jerusalem, while the Jews are said to be excluded from the City (or the Land) because they slew the Just One.

(c) an anti-cultic polemic.

In the *Dialogue,* we encounter this material once more, mainly in the sections *Dial.* 11-47 and 108-141. Justin makes a fuller use of it here, and especially adds substantial material on the «new people» theme (which is only hinted at in the *Apology*), and he has a much fuller anti-cultic material. In the Christological section, *Dial.* 48-107, the material used in *1.Apol.* 32ff is also used once more (*Dial.* 49-54; 72?; 84; 87; 97), but it does not carry the main burden of argument.

(B) In the Christological section of the *Dialogue* another source is employed which I have labelled the «anti-Hezekiah» or the «recapitulation» source. It is evident that this material has another profile than the Christological testimonies in *1.Apol.* 32 etc. For one thing, the *Dialogue* source does not seem to apply the two parousias scheme. Within *Dial.* 48-108, the two parousias scheme is only applied within *Dial.* 49-54; i.e. in chapters where material from *1.Apol.* 32 is employed once more. In the anti-Hezekiah and anti-Solomon polemic which is fundamental to the Christological section of the *Dialogue,* the two parousias scheme plays no role.

This corresponds to a further difference. In *1.Apol.* 32ff the point is to prove that Jesus so to speak has fulfilled one half of the Messianic prophecies, viz. the prophecies concerning the lowly appearance of the Messiah. This guarantees his fulfilling of the prophecies concerning his glorious coming.

The polemic and apologetic in *Dial.* 48-108 is different. The Jewish objection is that the main Christological prophecies are not Messianic at all, but refer to historic kings in Israel. The rebuttal consists in showing that the Christological testimonies envisage a king conquering Satan and demons -a thing never done by any Jewish king, because this is a super-human feat only accomplished by Christ, the second Adam, God's Son. Material from this «recapitulation» source is used also in *Dial.* 31-38; 43; 118:2?;124f.

To the testimonies and arguments deriving from this source, Justin has added more material from various sources, i.a. Matthew and Paul (cf. the table above). Two sections stand out as being his own original contributions: the one on the theophanies, *Dial.* 56-60; and the one on Psalm 22, *Dial.* 98-106.

Of minor importance are two hypothetical sources we meant to recognize. The one is the «tract on Greek mythology» already observed by Bousset. The other is the small apologetic tract in *1.Apol.* 59f. It is concerned with Plato's and other philosophers debt to Moses, an idea not unrelated to the theme of the tract on mythology. In both cases a dependence upon Moses - or more generally: OT prophecy - is posited. One should not exclude the possibility that we have to do with one and the same source, which might well be the *Apology* of Quadratus, but here we are on feeble grounds.

However, the subject-matter of this (or these) source(s) was hardly OT exegesis as such. The relevant OT passages are only quoted as explanations for certain striking «parallels» to Biblical ideas in Greek literature. There is little explicit exegesis of the OT passages. They do not, strictly speaking, function as part of Justin's proof from prophecy (with the exception of the healing testimony). I shall therefore not include this material in the analyses in Part III.

Before we conclude Part II, however, it is relevant to raise the question of the nature and the identity of the two main sources, the «kerygma source» and the «recapitulation» source.

## CHAPTER FOUR

THE NATURE AND IDENTITY OF THE RECONSTRUCTED SOURCES

*1. The «kerygma source».*

It may first be relevant to point out that the argument developed so far in the present study is not sufficient to prove that on the litterary level the «kerygma source» was a single, published work of litterature. This may have been the case, but there is nothing in the evidence surveyed above which contradicts the hypothesis of a connected series of tracts, perhaps circulating within a «school» tradition (this was Bousset's proposal). The above argument has concentrated mainly on the common and interconnected theological ideas contained in this material. For convenience, I have spoken about this material as a «source», but this is not meant to imply very precise notions about the literary format this material had.

We have made some relavant observations, however. One should not think of this material as mere anthologies or excerpts of OT texts. We have seen repeatedly that a minimum of exposition and in some cases (the Christological testimonies) fulfilment narratives were appended to the texts. And the OT texts as well as the exposition and fulfilment reports are so carefully worked out that one should probably think of something more than just casual lecture notes.

It is evident that in many respects this «kerygma source» is close to *Barnabas.* But there is no question of identity. Justin's non-LXX quotations tend to deviate from the LXX where Barnabas agrees, and vice versa. Many of the crucial testimonies in Justin's «kerygma» material are totally absent from *Barnabas.* Nor is any other preserved Christian writing prior to Justin a possible candidate for identification as the «kerygma source».

We are therefore led to seek possible candidates among other early Christian writings now lost. And here we come across the interesting fragments of the *Kerygma Petrou* preserved by Clement of Alexandria. Could it be that the *Kerygma Petrou* is identical with the «kerygma source» in Justin?

We came across the *Kerygma* in our study of Jer 31:31f in Justin (cf. above, pp. 72f). It seems that in *Dial.* 11:2 and *Dial.* 67:9 Justin alludes to the condensed, non-LXX version of this text found in the *Kerygma.* Let us review the existing evidence concerning the *Kerygma* to see if more material in Justin could possibly derive from it.[1]

Before we indulge in hypothesis, let me briefly state the general points of contact between Justin and the *Kerygma* (=KP).

(1) KP was a work of missionary apologetics (fragms. 1 and 2),[2] attaching great importance to OT prooftexts (fragm. 6). The same combination recurs in Justin.

(2) According to the KP, the twelve apostles have evangelized the whole world (fragms. 3 and 4). The idea recurs in Justin.

(3) KP: «We say nothing without (foundation in) the Scriptures» (fragm. 6). Justin takes the same line, *Dial* 28:2; 29:2; 32:2; 56:16; 58:1; 68:1; 80:1 etc.

(4) KP contains two important texts about Christ the Law (Is 2:3 cf. below) and the New Covenant, Jer 31:31. Both texts have a prominent position in Justin, and - as we have seen - he seems to know the non-LXX text of Jer 31:31 used in the KP.

(5) The KP seems to have arranged the Scriptural proof concerning Christ in a «creed» sequence not unlike Justin's (fragm. 6).

These points are sufficient to give the KP an important position in the tradition leading up to Justin's *Apology* and *Dialogue*, but they are hardly sufficient to establish a theory of literary dependence. So we shall have to consider some additional, more detailed observations.

We start in Clement of Alexandria, *Strom.* VI:48:7 - 49:1, and the largely parallel section *Protr.* 95:2 (cf. synopsis next page).

One first notices that Clement twice quotes Deut 30:15/19 and Is 1:19f together, and seemingly from the same source, because both texts are markedly non-LXX and almost identical. (The non-LXX addition καὶ πῦρ in Is 1:20 has been dropped in the *Strom.* quotation, but this may be due to a scribe noticing the «error»). The source is probably the KP, because in *Strom.* VI this writing has been quoted twice in the immediately preceeding context (fragm. 4 in VI:48:2f; fragm. 5 in 48:6). In fact, the Deut 30:15/19 quotation is joined immediately to fragment 5, and there is nothing which excludes the possibility that the two OT texts really are part of the excerpt from KP.

---

1. Concerning the *Kerygma Petrou*, see esp. E. von Dobschütz, *Das Kerygma Petri kritisch untersucht* (TU 11:1, Leipzig, 1893) (text and commentary); W. Schneemelcher, Introduction to the Kerygma in *NT Apoc.* II, pp. 94-98; P. Nautin, 'Les citations de la 'Prédication de Pierre' dans Clément d'Alexandrie, *Strom.* VI.V.39-41' *JTS* New Ser. 25 (1974), pp. 98-105; H. Paulsen, 'Das Kerygma Petri und die urchristliche Apologetik', *ZKG* 88 (1977), pp. 1-37; W. Rordorf, 'Christus als Logos und Nomos. Das Kerygma Petrou in seinem Verhältnis zu Justin', *Kerygma und Logos. Festschrift fur Carl Andresen zum 70. Geburtstag* (ed. A. M. Ritter, Göttingen/Zürich, 1979), pp. 424-434 (the last mentioned article is not concerned with the literary relation between the KP and Justin).

2. In the counting of fragments, I follow Schneemelcher in *NT Apoc.*

| 1. Apol. 44:1-4 | Protr. 95:2 = Strom. VI:48:7-49:1 | Deut 30:15.19 LXX |
|---|---|---|
| ᾿Ιδοὺ πρὸ προσώπου σου | ᾿Ιδοὺ τέθεικα πρὸ προσώπου ὑμῶν τὸν θάνατον καὶ τὴν ζωήν | ᾿Ιδοὺ δέδωκα πρὸ προσώπου σου σήμερον τὴν ζωὴν καὶ τὸν θάνατον |
| τὸ ἀγαθὸν καὶ τὸ κακόν ἔκλεξαι τὸ ἀγαθόν . . . | . . . ἐκλεξασθαι την ζωην . . . | τὸ ἀγαθὸν καὶ τὸ κακόν . . . καὶ ἔκλεξαι τὴν ζωὴν . . . |

| | | |
|---|---|---|
| καὶ ἐὰν θέλητε καὶ εἰσακούσητέ μου τὰ ἀγαθὰ τῆς γῆς φάγεσθε ἐὰν δὲ μὴ ᵃθέλητε μηδὲᵃ εἰσακούσητέ μου μάχαιρα ὑμᾶς κατέδεται τὸ γὰρ στόμα κυρίου ἐλάλησε ταῦτα | = Is 1:19f LXX = 1. Apol. 61:8 | ἐὰνᵃ ἀκούσητέ μου καὶ θελήσητε τὰ ἀγαθὰ τῆς γῆς φάγεσθε ἐὰν δὲ μὴ ὑπακούσητέᵇ μου μηδὲ θελήσητε μάχαιρα ὑμᾶς ᶜκαὶ πῦρᶜ κατέδεται τὸ γὰρ στόμα κυρίου ἐλάλησεν ταῦτα |

| a a) Om. 1. Apol. 44:4 = 61:8 | a) Protr. 95:2 adds γαρ b) Strom. VI:49:1: ακουσητε c-c) Om. Strom. VI:49:1 |
|---|---|

Now, let us compare Clement's quotations with Justin's. Justin's text of Deut 30:15/19 is hardly directly dependent upon Clement's. Justin's Is 1:16-20 quotation is much closer to the LXX than Is 1:19f in Clement. Yet there is a coincidence in the sequence of the two texts, and Justin seems to have known Clement's non-LXX text of Is 1:20.In his comment on this verse in *1.Apol.* 44:5 Justin says:«The phrase 'The sword will devour you' does not mean that the disobedient will be slain by swords, but the sword of God *is the fire* (ἡ μάχαιρα τοῦ θεοῦ ἔστι τὸ πῦρ), of which those who choose to do what is evil are made the fuel.» (Cf. also *1.Apol.* 44:6). This exegesis sounds as if Justin had known Clement's text: μάχαιρα ὑμᾶς καὶ πῦρ κατέδεται. There is thus a possibility that Justin may have known Clement's source - the KP.[3] His - largely - LXX text of Is 1:16-20 may be a substitute for the non-LXX text of his source.[4]

It deserves notice that both the Deut and Is texts are perfectly suitable in a missionary setting. *1.Apol.* 44 occurs in the middle of the «Law out from

3. I would here express myself a little more definite than Prigent, *Justin*, p.231: «*Certes il n'est pas impossible que Clément s'inspire de l'Apologie, mais dans la mesure où Justin dépend d'un écrit antérieur, rien n'interdit de chercher dans celui-ci la source où l'alexandrin a puisé.*» (Prigent of course thinks of the *Syntagma* as the source).

4. The deviations from the LXX in *1.Apol.* 44:3f look like casual omissions. Koester has a detailed analysis, *Schriftbeweis*, p. 5, and concludes that we have to do with a good LXX text. The fact that the same omissions (plus one more) recur in the second quotation, *1.Apol.* 61, may have the simple explanation that Justin in *1.Apol.* 61 is copying his earlier excerpt in *1.Apol.* 44.

Zion» section of the *Apology.* Let us pursue the comparison between Justin and Clement with reqard to some other texts within this section.

Justin's first testimony on the apostolic mission is Is 2:3b.4 (LXX text). In *Eclogae Propheticae* 58 Clement says: «The Saviour himself is called νόμος and λόγος, as Peter in the *Kerygma* and the prophet: 'Out of Zion shall go forth the νόμος, and the λόγος of the Lord from Jerusalem.'» Most commentators suppose that this reference to Is 2:3 was already present in the *Kerygma Petrou*,[5] this testimony being the Scriptural justification for calling Christ Law and Logos. It is thus reason to think that the *Kerygma* lurks in the background in the first chapters of Clement's *Protreptikos* also, where Is 2:3b is the programmatic opening quotation from Scripture, *Protr.* 2:3 (the same excerpt as in *Ecl. proph.* 58, and the very same words with which Justin's LXX excerpt in *1.Apol.* 39:1 begins!).

A dominant theme in the first chapters of the *Protreptikos* is «the New Song», τὸ ᾆσμα τὸ καινόν. No doubt this is partly inspired from Ps 96:1 (LXX): ᾄσατε τῷ κυρίῳ ᾆσμα καινόν. As we have seen, a conflated version of Ps 96 and 1 Chron 16 was one of Justin's main testimonies on the «Law out from Zion» in *1.Apol.* 41:1-4. Is it mere coincidence that Clement quotes *from the same conflated text* in *Protr.* 62:4 ? (Clement's citation reads: πάντες οἱ θεοὶ τῶν ἐθνῶν δαιμονίων εἰσὶν εἴδωλα ὁ δὲ θεὸς τοὺς οὐρανοὺς ἐποίησεν. Compare this with the synopsis above, p.36f). Shall we again suppose a common source - the KP?

Turning to another «Law out from Zion» testimony, Ps 110:2, we have seen reasons to suspect that behind the LXX text of Ps 110:1-3 ( *1.Apol.* 45 - the text quoted after Deut 30:15/19 and Is 1:16-20!) there lies an original non-LXX text which did not read ῥάβδον δυνάμεως ἐξαποστελεῖ *σοι* κύριος . . ., since Justin takes the κύριος to be Christ. Turning to Clement, we find in *Paed.* I:61:3 the following separate quotation of Ps 110:2a: ῥάβδον δυνάμεως ἐξαποστελεῖ κύριος ἐκ Σιων — i.e. exactly the text we supposed to be hidden behind the present LXX text in *1.Apol.* 45.[6]

In *Paed.* I:61 we find a small tract with ῥάβδος testimonies: Is 11:1.3f; Ps 118:18; Ps 2:9; Ps 110:2; Ps 23:4. Again: Is it accidental that Ps 2:9 may be hidden behind the large quotation of Ps 1f in *1.Apol.* 40:8-19, and that Is 11:1 and Ps 23:4 figure within the ῥάβδος catena in *Dial.* 86 - *ad vocem* ῥάβδος in Ps 110:2 in *Dial.* 83?

We have seen reasons to think that non-LXX versions of Is 3:10 and Is 5:20 belonged together in Justin's testimony source. Let us compare our two writers in this respect:

---

5. Cf. i.a. von Dobschütz, p. 29 (with a certain reservation), Daniélou, *Theology,* p. 164; Paulsen, *art. cit.,* pp. 24f; Rordorf, *art. cit.,* p. 425.
6. Note also the partial parallelism concerning testimonies against the Jews, *Paed.* 1:9 and *Dial.* 11-29, see Prigent, *Justin,* pp. 272f.

| Is 3:10 LXX | Clem. Alex. *Strom.* V:108:2 | *Dial.* 136:2/137:3 |
|---|---|---|
| δήσωμεν<br>τὸν δίκαιον<br>ὅτι δύσχρηστος<br>ἡμῖν ἐστι | ἄρωμεν ἀφ᾽ ἡμῶν<br>τὸν δίκαιον<br>ὅτι δύσχρηστος<br>ἡμῖν ἐστιν | ἄρωμεν<br>τὸν δίκαιον<br>ὅτι δύσχρηστος<br>ἡμῖν ἐστιν |

| Is 5:20f LXX | *Paed.* III:92:1 | *1. Apol.* 49:7 |
|---|---|---|
| οὐαὶ οἱ λέγοντες<br>τὸ πονηρὸν καλὸν<br>καὶ τὸ καλὸν πονηρόν<br>... οἱ τιθέντες<br>τὸ πικρὸν γλυκὺ<br>καὶ τὸ γλυκὺ πικρόν<br>οὐαὶ οἱ συνετοὶ<br>ἐν ἑαυτοῖς<br>καὶ ἐνώπιον ἑαυτῶν<br>ἐπιστήμονες | οὐαὶ τοῖς λέγουσι<br><br><br><br>τὸ γλυκὺ πικρὸν<br>καὶ τὸ πικρὸν γλυκύ<br>οὐαὶ οἱ συνετοὶ<br>ἐν ἑαυτοῖς<br>καὶ ἐνώπιον αὐτῶν<br>ἐπιστήμονες | οὐαὶ τοῖς λέγουσι<br><br><br><br>τὸ γλυκὺ πικρὸν<br>καὶ τὸ πικρὸν γλυκύ |

Of course it is possible to regard Justin as Clement's source for the non-LXX readings, but one gets a simpler explanation if one assumes that Justin excerpted Clement's source - the KP?

(A survey of the supposed KP testimonies in Irenaeus and Tertullian yields no unambiguous evidence of direct recourse to the KP.)

Returning to one of the texts from which we started - Is 1:16-20 in *1.Apol.* 44 - we notice that this text returns as a baptismal testimony in *1.Apol.* 61:7-8. Here the text is followed by this remark: «And we *learned* (ἐμάθομεν) *from the apostles* this reason for this. At our first birth we were born of necessity without our knowledge, ... and grew up in bad habits and wicked behaviour. So that we should not remain children of necessity and *ignorance* (ἀγνοίας), but of free choice and knowledge, and *obtain remission of the sins* we have already committed, there is named at the water, over him who has chosen to be born again and has *repented of his sinful acts*, the name of God ...» (*1.Apol.* 61:9f). This does not look like a direct quotation, but perhaps Justin is paraphrasing a passage from *an apostolic pseudepigraph* - the same source which prompted the Is 1:16-20 quotation, i.e. the KP? Compare fragments 2a; 4, and 5 (ὅσα ἐν ἀγνοίᾳ τις ... ἐποίησεν ... ἐὰν ... μετανοήσῃ, πάντα αὐτῷ ἀφεθήσεται τὰ ἁμαρτήματα, fragm. 5. ὥστε καὶ ὑμεῖς ὁσίως καὶ δικαίως μανθάνοντες ἃ παραδίδομεν ὑμῖν ..., fragm. 2).

Finally: In fragment 6 Peter says: «But we, unrolling *the books of the prophets which we possess* ...» The italicized words show clearly that Peter is speaking to a Gentile audience not familiar with the OT. And Peter's words would form a perfect sequel to the concluding remarks in Justin's version of the Aristeas legend: »... the books remain in the hands of the Egyptians down to the present: *the Jews everywhere (have) them too*» (*1.Apol.* 31:5). In other words: Did Peter in the *Kerygma* introduce his Scriptural proof with a version of the Aristeas legend? One should note the parallelism between Justin's and Peter's summary of the Scriptural proof:[7]

| *1.Apol.* 31:7 | KP fragm. 6 |
|---|---|
| We find (εὕρωμεν) it predicted in the books of the prophets that Jesus our Christ | We, unrolling the books of the prophets... find (εὕρωμεν) |
| would come (παραγινόμενον) born of a Virgin, grown to manhood, healing every sickness... | his coming (παρουσία) |
| be hated and unacknowledged and crucified, | and death and cross |
| dying | and all the rest of the tortures the Jews inflicted on him |
| and rising again (ἀνεγειρόμενον) | and his resurrection (ἔγερσιν) |
| and ascending into heaven | and assumption to heaven previous to the founding of [8] Jerusalem. |

Does this mean that the prooftexts for the »creed« in *Apol.* 32-35/50ff are also taken from the KP? There is, as far as I can see, no direct evidence in Clement to substantiate that hypothesis.

And it is time to mention some evidence which calls for caution. The anti-cultic polemic in the KP is different from Justin's.[9] And we have seen that Justin's anti-cultic polemic is closely related to the testimonies in *1.Apol.* 37 - and even to the New Law testimonies. The anti-cultic polemic in the KP shows that the distance to Judaism is considerable.[10] As we shall see, the same cannot be said about the material in Justin. The KP lays great stress on the concept of the Christians as the »third race«[11] and connects Jer 31:31 with this concept. This is utterly foreign to Justin. His entire material on the New People has another orientation, and he rather takes Jer 31:31 as a Christological testimony: Jesus is the new Covenant in person (see further below).

This is sufficient to warn against any temptation to make the *Kerygma* the source behind all the non-LXX texts in Justin. It seems obvious that we shall have to search for other testimony sources besides the KP.

---

7. On this parallelism, cf. Rordorf, 'Logos und Nomos', p. 430. Rordorf points to *Dial.* 85:2 as especially close to the KP, *ibid.*, n. 30.

8. Most commentators emend the reading of the text (κτισθῆναι), suggesting κριθῆναι (von Dobschütz); καθαιρηθῆναι or ληφθῆναι. But perhaps one should keep the text as it is - it may envisage the New Jerusalem (Rev 21f), cf. Rordorf, *art. cit.* pp. 430f.

9. The accusation that the Jews worship angels (fragm. 2a) recurs in Aristides (who here probably depends on the KP), but not in Justin. Neither has he a parallel to the polemic based on Jewish non-observance of the feasts when the moon does not appear. (This premiss in the KP is incorrect, by the way, - an indication that the author has no first-hand knowledge of Judaism, as pointed out by Nautin, *art. cit.*, p. 105).

10. Cf. the instructive remarks in Nautin, pp. 102/105.

11. For comments and bibliography relating to this important concept, see below, pp. 332/351 with notes.

Observing Justin's great familiarity with many of the non-LXX texts, especially in the Christological section of the *Apology,* one can hardly escape the impression that they derive from sources which Justin had not just happened to read. And the quite complex relation proved to exist in regard to all known and hypothetical sources excludes, I think, every theory which claims a single - or even a couple of literary sources - as the all-explaining source behind Justin's non-LXX texts and his non-LXX exegesis. The very complexity of the evidence, taken together with Justin's *great familiarity*[12] with much of the material, makes one inclined to believe that Bousset's proposal after all has much to be said for it: Some of Justin's testimony sources may have been *Schriftbeweistraktate* circulating within a «school» milieu. The KP may draw on such material, closely related to Justin's - or the KP may have been incorporated among other sources in the teaching activity of the school.

Final certainty is difficult to acheive here, but I think the observations above about possible dependence upon the KP should be seen as a supplement rather than as an alternative to Bousset's proposal.

## 2. *The «recapitulation» source*

I think the remarks made above concerning the «kerygma» source apply here as well: The arguments advanced so far are hardly sufficient to prove that we have to do with a single, published , work of literature. And yet I am more inclined to think that such was the case with this source, because here we seem to encounter a very consequent line of thought, and the material has a remarkable thematic concentration.

The suggestion I want to make here is that this source might be identical with the lost *Controversy between Jason and Papiscus* written by Aristo of Pella.[13] Not much is known about this writing or its contents. But the few scraps of information that *have* come down to us, are of considerable interest.

---

12. I am referring to the phenomenon - often observed in the textual analyses in Part I - that Justin in his allusions and expositions of a text presupposes the non-LXX readings of his testimony sources, despite the fact that he has copied large LXX excerpts in the immediate context. In the vast majority of cases this observation has reference to material deriving from the «kerygma» source, this is another indication that this material could well derive from some «school» tradition, and not from any writing Justin had happened to read.

13. For general information on Aristo, see O. Bardenhewer, *Geschichte der altkirchlichen Literatur* I (Freiburg im Breisgau, 1913 (repr. Darmstadt, 1962)); pp. 202-206; A. von Harnack, *Geschichte der altchristlichen Literatur bis Eusebius* I:1 (1893 (repr. Leipzig 1958)). Harnack once thought that Aristo's controversy could be reconstructed from Evagrius' *Altercatio (Die Altercatio Simonis Judaei et Theophili Christiani, nebst Untersuchungen über die antijüdische Polemik in der Alten Kirche* TU 1:3, Leipzig 1883 ). The criticism of this thesis by P. Corssen (*Die Altercatio Simonis Judaei et Theophili Christiani auf ihre Quellen geprüft* (Berlin, 1890)) and Th. Zahn (*Forschungen zur Geschichte des neutestamentlichen Kanons* 4 (1891), pp. 308-329), caused him later to retract from this hypothesis; cf. his *Geschichte* I:1, p. 95, and Bardenhewer, pp. 205f.

Origen has the following to say about this *Controversy:* «. . .a Christian is described as conversing with a Jew on the subject of the Jewish Scriptures, and proving that the predictions regarding Christ fitly apply to Jesus; although the other disputant maintains the discussion in no ignoble style, and in a manner not unbecoming the character of a Jew» (*Contra Celsum* IV:52).[14] We notice that according to Origen the only theme of the *Controversy* was the Messiahship of Jesus. Origen says nothing about a discussion of the Law, the people of God, etc. One should probably not press this silence unduly, and yet it is relevant to point out that in our analysis above we came across the «recapitulation» source only in sections concerned with Christology. It is striking that in *Dial.* 91:4 - 94:5 (brazen serpent - derived from the «recapitulation» source), the section dealing with the Law (*Dial.* 92f) is an obvious insertion.

We move on to some observations of details, taking into consideration relevant material in Irenaeus and Tertullian.

(1) Let us begin with Justin's combined allusions to Ps 110:3 and Ps 72:5/17. A similar but not identical quotation occurs in Irenaeus, *Dem.* 43, introduced as «Jeremiah».[15]

| *Dem.* 43 | *Dial.* 45:4 | *Dial.* 76:7 |
|---|---|---|
| Before the daystar ⌉ Ps 110:3 <br> I begot Thee ⌋ <br> Thy name ⌉ Ps 72:17 <br> is before the sun⌋ | ὃς καὶ <br> πρὸ ἑωσφόρου⌉ Ps 110:3 <br> καὶ σελήνης ⌋ Ps 72:5 <br> ἦν | πρὸ ἡλίου  Ps 72:17 <br> καὶ σελήνης  Ps 72:5 <br><br> ἐκ γαστρὸς ⌉ <br> γεὶννηθήσεσθαι ⌋ Ps 110:3 <br> αὐτὸν |

Justin's allusions are free and variable, and it is difficult to assess a possible dependence upon Irenaeus' source - granted that Irenaeus depends on a source for his «Jeremiah» quotation. This last surmise does indeed seem very probable. In *Dem.* 43 we find three testimonies on the pre-existence of the Son: (1) a *Targum* - probably Christian - of Gen 1:1: »*Baresith bara elovim basan benuam samenthares*«. J.P. Smith[16] has proposed to restore this to:

---

14. I have adopted the ANF translation.
15. J. P. Smith's surmise as to how this false ascription arose, is ingenious and not improbable:·The composite text and the attribution to Jeremias could .. be accounted for by supposing the source to have had, for instance: «Jeremias:'Before I formed Thee in the womb, I knew Thee'(Jer 1:5); also:'from the womb before the daystar I begot Thee; His name continueth before the sun'.» The text attributed correctly to Jeremias (Jer 1:5) has been omitted as less suitable for the present purpose, but the two Psalm-texts have been mistakenly supposed to be a single quotation from the same source as the preceeding one.» (*Demonstration,* p. 182, n. 206).
16. J. P. Smith, 'Hebrew Christian Midrash in Iren. Epid. 43', *Biblica* 38 (1957); cf. also P. Nautin, 'Genèse 1,1-2, de Justin à Origène', *In Principio. Interprétations des premiers versets de la Genèse* (Etudes Augustiniennes, Paris, 1973) (pp. 61-94)pp. 84-86. I find Prigent's comment on this text in Irenaeus, *Justin,* p. 129, rather misleading, cf. below p. 338, n. 29.

בראשית ברא אלהים (ברוך שמו) בן יאחר את השמים והארץ

»In the beginning God (blessed be his name!) created a Son, afterwards the
heaven and the earth.« This accords with Irenaeus' own translation:»A Son in
the beginning God established, then heaven and earth.« (2) Then follows
the »Jeremiah« quotation Ps 110:3/Ps 72:17; and (3) the third quotation is an
apocryphal »Jeremiah« logion: »Blessed is he who existed before he was
made man.« It is evident that Irenaues does not quote these texts from the
LXX, and their common theme points to a testimony source.

Tertullian seems to have known the same source: *Aiunt quidam et
Genesin in Hebraico ita incipere: in principio Deus fecit Filium (Adv. Prax.
5:1).* However, Tertullian may have this from the *Demonstration* of Irenaeus.

Turning to Jerome, we find the following remark in *Quest.Hebr. in Genes.
inc.: Plerique existimat, sicut in altercatione quoque Jasonis et Papisci
scriptum est, et Tertullianus in libro contra Praxeam disputat: necnon
Hilarius in expositione cujusdam Psalmi affirmat, in Hebraeo haberi: In
filio fecit Deus coelum et terram.*[17] If Jerome here carefully copies what he
read in the *Controversy between Jason and Papiscus,* this writing cannot be
the source behind *Dem.* 43. The source in *Dem.* 43 does not take בראשית
as *in filio,* but *adds* »the Son« as the first work »created« »in the beginning«.
However, there is reason to doubt Jerome's exactness, for he also says that
Tertullian in *Adv.Prax.* reads *in filio,* which is manifestly not the case.
Tertullian has the same reading as *Dem.* 43. It thus seems that Jerome took
the reading *in filio* from Hilary,[18] and included the two other writers for no
other reason than that they also had a «Son» in Gen 1:1. We have thus an
indication that the *Controversy between Jason and Papiscus* may well be
the source behind *Dem.* 43 (and *Adv.Prax.* 5:1, if this text is independent of
*Dem.* 43). The presence of a Hebrew Targum on Gen 1:1 in *Dem* 43 is
remarkable, and we have every reason to believe that the *Controversy*
argued from the Hebrew text of Gen 1. So - if Irenaeus depends on the
*Controversy* in *Dem.* 43, the same may be true of Justin in his combined
allusions to Ps 72:17/Ps110:3 in the «recapitulation» passages.

(2) Maximus Confessor[19] states that he has read the phrase »seven
heavens« in the *Controversy.* Compare *Dem.* 9: »But the earth is encompas-
sed by seven heavens, in which dwell Powers and Angels and Archangels,
giving homage to the Almighty God who created all things, not as to one
having need of anything, but lest they too be idle and useless and accursed.
Therefore the Spirit of God in his indwelling is manifold, and is enumerated by Isaias the prophet in the seven charismata resting on the Son of God,

---

17. PL 23, cols. 985-987.
18. What Hilary wrote, was the following: *Bresith* verbum Hebraicum est. Id tres significantias in
    se habet, id est *in principio,* et *in capite,* et *in filio. (Ibid,* note *ad loc.).*
19. PG 4, col, 422.

that is, the Word, in his coming as man. (Follows a quotation of Is 11:2f(LXX)) Hence the first heaven from the top, which encloses the others, is wisdom; and the one after it, that of understanding . . . and the seventh, this firmament of ours, full of the fear of this Spirit, who lights up the heavens.» There are several interesting features in this passage. I restrict myself to two. (A) The doctrine of the seven heavens[20] seems to be combined with Is 11:2f in the following way: In his descent through the heavens, the Son of God clothes himself successively with the seven *charismata* enumerated in Is 11:2f.[21] It is evident that in Justin's anti-Hezekiah source it was a major point to prove that Jesus was in full possession of his *dynamis* already from birth. This may well accord with the interpretation of Is 11:2f given in *Dem.* 9, but hardly with an application of Is 11:2f to Jesus' baptism. Now, in *Dial.* 87f Justin is very likely *also* drawing on a source which applied Is 11:2f to the baptism of Jesus (cf. above pp. 195 -199).

But Justin corrects this, and although his own idea is different from the one in *Dem.* 9, he may have been inspired to his refutation (of any connexion between Is 11:2f and Jesus' baptism) from the source behind *Dem.* 9. - Next (B) we notice the close connexion between the doctrine of the seven heavens and the angelology of the text. The fall of the angels is hinted at: «lest *they too* be idle and useless and *accursed*». This is taken up in *Dem.* 16: The archangel of the earth led Adam to sin, and because the angel «at the prompting of his nature . . . had rebelled and fallen away from God . . . was called in Hebrew Satan, that is, apostate (= ἀποστάτης); but the same one is also called the slanderer. So God rebuked the serpent, who had been the bearer of the slanderer, and this *curse* fell upon the animal itself, and the angel, Satan, lurking hidden within it . . .» J.P.Smith says that «this meaning for the word »Satan« is doubtless taken from Justin, who derives the word from *sata* »apostate« and *nas* »serpent« . . .»[22] The parallel in *Dial.* 103:5 is indeed close, but the connexion between angelology and the theme of the seven heavens is also close in Irenaeus - possibly already in Irenaeus' source material. That would suggest direct access to Justin's source at this point. Was this source the *Controversy?*

We have seen already that angelology played a major role in Justin's anti-Hezekiah source, cf. *Dial.* 79 and especially *Dial.* 85:6: «Now this is the saying by which I signified that God made it clear that there are *angels* and *powers* (δυνάμεις) in heaven: »Praise the Lord from the heaven; praise him in the highest; praise him all ye his angels; praise him all ye his powers«(Ps

---

20. There is an obvious parallel in *Asc. Ies.,* pointed out i.a. by J. A. Robinson in his Introduction, pp. 41-43, and by J. P. Smith, note *ad loc. (Demonstration,* p. 146). But there is nothing corresponding to the peculiar juxtapposition of the seven heavens and Is 11:2f - this is peculiar to *Dem* 9.

21. I take this to be the meaning of the quite enigmatic chapter. It seems Irenaeus is here reproducing a tradition with which he himself was not utterly at home.

22. *Demonstration,* p. 153, n. 90.

148:1) .» *Dem.*9 also speaks of *powers* and *angels* (and archangels, preparing the description of Satan's fall). Is there a common source behind *Dem.*9 and *Dial.* 85:6?[23]

(3) In his commentary on Gal 3:13 Jerome[24] says that he has read in the *Controversy*: λοιδορία θεοῦ ὁ κρεμάμενος. This reading of Deut 21:23 has one obvious implication: Whatever Aristo may have made of Deut 21:23, he could not share the Pauline argument in Gal 3:13, and he must have refused to apply Deut 21:23 to Jesus. Aristo's reading corresponds to Aquila's and the rabbinic understanding of the passage ( קללת אלהים does not mean «accursed by God» but «an insult against God»).[25] Of course there could be no question of Christ bearing (vicariously) a λοιδορία θεοῦ!

As I have argued above (p. 218f), the «recapitulation» source employed in Dail. 91/94 refused to apply Deut 21:23 to Jesus. The argument seems to have been something like this: When Moses made an image of the serpent, he broke one of God's commandments (Ex 20:4). In a similar way, the Law (Deut 21:23) will be suspended at the realization of this type, namely when Jesus is nailed to the tree. By fixing the serpent to a type of the cross, Moses proclaimed that death was to come to the serpent through the cross. As we have seen, this idea is closely related to other «recapitulation» passages in which Christ is potrayed as the second Adam conquering Satan. Here it is relevant to point out that in Justin's material on the temptation story (*Dial.* 103:5 and 125:3f), the identification of Satan with the serpent and the naming of Christ as his conqueror («Isra-el») is brought out by means of two Hebrew-Aramaic etymologies, and these are the only ones in the *Dialogue:* 'Satanas' means «apostate serpent» (*Dial.* 103:5), «Israel» means «a man overcoming power» (= Christ overcoming Satan, *Dial.* 125:3f). One may suggest that the non-Pauline treatment of Deut 21:23 in *Dial.* 91:4; 94 - so closely connected with the material in *Dial.* 103:5 and 125 - derives from the same source from which Justin got his Hebrew etymolopies for Satanas and Israel. We know one thing about the *Controversy*: It sometimes argued from the Hebrew text.[26]

---

23. In *Dem.* 8 Irenaeus says that God is *creator* of heaven and earth and the whole world, and *maker* of *angels* and men. Ps 148:5 reads: ὅτι αὐτὸς εἶπεν καὶ ἐγενήθησαν, αὐτὸς ἐνετείλατο καὶ ἐκτίσθησαν. The two verbs refer to i .a. ἄγγελοι and δυνάμεις in vs. 2.

24. PL 26, col. 387.

25. On the different readings and interpretations of Deut 21:23, cf. the convenient collection and discussion of the relevant material in Gert Jeremias, *Der Lehrer der Gerechtigkeit* (Studien zur Umwelt des Neuen Testaments 2, Göttingen, 1963), pp. 133-135. Of special interest is the reading of Symmachus: διὰ τὴν βλασφημίαν τοῦ θεοῦ ἐκρεμάσθη. This is of course utterly un-Pauline.

26. One might object against this proposal that the non-Pauline material in *Dial.* 91/94 seems to share the catchword «curse» with the Pauline (and LXX) reading of the text. But this consequent reference to the «curse» might be Justin's conscious modification of the λοιδορία of his source, since this latter reading would have made his intended synthesis with the Pauline point of view utterly complicated.

(4) A main point in Justin's anti-Hezekiah source is an anti-Hezekiah polemic (apropos Is 7:14) based upon Is 8:4, which is interpolated into Is 7:16.[27] Let us compare a passage in Tertullian's *Adv. Marc.*: *Prouoca nunc, ut soles, ad hanc Esaiae comparationem Christi, contendens illam in nullo conuenire. Primo enim, inquis, Christus Esaiae Emmanuhel uocari habebit. Dehinc uirtutem sumere Damasci et spolia Samariae aduersus regem Assyriorum. Porro iste, qui uenit, neque sub eiusmodi nomine est editus, neque ulla re bellica functus est* (III:12:1). In order to evaluate this passage, one has first to notice that chs. 12f of *Adv.Marc.* III evidently depend on *Dial.* 77f. One could therefore imagine that Tertullian here ·hypothetically· ·makes his adversary object to Justin's treatment of Is 7:10ff in *Dial.* 77f. (Marcion cannot for chronological reasons have gainsayed Justin in the *Antitheseis* ). In that case the combination of Is 7:14 and 8:4 in *Adv.Marc.* III:12:1 derives from Justin, not from Marcion. The parallel passage in *Adv.Jud.* 9:1f might be adduced in support of this: '*Sic ut Esaias praedicat: audite, domus Dauid . . . ecce uirgo concipiet et pariet filium: et uocabitis nomen eius Emmanuel . . . Butyrum et mel manducabit, quoniam, priusquam cognoscat infans uocare patrem aut matrem, accipiet uirtutem Damasci et spolia Samariae aduersus regem Assyriorum'*, *sic itaque, dicunt Iudaei, prouocemus ad istam praedicationem Esaiae et faciamus compaarationem, an Christo qui iam uenit competat illi nomen, quod Esaias praedicauit . . . Et primo quidem Esaias praedicat eum Emmanuel uocitari oportere, dehinc uirtutem sumpturum Damasci et spolia Samariae aduersus regem Assyriorum. Porro iste, dicunt, qui uenit, neque sub eiusmodi nomine est dictus neque re ulla bellica functus.* Here the dependence on Justin seems patent: The quoted text is a condensed version of Justin's interpolated text. And the objections against Justin's argument is here put into the mouth of the Jews, not Marcion - another indication that the argument attributed to Marcion is not authentic.[28]

But there are some observations which tell against this explanation. In *Adv.Jud.* the Jews are made to argue that Is 7:14/8:4 do not fit *Christo qui iam uenit* - the Messiah who has already come. The implication must be that the Messiah spoken of in Isaiah has not yet come. But this is the position of Marcion - not of the Jews. As we shall see below (p.380f), there is Jewish evidence confirming Justin's assertion that the Jews did not refer Is 7:14/8:4 to a future Messiah, but to Hezekiah. This means that whatever literary relation there may be between *Adv.Jud.* and *Adv.Marc.* III in the

27. For the following, cf. Prigent *Justin*, pp. 149-155.
28. According to Prigent, *loc. cit.,* Tertullian depends on Justin, viz. Justin's *Syntagma.*

passages where they run parallel,[29] this argument has its authentic setting in the anti-Marcion debate.

This suggests that *Adv.Marc.* III:12:1 may relate something actually written by Marcion in his *Antitheseis*. In the context, Tertullian is no doubt referring points actually made by Marcion (III:8ff), and in III:15 the discussion on Emmanuel is mentioned on a line with the discussion on Marcion's docetic Christology. Concerning Marcion's argument about the warlike acts of the Messiah, it would not hit Justin's exposition in *Dial.* 77f, and Tertullian obviously considers a mere repetition of Justin's exegesis a sufficient rejoinder.

I take this to point to the conclusion that the *prouoca nunc, ut soles* in *Adv.Marc.* III:12:1 refers to something actually written by Marcion.[30] Justin may be silently answering Marcion concerning the meaning of Is 8:4 in *Dial.* 78:8f. But if the combined, interpolated version of Is 7:14ff was already known to Marcion, there is every reason to think it was pre-Justinian, known to Marcion from the same source which Justin employs in *Dial.* 66/77f. Marcion's objection, as stated by Tertullian, is obviously an objection to a given Christian exegesis of the combined text. Did Marcion find this in the *Controversy?*

(5) One final observation. In the sections where we have surmised that the ·anti-Hezekiah· source is employed, there is a remarkable great number of Jewish objections *stated by Justin himself.* The following list gives the evidence:

| | |
|---|---|
| 32:4 | Jewish exegesis of Dan 7:25 |
| 33:1 | Jews say Ps 110 is spoken about Hezekiah |
| 34:1f ⎫<br>34:7 ⎭ | Jews say Ps 72 is spoken about Solomon |
| 36:2 | Jews say Ps 24 is spoken about Solomon |
| 43:8 | They say that Is 7:14 reads νεᾶνις and is spoken about Hezekiah |

---

29. There are in the main three theories: (1) The parallel passages in *Adv.Marc.* III are Tertullian's own better re-statements of his first attempts in *Adv.Jud.* (So H. Tränkle, *Q. S. F. Tertulliani Adversus Iudaeos. Mit Einleitung und kritischer Kommentar* (Wiesbaden, 1964), pp. XIV - XLIV). (2) *Adv.Jud.* is the ·pirate· edition of Tertullian's second draft of the *Adv.Marc.* mentioned in Tertullian's preface (so G. Quispel *De Bronnen van Tertullianus Adversus Marcionem* (Leiden, 1943), pp. 56-79), or *Adv.Jud.* and *Adv.Marc.* III both draw on this earlier edition of the *Adv.Marc.* (so P. Prigent, *Justin* pp. 138-140('Excursus: La commune origine d'Adversus Marcionem III et d'Adversus Iudaeos'). (3) The passages parallel to *Adv.Marc.* III in *Adv.Jud.* are scribal interpolations into the text of the latter treatise (so recently P. Nautin, *Annuaire*, pp. 162f). It is not my intention here to enter this discussion; it is not necessary for my purpose. The two last mentioned theories both lend support to my contention that the setting of the parallel passages is primarily the anti-Marcion polemic; and even the first theory does not exclude this view, if one takes it that *Adv.Jud.* is an ·exercise· piece, preparing for the *magnum opus.*

30. Harnack accepts this without question, *Marcion,* p.114

52:3     Jews say that Herod was not a Jew
64:5     They say Ps 72 is spoken of Solomon
77:2f    Jews say that Hezekiah waged war on the men in Damascus (Is
       8:4).
83:1     Jews say Ps 110 is spoken about Hezekiah
85:1     Jews say Ps 24 is spoken about Hezekiah or Solomon.

One easily observes that the polemic against these objections is deeply integrated into Justin's source material, and by these objections the exposition is not side-tracked or delayed (except in *Dial.* 32:4 - but there the material has been put to a use different from the one in the source). It is otherwise with the objections *raised by Trypho*. They normally serve to introduce excurses which seem like insertions into a continuous exposition (cf. the table above, p. 192f):

32:1    Objection concerning Dan 7:13f  ⟶  excursus on the motive on the two parousias, not contained in the anti-Hezekiah source.
35:1    Objection concerning Christian heretics  ⟶  excursus on this theme, partly anti-Marcion.
38:1    Objection concerning Christ's pre-existence - preparing the section on the theophanies, *Dial.* 55ff, which thus was not part of the anti-Hezekiah source. As we have seen already, the whole treatment of the theophanies may be originally anti-Marcion.
48:1    Trypho introducing the theme of *Dial.* 55ff.
49:1    Elijah has not yet come - section on the precursor. *Dial.* 49-54, using once more material behind *1.Apol.* 32.
49:6    How could Elijah's spirit be in John?  ⟶  analogy:Moses/Joshua.
51:1    The (synoptic!) testimony on John, Is 40:1ff, is ambiguous.
55:1    Does Scripture know another God besides the Maker of the universe?  ⟶  introducing *Dial.* 55ff on theophanies.
64:1    Jesus Messiah for the Gentiles only.
65:1    What about Is 42:8?  ⟶  excursus on this text.
67:1    Is 7:14:  (a) νεᾶνις, not παρθέος ⎫ formulated *by Justin*
               (b) spoken of Hezekiah ⎭ in *Dial.* 43:8!
               (c) Virgin birth reminiscent of Greek mythology  ⟶  excursus on Greek mythology, 69f.
               (d) Adoptionist Christology the only acceptable  ⟶  excursus on obedience to the Law, 67.
68:1    God becoming man is incredible  ⟶  Justin answering by connecting *Dial.* 55ff with *Dial.* 63.76ff (Virgin birth).
71:4    Which passages have been left out by the Jewish scribes?
       ⟶  *Dial.* 72f excursus on left-out passages.
74:1    Ps 96 spoken about the Father  ⟶  exposition of Ps 96.

77:1    Is 7:14 spoken about Hezekiah.
79:1    Blasphemous to say that angels have fallen $\longrightarrow$ excursus on angelology.
80:1    Is your millennialism sincere?
87:2    How is Is 11:2f to be understood? $\longrightarrow$ excursus on this text and the baptism of Jesus.
89:2    How is a death that is accursed in the Law (Deut 21:23) compatible with Messiahship? $\longrightarrow$ pointing forward to Pauline argument in *Dial.* 95.

Looking through this list, one observes that for the most part these objections by Trypho introduce material which we on other, independent grounds have deemed additions to the anti-Hezekiah source. I think there is a simple explanation to both the above lists. If Justin's source was a *dialogue,* he would not want simply to reproduce the questions and answers of his source. The objections and questions raised in the source he would include in his own exposition of the text - hence the many objections *stated by Justin himself.* But he would show his independence of his source, and his greater mastery of the debate, by letting Trypho ask *new* questions - questions not asked or answered in Justin's source. That may be the reason why the direct answers to Trypho's objections so often look like excurses and deviations which interrupt the *ductus* of the exposition. This would provide an elegant explanation for the excessive «excursus technique» of the *Dialogue.*

This argument that the anti-Hezekiah source was a *dialogue* is quite independent of the arguments advanced above, pointing to the *Controversy between Jason and Papiscus.*

Taken together, I think the arguments advanced above lend some plausibility to the hypothesis that the anti-Hezekiah or «recapitulation» source employed in *Dial.* 32-38 and 63ff is identical with Aristo's *Controversy between Jason and Papiscus.* If Marcion had critical comments about the *Controversy* in his *Antitheseis,* it would provide an elegant explanation of the fact that some of Justin's additions to his source are partly anti-Marcion (*Dial.* 35; 56-60/75; 82).

# PART THREE:

# THE SETTING, PROFILE, AND PROVENANCE OF JUSTIN'S EXEGETICAL MATERIAL

# INTRODUCTORY REMARKS

*1. On purpose and method; and a brief survey of previous research*

My purpose in this third part of my study is to learn as much as possible about the following two questions: (1) What is the theological profile of Justin's exegetical traditions, and (2) from which quarters within the Early Church do they come? The two questions are of course closely interconnected. An answer to one of them helps in answering the other one. Let me submit some considerations which may add some precision to the two basic questions. We know that the Christian Church in its two first centuries was caught up in a difficult process with farreaching consequences: There took place a gradual transition from a predominantly Jewish to a predominantly Gentile setting. Parallel with this, the geographical scene was enlarged and got new centres of gravity. While Palestine (Jerusalem) and Syria (Antioch) continued to be important mainlands, there developed new centras in Rome, Asia Minor, and Alexandria. To some extent this geographical expansion may be seen to correspond to theological diversification, but there is no obvious one-to-one correspondence between geographical location and theological outlook.

In trying to characterize Justin's exegetical traditions, I have both of the above processes in mind. Justin is a Gentile by birth; according to his stylized autobiography in *Dial.* 2-8 he was not familiar with the Bible before his conversion to Christianity as an adult. He thus had another background than the typical Gentile Christian of an earlier generation, who would normally have a prehistory as a God-fearer and visitor of the Synagogue - let say Timothy, who «from childhood had been acquainted with the sacred writings» (2 Tim 3:15). We cannot be wrong in taking Justin to be a Gentile Christian theologian in the full sense of the word. But this makes me all the more interested in the tradition which he inherited. Was a Gentile theology a fresh phenomenon in Justin's days? How «Jewish» is Justin's tradition?

Justin was a Gentile; but he was born and presumably brought up in Palestine. This makes him all the more relevant for a case-study of the transition described above. It is commonly assumed that the philosophical itinerary and the conversion to Christianity described in *Dial.* 2-8 occurred outside Palestine, after Justin left Samaria for Ephesus or other cities on the route to Rome. But of that we know nothing, and there is no necessity in assuming that the events described in *Dial.* 2-8 occurred outside Palestine.[1] If we are right to regard the encounter with the Old Man as in some sense historical,[2] it seems to me we are free to locate it anywhere on the coastline from Palestine to Rome. This leaves us with the fascinating possibility that the Old Man may have been a Palestinian or Syrian Christian, and that Justin's theological traditions may have a Palestinian or Syrian provenance. A closer look at his exegetical traditions may confirm or rule out that possibility.

The method adopted to persue the aims delineated above is thought to be the most simple and straightforward one. After grouping together the material which seems to belong together at a stage prior to Justin (Part II), I compare it with the closest available parallels in Christian literature earlier than Justin, or contemporary or later than him but independent of him. In this way we get material to characterize the theological outlook of Justin's traditions, and we may get some clues to its provenance.

Supporting evidence in both respects is gained by constant comparison with contemporary and later Jewish - especially rabbinic - exegesis. How close is Justin's exegetical traditions to the exegesis of the Rabbis? If it is so close that it seems developed in constant dialogue with rabbinic exegesis -how should we visualize the setting in which this tradition developed?

Anyone occupied with the phenomenon of early Christian exegesis of the Scriptures has to wrestle with the elusive concept of Jewish Christianity. Many and diverse attempts have been made to provide working definitions

---

1. In the Hellenistic cities of Palestine - most of them on the coastline - Greek philosophy had flourished since the days of the Ptolemies. M. Hengel (*Judentum und Hellenismus* (WUNT 10, Tübingen, 1969) has an interesting survey of well-known philosophers from the Palestinian and Syrian cities during the two last centuries BC (pp. 152-161). *Es waren in Palästina und Phönizien . . . sämtliche Philosophenschulen vertreten . . .* (p. 160). It is not without interest to notice that R. Joly has made a good case for the view that Justin in his *history of philosophy* in *Dial.* 2:1f may be influenced by Antiochus *of Asqalon* (Joly, *Christianisme et Philosophie*, 32-38. In Justin's days, a young man in Flavia Neapolis would probably have no problems in finding himself private tutors of philosophy without going abroad (cf. *Dial.* 2:3-6). In fact, Justin says that the Platonist who converted him to Platonism had *recently come to live in our city* (2:6). Williams in his note *ad loc.* says *Hardly . . . Flavia Neapolis . . .*, arguing from *Dial.* 3:1 that *our city* should be placed near the sea, which is obviously not the case with Neapolis/Nablus. But *Dial.* 3:1 does not necessarily imply that the seaside where Justin sought solitude was on the outskirts of *our city* in 2:6. One thus cannot exclude the possibility that Justin finished his philosophical itinerary by being converted to Platonism in his native town of Neapolis. Hyldahl in his comment on *Dial.* 2:6 leaves this possibility open (p. 146); likewise Barnard, *Justin.*

2. Cf. my article 'The conversion of Justin Martyr', StTh 30 (1976), pp. 53-73, with references to relevant literature.

of this unavoidable but difficult term.[3] It is not necessary to my purpose here to enter on an extensive discussion of this complex problem. Suffice it to say that I take the word «Jewish» in the composite term «Jewish Christian» to be primarily a term describing Jewish descent and Jewish national identity. I have avoided to speak of Jewish *Christianity* or Judaeo- *Christianity* . I believe these terms too easily suggest a distinctive and uniform *theology* , or at least a set of doctrines, shared by all or most Jewish Christians. The available evidence rather points to great theological diversity. I shall use, however, the term Jewish *Christian* (noun), meaning by this a Christian of Jewish descent who after his adherence to the Christian faith still keeps a consciousness of his Jewish identity. He may be a member of one of the Jewish Christian splinter groups deemed heretical by the Great Church, but he may also be a member of the Great Church. Various groups of Jewish Christians may perhaps be further characterized by specific *theologoumena* (e.g. adoptionist Christology, eternal validity of the Law), but hardly all Jewish Christians. On a priori reasons, I believe one should not so much seek the common denominator in specific doctrines as in certain theological *concerns*. In my definition a Jewish Christian has not abandoned his Jewish identity. He is still an Isrealite, a member of his people. For him the people of Israel, the Jewish nation, is still central in God's history of salvation. I think there is reason to believe that one of the main concerns of Jewish Christians precisely originated from their Jewish identity: The concern for Israel.[4]

I submit these a priori considerations as first pointers to a meaningful use of this term in characterizing parts of Justin's inherited tradition. We shall have to inquire in the course of the present study if specific concepts or thought-patterns can be related to typically Jewish Christian concerns. (I use the adjectives «Judaeo-Christian» or «Jewish Christian» in the simple meaning «deriving from or pertaining to Jewish Christians».)

---

3. Cf. i.a. R. N. Longenecker, *The Christology of Early Jewish Christianity* (Studies in Biblical Theology, 2nd Ser. 17, London, 1970), pp, 1-24; A. F. J. Klijn, 'The Study of Jewish Christianity', *NTS* 20 (1974), pp. 419-431; R. Murray, 'Defining Judaeo-Christianity', *The Heythrop Journal* 15 (1974), pp, 303-310; M. Simon, 'Réflexions sur le judeo-christianisme', *Christianity, Judaism and other Greco-Roman Cults. Studies for M. Smith at Sixty* (Studies in Judaism in Late Antiquity 12:2, Leiden, 1975) pp. 53-76; B. J. Malina, 'Jewish Christianity or Christian Judaism: Toward a hypothetical Definition', *JSJ* 8 (1976), pp. 46-57; S. K. Riegel,'Jewish Christianity: Definitions and Terminology', *NTS* 24 (1978), pp. 410-15. One can hardly say that a reasonable degree of unanimity has been reached in the definition of the terms.

4. In this way of defining Jewish Christian concerns I partly join issue with J. Jervell,'The Mighty Minority', *StTh* 34 (1980), pp. 13-38. Cf. esp. his definition p. 21:«The Jewish Christians refuse to separate Christianity from the religious, political, and cultural fate of Israel - and there is but one Israel. I am inclined to call this the common denominator which keeps Jewish Christians groups and churches and parties together. There is but one people of God, namely Israel. The significant mark of this people of God is the circumcision of the mosaic torah. So they stick to circumcision. The mosaic torah is a seal and characteristic for the people of the covenant and the salvation. Therefore the law is permanently valid.» In the light of the Jewish Christian material studied in the present work, I should like qualify the latter part of this statement, but essentially I believe Jervell to be right.

The reader will notice that while prime importance is accorded to early Christian and rabbinic parallel material, the Gnostic texts are largely neglected in the present study. A perusal of the relevant Gnostic literature has convinced me that while the Gnostics were often keen interpreters of OT texts, they were foreign to that kind of prophecy/fulfilment exegesis which is basic to Justin's tradition.[5] In the relatively few cases of overlapping between Justin's proof-text dossier and the OT quotations in the Gnostic writings, the latter seem to have a much greater distance to the tradition employed by Justin than Justin has himself.

It has been claimed that Justin's exegesis concerning the Law is inspired from Gnostic sources. I take that suggestion up in the proper place. Concerning the Christian and Jewish parallel material, it may be useful to place some further reflections on problems and method within the framework of a brief survey of previous research.

Until now, the Jewish sources have received most attention, partly by Jewish experts in rabbinic exegesis. The classic study of Justin's debt to rabbinic *haggadah* is A. H. Goldfahn's.[6] Patristic scholars have for the most part been satisfied merely to repeat Goldfahn's material,[7] with one notable exception: A. Lukyn-Williams in the notes to his translation often adds new material based on his own knowledge of the rabbinic literature.[8] It seems that scholars have often overlooked the fact that Goldfahn's aim was rather limited. He would only collect rabbinic parallels to *aggadoth* which Justin reported *as being Jewish* - either by putting them into the mouth of Trypho, or by reporting what the Jewish teachers taught. Rabbinic parallels to Justin's own exegesis are thus neglected by Goldfahn. It goes without saying that these parallels are often the most important, especially for our purpose.

The patristic scholar with no thorough knowledge of rabbinic literature will only hesitantly enter the extremely difficult field of rabbinica. He will rely heavily on the recognized experts in the field, using their references as his guide to important rabbinic material. Invaluable tools in this respect are also the indexes in Billerbeck's and Ginzberg's collections of rabbinic *haggadah*. Ginzberg's volumes of notes have the additional advantage of

---

5. A convenient survey of the Gnostic OT dossier is provided in the Scriptural Index in W.Foerster, *Die Gnosis* 1/2 (Die Bibliothek der Alten Welt I, Zürich-Stuttgart, 1969/71). Cf. also B.A. Pearson,'Biblical Exegesis in Gnostic Literature', *Armenian and Biblical Studies* (ed. M.E. Stone, Jerusalem, 1976), pp. 70-80; R. McL. Wilson,'The Gnostics and the Old Testament', *Proceedings of the International Colloquium on Gnosticism, Stockholm Aug. 20-25 1973* (ed. G. Widengren, Stockholm, 1977), pp. 164-68.
6. A. H. Goldfahn, 'Justinus Martyr und die Agada', *Monatsschrift fur Geschichte und Wissenschaft des Judentums* 22 (1873), pp. 49-60/104-115/145-153/193-202/257-69,
7. See i.a. L. W. Barnard, 'The Old Testament and Judaism in the Writings of Justin Martyr', *VT* 14 (1964), pp. 395-406; W. A. Shotwell , *Exegesis*, pp. 71-93.
8. Samaritan material is adduced by P. R. Weis, 'Some Samaritanisms of Justin Martyr', *JTS* 45 (1944), pp. 199-205.

frequent references to patristic parallels. One also finds great help in the Index volumes to the Soncino translations of the *Babylonian Talmud* and the *Midrash Rabba*, likewise the indexes in W. Braude's midrash translations.[9] A Jewish study especially devoted to Justin seems to have passed almost unnoticed among Justin experts: M. Friedländer, *Patristische und Talmudische Studien*.[10] This study adds much relevant material not found in Goldfahn.

I cannot claim to have exploited these sources to the full; even less can I claim any completeness in the collection and treatment of the Jewish material. Nevertheless, I have found it of some importance to include this material in the present study. As was said already: If a close contact with Jewish - especially rabbinic - exegesis can be found in Justin, this is a first pointer to the provenance of his exegesis.

But this at the same time poses a problem. Did Justin get his Jewish ideas directly from Jews, or were they already part of the Christian exegetical tradition which he inherited? When Justin says that God commanded that the two goats on Atonement Day should be alike (*Dial.* 40:4), one could easily imagine that he had this rabbinic *haggadah*[11] from some Jew. But the same *haggadah* appears in *Barn.* 7:6 - it was in other words already part of the Christian tradition treating the two goats as Christological types. It is difficult to decide similar questions in cases where no prior Christian sources are available. One shall here have to resort to other indications. If the rabbinic *haggadah* is deeply integrated into an exegetical argument which in other respects seems to be traditional, it probably came down to Justin as part of that tradition.

Shotwell's study on Justin's exegesis derserves special mention in this context. In addition to repeating and sifting the material gathered by Goldfahn, Lukyn-Williams, and others, Shotwell adds a new point of view: Justin is dependent upon the (Palestinian) rabbis for his exegetical *method*. His exegetical procedures correspond roughly to Rabbi Hillel's seven principles for exegesis. I have two problems with this thesis. First, it is not at all clear to me that all the arguments in Justin which Shotwell subsumes under Hillel's rules really are examples of those rules. (Some detailed comments on particular examples will be given in due place.) But, secondly, even if one grants Shotwell's characterization of Justin's procedures, it still does not tell us much about Justin's contact with Judaism. There is

---

9. In the present study, I have relied heavily on these and other available translations of rabbinic texts. Only in a few cases have I checked the Hebrew original of rabbinical sayings - as quoted in relevant secondary literature. Concerning questions of method, one can get useful hints in R. Loewe, 'The Jewish Midrashim and Patristic and Scholastic Exegesis of the Bible', *Studia Patristica* I (TU 63, Leipzig, 1957), pp. 492-514.

10. M. Friedländer, *Patristische und talmudische Studien* (Wien, 1878 (repr. Westmead, 1972)), esp. pp. 80-137 ('Justins Dialog mit dem Juden Tryphon').

11. Cf. *M. Yoma* 6:1.

nothing especially rabbinic or Palestinian about Hillel's seven rules when they are taken one by one. They all correspond to usual ways of reasoning in the Hellenistic world.[12] It would hardly call for an explanation if Justin reasoned the same way. There is, however, another element in Shotwell's study which I believe the present study may confirm: In his type of allegory, Justin is much closer to the rabbis than to Philo. Opinions have differed widely concerning Justin's debt to Philo. P. Heinisch [13] and E. R. Goodenough deemed it to be extensive and substantial, while Shotwell comes to the conclusion that it is minimal. One should compare this with D. C. Trakatellis' recent monograph on divine pre-existence in Justin.[14] Trakatellis once again points to Philo as a main influence on Justin. The whole issue thus calls for a renewed treatment.

Let me add a final remark on the rabbinical sources. I am painfully aware of the extreme difficulties concerning the dating of rabbinic texts and sayings. I have adopted a rather conservative attitude concerning the attribution of rabbinical sayings to named rabbis after 70 AD in the *Mishnah* and the *Talmuds*. I am more sceptical concerninq attributions in the *Midrashim*, but in cases where Justin's material is very close to rabbinical sayings attributed to roughly contemporary rabbis, this fact in itself may indicate that the attributions are not entirely anachronistic. In cases where the rabbinic sayings are anonymous and occur in late texts, I have tried to exert due caution.

There is no comprehensive treatment of the Christian sources of Justin's OT exegesis. In the former century, the Tübinger school generated a debate as to whether Justin was an «ebionitic» or a «paulinist» Christian.[15] It has turned out that this was a rather misleading way of posing the problem. The tendency in this century has been, roughly speaking, to make Justin a «mainstream» theologian not particularly dependent on any specific branch of early Christian theology.[16] The only precision which has been proposed is that Justin is dependent upon a Lukan tradition. This position was taken by F. Overbeck in 1872[17] and has since been revived by J. C. O'Neill[18] and N.

---

12. See esp. D. Daube, 'Rabbinic Methods of Interpretation and Hellenistic Rhetoric', *HUCA* 22 (1949), pp. 239-264; *idem*, 'Alexandrian Methods of Interpretation and the Rabbis', *Festschrift Hans Lewald* (Basel, 1953), pp. 27-44 B. Salomonsen,'Om rabbinsk hermeneutik' (Danish,'On rabbinic hermeneutics'), *DTT* 36 (1973), pp, 161-173, esp. pp. 168-173, with relevant literature.

13. P. Heinisch, *Der Einfluss Philos auf die älteste christliche Exegese (Barnabas, Justin und Clemens von Alexandria)* (Alttestamentliche Abhandlungen, Heft 1/2, Münster i. W., 1908). Cf. also the same point of view in C. Siegfried, *Philo von Alexandria als Ausleger des Alten Testaments* (Jena, 1875 (repr. Amsterdam 1970)), pp. 332-340.

14. D. C. Trakatellis, *The Pre-Existence of Christ in the Writings of Justin Martyr* (Harvard Dissertations in Religion 6, Missoula, 1976).

15. Cf. the review of the debate in von Engelhardt, *op, cit.*, pp. 30-68.

16. One could name the studies of L. W. Barnard and E. F. Osborn as representatives of this trend.

17. F. Overbeck, 'Über das Verhältniss Justins des Märtyrers zur Apostelgeschichte', *ZWTh* 15 (1872), pp. 305-349.

18. J. C. O'Neill, *The Theology of Acts in its historical Setting* (London 1961), esp. pp. 10-53.

Hyldahl,[19] though on partly different premises. For Overbeck, however, this amounts to no more than saying that Justin represents mainstream Gentile Christianity - like Luke. Both writers, according to Overbeck, represent a Gentile Christianity profiting from the practical results of Paul's struggle for freedom from the law, but deeply alienated from his theology. O'Neill is mainly interested in Justin as a witness to the late date of the theology of Acts. Hyldahl concentrates mainly on the politic apologetic in Acts and Justin. But he has also some suggestions about a continuity in the «Schrift-beweis»[20] (cf. his emphatic statement to this effect quoted in the Introduction above, p.6). However, Hyldahl's arguments are of a formal nature, he has no investigation of Justin's proof-text tradition compared with Luke's.[21]

We are thus still left with the impression that Justin represents «main-stream» theology. I hold this proposition to be true. In any case Justin *became* a mainstream theologian: His writings seem to have become so influential that he partly decided where the stream was to flow - witness Irenaeus and Tertullian. But the question is still to be asked: Which forces shaped this mainstream theology, on which traditions was it built up? Overbeck tends to explain all differences between Luke and Justin by referring to «development». This is too simple. Much had happened in the intervening years. And as I am trying to show in the present study, some of the things that had happened had important theological repercussions.

Concerning the massive bulk of exegetical traditions in Justin, the above-mentioned studies leave us with next to nothing. In that respect one should rather turn to monographs concerned with the exegesis of the Early Church. J. Daniélou often touches upon material found in Justin in his *Théologie du Judéo-Christianisme*. Daniélou makes us understand that he deems part of Justin's material to be of Judaeo-Christian origin,[22] but he has no evaluation of Justin's tradition as a whole. One should also consult the great number of monographs and articles which map the trajectory of a single theme or text through the patristic period.[23] Much valuable insight can be gained from these, but again we are left without an integrated synthesis concerning Justin, and for the second century many of these studies tend to be rather summary.

W. A. Shotwell in his study of Justin's exegesis has a chapter on Justin and his Christian precursors.[24] But Shotwell largely contents himsef with poin-

---

19. *Op.cit.* pp. 261-272.
20. *Ibid.,* p. 269.
21. A first step in this direction is the unpublished dissertation of W. S. Kurz, referred to in the Introduction, p.6, n.16. The evidence displayed by Kurz is sufficient to show that in proof-text dossier there is little overlap between Luke and Justin.
22. Cf. above, Introduction, 6f.
23. The ones most relevant for Justin are listed in the notes and the Bibliography. For a survey and evaluation of this kind of studies, see W.-D. Hauschild, 'Der Ertrag der neueren auslegungsgeschichtlichen Forschung für die Patristik', *Verkündigung und Forschung* 16 (1971), pp. 5-25.
24. *Op. cit.,* pp. 48-70.

ting out some parallels to Justin's exegesis in the NT, *1. Clement*, Ignatius, *Barnabas*, Papias, and the «Testimony Book». He makes some proposals as to direct dependence on the part of Justin, but the whole chapter has the nature of a sketch, and offers little to our purpose. The conclusion is meagre: «. . . the Apostolic Fathers added little to what Justin had received from the New Testament writers. Even Barnabas, if known and used by Justin, could have contributed little to his exegesis.»[25] I hold this to be essentially true - but then, where does Justin's surplus *vis-a-vis* the NT come from?

With these remarks, I believe I have sufficiently delineated the setting and the approach of the following pages, and I turn to some brief but necessary words on two early Christian ducuments found to be of great importance as parallel material to Justin's tradition.

*2. Two important sources for comparison:* The Anabathmoi Iakobou *and the* Testaments of the Twelve Patriarchs

The first source is labelled *Anabathmoi Iakobou II* by G.Strecker in his monograph on the *Pseudo-Clementines*.[26] This name is as good as any other and seems to have gained some acceptance.[27] I shall therefor use AJ II as a short reference to this source. It is found in the Pseudo-Clementine *Recognitions* (henceforward *Rec.*), Book I:33-71 (44:4 - 53:3 being an insertion).[28] Whatever one may think of the complex problems of literary criticism within the Pseudo-Clementine literature, it is evident that these chapters in *Rec.* I stand out by their peculiar theology which is markedly different from that of the rest of the *Pseudo-Clementines.* This has been seen by several commentators,[29] and is argued minutely and convincingly by Strecker.

Strecker tentatively dates this source to the second half of the second century: It knows the Hadrianic decree, on the other hand, it was used by Strecker's *Grundschrift* redactor (first half of the third century)».[30] J.L. Martyn suggests »near the mid-point of the second century«.[31] I provisionally

---

25. *Ibid*, p. 70.
26. G. Strecker, *Das Judenchristentum in den Pseudoklementinen* (TU 70, Berlin, 1958), pp. 221-254. cf. further H. J. Schoeps, *Theologie und Geschichte des Judenchristentums* (Tübingen, 1949), pp. 384-417; J. L. Martyn, 'Clementine Recognitions 1,33-71, Jewish Christianity, and the Fourth Gospel', *God's Christ and his People. Studies in Honour of Nils Alstrup Dahl* (ed. by J.Jervell/W. A. Meeks, Oslo-Bergen-Tromsø, 1977), pp. 265-295.
27. Cf. e.g. Martyn, *art. cit.;* A. Lindemann, *Paulus im ältesten Christentum* (BHTh 58, Tübingen, 1979), pp. 108f.
28. Cf. Strecker, *op.cit,* p. 236.
29. See the survey of previous research in Strecker, and cf. esp. Schoeps, *loc.cit.*, who works with literary theories different from those of Strecker.
30. Strecker, *op. cit,* pp. 253f .
31. *Art. cit*, p. 272.

accept this dating - we shall have opportunity to add some independent arguments on the matter as we proceed with the analysis of some parallels between Justin and the AJ II.

No doubt the AJ II is written by a Jewish Christian. He traces salvation history from Abraham to the Jerusalem Church under leadership of James. He seems to accept circumcision, at the same time emphasizing baptism as a substitute for Temple sacrifices. He is friendly to mission among the Gentiles, but apparently rejects Paul (the narrative breaks off before Paul's conversion outside Damascus, but there are indications that the author would not accept the Christian Paul).[32] We shall have ample opportunity to characterize aspects of his theology below.

It is relevant to notice that the great interest invested in Jerusalem in this source is matched by two obscure references to the Pella flight (Rec I:37:2 and I:39:3). Strecker and Martyn take this as an indication that the writer saw his own community as the heir of the Jerusalem community, and that he should be located among the Christians in or near Pella who traced their descent from the Jerusalem community by means of the legend about the flight to Pella.[33]

The other source which will often be adduced in the following, is the Christian redaction or interpolation of the *Testaments of the Twelve Patriarchs* (henceforward TP).[34]

A patristic scholar feels rather hesitant when he enters a field where the competent specialists are in such disagreement as with regard to the TP. On the one hand, the entire writing is considered a Christian composition employing Jewish traditions (M. de Jonge); on the other hand, it is deemed an entirely Jewish writing, with Christian interpolations only in secondary strata of the textual transmission (e.g. M.Philonenko, to some extent A.Hultgård).[35] What complicates the question is especially the intricate interconnexion between redaction history and textual transmission. The non-expert certainly has good reason to suspend judgement on the issue.

Nevertheless, I have found the material in the TP of such relevance that it had to be included in the present study. This calls for some preliminary remarks on the position adopted concerning the disputed questions. The following statements are not meant as a contribution to the study of the TP,

---

32. Cf. esp. Martyn, *art. cit.*, p. 271.
33. Cf. Strecker, *op.cit.*, p. 253, and Martyn, *art. cit.*, p. 272. Cf. also M. Simon, 'La migration à Pella: Légende ou réalité? *RSR* 60 (1972), pp. 37-54, esp. pp. 40f.
34. Useful surveys of the history of research are given in M. de Jonge, *The Testaments of the Twelve Patriarchs. A Study of their Text, Composition and Origin* (Assen, 1953),pp. 9-12; *idem*, 'Recent studies on the Testaments of the Twelve Patriarchs', *SEÅ* 36 (1971), pp. 77-96; J. Becker, *Untersuchungen zur Entstehungsgeschichte der Testamente der Zwölf Patriarchen* (Arbeiten zur Geschichte des antiken Judentums und des Urchristentums 8, Leiden, 1970), pp. 7-15.
35. De Jonge, *op.cit.*; M. Philonenko, *Les Interpolations chrétiennes des Testaments des Douze Patriarches et les Manuscrits de Qoumrân* (Paris, 1960); A. Hultgård, *Croyances messianiques des Test. XII Patr. Critique textuelle et commentaire des passages messianiques* (Uppsala, 1971).

their only purpose is to delineate the position taken by the present writer, and to supply some sparse arguments.

(1) I hold the TP to be a Jewish work with Christian interpolations. These interpolations cannot be eliminated by sheer textual criticism - they are present in all strata of textual transmission.[36]

(2) In the passages which contain Messianic or Christological sayings,[12] I believe one can roughly discern three main strata in the TP. (a) There are several passages which speak of an eschatological restoration of Levi's priesthood and Juda's kingship.[38] The priesthood is given dominance over the kingship.[14] The two offices are not united in one Messianic person. This stratum must be Jewish, and can be seen to exhibit structural parallels to the bipolar Messianism of the Qumran community.[40] (b) A second stratum speaks of the salvation of God arising from Levi and Judah.[41] This is still Jewish, but the idea has been Christianized by the identification of this «salvation» with *one* Messianic figure (i.e. Christ), resulting in the illogical idea of a Messiah from Levi *and* Judah.[42] One can observe this process i.a. in the following passage (*T.Jos.* 19:11):[43]

| Armenian | Greek |
|---|---|
| And do you my children honour Levi and Judah, for from them shall arise the salvation of Israel. | Do you therefore my children observe the commandments of the Lord, and honour Levi and Judah, for from them shall arise unto you the lamb of God who shall take away the sin of the world saving all the nations and Israel. |

36. Cf. esp. Becker, *op. cit*, pp. 44-68. Cf. also de Jonge, *Testaments*, pp. 23-34.

37. On the Messianism of the TP, see i.a. Hultgård, *op. cit*; A. S. van der Woude, *Die messianischen Vorstellungen der Gemeinde von Qumran* (Studia Semitica Neerlandica 4, Assen, 1957), pp. 190-216; J. Liver, 'The Doctrine of the two Messiahs in sectarian Literature in the Time of the second Commonwealth', *HTR* 52 (1959, pp. 149-185), pp. 163-185.

38. E. g. *Test. Rub.* 6:7-12; *Test. Sim.* 7:1; *Test. Jud.* 21:1f; *Test. Iss.* 5:7; *Test. Dan* 5:4; *Test. Naph.* 8:2f. The eschatological aspect is more implicit than explicit in some of these passages. De Jonge first isolated this group of texts as a distinctive category of «Levi-Judah-passages», *Testaments*, pp. 83/86-89, cf. Becker, *Testamente*, pp. 178-82. One should probably not speak of «Messianism» at all concerning these passages (against J. Liver, *art. cit.*).

39. Cf. Liver, *art. cit*, pp. 163ff; van der Woude, *Messianische Vorstellungen*, pp. 195-198.

40. This is rightly pointed out by Liver, *art. cit.*, but he reads too much of Qumran Messianism into the Levi-Judah passages. Cf. also B. Otzen's Introduction to his translation in *De gammeltestamentlige Pseudepigrafer* ('The Old Testament Pseudepigrapha'(Danish)) Copenhagen, 1974), p. 682.

41. E.g. *Test. Gad* 8:1; *Test. Dan* 5:9f; *Test. Naph.* 8:2f; *Test. Sim.* 7:2, cf. van der Woude, *Messianische Vorstellungen*, p. 190; de Jonge, *Testaments*, p.88.

42. Apart from *Test. Jos.* 19:11 quoted in the text, cf. *Test. Dan.* 5:9-12. I take also *Test. Sim.* 7:1f to belong to this category, although the identity of the High Priest and the King is not clearly stated.

43. I have adapted the translation of Liver, *art. cit.*, pp. 176f. On *Test.Jos.* 19:11f, cf. Hultgård, pp. 169/174-178; van der Woude, pp. 201-204. Both writers judge the Armenian text to be more original - van der Woude by the striking argument that ἀνατέλλειν suits «the salvation of Israel», not a lamb.

(c) A more thorough Christian redaction is acheived in *T.Lev.* 18 and *T.Jud.* 24. Here the Messiah is from Judah, not from Levi, and his priesthood substitutes the Levitic priesthood, *T. Lev.* 18:1f.[44] There is in these texts, in their present form, no question of a restoration of the priestly and kingly dynasties, but only of a single person whose combined kingship and priesthood is eternal. I hold these texts to be so thoroughly Christianized that whatever one may think of a Jewish substratum shining through in different verses and phrases,[45] in their present form these texts should be read as Christian texts in their entirety.[46]

(3) This last remark brings me to a point made by J.Jervell concerning the TP as a whole.[47] «*Man sollte einmal versuchen, wo Interpolationen sicher vorliegen, die ganze Schrift mit den Augen des Interpolators zu lesen, um zu sehen, was dann herauskommt*».[48] The interpolator did not want us to detect his work as an interpolator; he wanted us to read and understand the whole book as it resulted from his editorial work. This means that the interpolations should not be read in isolation when we ask what was the theology of the interpolator. The interpolations should be read as interpretations of the context into which they are inserted.

This point of view in some cases reduces the necessity of exactly delineating what is interpolation and what is *Grundschrift.*

(4) The Christian interpolations tend to come in two sorts of passages: (a) the sayings about restoration of priesthood and kingship, and (b) the sayings about judgement, exile and final redemption for Israel.[49] The work of the interpolator with respect to the last category of texts is most helpful in determining his theological outlook. This aspect has been stressed by Jervell. We shall have opportunity to return to this below.

(5) There is certainly more than one Christian interpolator. Some of the Christological interpolations seem late, reflecting a developed Christology.[50] But I think one can discern a basic stem of early interpolations which seem to reflect a consistent theology, centering on Christ as the teacher of God's Law, bringing salvation to the Gentiles and Israel.[51] This interpolator seems close to a certain stratum of Justin's material. Jervell deems him a Jewish Christian writing at the turn of the first century.

---

44. This is well observed by M. de Jonge, *Testaments,* p. 89, and M.-A. Chevallier, *L'Esprit et le Messie dans le bas-judaïsme et le Nouveau Testament* (EHPhR 49, Paris, 1958), p. 131, n. 1.

45. There are good reasons to think that in *Test. Lev* 18 and *Test. Jud* 24 sayings about God have been given a Christological interpretation, cf. van der Woude pp. 205f.

46. So of course de Jonge, but cf. also Chevallier *op. cit.* pp. 125-132. Becker, *Testamente,* also deems the Christian redaction to be substantial (pp. 291-300 on *Test. Lev.* 18, pp. 319-323 on *Test. Jud.* 24).

47. J. Jervell, 'Ein Interpolator interpretiert. Zu der christlichen Bearbeitung der Testamente der zwölf Patriarchen', *Studien zu den Testamenten der Zwölf Patriarchen* (BZNW 36, ed. W. Eltester, Berlin, 1969), pp. 30-61.

48. *Op. cit.* p. 31.

49. De Jonge recognized the common characteristics of these passages, and labelled them «S.E.R.-passages» («Sin-Exile-Return»), *Testaments,* pp. 83-86.

50. Jervell, *art. cit.,* distinguishes between an early stratum of interpolations, reflecting a Judaeo-Christian outlook, and later, more extensive Christological interpolations (pp. 49f/56-59).

51. Cf. again Jervell, *art. cit.*

## CHAPTER ONE

## THE SETTING OF JUSTIN'S EXEGESIS

As I have pointed out earlier (above, pp. 11 - 13), Justin thinks of himself as one who carries on an exegetical tradition handed down to the Church from the risen Christ via the apostles.

There can be no doubt about the source of this impressive conception in Justin: it is Lukan. According to Luke, Christ after his resurrection «opened» the meaning of the Scriptures to his disciples (not so exclusively the 12 apostles, as in Justin). And while so doing, he referred back to his passion predictions: «These are my words which I spoke to you, while I was still with you, that everything written about me in the Law of Moses and the prophets and the psalms must be fulfilled» (Lk 24:44, cf. 24:6f). This cross reference to the passion predictions corresponds to a Lukan peculiarity in the third passion prediction. While the other passion predictions have no explicit reference to the fulfilment of the Scriptures, Luke adds this in the third prediction: «Behold, we are going up to Jerusalem, *and everything that is written of the Son of Man by the prophets will be accomplished.* For he will be delivered . . .»(Lk 18:31f).[1]

Justin has the same cross reference between postresurrectional instruction and passion prediction: «For these (the apostles), after he had risen from the dead, and they had been convicted by him that even before his passion he told them that he must suffer these things, *and that these things had been proclaimed beforehand by the prophets . . .» (Dial.* 106:1). The text from *Dial.*76:6 quoted above (p. 11) is immediately followed by 76:7: «For he cried before he was crucified: The Son of Man must suffer many things, and be rejected by the Scribes and Pharisees . . .» Cf. also *Dial.* 100:2f.

Luke no doubt wanted his readers to see the fruit of this instruction of the disciples in the missionary and apologetic speeches in Acts: The OT proof here presented derives from the instruction given by the risen Christ. We have seen already how Justin carries on this point of view.

This correspondence between Luke and Justin can be traced further in at least two respects.

(1) There is a striking similarity with regard to the purpose of the Scriptural proofs in Acts and Justin. The aim of the missionary speeches in

---

1. The importance of the proof-from-prophecy in Luke-Acts is rightly emphasized and clearly demonstrated in P. Schubert, 'The Structure and Significance of Luke 24', *Neutestamentliche Studien für R. Bultmann* (BZNW 21 , Berlin, 1954), pp. 165-186, esp.pp. 174-186. (On the Lukan passion predictions, see *ibid.*, pp. 180-182).

Acts is - generally speaking - to prove from the OT and the resurrection of Jesus that he is the Messiah and that by his resurrection the Messianic age has been ushered in. When Luke in a summary way shall describe the contents of the preaching, it is quite simply said that the missionaries proved from the Scriptures that Jesus is the Messiah. «Saul increased all the more in strength and confounded the Jews who lived in Damascus by proving that Jesus was the Christ», 9:22; «. . . Paul went in (to the synagogue) as was his custom, and for three weeks he argued with them from the Scriptures, explaining and proving that it was necessary for the Christ to suffer and to rise from the dead, and saying, 'This Jesus, whom I proclaim to you, is the Christ'», 17:2f; «. . . Paul was occupied with preaching, testifying to the Jews that the Christ was Jesus», 18:5; «. . . he (Apollos) powerfully confuted the Jews in public, showing by the Scriptures that the Christ was Jesus», 18:28, cf. also 28:23. According to his own understanding, Justin is doing exactly the same.

(2) The *setting* of Paul's missionary activity in Acts roughly corresponds to the setting of Justin's dialogue with Trypho. In Acts, the setting of Paul's missionary preaching and teaching is the *dialogue,* the *debate* with the Jews in the synagogues, Acts 13:5.15; 14:1; 17:4.12.17; 18:4. These dialogues are not only aimed at the Jews, but also at an interested audience of God-fearing Gentiles[2] present in the synagogues, Acts 13:16.26.43; 14:1 etc. And when Paul is rejected by the Jews, one has to imagine that it is primarily to these God-fearers he turns, as indicated in Acts 13:46-48; 14:1f; 16:13f; 18:7; 19:9f; 28:17-31. In the case of Apollos, one even gains the impression that his refutation of the Jews «in public» is primarily aimed at the conversion - not of the Jews, but of the benevolent audience of such discussions. Luke nowhere indicates that Paul's turning from the Jews to the God-fearing Gentiles implied a basic change in the mode of presenting the kerygma: The proof from the Scriptures is addressed also to these people, Acts 13:16.26, because they believe in the God of the Jews and are supposed to know the Scriptures - cf. also Acts 8:26-40 and 10:34-43.

The dialogue, the debate, the polemic exposition is mentioned as the mode of proclamation. διελέξατο αὐτοῖς ἀπὸ τῶν γραφῶν, 17:2; διελέγετο . . . τοῖς Ἰουδαίοις καὶ τοῖς σεβομένοις 17:7; διελέγετο δὲ ἐν τῇ

---

2. On this important group in Jewish and early Christian mission, see esp. K. Lake, 'Proselytes and God-Fearers', *The Beginnings of Christianity,* Part I, Vol.,V (ed. F. Jackson/K. Lake, London, 1933), pp. 74-96; F. Siegert, 'Gottesfürchtige und Sympathisanten', *JSJ* 4 (1973), pp. 109-164; N.J. Mc Eleney, 'Conversion, Circumcision, and the Law', *NTS* 20 (1974), pp. 319-341; E. Every, 'Jews and God-Fearers in the New Testament Period', *Immanuel* 5 (1975), pp. 46-50. Concerning the relation between Luke's portrait and Paul's actual missionary procedure, one should probably say with M. Hengel: There is fundamentally no contradiction between Paul's selfunderstanding as an apostle to the Gentiles, and Luke's claim that Paul chose the synagogues as his base of preaching. «*Dort fand Paulus die 'Heiden', bei denen er am meisten Erfolg hatte und die er darum in erster Linie ansprechen konnte, die 'Gottesfürchtigen'*. . . (M. Hengel, 'Die Ursprünge der christlichen Mission', *NTS* 18 (1971/72), pp. 15-38, quot. p. 21, n. 23a).

συναγωγῇ κατὰ πᾶν σάββατον, ἔπειθέν τε Ἰουδαίους καὶ Ἕλληνας ,
18:4 - cf. 18:19; 19:8f.[3]

If one tries to visualize this picture of Paul's mission in Acts, the following
scene emerges: Paul is proving the Messiahship of Jesus from the OT in
debate with the Jews, the God-fearing Gentiles being a more or less
interested audience.

The parallel to the setting of Justin's dialogue with Trypho is also in this
respect striking. Already the *mise en scène* of the dialogue in *Dial.* 1:1 and
9:3 is not very unlike the scene in Acts 19:9: After his break with the
synagogue, Paul daily lectures and holds discussions in the «school» of
Tyrannos, not unlike the «philosopher» Justin, who in the fiction of the
*Dialogue* spends his time expounding the Christian doctrine in the «Colon-
nades» (of Corinth or Ephesus?).[4] N.Hyldahl observes on *Dial.* 1:1: «*Die
σχολή (vgl. Dial. 9:2: ἀσχολία), die ihm zur Verfügung steht, vermittelt
sofort den Eindruck erhabener Ruhe und Würde.*»[5] In the *Matyrdom* Justin
tells us that during his second stay in Rome »anyone who wished could
come to my abode and I would impart to him the words of truth.«[6] Compare
Paul in Acts 28:30f:»And he lived there two whole years . . . and welcomed
all who came to him, preaching the kingdom of God and teaching about the
Lord Jesus Christ quite openly and unhindered.«

Further, there can be no doubt that the companions of Trypho, at least
some of them, are meant to be Gentiles believing in the God of the Jews,
and to some extent familiar with the LXX. In *Dial.* 23:3, the phrase »to you,
Trypho, and to those who wish to become proselytes, I proclaim . . .«
probably characterizes Trypho's friends as *would-be proselytes.*[7] This corresponds with the picture of Trypho as *a proselytizing Jew* in *Dial.* 8:4.[8]
Trypho's friends become particularly engaged when Justin says that Is 42:6f
does not refer to the (Jewish) proselytes, *Dial.* 122:4: It looks as if they are
personally involved! It is a very reasonable surmise that the *Dialogue* itself
is addressed primarily to the same kind of people,[9] or at least that these

---

3. Cf. G. Schrenk, art. 'διαλέγομαι', *ThDNT* II pp. 93-95. The term is most often used in the
   meaning 'having a dialogue, a debate' in Greek Hellenistic and Jewish writings from the
   period, but can also be used of more monologic expositions. I doubt that the element of
   debate and dialogue is so absent from the Acts passages as assumed by Schrenk, p. 95. It is
   difficult to imagine Paul preaching Christ in a synagogue for three months (Acts 19:8)
   without any debate taking place!
4. See the extensive discussion in Hyldahl , *Philosophie und Christentum*, pp. 91f/96f.
5. *Op. cit.*, p. 88,
6. *Martyrdom,* § 3, Musurillo pp. 44f.
7. This is argued convincingly by Th. Zahn,'Studien zu Justinus Martyr', *ZKG* 8 (1886, pp. 1-84),
   pp. 57-61; cf. also Hyldahl, *op. cit.* pp. 19f, and Donahue, *Controversy,* pp. 183-185. J. Nilson,
   'To whom is Justin's *Dialogue with Trypho* addressed?', *Theological Studies* 38 (1977, pp.
   538-46), wrongly states that Trypho's companions are 'committed Jews' (p. 542),
8. Cf. Zahn, *art. cit.*, p. 57, and Nilson, *art. cit.*, p. 541.
9. Cf. Hyldahl, pp. 19f, who accepts Zahn's comments about Trypho's friends, and adds, «*dass
   Tryphons Freunde im Grunde nichts anderes sind als die Leser des Dial.*» (p. 20). Th.
   Stylianopoulos *(Justin Martyr and the Mosaic Law* (SBL Diss. Ser. 20. Missoula, 1975)) in

were the original addressees of the exegetical exposition of the *Dialogue*.[10]

The dialogue setting in the *Dialogue* is thus rather similar to many of Paul's missionary dialogues in Acts: The interlocutors are the Christian missionary and a (the) Jew(s), the audience (and in gradually increasing measure the addressees of the exposition) are the God-fearing Gentiles.

To conclude: Concerning his understanding of the origin and purpose of the Scriptural proof, and concerning its setting, Justin exhibits striking parallels with Luke-Acts. This is especially true of the *Dialogue*. It can be said to represent a specimen of the long missionary dialogues hinted at in Acts, both for its purpose and its setting. In the *Dialogue* we encounter not so much a Christian apologist as a Christian missionary. He is trying to convert - not primarily Trypho, his interlocutor, but his audience, i.e. his readers.

In the *Apology*, Justin is more of an apologist. But in *1.Apol.* 31ff he goes on to present, in a more elementary form, the apostolic kerygma and its proof from the Scriptures. He again falls into the role of the Christian missionary basing himself on the argument from prophecy - much in the same way as the Old Man addressed Justin.

Two questions are suggested by these observations.

(1) Is the missionary setting also valid for the tradition upon which Justin depends?

(2) Do the parallels with Acts in setting and purpose for the Scriptural proof correspond to a continuity between Luke's and Justin's proof-text tradition? We have seen already that there is no great overlap in proof-text dossier between the two writers. If there nevertheless is continuity of theological ideas between Luke and Justin's proof-text tradition, we have a sure indication that Justin's Lukan peculiarities are not simply a product of his reading Luke, but was already part of the tradition on which Justin depends.

---

his 'Appendix: Are Pagans the addressees of the Dialogue?' (pp. 169-195), argues that the primary addressees are the Jews. But his arguments are hardly convincing, cf. my review in *TTK* 49 (1978), pp. 151f. He does not seriously consider the setting which the *Dialogue* itself suggests - viz. the Jewish and Christian missions *to the same group*, Gentile God-fearers. Donahue in his abovementioned dissertation, has argued with great force that this is the setting for the *Dialogue*. He makes the interesting proposal that Pompey, to whom the *Dialogue* is addressed, may be a God-fearing Roman who had Jewish friends exhorting him to become a Jew. J. Nilson makes the same point concerning the setting of the *Dialogue*, apparently without knowledge of Donahue's dissertation: «More likely than not, Jewish and Christian evangelizers would find themselves competing for the same group of potential Gentile converts.» (p. 544). «Justin's *Dialogue* ... is addressed primarily to a non-Christian Gentile audience at Rome which is favourably disposed towards Judaism and Christianity, yet is unable to adequately distinguish the one from the other.» (p. 539).

10. I would like to underline the word 'primarily' in the quotation from Nilson (in the preceeding note). As I have argued , Justin may have written at least parts of the *Dialogue* with a side-glance to inner-Christian controversies. The opening chapters may also indicate that Justin had a wider audience in mind than God-fearers in the strict sense. Perhaps he wanted to extend his audience to include Platonists and others sympathetical towards monotheism on purely philosophical grounds.

## CHAPTER TWO

THE MAIN EXEGETICAL TRADITIONS BEHIND THE *APOLOGY* AND
*DIAL.* 11-47/108-141: THE «KERYGMA SOURCE».

*1. The Christological testimonies*

It may be useful first to summarize the analysis in Parts I and II in a brief
table:

(1) Gen 49:10f (Zech 9:9): The coming of the Messiah
(2) Num 24:17/Is 11:1/Is 51:5: *Anatellein* motif I
(3) Ps 72:17; Zech 6:12: *Anatellein* motif II
(4) Is 7:14: The birth of the Messiah
(5) Is 9:5a: The hidden growth of the Messiah
(6) Is 11:2f: The Messianic anointing with the Spirit
(7) (a) Ps22; Is 53: The passion and death of the Messiah
     (b) *Dial.* 72: Paschal lamb (Ps. Ezra; Jer 11:19: Is 53:7); descent to
     Sheol (Ps. Jer).
(8) Ps 24:7f: The ascension of the Messiah
(9) Ps 110:1: Enthronement
(10) Dan 7:13: Return of the Messiah
(11) Zech 12:10-12: Recognition of the Messiah

Let me begin with a consideration of the profile of this dossier of
taken as a whole. J. Brierre-Narbonne submits the following list of Messianic prophecies most often referred to in the Talmuds:[1]

| | |
|---|---|
| Gen 49:10f | *(Sanh.* 5a; 98b; *Ber.* 57a; *Yom.* 53b) |
| Is 11:1-4 | (p *Ber.* 5a; *Sanh.* 93a) |
| Mic 5;1-4 | (p *Ber.* 5a; *Yom.* 10a; *Sanh.* 98b; *Sukk.* 52b) |
| Zech 9:9f | *(Sanh.* 98a; 99a) |
| Zech 12:10-12 | (p *Sukk.* 55a; *Sukk.* 52b) |
| Ps 2:1-8 | *(Ber.* 7b; *A. Zar.* 3b (2x); *Sukk.* 52b) |
| Ps 72:5/17 | *(Sanh.* 99a; 98b; *Pes.* 54a; *Ned.* 39b). |

Two facts about this list are rather striking: (1) its minimal correspondence with the central Christological testimonies of the NT writers, Matt-

---

1. J. Brierre - Narbonne, *Exégèse talmudique des prophéties méssianiques* (LOPG, Paris, 1934),
pp. 34f. There are other OT passages quoted as often as the ones in the above list, but they are
more concerned with the Messianic age than with the coming of the person of the Messiah,
cf. *ibid.*

hew excepted; and (2) its remarkably great correspondence with the Christological testimonies of the «kerygma» tradition in Justin. This correspondence is increased if we add to the above list some testimonies quoted only once (e.g. Num 24:17 - and cf. detailed comments immediately below).

In other words: Compared with the NT writings, Justin's «kerygma» dossier is remarkably «Jewish». Why so? I believe the following considerations are relevant. From the beginning, Christians had to stress what was startlingly new and unexpected about their Messiah: his death on the cross and his glorious resurrection and ascension: 1 Cor 15:3f; Lk 24:26f.46f; Acts 2:22-36. This focus was the distinctive *novum* of NT Messianism, and the Scriptural texts chosen to prove that this had been predicted by Scripture were to a large extent others than the traditional Messianic testimonies of Judaism.

However, at a later stage, and in a milieu still in living contact with Jewish Messianic expectations, one should expect that Christians tried to make their proof-text dossier more «complete» and comprehensive by including the traditional Jewish testimonies. It seems it is this process which can be discerned in late strata of NT literature: the infancy narratives, Hebrews, and Revelation.

The star seen ἐν τῇ ἀνατολῇ by the Magi, Mt 2:2, may very well be an allusion to Num 24:17.[2] Perhaps an allusion to the same text (and/ or Zech 6:12?) is contained in Lk 1:78: ἐπισκέψεται ἡμᾶς ἀνατολὴ ἐξ ὕψους.[3] Common to the Matthean and Lukan allusions is the emphasis on the catchword ἀνατολή. As we have seen, this emphasis is carried on in Justin's material: Here Ps 72:17 is modified to suit the rest of the ἀνατολή testimonies by the introduction of a non-LXX ἀνατέλλειν in the text (see above, pp.84f.). Hebrews 7:14 seems to have a joint allusion to Gen 49:10 and Num 24:17: ἐξ Ἰούδα ἀνατέταλκεν ὁ κύριος ἡμῶν.[4]

Perhaps the most interesting allusions come in Revelation:[5]

| | | |
|---|---|---|
| 5:5: | ἰδοὺ ἐνίκησεν ὁ λέων ὁ ἐκ τῆς φυλῆς Ἰούδα | (Gen 49:9f) |
| | ἡ ῥίζα Δαυίδ | (Is 11:1) |
| | | |
| 22:16: | ἐγώ εἰμι ἡ ῥίζα καὶ τὸ γένος Δαυίδ | (Is 11:1) |
| | ὁ ἀστὴρ ὁ λαμπρὸς ὁ πρωϊνός | (Num 24:17) |

---

2. A recent and most exhaustive discussion is found in Brown, *Birth of the Messiah*, pp. 195f. Brown aptly parallels several motifs in the Baalam story with the Magi story in Mt 2.

3. In the LXX, ἀνατολή is used as the Greek equivalent for Hebrew צמח in some of the Messianic «Branch» prophecies, Jer 23:5; 33:15; Zech 3:8; 6:12. «*Aber schliesslich kommt ein Spross nicht aus der Höhe, und er leuchtet auch nicht. Im griechischen Raum konnte der verfestigte Messiasname* ἀνατολή *auch vom Verbum* זרח = ἀνατέλλω = «*aufgehen*» *her verstanden werden.* ἀνατολή *ist dann der «Aufgang» eines Gestirns oder hier dieser aufgehende Stern selbst. In Anknüpfung an Bilder wie Num 24,17 und Is 9,1; 60:1ff hat man im Spätjudentum, besonders in Qumran, das Auftreten des Messias gern mit dem Aufstrahlen eines Gestirns verglichen...*» (H. Schürmann, *comm. ad loc.,* p. 92). Cf. also Brown, *Birth of the Messiah,* pp. 373f /388-391 .

4. Cf. 0. Michel, *comm. ad loc.,* p. 271, and P. Prigent, 'Testimonia messianiques', p. 422. ἀνατέλλειν here is a *hapax leg.* in Hebrews.

5. Cf. esp. Daniélou, *Theology,* p. 219, n. 42; and Prigent, 'Testimonia messianiques', p. 426.

These traditional Jewish proof-texts on the Messiah (Gen 49:10f and Num 24:17 are the only passages of the entire Pentateuch which receive a Messianic interpretation in the Targum Onqelos!) are not yet treated as major Cristological proof-texts in the NT, but their appearance indicates an ongoing process.

It is this process of enriching the dossier of Christological proof-texts with more of the traditional Jewish testimonies which comes to its climax in Justin's material. This will be confirmed as we review the main texts in Justin's dossier which have been added to the basic NT testimonies and ask whether there be points of contact with Jewish exegesis in each case.

## (A) A rewiew of Jewish parallels

### (a) Gen 49:10f (Zech 9:9)

We have observed already that Justin's «testimony» version of Gen 49:10f seems influenced by a targumic tradition also represented in the *Targum Onqelos*, and we may therefore begin with a fuller review of the targumic evidence. The text is an important Messianic testimony in all the Targums.[6]

In *Targum Onqelos*, the most relevant passage runs like this:[7] «The ruler shall never depart from the House of Judah, nor the scribe (or: teacher) from his children's children for evermore until the Messiah comes, whose is the kingdom,[8] and him shall the nations obey.» One can see how the Targumist in vs. 10 grapples with the problem of the cessation of kingship in Israel. מחקק is interpreted as «scribe», i.e. he who studies the חקים The problem is thus solved by transferring the idea of dominion from the Davidic dynasty to the spiritual leaders of Israel, the succession of rabbinical teachers. One of the factors which helped to create this exegesis, may have been Christian exegesis of this text along Justin's lines.[9]

---

6. Cf. esp. J. Brierre-Narbonne, *Exégèse targumique des prophéties messianiques* (LOPG, Paris, 1935), pp. 15-27; S. H. Levey, *The Messiah: An Aramaic Interpretation. The Messianic Exegesis of the Targum* (Monographs of the Hebrew Union College 2, Cincinatti, 1974), pp. 5-10; M. Aberbach and B. Grossfeld, *Targum Onqelos on Genesis 49* (SBL Aramaic Studies 1, Missoula, 1976), pp. 12-27.

7. Rendered here according to the translation in Aberbach and Grossfeld.

8. This is a rendering of the famous שׁילה read as אשר לו = שׁלו «to whom it (= the kingdom) belongs». Cf. above, p. 25. The same reading is presupposed in *Gen.Rab.* 99:8, p. 982.

9. Cf. Levey's remark ad loc.: «The perpetuation of the scribe-educator in the descendants of Judah is probably designed to fill the historical gap between the end of the political rule of the Davidic line and the advent of the Messiah in the remote future, the Messiah becoming a combination of the two - a king-educator.» ( *Op. cit*, p. 149, n. 21). Note also the words «for evermore» (          ) added to the Hebrew text. «This additional stress on the *permanent* nature of Judah's pre-eminence may have been designed to counter Christian polemical attacks on the Jews which repeatedly emphasized that the Law had been superseeded, and that the Jews had been deprived of their exalted status as the chosen people.» (Aberbach and Grossfeld, p. 13). As we shall see, however, this way of «saving» the continuity of kingship is anticipated in the Qumran scrolls - it therefore cannot be explained solely as an apologetic concept in the debate with Christians.

In *Targum Ps. Jonathan*, שבט is paraphrased «kings and rulers», while מחקק is taken as «scribes who teach the Torah». This Targum has a very militant Messianism in Gen.49:11. S.H.Levey takes this as a reflex of the Bar Kokhba revolt.[10] The *Fragmentary Targum* takes שבט as «kings», מחקק as «scribes». עד יבא שילה is paraphrased as in *Targum Onqelos*: «until the coming of the king Messiah, to whom belongs the kingdom».[11] Gen 49:12 in *Ps. Jonathan* and the *Fragmentary Targum* ascribes to the Messiah a restoration of the *halakah*. - Levey thinks this also points to the Bar Kokhba uprising.[12]

We thus see that the Targums see the royal succession continued in the line of rabbinical teachers. There are also possible reflexes of the Bar Kokhba revolt.

The Targumist exegesis is carried on in the *Babylonian Talmud*. Here both שבט and מחקק are referred to the succession of rabbis: «The authority in Babylon is designated 'sceptre', but that of Palestine, 'lawgiver', as it has been taught: 'The sceptre shall not depart from Judah', this refers to the Exilarchs of Babylon who rule over Israel with sceptres, 'and a lawgiver...', this refers to the descendants of Hillel who teach the Torah in public» (*Sanh*. 5a,pp. 15f).[13] *Midrash Rabba* interprets in a similar vein: «'The sceptre shall not depart from Judah' alludes to the Sanhedrin,[14] which punished and kept in order; 'nor a ruler from between his feet', to the two clerks of the judges who stand before them...» (*Gen.Rab*.98:8, p. 956).[15] The date and significance of a Messianic interpretation of Gen 49:10 is attested by two independent sources. Josephus seems to have known that this verse was applied to the Messiah. He remarks that the Jews interpreted «an ambiguous oracle... found in their sacred Scriptures to the effect that... one from their country would become ruler of the world.» (*Bell.Jud.* VI:312f).[16] This early date for a Messianic interpretation of Gen 49:10 is now confirmed by the Dead Sea scrolls. *4Q patr.* is a fragment of a midrash on Gen 49: «(There shall not) cease a ruler ( שליט ) from the tribe of Judah when there be dominion for Israel (and there will not) be cut off an

---

10. Levey, *op. cit.*, pp. 9f.
11. The same reading occurs in the *Targum Neofiti*: «Kings shall not cease from among those of the house of Judah, and neither (shall) scribes teaching the Law from his son's sons until the time King Messiah shall come whose is the kingship; to him shall all the kingdoms be subject.» (Translation according to A. Diez Macho's edition, p. 635).
12. Levey, *op. cit.*, p. 11. On Bar Kokhba's zeal for the Law, cf. below p. 294
13. Messianic exegesis of Gen 49:10 is evidenced also elsewhere in the Babylonian *Talmud*, see *Yoma* 53b (p. 251); *Ber*. 57a (p. 352).
14. The premiss of this exegesis is given in a midrash attributed i.a. to R. Jose b. Hanina (ca 270): «The majority of the Sanhedrin were descended from Judah.» (*Gen.Rab*. 98:10, p. 958).
15. It is interesting to note that *ad* vs. 11 the Midrash makes the same combination between Gen 49:11 and Zech 9:9 as I have posited for Justin's source: «'His foal and his colt' intimate: when he will come of whom it is written,'lowly, and riding upon an ass, even upon a colt the foal of an ass'.»(*Gen.Rab*. 98:8, p. 957. The same connexion is repeated in *Gen.Rab*. 99:8, p. 983).
16. Cf. also *Bell. Jud.* III:401.

enthroned one (belonging) to (the line of) David, for the staff ( מחקק ) is the covenant of kingship and the families of Israel are the feet until the coming of the anointed of righteousness, the shoot ( צמח ) of David. For to him and to his seed has been given the covenant of kingship over his people for everlasting generations . . .» [17]

This no doubt is a straightforward Messianic interpretation of the text. But it is difficult to know exactly how the author conceived of the succession of rulers leading up to the Davidic Messiah, partly due to the fragmentary character of the text. J.Liver's interpretation deserves notice: «. . . the dominion of the Shoot of David is presented as a promise which will be fulfilled only in the expected future, in the present this authority is vested in the families of Israel, i.e., in the community as a corporate body.»[18] This may well be a more primitive version of the later rabbinic idea of a succession of scribes or teachers. The rabbinic idea is, moreover, directly anticipated in CD 6:7, where מחקק is interpreted as דורש התורה.[19]

To conclude: There is an unanimous exegetical tradition in Jewish sources which takes Gen 49:10f as a Messianic prophecy. The cessation of royalty prior to the coming of the Messiah is a problem which has been felt -and solved, in different ways.

(b) Num 24:17/ Is 11:1 /51:5

As is well known, Num 24:17 was attached to Bar Kokhba. «R. Schimon b. Jochai (um 150) hat gelehrt: Mein Lehrer Aqiba hat vorgetragen: Hervorgetreten ist ein Stern aus Jakob; hervorgetreten ist Kozeba aus Jakob. Als R.

---

17. Text: Lohse, p. 246. I have rendered the text according to the translation in Liver, 'Two Messiahs', pp. 156f. A slightly different translation is offered by D.R. Schwartz in his article 'The Messianic Departure from Judah (4Q Patriarchal Blessings)' ThZ 37 (1981) pp. 257-266), pp. 265f. The main difference is that Schwartz takes «Israel» to be a negative concept (= apostate Israel), and therefore takes the rule of Israel to be present, not future:» 'A ruler will (not) depart from the tribe of Judah' : (this means that) while Israel rules there will (not) be cut off a Davidic (heir to) the throne . . .» (ibid.) For general information on the Messianism of the Qumran scrolls, cf. i.a. R. E. Brown,' The Messianism of Qumran', CBQ 19 (1957), pp. 53-82; K. Schubert,'Die Messiaslehre in den Texten von Chirbet Qumran', BZ Neue Folge 1 (1957), pp. 177-197; A. S. van der Woude, Messianische Vorstellungen; J. Liver,'Two Messiahs', pp. 149-163.

18. Liver, art. cit., p. 160. Schwartz, art. cit., comes out with a somewhat different interpretation: «. . . the Qumran exegete took Gen 49.10 as prophesying the exile of the Davidic monarchic line among the sect itself, while Israel (usurpers) ruled, until the birth of the Davidic Messiah who will «depart» from his exile and establish his monarchy» (p. 263). On both interpretations , however, it is evident that the cessation of the Davidic monarchy before the Messiah had come was a major difficulty felt with regard to this Biblical verse. The Christian theologians responsible for making Gen 49:10 a major Christological testimony no doubt were aware of this.

19. Lohse, p. 76; cf. van der Woude, Messianische Vorstellungen, pp. 69f.

*Aqiba den Bar Kozeba erblickt hatte, rief er aus: Das ist der König, der Messias* ( p *Taan.* 4:5) [20]

The Messianic exegesis of the passage is older than Bar Kokhba, however, and again we find the decisive evidence in the Dead Sea Scrolls. *4Q test.* 9-13 quotes Num 24:15-17 as a Messianic testimony,[21] and CD 7:19ff; 1QM 11:6f, and 1Q Sb 5:27f allude to the same text in a Messianic vein.[22] In the *Babylonian Talmud* this testimony disappears, possibly because of its association with Bar Kokhba. It is given prominent attention, however, in the Targums.[23] *Onqelos* reads: «. . . a king shall arise out of Jacob and be anointed the Messiah out of Israel. He shall slay the princes of Moab and reign over all mankind.» *Targum Ps. Jonathan* is even more exuberant in its triumphant Messianism to this verse. The *Fragmentary Targum* is more reticent and only speaks of a king, redeemer and ruler.

Let me add in the passing that Gen 49:10ff and Num 24:17ff are the only texts in the Pentateuch which receive a Messianic interpretation in *Targum Onqelos.* The same two passages have prominent position as the opening testimonies in Justin's material in *1.Apol.* 32!

Is 11:1ff is treated as a Messianic prophecy in 1Q Sb 5:21f.25f;[24] 4Q p. Isa. [a][25] It is relevant to note that in 1Q Sb 5:25-29 allusions to Is 11:1ff; Num 24:17, and Gen 49:9 are combined - cf. again *1.Apol.* 32.

Is 11:1ff recurs as a Messianic testimony in an anti-Bar Kokhba polemic in the *Babylonian Talmud, Sanh.* 93b, pp. 626f.[26]

It is rather striking that even the third element in Justin's composite quotation - viz. Is 51:5 - was probably taken as a Messianic prophecy by the Qumran exegetes. This may be deduced from the reading of this verse in the Isa scroll, which changes the verse from 1st person (God speaking) to 3rd person (the Messiah). Justin's deviant text of Is 51:5 has the same reading! (Cf. above, p.50 with note).

---

20. Quoted according to the translation of Str. Bill. I, p. 76. Cf. the parallel in *Lam.Rab.*11:2 § 4 (p. 157):«R. Johanan said: Rabbi used to expound 'There shall step forth a star (*kokab*) out of Jacob (Num 24:17) thus: read not *kokab* but *kozab* (= lie). When R. Akiba beheld Bar Koziba he exclaimed,'This is the King Messiah!' R. Johanan b. Tortha retorted:'Akiba; grass will grow in your cheeks and he will still not have come.» On the previous interpretation of this testimony, cf. esp. P. Schäfer, *Der Bar Kokhba-Aufstand* (Texte und Studien zum Antiken Judentum 1, Tübingen 1981), pp. 55-57.
21. Lohse, p. 250. Cf. van der Woude, pp. 182-185.
22. Lohse, pp. 80; 204; 60. Cf. relevant comments in van der Woude, pp. 53-61; 116-120; 113-116.
23. Cf. esp. Levey, pp. 21-27. The Targumic renderings of Num 24:17 are also conveniently gathered in R. E. Brown, *The Birth of the Messiah. A commentary on the Infancy Narratives in Matthew and Luke* (Garden City, New York, 1977), p. 195, n. 48. (I quote the Targums according to Levey's translation, *loc. cit.*).
24. Lohse, pp. 58/60.
25. Text: J. M. Allegro, 'Further Messianic References in Qumran Literature',*JBL* 75 (1956, pp. 174-187), p. 181. For comment, see Brown,'Messianism', p. 81; van der Woude, *Messianische Vorstellungen,* pp. 175-182; J. Liver, *art.cit.,* pp. 160f.
26. Rabbinic parallels are listed in J. Brierre-Narbonne, *Le Messie souffrant dans la litterature rabbinique* (LOPG, Paris, 1940), p. 12.

(c) Ps 72:17 ; Zech 6:12

The rabbis took Ps 72:17 as a testimony for the pre-existence of the Messiah's name (*Pes.* 54a, p. 265),[27] or as a proof that his name shall be Yinnon (*Sanh.* 98b, p. 667). In *Sanh.* 99a,[28] Ps72 vss. 5 and 17 are combined in a way reminiscent of Justin. (Question: How long will the days of the Messiah last?) «Rabbi (ca 200) said: Three generations, for it is written, 'They shall fear thee with the sun, and before the moon (they shall fear thee), a generation and generations» (p. 669). The *Targum ad loc.* also has the idea of the Messiah's pre-existent name:«. . . his name which was made ready even before the sun came into being.»[29]

Finally, Zech 6:12 may be included among the intended testimonies in *4Q flor* 1:11; *4Q patr* 3f, where the Messiah is called     צמח דויד     .[30] The rabbis also applied this text to the Messiah, p *Ber.* 2:4;[31] *Lam.Rab.* 1:16 § 51, p. 136; *Num.Rab.* 18:21, p. 734.

(d) Is 9:5a.[32]

For Justin, this text (in its deviant form!) proves that the Messiah «after his birth was to live hidden from other men until he grew to manhood» ( *1.Apol.* 35:1). The only point I want to make here is that the similar idea of the hiddenness of the Messiah prior to his proclamation, is well-known in Jewish sources. Justin himself puts this view in the mouth of Trypho: «Messiah, if indeed he has ever been and now exists anywhere, is unknown, and does not even know himself at all . . . until Elijah shall have come and anointed him, and shall have made him manifest to all» (*Dial.* 8:4f, cf. *Dial.* 110:1). L.Williams[33] has pointed out the relevant parallels. «Just as no one can explore or know what is in the depths of the sea, so no one on earth can see my Son or those who are with him, except in the time of his day», 4 Ezra 13:52. «R. Nahman (4th cent.) said: If he (the Messiah) is of those living (to day) , it might be one like myself, as it is written . . . (Jer 30:21) . Rab (died 247)[34] said: If he is of the living, it would be our holy Master (i.e. Judah

---

27. Parallel: *Ned.* 39b (p. 125); Pes. 54a (p. 265). Both passages are *Baraitahs.* cf. J. Brierre-Nar-bonne, *Les Prophéties messianiques de l'Ancient Testament dans la littérature juive en accord avec le Nouveau Testament* (LOPG, Paris, 1933), pp. 24-26.

28. A parallel occurs in *Lam.Rab.* 1:16 § 51 (p. 138).

29. Levey, *op.cit.,* p. 117.

30. Cf. van der Woude, *Messianische Vorstellungen,* pp. 169-172.

31. Str. Bill. I, p. 66.

32. In rabbinic literature this text is applied to the Messiah. Cf. Klausner, *op. cit.,* p. 462, who quotes a saying attributed to the pre-Hadrianic Tanna R. Jose the Galilean:«Also, the Messiah's name is called Peace, for it is written,'Everlasting Father, Prince (called) Peace.» However, the text is also applied to Hezekiah, *Sanh.* 94a (p. 632).

33. In his translation, p. 18, n. 2. The authenticity of Justin's report on Jewish concepts about the hidden Messiah is argued also by E. Sjöberg, 'Justin als Zeuge vom Glauben an den verborgenen und den leidenden Messias im Judentum', *Interpretationes ad Vetus Testamentum pertinentes Sigmundo Mowinckel septuagenario missae* (Oslo, 1955, pp. 173-183), pp. 173-175.

34. «347» in L.Williams' note is a misprint.

han-Nasi) », *Sanb.* 98b, p. 668. In *Sanb.* 98a the Messiah is pictured as sitting among the lepers at the citygate.

(e) Ps 24:7f.[35]

The relevant Jewish material on this text has been gathered and discussed at great length by E. Kähler,[36] and it is sufficient here to point out only the most important texts.

Two Jewish interpretations can be discerned in the available sources: one historical and one eschatological. The historical interpretation refers Ps 24:7ff to Solomon, when he carried the holy Ark into the temple, *Moed Kat.* 9a, p. 48.[37] More relevant in our context is the eschatological interpretation. This is found in the *Targum,* in some midrashes and probably already underlies the translation of the LXX.[38] According to the *Targum,* the gates of Ps 24:7.9 are the gates of *Gan Eden.*[39] Underlying this identification is probably an idea similar to the one found in *Midrash Leqah Tob.* Here the ten voices from heaven are enumerated which accompany Israel's eschatological conquest of Jerusalem, the Messiah being their leader.[40] At the gates of Jerusalem, Is 26:2 and Ps 24:7 are spoken. Kähler reasonably proposes that the demonological flavour of the LXX translation (οἱ ἄρχοντες) also implies an eschatological perspective.[41]

Another factor may also have facilitated the Christian application of Ps 24:7ff to Christ's ascension. According to the *Mishnah,* this Psalm was sung on Sunday morning in the Temple service. «This was the singing which the Levites used to sing in the Temple. On the first day they sang: »The earth is the Lord's . . . (Ps 24)«, M *Tam.* 7:4.[42] This is reflected in the superscription to this Psalm in the LXX: Ψαλμὸς τῷ Δαυιδ τῆς μιᾶς σαββάτων.[43] Perhaps the Temple practice was reflected in the synagogues of the Diaspora.

---

35. On this text in Justin, cf. P. Beskow, *Rex Gloriae,* pp. 103-106.
36. E. Kähler, *Studien zum Te Deum und zur Geschichte des 24. Psalms in der Alten Kirche* (Veröffentlichungen der Evangelischen Gesellschaft für Liturgieforschung 10, Göttingen, 1958), pp. 44-50.
37. Cf. Goldfahn, 'Aggada', pp. 104-106, with further references. Cf. also B. Z. Bokser, 'Justin Martyr and the Jews', *JQR* New Ser. 64(1973/74) (pp. 97-122/204-211), pp. 112f.
38. One should also compare the concept of *3 Enoch* 48(D):6-9, according to which the angels of heaven opposed the ascension of Enoch, cf. Beskow, *op. cit.,* p. 105.
39. Cf. Str. Bill. IV, p. 1151.
40. Kähler, *op. cit,* pp. 47f; Str. Bill. I, pp. 96f/960. The midrashic exposition is attributed to R. Levi, ca 300.
41. Kähler: «*Konnte für die aramaisch sprechende Synagoge die eschatologische Deutung des Psalms eine unter anderen sein, für die hellenistische Synagoge gab es keine andere Deutung als diese.*» (p. 50).
42. This was also pointed out by Kähler, *op. cit,* pp. 44f.
43. Cf. A. Rahlfs' preface to the Göttingen LXX of Psalms, pp. 72f. The superscription is pre-Christian.

Christians used to this must have come to think of their Messiah's triumphant resurrection/ascension on the first day of the week, especially if they had the Jewish eschatological interpretation of the Psalm in mind.[44]

In the case of Ps 24:7f, we are in a position to follow the transition from Jewish exegesis to the one we meet in Justin, because we possess an intermediate link in the *Apocalypse of Peter.*[45] In chs. 15ff we find an expanded version of the Transfiguration story (primarily according to the Lukan version, but also some Matthean peculiarities).[46] This paraphrase ends in a proleptic description of Christ's ascension at the head of his elect. The text runs: »And I (Peter) trembled and was afraid, and we looked up and the heavens opened and we saw men in the flesh, and they came and greeted our Lord and Moses and Elias, and went into the second heaven. And the word of Scripture was fulfilled: 'This generation seeketh him and seeketh the face of the God of Jacob' (Ps 24:6). And great fear and great amazement took place in heaven; the angels flocked together that the word of Scripture might be fulfilled which saith: 'Open the gates, ye princes.'(Ps 24:7).«[47]

This is only a slight Christianisation of the Jewish exegesis quoted above, especially as found in the Targum. One should notice that the righteous men who accompany Christ in his ascent to the second heaven, in ch. 16 (= chs. 12-20 in the Akhmim fragment) are seen as dwelling in the garden of Paradise, cf. the Targumic exegesis quoted above. The closeness to *Midrash Leqach Tob* is also striking: In both cases Ps 24:7 is referred to the entry of the Messiah *and his people* into Jerusalem/the second heaven.

The *Apocalypse of Peter* thus seems to stand midway between the Jewish tradition and Justin's material, which concentrates on Christ alone. That the gates are the gates *of heaven,* is implied in the *Apocalypse of Peter,* and expressly stated in Justin's deviant text: ἄρατε πύλας οὐρανῶν.

(f) Dan 7:13 and Zech 12:10-12

While these two texts are often combined as two complementary ways of describing the Messiah's return for judgement in the Christian tradition,

---

44. I believe there is every reason to think that the Christological application of Ps 24:7ff is primary, and the (Gnostic) application of the Psalm to the ascent of the individual soul after death secondary. We find this Gnostic exegesis i.a. in the *Naassene Sermon,* cf. Beskow, *Rex Gloriae,* p. 105.

45. It is possible that 1 Cor 2:8 echoes a Christological interpretation of Ps 24:7.9 (cf.Kähler, pp.50-53): The ἄρχοντες did not recognize Christ and (therefore) crucified the κύριος τῆς δόξης. This would be in line with later apocalyptic and gnostic speculations about the hidden descent of the saviour (hence the surprised question at his ascent, »Who is this King of Glory?«), but the scanty indications in Paul are hardly sufficient to warrant any probability to this hypothesis. (It was propounded in great detail by M. Dibelius, *Die Geisterwelt im Glauben des Paulus*(Göttingen, 1909), pp. 92-99. He interpreted the Pauline text in the light of the descent motif in *Asc.Ies.* But cf. E. Kähler, *op. cit.,* p. 53.)

46. Cf. E. Massaux, *Influence,* pp. 255-58.

47. *NT Apoc.* II, pp. 682f.

they are never combined in the rabbinic sources, because Zech 12:10ff is referred to the Messiah ben Ephraim. The rabbinic conception of Dan 7:13[48] is found i.a. in *Sanh* 98a (p. 664): «R. Alexandri (ca 270)said: R. Joshua (ca 250) opposed two verses: it is written,'And behold, one like the son of man came with the clouds of heaven;' whilst (elsewhere) it is written,'(behold, thy king cometh unto thee . . .), lowly, and riding upon an ass!' - If they (Israel) are meritorious,(he will come) 'with the clouds of heaven;' if not,'lowly and riding upon an ass'.»

Zech 12:10-12 was taken to be a passage describing the mourning over the slain Messiah ben Ephraim[49] (on this figure, cf. further below, p. 395f).

Conclusion:

This review of Jewish parallels to Justin's material[50] shows that all the main texts were familiar Messianic testimonies within Jewish exegesis prior to, contemporary with, and later than Justin. There are even parallels and points of contact in some textual and exegetical details, and in the combination of texts. This would seem to indicate that Justin's material evolved in a milieu being in close contact with Jewish exegesis. This close contact may also be indirectly witnessed in some possibly anti-Christian motifs in the rabbinic exegesis, or in the grappling with problems raised by Justin.

(B) Theological concerns and ideas

(a) The Star from Jacob - the light of the world (Gen 49:10f; Num 24:17 etc.)

The «kerygma» sequence of Christological testimonies is characterized i.a. by the prominent position accorded to Gen 49:10f and Num 24:17 as

---

48. Rabbinic interpretations of Dan 7:13 are conveniently gathered in Brierre-Narbonne, *Prophé-ties messianiques*, pp. 78f. cf. also Str. Bill. I, pp. 956f. Justin's tradition does not seem to be particularly affected by the «Son of Man» concept of *1 Enoch* 37ff.

49. Cf. the two Talmuds on Zech 12:10: «*Il y a 2 manieres différentes d'expliquer ce verset: d'apres un avis le prophète déplore la mort future du Messie; d'apres l'autre, il s'agit de la ruine du mauvais penchant.*» (*p. Sukkah* V:2 (transl. Schwab, vol. IV, p.43)). «What is the cause of the mourning. R. Dosa (ca 180) and the Rabbis differ on the point. One explained, The cause is the slaying of Messiah the son of Joseph, and the other explained: the cause is the slaying of the Evil Inclination. It is well according to him who explains that the cause is the slaying of Messiah the son of Joseph, since that well agrees with the Scriptural verse . . . (Zech 12:10)», *Sukkah* 52a (p. 240). For comments on these passages, cf . Brierre-Narbonne, *Le Messie souffrant*, pp. 9-11; J. Klausner, *Messianic idea*, pp. 490-92 («an Amoraic transmission of a Tannaitic interpretation»); and esp. S. Hurwitz, *Die Gestalt des sterbenden Messias. Religionspsychologische Aspekte der jüdischen Apokalyptik* (Studien aus dem C. G. Jung-Institut, Zürich, 8, Zürich/Stuttgart, 1958), pp. 89-121. Cf. also further literature on the Messiah ben Joseph listed below, p.395, n.49.

50. For general surveys of Talmudic Messianic prooftexts and exegesis, cf. J. Brierre-Narbonne, *Exégèse talmudique des prophéties messianiques* (LOPG, Paris, 1934), esp. pp. 27-33; and K. Hruby,'Der talmudische Messianismus', *Emuna* 9 (1974), pp. 324-332.

major texts announcing the coming of the Messiah (as in Targum Onqelos). The most clarifying parallel to this is found in the Christological passages of the TP.

One first notices that a Messianic interpretation of Gen 49:10 - possibly also Num 24:17 - is clearly presupposed in the Jewish *Grundschrift* with which the interpolator is working. In *Test. Reub.* 6:11; *Test.Sim.* 7:1; *Test. Jud.* 21:1f; *Test. Iss.* 5:7; *Test. Dan* 5:4; *Test. Napht.* 8:2f we find passages where the Jewish author clearly refers to Gen 49:10 (kingdom for Judah), possibly also Num 24:17 (ἀνατέλλειν occurs in *Test. Sim.* 7:1; *Test. Napht.* 8:2). There can be no doubt about the Jewish provenance of these passages: The king of Judah and the priest of Levi are different persons, and the kingdom is subordinated to the priesthood.

The Christian redactor has modified this. In *Test.Jud.* 24 and *Test. Lev.* 18, the king of Judah and the priest of Levi is the same person, and he issues from Judah, not from Levi. One further observes that the references to Num 24:17 have become more explicit. Let us review some of the passages where the Christian redaction is evident. (The square brackets indicate passages deemed interpolations by Becker).[51]

«[And after these things shall a star arise to you from Jacob in peace and a man shall arise from my seed like a sun of righteousness walking with the sons of men in meekness and righteousness, and no sin shall be found in him . . . And you shall be unto him sons in truth, and you shall walk in his commandments first and last. This (is) the branch of the most high God, and this (is) the fountain giving life unto all]. Then shall the sceptre of my kingdom shine forth, and from your root shall arise a stem and from it shall grow a rod (ῥάβδος) of righteousness to the nations, to judge and to save all that call upon the Lord« *(Test. Jud.* 24). One first notes the biblical allusions in this text. *Judah* is speaking, which means that »from my seed« and »the sceptre of my kingdom« (σκήπτρον = שבט ) are allusions to Gen 49:10. This reference is present in other interpolated passages also. *Test.Reub.* 6:11f: ». . . because him (i.e. Judah) hath the Lord chosen to be king over all the nation. And bow down before his seed, for [on your behalf he will die in wars visible and invisible] and will be king forever«; *Test. Sim.* 7:2: «[For the Lord shall make arise from Levi as if it were a High Priest, and from Judah as if it were a king, God and man, and he shall save all the nations and the race of Israel].»; *Test. Lev.* 8:14: [«. . . a king shall arise from Judah and shall establish a new priesthood . . .]»

---

51. As a rule, I have followed Becker's judgement on textual questions. I have adjusted existing English translations accordingly or made my own. Among the numerous studies of *Test. Jud.* 24, special mention should be made of the following: K. Schubert, 'Testamentum Juda 24 im Lichte der Texte von Chirbet Qumran', *WZKM* 53 (1957), pp. 227-236; A. Hultgård, *Croyances messianiques*, pp. 149-162; de Jonge, *Testaments*, pp. 89-91; Becker, *Testamente*, pp. 319-323; Chevallier, *L'Esprit et le Messie*, pp. 126-132. Becker's analysis of the textual material is conveniently expressed in his German translation, *JSHRZ* III:1 (Gütersloh, 1974).

The reference to Num 24:17 in *Test. Jud.* is easily recognized (it is most extensive in the Greek version, but is present also in the Armenian).[52]

Of great interest is the reference to Mal. 3:20: ὡς ἥλιος δικαιοσύνης. The full text of Mal 3:20 makes plain why this text was joined to Num 24:17: καὶ ἀνατελεῖ ὑμῖν . . . ἥλιος δικαιοσύνης . . . With this one should again compare Justin's deviant version of Ps 72:17 in *Dial.* 121:1: τὸ ὄνομα αὐτοῦ εἰς τὸν αἰῶνα, ὑπὲρ τὸν ἥλιον ἀνατελεῖ . . . Compare also Justin's comment: »For his word of truth and wisdom is more blazing and *more enlightening* (φωτεινότερος) *than the sun's rays*, and entereth into the very depths of the heart and of the understanding« (*Dial.* 121:2). Both in *Test.Jud.* 24 and in *Dial.* 121:1f the idea of enlightenment through the Messiah is prominent. In both passages this enlightening is expressed in Law terms. We shall see the significance of that later (see below, pp. 353ff).

The second major Christological passage in TP is *Test. Lev.* 18. I quote the most relevant clauses: »Then shall the Lord raise up a new priest. And to him all the words of the Lord shall be revealed; and he shall execute a righteous judgement upon the earth for a multitude of days. [And his star shall arise in heaven as of a king, lighting up the light of knowledge as the sun the day . . .] He shall shine forth as the sun on the earth, and shall remove all darkness from under heaven . . . And in his priesthood the Gentiles shall be multiplied in knowledge upon the earth, and enlightened through the grace of the Lord. In his priesthood shall sin come to an end, and the lawless (οἱ ἄνομοι) shall cease to do evil . . .«

Here the idea of enlightening is even more pronounced, and again we encounter typical Law terms.

This may throw light on the third element in Justin's composite quotation in *1.Apol.* 32:12, viz. Is 51:5. In *Dial.* 11:3 a larger excerpt from the same Isaiah passage recurs, and here we read the following: . . . νόμος παρ' ἐμοῦ ἐξελεύσεται καὶ ἡ κρίσις μου εἰς φῶς ἐθνῶν . . . καὶ εἰς τὸν βραχίονά μου ἔθνη ἐλπιοῦσιν. This text expresses the idea of enlightenment by the Law, and if Justin's material enshrined the concept of Christ as the Law enlightening the Gentiles, it was a natural step to include Is 51:5 in the composite quotation in *1.Apol.* 32:12. [53]

---

52. If Hultgård is right that the Armenian version is closer to the Jewish »Grundschrift«, it would mean that the Christian interpolator at work in the Greek version introduced more features from Num 24:17 - obviously because the text was an important Christological testimony for him (Hultgård, *op.cit.*, pp. 149f). But the presence of an allusion to Num 24:17 in the Armenian version may tell against Hultgård's thesis that *Test.Jud.* 24:1-3 originally envisaged *God's* reign. Becker argues that in *Test.Jud.* 24 the Armenian version is an abridgement of the Greek which in 24:1-3 in its entirety is Christian, *Testamente*, pp. 321f. I believe there is much to be said for Becker's thesis.

53. One should observe that Is 51:3 was interpreted as a Messianic prophecy by the rabbis, Str. Bill. II, p. 113. It is also relevant to note that Is 51:4f is rendered in a form which may indicate Messianic interpretation in the Qumran Is^a scroll, cf. R. Longenecker, *Christology*, pp. 99f.

To conclude: It seems that the tradition embodied in *1.Apol.* 32 is closely related to the tradition represented by the Christian redactor responsible for *Test.Lev.* 18 and *Test. Jud.* 24 as quoted above.

Let me add that this redactor at all appearances was a Jewish Christian: He is intensely concerned about the final salvation of Israel (see below, pp. 283f)

A final observation may help to clarify the provenance and profile of Justin's material. We have seen repeatedly above that other parts of Justin's tradition show reflexes of the Bar Kokhba revolt and its consequences (the Hadrianic decree). Is the same reference implied in *1.Apol.* 32? Let me make some a priori suggestions. The Bar Kokhba revolt must have been a startling experience to Christians immediately affected by it - especially Jewish Christians and especially as long as the revolt was successful. It seemed the Jews had got a Messiah corresponding to their expectations, a Messiah doing what Jesus had not done. Christians must have felt an urgent need to prove Bar Kokhba a false Messiah, even before his failure.[54]

These a priori considerations can be confirmed from the *Apocalypse of Peter.*[55] In ch. 1 Jesus' warning against false Messiah's are quoted with great emphasis (Mt 24:5 par.). In ch. 2 one is not left in doubt as to who is envisaged. «Hast thou not grasped that the fig-tree is the house of Israel? Verily, I say to you, when its boughs have sprouted at the end, then shall deceiving Christs come, and awaken hope (with the words): 'I am the Christ, who am (now) come into the world.' And when they shall see the wickedness of their deeds (even of the false Christs), they shall turn away after them and deny him to whom our fathers gave praise (?), the first Christ whom they crucified and thereby sinned exceedingly. But this deceiver is not the Christ. And when they reject him, he will kill with the sword (dagger) and there shall be many martyrs. Then shall the boughs of the fig-tree, i.e. the house of Israel, sprout, and there shall be many martyrs by his hand: they shall be killed and become martyrs.»[56] We observe here the deep concern about the fate of Jewish Christians during the Bar Kokhba uprising shown by an author embedded in Jewish apocalyptic traditions.

When Christians should counter Bar Kokhba's Messianic claim, what would they say? They would probably point out (1) that Bar Kokhba was

---

54. Cf. Schäfer, *op. cit*, p.60.
55. I.e. the Ethiopic version.
56. Translation of H. Duensing and D. Hill in *NT Apoc* II, p. 669. I hold the reference to Bar Kokhba to be evident, cf. Ch. Maurer's introduction, *ibid* p. 664. Schäfer, *op.cit.,* thinks the picture of the false Messiah is too traditional to entail any reference to Bar Kokhba (p. 62). But an author so close to Bar Kokhba's days as the author of the *Apocalypse of Peter* could hardly fail to apply the traditional picture to Bar Kokhba.

not of Davidic descent,[57] (2) that Bar Kokhba did not fulfil the universal tasks of the Messiah.

This corresponds to the two additions to Num 24:17 in *1.Apol.* 32:12. The »star« shall be the ἄνθος . . . ἀπὸ τῆς ῥίζης Ἰεσσαί, Is 11:1, and the Gentiles have put their hope on Jesus, Is 51:5.

As we have seen, Num 24:17 and Is 11:1 are joined in allusions prior to Justin, but the production of a deviant *text* to Num 24:17 which fused Is 11:1 and Is 51:5 to the very text of Num 24:17, may very well have been prompted by polemic concerns about Bar Kokhba. If this surmise is right it adds another argument for the Judaeo-Christian provenance of Justin's material. Such an intense concern about the Bar Kokhba incident is most likely to be sought among Jewish Christians.

Besides, this surmise points to a *terminus post quem* for Justin's material in its present form.

(b) The Son of the virgin - the anointed Messiah (Is 7:14; Is 11:2f)

As far as one can glean from Justin's text, his source did not have any explicit OT proof for the theme of divine pre-existence. In fact, the fulfilment report is very close to Luke's theological understanding of the virgin birth: While there is no explicit reference to the pre-existence idea, the emphasis is laid on the Son of God concept: συλλήψῃ . . . ἐκ πνεύματος ἁγίου καὶ τέξῃ υἱὸν καὶ υἱὸς ὑψίστου κληθήσεται (*1.Apol.* 33:5). The second καὶ here is very likely meant to indicate a causal relationship between Jesus' status as God's Son and his supernatural conception by the Spirit (Luke in 1:35 has διὸ!). But this is not further elaborated, neither in Luke, nor, apparently, in Justin's source. (Whether Justin's identification of the Spirit with the Logos in *1.Apol.* 33:6 was also present in Justin's source, is open to doubt. The opening phrase of *1.Apol.* 33:6 reads like an added comment).

If we grant my previous analysis of *Dial.* 49-51 and 87f, we may add another parallel with Luke: It seems reasonable to suppose that the idea of the Messiah being anointed with the Spirit (at his baptism) was combined with the concept of his virgin birth in Justin's source material. Exactly the same combination is found in Luke (anointing with the Spirit: Lk 4:18ff; Acts 4:27; 10:38), and in both cases the inherent adoptionist tendency of the anointing concept is only implicitly modified by the virgin birth motif.

---

57. On Bar Kokhba's non-Davidic descent, cf. i.a. J. Klausner *The Messianic Idea in Israel: From Its Beginnings to the Completion of the Mishnah* (New York, 1955), p. 395, and E. E. Urbach, *The Sages: Their Concepts and Beliefs I & II* (Jerusalem, 1975), I p. 674; II, p. 999, n. 82. Apparently, Bar Kokhba's non-Davidic origin was the subject of controversy among the rabbis. Urbach, *loc. cit.*, interprets the Midrash passage quoted in note 20 above on this background: R. Johanan b. Torta's sharp reaction against R. Akiba's claim that Bar Kokhba was the Messiah, »emanated apparently from his view that the Messiah must necessarily be descended from the House of David.« (I, p. 674).

It is relevant to notice that the Christian interpolator(s) of the TP has the same combination of motifs. In *Test. Jos.* 19:8 the Armenian text may have preserved a pre-Christian Virgin motif[58] - in any case this has been Christianized in the Greek text: καὶ εἶδον ὅτι ἐκ τοῦ᾽ Ἰούδα ἐγεννήθη παρθένος, ἔχουσα στολὴν βυσσίνην, καὶ ἐξ αὐτῆς ἐγεννήθη ἀμνὸς ἄμωμος . . . The Messianic anointing with the Spirit is described in *Test.Lev.* 18:6f and *Test.Jud.* 24:1-3. «The heavens shall be opened, and from the temple of glory shall come upon him sanctification, with the Father's voice as from Abraham to Isaac. And the glory of the Most High shall be uttered over him, and the Spirit of understanding and sanctification shall rest upon him in the water (καὶ πνεῦμα συνέσεως καὶ ἁγιασμοῦ καταπαύσει ἐπ᾽ αὐτόν ἐν τῷ ὕδατι.» (*Test.Lev.* 18:6f).[59] The allusion here to Is 11:2f is evident; we thus are facing a Christian theologian applying this testimony to the baptism of Jesus.

It seems to me that M.-A. Chevallier is right to claim that *Test.Lev.* 18:6f in its entirety is dependent on the synoptic account of Jesus' baptism. The reference to Jesus' baptism is thus not present only in the words ἐν τῷ ὕδατι,[60] but in the combination of motifs in the passage as a whole: the opening of the heavens, the fatherly voice, the descent of the Spirit.[61]

How is this endowment with the Spirit understood? The text does not give us many clues, but let me adduce the parallel in *Test. Jud.* 24:2f:«And the heavens shall be opened unto him, to pour out the spirit, the blessing of the Holy Father; and he (the Messiah) shall pour out the spirit of grace upon you; and you shall be unto him sons in truth, and ye shall walk in his commandments first and last.» On the last part of this passage I have commented above. Here I shall emphasize the idea that because the Messiah is endowed with the Spirit, *he himself becomes the spender of the Spirit* to his believers - his «sons».

This corresponds exactly to the exegesis of Is 11:2f which we meant to discern traces of in *Dial* 87:5: «. . . those gifts . . . when they had taken their rest in Christ (ἀνάπαυσιν λαβόντα), should . . . be given by the grace of the power of that Spirit to them that believe on him.» As we have seen, this is not Justin's own exegesis of the 'rest' motive in Is 11:2 (see above, p. 197), but it agrees perfectly with the ideas in *Test.Lev.* 18 and *Test.Jud.* 24. One also notices a trace of the same tradition when Justin in *Dial* 39:2 enumerates

---

58. This is argued i.a. by B. Murmelstein,'Das Lamm in Test.Jos. 19,8,' *ZNW* 58 (1967), pp. 273-79; Hultgård, *Croyances messianiques,* pp. 167-69/176-79. J. Becker, on the other hand, regards the Armenian text as Christian and secondary, *Testamente* pp. 59-66. Essentially the same position is taken by J. Jeremias,'Das Lamm das aus der Jungfrau hervorging (Test. Jos. 19:8)', *ZNW* 57 (1966), pp. 216-219.

59. Cf. i.a. Becker, *Testamente,* pp. 293ff; M. -A. Chevallier, *l'Esprit et le Messie,* pp. 127-132.

60. This was deemed the only Christian element in the text by Charles in his ed. of the text, cf. also Hultgård, p. 116. Becker takes the whole of vss. 6f to be a Christian interpolation, cf. his translation *ad loc.* (p. 60)

61. *Loc. cit,* esp. p.129.

Christian *charismata* in partial agreement with Is 11:2. The idea in *Dial.* 87:4 may also be part of the same concept: Before Christ there was only a partial giving of the Spirit.

The distinctive feature of this tradition in Justin and its parallel in Test. XII Patr., is that it connects the motif of Jesus as the spender of the Spirit/*charismata* with his *baptism*. In the NT the same motif is connected with Christ's ascension, Eph 4:8; Acts 2:32-36.[62]

Justin can be said to re-introduce this NT point of view in *Dial.* 39:4 and *Dial.* 87:6, where he quotes the testimony from Eph 4:8: Ps 68:19. (In *Dial.* 87:6 also the programmatic testimony from Acts 2: Joel 3:1f).

On the other hand, the concept of Jesus being anointed with the Spirit is not entirely foreign to the NT. Luke alludes to this idea in Lk 4:18f and Acts 10:38, perhaps also in Acts 4:21, and he certainly has Jesus' baptism in mind.[63] But the OT testimony envisaged by Luke is Is 61:1. (Justin alludes to this text in *Dial.*12:2, but there is no reference to Jesus' baptism.) The only NT writer who probably refers Is 11:2 to the baptism of Jesus, is John (Jn 1:32f: the Spirit remained on him (ἔμεινεν ἐπ᾽ αὐτόν).[64] The presence of this motif in John serves to underline the fact that an application of Is 11:2f to the baptism of Jesus need not imply adoptionist Christology in any strict sense.

To conclude: This survey of relevant parallel material has shown that the closest parallel to Justin's source for Is 11:2f and the anointing idea is to be found in the TP.

Let me add here that an independent confirmation that this application of Is 11:2f to the baptism of Jesus was popular among Jewish Christians is to be found in the *Gospel of the Hebrews*: «And it came to pass when the Lord was come out of the water, the whole fount of the Holy Spirit descended upon him and rested on him (*requieuit super eum*) and said to him: My Son, in all the prophets was I waiting for thee that thou shouldst come and I might rest in thee (*requiescerem in te*). For thou art my rest (*tu es enim requies mea*), thou art my first-begotten Son that reignest for ever» (*Gospel according to the Hebrews*, fragm. 2).[65] The fragment from the *Gospel of the Hebrews* embodies a Judaeo-Christian concept with Gnosticising features, resembling the theology of the *Kerygmata Petrou* underlying the *Pseudo-Clementines*.[66] The Holy Spirit seeks «rest» - this is the dominant motif - in all

---

62. Cf. esp. J. Dupont,'Ascension du Christ et don de l'Ésprit d'après Actes 2:33', *Christ and the Spirit in the New Testament. In Honour of C.F.D. Moule* (ed. by B. Lindars and S. S. Smalley, Cambridge, 1973), pp. 210-228.

63. Cf. i.a. M. Dorner,*Das Heil Gottes*, pp.45-68. Kurz, *Christological Proof*, p. 158, emphasizes the contrast between Luke and Justin in their respective treatments of Jesus' baptism, cf. also pp. 187-189. But he does not consider the possibility that one of Justin's sources in *Dial.* 87f was much closer to Luke than Justin himself.

64. Cf. Brown, *comm. ad. loc.* (p.66).

65. Text: Preuschen, *Antilegomena*, p. 4; translation according to *NT Apoc.* I, pp. 163f. The fragment is preserved in Jerome, *Comm. in Is.* IV (on Is 11:2).

66. Cf. Ph. Vielhauer's remarks in his Introduction to the *NT Apoc.* translation, I, pp. 159-161.

the prophets, but only finds rest in her own Son, Jesus. The concept of Messianic anointing is not clearly contained here. On the other hand the text is of considerable interest in so far as the *Gospel of Hebrews* combines the ideas of pre-existence of Christ and an understanding of Christ's baptism as an endowment with the Spirit. «The whole fount of the Holy Spirit» is very likely a reference to the sevenfold Spirit enumerated in Is 11:2f, and *requieuit super eum* recalls the ἀναπαύσεται ἐπ᾽ αὐτόν of Is 11:2.

We have now, finally, to take a closer look at another element in Justin's treatment of the baptism of Jesus, viz. the idea of John the Baptist as «Elijah» anointing the Messiah. The relevant material is to be found in *Dial.* 49:3.6f; 52:3; 86:2b.3, and may be summarized thus:

(a) «The Spirit in the prophets used to anoint and appoint even your kings» (*Dial.* 52:3).

(b) The two supreme examples of this are Elijah and John: The anointing spirit of Elijah was also present in John (*Dial.* 49:3.6f)

(c) Jacob's anointing of the stone in Bethel is a type of Christ's anointing; Ps 45:8 is a direct testimony: «Therefore God, thy God, hath anointed thee (ἔχρισέν σε) with oil of gladness.»(*Dial.* 86:2f.)

It is not difficult to find the origin of the concept that John is «Elijah». Justin himself quotes Mt 17:11-13 in *Dial.* 49:5, and the topic is common to the three synoptics; although Luke has a certain reserve against the Elijah-John typology, because he applies several Elijah motifs to Jesus himself.[67] It is Luke, however, who has the closest parallel to Justin's idea that Elijah's spirit was in John: καὶ αὐτὸς προελεύσεται ἐνώπιον αὐτοῦ ἐν πνεύματι καὶ δυνάμει ᾽Ηλίου , Lk 1:17.

But the concept of John/«Elijah» *anointing* Jesus is not explicitly stated in the NT. Here we shall have to turn to Jewish sayings about Elijah. In Sirach 48:8 Elijah is called ὁ χρίων βασιλεῖς εἰς ἀνταπόδομα καὶ προφήτας διαδόχους μετ᾽ αὐτόν. Although this text has historical incidents in mind (1 Kings 19:15f), it has also an eschatological perspective:«... you (Elijah) who are ready at the appointed time, it is written, ... to restore the tribes of Jacob.» (*ibid.*, vs. 10). This text may thus point forward to the rabbinic idea that Elijah shall restore the bottle of anointing oil: «And this (viz. the bottle of manna) is one of the three things which Elijah will, in the future, restore to Israel: The bottle of manna, the bottle of sprinkling water, and the bottle of anointing oil.» (*Mekh.* Vayassa VI:81-83, p. 126).[68]

In the *Dialogue*, it is Trypho who states that Elijah shall anoint the Messiah. No more than hints at this idea are found in the Jewish material

---

67. Cf. J.-D. Dubois, 'La figure d' Elie dans la perspective lucanienne', *RHPhR* 53 (1973), pp. 155-76.
68. More rabbinic texts quoted in Str. Bill. IV, p. 797.

quoted above.[69] It seems, however, that Justin's source portrayed John as a new Elijah anointing Jesus. It is thus possible that the idea put in the mouth of Trypho was transmitted to Justin via this source. But here we enter into the realm of speculation.

The conclusion I think we can state with some certainty is that Justin in the passages reviewed above seems to draw on a source which made John a second Elijah, anointing Jesus with the the Holy Spirit at his baptism, thus fulfilling Is 11:2f. This endowment with the Spirit makes Jesus the spender of the Spirit. We have found elements of this idea in Jewish literature and the NT, but in the description of Jesus' baptism and its effects we find the closest parallel in the Chistian interpolations of *Test.Lev.* 18 and *Test.Jud.* 24.[70]

(c) The slaying of the Just One and the guilt of the Jews.

Let us take a closer look at the «fulfilment reports» in *1.Apol.* 35 and 38. Here it is said that the Jews crucified Jesus. The ones who mocked him, also were Jews. One might say that this is no peculiarity in Justin. The tendency to put the blame for Jesus' crucifixion on the Jews alone is evident from a very early stage in Christian literature ( 1 Thess 2:14f; the passion narratives; Acts 7:51f etc.). «It was obviously in the interest of the Christian Church, seeking tolerance from the Roman authorities under whom it had to live, to avoid blaming the Romans for the death of Jesus . . . The process of bettering Pilate's image continues beyond the NT period until the time of Eusebius.» These statements by R.E.Brown may be taken as representative[71] for an often expressed opinion among NT scholars.

---

69. Ginzberg's statement is perhaps a little too definite: «. . . the old rabbinic writings know nothing of this function of Elijah's, and the prevalent opinion in these works is that the Messiah will not be anointed at all.» (VI, p. 340 - an equally definite statement in Goldfahn, p. 194). But cf. the opposite point of view in A. J. B. Higgins,'Jewish messianic belief in Justin Martyr's *Dialogue with Trypho',* Nov. Test. 9 (1967); pp. 298-305.

70. One should also note the interesting tradition in *Rec.* 1:45-48. «Although .. he was the Son of God, and the beginning of all things, he became man; him first God anointed with oil which was taken from the wood of the tree of life; from that anointing therefore he is called Christ. Thence, moreover, he himself also .. anoints with similar oil every one of the pious when they come to his kingdom .. and being filled with the Holy Spirit, they may be endowed with immortality.» ( 1:45:4f). As is evident from the context, the author is thinking of a spiritual anointing, of which the anointing chrism of the OT is a shadow. There is probably an Adam/Christ typology involved here, cf. P. Beskow, *Rex Gloriae,* p. 117. In its present form the passage *Rec.* 1:45-48 probably is composed by the «Grundschrift» author, but he may have employed traditional material, cf. G. Strecker, *Pseudoklementinen,* p. 236. One should note here also the combination af pre-existence and anointing concepts.

71. R. E. Brown, *The Gospel according to John I & II* (The Anchor Bible 29 & 29A, New York, 1966/70), p. 794. Some other representative statements: «. . . *die Haupttendenz des ganzen matthäischen Berichtes. . .: Es geht um die Alleinschuld der Juden an dem Tode Jesu.»* (W. Trilling, *Das wahre Israel. Studien zur Theologie des Matthäus-Evangeliums* (StANT 10, 3rd ed., München, 1964) , p. 73). «The Jews are presented as being wholly responsible for the crucifixion. Their leaders took the initiative at his capture; they were the prosecutors at his trial; recognizing him for what he was, they nevertheless deliberately turned their backs

However, one can reasonably doubt the explanation here given. And I think one misses in important aspect of the whole development if one takes apologetic concerns about the Romans as the main motive. Reading the texts, one observes that the main point is to put the guilt on the Jews - not to exculpate Pilate or the Romans. The Jews are guilty, but that does not mean that Pilate is innocent. He is corrupt, and corrupt is not the same as innocent. It seems to me that apologetics *vis-a-vis* the Romans is a minor concern for the early writers - if a concern at all.[72] But why then this concentration of guilt on the Jews?

There is in late OT and intertestamental literature a quite distinct «deuteronomistic» scheme of preaching penitence to Israel.[73] It often comprises the following elements: (1) Israel's guilt is their rejection of God's word, expressed in their killing of the prophets; (2) Israel is now in a state of punishment, usually exiled, and/or under foreign rule; (3) the way to salvation is recognition of Israel's guilt and conversion to God.[74]

---

upon him; they constrained the weak political power to hand him over to them; and they are virtually stated to have crucified him.»(E. Franklin, *Christ the Lord. A study in the Purpose and Theology of Luke-Acts* (London, 1975), p. 93). «An sich stehen so in der Passionsdarstellung *(des Lukas) zwei Tendenzen nebeneinander: die dogmatische von der Notwendigkeit des Leidens und die «historische» von der Schuld der Juden - und der Unschuld des Imperiums, das den unpolitischen Charakter des Evangeliums und Königtums Jesu durchschaut.» (H. Conzelmann, *Die Mitte der Zeit. Studien zur Theologie des Lukas* (BHTh 17, 5th ed., Tübingen, 1964), p. 131). Cf. for the Patristic period, M. Simon, *Verus Israel. Étude sur les relations entre chrétiens et juifs dans l'Empire Romain (115-425)* (Paris, 2nd ed., 1964), pp. 147ff.

72. This is seen by many commentators. cf. Trilling on Matthew: «Pilatus hat die Funktion eines Statisten oder etwa eines Katalysators ... Ein spezielles Interesse an Pilatus, an seiner Entlastung und damit eventuell verbundene apologetische Motive für die Heidenmission sind für Matthäus nicht anzunehmen. Ihm geht es um «die Juden» und damit um das Schicksal Israels.» (*Op. cit.*, p. 74). Franklin writes on Luke:«Political apologetic does not of itself supply sufficient motive ... Pilate does not appear as an impressive figure and, since he does give way to Jewish pressure, Roman discrimination and justice are hardly presented as a matter in which confidence can be placed. In Luke 13.1 Pilate is presented as tyrant and, though in Acts 3.13 he is described as wishing to release Jesus, this fact is brought out only to emphasize the obduracy of the Jews. On the other hand, in Acts 4.27 he is named among the opponents of Jesus. In Luke, the Romans alone actually condemn Jesus and the final resposibility is very definitely stated to be theirs (23.24-5, and compare 18.32-3 with Mark 10.33-4) ... Apologetic motives are secondary here, and Luke would seem to have scarcely more desire to vindicate Pilate than he would have to present Herod in a favourable light. The reason for his changes can only be that he wishes to lay the blame for the death of Jesus firmly upon the Jews.»(*Op. cit.*, p. 93). Cf. also J. Jervell's sharp criticism of the traditional theory that a main concern for Luke was apologetics *vis-a-vis* the Romans, *Luke and the People of God. A New Look at Luke -Acts* (Minneapolis, 1972), pp. 154-158.

73. The authoritative treatment of this theme is O. H. Steck, *Israel und das gewaltsame Geschick der Propheten. Untersuchungen zür Überlieferung des deuteronomistischen Geschichtsbildes im Alten Testament, Spätjudentum und Urchristentum* (WMANT 23, Neukirchen-Vluyn, 1967).

74. Examples of this scheme: Ps 79; Ezra 9:6-15; Neh 1:5-11; 9:5-37; Ps 106; Tobit 3:1-6; Dan 9:4-19; Baruch 1:15-3:8; *Jub.* 1:7-26; 1QS I:24- II:1; *Pesiqta Rabbati* 138a. Texts in which Israel's sin is specified as the killing of the prophets: Neh 9:26; Ezra 9:11; Ant. IX:13:2; X:3:1; Jub. 1:12. A rich material is treated in Steck, *op. cit.*, pp. 60-195.

One can observe in the NT how this scheme is applied to the persecution of Jesus and his followers (Mt 5:11f par; Mt 23:29-36 par; Mt 23:37-39 par; Acts 7:51f *et al.*). The scope and purpose of these NT passages vary. Element 3 in the scheme is usually lacking - this is sometimes the case in the Jewish material. Exhortation to conversion is then turned to proclamation of judgement, but still a deep concern for Israel and its fate is felt. «*Israel selbst ist es, das die Vorstellung ausgebildet und überliefert hat, es ist darin in einer Tiefe mit sich zu Gericht gegangen . . .*»[75]

When Jewish Christians applied this scheme of judgement and penitence preaching in their approach to their fellow Jews, there is no question of apologetics to the Romans. We have to do with a deeply felt address to Israel, employing the most searching model of penitence preaching known from Jewish tradition. It is probably more than a rhetorical device that one of the most harsh statements on Jewish guilt in the whole literature of the second century - Melito's *Paschal homily* vss. 72-99 - is addressed directly to Israel. I believe this reflects the original and creative setting for the sayings about Israel's guilt: the missionary approach - to the Jews!

It goes without saying that in the hands of the triumphant Gentile Christian Church this tradition soon deteriorates into a slogan[76] which -deprived of its original setting and purpose - might easily express or promote Christian anti-Semitism. Melito's homily is instructive in that respect also.

One good example of this tradition in its original setting and concern is again the Christian interpolator of the TP. More than once, he makes the Jews guilty of crucifying Jesus, and for this their greatest sin they are punished by exile. But the author believes in final salvation for Israel, and makes the patriarchs exhort their descendants to true conversion and repentance. The deuteronomistic scheme is already present in the Jewish source; the interpolator applies it to Jewish rejection of Jesus.[77]

The only relevant guilt within this scheme, is *Israel's* guilt. What I want to suggest is that Justin's material in *1.Apol.* 35.38 derive from a similar setting, that it was formed by theologians deeply concerned with Israel. At this stage, this can be no more than a proposal. We shall see if other parts of Justin's material can substantiate this surmise.

Let me add one final observation. When Jesus is seen as the last in a line of prophets killed by Israel - as required by the deuteronomistic scheme -he is often portrayed as the «Just One», ὁ δίκαιος.[78] Ps 22 is an ideal field of testimonies on the suffering Just One, and it may be more than a coinci-

---

75. Steck, *op. cit.*, p. 321.
76. For a survey of the patristic material, cf. D. Judant, *Judaisme et Christianisme. Dossier patristique* (Paris, 1969), pp. 78f.
77. Cf. esp. J. Jervell, 'Interpolator' pp. 41-47. The most relevant texts are given below, p.291.
78. Acts 3:14; 7:52; 22:14; Jas 5:6. I return to this theme more fully below.

dence that Justin in his fulfilment reports to the testimonies from Ps 22 shows contact with the tradition behind the *Gospel of Peter.* This Gospel gives prominence to the idea of Jesus as ὁ δίκαιος and is also very concerned about the guilt of the Jews.

To pursue these suggestions, we should have to study Justin's material on the «slaying of the Just One» in its entirety. But this would take us too far from the track we are now following, and I therefore postpone that discussion to a later heading (see below, pp. 288ff). Here I am content to point out this possible cross-connexion within Justin's material.

(d) The ruling Messiah (Ps110:1f)[79]

In the NT, one can roughly classify three uses of Ps 110:1:[80]

(1) The κύριος title for the Messiah shows that the Son of David Messianism of the rabbis is insufficient, Mk 12:35-37 par.

(2) Christ's session at the right hand of God will be revealed at Christ's *parousia,* Mk 14:62/Mt 26:64;[81]

(3) Christ's enthronement at God's right hand is a present fact to be proclaimed and experienced in the life of the Church, Rom 8:34; Col 3:1; Eph 1:20; Lk 22:69; Acts 2:33-35; 5:30-32; 1 Pt 3:22; Heb 1:3.13; Polyc. *ad Phil.* 2:1.

In the tradition we can discern behind the *Apology,* it is the third line which is carried on. Christ's ongoing subduing of his enemies is seen in a demonological framework: Christ reigns by liberating men from servitude under the demons, *1.Apol.* 45:1. Justin's tradition has elegantly combined this with the idea of the apostolic kerygma by making Ps 110:2 a major testimony to the latter idea.[81] This means that in order to characterise Justin's material further, we shall have to study his ideas on the apostolic mission. To this we return below (pp. 359ff).

(e) The Saviour of Israel (Zech 12:10-12).

Matthew and Revelation refer Zech 12:10-12 to the reaction of all men at the *parousia* (πᾶσαι αἱ φυλαὶ τῆς γῆς), while Justin's text clearly has the

---

79. It is hardly relevant to my purpose to enter upon a full discussion of the rabbinic interpretation of Ps 110. See D. M. Hay, *Glory at the Right Hand: Psalm 110 in Early Christianity.* (SBL Mon. Ser. 18, Nashville /New York, 1973), pp. 21—33, largely confirming the suggestions of Billerbeck, Str. Bill. IV, pp. 452ff.

80. The literature on Ps 110 in the NT is extensive. Cf. i.a. Hay, *op. cit.,* W.R.G. Loader, 'Christ at the Right Hand - Ps CX. 1 in the New Testament', NTS 24 (1978), pp. 199-217; M. Guorgues, *À la droite de Dieux. Resurrection de Jesus et actualisation du Psaume 110:1 dans le Nouveau Testament* (EB, Paris, 1978). My classification of the three main uses is a simplification of the more refined classification employed by these authors; cf. esp. Loader.

81. This tradition is carried on in *Apoc. Petr.* 6; *Sib.* II: 238-244; Hegesippus (*apud* Eus. *E. H.* II:23:13).

82. Cf. esp. the instructive treatment of Ps 110:1f in the NT and Justin by Daniélou, *Études,* pp. 46-49. Daniélou rightly stresses that Justin's tradition embodies the idea expressed in the sequence ascension - session - mission, and points to Acts and Mk 16:19 as NT predecessors.

Jews in mind. This agrees with the original meaning of the text, and with the rabbinic interpretation.[83]

Justin's combined text presupposes a dispersion of the Jews (strophe 1 on the table p. 76). Their holy city with its Temple is devastated: ἡ δόξα ἣν εὐλόγησεν οἱ πατέρες ἡμῶν ἐγενήθη ἡμῖν εἰς ὄνειδος (Is 64:10 non-LXX - cf. the context in Isaiah: πόλις τοῦ ἁγίου σου ἐγενήθη ἔρημος (vs. 9)). One can see here a reference both to a post-70 and a post-135 situation. The analogy with other texts in Justin would point to the latter alternative.

Another remarkable feature of the text, is the elaborate description of Israel's repentance. It is obviously meant to be sincere, and probably salvific, since the text speaks of the ingathering of the Jewish diaspora in a friendly tone (τέκνα, φέρειν, μὴ προσκόπτειν). Where are we to seek parallels to this conception in Christian literature prior to or contemporary with Justin?

It seems once again that the closest parallel is to be sought with the redactor of the TP. A considerable number of his interpolations occur within the passages dealing with the deuteronomistic pattern of sin - exile -redemption. For the author of the Jewish source, the reference (fictionally) is to the Babylonian exile. The Christian interpolator, however, identifies Israel's sin as their guilt in the crucifixion of Jesus. J.Jervell is probably right when he assumes that the Christian redactor took the resultant text seriously: The crucifixion of Jesus is followed by exile and final redemption for Israel.[84] One can observe this «interpretation by interpolation» process in a number of texts: *Test. Lev.* 10:1-4; 14f; 16; *Test. Jud.* 22; *Test. Zeb.* 9:5; *Test Ben.* 9f; *Test. Asher* 7:1-3.

Beyond this general parallelism, there may be some terminological links between Justin's combined, non-LXX text to Zech 12:10-12 and the relevant passages in the TP, but they are hardly very significant.[85]

I think Justin's text to Zech 12:10-12 definitely proves the genuine concern for Israel's conversion and redemption which we posited was inherent in his tradition above.

---

83. The rabbis evidently took the mourners to be Israel, cf. the two talmudic passages quoted above (p.269,n.49).

84. Cf. Jervell, 'Interpolator', pp. 41-47 - and chapter 2 below.

85. In Is 64:10, Justin's deviant text in *1.Apol.* 52:12 reads: ἡ δόξα, ἣν εὐλόγησαν οἱ πατέρες ἡμῶν, ἐγενήθη ἡμῖν *εἰς ὄνειδος* (LXX: ἐγενήθη πυρίκαυστος). Cf. *Test. Lev.* 10:3f: σχισθήσεται τὸ καταπέτασμα τοῦ ναοῦ, ὥστε μὴ καλύψαι τὴν ἀσχημοσύνην ὑμῶν . . . καὶ ἔσεσθε *εἰς ὄνειδος* καὶ εἰς κατάραν ἐκεῖ. Cf. also *Test Lev.* 15:2: . . . καὶ λήψεσθε *ὄνειδος* καὶ αἰσχύνην αἰώνιον . . . In Zech 2: 10 Justin's non-LXX text in *1.Apol.* 52:10 reads: . . . συνάξαι *τὰ ἐσκορπισμένα τέκνα* (LXX: συνάξω ὑμᾶς . . .) Cf. *Test. Lev.* 16:5: ἔσεσθε ἐν τοῖς ἔθνεσιν εἰς κατάραν καὶ εἰς *διασκορπισμόν* (MS e reads : διεσκορπισμένοι), ἕως αὐτὸς πάλιν ἐπισκέψηται . . . καὶ προσδέξηται ὑμᾶς ἐν πίστει καὶ ὕδατι. Cf. also *Test.Ash.* 7:2: καὶ ὑμεῖς *διασκορπισθήσεσθε* εἰς τὰς τέσσαρας γωνίας τῆς γῆς. The shared terms are not uncommon LXX words, however, and I do not want to make much out of these parallels. The composer of Justin's text may have been familiar with the ideas and terminology of the Testaments - more one can hardly say.

In Justin's own theology there is no corresponding concern. He hopes for the conversion of a few individual Jews, but for the Jewish nation as such he has no hope, *Dial* 120:2; 32:2.

(f) The testimonies in *Dial* 72: The paschal lamb.

We have surmised above (p. 178f) that *Dial* 72 draws on a source with passion testimonies which had the paschal lamb typology as their common denominator, emphasizing the purifying, propitiary blood of Christ (*Dial* 13f; *Dial* 40:1-3), and placing this concept in a baptismal setting - cf. *Barn.* 5:1f. The baptismal setting may also explain the last testimony in *Dial* 72: the Ps. Jer text on Christ's descent.[86]

It is time here to point out some features which connect the material in *Dial* 72 with Justin's Christological testimonies in the *Apology*.

(1) The paschal lamb concept in the *Dialogue* (*Dial* 13f; 40:1-3; 72; 111:3f) is centered upon the idea of *remission uf sins through Christ's blood.* (Cf. on Gen 49:11 and Is 7:14 above). Is 53:7 (paschal lamb) may be another testimony nucleus behind *1.Apol* 50f. I suspect we have here material drawn from the same source which is behind the long Is 53 excerpt in *1.Apol* 50f. The soteriological concepts implied in this will be analysed in some detail when we turn to the cultic typology in Justin (below, p. 299ff). The only direct trace of testimony material in *1.Apol* 50f is the deviant version of Is 53:12 in *1.Apol* 50:2. This text expresses the idea of expiatory suffering, and blames the Jews for Jesus' death (see discussion of the text above, p. 62f). It may be relevant to point out that in the preceeding verse, Is 53:11, the concept of the Just One occurs: δικαιῶσαι δίκαιον εὖ δουλεύοντα πολλοῖς.

Since we have seen close parallels between Justin's material and the Christian interpolator of the TP, it may be relevant to point out that this interpolator was familiar with a «lamb» Christology which alludes to Is 53 and John 1:29.36. «And I saw: [there was born a virgin from Judah. She carried a robe of byssus, and from her was born an unblemished lamb] (ἀμνὸς ἄμωμος )», *Test. Jos.* 19:8 (Greek). «... [honour Levi and Judah. For from them shall arise (ἀνατελεῖ) unto you the lamb of God (ὁ ἀμνὸς τοῦ θεοῦ), who shall take away the sins of the world, saving all the nations and Israel»], *Test. Jos.* 19:11. Perhaps the most interesting «lamb» passage comes in *Test.Ben.* 3:8 (Greek): [«On you (i.e. Joseph) shall be fulfilled the heavenly prophecy about the lamb of God and the saviour of the world, viz. that the lamb will be delivered (παραδοθήσεται) by the lawless (ἄνομοι), and that the sinless will die for the ungodly through the covenant blood for

---

86. On the connexion between the ideas of baptism and descent, cf. esp. B. Reicke, *The disobedient spirits and Christian baptism. A study of 1. Pet. III:19 and its context* (ASNU 13, Copenhagen, 1946), pp. 245-47; P. Lundberg, *La Typologie baptismale dans l'ancienne église* (ASNU 10, Leipzig/Uppsala, 1942), pp. 64-116. The theme is treated more fully below, pp. 378f

the salvation of the Gentiles and Israel, and he shall destroy Beliar and his servants»].[87] The special relevance of this text is its allusions to Is 53:12. The idea expressed in these allusions - viz. that the lamb was delivered (to death) *by the* ἄνομοι (no doubt the Jews) - is in accordance with Justin's non-LXX text, against the LXX text of Is 53:12.[88] I am therefore inclined to believe that these interpolations are related to Justin's material, and that they are old, despite their absence in the Armenian version.[89]

(2) The Ps. Ezra quotation in *Dial.* 72:1 shows a concern for the devastation of Judaea and Jewish calamity: «And if ye understand ... that we are about to humble him on a cross, and afterwards put our hope in him, this place will never be laid desolate ... But if ye do not believe on him ... ye shall be a laughing stock to the Gentiles.» One should notice the terminological links between this text and the Zech 12:10-12 quotation studied above, and also with the «devastation» testimonies in *1.Apol.* 47:

| Ps. Ezra | *1. Apol.* 52:11f | *1. Apol.* 47 |
|---|---|---|
| καὶ ἐὰν *διανοηθῆτε* καὶ ἀναβῇ ὑμῶν ἐπὶ τὴν *καρδίαν*... | καὶ τότε ἐν Ἰερουσαλὴμ κοπετὸς μέγας, οὐ κοπετὸς στομάτων... ἀλλὰ κοπετὸς *καρδίας* καὶ... σχίσωσιν... τὰς *διανοίας*... | (Is 64:9): |
| οὐ μὴ *ἐρημωθῇ* ὁ *τόπος οὗτος*... | | ἐγενήθη *ἔρημος* Σιών, ὡς *ἔρημος* ἐγενήθη Ἰερουσαλὴμ (Is 1:7): ἡ γῆ αὐτῶν *ἔρημος*... |
| ἂν δὲ μὴ πιστεύσητε... ἔσεσθε ἐπίχαρμα τοῖς ἔθνεσι | ἡ δόξα... ἐγενήθη ἡμῖν] εἰς ὄνειδος | = Is 64:10 non-LXX |

The Ps. Ezra text expresses the same deuteronomistic pattern of preaching as is contained in *1.Apol.* 52:10-12: Israel's guilt and disbelief concerning Jesus result in exile and calamity (devastation of «this place» - Jerusalem!), but the author of the text has hope for Israel - he puts an urgent call to conversion in the mouth of Ezra, and promises national restoration if Israel will believe. Justin himself has no similar hope for the Jewish nation.

(3) The Ps. Jer logion shows a deep concern for the situation of the OT pious men. Whether or not ἀπὸ Ἰσραὴλ τῶν νεκρῶν αὐτοῦ is the original

87. Becker, *Testamente*, pp. 52f, points out the strange feature that the lamb (Christ) is said to descend from Joseph. He takes this to be a clear indication that the present text was not created in its entirety by a Christian author but that the idea resulted from a somewhat unhappy interpolation into a Jewish text. Cf. also the extensive discussion of Test. Benj. 3:8 in W.Popkes, *Christus Traditus. Eine Untersuchung zum Begriff der Dahingabe im Neuen Testament* (AThANT 49, Zürich/Stuttgart, 1967), pp. 47-55.
88. Popkes, in his otherwise excellent treatment of this passage, seems to have overlooked this, cf. esp. his discussion of the reference to Is 53 on p. 49.
89. Cf. the literature listed in the notes, pp. 254f.

reading,[90] there can hardly be any doubt that the ones in Hades to whom Christ descended[91] are thought to be the pious of the OT. The text in its Christian use is concerned about the pious Israel of the OT: Are they reached by Christ's salvation?[92]

This *descensus* concept may be hinted at in 1 Pt 4:6.[93] It is clearly presupposed in the *Gospel of Peter* 41: ἐκέρυξας τοῖς κοιμωμένοις; Ignatius may also presuppose the idea, *Magn.* 9:2: *Philad.* 9:1; *Trall.* 9:1.[94] The most extensive treatment of the theme is found in Hermas, *Sim.* IX:16:5, but here the descent is transferred from Christ to the apostles: «. . . these apostles and teachers, who preached the name of the Son of God, having fallen asleep (κοιμηθέντες) in the power and faith of the Son of God, preached also to those who had fallen asleep before them (ἐκήρυξαν καὶ τοῖς προκεκοιμημένοις) . . .» The last mentioned are the patriarchs and the prophets and other righteous men of the OT, cf. *Sim* IX:15:4. Perhaps a more original version of Hermas' idea is to be found in a «presbyter» tradition in Irenaeus, *Adv.Haer.* IV:27:2: «It was for this reason, too, that the Lord descended into the reigns beneath the earth, preaching his advent there also, and (declaring) the remission of sins received by those who believe in him. Now all those believed on him who had hope towards him, that is, those who proclaimed his advent and submitted to his dispensations, the righteous men, the prophets, and the patriarchs, to whom he remitted sins in the same way as he did to us . . .»[95]

It seems a similar concept is embodied in three interpolated passages in the TP. *Test. Lev.* 4:1 reads: καὶ τοῦ ᾅδου σκυλευομένου ἐπὶ τῷ πάθει τοῦ ὑψίστου. The closeness to Mt 27:52 may point to the OT pious men as the ones who are saved by this plundering of Hades.[96] In *Test.Dan* 5:10f the interpolator has made the text speak about Christ plundering Beliar, καὶ τὴν αἰχμαλωσίαν λήψεται ἀπὸ τοῦ Βελίαρ, τὰς ψυχὰς τῶν ἁγίων.[97]

---

90. Cf. the discussion below, p. 452.
91. There can hardly be any doubt that the apocryphal text is of Christian origin - one can hardly imagine a Jew speaking about Jahve descending *to Sheol.* This is rightly pointed out by Hilgenfeld, 'Citate', pp. 391f, n. 1, against Credner, p. 250, who posited a Jewish origin. Christian origin is also posited by A. Resch, *Agrapha. Ausserkanonische Schriftfragmente* (TU 30:3/4, 2nd ed., Leipzig, 1906), pp. 320-322; Koester, *Schriftbeweis,* p. 33; Daniélou, *Theology,* p. 102.
92. This is emphasized by Daniélou, *Theology,* pp. 102f. cf. also the instructive comments in W. Bieder, *Die Vorstellung von der Höllenfahrt Jesu Christi* (AThANT 19, Zürich, 1949), pp. 135-153.
93. Cf. e.g. Schelkle's *comm. ad. loc.* (p. 116).
94. On these passages, see esp. Bieder, *op. cit.,* pp. 141-143. Bieder argues that only *Magn.* 9:2 testifies to the *descensus* motif, and that Ignatius himself was unconcerned about this (traditional) concept.
95. On this passage, cf. Bieder, *op.cit.,* pp. 182f.
96. Cf. i.a. Becker, *Testamente,* p. 268: «. . . *liegt doch eine sachliche Aufnahme von Mt 27:52 vor.»* Cf. also Bieder, *op. cit.,* pp. 162f.
97. Bieder, *op. cit.,* p. 165, doubts that the reference is exclusively to the OT righteous men, but I cannot escape the impression that this is the author's meaning.

Taken together with *Test. Benj.* 9:5 (Greek), we have here a *descensus* concept close to the Ps. Jer logion, except that the «plundering of Hades» motif is not stated in Ps. Jer. This concern for the OT pious men may be seen as another Judaeo-Christian characteristic of Justin's tradition, shared with Hermas, the *Gospel of Peter*, the TP, and Irenaeus' «Presbyter».

It remains to be remarked that in Justin's own theology this idea seems to have found no echo, at least not in his preserved writings. The patriarchs shall be saved, but Justin has nothing to say about Christ's descent to preach the Gospel to them. The Ps. Jer. text is quoted without the slightest comment.

(g) The two *parousias*.[98]

In the NT, only Christ's glorious return is called a παρουσία (Mt 24:3.27.37.39; 1 Cor 15:23; 1 Thess 2:19; 3:13; 4:15; 5:23; 2 Thess 2:1.8; Jas 5:7f; 2 Pt 3:4; 1 Jn 2:28 - see also Herm. *Sim.* V:5:3) - never his first coming. H. Conzelmann may be right that Luke comes close to the idea of two comings.[99] The first who calls Christ's coming in the flesh a *parousia* is apparently Ignatius. *Philad.* 9:2.

The idea and terminology of Justin is present very clearly in another source, however, viz. the AJ II.

Here we read the following: «He (Moses) therefore intimated that he (Christ) should come, humble indeed in his first coming (*primo... adventu humilem*), but glorious in his second (*secundo vero gloriosum*). And the first, indeed, has already been accomplished; since he has come and taught, and he, the judge of all, has been judged and slain. But at his second coming he shall come to judge, and shall indeed condemn the wicked, but shall take the pious into a share and association with himself in his kingdom. Now the faith in his second coming depends upon his first. For the prophets - especially Jacob and Moses - spoke of the first, but some also of the second... It was to be expected that Christ should be received by the Jews... but that the Gentiles should be averse to him... Yet the prophets, contrary to the order and sequence of things, said that he should be the expectation of the Gentiles (Gen 49:10), and not of the Jews (*dixerunt eum expectationem gentium et non Iudaeorum...*). And so it happened... And thus in all things prophecy appears faithful, which said that he was the expectation of the Gentiles» (*Rec.* I:49:2 - 50:4). Parallel to

---

98. On this theme in Justin, cf. J. Leclerq,'L'idée de la royauté du Christ dans l'Oevre de Saint Justin', *L'Année Théologique* 7 (1946, pp. 83-95), pp. 87-91; P.Beskow, *Rex Gloriae*, pp. 98f.

99. *Mitte der Zeit*, p. 10, n. 1: «*Es ist sachlich berechtigt, bei Lc von «zwei Adventen» zu sprechen, wenn sich diese Terminologie so auch nicht findet.*» Cf. also *ibid.*, p. 182, n. 1. L. Goppelt takes the two parousias pattern as an example of the rationalistic tendency of Frühkatholizismus: «*Hier ist Jesu Erscheinung nicht mehr das eschatologische Ereignis schlechthin, sondern nur mehr die anhebende teilweise Erfüllung.*» (*Christentum und Judentum im ersten und zweiten Jahrhundert. Ein Aufriss der Urgeschichte der Kirche* (BFChTh 2. Reihe 55, Gütersloh, 1954), p. 298). I wonder whether such sweeping statements are justified.

this is a passage in *Rec.* I:69:3f: »He (James) showed by most abundant proofs that Jesus is the Christ, and that in him are fulfilled all the prophecies which relate to his humble advent. For he showed that two advents of him are foretold: one in humiliation, which he has accomplished; the other in glory, which is hoped for to be accomplished, when he shall come to give the kingdom to those who believe in him, and who observe all things which he has commanded.«

According to G. Strecker,[100] both passages derive from the AJ II source. Let us note the most relevant elements in these two passages:

(1) Gen 49:10 - and in this verse the words *expectatio gentium* - is given prominent position in the doctrine of the two *parousias.* Cf. i.a. *Dial.* 52.

(2) Jacob and Moses are prominent among the prophets. Cf. the position of testimonies like Gen 49:10f; Num 24:17 in Justin's material.

(3) The second advent is *glorious.* Cf. Justin: . . . τῇ ἐνδόξῳ . . . παρου-σίᾳ, *Dial.* 31:1, further *1.Apol.* 52:3; *Dial.* 14:8; 34;2; 36:1; 49:2; 110:2; 121:3 (and the synoptic table above, p. 155).[101]

(4) In his second coming Christ comes to judge, *iudicaturus adveniet.* He is the judge of all, *iudex omnium.* Cf. Justin: In his second coming Christ κριτὴς ἁπάντων ἐλεύσεται, *Dial.* 49:2, further *Dial* 36:1; 46:1; 118:1; 132:1.[102]

(5) At his second coming Christ will condemn the wicked (*impios. . . condemnabit*), but share his kingdom with the pious (*pios. . . in consortium regni societatemque suscipiet, Rec.* I:49:4; *veniet dare regnum credentibus in se . . . Rec.* I:69:4). Cf. *1.Apol.* 52:3: At his second coming Christ «will raise the bodies of all men who have ever lived, and will clothe the worthy with incorruption, but send those of the wicked, eternally conscious, into eternal fire with the evil demons»; *Dial.* 34:2 = *Dial.* 39:7: Christ shall come again with glory, having his kingdom for ever; «. . . to him it has been given to judge . . . all men, and . . . the everlasting kingdom is his», *Dial.* 46:1; Christ shall raise all up, «and sets some as incorruptible and immortal and free from all sorrow in an everlasting kingdom . . . and sends others away into eternal punishment by fire», *Dial.* 117:3; cf. also *Dial.* 120:5f.

(6) The fulfilment of the prophecies concerning the first coming guarantees the fulfilling of the prophecies concerning the second coming. Cf. *1.Apol.* 52:1: «Since we have shown that all these things that have already happened were proclaimed in advance through the prophets . . . it must similarly be believed that those things which were similarly prophesied and are yet to happen will certainly take place.»

---

100. Strecker, *Pseudoclementinen*, pp. 236/247-49. Although *Rec.* 1:49:2-50:4 occurs within the insertion 1:44:3 - 54:4a, Strecker is certainly right to argue that the two parousias motif derives from the AJ II source, cf. also Schoeps, *Judenchristentum*, pp. 409f.

101. This fixed terminology in Justin is striking, because none of his OT testimonies concerning the second parousia contain the catchword δόξα.

102. Here the same remark applies as in the foregoing note.

This series of coincidences cannot be accidental: Justin and AJ II are following a common tradition. We have surmised above that the two *parousias* scheme reflects a situation in which dialogue with Jewish Messianism was vivid. The scheme is relevant as a main answer to Jewish complaints about Jesus not fulfilling the triumphant Messianism of the OT.[103] This - together with the occurrence of the same scheme in AJ II - point to Judaeo-Christian provenance.[104]

*Conclusions:*

(1) The Christological testimonies in the *Apology* stem from a Judaeo-Christian milieu in close contact with Jewish Messianic exegesis of the OT. The NT dossier of Christological prooftexts has been modified and supplemented by texts which loomed large in Jewish Messianism.

The Gospel narratives in the fulfilment reports represent a fusion of Matthean and Lukan elements, with some extra-canonical features added -these are parallelled in the *Gospel of Peter* and the *Protevangelium of James*.

(2) Some of the testimonies seem to reflect the Bar Kokhba uprising and its effects: Jews excluded from Jerusalem. There is an implicit polemic against the false Messiah in whom the Jews had placed their hope.

One may suggest that in the tragic years following immediately upon the uprising, Jewish Christians addressed their fellow Jews with new missionary zeal and urgency: The false Messiah had failed - it was time to turn to the true Messiah, the true Star from Jacob, the root from Jesse, the expectation of the nations.

(3) This tradition is deeply concerned with the fate of Israel. The Jews are in a state of exile and calamity because they rejected and crucified Jesus. But there is still hope. God shall once turn the diaspora of the people, and they shall recognize the true Messiah whom they pierced.

(4) The scheme of the two *parousias* and Gen 49:10 as a basic Messianic testimony connects Justin's material with AJ II. But the closest parallels are to be found in the Christian interpolations of the TP. Both of these Judaeo-

---

103. Cf. B. Z. Bokser: »Justin was aware that for the Jews there was a glaring contradiction between the realities of the world as they knew it and the conditions which for them constituted the criteria of messianic redemption. He had a ready answer: there were to be two advents of Christ, one in which he would suffer and die an ignominious death, the other when he would return in glory and when the golden age pictured by the prophet would be inaugurated.« ('Justin Martyr and the Jews', *JQR* New Ser. 64 (1973/74, pp. 97-122/204-211), p. 109). P. Beskow also places the two parousias pattern in the same setting, *Rex Gloriae*, pp. 98f. Friedländer, *Studien*, pp. 92f, takes the well-known rabbinic juxtaposition of Dan 7:13 and Zech 9:9 as counter-polemic against the two parousias scheme. (The rabbinic passage is quoted above, p. 269)

104. Cf. Schoeps, *Judenchristentum*: »hier liegt ein Stück früher (juden)christlicher - speziell protolukanischer - Theologie vor«. (p. 410).

Christian sources share with Justin's material a deep concern for Israel. And the Christian Messianism of the TP has much the same Christological profile as Justin's material: Virgin birth combined with anointing with the Spirit in baptism; «lamb» Christology (Is 53); Jesus' death understood as expiatory suffering.

(5) The theme of divine pre-existence is not included in the OT proof. I should like to add two remarks on this. The first is that this hardly is due to Justin's selective use of this tradition. For Justin the pre-existence idea is of paramount importance, and he would have no reason to exclude it if it was present in his source. It deserves notice that one of the testimonies - viz. Ps 72:17 - in the LXX text contains the notion of pre-existence (cf. also the rabbinic exegesis). But in Justin's deviant «testimony» version of the text this aspect has been sacrificed in favour of the *anatellein* motif.

My second remark is a suggestion concerning the reason for this. It seems that this tradition is mainly occupied with those Messianic prophecies of the OT which foretell the *task* accomplished by the Messiah. It is more interested in his career than in his person. In this respect it shares a characteristic of rabbinic Messianism. One should not press the argument from silence unduly. The authors of this tradition may or may not have shared the concept of Christ's divine pre-existence. But they did not make it part of their Christological *proof from prophecy.*

(6) In more than one respect, this Christological tradition has a profile similar to Luke's in the NT. But the proof-texts are partly others, and it looks as if we are facing independent theologians working on their own.

I am satisfied with these preliminary conclusions at this stage. Much of the material treated in the following sections is so close to these Christological testimonies that the picture can be completed and nuanced as we proceed with the analysis.

### 2. The slaying of the Just One and the devastation of Judaea.

We have located this tradition in *1. Apol.* 47-49; *Dial.* 16f; 108:2f; 133; 136f. Let us briefly resume the two main elements:

(1) The Jews slew the Just One, as they did with the prophets before him and his believers after him: Is 57:1f; Is 3:10; Is 5:20.

(2) As a punishment for this, Judaea has been laid waste and Jerusalem is destroyed, and no Jew is allowed to enter there (Hadrianic decree): Is 1:7/Jer 50:3; Is 64:9-11.

I have commented above (p. 160) on the combined testimony Is 1:7/Jer 50:3. The addition of Jer 50:3 in all probability directly refers to the Hadrianic decree. We have also seen that only Justin's deviant version of Is 3:10 is fit as a testimony on the *killing* of the Just One. It is now time to make some more general comments on the whole complex.

In the deuteronomistic pattern of sin - exile - conversion-return, the sin of Israel is sometimes expressed in the statement that they *killed all the*

Dr. Mark 3442

Nov. Oct. 19

**PLEASE ORDER FROM
MIDWEST LIBRARY SERVICE**

**Halpern, Ruth.**
Getting the most from WordPerfect / Ruth Halpern. —
Berkeley : Osborne McGraw-Hill, c1988.

xv, 606 p. : ill. ; 24 cm.

Cover title: Getting the most from WordPerfect 5.
ISBN 0-07-881364-6

395

1. WordPerfect (Computer program)  2. Word processing.  I. Title.

Z52.5.W65H33  1988  652.5′536—dc20  89-182992
AACR 2  MARC

*prophets* (Neh 9:26; 1 Kings 19:14; *Jub.* 1:12; Josephus *Ant.* IX:13:2; X:3:1; *Pes. Rab.* 138a;146a). O.H. Steck has shown with great force that this is not intended as a historical statement about the prophets, but as a theological statement about Israel's obdurate response to God's word.[105]

In the NT, this traditional topic receives a new aspect. It is now not only used to accuse Israel for obstinacy and unwillingness to accept Jesus as God's messenger - it also takes on an apologetic aspect: To be killed by the people was always the fate of the true messenger from God! The apologetic value of this topic has to do, of course, with the harsh notion of a Messiah killed by his own people - a thing unheard of in Jewish Messianism. Jesus as the Just One and his killing by the Jews are thus correlative ideas. In the NT Luke perhaps brings this out with most emphasis. In Mark, the words of the centurion watching the death of Jesus are: «Truly this man was the son of God», 15:39. Matthew has retained this (Mt 27:54), while Luke significantly alters: «Certainly this man was δίκαιος», Lk 23:47. In Acts 3:14 Peter reproaches the Jews: «You denied the Holy and Just One.» The passage most relevant in our context occurs in Acts 7:51f. Here we find the concept of the slaying of all the prophets combined with the idea of Jesus as the Just One: «Which of the prophets did not your fathers persecute? And they killed those who announced beforehand the coming of the Just One, whom you have now betrayed and murdered.»[106] Mention should also be made of Acts 22:14, where Ananias is reported to have said to Paul: «The God of our fathers appointed you to know his will, to see the Just One and to hear a voice from his mouth.»[107]

One feature of the Just One Christology deserves to be underlined: Implicitly or explicitly Jesus is here included in *a succession of righteous men* who were killed - first and foremost the prophets. Sometimes also Jesus' disciples are included in this succession of righteous men, Mt 5:11f; 23:34.

Now let us turn to Justin's material. «Ye slew the Just One and his prophets before him, and now ye reject, and, as far as in you lies, dishonour those that set their hope on him», *Dial.* 16:4, cf. *1.Apol.* 48:4 ; *Dial.* 17:1; 133:1 (cf. also synopsis above, p. 160). We see how Justin preserves the characteristic features of this tradition: «Just One» Christology is coupled to

---

105. Cf. note 73, p.278.
106. On the concept of Christ as ὁ δίκαιος in the NT, cf. esp. R. N. Longenecker, *Christology*, pp. 46f. Cf. also the comment of Steck, *op. cit.*, pp. 265-69. «... *es hat im hellenistischen Christentum an Israel gerichtete Verkündigung gegeben, die die Tradition der dtr. P(propheten)A(ussage) aufgegriffen hat, um die Tötung Jesu in die Geschichte der von Mose über die Propheten bis in die Gegenwart permanenten Halsstarrigkeit des Gottesvolkes zu stellen.*» (Steck, p. 267).
107. There are some precedents for a «Just One» Messianology in Jewish literature: *Ps.Sal.* 17:32. «The Just One» is also used as a Messianic designation in the similitudes of *1 Enoch* 38:2; 53:6. Cf. Longenecker, *loc. cit.*

the motif of Jewish murder of the prophets, and Christ's believers are included in the succession of persecuted men.

Further: In Justin, as in the tradition before him, the accusation is addressed directly to Israel - the Jewish guilt is emphasised in an effort to bring Israel to repentance.

Let us add some details concerning Justin's OT quotations. Is 3:10 is an ideal testimony on the death of the Just One (in Justin's deviant version). In Justin's contemporary, the Jewish Christian Hegesippus, we encounter the same deviant text as a testimony on the murder of James ὁ δίκαιος: «And the Scripture written in Isaiah was fulfilled, ῎Αρωμεν τὸν δίκαιον, ὅτι δύσχρηστος ἡμῖν ἐστιν.» (*apud* Eus. E.H. II:23:15).

Is 5:20 is a testimony on Jewish slandering of Christians, according to Justin (*1.Apol.* 49:6). In *Dial.* 16:4 he returns to this: «. . . cursing in your synagogues them that believe on Christ», cf. also *Dial.* 47:4; 93:4; 108:3; 117:3; 137:2. It is very likely the *Birkat Minim* [108] in the Eighteen Benedictions Justin has in mind.[109] The prayer was introduced between 70 and 100 AD,[110] and had for its purpose to prevent Jewish Christians and other heretics from staying within the synagogue community.[111] Justin's material

---

108. There is a vast literature on this *Berakah* of the *Shemoneh Esreh.* Cf. i.a. I. Elbogen, *Der jüdische Gottesdienst in seiner geschichtlichen Entwicklung* (Leipzig, 1913), pp. 252-54; Str. Bill. IV, pp. 208ff; J. Jocz, *The Jewish People and Jesus Christ. A study in the Relationship between the Jewish People and Jesus Christ* (London, 1949), pp. 51-57; M. Simon, *Verus Israel,* pp. 235-37; K. Hruby, *Die Stellung der jüdischen Gesetzeslehrer zur werdenden Kirche* (Schriften zum Judentumskunde 4, Zürich, 1971), pp. 22-24; G. Stemberger, 'Die sogenannte «Synode von Jabne» und das frühe Christentum', *Kairos* 19 (1977), pp. 14-21; P. Schäfer, 'Die sogenannte Synode von Jabne', in *idem, Studien zur Geschichte und Theologie des rabbinischen Judentums* (Leiden, 1978), pp. 45-64 (esp. pp. 46-55); R. Kimelman, '*Birkat Ha-Minim* and the Lack of Evidence for an Anti-Christian Jewish Prayer in Late Antiquity', *Jewish and Christian Self-Definition,* Vol. II (eds. E.P. Sanders, A.I. Baumgarten, A. Mendelson, London, 1981), pp. 226-44; W. Horbury, 'The Benediction of the *Minim* and Early Jewish-Christian Controversy', *JTS* NS 33 (1982), pp. 19-61.
109. So S. Krauss, 'The Jews in the Works of the Church Fathers', *JQR* 5 (1893, pp. 122-157 (continued in 6 (1894), pp. 82-99/225-261 )) pp. 130-34. cf. also Jocz, *op. cit,* pp.53ff - and already Goldfahn, 'Agadah', pp. 56f.
110. The Talmudic evidence is *Ber.* 29a, quoted in L. Williams' note *ad Dial* 16:4 ( p. 33). The *Berakah* is here attributed to Samuel the Small. On the date of the prayer cf. Jocz, *op. cit.,* pp. 55f.
111. Cf. Elbogen: «*Es war der ausgesprochene Zweck dieses Gebetes, den Juden-Christen den Aufenthalt in der Synanoge zu verleiden oder ganz unmöglich zu machen.* » (*Op. cit.,* pp. 252f ). This traditional theory - carefully argued anew by Jocz, *loc. cit.* - has recently been challenged by Stemberger, Schäfer, and Kimelman (cf. references given above). While allowing that Christians might be included in the scope of the Benediction, they argue that it is not primarily directed against Christians (Jewish or Gentile). However, the very time for the introduction of this Benediction, and the general picture of the *Minim* in the Talmuds, are strong indications that the traditional theory is correct, and the patristic evidence cannot easily be dismissed. Cf. the careful and extensive examination of the entire material, Jewish and Christian, in Horbury's article. Horbury thinks Justin's evidence should be take at face value, and he makes the interesting proposal that the *Birkat Ha-Minim* was intended not only to exclude Jewish Christians, but also to be heard by Gentile visitors in the Synagogues, thus disouraging them from becoming Christians. I think Horbury is right to place the whole phenomenon within the context of *missionary competition.*

betrays deep concern about the *Birkat Minim,* and it seems likely that it is the response of those immediately affected by it - the Jewish Christians - we have preserved in the testimony, Is 5:20: «Woe to those who call sweet bitter and bitter sweet.»[112]

We now turn to the second main element in Justin's tradition, the devastation of Judaea. In many of the OT, intertestamental and NT texts treating the murder of the prophets, the punishment is said to be foreign rule and/or exile.[113] Justin's material is thus not without precedents when the devastation of Judaea and the expulsion from Jerusalem is seen as a punishment for the killing of the Just One, *1.Apol.* 47; *Dial.* 16f*; Dial.* 108:2f.

Apart from the NT, we shall again have to go to the Christian interpolator of the TP to find a Christian writer intensely concerned with the catastrophe of Israel, and taking it as a punishment for the crucifixion of Jesus, *Test. Lev.* 10:1-4; 14f; 16*; Test. Jud.* 22*; Test. Zeb.* 9:5-9*; Test. Asher* 7:1-3; *Test. Ben.* 9f. The punishment is described as destruction of the Temple and dispersion of Israel (in the Jewish source this of course refers to the incidents in 587 BC). There are some allusions in the description of these catastrophes which may point to Is 1:7 and Is 64:6-11 - the testimonies chosen by Justin's tradition:

Is 64:9-11 LXX: ἐγενήθη *ἔρημος* Σιων ὡς *ἔρημος* ἐγενήθη Ιερουσαλημ *εἰς κατάραν* ὁ οἶκος *τὸ ἅγιον* ἡμῶν καὶ ἡ δόξα ἣν ηὐλόγησαν οἱ πατέρες ἡμῶν ἐγενήθη πυρίκαυστος . . . ( *1.Apol.* 52:12 non-LXX: ἐγενήθη ἡμῖν *εἰς ὄνειδος*). Is 1:7: ἡ γῆ αὐτῶν *ἔρημος* . . . Cf. the following passages in TP: καὶ διασπαρήσεσθε αἰχμάλωτοι ἐν τοῖς ἔθνεσιν, καὶ ἔσεσθε *εἰς ὄνειδος* καὶ *εἰς κατάραν* ἐκεῖ, *Test. Lev.* 10:4. διὰ τοῦτο ὁ ναός ὃν ἐκλέξεται κύριος *ἔρημος* ἔσται . . . καὶ λήψεσθε *ὄνειδος* καὶ αἰσχύνην αἰώνιον . . ., *Test.Lev.* 15:1f. δι᾽ αὐτὸν ἔσονται *τὰ ἅγια* ὑμῶν *ἔρημα* ἕως ἐδάφους. καὶ τόπος ὑμῖν καθαρὸς οὐκ ἔσται, ἀλλ᾽ ἔσεσθε ἐν τοῖς ἔθνεσιν *εἰς κατάραν,* *Test.Lev* 16:4f. καὶ παραδοθήσεσθε εἰς χεῖρας ἐχθρῶν ὑμῶν καὶ ἡ γῆ ὑμῶν *ἐρημωθήσεται* καὶ *τὰ ἅγια* ὑμῶν καταφθαρήσονται, καὶ ὑμεῖς διασκορπισθήσεσθε εἰς τὰς τέσσαρας γωνίας τῆς γῆς, *Test.Asser* 7:2.

One may suggest that the ones responsible for Justin's material chose their proof-texts under influence from the description of Israel's punishment current within the deuteronomistic pattern in Jewish literature of their day. One Christian writer intimately familiar with this pattern was the interpolator of the TP. He has actualized this Jewish pattern to fit a post-70, or, perhaps more likely, a post-135 situation. The testaments are thus turned

---

112. Cf. Jocz, *op. cit.,* p. 57:«We would therefore, assume that Justin knew that the *Birkat ha-Minim* had primarily Christians in view. This he could easily have learned from Hebrew Christians or from sources related to them».

113. Foreign rule: Neh 9:26f; Josephus *Ant.* IX:266; X:38-40; 1 Thess 2:15f. Exile: *Jub.* 1:12f; Mk 12:1-9.

into a call to repentance addressed to non-Christian fellow Jews.[114] Justin's material very likely has the same background and purpose.

There is another interesting parallel, viz. the AJ II. Here Peter says: «. . . everyone who, believing in this prophet who had been foretold by Moses, is baptized in his name, shall be kept unhurt from the destruction of war which impends over the unbelieving nation, and the place itself; but those who do not believe shall be made exiles from their place and kingdom, that even against their will they may understand and obey the will of God» (*Rec.* I:39:3). It is customary to see here a reference to the migration to Pella.[115] The reference is not very explicit, however, and Strecker observes that in *Rec.* I:39:3 «*offenbar die erste und zweite Belagerung Jerusalems nicht mehr unterschieden wird; denn erst Hadrian erliess das Edikt zur Vertreibung der Juden aus Jerusalem, das hier anscheinend vordatiert ist.*»[116]

The parallel passage in *Rec.* I:37:2 says: «. . . that . . . they might hear that this place, which seemed chosen for a time . . . was at last to be wholly destroyed.»[117]

In the AJ II this idea is combined with the anti-cultic polemic: The main task of Jesus was to abolish sacrifices, institute baptism instead of sacrifices, and teach that God wants mercy and righteousness instead of bloody victims (*Rec.* I:37-39). Disbelief in Jesus and continuance with the sacrificial cult is thus one and the same sin, according to the AJ II. The reason for Israel's exile can therefore also be said to be the sacrificial cult. «And in order to impress this upon them, even before the coming of the true prophet, who was to reject at once the sacrifices and the place, it was often plundered by enemies and burnt with fire (cf. Is 64:10: ἐγενήθη πυρίκαυστος), and the people carried into captivity among foreign nations . . . that by these things they might be taught that a people who offer sacrifices are driven away and delivered up to the hands of the enemy, but they who do mercy and righteousness are without sacrifices freed from captivity, and restored to their native land» (*Rec.* I:37:3f). This is carried on in *Rec.* I:38:5: «But when they sought for themselves tyrants rather than kings, then also with regal ambition they erected a temple in the place which had been appointed to them for prayer.» With this background one can ask if it is mere coincidence that Justin in *Dial.* 17:3 - after the OT testimonies on the devastation of Judaea and the slaying of the Just One in the preceeding context - goes on to quote the following saying of Jesus: »It is written, 'My house is a house of prayer, but ye have made it a den of robbers'« (a

---

114. Cf. esp. J. Jervell,'Ein Interpolator', pp. 52-54.
115. Cf. e.g. Schoeps, *Judenchristentum*, pp. 47/267; J. L. Martyn, 'Clementine Recognitions', p. 272.
116. Strecker, *Pseudoklementinen*, p. 231.
117. So the Latin text. The Syriac text has a closer parallel to *Rec.* 1:39:3: «*Durch die Weisheit Gottes sollten dann die Glaubenden an einem sicheren Ort des Landes zur Rettung versammelt und vor dem Krieg bewahrt werden . . .*» (Strecker's paraphrase, *op. cit*, pp. 226f).

conflation of Mt 21:13 (or Lk 19:46) and Mk 11:17). Four facts claim our attention:

(1) There is in Justin's own theology no direct juxtaposition of exile motif and anti-temple polemic. Nevertheless these motives are joined in *Dial.* 16f, and the AJ II provides a perfect explanation.

(2) The Jesus logion in *Dial.* 17:3 may have been taken to express the same anti-temple polemic which is found in AJ II.

(3) Justin is not quoting directly from one of the Gospels, but seems to follow a harmonistic source.[118]

(4) Justin violates his own principle of quoting only Scripture in his debate with Trypho. (He apologizes for this in *Dial.* 18:1). I think a conclusion imposes itself: The Jesus logion was included in the source Justin employs in *Dial.* 16f,[119] and this source represents the same tradition as the one we find in AJ II.

It thus seems that Justin's material in all the elements studied so far, point to Judaeo-Christian provenance: »Just One« Christology, murder-of-the-prophets motif, deuteronomistic sin-exile pattern, coupling of exile motif and anti-temple polemic.

It remains to examine a last motif which in Justin is attached to this material, viz. his anti-circumcision polemic. I emphasize that I do not at this stage enter upon a full review of all anti-circumcision polemic in Justin - I only treat two passages immediately attached to the material studied above. These two passages are *Dial.* 15:7 - 16:2, and *Dial.* 28:2-4. The texts have been synoptically analysed above (pp. 70 - 72). As one can easily see from the parallel in *Barnabas* (9:5), Justin's anti-circumcision testimonies (Jer 4:3f; 9:24f; Deut 10:16f) are decidedly pre-Bar Kokhba. Strictly speaking, they are not anticircumcision texts at all. They exhort to true circumcision, i.e. circumcision of the heart, - they do not speak against carnal circumcision as such. Both *Barnabas* and Justin tacitly admit this. None of the two writers launch their attack on circumcision directly from these texts. In *Barnabas* the main anti-circumcision argument is the non-Scriptural idea that an evil angel misled the Israelites to take the commandment of circumcision literally, and further the fact that other peoples also are circumcised, *Barn.* 9:4.6. In Justin, the decisive argument against circumcision is the fact that circumcision now excludes from Jerusalem.

This means that while Justin's testimonies are pre-Bar Kokhba, his argument is decidedly post-Bar Kokhba.

Before we go on to comment on this observation, it may be useful to add some words on the political and religious background for a theological debate about circumcision in the years around the Bar Kokhba revolt.

---

118. Cf. the analysis in Bellinzoni, *Sayings*, pp. 111-113.
119. This may be the case with the two logia quoted in *Dial.* 17:4 also. Both sayings are 'woe!' oracles, and thus fit Is 3:9 and Is 5:18. Bellinzoni argues for a written harmonistic source behind these logia, *op. cit*, pp 33-37.

There are good reasons to believe that Hadrian promulgated a general ban on the rite of circumcision not very long before the uprising.[120] This prohibition was in force before, under and after the revolt - it was withdrawn for the Jews only by Antoninus Pius at a later date.[121] It may very well have been one of the factors which gave rise to the revolt.

One would naturally expect that the Jews reacted to this with a renewed zeal for the rite of circumcision[122] - and for the Law in general. The newly found Bar Kokhba documents confirm this. Bar Kokhba and his men were strict observers of the Law,[123] and there is a rabbinic passage which state that many Jews were re-circumcised in the days of Bar Kokhba (i.e. they had probably formerly tried to annul their circumcision by *epispasmos*).«It was taught: He whose circumcision is disguised must re-circumcise. R. Judah said: He does not re-circumcise, because it is a suppressed foreskin. (The parallel in Yeb. 72a says: because it endangers his life) Said they to R. Judah: Yet there were many in the days of the son of Kosiba who re-circumcised and yet gave birth to children after that», *Gen.Rab.* 46:13, p. 397.

One can easily imagine Jewish Christians addressing their fellow Jews in those turbulent days with the following message: Your zeal for circumcision we appreciate, but the carnal rite only will not save you. What matters is the circumcision of the heart, and this circumcision consists in faith in Jesus the Messiah.

In fact, we do find among the rabbis contemporary with the Bar Kokhba revolt a counter-attack on those who used texts like Jer 4:3f; Deut 10:16f etc. to play down the significance of outward circumcision. «R. Akiba said: There are four kinds of *'orlah*. Thus, *'orlah* is used in connection with the ear, ... the mouth, ... the heart: For all the house of Israel are *'arle* in the heart (Jer 9:25). Now, he (Abraham) was ordered, 'Walk before me, and be thou whole' (Gen 17:1). If he circumcised himself at the ear, he would not be whole; at the mouth, he would not be whole; at the heart, he would not be whole. Where could he circumcise himself and yet be whole? Nowhere else than at the *'orlah* of the body». *Gen. Rab.* 46:5, p. 392.

With this background, there is strong reason to beleive that the circumcision testimonies were part of the tradition behind *Dial.* 16f etc.as it reached Justin. This tradition may have regarded circumcision as a rite of minor importance - related mainly to the question of Jewish identity. In any case, this seems to have been the position adopted by the milieu behind AJ II.

---

120. Cf. G. Vermes and F. Millar, *The History of the Jewish People* (»New Schürer»)I (Edinburgh, 1973), pp. 536-540; J. A. Fitzmyer,'The Bar Cochba period', in *idem, Essays on the Semitic Background of the New Testement* (London, 1971 ) pp. 305-354, esp. pp. 320-324 with further literature; P. Schäfer, *Bar Kokhba,* pp. 38-45.
121. »New Schürer», p. 539; P. Schäfer, pp. 40-43.
122. Cf. Goldfahn, 'Aggada', p. 55. Bar Kokhba probably enforced circumcision of assimilated Jews, cf. P. Schäfer, *Bar Kokhba,* p. 46.
123. Cf . Fitzmyer, *art. cit.* p. 341; Schäfer, *op.cit.,* pp. 75f.

This Judaeo-Christian community almost certainly practised circumcision -there is no anti-circumcision polemic in AJ II.[124] But the decisive rite is baptism. In order to regain their land and city, in order to be saved, Israel must accept baptism. In AJ II baptism is not said to be the spiritual circumcision of the heart, but this is a clearly expressed topic in Justin, *Dial.* 18:2; 43:2, and was probably handed down to him as part of the same tradition.

Now, the point where Justin definitely transcends this Judaeo-Christian tradition, is his anti-circumcision polemic based on Hadrian's decree. God gave the rite of circumcision to the Jews *with the very purpose* of excluding them from Jerusalem, *Dial.* 16:2. «To you therefore alone was this circumcision necessary, that the people may not be a people, and the nation not a nation.» *(Dial.* 19:5).

Certainly the author of AJ II could not have followed Justin in this kind of reasoning, and I doubt if any Judaeo-Christian could. I cannot escape the impression that we hear the triumphant Gentile Christian Church speaking: You Jews are excluded from Jerusalem, we Gentiles are admitted - we take your place . . . It remains to be asked whether this is Justin's own twist on the tradition, or if this idea was already part of the tradition as it reached him. The latter alternative would mean that a basically Judaeo-Christian deposit had passed through Gentile Christian hands before it reached Justin.

At the present stage it seems wise to keep both alternatives open. We shall try to gather cumulative evidence in the following sections which may help to point out an answer.

In any case, the material presented in this section has been shown to be closely related to the Christological testimonies studied above, and it confirms our surmises about the setting and provenance of the tradition. We hear Jewish Christians addressing their fellow Jews with an urgent missionary appeal in the years when the catastrophe of Bar Kokhba was still a fresh experience.

### 3. The law of Moses.

(a) Anti-cultic testimonies and cultic typologies.

We have seen in Part One (pp. 168f/178f) that the cultic typologies in *Dial.* 13f; 40f; 111:3f, seemed to be related to the anti-cultic testimony in *1.Apol.* 37:5-8. It may seem contradictory to connect anti-cultic polemic with cultic typology, but this connexion is undeniably present in Justin's material.

I shall first briefly list the main correspondences between anticultic polemic and cultic typology, then I shall discuss the meaning and scope of the anti-cultic texts. Lastly I shall treat the main cultic typologies.

---

124. Cf. esp. J. L. Martyn, 'Clementine Recognitions', pp. 270f.

| Anti-cultic polemic | Cultic types |
|---|---|
| *1.Apol.* 37:5-8 = Is 1:11-15/58:6f<br>«My soul hates:<br>(1) your new moons<br>(2) and sabbaths  —————→<br>(3) ... the great Day of the Fast  —————→<br>   (= Atonement day)<br>(4) ... offerings of σεμίδαλις  —————→<br><br><br>(5) ... fat of lambs and<br>   blood of bulls ...» | <br><br><br>*Dial.* 12:3 Continual sabbath<br>*Dial.* 40:4f: The two goats at<br>the Fast (= Atonement day)<br>*Dial.* 41:1-3: Offering of<br>σεμίδαλις (Lev 14:10) a type<br>of the eucharist |
| *Dial.* 13:1 = Heb 9:13/Is 1:13<br>Christians no longer cleanse themselves<br>with<br>(a) ritual baths  —————————→<br>(b) blood of goats  —————————→<br><br>(c) blood of sheep —————————→<br><br>(d) ashes of an heifer  —————————→<br><br>(e) offerings of σεμίδαλις —————————→ | <br><br><br>Dial 13 etc.:Baptism<br>Dial. 40:4f: The two goats<br>on Atonement Day<br>Dial. 40:1-3 etc.: Paschal<br>lamb<br>Red heifer, Num 19:1-10,<br>cf. Barn. 8<br>*Dial.* 41:1-3: Eucharist |

Justin hints in *Dial.* 42:4 that his dossier of cultic types is richer than the selection included in the *Dialogue. Dial.* 13:1 suggests that he knew the typology on the Red Heifer, and *Dial.*12:3 suggests that he could have said more about the sabbath. Two types fall outside the above lists: Circumcision as a type of baptism in *Dial.* 41:4f; and the twelve bells on the High Priest's robe in *Dial.* 42:1. We shall have to investigate whether these were parts of the same tradition.

But for the present, we first turn to the anti-cultic texts. In the *Apology*, the main testimony is Is 1:11-15/58:6f (on the deviant text, see above, pp. 55f). The text contains polemic against New Moons, sabbath, the great Fast (Atonement day), Temple worship and sacrifices. The positive counterpart is the *true fasting* described in Is 58:6f. The same contrast is contained in *Dial.* 40:4: True fasting (Is 58:6) substitutes the offerings of the Atonement Day («the Fast»).

It is relevant first to note that structurally this idea has parallels in rabbinic literature. «When R. Sheshet (ca 260) kept a fast, on concluding his prayer he added the following: Sovereign of the Universe, Thou knowest full well that in the time when the Temple was standing, if a man sinned he used to bring a sacrifice, and though all that was offered of it was its fat and blood, atonement was made for him therewith. Now I have kept a fast and my fat and blood have diminished. May it be Thy will to account my fat and blood which have diminished as if I had offered them before Thee on the altar, and do Thou favour me», *Ber.* 17a, pp.100f.

Very close to Justin is the sequence in *Barn.* 2:4 - 3:6: Is 1:11-13; Jer 7:22f/Zech 8:17 (rejection of sacrifices etc) —→ Ps 51:19 etc. (true sacrifice); Is 58:4-10 (true fasting). One should to this sequence also compare *Dial.* 22:6-10: Jer 7:21f ⟶ Ps 50. (In *1.Clem.* 52:3f, Ps 50:14f and Ps 50:19 are combined to one testimony, and the context suggests an original setting within anti-cultic polemic, although this is not the purpose of the present text in *1.Clem.*) There is no question of direct literary dependence of Justin on *Barn.*; there must therefore have existed some kind of common proof-text tradition on which both authors were drawing.

Now, true fasting is not the only contrast motive implied in Justin's anti-cultic polemic. In *Dial.* 13 *the blood of Christ* (our Paschal Lamb - Is 53), applied to the believer in baptism, is contrasted with the blood of goats and sheep etc.(cf. the table on the preceeding page). The idea of propitiation and forgivenness of sins is here prominent. Propitiation is now not to be obtained from the sacrificial cult, but in baptism. The same idea can be discerned in *Barnabas'* material (it is somewhat blurred in his own exposition by the insertion of *Barn.* 4, treating the author's personal favourite idea of the one covenant): The testimonies on sacrificial cult and fasting in *Barn.* 2f are followed by this passage in 5:1f: «For it was for this reason that the Lord endured to deliver up his flesh to corruption, that we should be sanctified by the remission of sin, that is, by his sprinkled blood (Is 53:5/7)» There are baptismal overtones in this this text,[125] and this makes the parallel to *Dial.* 13 almost perfect.

In Justin's testimony material, this contrast can also be read out of the Isaiah text itself: baptism, Is 1:16-20, now takes the place of sacrifices etc., Is 1:11-15; cf. *Dial.* 12:3 ⟶ *Dial.* 13; *Dial.* 18:2.

Turning to AJ II, we meet in plain words the very idea implied in Justin's and *Barnabas'* material: «Lest they (the Jews) might suppose that on the cessation of sacrifice there was no remission of sins for them, he (Christ) instituted baptism by water among them, in which they might be absolved from all their sins on the invocation of his name ... being purified not by the blood of beasts, but by the purification of the Wisdom of God.»(*Rec.* I:39:2). In one respect, this text may be seen to express the common idea in a simpler and probably more original form than Justin and *Barnabas.* In AJ II *only the sacrificial cult* is envisaged. Baptism replaces sacrifices, and the common denominator is remission of sins.[126] In Justin and *Barnabas* the scope has become wider; Is 1:13 carries with it a polemic on Jewish sabbath and the festal calendar also. This perhaps reflects a difference in setting. AJ

---

125. Cf. Prigent, *Épître,* n. 105, p.7.
126. The AJ II here comes very close to the theology of the Jewish *IV Sib.* which is remarkably anti-temple and anti-sacrifice, and exhorts to baptism and conversion as the means to obtain remission of sins. «Baptism and repentance functionally replace the temple cult in Sib IV, and even greater weight is placed on them as a means of salvation.» (J. J. Collins, 'The Place of the Fourth Sibyl in the Development of the Jewish Sibyllina', *JJS* 25(1974, pp. 365-80), p. 378). Collins speculates that the 4th Sibyl derives from a Jewish baptist sect in the Jordan Valley -this would provide a geographical link to the AJ II (Pella!). Cf. also W. Brandt, *Die jüdischen Baptismen* (BZAW 18, Giessen, 1910), pp. 87-90.

II represents an address to pious Jews, observing the Law. Justin's tradition seems more adapted to Gentile God-fearers as the addressees - one has to tell them that they do not have to become Jews in order to be members of God's elect people. This would naturally lead to a more total polemic against the ritual practises of the Jews.

But this is a difference of nuance rather than a fundamental change. There is nothing to suggest that the tradition behind AJ II would require of the Gentiles that they should become Jews in order to become Christians -on the contrary. This tradition recognizes the mission to the Gentiles but concentrates on the mission to Israel.

One final remark on the setting of Justin's material. When the Church addressed Gentile God-feares who were fascinated by Judaism and perhaps contemplated conversion to Judaism, one of the first things to be clarified must have been the question of baptism - especially with women who had no problems with circumcision. The Church offered an alternative to Jewish proselyte baptism but on what Scriptural support?

Here Jer 2:12f must soon have suggested itself as the ideal polemic testimony. The combined version in *Barn.* 11:2 shows that the text already had a history in the testimony tradition prior to *Barnabas*. In Justin the text seems to have been brought up to date with the addition of a third element -very likely a reference to the Hadrianic decree: «for I have given Jerusalem a bill of divorce in your presence» (Jer 3:8).

It is now time to ask how this anti-cultic polemic can accord with the exploitation of the same practices as types of NT events or practices. Justin himself provides an answer on several occasions: Before Christ's coming, the cultic commandments were useful and necessary to keep for the Jews (see esp. *Dial.* 27:2.4; 46:5; but also *Dial.* 20:1; 23:3).The cultic practices were not in themselves reprehensible or abhorrent to God. But this changes with the coming of Christ. To *continue* with these practices after Christ's-coming, as if salvation still depended upon them, is abhorrent to God. It would seem that the anti-cultic texts were understood in this vein not only by Justin, but also by the tradition he is following. The harsh rejectory words in Is 1:11ff[127] and the other texts were thus very likely taken as *prophecies* about the status of the Jewish cult *post Christum*. Taken in this vein, the anti-cultic texts are entirely compatible with a positive, typological exploitation of the very same cultic observances. Roughly speaking, the same double attitude is taken by Hebrews, and no contradiction is seen.

We now turn to an analysis of these cultic typologies.

---

127. It is interesting to notice that the anti-cultic polemic based on Is 1:11ff seems not to have passed unnoticed among the rabbis. «*R. Akiba, questionné un jour par un chrétien sur ce versets, répondit: S'il était ecrit: Mes néoménies et mes fêtes, je te donnerais raison; mais tel quel, le verset parle des néoménies et des fêtes instituées par Jéroboam.*» (A. Marmorstein, 'L'Épître de Barnabé & la polemique juive', *REJ* 60 ( 1910, pp. 213-220), p. 219, paraphrazing *Tanhuma* (Buber, p. 156)).

(α) Paschal lamb and unleavened bread.

The most elaborate exposition of the paschal lamb typology is to be found in *Dial.* 40:1-3 and *Dial.* 111:3f. If we synthesize these two passages, the following elements emerge:

| Type | Realization |
|---|---|
| (1) As the blood of the passover lamb saved them that were in Egypt (111:3) | so also will the blood of Christ rescue from death them that have believed (111:3). |
| (2) The blood was smeared (χρισθέν) on the houses (111:3) | They who believe on Christ anoint (χρίονται) their «houses», i.e. themselves (40:1) |
| (3) The blood on the doorposts and the upper lintel formed the sign of the cross *(Dial.* 111:3f by implication) | Christ was crucified (111:4) |
| (4) The lamb was roasted in a cross-like fashion (40:3)[128] | Christ was crucified (40:3) |

Justin says that Christians anoint their «houses», i.e. themselves, with the blood of Christ. To justify this designation of man as a house, he appeals to Gen 2:7. «For that the form (τὸ πλάσμα) in which God formed (ἔπλασεν) Adam, became the house of the inbreathing that God gave, you can all perceive.»

I think two texts in *Barnabas* can elucidate this seemingly farfetched combination of paschal lamb typology and Gen 2:7. In *Barn.* 6:8-19 there is a baptismal midrash on Ex 33:1.3 («Enter into the good land ... flowing

---

128. In *Dial.* 40:3 Justin speaks in the present tense about the manner of roasting the paschal lamb. J. Jeremias, *Die Passahfeier der Samaritaner* (BZAW 59, Giessen, 1932), pp. 55/96, accepts this report without question as evidence about the Samaritan practice in Justin's days. It is indeed probable that Justin is drawing on memories from his early years in Neapolis by Gerizim. However, the fact that the Samaritan practice in modern times accords with the prescriptions in the Mishnah (Pes. 7:1), should warn against accepting Justin's report at face value. The Samaritans roast the lamb on a *single* spit which is thrust through from the head and backwards (as prescribed in the Mishnah), and to this same spit the hind legs are fastened. The lamb is roasted with the head downwards (see pictures and text in Jeremias, *op. cit.,* pp. 33-37). However, during the spitting of the lamb, it is fastened to a horizontal bar carried by two men, and for some moments during this process, a distant observer might be reminded of a crucifixion, cf. pictures in Jeremias, pp. 32f. It seems a modern observer has made the same mistake as Justin, cf. the quotation in L. Williams *ad. loc.* (p. 80, n.2):«A recent traveller describing in some detail the present method of sacrificing the Paschal lambs among the Samaritans, says the slain lambs 'are crucified on rough wooden crosses, head downwards, with the hind legs on the arms of the crosses'(J. E. Wright, *Round about Jerusalem* 1918, p. 91).» It is thus probable that Justin *bona fide* recalled the Samaritan practice as a crucifixion of the lambs.

with milk and honey»).[129] The relevant points in our context are found in vss. 9; 11f, and 14f. In vs. there is established a connexion between the words σάρξ (i.e. the σάρξ of Jesus) and γῆ by means of an allusion to Gen 2:7: ἄνθρωπος γὰρ γῆ ἐστιν πάσχουσα. ἀπὸ προσώπου γὰρ τῆς γῆς ἡ πλάσις τοῦ 'Αδὰμ ἐγένετο. This implies an Adam - Christ typology.[130] Further, in vss. 11f the new creation of Christians in baptism is described in the following way: «Since then he made us new(ἀνακαινίσας) by the remission of sins, he made us another type, that we should have the souls of children, as though he were creating us afresh (ἀναπλάσσοντος). For it is concerning us that the scripture says: (Gen 1:26).» The idea contained in this passage is that the process effected in baptism is really the creation spoken of in Gen 1:26. The terminology of πλάσσειν and πλάσμα (6:12) even recalls Gen 2:7. This implicit reference to Gen 2:7 is perhaps also contained in vss. 14f: «... we have been created afresh (ἀναπεπλά-σμεθα)... (Ezek 36:26), for, my brethren, the habitation (τὸ κατοικητή-ριον) of our hearts is a shrine (ναὸς) holy to the Lord...» At their ἀνάπλα-σις, the believers' hearts become temples of the Lord - probably an allusion to the indwelling of the Holy Spirit, thus again recalling Gen 2:7.

This is brought out more clearly in *Barn.* 16:7-10,[131] where the human heart is again spoken of as a κατοικητήριον for God: «When we received[132] the remission of sins, and put our hope on the Name, we became new, being created again from the beginning, wherefore God truly dwells in us, in the habitation which we are... This is a spiritual temple being built for the Lord.» We meet in these passages an implied Adam/believer typology, drawing upon Gen 1:26 and Gen 2:7. I suggest that Justin in *Dial.* 40:1 is briefly hinting at the same idea: In his baptism the believer is created anew and becomes a «house for the inbreathing of God».

This raises the question whether there be a reference to a baptismal anointing in *Dial.* 40:1. Only 20-25 years afterwards, Melito in his Paschal Homily gives a paraphrase of Ex 12 replete with terms related to Christian baptism and unction (vss. 14-17).[133] Justin's idea that Christians anoint

---

129. On this text, cf. esp. N. A. Dahl,'La terre où coulent le lait et le miel selon Barnabé 6,8-19', *Aux Sources de la tradition chrétienne* (Mélanges M. Goguel, Neuchâtel-Paris, 1950), pp. 62-70; L. W. Barnard, 'A Note on *Barnabas* 6,8-17, *Studia Patristica* IV:2 (TU 79, Berlin, 1961), pp. 263-267. I have commented on the passage in some detail in my article (Norwegian), 'Tidlig kristen dåpsteologi i Barnabas' brev' ('Early Christian baptismal theology in the Epistle of Barnabas') TTK 47(1976) (pp. 81-105), pp. 93-97. Cf. also Prigent, *Les Testimonia,* pp. 84-90.
130. Cf. esp. Barnard, *art. cit.,* p. 264.
131. On this text, cf. Prigent, *Les Testimonia,* pp. 80-82; and my article, pp. 97-99.
132. I take the aorist participle as a reference to baptism.
133. St. G. Hall points them out in the notes to his edition of Melito's text, pp. 8f. See esp. vs. 14: λαβόντες δὲ τὸ τοῦ προβάτου αἷμα *χρίσατε* τὰ πρόθυρα τῶν οἰκιῶν ὑμῶν ... Vs. 17: ...ἐσφραγισμένον τῷ τοῦ προβάτου αἵματι ... Theophilus *Ad Autol.* 1:12 seems also to refer to an anointing of Christians, cf. L. L. Mitchell, *Baptismal Anointing* (Alcuin Club Collections 48, London, 1966), pp. 12f.

themselves with Christ's blood may well reflect a baptismal anointing practised already at his time, although no direct evidence of baptismal unction for such an early date is preserved.[134]

It thus seems that for Justin the paschal lamb typology is intimately connected with the theme of baptism. This may have been the case with *Barnabas'* material also. In 5:1f the paschal lamb motif may be implicit in the Is 53:5/7 quotation. In any case, Is 53:7 is a testimony on Christ the paschal lamb in Justin: «For Christ was the passover, who was sacrificed later, as also Isaiah said:'He was led as a sheep to slaughter'». *Dial.* 111:3. We have seen already that πάσχα and ἄρνιον/πρόβατον are the connecting catchwords in *Dial.* 72:1-3 ( Ps. Ezra.; Jer 11:19; Is 53:7). In *Dial.* 13f we find the following sequence of elements: Baptism; purifying blood of Christ; Is 52:10 - 54:6; baptism; typology on unleavened bread. On the background of the above observations, I think P.Prigent is wrong when he suggests that the long Is 53 quotation has been secondarily introuced into the baptismal context of *Dial.* 13f.[135] I should say: Is 53 was for Justin a saying on the paschal lamb, whose blood was applied to the believer in baptism. This explains the juxtaposition of baptism and Is 53, it also makes plain why a typology on the unleavened bread is added in *Dial.* 14:2f.

There are some NT «lamb» passages over which there has been much debate as to whether the paschal lamb or the Isaian «Servant» (Is 53:7) is being envisaged: John 1:29.36;[136] Rev 5:6. The material here presented may indicate that those scholars are right who think one should not posit an either/or alternative.[137] Already 1 Pt 1:18f testifies to an early fusion of paschal lamb and Is 53 motives.[138] One should note also the prescript in 1 Pt (1:2). Terminologically, it points forward to *Barn.* 5:1f: «. . . chosen and

---

134. The earliest direct evidence for a baptismal anointing is found in Tertullian, *De Bapt.* 7. Cf. G. Kretschmar,'Die Geschichte des Taufgottesdienstes in der Alten Kirche', *Leiturgia. Handbuch des evangelischen Gottesdienstes V* (ed. K. F. Müller and W. Blankenburg, Kassel, 1970) (pp. 1-348), pp. 28f. A. H. Couratin, 'Justin Martyr and Confirmation - A Note', *Theology* 55 (1952), pp. 158-60, argues that a separate rite of baptismal unction is hinted at in *Dial.* 41. I believe there is much to be said for L. L. Mitchell's cautious conclusion, based on a balanced review of the evidence: «. . . we cannot state definitely that Justin knew the sequence of water, oil, Spirit found in Tertullian, but there is certainly nothing in his manner of writing incongruous with his having known it . . .» *(Baptismal Anointing,* p. 15. Cf. his discussion pp. 13-15.). Mitchell has an interesting chapter on the use of oil in ordinary bathing in antiquity, pointing out that oil was considered an almost obligatory prerequisite:«The use of oil corresponded to the modern use of soap.» (*Op. cit.,* p. 25, the whole chapter pp. 25-29). Perhaps the right question to ask is not: when was anointing introduced into the baptismal rite, but: When and how was the secular rite of anointing given a theological, if not to say sacramental, significance?

135. *Justin* p. 247.

136. Cf. i.a. Barrett,*comm. ad loc.,* pp. 146f; Brown, *comm. ad. loc.,* pp. 58-63; and Schnackenburg, *comm. ad loc.,* pp. 285-288.

137. Brown in his comm. refers to Melito's fusion of the two motifs as an argument that the same fusion is present in John (p. 63). He seems to be unaware of the earlier evidence in *Dial.* 111:3.

138. Cf. Schelkle, *comm. ad loc.,* pp. 48-50; Kelly, *comm. ad loc.,* pp. 73-75.

destined by God the Father and sanctified by the Spirit for obedience to Jesus Christ and for sprinkling (ῥαντισμός) with his blood.» Paschal lamb typology is evidenced also in the well-known testimony in John 19:36, and in the Johannine chronology for the passion.

But regarding the age of Justin's tradition in *Dial.* 13f, we have the most significant precedent in Paul, 1 Cor 5:7f. Paul[139] here seems to expand a Jewish Passover *Haggadah* formula by some Christian additions (italicized here):[140] «Cleanse out the old leaven

> *that you may be a new lump, as you really are unleavened.*
> *For Christ,*

our paschal lamb has been sacrificed. Let us therefore celebrate the festival, not with the old leaven,

> *the leaven of malice and evil,*

but with the unleavened bread

> *of sincerity and truth.»*

Compared with Paul, the new element in *Dial.* 14 is an anti-Jewish note in the typologizing of the unleavened bread:«For this is the inner meaning of the unleavened bread, that you do not practice the old deeds of the bad leaven. But you have thought of all things in a carnal way, and consider it to be piety, even though when you do such things, your souls are filled with guile, and, in fact, evil of every kind. Therefore also after seven days of eating unleavened bread God charged you to knead new leaven for yourselves, that is, the practice of other deeds, and not the imitation of the old and worthless.» This anti-Jewish twist to the idea may well have been part of the tradition as it reached Justin, for it is anticipated in Ignatius, *Magn.* 10:2f: «Put aside then the evil leaven which has grown old and sour, and turn to the new leaven, which is Jesus Christ . . . It is monstrous to talk of Jesus Christ and practice Judaism.»[141]

Justin's typology also contains another element not found in Paul, viz. the new leaven to be knead after the seven days of *mazzot.* An explicit command to knead this leaven is not contained in the OT, but may have been part of rabbinic *halakah* in Justin's days.[142] If so, we have here another

---

139. Or was the Christianized version already pre-Pauline? This view is taken by i.a. J. Jeremias, *Die Abendmalsworte Jesu* (4th ed., Göttingen, 1967), pp. 53f, and B. Lohse, *Das Passafest der Quartadecimaner* (BFChTh 2.Reihe 54, Gütersloh, 1953), pp. 101-105.

140. Cf. H. Windisch, art. 'ζυμη', *ThDNT* II, pp. 902-906. Windisch also takes the adjective «old» to be an interpretative addition.

141. On the interpretation history of the Pauline idea, cf. W. Huber, *Passa und Ostern. Untersuchungen zur Osterfeier der alten Kirche* (BZNW 35, Berlin, 1969), pp. 108ff.

142. Goldfahn, 'Aggada', pp. 55f denies this, and suspects a mistake in Justin. But cf. P. R. Weis, 'Some Samaritanisms of Justin Martyr', *JTS* 45 (1944, pp. 199-205), pp. 200f. Weis points to *Targum Ps. Jonathan ad Ex* 12:18. The Targum here adds: On the night of the twenty-second ye shall eat leaven. Weis takes this to reflect Samaritan rather than rabbinic halakah. This I am not competent to judge.

proof of the close contact with Judaism preserved throughout the development of Justin's tradition.[143]

As a transition to the next section, let us finally note that the rabbis can put the blood of the passover lamb in immediate connexion with the blood of circumcision, and that both «bloods» can be seen as propitiary. «*Vous mélangerez le sang du sacrifice de la Pâque et de la circoncision pour en faire un signe sur les demeures où vous résidez; je verrai le mérite du sang et je vous éparagnerai*», (*Targum Ps. Jonathan* to Ex 12:13).[144]

### (β) Circumcision

Before we turn to the main passage in *Dial.* 41:4, let us note the way Justin speaks about circumcision in *Dial.* 24:1: »Understand that the blood of that circumcision is rendered useless, and we have believed the blood that bringeth salvation.« This seems to imply that the Jews regarded the blood of circumcision as in some way a propitiary bloodshed, and this can be substantiated from rabbinic sources.[145]

---

143. It would be of some relevance for the characterization of Justin's tradition, if he could be shown to depend on quartodeciman ideas. This has been claimed, and a brief note on the issue may be required. I take as a premiss that the quartodecimans followed the Johannine chronology concerning the death of Jesus. This has been argued in some detail by Huber, *op. cit*, and J. Blank, *Meliton von Sardes: Vom Passa* (Sophia. Quellen Östlicher Theologie 3, Freiburg im Breisgau, 1962), pp. 35-41; and I accept their conclusions. Does Justin reflect this Johannine/quartodeciman chronology in his treatment of the passion story? W. O. E. Oesterley thinks so (*The Jewish Background of the Christian Liturgy* (Oxford, 1925), pp. 191f). The most relevant passage is *Dial.* 111:3:«And it stands written that on the day of the Passover (ἐν ἡμέρᾳ τοῦ πάσχα) you took him and likewise (ὁμοίως) at the passover (ἐν τῷ πάσχα) you crucified him.» As far as I can see, this text is ambiguous on the chronological issue. Justin seems to have been aware that among the Jews the days were reckoned from evening to evening, cf. *Dial.* 97:1; 99:2; 103:7. The passage in *Dial.* 111:3 could then be paraphrased in the following two ways: (1) On the seder night you took him, and likewise during the following day of Passover you crucified him (i.e. synoptic chronology). (2)You crucified him on the seder night day (14th Nisan) and arrested him on the evening of the same day, i.e. the preceeding evening. On the whole, I think the first alternative recommends itself. Justin only has synoptic allusions in his renderings of the Passion story, and alternative 2 looks a little more forced as a rendering of Justin's text. (Oesterley supports his claim with a rather misleading translation of *Dial.* 111:3: «It is written that ye took Him and crucified Him on the day of the Passover . . .» In Justin's text ἐν ἡμέρα τοῦ πάσχα only refers to Christ's arrest, and this would be a strange designation of the evening preceeding the seder night). I thus conclude that Justin rather seems to follow synoptic than Johannine chronology, and we are thus hardly in a position to say anything with certainty about possible quartodeciman provenance for his paschal lamb typology and other paschal motifs. Paschal lamb typology was no doubt of paramount importance in the quartodeciman Passover celebration - witness Melito's homily - but the motif may have been popular in other quarters also.

144. Translation of R. le Déaut in *idem, La Nuit Pascale* (Analecta Biblica 22, Roma, 1963), p. 210. On the whole topic, see le Déaut's excursus 'Paque et circoncision', *ibid*, pp. 209-212, with more rabbinic material.

145. E.g. *Ex. Rab.* 15:12 (pp. 174f), a passage in which Passover lamb and circumcision are also taken together: «(God says) 'I am now occupied in judging souls, and I will tell you how I will have pity on you, through the blood of the Passover, and the blood of circumcision, and I will forgive you.» Cf. also *Ex.Rab.* 17:3 (p. 213): «On account of two kinds of blood were Israel redeemed from Egypt - the blood of the Passover and the blood of circumcision.» Cf. L. Morris, 'The Passover in Rabbinic Literature', *Australian Biblical Review* 4 (1954/55, pp. 59-76), p. 65.

*Dial.* 41:4 is a very condensed passage. »Further, the commandment of circumcision, commanding you to circumcise all infants on the eighth day without fail, was a type of the true circumcision with which we were circumcised . . . by him who rose from the dead on the first day of the week, Jesus Christ our Lord. For the first day of the week, the first indeed of all the days that ever were, is further called the eighth according to the number of all the days of their cycle . . .«

Justin seems to presuppose here a connexion between Christ's resurrection and Christian baptism, a connexion he takes for granted and which he does not explicate. One is led to think of Col 2:11f: »In him also you were circumcised with a circumcision made without hands, by putting off the body of flesh in the circumcision of Christ; and you were buried with him in baptism, in which you were also raised with him through faith in the working of God, who raised him from the dead.« How much of this Pauline baptismal theology was preserved in Justin's material is difficult to say. A simple coupling between baptism and Christ's resurrection is probably contained in 1 Pt 1:3, and may have been a commonplace notion in several quarters of the early Church.

The somewhat elaborate juxtaposition of circumcision and baptism via the eighth day motif immediately recalls *Dial.* 138:1f. Here we meet a typology built on the eight souls in Noah's ark. They were, we are told, »a symbol of the day that is indeed eighth in number, in which our Christ appeared as risen from the dead . . . For Christ, being the Firstborn of every creature, has also become again the head of another race, which was begotten anew of him by water and faith and wood . . .« The remarkable echo of Col 1:15-18 contained in this passage - probably already contained in the tradition as it reached Jusin[146] - should encourage us to think that important motifs in the Pauline baptismal theology may even be found between the lines in *Dial.* 41:4.

To conclude: Justin's material on circumcision as a type of baptism clearly echoes Pauline *theologoumena* which may, however, not have been Pauline peculiarities, but well-known notions the early Church. Justin's way of speaking about the «blood of circumcision» may testify to continued contact with Jewish theology. And there is nothing which tell against the assumption that the typology of circumcision was part of the same dossier which Justin is employing for the rest of *Dial.* 40f. On the important topic of the «second» circumcision, see below pp. 334ff.

(γ) The σεμίδαλις offering (Lev 14:10)

As was remarked above, this is a rather out-of-the-way type. The σεμίδαλις is only one of several elements making up the cleansing sacrifice for a healed leper. I suggested that the occurrence of σεμίδαλις within the anti-cultic polemic in Is 1:11ff may have helped to direct the attention of

---

146. Noah as the beginning of a new race was known to Philo, cf. below, p.339.

Christian theologians to this remote text in Lev 14. But maybe there is more to it. It is possible with the help of Hebrews to reconstruct a tradition which might have made more extensive use of Lev 14 than is presently the case in Justin.

In Hebrews 9, the author has an extensive discussion on the various cleansing ceremonies of the old covenant. Among these, he treats also the purifying covenant blood sprinkled by Moses, Ex 24:3-8. But in his paraphrase of this incident, the author has included features belonging to the Atonement day (Lev 16); the Red Heifer (Num 19); and the purification of lepers (Lev 14). In the following table these additions to the Ex text are spelled out in the column to the right.

Table: Ex 24:3-8 as paraphrased in Heb 9:19-21 (text of Nestle 25)

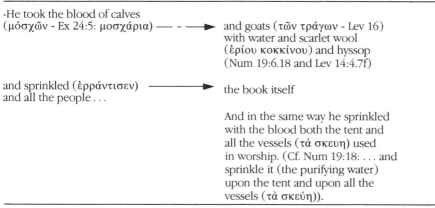

«He took the blood of calves
(μόσχων - Ex 24:5: μοσχάρια) ──── - ──⟶ and goats (τῶν τράγων - Lev 16)
with water and scarlet wool
(ἐρίου κοκκίνου) and hyssop
(Num 19:6.18 and Lev 14:4.7f)

and sprinkled (ἐρράντισεν) ──────⟶ the book itself
and all the people . . .

And in the same way he sprinkled
with the blood both the tent and
all the vessels (τὰ σκευη) used
in worship. (Cf. Num 19:18: . . . and
sprinkle it (the purifying water)
upon the tent and upon all the
vessels (τὰ σκεύη)).

The important point now is to see which catchwords prompted the inclusion of this added material. First, cleansing with *hyssop* is mentioned in the entire Pentateuch only in Lev 14:4.6.49-52, and Num 19:(6).18. In the rest of the OT cleansing with hyssop is mentioned only in Ps 51:9 - a text one can easily imagine as a baptismal testimony:«Purge me with hyssop, and I shall be clean; wash me (πλυνεῖς με), and I shall be whiter than snow».

Further, the common stock of catchwords in Lev 14 and Num 19 extends beyond this. There is in fact a striking similarity of terminology in the two passages:

| Lev 14:6-8 | Num 19:6 |
|---|---|
| The priest shall take<br>the living bird<br>καὶ τὸ ξύλον τὸ κέρδινον<br>καὶ τὸ κλωστὸν κόκκινον<br>καὶ τὸ ὕσσωπον<br>and dip them (βάψει)<br>and the living bird<br>in the blood of the bird<br>that was killed over the<br>running water (ἐφ᾽ ὕδατι ζῶντι)<br>and he shall sprinkle (περιρρανεῖ)<br>... on him who is to be<br>cleansed (τὸν καθαρισθέντα) ...<br>and he who is to be cleansed<br>shall wash (πλυνεῖ) his<br>clothes ...<br>and bathe (λούσεται) himself<br>in water, and he shall be clean ... | The priest shall take<br><br>ξύλον κέρδινον<br>καὶ ὕσσωπον<br>Num 19:18f<br><hr><br>A clean person shall take hyssop<br>and dip it in the water<br><br><br>(βάψει εἰς τὸ ὕδωρ<br>and sprinkle (περιρρανεῖ) ...<br><br><br><br>... and shall wash (πλυνεῖ) his<br>clothes<br>and bathe (λούσεται) himself<br>in water, and he ... shall be clean. |

As is easily seen, both passages are replete with terminology that could easily be given a baptismal connotation.[147] This may be implied in Heb 9:18ff; in *Barn.* 8 a baptismal interpretation of the Red Heifer ceremony is explicit enough.

What I want to suggest is that Justin may have known the typological tradition discernible in Hebrews and *Barnabas*, and that a baptismal interpretation of Lev 14:2-9 may easily have suggested an eucharistic interpretation of Lev 14:10:[148] After his cleansing the leper offers a sacrifice (including σεμίδαλις) ⟶ after his cleansing by baptism, the sinner partakes of the eucharist (cf. the sequence of the baptismal liturgy, reflected

147. One should also notice that cleansing from leprosy (Lev 14) and from corpse defilement (Num 19:1-13) are the only rites (besides cleansing from semen pollution) which according to rabbinic halakah should be performed in *running water* only ( מים חיים = ὕδωρ ζῶν, the «highest» kind of purifying water, cf . Str. Bill. I, pp. 108f). The earliest Christian source which specify the water of baptism, *Did.* 7:1f, also speaks about ὕδωρ ζῶν as preferable. If Gentiles at their conversion were regarded as affected with corpse defilement or leprosy defilement because of their idolatry, it would be quite natural to think of their cleansing in terms of Num 19 and Lev 14. And it seems the rabbis applied exactly these analogies. G. Alon, 'The Levitical Uncleanness of Gentiles'(in *idem, Jews, Judaism and the Classical World* (Jerusalem, 1977), pp. 146-189), adduces i.a. the following passages: «The uncleanness of idols has been made equivalent to that of one unclean through gonorrhea or leprosy.» (p Pes. IX:36c). «It is taught (in a *Baraita*), R. Judah b. Bathyra said:'Whence do we learn that offerings to idols defile whatever is in the same tent? For it is stated in Scripture, 'They joined themselves also unto Baal of Peor and ate sacrifices of the dead'- just as a corpse defiles all that is in the same tent, even so do offerings to idols defile whatever is in the tent.» (A. Zar. 32b; *Hull.* 13b). (Rendered after Alon, p. 170). To treat Lev 14 and Num 19 as relevant texts on proselyte baptism, and, *mutatis mutandis,* on Christian missionary baptism, would thus be in accordance with the rabbinic theory of Gentile uncleanness.

148. This was proposed by A. H. Couratin, *art. cit.* (note 134 above), pp. 458f, but he did not substantiate his proposal with the pre-Justinian material I have adduced here.

also in *1.Apol.* 61/65 and *Dial.* 115f/117). In *Dial.*41:2 the exposition of the σεμίδαλις offering is followed by the classic testimony on the eucharistic offering of the new people, Mal 1:10-12.

To conclude: It may well be that Justin in *Dial.* 41:1 is hinting at a typological tradition richer than the present text, a tradition one can suspect behind Hebrews, and which partly comes to light in *Barnabas*.

If the hypothesis expounded in this section is right, it serves to underline an impression gained from the material in the preceeding sections, viz. the paramount importance of *baptism* in the typologizing of OT cultic precepts. This accords with the point of view found in the AJ II and also implied in Justin's and *Barnabas'* material (cf. above, p. 297). that *baptism takes the place of OT sacrifices.* This would seem to indicate that the tradition as we meet it in Justin, has developed in a milieu whose thinking was very close to the model found in AJ II.

(δ) The two goats and the High Priest.

I have found it convenient to start this section with an examination of the chapter on the two goats in *Barnabas, Barn.* 7. The intricate web in this passage has been analyzed in great detail by P.Prigent[149] and K.Wengst,[150] and I content myself with only the most relevant points to our purpose.

First: It seems that *Barnabas* - or his source - had some knowledge of rabbinical *halakah* concerning the two goats of the Day of Atonement.

---

149. Prigent, *Les Testimonia,* pp. 99-110; partly repeated and corrected in *idem, Épitre,* notes *ad loc.*

150. K. Wengst, *Tradition und Theologie des Barnabasbriefes* (Arbeiten zur Kirchengeschichte 42, Berlin, 1971), pp. 30-33.

| Barnabas | Rabbinic parallel |
|---|---|
| «And let them eat of the goat which is offered in the fast for all their sins... and let the priests alone eat the entrails unwashed with vinegar....»[151] | «If it (Atonement Day) fell on a Friday, the he-goat (Num 29:11) of the Day of Atonement was consumed at evening. The Babylonians[152] used to eat it raw since they were not squeamish», M. Menahot 11:7. |
| «Take two goats, goodly and alike, and offer them....» | «The two he-goats of the Day of Atonement should be alike in appearance, in size, and in value», M. Yoma 6:1. |
| «And do ye all spit on it, and goad it, and bind the scarlet wool about its head, and so let it be cast into the desert.» | «... the Babylonians... used to pull its hair...», M. Yoma 6:4. «He bound the thread of crimson wool on the head of the scapegoat and he turned it towards the way by which it was to be sent out», M. Yoma 4:2. |
| «He who takes the goat into the wilderness drives if forth, and takes away the wool, and put it on a shrub which is called Rachel....»[153] | «They delivered it to him that should lead it away...», M. Yoma 6:3. «He divided the thread of crimson wool and tied it to the rock and the other half between its horns, and he pushed it down into the ravine from behind...», M. Yoma 6:6. |

Secondly, *Barn.* 7:3-11 is clearly divided into two parts: 7:3-5 is concerned with the sin-offering goat, 7:7-11 with the scapegoat, 7:6 being a transitional passage stating that the two goats should be alike (this is taken up in 7:10) The exposition about the sin-offering goat can be summarized thus: Just as the sin-offering goat was to be moistened with vinegar before it was eaten by the priests, so Christ, the real sin-offering, was given vinegar

---

151. L. Ginzberg calls this «an old Palestinian tradition» (article 'Allegorical Interpretation of Scripture' in *idem, On Jewish Law and Lore* (Philadelphia, 1955, pp. 127-150), p. 148). He gives no reference, however, and if he has the parallel in *M. Men.* 11:7 in mind, there is, strictly speaking, no parallel to Barnabas' statement that the «entrails» were eaten «unwashed with vinegar». I have not been able to find other parallels which could substantiate Ginzberg's statement.

152. Cf. Danby's comment *ad loc.,* based on the babylonian *Gemara* 100a: «They were not, actually, priests from Babylon, but Alexandrians; and the Palestinian Sages called them Babylonians in hatred of them.» (p. 509, n. 2).

153. The text is uncertain. H reads ραχη; S ραχηλ; G ραχιλ; L *rubus.* Windisch in his commentary (*Handbuch,* p. 346) made the ingenious proposal that we have to do with a corruption of ραχίς = cliff, matching the rabbinic parallel. If this is correct, the word ραχίς must have been misunderstood already by the author of Barnabas, or corrupted prior to him, since he clearly takes ραχη (or whatever he wrote) to mean «a shrub». Cf. also Prigent, *Les Testimonia,* p. 105.

(and gall) at his crucifixion. The 'priests' are the Christians. Probably an eucharistic motif is implied in this typology. As a side-motif, the author briefly alludes to the offering of Isaac, 7:3 fin.

Even more elaborate is the development of the scapegoat motif in 7:6ff. The scapegoat is ἐπικατάρατος, probably an allusion to Deut 21:23. The people should spit (ἐμπτύσατε) on it and *goad* (κατακεντήσατε) it. The first term recalls Is 50:6 and Mt 26:67; 27:30 par.; the second Zech 12:10.[154] In 7:9 this application of Zech 12:10 to the scapegoat is carried further: «Listen:'the first goat is for the altar, but the other is accursed', and note that the one that is accursed is crowned (with scarlet wool), because then 'they will see him'(Zech 12:10) on that day with the long scarlet robe (τὸν ποδήρη ... τὸν κόκκινον) on his body, and they will say: 'Is not this he whom we once crucified and rejected and pierced (κατακεντήσαντες, Zech 12:10) and spat upon? Of a truth it was he who then said that he was the Son of God.»

This passage calls for some comments. First, we note again the significance of the catchword κόκκινος, cf. above on Num 19 etc. Secondly, the saying about Christ's return deserves close attention. It seems clear that the scarlet wool «crowning» the head of the scapegoat is a figure of the returning Christ. But the vivid imagery of Christ «crowned» and dressed in a scarlet robe (ποδήρη) at his return, cannot be derived from Lev 16 nor Zech 12:10. To find the background we shall have to look in two directions. (1) It is implied that this dressing is the reason why the Jews recognize Jesus in his return. This points to the passion story of the Gospels. «And they stripped him and put a scarlet robe (χλαμύδα κοκκίνην) upon him, and plaiting a crown of thorns they put it on his head.» (Mt 27:28f; cf. Jn 19:2 [ἱμάτιον πορφυροῦν]). At his return Jesus shall wear the royal dressing which was put on him in mockery during his passion. But there is probably a further reference. (2) Jesus shall be dressed in a ποδήρη. In the LXX this is the robe of the High Priest, Ex 25:7; 28:4.31; 29:5; 35:9; Zech 3:5. I think one should consider the possibility that *Barnabas* may be alluding specifically to Zech 3:5: ἐνδύσατε αὐτὸν ποδήρη καὶ ἐπίθετε κίδαριν καθαρὰν ἐπὶ τὴν κεφαλὴν αὐτοῦ. Here we have both the ποδήρη and - if not terminologically - the «crowning». Barnabas would not be the first Christian writer to allude to Zech 3:5. In Rev 1:13 the Son of Man is seen dressed in a ποδήρη and standing among seven lampstands. The last feature is certainly an allusion to Zech 4:2. In Zech 4:11-14 the prophet sees Joshua the High Priest and Zerubbabel standing by the lampstand. So it is not unreasonable to think that Joshua the High Priest is also in mind when Rev 1:13 talks about the ποδήρη.

---

154. NB: in the non-LXX version found in the NT and Justin: ὄψονται εἰς ὃν ἐξεκέντησαν (Jn 19:37 - cf. Rev 1:7; *1.Apol.* 52:12; *Dial.* 14:8; 64:7; 118:1).

To conclude: I think there are good reasons to see a High Priest (Zech 3:1-6) typology behind Barn 7:9: In his return, Christ, like Joshua the High Priest, will be crowned and dressed in the highpriestly robe.[155] This inclusion of motifs related to the robe of the High Priest, and a possible Joshua typology (Zech 3:1-5) in a chapter devoted to Lev 16, suggests that Justin's treatment of the High Priest's robe in *Dial.* 42:1, and Joshua the High Priest in *Dial.* 115f, is not without foundation in previous tradition.[156]

Returning to *Barnabas*, we must thirdly underline the combination of scapegoat typology and the two *parousias* motive. The terminology of two *parousias* is not found in *Barnabas*, but the idea is contained in *Barn.* 7. Let us notice that Barnabas' logic is somewhat strained here. It seems that both goats serve as types of Christ's suffering, while the scapegoat also typifies Christ in his return. At the same time, the likeness of the two goats seems to be used as a pointer to the identity of Christ in his two comings.

Now let us turn to Justin's texts.

(1) *Dial.* 40:4f.:«Likewise, the two identical goats which had to be offered during the Fast - one of which was to be the scapegoat and the other the sacrificial goat - were an announcement of the two advents of Christ: of the first advent, in which your priests and elders sent him away as a scapegoat, seizing him and putting him to death; of the second advent, because in that same place of Jerusalem you shall recognize (Zech 12:10) him whom you had subjected to shame, and who was a sacrificial offering for all sinners who are willing to repent . . .»

One immediately observes that this typology is much poorer in detail than *Barnabas'*. But Justin has added one of his favourite ideas: The (second) coming of Christ is to take place *in Jerusalem*. On one point he has a feature not found in *Barnabas*: The Jewish priests and elders should seize, literally: «lay their hands on» (ἐπιβαλόντες . . . τὰς χεῖρας) him. This may recall Lev 16:21: καὶ ἐπιθήσει Ααρων τὰς χεῖρας αὐτοῦ ἐπὶ τὴν κεφαλὴν . . . On the other hand, Justin shares with *Barnabas* the somewhat strained logic of the argument on the two advents. But he has reversed the goats: For Justin the *sin-offering goat* is a type of Christ in his passion and return.

I think the deviations from *Barnabas* are so substantial as to exclude direct borrowing. It seems both authors depend on a common tradition

---

155. Prigent has neglected the motif of the ποδήρη in his analysis of *Barn.* 7 (*Les Testimonia*, pp. 99ff). That my interpretation is not fortuite, is indicated in Tertullian's restatement of Barnabas' idea. In *Adv. Marc.* III:7:6 he says: «Then those who pierced him will know who he is, and will smite their breasts . . . So also in Zechariah, in the person of Jeshua . . . the veritable High Priest of the Father, Christ Jesus, is by two styles of raiment marked out for two advents . . . : (in his second advent) he is .. arrayed in *podere et mitra et cidari munda*, which means the glory and dignity of his second coming.»

156. This would suggest that *Dial.* 41f and *Dial.* 115f may derive from the same source. There are signs of rabbinic haggadah concerning Joshua the High Priest in *Dial.* 116:3, cf. Goldfahn, 'Aggada', 'pp. 198f, and L. Williams, note *ad loc.* (p. 240).

which included elements derived from rabbinic *halakah*. It also seems that the theme of Christ's return (Zech 12:10) was an integral part of this tradition. This suggests that this topic is related to the tradition behind Justin's Christological testimonies in the *Apology,* which also express the idea of two comings and take Zech 12:10ff as a main testimony on the second coming.

(2) *Dial.* 42:1: «The order that twelve bells were to be pendent on the robe (ποδήρη) of the High Priest was a symbol of the twelve Apostles, who were dependent on the power of Christ the everlasting Priest, by whose voices all the earth was filled with the glory (cf. Is 6:3) and grace of God and his Christ.»

The number of the bells is not given in the OT (Ex 28:33f). The rabbinical sources say 36 or 72,[157] i.e. multiples of 12. Probably the number 12 in Justin's text has been reached by combining Ex 28:33f with vss. 17-21 of the same chapter.[158] Independently of Justin we find the same tradition in the *Protevangelium of James*: «And the High Priest took the vestment with the twelve bells . . .», 8:3. It may well go back to Jewish sources.

Let us next pay attention to the phrase δἰ ὧν τῆς φωνῆς ἡ πᾶσα γῆ τῆς δόξης καὶ χάριτος τοῦ θεοῦ . . . ἐπληρώθη. Two Biblical passages are called to mind. First, after the narrative of how Aaron consecrated the High Priest's robe in Ex 39, we read in Ex 40 how God's δόξα filled the tabernacle: καὶ δόξης κυρίου ἐπλήσθη ἡ σκηνή (vss. 34f). It is plain that Justin knew these verses - he alludes to them in *Dial.* 127:3: «. . . nor had Moses himself power to enter into the tabernacle which he made, if it was filled with the glory from God.« Justin or his tradition may have seen a connexion between the High Priest's robe and the glory which filled the Temple, cf. the remarks in Ex 28 about the robe: It shall be for honour and δόξα (vss. 2 and 40). It is interesting to note that in Is 6:1, where the Hebrew text reads: »and his (God's) *robe* filled the whole Temple«, the LXX reads: καὶ πλήρης ὁ οἶκος *τῆς δόξης* αὐτοῦ. The special relevance of this is that the second Scriptural passage which closely resembles Justin's phrase quoted above, is Is 6:3: πλήρης *πᾶσα ἡ γῆ* τῆς δόξης αὐτοῦ.

Let me provisionally formulate a hypothesis: *Dial.* 42:1 embodies a High Priest typology, where the world is Christ's tabernacle, and as the bells on the High Priest's robe filled the tabernacle with their sound, so now Christ's »bells«, the apostles, have filled Christ's tabernacle, the world, with their voice.

---

157. Cf. L. Williams, note *ad. loc.* (p. 83).
158. Or perhaps one should accept the proposal of Heinisch, *Einfluss Philos,* p.235, viz. that Justin (I would say: his source) derives the number 12 from the typological counterpart: the apostles.

One does in fact find Jewish precedents to this idea, or, to be more precise: We find the High Priest's robe treated as a *cosmic symbol*.[159] »For upon his (Aaron's) highpriestly robe (ποδήρη) was the whole world pictured.« (*Sap. Sal.* 18:24).»We have in it (the vesture of the High Priest) as a whole and in its parts a typical representation of the world and its particular parts.«[160] (Philo *Vita Mos* II 24(117)) Beginning with the ποδήρη, Philo explains that the violet colour of the gown is a symbol of the air, the flowers at the bottom of it represents the earth, the pomegranates mean the water, »while the bells represent the harmonious alliance of these two« (*ibid.*; 118-121). Josephus tells his readers that the tabernacle itself and all its equipment had a cosmic significance. »For if one reflects on the construction of the tabernacle and looks at the vestments of the priest and the vessels . . . he will discover that our lawgiver was a man of God . . . In fact, every one of these objects is intended to recall and represent the universe . . .« The tabernacle symbolises earth and heaven, »the High Priest's tunic likewise signifies the earth, being of linen, and its blue the arch of heaven, while it recalls the lightnings by its pomegranates, the thunder by the sound of its bells.« *(Ant.* III:180-84).

On this background one can see that there is good sense in the typology in *Dial.* 42:1 - and one can add a further observation. Ps 19:5 is quoted as a testimony on the apostolic mission *Dial.* 42:1: «Into all the earth did their sound go forth, and their sayings unto the ends of the world.» Looking at the context of this verse in Ps 19, we find a phrase which could easily be taken to express the idea of the world as Christ's tabernacle: ἐν τῷ ἡλίῳ ἔθετο τὸ σκήνωμα αὐτοῦ (vs. 5b, immediately following Justin's excerpt); we also meet the concept of the world being filled with δόξα: vs. 2.

Ps 19:5 is a Pauline testimony on the apostolic mission, and Justin probably quotes directly from Rom 10:18. But one may suggest that this Pauline text was taken as a point of departure for a richer exploitation of motives in Ps 19, and that such a tradition is evidenced in *Dial.* 42:1. What is certain is that the tradition contained in *Dial.* 42:1 shows every sign of close contact with Jewish speculation on the High Priest's robe and the tabernacle.

One last remark: Justin's Christological material in *1.Apol.* 32 contains the saying that Christ washed his robe (στολή) i.e. his believers, in his own blood, 32:7. The idea here is somewhat different - here Christ's robe is the Church. But still a High Priest typology may be implied, and in *1.Apol.* 32:8 a kind of Temple imagery is employed: ἐν οἷς οἰκεῖ τὸ παρὰ τοῦ θεοῦ

---

159. See esp. F. J. Dölger, 'Die Glöckchen am Gewande des jüdischen Hohenpriesters nach der Ausdeutung jüdischer, heidnischer und frühchristlicher Schriftsteller', in *idem, Antike und Christentum* 4 (Münster, 1934), pp. 233-242.
160. On the symbolism of the High Priest's robe in Philo (and Justin), cf. also Heinisch, *Einfluss Philos*, pp. 233-237.

σπέρμα, ὁ λόγος. There is, perhaps, a cross-connexion here which would point to a common provenance for the material in *1.Apol.* 32 and *Dial.* 42:1.

(3) *Dial.* 115f. As we have seen, there are great chances that Zech 3:5f is given a Christological interpretation in *Barn.*7:9, cf. Rev 1:13. In *Dial.* 115:1, Zech 2:14 - 3:2 is quoted, but the comment afterwards concern Zech 3:1-5. A Christological typology is only hinted at in *Dial.* 115:3f - Justin's main thrust is an ecclesiastical typology: Joshua foreshadows Christian believers.

It is evident that Justin has turned directly to the Zechariah text in his rendering of this material. But one suspects a substratum: A Christological interpretation centered on Zech 3:5. This would be a tradition shared with *Barnabas* - not taken directly from him.

As a general conclusion to this paragraph, let me emphasize two points.

The first is the major position accorded to *baptism* in the typologizing of OT cultic precepts in this material. This accords with the point of view stated explicitly in AJ II: Baptism now accords remission of sins, and in that capacity replaces the sacrificial cult.

The second point is the possibility of crossconnexions with the Christological materials in the *Apology.*

It seems we are still facing material deriving from the same theological milieu as the testimonies in *1.Apol.* 32ff.

(b) The ceremonial laws as an accommodation.

Justin's idea is this: The ceremonial laws were enjoined upon Israel as an accomodation to their hardness of heart, which was first and foremost displayed in the making of the golden calf.

Reviewing the relevant passages, one soon observes a rather constant terminology and a common stock of motives: *Dial.* 18:2: circumcision, sabbath and festivals enjoined on the Jews because of their ἀνομίαι and σκληροκαρδία. *Dial.* 19:5f: Israel was ἄδικος and ἀχάριστος when they made the calf (μοσχοποιήσας). God allowed sacrifices to be brought to him ἵνα μὴ εἰδωλολατρῆτε. But Israel even *sacrificed their children to demons. Dial.* 20:4: God commanded the Jews to abstain from unclean things, for although Israel ate manna, the*y made the golden calf. Dial.* 22:1: God commanded offerings διὰ τὰς ἁμαρτίας . . . καὶ διὰ τὰς εἰδωλολατρείας. *Dial.* 27:2: God enjoined the same things through Moses and the Prophets (sabbath etc.), διὰ τὸ σκληροκάρδιον . . . καὶ ἀχάριστον . . . *Dial.* 43:1: Sabbath and sacrifices and offerings and feasts enjoined διὰ τὸ σκληροκάρδιον. (The same formula in *Dial.* 44:2; 45:3; 46:5.7; 47:2; 67:4.10). *Dial.* 67:8: Offerings and sacrifices enjoined διὰ τὸ σκληροκάρδιον . . . καὶ εὐχερὲς πρὸς εἰδωλολατρείαν. *Dial.* 73:6: Changing of the Scripture's text even more awful than the μοσχοποιΐα, after being fed with manna, and worse than *sacrificing children to demons,* and *slaying the prophets. Dial.* 102:6: Jews μοσχοποιήσαντες, ἀεὶ δὲ ἀχάριστοι καὶ φονεῖς τῶν δικαίων. *Dial.* 131:4: Jews always ἀχάριστοι. *Dial.* 132:1: You Jews ἐμοσχοποιήσατε, *committed fornication* with the daughters of the aliens, καὶ εἰδωλολατρῆσαι ἐσπουδάσατε . . . *Dial.* 133:1: You *sacrificed your children to demons* . . . (Is 3;10etc). *Dial.* 136:3: The Jewish forefathers offered caces τῇ στρατιᾷ τοῦ οὐρανοῦ.

In his description of Israel's sin, Justin is close to Paul, 1 Cor 10, and Stephen in Acts 7. Paul: «Do not become εἰδωλολάτραι as some of them were; as it is written, 'The people sat down to eat and drink and rose up to dance'. We must not *commit fornication* as some of them did..», 1 Cor 10:7f. Stephen: «καὶ ἐμοσχοποίησαν¹⁶¹ . . . καὶ ἀνήγαγον θυσίαν τῷ εἰδώλῳ . . . λατρεύειν τῇ στρατιᾷ τοῦ οὐρανοῦ . . . (Acts 7:41f); σκληροτράχηλοι καὶ ἀπερίτμητοι καρδίαις . . . τίνα τῶν πρωφητῶν οὐκ ἐδίωξαν οἱ πατέρες ὑμῶν . . . καὶ φονεῖς ἐγένεσθε [τοῦ δικαίου] Acts 7:51f. We have noticed already that Stephen's polemic testimonies, Am 5:25-27 and Is 66:1f, recur in *Dial.* 22. If we include also some of the possible allusions in Acts 7:51, the amount of common material becomes considerable: Lev 26:41 (ἡ καρδία αὐτῶν ἡ ἀπερίτμητος), cf. *Dial.* 16:1; Jer 9:25 (᾽Ισραὴλ ἀπερίτμητοι καρδίας αὐτῶν . . .), cf. *Dial.* 28:3.

The elements not found in Paul or Stephen are: σκληροκαρδία as the word describing Israel's sinful condition; the sacrificing of children to demons; and the motive of ἀχαριστία. The term σκληροκαρδία is, however, not far from σκληροτράχηλος in Acts 7:51, and one can suggest several reasons why σκληροκαρδία became a favourite term in Justin. It is a central catchword in some of the anti-circumcision testimonies used by Justin, and it occurs in Jesus' polemic against the Pharisees in Mk 10:5 = Mt 19:8: Moses introduced a temporary accommodation in the Law πρὸς τὴν σκληροκαρδίαν ὑμῶν. (Jesus has not the ceremonial law in mind, but formally his argument is close to Justin's: The original will of God was later modified because of the hard hearts of the people).¹⁶²

The sacrifice of children to demons is mentioned in some OT summaries of Israel's history, e.g. Ps 106:37: καὶ ἔθυσαν τοὺς υἱοὺς αὐτῶν καὶ τὰς θυγατέρας αὐτῶν τοῖς δαιμονίοις. It is worthwhile to notice that another testimony on Israel's sacrifices to demons, Deut 32:17, figures in the context in 1 Cor 10 (vs. 20).

The ἀχαριστία of Israel (a non-Biblical term), is a natural contrast motive inherent in the OT material.

It thus seems that Justin's description of Israel's sin is a natural development of motives already found in the NT. We can follow the growth of this tradition in *1. Clem.* 51-53. We find here a parainetic section comprising motives from exodus and desert wandering. It seems *1.Clem.* is using quotation material which originally had another orientation, viz. anti-cultic

---

161. Μοσχοποιεῖν is a *hapax leg.* in the NT, and recurs in the quoted passages in Justin. Cf. Lake and Cadbury, *Beginnings* IV, pp. 78f.

162. Cf. esp. K. Berger, 'Hartherzigkeit und Gottes Gesetz. Die Vorgeschichte des antijüdischen Vorwurfs in Mc 10,5', *ZNW* 61 (1970), pp. 1-47.

polemic. The passage runs like this: Ch. 51:3: warning not to harden the heart, σκληρῦναι τὴν καρδίαν, like the transgressors of Num 16. Ch. 52: The Lord demands confession of sins, not animal sacrifices. The quotation sequence proving this looks as if derived from a cluster of anti-cultic testimonies: Ps 69:31-33; Ps 50:14f/ Ps 51:19a. In ch. 53 follows a warning description of the golden calf incident: «Go down hence quickly, for thy people, whom thou didst bring out of the land of Egypt, have committed iniquity (ἠνόμησεν) . . . they have made themselves molten images'. And the Lord said to him: 'I have spoken to thee once and twice, saying, I have seen this people, and behold, it is stiffnecked (σκληροτράχηλος) . . .» The quotations are taken from Deut 9:12-14, the deuteronomic parallel to Ex 32:7-9. We notice again the designation of Israel as σκληροτράχηλος in connexion with the golden calf episode. Whether the juxtaposition of anti-cultic testimonies in ch. 52 and golden calf incident in 53 implies a theory that the cultic observances were enjoined on Israel as a reaction to the golden calf incident is impossible to say. If *1.Clem.* is using an anti-cultic source in chs. 52f, this source may well have expressed such a view, but this must remain pure hypothesis.

In the texts reviewed so far, we have found no clear expression of the idea that the cultic observances were given subsequent to the golden calf episode as an accommodation to Israel's proneness to idolatry. Acts 7 perhaps comes closest; here we find the idea that God punished Israel by letting them indulge in pagan sacrificial cult: παρέδωκεν αὐτοὺς λατρεύειν τῇ στρατιᾷ τοῦ οὐρανοῦ (7:42). But it would be foreign to Stephen (Luke) to include Mosaic precepts in God's punitive action.[163]

Coming next to *Barnabas,* we notice a peculiar treatment of the golden calf incident (4:7f and 14:1-4): Moses offered God's covenant to the people, but when learning about their idolatry, broke the tables of the covenant. The covenant was thus withdrawn, but is now offered anew through Christ. There is no saying here that the ceremonial laws are an accommodation to Israel's hardness of heart. Nevertheless, a not totally different idea lingers in the background in *Barn.* 9:4. *Barnabas* here says that an evil angel mislead the Jews to take the commandment of circumcision literally. Perhaps *Barnabas* is here exploiting the Jewish idea that angels were mediating at

---

163. On the law in Luke-Acts, cf. i.a. J. Jervell, 'The Law in Luke-Acts', in *idem, Luke and the People of God. A New Look at Luke-Acts* (Minneapolis, 1972), pp. 133-151. I believe M. Simon unduly reads later concepts into Stephen's speech when he writes:«. . . *la loi rituelle est née des mauvais penchants des Juifs. L'idée apparaît déja chez Etienne, lorsqu'il dénonce le culte du Temple comme indigne du vrai Dieu et simplement toléré par lui, comme une concession fait aux Juifs pour éviter un mal pire.»* (*Verus Israel,* p. 112). Schoeps, *Judenchristentum,* pp. 222/236-40/440-445, goes even further than Simon in reading Acts 7 on a line with *Rec.* 1:33ff.

the giving of the Law at Sinai,[164] turning it into a radically anti-Jewish conception. In any case his idea implies that the literal observance of a ceremonial precept is seen as a misfortune or a punishment. One can speculate whether *Barnabas* is dependent on the same tradition as Justin, but modifying it thoroughly because he does not accept the «two covenants» framework inherent in the tradition.[165]

Turning, finally, to the AJ II, we find for the first time Justin's idea in plain words. The relevant passages can be summarized like this: Moses led the people through long windings for forty years to root out Egyptian influence. At Sinai the ten commandments were given, the first commandment being to worship God alone. «But when Moses had gone up to the mount, and was staying there forty days, the people, although they had seen Egypt struck with the ten plagues . . . manna also given to them from heaven . . . (there follows an enumeration of God's beneficial miracles reminiscent of *Dial.* 131:3.6 )[166] those very people . . . made and worshipped a golden calf's head, after the fashion of Apis, whom they had seen worshipped in Egypt; and after so many and so great marvels which they had seen, were unable to cleanse and wash out from themselves the defilements of old habit. On this account, leaving the short road . . ., Moses conducted them by an immense circuit of the desert, if haply he might be able . . . to shake off the evils of old habit by the change of a new education. [167] When meantime Moses, that faithful and wise steward, perceived that the vice of sacrificing to idols had been deeply ingrained into the people from their association with the Egyptians, and the root of this evil could not be extracted from them, he allowed them indeed to sacrifice, but permitted it to be done only to God, that by any means he might cut off one half of the deeply ingrained evil, leaving the other half to be corrected by another, at a future time . . .» *(Rec* I:35:1 - 36:1).

It is not difficult to recognize the same idea here as in Justin, neither is it difficult to see that the AJ II has preserved it in a simpler and more original

---

164. Hints in the NT: Gal 3:19; Acts 7:38.53; Heb 2:2. Some Jewish texts: Deut 33:2 LXX, *Jub.* 1:27ff; Philo *De Somn.* I:142f; Josephus *Ant.* XV:136; *Cant.Rab.* I:2 § 2 (pp. 21f); *Pes. Rab.* 21 (103b/104a). For comments, see i.a. Schlier, *comm. ad* Gal 3:19; E.E. Ellis, *Paul's Use of the Old Testament* (Edinburgh/London, 1957), pp. 65f. Concerning the rabbinic material, cf. P. Schäfer, *Rivalität zwischen Engeln und Menschen. Untersuchungen zur rabbinischen Engelvorstellung* (Studia Judaica 8, Berlin/New York, 1975), pp. 44-51. Schäfer demonstrates how the rabbis later tended to diminish or exclude the mediating role of the angels - probably in reaction to Christian exploitation of the idea.

165. On the relationship between Barnabas and Justin on this point, cf. P. G. Verweijs, *Evangelium und neues Gesetz in der ältesten Christenheit bis auf Marcion* (Utrecht, 1960), p. 229.

166. Justin's enumeration of the miracles during the desert wandering has an element of rabbinic haggadah: The clothes of the children grew along with them (*Dial.* 131:6) - cf. the rabbinic parallels gathered by Ginzberg, III, p. 237; VI, p. 83; and L Williams, note *ad loc.* (p. 272).

167. This is not the reason for the 40 years given in the OT, but it agrees with *Ex.Rab.* 30:7 (p. 354); *Cant.Rab.* 5:5 (p. 236). Cf. esp. L. Smolar and M. Aberbach, 'The Golden Calf Episode in Postbiblical Literature', *HUCA* 39 (1968, pp. 91-116), p. 105.

version. *Only the sacrificial cult is envisaged* - there is in AJ II no anti-sabbath or anticircumcision polemic (cf. above, p. 297). The correspondence between Israel's sin and the remedy is thus much simpler than in Justin: The *vitium idolis immolandi* is temporarily and partly repaired by *the sacrificial cult.*

There is no question in AJ II of a special, inherent sinfulness of the Jews -their tendency to idolatry is a product of bad influence from the Egyptians. There is nothing like Justin's gross anti-Jewish twist to the idea (viz. Israel inherently more sinful than the rest of mankind). The catchword σκληρο-καρδία is lacking.[168]

It seems we have in AJ II, in a more primitive, original version, the Judaeo-Christian conception underlying Justin's polemic in *Dial.* 19:5f etc.[169]

The Judaeo-Christian character of this tradition is rendered likely also by the fact that the conception very likely is of Jewish origin. The Amora R. Levi (3rd cent.) explained the sacrificial cult in a vein very similar to AJ II: «Because Israel were passionate followers after idolatry in Egypt and used to bring their sacrifices to the satyrs, as it is written, 'And they shall no more sacrifice their sacrifices unto the satyrs' (Lev 17:7) - and these satyrs are nought but demons, as is borne out by the text which says, 'They sacrificed unto demons, no-gods' (Deut 32:17), these demons being nought but satyrs . . . - and they used to offer their sacrifices in the forbidden high places, on account of which punishments used to come upon them, the Holy One, blessed be he, said:' Let them offer their sacrifices to me at all times in the Tent of Meeting, and thus they will be separated from idolatry and saved from punishment.» (*Lev.Rab.* 22:8, pp. 286f - the text is a midrash on Lev 17:3).[170] Although this text is later than AJ II and Justin, it seems unreasonable to suppose that the idea was taken over from Christian sources by the rabbis. It was probably the other way round.[171] Mildly

---

168. K. Berger's attempt to read the concept of σκληροκαρδία into the *Rec.* I text is hardly convincing, *art. cit.* pp. 21f. Berger streamlines the material unduly, cf. the justified criticism in H. Hübner, 'Mark. VII:I-23 und das 'jüdisch-hellenistische Gesetzesverstandniss'', *NTS* 22 (1976), pp. 319-345.

169. It is interesting to notice that the idea of AJ II is carried on independently of Justin - in the Syrian *Didascalia*. The *Didascalia* on this point may betray continued contact with rabbinic ideas. Cf. Simon, *Verus Israel*, pp. 114116; Schoeps, *Judenchristentum*, pp. 61f/224f.

170. Cf. A. Marmorstein, *The Old Rabbinic Doctrine of God II: Essays in Anthropomorphism* (1937 (repr. New York, 1968)), pp. 89f; E. E. Urbach, *The Sages* I, p. 368. Essentially the same reason for the sacrificial cult is repeated in Maimonides, *Guide of the Perplexed*, IIII:32.44.

171. Marmorstein, *op.cit.*, pp. 90f, speculates that already Philo in *De Vita Mos.* 15:87 attacks a similar idea. Philo writes: «They (the Jews) told him (Pharaoh) that their ancestral sacrifices must be performed in the desert, as they did not conform with those of the rest of mankind, but so exceptional were the customs peculiar to the Hebrews that their rule and method of sacrifices ran counter to the common course.» One has to agree with Marmorstein that such a passage would be perfectly suited as an indirect polemic against Rabbi Levi's idea; but Philo's passage does not call for any counter-position to be intelligible, and Marmorstein may be reading into the text a polemic intention foreign to Philo.

anti-temple and antisacrificial tendencies are not unknown among the Pharisees even prior to 70 AD,[172] and may have been strenghtened after the abolition of the Temple cult.[173]

It is evident that in AJ II the fall of the Temple has played a major role; it is seen as the final proof that God repudiates the sacrificial cult: The whole Jewish history teaches that «a people who offer sacrifices are driven away and delivered up into the hands of the enemy, but they who do mercy and righteousness are without sacrifices freed from captivity, and restored to their native land.» (*Rec.* I:37:4).

This same chapter of AJ II contains the notion that God chose Jerusalem as the only legitimate place of sacrificing *in order* to put an end to sacrificing through the destruction of the city. This idea also recurs in Justin, *Dial.* 40:2: «God does not allow the sheep of the Passover to be sacrificed at any other place than that on which his name has been called, knowing that there would come a time ... when even the place of Jerusalem would be handed over to your enemies, and all offerings should completely cease to be.» In *Dial.* 46:2 Trypho recognizes that all offerings (προσφοράς) are now come to an end.

The same paragraph in the *Dialogue* is very instructive concerning Justin's use of the anti-sacrificial argument in AJ II. Justin is aware that the issue between him and Trypho is not really the sacrificial cult. The disputed matters are well summarized by Trypho in *Dial.* 46:2: the observance of the sabbath, and circumcision, and keeping the monthly feasts, and washing (cf. the corresponding enumerations in *Dial.* 8:4; 10:1.3; 18:3). These practices are entirely outside the scope of the argument advanced in AJ II. But Justin *has stretched the argument to somehow cover these practices also!* «For we should, in fact, be keeping even this circumcision ... and the sabbaths, and all the festivals, if we did not know the reason why it was enjoined ... on you, namely, because of your transgressions and hardness of heart» (*Dial.* 18:2). In *Dial.* 19:6 he keeps closer to the original idea: sacrifices commanded by God - but then Justin smuggles in the sabbath under the same heading, and in *Dial.* 20:1 continues with the dietary laws.

It is evident that Justin's use of the argument here is secondary compared with the AJ II. One further observation corroborates the impression that Justin is handling an idea coming to him from previous tradition: Justin strictly speaking never *establishes* his point by any kind of argument. He never argues that God enjoined the ceremonial laws as an accommodation to Israel's tendency to idolatry and apostasy - he simply takes this for granted.

One should observe, however, that even in his development of the primitive idea, Justin may not have been without contact with rabbinic

---

172. Cf. Schoeps, *Judenchristentum*, p. 228.
173. Cf. A. Guttmann, 'The End of the Jewish Sacrificial Cult', *HUCA* 38 (1969), pp. 137-148.

theology. Justin's contemporary, R. Meir, is reported to have said: «Why was the Torah given to Israel? Because they are impetuous» ( עזים , Str.Bill.III, p.97 translates: *starrsinnig*), *Betz.* 25b, p.130. This is a midrash on Ex 32:9 ('Behold, it is a stiffnecked people') as one can see from the parallel in *Ex. Rab.* 42:5.[174] R. Meir thus conceives of the Law as a means to discipline Israel. The same idea is contained in the continuance of the *Betzah* 25b passage: «The school of R.Ishmael (died ca 135) taught: 'At his right hand was a fiery law unto them'(Deut 33:2); the Holy One, blessed be he, said: These are worthy to be given a fiery law. Some say: The laws of these are like fire, for had not the Law been given to Israel no nation or tongue could withstand them. And this is what R. Simeon b. Lakish (ca 250) said: There are three distinguished in strength (or: impetuousness, עזים ): Israel among the nations, the dog among the animals, the cock among the birds.» In the somewhat parallel passage, *Ex.Rab* 42:9, p.493, one can observe how later rabbis tried to turn this motive into a positive saying about Israel: «R. Jakim (ca 350) said: Three are undaunted (impudent): among beasts, it is the dog; among birds, it is the cock; and among the nations it is Israel. R.Isaac b. Redifa (ca 330) said in the name of R. Ammi (ca 300): You think this is said disparagingly (viz. Ex 32:9: a stiffnecked people), but it is really in their praise; for it means: 'Either be a Jew or be prepared to be hanged'» (i.e. 'stiffnecked' = stubborn in their loyalty!).

But R. Meir's saying was certainly not meant in this vein. None among the rabbis was so harsh in his condemnation of the sin of the golden calf as R. Meir:[175] «It was not even one complete day (before they sinned), for while they were yet standing near Sinai, exclaiming 'We will do and obey', their hearts were already concentrated on idolatry, for it says, 'But they beguiled him with their mouth, and lied unto him with their tongue'» (Ps 78:36). (*Ex.Rab.* 42:8,pp.489f).In short, R. Meir seems to mean: Israel is an especially stiffnecked people; they therefore need special discipline: the Torah. There is no question here of the ceremonial components of the Torah, the Torah in its entirety is envisaged. Yet, if Justin was aware of this rabbinic conception - and he may well have been - he could take it as an argument for his amplification of the anti-sacrificial argument handed down to him by the Judaeo-Christian tradition. He would even find some support for his σκληροκαρδία argument.

---

174. The passage reads:«Another explanation of 'Go, get thee down'. R. Meir said: They need chastisement (*Red* = go down is connected by a play on words with *marduth*, chastisement). Whence do we know that this is what He said to him? You may know this from what God said to him, for it says 'And the Lord said unto Moses:'I have seen this people, and, behold, it is a stiffnecked people' (Ex 32:9). One does not say: 'So-and-so is stiffnecked' unless he needs chastisement. Our Sages too said: 'Go, get thee down' means, as R. Meir said, they need chastisement.» (p. 486). Cf. Urbach, *The Sages,* pp. 540f.
175. Cf. the survey of the rabbinic material in Smolar and Aberbach,'Golden Calf', *passim.*

To conclude: In his argument against the ceremonial laws as an accommodation necessitated by Israel's hardness of heart (golden calf episode),
Justin is dependent on a Judaeo-Christian idea concerning the sacrificial
cult.[176] Justin has extended the range of the argument to cover ceremonial
precepts originally not envisaged by the argument, and has sharpened the
criticism of Israel inherent in the argument. In so doing, he is not without
contact with contemporary Jewish exegesis.

It remains to be noted that the rabbis seem to have responded to the
challenge contained in Justin's argument. In a midrash on Deut 32:9, Deut
14:2 is quoted as a testimony to the continuing validity of Israel's election.[178]
E. Mihaly[178] remarks that this text was ideal in two respects: It is spoken after
the golden calf incident,[179] and it forms the introduction to dietary laws - i.e.
these are not punitive. This would accord perfectly with the sequence in
*Dial.* 19:6 - 20:1, although Mihaly concentrates on the parallels in *Barnabas.*

In order further to characterize Justin's concept, I must add a few words
on the positive counterpart to the «accommodation» theory, viz. the concept
that the Law also contains another element, «the eternal acts of righteousness» (τὰ αἰώνια δίκαια, *Dial.* 28:4; τὰ ἀεὶ καὶ δὶ ὅλου δίκαια, *Dial.* 93:1);
«the acts good, pious and righteous by nature» (τὰ φύσει καλὰ καὶ εὐσεβῆ

---

176. In his otherwise instructive discussion of Justin's concept of the law and of corresponding
    stages within salvation history, H. von Campenhausen has largely neglected the traditional
    background for Justin's concept of the law (*Die Entstehung der christlichen Bibel* (BHTh 39,
    Tübingen, 1968), pp. 115-120). He therefore takes Justin's concept to be his own invention
    -inspired from Paul and Luke, necessitated by Marcion and the Gnostics. «*So ist der
    gewaltsame Ausweg verständlich, zu dem sich Justin entschliesst. Er hält am göttlichen
    Ursprung des ganzen Gesetzes fest; aber er stellt den zeremoniellen Teil für sich, indem er
    ihn nicht wie bisher nur prophetisch deutet, sondern als eine partikulare, allein die Juden
    angehende Lebensordnung interpretiert.*» (*Op. cit.*, p. 115). «*Justin hat seinen Weg unter dem
    Druck der neuen Fragestellung offensichtlich selbst gefunden. Der einzige Theologe, mit
    dem er sich ernstlich vergleichen lässt ist der Valentinianer Ptolemäus(!)*» (*Ibid.*, p. 118). I
    believe that Justin is here made much more creative than he really was. His conception of the
    law is no «*Ausweg, zu dem er sich entschliesst*». It is a piece of received tradition, ultimately
    deriving from Judaeo-Christian sources.
177. The passage is *Sifre Deut* to Deut 32:9. After Israel's election through Jacob has been
    established by means of Deut 32:9 and Ps 135:4 (this part of the midrash is quoted below,
    346f.), the midrash continues: «But the matter is still in doubt and we do not know whether the
    Holy One, blessed be he, chose Israel for himself as his treasure, or whether Israel chose the
    Holy one, blessed be he. It is said in Scripture,'And the Lord your God has chosen you to be
    his own treasure' (Deut 14:2). And from where in the Bible do we know that Jacob also
    chose God? It is said in the Scriptures,'Not like these is the portion of Jacob, for he (God) is
    the one who forms all things ... (Jer 10:16).» (Translation taken from E. Mihaly's article (next
    note), p. 114).
178. E. Mihaly,'A Rabbinic Defense of the Election of Israel. An Analysis of Sifre Deuteronomy 32:9,
    Pisqa 312', *HUCA* 35 (1964), pp. 103-143.
179. Mihaly takes «the matter still in doubt» to be whether Israel's election still was valid after the
    golden calf episode, *art. cit.*, pp. 119-123. He believes the author of the midrash is answering
    challenges presented by *Barnabas* and Justin.

καὶ δίκαια, *Dial.* 45:3, cf. *Dial.* 93:1); or simply τὰ δίκαια, *Dial.* 23:1.5; 30:1. In *Dial.* 93:1, Justin is grappling with the idea of a νόμος φύσεως althouth he does not employ this term, which was formed by Philo,[180] and may have been widespread in Hellenistic Judaism in Justin's day. But for Philo the νόμος φύσεως is the entire Mosaic Law. Justin's idea of a bipartite division within the Law, only one part representing the νόμος φύσεως, may have been preformed in Judaeo-Christian tradition. In AJ II we meet a similar division within the Law: The ten commandments, and especially the first, are eternally valid, while the ceremonial law is only a temporary admission.

Justin never gives a complete enumeration of the eternal components of the Law, but he has some hints:

(1) Every race of men is aware that adultery (μοιχεία) is evil, and fornication (πορνεία), and murder (ἀνδροφονία), and all suchlike things, *Dial.* 93:1.

(2) The double commandment of love and the Golden Rule, *Dial.* 93:2f.

One is reminded of the proselyte catechism in the *Didache*. If one subtracts the Jesus *logia* in *Did.* 1:3-6, one is left with the following text: (1) The way of life is this: «First, thou shalt love the God who made thee, secondly, thy neighbour as thyself; and whatsoever thou wouldst not have done to thyself, do not thou to another» (*Did.* 1:2); (2) «But the second commandment of the teaching is this: οὐ φονεύσεις, οὐ μοιχεύσεις, οὐ παιδοφθορήσεις, οὐ πορνεύσεις . . .

Except for the inversion of the two components, Justin's text in *Dial.* 93:1-3 reads like a paraphrase and comment on a proselyte catechism like the one in *Didache.*

This would be another indication of the missionary setting from which Justin's material derive. It may be more than a coincidence that it is in a missionary text we find perhaps the closest Jewish parallel to this rejection of the sarificial cult. In the *Fourth Sibyl* we read the following: »Happy shall those men be throughout the earth who shall truly love the Mighty God, blessing Him before eating and drinking, staunch in their godliness. Who, when they see them, shall disown all temples and altars, vain erections of senseless stones, befouled with constant blood of living things and sacrifices of four-footed beasts. But they shall look to the great glory of the one God, neither comitting dastard murder, nor bartering for dishonest gain . . .« (vss. 24-31). I believe those scholars are right who here find a general rejection of *all* temple cult, the (now fallen) Jerusalem Temple not excep-

---

180. This is shown by H. Koester, 'Νομος φυσεως. The concept of Natural Law in Greek Thought', *Religions in Anitquity. Essays in Memory of E. R. Goodenough* (Studies in the History of Religions, Suppl. to Numen 14, Leiden, 1968), pp. 521-41. Concerning the concept of natural law in Justin, cf. the valuable discussion in C. Andresen, *Logos und Nomos*, pp. 327-334.

ted.[181] (One may also suggest that some Diaspora Jews who had learnt to despise the pagan sacrifices in their surroundings could have reacted with very mixed feelings when they came to Jerusalem and watched the sacrificial cult of the Temple). [182] Another testimony of such a-cultic, purely ethical Jewish preaching to Gentiles, are the sentences of Pseudo-Phokylides.[183]

I have indicated above that Acts 7 in some respects contains anticipations of Justin's tradition concerning the sacrificial cult. The interpretation of Acts 7 is notoriously difficult and controversial. If one follows the lead of i. a. M. Simon, one would seek the originators of Justin's tradition among the «Hellenists» of the early community in Jerusalem.[184] I am not prepared in the context of the present study to enter on anything like a full discussion of the complex issues involved in the interpretation and traditio-historical analysis of Stephen's speech. Let me just make the following brief remarks:

(1) While there are points of contact between Justin's tradition and Acts 7, there is no trace in Acts 7 of the idea that some Mosaic commandments were punitive and temporary, and this idea is basic to Justin's tradition. (2) In its most pure and primitive version we meet Justin's tradition in the AJ II, and here the authority claimed is *James,* not any of the «Hellenists». (3) We are hardly in a position which allows very definite statements about the relationship between the «Hellenists» and the rest of the Jerusalem community with regard to their position *vis à vis* the sacrifices of the temple service. Obviously Stephen was taken by his adversaries to denigrate the temple, but so was Jesus, and we have no suffficient evidence to claim that only the «Hellenists» understood and carried on the position of Jesus with regard to the temple and its sacrifices.

While the sources hardly allow us to get a very clear picture of the various factions in the Jerusalem community, they do indicate that the kind of criticism of the sacrificial cult we meet in Justin somehow can be traced back to the early community in Jerusalem. The «Pella connexion» provided

---

181. Cf. i.a. B. Noack,'Are the Essenes referred to in the Sibylline oracles', *StTh* 17 (1963, pp. 90-102), pp. 97f; V. Nikiprowetzky, 'Reflexions sur quelques problémes du quatrième et du cinquième livre des Oracles Sibyllins', *HUCA* 43 (1972, pp. 29-76), pp. 56f; and esp. J. J. Collins, 'The Place of the Fourth Sibyl in the Development of the Jewish Sibyllina', *JJS* 25 (1974, pp. 365-80), pp. 368f. «We should emphasise that Sib IV is not directly attacking the Jerusalem temple on any interpretation. Rather the author ignores it, to the extent that he fails to distinguish it from pagan temples. This neglect is itself a form of attack . . .» (Collins, p. 369). As we have noticed already (above, note 126), the Fourth Sibyl puts conversion and baptism in the place of sacrifices - again a striking parallel to the conception of the AJ II.
182. M. Hengel ('Die Ursprünge der christlichen Mission', *NTS* 18 (1971/72), pp. 15-38) suggests that this reaction was common among Diaspora Jews visiting Jerusalem (pp. 27-29). But we lack evidence to substantiate such a generalization.
183. Cf. A. Kurfess, 'Das Mahngedicht des sogenannten Phocylides im zweiten Buch der Oracula Sibyllina', *ZNW* 38 (1939), pp. 171-181; P. W. van der Horst, *The Sentences of Pseudo-Phocylides. With Introduction and Commentary (Studia in Veteris Testamenti Pseudepigrapha* 4), Leiden, 1978, esp. pp. 64-67.
184. Cf. above, p.315, n.163.

by the AJ II is in this perspective of considerable relevance. At the same time one can hardly escape the impression that the catastrophe of the year 70 AD has left such a deep imprint on the tradition in Justin's and the AJ II version, that the attempt to trace it to specific milieus prior to 70 is utterly delicate.

Excursus I: *A tripartite division of the Law in Justin?*

In his instructive monograph on Justin Martyr and the Mosaic Law, Th. Stylianopoulos argues that there is a tripartite division of the Law in Justin.[185] He complains that "the tripartite division of the Law has not received much attention by students of Justin."[186] According to Stylianopoulos, Justin divides the Law into the following three components:
(1) The ethical commandments, "those things that are by nature good and pious and just" (*Dial* 45:3).
(2) Commandments intended as types, prophecies.
(3) Commandments given as accommodations to Israel's hardness of heart.
Stylianopoulos relates this tripartite pattern to the Gnostic theory propounded in Ptolemy's letter to Flora: The Law has three parts according to its three authors, God, Moses, and the Jewish elders. There is a decreasing religious value in the three parts. Within God's Law, Ptolemy differentiates between (1) the Decalogue, (2) the law of defense and retaliation, and (3) the ritual commandments.
On this background, Stylianopoulos thinks that Justin's tripartite division is meant as an orthodox rebuttal, mainly directed against the Gnostics and Marcion, and shaped in the battle on that front.[187] Justin's scheme is hailed by Stylianopoulos as a "landmark in the history of Christian exegesis."[188]
I find Stylianopoulos' thesis misleading. Even if one grants the existence of a tripartite scheme in Justin, it has only a very superficial similarity to Ptolemy's theory - a fact which Stylianopoulos himself fairly points out.[189] But there is no tripartite division of the Law in Justin. The commandments given because of σκληροκαρδία and the commandments with a typological significance are not two different classes of precepts - they are, largely, *the same precepts viewed from two different angles.*
Stylianopoulos' argument for the thesis that two categories are envisaged by Justin can be summarized thus:
(1) The ἤ - ἤ in *Dial.* 44:2 should be read as an exclusive alternative: "... one commandment was appointed for piety and the practice of righteousness, and another command and action was in the same way spoken *either* as referring to the mystery of Christ *or* on account of the hardness of your peoples heart."[190]
(2) This either/or alternative is observed by Justin in his treatment of the different precepts: one and the same precept is never said to be given due to σκληροκαρδία, and at the same time given a typological interpretation (circumcision excepted).[191]
The second of these statements is not correct. Apart from circumcision, Justin can treat the sabbath; the festivals, including Atonement Day; the sacrifices in general; and the Temple, in both ways: as types, *and* as accommodations to Israel's hardness of heart. Both points of view are meant to comprise the entire ceremonial law, cf. e.g. *Dial.* 18:2 (*all* ritual commandments an accommodation) with *Dial.* 42:4 (*all* Mosaic precepts capable of a typological interpretation). Stylianopoulos has to admit this, and says that *Dial.* 42:4 is "inconsistent with Justin's tripartite division of the Law."[192] True - but the tripartite division is Stylianopou-

---

185. Th. Stylianopoulos, *Justin Martyr and the Mosaic Law* (SBL Diss. Ser. 20, Missoula, 1975).
186. *Ibid.*, p. 53.
187. *Op.cit.*, pp. 68/74-76. Stylianopoulos develops suggestions made by von Campenhausen, *op. cit.*, pp. 118f, cf. the quotation above, p.320, n.176.
188. *Op.cit.*, p. 53.
189. *Ibid.*, p. 55, esp. n. 27.
190. *Ibid.*, p. 61.
191. *Ibid.*, pp. 61-63.
192. *Ibid.*, p. 60.

los', not Justin's. I believe Stylianopoulos has had a right feeling when he qualifies his theory with the following wise reservation: «There is, therefore, a material unity between these two categories which . . . constitute one ritual law having two functions rather than two «divisions».»[193] Exactly!

His argument concerning the ἤ - ἤ alternative in *Dial.* 44:2 is equally difficult to grant. According to the Greek grammars I have consulted, this construction need not always express an absolute alternative.[194] In any case, the syntax of Justin's sentence would seem to imply no more than that there are two possible aspects to every command belonging to the ceremonial law. The passage as a whole speaks about a two-fold, not a three-fold division of the Law.

## (c) The righteous Patriarchs.

The material we are here going to investigate, is summarized above, 171. As one can easily see, there are several interconnected arguments, but the two most important ones can be branded the »Patriarch« and the »nature« argument respectively: (1) The Patriarchs were righteous without any ceremonial observances (esp. circumcision and sabbath); (2) Nature (or God) does not observe circumcision or sabbath.

One should note especially the passage in *Dial.* 23:3: »To you, Trypho, and to those who wish to become proselytes, I proclaim a Divine word which I heard from that Old Man. You see that nature does not idle nor keep sabbath. Abide as ye have been born. For if before Abraham there was no need of circumcision, and before Moses none of keeping the sabbaths, and of festivals, and of offerings, neither in like manner is there any need now, after . . . Jesus Christ has been born . . .« I think the very setting here is telling: This kind of argument is used to prove to would-be proselytes, i.e. Gentile God-fearers, that they need not worry about circumcision or the other ceremonial observances of the Torah. This probably reflects the original *Sitz im Leben* of this kind of argument within the Christian tradition.

It seems the argument is older than Christianity. The indirect polemic against the »Patriarch« argument in the *Book of Jubilees* may indicate that the argument was used by extreme »hellenizers« within the Jewish community as early as the second century B.C. *Jubilees* ascribes observance of several Mosaic practices to the Patriarchs,[195] *Test. Lev.* 9:6ff likewise. Philo knows of Jews who discard literal observance of the ceremonial precepts. Philo himself - as a rebuttal? - tends to project the Mosaic law back to the patriarchal period. The Patriarchs not only observed the law before it was

---

193. *Ibid.*, p. 63.
194. Blass-Debrunner-Rehkopf, § 446 (pp. 375f); Kühner-Gerth II:2, § 538:2 (p. 297): η sometimes = Latin *sive*.
195. Even the angels observe the Sabbath, *Jub.* 2:17f. Noah observed the festal calendar, *Jub.* 6:1ff. Abraham observed the sacrificial commandments, *Jub.* 15:1ff, celebrated the feast of tabernacles, 16:21-31 (it is an eternal, timeless command ordained in the heavenly tables). He celebrated the feast of Passover, 18:18f, and enjoined (partly Mosaic) commandments concerning sacrifice upon Isaac, 21:7ff - etc.

given - they were themselves νόμοι ἔμψυχοι.[196] The Rabbis also state that the Patriarchs observed the Torah. «We find that Abraham our father had performed the whole Law before it was given . . .», *M. Kid.* 4:14.[197]

The «nature» argument is also known to the rabbis. «A pagan sage asked Rabbi (Judah) : If circumcision is so beloved (of God), why was the mark of circumcision not given to Adam at his creation?», *Pes. Rab.* 23:4.[198] A *min* in Rome asked R. Gamaliel, R. Joshua, R. Eliezer b. Azariah, and R. Akiba why God did not keep his own commandment concerning the sabbath, *Ex.Rab.* 30:9, pp.355f. The rabbis answer that God does in fact observe the sabbath - the world is his courtyard, and the blowing of winds on the sabbath is therefore no violation of the sabbath rest.[199] The answer to the «Patriarch» argument concerning circumcision was to state that the Patriarchs in fact were born circumcised.[200] One can easily see from this that the rabbis took great pains to refute these arguments, and the forced statements to which they were driven, show the considerable strength of Justin's exposition.[201]

Let us finally emphasise the implication in *Dial.* 23:3, viz. that this kind of argumentation was something handed down to Justin by his Christian teacher - or teachers. It seems we are right to conclude that Justin draws upon a tradition which had its setting in the mission to Gentile God-fearers.

---

196. *De Abr.* I :5: οἱ γὰρ ἔμψυχοι καὶ λογικοὶ νόμοι ἄνδρες ἐκεῖνοι γεγόνασιν. The patriarchs «before any at all of the particular statutes was set in writing followed the unwritten law with perfect ease, so that one might properly say that the enacted laws are nothing else than memorials of the life of the ancients, preserving to a later generation their actual words and deeds.» (*Ibid.*). Cf. also *De Dec.* I:1: The patriarchs are νόμοι ἄγραφοι. Philo's polemic against non-observant Jews is found in *De Migr.* I:150. J. Bergmann describes the attitude of these Jews in the following words: «*Sie suchten den Konflikt zwischen philosophischer Bildung und jüdischer Religionsübung zu lösen, und wenn sie sich nicht zu dem Kompromiss der allegorischen Gesetzesauslegung entschlossen, fanden sie die Lösung in der Verwerfung des jüdischen Zeremonialgesetzes. Sie beriefen sich dabei auf die Erzväter die das Gesetz nicht gekannt und nicht geübt und dennoch um ihres frommes Wandelns willen Gottes wohlgefallen erlangt hatten.*» (J. Bergmann, *Jüdische Apologetik im neutestamentlichen Zeitalter* (Berlin 1908), p. 98). Bergmann here hypothetically reconstructs their position from the indirect and direct polemic in *Jubilees* and Philo. I know of no direct, contemporary witness to this point of view, but Bergmann's proposal seems likely enough.
197. Cf. A. Marmorstein, 'Quelques problèmes de l'ancienne apologétique juive', *REJ* 67 (1914, pp. 161-173), pp. 161-163. Marmorstein i.a. refers to *Sifre Deut* 336 (Jacob observed all the ordinances of the Torah; the same in *Gen.Rab.* 63:15); *M. Kid.* 4:14: «And we find that Abraham our father had performed the whole Law before it was given, for it is written:(Gen 26:5)»; cf. the parallel in *Yoma* 28b (pp. 133f) and cf. further *Gen.Rab.* 95:2; *Lev.Rab.* 2:9. One also finds rabbinic attempts to denigrate the righteousness of the patriarchs, cf. Goldfahn, p. 260, who refers to *Gen.Rab.* 25 *ad* Gen 5:24. Cf. also Friedländer, *Studien*, p. 98.
198. Braude, p. 478. In *Gen. Rab.* 46:3 (p. 390) the same question is asked by Abraham.
199. Cf. Marmorstein, *art. cit.*, p. 165.
200. Cf. Friedländer, *Studien*, pp. 97f, who refers to *Gen. Jalkuth* 1. Cf. also K. Hruby, 'Exégèse rabbinique et exégèse patristique', *RSR* 47 (1973, pp. 341-372), p. 349; and Ginzberg V, pp. 268f. Another rabbinic rebuttal is to deny the righteousness of patriarchs like Enoch, cf. e.g. *Gen.Rab.* 25:1 (p. 205).
201. I believe Friedländer , *loc. cit*, is right to stress this.

*Conclusions:*

It seems one can discern two layers in Justin's material on the Law. We find a typologizing of the OT cult centered around baptism, and an argument concerning the sacrificial cult as an accomodation made necessary by Israel's proneness towards idolatry. This is close to the Judaeo-Christian tradition encountered in the AJ II. But in Justin there is a radicalization of this. The anticultic polemic is made to cover all ritual concepts in the OT - sabbath and circumcision included. The argument concerning the uncircumcised patriarchs clearly belongs to this second stratum - it would be unthinkable in the AJ II. But Justin handles it as a selfexplanatory, compelling argument. This speaks for a received tradition - cf. his own statement about the «divine word» he received from the Old Man, *Dial.* 23.

It seems we are facing a Judaeo-Christian substratum which has passed through Gentile Christian hands before it reached Justin. The setting seems to be the mission to Gentile God-fearers.

## 4. *The new people in the new Jerusalem.*

In this chapter I am going to discuss two closely interrelated concepts in Justin: his people of God idea and the eschatology of the «kerygma» tradition. Let me begin with some remarks on the people of God problem.

In a recent study,[202] P. Richardson has argued that Justin is the first who claims that the Church is «Israel». Richardson's thesis contradicts the view that this claim was regarded as evident and selfexplanatory by almost all early Christians.[203] I shall take this question is a point of departure in the following analyses. Richardson has compared Justin with his Christian precursors, but he has not asked the question how the «Israel» concept is applied in Justin's inherited tradition. Is Justin an innovator, or is his conception already part of the tradition on which he depends? Which motive led to the idea that the Church is «Israel»?

I shall thus use the «Israel» concept as one tool to characterize Justin's material concerning the people of God. Besides, I shall use two somewhat stylized schemes which I believe can be discerned already in the NT. They concern the relationship between Jews and Gentiles, and may be called the «association model» and the «substitution model» respectively. The association model may be delineated like this: The Jews who have come to belief in Jesus as the Messiah constitute the true Israel, the restored people of God, the continuance of the Israel of the OT. The believing Gentiles are *added* to this restored people of God. They become co-heirs, while the

---

202. P. Richardson, *Israel in the Apostolic Church* (SNTSt Mon. Ser. 10, Cambridge, 1969).
203. Cf. as a representative example von Harnack's statement: «*Sofern man sich aber als Volk fühlte, wusste man sich als das wahre Israel, als das neue Volk und als das alte zugleich.*» (*Mission* I, p. 259).

Jews remain the heirs. The substitution model, on the other hand, focuses on the unbelief of the Jews. As a whole, the Jewish nation has rejected the Gospel of the Kingdom, thereby forfeiting their right to the Kingdom. It is taken from them and given to the Gentiles, who thus take the place of the Jews as God's chosen people, while individual Jews join this people.

There need be no absolute contradiction between these two models. The one focuses on the relationship between Gentiles and *believing* Jews, the other on Gentiles and *disbelieving* Jews. Yet there is a marked difference which has to do with the evaluation of Israel's response to the Gospel. In the substitution model, Israel is seen as essentially disbelieving. In the association model, only a part of Israel is disbelieving - and not forever.

One may name Paul a proponent of the »association« type, especially in Romans 11 (cf. also Eph 2). Matthew is perhaps the most profiled substitution theologian.[204] Judgements on Luke vary,[205] possibly because the historian Luke has taken up traditions pointing in both directions.

I now turn to Justin's material, and as usual I start in the *Apology.*

(a) Gentiles instead of Jews.

That men of the Gentiles rather than the Jews would believe in Jesus, the Messiah, was for Justin part of the traditional proof from prophecy, *1.Apol.* 31:7. He takes this up in *1.Apol.* 49:1: »It was said . . . that the peoples of the Gentiles who were not looking for him would worship him, and that the Jews who were constantly looking for him would not recognize him when he came« (introducing Is 65:1-3). In the *Apology,* the theme is brought up once more in 53:3-12: » . . . we know that the Christians ἐξ ἐθνῶν are more numerous and truer than those from among the Jews and Samaritans. For all the other nations of mankind are called ἔθνη by the prophetic Spirit, while the Jewish and Samaritan tribes are called Ἰσραηλ and οἶκος Ἰακὼβ«, *1.Apol.* 53:3f. The last quoted passage may conveniently be taken as a point of departure for our enquiry.

First, Justin states that the Jewish people is called »Israel« and »House of Jacob« by the prophets, while the Gentiles are called ἔθνη. I suspect this

---

204. At least as interpreted by W. Trilling, *Das Wahre Israel, passim.*
205. J. Jervell in his essay 'The Divided People of God' (*Luke,* pp. 41-74) interprets Luke as a profiled »association« theologian, cf. Jervell's succinct statement: »The idea is that of a people (the true Israel = the believing Jews) and an associate people (= believing Gentiles)« (*Luke,* p. 143). S. G. Wilson, on the other hand, tends to take Luke as a »substitution« theologian, *The Gentiles and the Gentile Mission in Luke-Acts* (SNTS Mon. Ser. 23, Cambridge, 1973). Jervell emphasizes the importance of the mass conversion of Jews in the first chapters of Acts, but perhaps unduly neglects »substitution« motifs in Luke's Gospel. Cf. also the complex and balanced treatment of the subject in G. Lohfink, *Die Sammlung Israels. Eine Untersuchung zur lukanischen Ekklesiologie* (StANT 39, München, 1975) E. Franklin also stresses the importance of the idea of continuity for Luke: »The Gentiles are to be incorporated into the renewed Israel and so the continuity with God's initial covenant is to be maintained.« (*Christ the Lord,* p. 125).

little instruction on prophetic parlance is a piece of received tradition, and
for two reasons. (1) The instruction has no application to the two texts
quoted immediately afterwards, Is 54:1 and Is 1:9. None of the relevant
terms is contained in these texts. It is only when we come to the last text in
*1. Apol* 53, Jer 9:25, that we encounter Israel contrasted with the nations,
but still there is no mention of the House of Jacob. I think this indicates that
the little instruction in *1.Apol* 53:3f was not created *ad hoc* - it does not suit
the texts to which it has been attached. (2) Justin himself does not always
refer Israel and House of Jacob in the prophetic texts to the Jews (and
Samaritans). He sometimes takes these terms as designating the Christian
Church, *Dial* 11:5; 123:5-9; 135:3.5f; 136:1. This point granted, the next
thing to be observed is that this tradition includes the Samaritans in «Israel«.
I think this at once helps us to characterize the tradition a little more. In the
NT there are three writers who make explicit mention of the Samaritans:
Matthew, John, and Luke. For Matthew and John, the Samaritans do defini-
tely not belong to Israel; they are non-Jews, Mt 10:5f; John 4:9.22.

With Luke it is different. J.Jervell has argued - to my mind convincingly
- that Luke regarded the Samaritans as a part of the people of God.[206] They
may be unorthodox Jews (Lk 9:51-53), but they are not Gentiles. In Acts, the
first Gentile to be baptized is Cornelius in ch. 10 - and his conversion and
baptism raise the cardinal problem in a mission to uncircumcised Gentiles:
Must they be circumcised to become participants in God's salvation? The
Samaritans in ch. 8 create no similar problem. The border between Israel
and the Gentiles is crossed in ch. 10, not in ch. 8.

Justin's tradition in *1.Apol* 53:3f is not alone in sharing this Lukan point of
view. AJ II includes the Samaritans among the Jewish sects, on a line with
Saducees, Pharisees, and disciples of John, *Rec.* I:54, cf. I:57. Hegesippus
likewise includes the Samaritans among Jewish sects (*apud* Eus. E.H.
IV:22:6). Hegesippus was a Jewish Christian, the author of AJ II likewise. As
we noticed, the instruction in *1.Apol* 53:3f does not suit the texts to which it
has been appended. This encourages us to took for other texts or passages
which may have been joined to this instruction. In *Dial* 24:3 we read: «. . .
he has dismissed[207] his people, *The house of Jacob* (= the Jews), . . . come,
πάντα τὰ ἔθνη.» As the passage in *1.Apol* 53 requires, «House of Jacob»
here means the Jews, who are contrasted with «all ye nations». Toghether
with Jer 9:25 - quoted in *Dial* 28:3 - this passage thus forms a perfect

---

206. Cf. Jervell, *Luke*, pp. 113-132 ('The Lost Sheep of the House of Israel. The Understanding of
the Samaritans in Luke-Acts').
207. I think the parallel in *Dial* 135:6 proves that ἀνῆκε in the Isaiah quotation in *Dial* 24:3
should be taken to mean «sent away«, «rejected« (= Archambault:'laisse allér', Prigent:
'rejeté'(*Justin*, p. 267)), not «set free« (= L. Williams), «liberated« (= Falls) (Haeuser
ambiguous:'entlassen'); in any case «rejected« must have been Justin's understanding of the
text. But even if Justin's source took a more positive view of the salvation of Israel than Justin
himself, it could hardly speak of the salvation of the «House of Jacob» as a present,
accomplished fact.

counterpart to *1. Apol* 53:3f. We have seen already (above, 72/291f) that Jer 9:25 very likely belonged to the tradition treating the devastation of Judaea: Expulsion of Jews from Jerusalem. *Dial.* 24:3 forms a perfect counterpart: Invitation to «the nations» to enter Jerusalem.

This is clearly «substitution» theology. It should be emphasized that it does not automatically imply a transfer of the *term* «Israel» to the Church.

It may be useful to pause here and include a brief note on the use of «Israel» in Justin's precursors. Although the idea of the Church as the New Israel may not be entirely foreign to e.g. Matthew[208] - or the author of 1 Peter[209] - the term Israel is reserved for the Jews throughout the NT.[210] The same is true in Barnabas; here Israel is contrasted to «us» = the Christians. «For the scripture concerning him (= Christ) relates partly to Israel, partly to us» (5:2 - cf. 6:7.13; 8:1f.7; 11:1). «Israel» is often replaced by a simple «they». Turning to the *Kerygma Petrou*, we find the same: «any one of Israel» (Fragm 3) means a Jew; in the text of Jer 31:31 the author has had to change διαθήσομαι τῷ οἴκῳ Ισραηλ καὶ τῷ οἴκῳ Ιουδα διαθήκην καινήν (LXX) into διατίθεμαι ὑμῖν καινὴν διαθήκην - in order to be able to apply this text to the Christians. (It is significant that Justin has no similar problems in *Dial.* 11:3. For him the full LXX text is a testimony on Christians as it stands -i.e. «the house of Israel and Judah» refer to Christians! But even for Justin this was not self-explanatory. On this, see further below).

As far as I can see, the only Christian writer prior to Justin who refers «Israel» directly to the Church as such, is *1.Clem.* But even here, this is not his own language. «Israel» occurs within OT quotations applied to Christians.[211] We shall return to these passages below.

---

208. Cf. Richardson, *Israel*, pp. 188f; Trilling, *Das wahre Israel*, p. 213. Richardson emphasizes that Matthew never transfers the term Israel to the Church. cf. also S. Schulz, *Die Stunde der Botschaft. Einführung in die Theologie der vier Evangelisten* (Hamburg/Zürich, 1970), p. 234.

209. «The Church has taken over the inheritance of Israel.» (Richardson, p. 174).

210. With the single possible exception Gal 6:16. Most interpreters take Paul's «the Israel of God» to refer to the Church, cf. esp. N. A. Dahl, 'Der Name Israel. Zur Auslegung von Gal. 6,16', *Judaica* 6 (1950), pp. 161-170. Dahl here defends this traditional interpretation against the argument of G. Schrenk that Paul has the Jewish believers in mind; Schrenk, 'Was bedeutet «Israel Gottes-?', *Judaica* 5 (1949), pp. 81-94. Schrenk in his turn answers Dahl in *Judaica* 6. pp. 170-190: 'Der Segenswunsch nach der Kampfepistel'. The present writer is inclined towards Schrenk's point of view. But one should also take seriously the interesting proposal of P. Richardson, viz. that Paul speaks about the Jewish nation in their capacity as future believers. Richardson suggests that καὶ ἐπὶ τὸν 'Ισραὴλ τοῦ θεοῦ may be a conscious allusion to the Jewish prayer formula וְעַל כֹּל יִשְׂרָאֵל as it is found e.g. in the 19th *beraka* of the *Shemoneh Esreh* (p. 79). «The change from *kol yisrael* to *Israel tou theou* can only be interpreted on the grounds that for Paul 'all Israel' is too ambiguous (though he uses it in Romans after a long discussion of his meaning); he expects that only a part, *Israel tou theou*, will be blessed in the way he says. There is an Israel (of God) within (all) Israel.» (p. 82).

211. In *1.Clem.* 29:2, Deut 32:8f is applied to the Church; in 8:3 an apocryphal OT exhortation to conversion, addressed to Israel, is quoted.

Let us state a provisional conclusion. Justin's little tract on the terms «Israel», «House of Jacob» and «the nations» in *1.Apol.* 53:3f seems to be related primarily to the texts in *1.Apol.* 53:11 and *Dial.* 24:3, and can thus be seen to form part of a traditional complex treating the devastation of Judaea. In its way of reserving «Israel» for the Jews, this tract shares the traditional way of speaking.

This warns us that the application of «Israel» etc. to the Church in Justin is not so self-explanatory as a modern theologian is apt to think.[212] This becomes even more striking when we observe that the tradition we have here studied, quite clearly belongs to the «substitution» type. «The nations» *take the place* of the House of Jacob.

This is not Pauline, and hardly Lukan. One is rather reminded of Matthew.[213] For Matthew, Israel (or«the Jews», 28:15) has rejected the Gospel, and τὰ ἔθνη are invited to take their place: 8:10f; 21:41.43; 22:1-10; 28:18-20. It should be noted that in Matthew - as in Justin's material - this theme is coupled to the theme of the murder of the Just Ones, Mt 22:1-10; 21:33-43; 23:29-39. Like Justin's tradition, Matthew does not express this substitution idea by transferring the *term* Israel to the Church.[214]

So far, we are entitled to speak of a tradition in Justin which uses «Israel» the same way as Luke (viz. including Samaritans), the AJ II and Hegesippus, and which thinks in «substitution» categories. In order to nuance the picture, I shall pursue the suggested parallel in AJ II a little further.

The idea that believers should be more numerous among the Gentiles than among the Jews, is a thought not foreign to AJ II (*Rec.*I:42:1; 50:2 (quoted above, 285); 63:2; 64:2). As we saw, there is an apologetic motive at play: The fact that Jesus has been accepted by the Gentiles rather than by his own people, does not disprove his Messiahship - on the contrary (see esp. *Rec.*I:50). But AJ II has more to say. The calling of the Gentiles is a motive with its own weight.

First we encounter the idea that believing Gentiles replace - not the Jews as a nation, but the unbelieving Jews within the Jewish nation. «Inasmuch as it was necessary that the *gentes* should be called into the room of those who remained unbelieving (among the Jews) , so that the number might be filled up which had been shown to Abraham, the preaching of the blessed kingdom of God is sent into all the world.»(*Rec.*I:42:1). According to AJ II the believing Jews became more numerous than the unbelieving (*Rec.*I:43; 71:1), nevertheless the unbelieving Jews have to be replaced, compensated by believing Gentiles.

---

212. P.Richardson also reaches the conclusion that Justin is the first in Christian literature to claim that Christians are «Israel», *op. cit.*, pp. 9/15f.
213. Cf. Trilling, *Das wahre Israel*, and Schulz, *op. cit.*, pp. 209-234.
214. Cf. Schulz, *ibid.*, p. 216: «*Matthäus wendet nirgends die Würdenamen Israels und der damit verbundenen Vorstellungen des Gottesvolkes auf die Kirche an. . . . Kirche ist vielmehr nach Matthäus als die Gemeinde des Messias (16:28) und als «Reich des Menschensohnes» (13:41) christologisch bestimmt und Israel gegenüber etwas Neues.*»

And in *Rec.*I 64:2 we meet one more viewpoint on the relation Jews/Gentiles: «Then (after the destruction of the Temple) the Gospel shall be preached to the Gentiles *for a testimony against you, that your unbelief may be judged by their faith.*» Some of Justin's testimonies on the New People theme would fit the material in AJ II perfectly. Jewish sacrifices are no longer pleasing to God, but the offerings of thanksgiving among the Gentiles are: Mal. 1:10-12. The faith of the Gentiles - who did not expect Christ - is an example to the Jews: Ps 18:45f (these two texts are quoted together in *Dial.* 28:5f). The Pauline testimony Is 65:1f also suits this context, cf. *Rec.*I:50.

All I want to suggest by this, is the possibility that there may be a substratum in Justin's material which only spoke of a partial rejection of the Jews - more in line with the AJ II. The close parallels to AJ II in other parts of the same tradition complex in Justin may indicate this. In its present shape, however, Justin's tradition has sharpened this rejection motive - now the Jewish nation as such is rejected. To put it bluntly: While in AJ II «the people» believe and only individual Jews are unbelieving, in Justin the people are disbelieving and only individual Jews are saved.

Let us pursue the idea of Christians as a «people» in Justin and his predecessors.

(b) The New People

Luke once speaks of the Gentile Christians as a λαός in a significant manner: . . . λαβεῖν ἐξ ἐθνῶν λαὸν τῷ ὀνόματι αὐτοῦ, Acts 15:14.[215] In Paul this parlance occurs within one of his Scriptural quotations: Hos 2:25 in Rom 9:25; but cf. also 2 Cor 6:16 and Tit 2:14.[216] With most emphasis, however, this is carried out in 1 Pt 2:9f (with allusions to Ex 19:6 and - again - Hos 2:25). Turning to the term ἔθνος, we find this applied to the Gentile Christians in 1 Pt 2:9 and, probably, Mt 21:43.

*1.Clem.* has in 8:3 a non-canonical Scripture quotation which contains the terms «house of Israel» and «holy people» (λαὸς ἅγιος). There can hardly be any doubt that *1.Clem.* applies these words to the Corinthian community. In the prayer at the end of the letter, the congregation applies to itself several OT terms: «. . . turn again the wanderers of thy people (τοῦ λαοῦ σου) . . . let all the nations know thee, that thou art God alone . . . and that we are thy people (λαός σου) and the sheep of thy pasture», 59:4. Here the Christian congregation prays in OT and Jewish prayer language.

---

215. On this text, see i.a. N. A. Dahl, 'A People for his name', *NTS* 4 (1957), pp. 319-327; J. Jervell, *Luke*, p. 72, n. 22; G. Lohfink, *Die Sammlung Israels*, pp. 58-60; S. G. Wilson, *Gentile Mission*, pp. 224f. - Acts 18;10 is more vague.

216. On the term λαος in Paul, cf. Richardson's excursus 'Paul's use of ΛΑΟΣ, *op. cit.*, pp. 211-216. «*Laos* is used .. to show how Gentiles can become incorporated into the people of God: they move from 'not my people' over into the *laos.* The term is not transferred to the Gentiles or even the Church as such; it is used in a universal sense, the point of the whole section being joint inheritance, with Israel still central.» (*Ibid*, p. 215 on Rom 9:25).

*2.Clem.* can also talk about Christians as a people, and does this apropos Is 54:1:« Our people seemed to be deserted by God, but . . . now we who have believed have become many more than those who seemed to have God», 2:3.

In Hermas the term λαός for Christians is quite frequent: *Sim.* V:5:2f; V:6:2f; *Sim.* VIII:1:2.5; 3:3; *Sim.* IX:18:4. Except for *2.Clem.*, none of these passages in the Apostolic Fathers contrasts the Christians with the Jews, or speaks about Christians as a *new* people or *another* people. It is only when we come to *Barnabas* that we meet a concept which is profiled in this respect. Christ suffered in order to «prepare for himself τὸν λαὸν τὸν καινὸν», 5:7. The Jewish priests will give Christ gall and vinegar to drink »when I am on the point of offering my flesh for my new people . . .», 7:5; «now let us see whether this people (= the Christians) or the former people is the heir, and whether the covenant is for us or for them», 13:1. The Christians, not the Jews, have received the covenant because they are λαός κληρονομίας, 14:4. Christ «should redeem us from darkness and prepare a λαὸς ἅγιος (Is 62:12) for himself», 14:6. Who these Christians - the «us» - are, is said in plain words in 13:7: «'Behold I have made thee, Abraham, the father of the Gentiles (πατέρα ἐθνῶν) who believe in God in uncircumcision'.»

Barnabas tries to find Scriptural support for the idea of two peoples, the Christians and the Jews. In 13:2-6 he offers two typologies: the two babies in Rebekah's womb (13:2f), and Jacob blessing the younger Ephraim to the disadvantage of the elder Manasseh (13:4-6). This kind of reasoning can be said to be carried on in Justin's typology in *Dial.* 134: Jacob's two wives. (A common feature in *Barnabas* and Justin is that the typologies are found in OT material relating to *Jacob.* The significance of this will be treated in the section on Christians as Jacob/Israel (below, pp. 346f).

In *Barnabas,* there are as yet only sparse allusions to direct prophecies about the new people. In 14:6 there is probably a reference to Is 62:12 - this text recurs in Justin.

Before we turn to Justin's material, let me remark briefly that the *Kerygma Petrou* has a profiled idea of the Christians as a third people (τρίτος γένος),[217] distinct from Greeks and Jews. This idea is not found in Justin, nor, as far as I can see, in his testimony material.

---

217. I have here followed the translation of *NT Apoc.* II, which takes τρίτῳ γένει as «as a third race». One could also contemplate the translation «in a third way», and in that case A. von Harnack's comment holds good:«*Das bemerkenswerte ist . . . dass er (der Verfasser) ganz bestimmt drei Arten feststellt . . . und das Christentum ausdrücklich als das neue, dritte genus der Gottesverehrung bezeichnet. . . . Nicht in drei Völker teilt unser Verfasser die Menschheit, sondern in drei Klassen von Gottesverehrern.*» (*Idem, Die Mission und Ausbreitung des Christentums* I (4th ed., Leipzig, 1924), n. 265). This concept of the KP is taken over by the *Apology* of Aristides, the *Epistle to Diognetus,* and in Ps. Cypr. *De Pascha Computus,* ch. 17. Cf. Harnack, *op. cit.,* pp. 265-267/281-289; H. Paulsen, 'Kerygma Petri', pp. 20f/26f. .

Justin's testimony dossier on the new people can be tabulated in the following way:

| | | |
|---|---|---|
| *Dial.* 24:2 | ἔθνος δίκαιον, λαὸς φυλάσσων πίστιν<br>ἀντιλαμβανόμενος ἀληθείας<br>καὶ φυλάσσων εἰρήνην | } Is 26:2f |
| *Dial.* 26:3 | καὶ καλέσει αὐτὸν λαόν ἅγιον . . . | =Is 62:12<br>(within long<br>quot. Is 62:10 - 63:6) |
| *Dial.* 119:3 | ἡμεῖς λαὸς ἕτερος . . .<br>καταφεύξονται ἔθνη . . . εἰς λαόν ⎤<br>καὶ λαὸς ἅγιός ἐσμεν . . .<br>καὶ καλέσουσιν αὐτὸν λαὸν ἅγιον ⎤ | =Zech 2:15<br><br>=Is 62:12 |

Let us first take a look at the Is 26:2f allusion in *Dial.* 24:2. It clearly presupposes a non-LXX version of the text, based on the Hebrew:

| MT | *Dial.* 24:2 | Is 26:2 LXX |
|---|---|---|
| גוֹי צַדִּיק<br>שֹׁמֵר אֱמֻנִים | ἔθνος δίκαιον<br>λαὸς φυλάσσων πίστιν | ἀνοίξατε πύλας<br>εἰσελθάτω<br>λαὸςᵃ φυλάσσων<br>δικαιοσύνην<br>καὶ φυλάσσων ἀλήθειαν |
| | Aquila:<br>ἀνοίξατε πύλας<br>[καὶ] εἰσελθετω<br>ἔθνος δίκαιον<br>φυλάττον πίστιν | a) Lucianic MSS pre-<br>fixe δίκαιος, MS 233<br>has δίκαιος after λαός.<br>This creates a double<br>rendering of צדיק<br>and is obviously a<br>later contamination. |

We have seen above that Zech 2:15 in *Dial.* 119:3 represent a deviant »testimony« version (above, p.73f). Is 62:12 in *Dial.* 119:3 also has a deviant reading: καλέσουσιν versus *Dial.* 26:3 = Is 62:12LXX: καλέσει. All this points to a testimony source. Is 26:2f is a text about the eschatological entry into Jerusalem. Zech 2:15 talks about Gentiles who go to live in Jerusalem when God has taken his abode there. In the deviant »testimony« text the Jerusalem motif is perhaps indicated in the reading καὶ κατασκηνώσουσιν ἐν μέσῳ τῆς γῆς πάσης. Is 62:12 also treats eschatological salvation in Jerusalem.

We thus see that the testimonies on the new people are not chosen at random. They display the same Jerusalem-centered idea which we met in the former section («Gentiles instead of Jews»). *Dial.* 24:2f indicates the unity of the tradition treated in this and the former section: The Gentiles = the new people will take the place of the Jews in Jerusalem. The whole tradition complex is related and complementary to the «devastation of Judaea» theme, and represents a «substitution» theology.

As in *Barnabas,* Christians are called the new people, the holy people of God. But they are not called «Israel». To complete my analysis of this strand of tradition in Justin, I include here some remarks on the *Jerusalem* and *land* motif.

(c) New circumcision and the conquest of the land.

(α) We begin in *Dial.* 113f.

Justin here says that just as a second circumcision was performed by Joshua before Israel could enter the land, so now a second circumcision is necessary to enter the land. We shall leave out for the moment the Joshua/Jesus typology involved in this idea, and concentrate on the «second» circumcision as a necessary prerequisite to enter the land. In fact, the rabbis were quite concerned about the circumcision performed by Joshua.«'And I will give unto thee, and to thy seed after thee, the land of thy sojournings' (Gen 17:8). R. Judan (ca 350) gave five interpretations of this... (The fourth:) If thy children accept circumcision, they will enter the promised Land; if not, they will not enter... R.Berekiah and R.Helbo (ca 300) in the name of R.Abin b.R.Jose[218] said: It is written, 'And this is the cause *(dabar)* why Joshua did circumcise'(Josh 5:4): Joshua spoke a word (dabar) to them, and circumcised them. 'What think you', said he upbraiding them, 'that you will enter the Land uncircumcised?'[219] Thus did the Holy One, blessed be he, say to Abraham, 'And I will give unto thee, and to thy seed after thee ..., providing that you fulfil the condition,' And as for thee, thou shalt keep my covenant.»*(Gen. Rab.* 46:9 pp. 394f).[220]

This passage can be read as a counter-polemic directed towards the kind of argument brought forward by Justin: circumcision now excludes from Jerusalem. The rabbi sticks to the literal meaning of the Joshua text: The ones circumcised by Joshua were not formerly circumcised, and the rite performed by Joshua was the same circumcision which was enjoined upon Abraham in Gen 17.

According to Justin, the ones circumcised by Joshua were already circumcised with the circumcision given to Abraham - that is why the Biblical text speaks about a *second* circumcision, *Dial.* 113:7. The second circumcision points forward to the spiritual circumcision abolishing the carnal rite, and being necessary also for those who are carnally circumcised.

---

218. Str. Bill. IV, p. 38:«*In diesem Namen steckt ein Fehler.*»
219. Ginzberg VI, p.172, n .6, suggests that already Josephus knew the rabbinic haggadah which made circumcision a prerequisite for entering the land. He refers to *Ant.* V:1:11: «This name (Galgala = Gilgal) signifies «freedom»; for, having crossed the river, they felt themselves henceforth free both from the Egyptians and from their miseries in the desert.» I quote Ginzberg's comment: «perhaps presupposes the view... that by performing the rite of circumcision at that place they definitely won their liberty.» An overinterpretation?
220. Rabbinic parallels listed in Ginzberg, *loc. cit.,* and Str. Bill. IV, p. 38.

There is a rabbinic passage which suggests that even some of the rabbis regarded the ones circumcised by Joshua as already circumcised with «Abrahamic» circumcision. «Rabbah b. Isaac stated in the name of Rab (died 247): The commandment of uncovering the corona at circumcision was not given to Abraham; for it is said, 'At that time the Lord said unto Joshua: Make thee knives of flint' etc. (Josh 5:2). But is it not possible (that this applied to) those who were not previously circumcised; for it is written, 'For all the people that came out were circumcised; but all the people that were born' etc. (Josh 5:5). - If so, why the expression 'Again'? (Josh 5:2). Consequently it must apply to the uncovering of the corona. Why, then, the expression 'A second time'? - To compare the termination of the circumcision with its commencement . . .« (*Yeb.* 71b, pp. 484f). There is thus reason to think that Justin's reasoning concerning the circumcision performed by Joshua was not without pretext in Jewish exegesis. The occurrence of a non-LXX allusion[221] may indicate a testimony source at play.

In order to bring Justin's material into sharper relief, let us review his Christian precursors. In several NT passages there is a general connexion between becoming a Christian and becoming heir to the »inheritance« - a term belonging to the »land« terms[222] in the OT: Eph 1:13f.18; Tit 3:5-7; 1 Pt 1:3-5. In these texts, however, the concept of the inheritance is to a high degree spiritualized - there is no reference to the concrete land of Palestine.[223]

The first writer who comes close to Justin's idea is the author of Hebrews. In 3:7 - 4:13 we find the great exposition of Ps 95:7-11, which has for its theme the entrance into the κατάπαυσις - another OT term for the land.[224] We first notice an antitypical juxtaposition of Joshua and Jesus. »For if Joshua had given them the rest, God would not speak later of another day«, 4:8. Jesus, not Joshua, brings his people into the »rest«.[225]

The same juxtaposition recurs in Justin, but with two modifications: In Justin the »rest« (ἀνάπαυσις) seems not to be spiritualized at all - the »rest« is the land, the promised land. And Joshua is not pictured so antitypically. While in Hebrews he did not bring the people into the »rest«, in Justin he did so, but only in a temporary fashion. »(Joshua) led the people into the Holy Land. And as he divided it by lot to them that entered with him, so also will

221. Viz. καὶ θημωνιὰς ποιήσας in *Dial.* 113:6. The standard LXX reading is βουνός, corresponding to MT גבעת . Cf. L.Williams, note *ad. loc.* (p. 234).
222. On the «inheritance» as a term for the land in the OT, see J. Hermann, art.' נחלה and נחל in the OT', *ThDNT* III, pp. 769-776.
223. Cf. i.a. W. Foerster, art.' κλῆρος etc. (E.)The Word Group in the New Testament', *ThDNT* III, pp. 781-785.
224. Cf. Michel, *comm.* p. 195; and esp. O. Hofius, *Katapausis. Die Vorstellung vom endzeitlichen Ruheort im Hebräerbrief* (WUNT 11. Tübingen, 1970), pp. 29-41.
225. «*Das, was Josua erreichte, war wohl ein Vorzeichen, aber nicht mehr; denn Israel blieb in der Anfechtung und im Nichtvollendetsein.*» (Michel, *loc. cit.*). Cf. also Daniélou, *Sacramentum Futuri,* pp. 204f.

Jesus the Christ turn the dispersion of the people, and will distribute the good land to each, though not again in the same manner. For the one (Joshua) gave them the inheritance for a time . . . but the other (Jesus) will, after the holy resurrection, give us our possession for ever.«*(Dial.* 113:3f).

There may be a further echo of the Joshua story in Heb 4:12: »The word of God is living and active, sharper (τομώτερος) than any two-edged sword (μάχαιραν) . . .« This may echo Joshua's »swords« in Josh 5:2f, the knives with which he circumcised the people.[226] It is said in Josh 5:3LXX that Joshua made μαχαίρας πετρίνας ἀκροτόμους. The idea in Heb 4:12 may be that the spiritual circumcision observed by Christians cuts much deeper than the carnal circumcision performed by Joshua's sharp swords - and this spiritual circumcision is necessary to enter the »rest«.

The parallel in Justin says: Christians are circumcised with »swords of stone« (Josh 5:2f), i.e. the words of Jesus, *Dial.* 113:6f; 114:4. Here we have the same antitypic relation between sword and word, although the typology is again more positive in Justin.[227]

Certainly Justin has not read his own material out from these rather cryptic allusions in Hebrews. What Hebrews proves, is the early date of the idea enshrined in Justin's material.

The next writer to claim our attention is *Barnabas.* In 6:8-19 we find a self-contained unit which seems inserted into the present context on feeble catchword connexions. The text is a kind of midrash on Ex 33:1.3,[228] which is quoted in a very modified mixed version (influence from Deut 1:25 and Lev 20:24): «Lo, thus saith the Lord God, enter into the good land which the Lord sware that he would give to Abraham, Isaac and Jacob, and inherit it, a land flowing with milk and honey.» It is irrelevant to our purpose to indulge in a full analysis of the intricate exposition following this text. It is enough to state that it operates with OT material which for the most part is not found in Justin. All the more striking are some coincidences in ideas.

(1) There is probably a Joshua/Jesus typology implied in the text. «Hope . . . on that Jesus who will be manifested to you in the flesh» (6:9) - because that Jesus, not Joshua, will bring you into the good land. This

---

226. This OT background was suggested by J. R. Harris, *Testimonies* II, p. 54; and the suggestion is taken up by R. Murray, 'The Exhortation to candidates for Ascetical Vows at Baptism in the Ancient Syriac Church', *NTS* 21 (1975, pp. 59-80), p. 67: »Though the suggestion has been largely ignored or rejected, I believe that he was right.« The present writer is inclined to do the same.

227. One may suggest that the Rahab typology in *Dial.* 111:4 is related to the Joshua typology of *Dial.* 113f. (The Joshua typology is present in the context of *Dial.* 111:4 also: *Dial.* 111:1f.4). In Jewish tradition, Rahab is one of the model *proselytes* of the OT (Str. Bill. I, pp. 20-23; cf. in the NT:Mt 1:5; Jas 2:25; Heb 11:31. Cf. also Daniélou, *Sacramentum Futuri,* pp. 217-221), and she became the *wife of Joshua* (Daniélou, *loc. cit,* does not mention this, but cf. Str. Bill. I, p. 23, and Ginzberg V; p. 171). For Christians versed in rabbinic haggadah, Rahab would thus be an ideal type of the Church: The Church is the bride of Jesus; Christians have turned from idolatry and immorality to true piety.

228. For literature, see above, p.300, n.129.

completion of *Barnabas'* sentence seems justified by 6:16: «We then are they whom he (Jesus) brought into the good land.»

(2) The entrance to the land comes through baptism. The land is a land flowing with milk and honey; milk and honey are the nourishment of newborn children; one has to become a newborn child to enter the land; one becomes a newborn child in baptism. This is the train of thought in the complex passage 6:10-17, as far as I am able to understand it. There is in this midrash no anticircumcision polemic, but instead of circumcision, baptism is the necessary condition for entering the land.

(3) The baptismal theology is embedded in the concept of a new creation. «See, I make the last things as the first.» (6:13). In *Barnabas'* midrash this motive is deeply integrated into the whole argument on baptism and the land.

In his exposition of the Jesus/Joshua typology in *Dial.* 113:3-7, Justin has a passage which seems to interrupt the exposition: «For this is he after whom (?)[229] and by whom the Father will renew the heaven and the earth.» (*Dial.* 113:5). The evidence in *Barnabas* may suggest that this motif of the new creation was more integral to Justin's material than his present text shows. As we shall see, his material in *Dial.* 138 confirms this.

It is only natural in connexion with Joshua to concentrate on the land. But I think it may be significant that even in *Dial.* 113 the Jerusalem motif breaks through. «This (Jesus) is he who is to shine in Jerusalem as an everlasting light. This is he who is always king of Salem and everlasting priest of the Most High, according to the order of Melchizedek.» ( *Dial.* 113:5).

In fact, the land and Jerusalem are to some extent interchangeable concepts in the tradition Justin is following. We observe this in the testimonies in *1.Apol.* 47: Is 64:9-11 speaks about Zion and Jerusalem, while the testimony which in its very text is adapted to the Hadrianic decree, Is 1:7/Jer 50:3, speaks about «the land». Justin in his comment could also be taken to mean that the Hadrianic decree excluded the Jews from the whole land, although *Dial.* 16:2 proves that he is fully aware that only Jerusalem is

---

229. I have rendered this passage quite literally, like the *ANF* translator (p.255). The text may be corrupt: οὖτος γάρ ἐστιν ἀφ' οὖ καὶ τὸν οὐρανὸν καὶ τὴν γῆν καὶ δι' οὖ ὁ πατὴρ μέλλει καινουργεῖν. L. Williams translates: «For this is He of whom the Father (made) the heaven and the earth, and by whom He will restore them.» But he also contemplates the alternative «at whose coming, and by whom, the Father will restore. . .» (cf. his note *ad loc.*, p. 233). Falls prefers the latter alternative: «After His coming the Father will, through Him, renew . . .» (p. 323). (Archambault similar, p. 183). Neither alternative seems entirely satisfactory. If one accepts the transmitted text, Haeuser's interpretation seems preferable: The renewal of heaven and earth *takes its beginning* in Christ's incarnation (this makes sense of the ἀπό): *«Jesus ist seiner menschlichen Natur nach das erste Geschöpf der neuen Weltordnung»* (note *ad loc.*, p. 183). Accordingly Haeuser translates:*«Bei der Erneuerung von Himmel und Erde nämlich fängt der Vater bei ihm an, und durch ihn will er die Neuschaffung bewerkstelligen.»* In any case, it is evident that the text enshrines a «recapitulation» idea of some sort, related to Col 1:18. Cf. below on *Dial.* 138.

concerned. The point is that to Justin's tradition and to Justin himself this distinction is immaterial. Jerusalem represents the whole land. The land is· «Jerusalem and the countryside round it» ( *Dial* 123:6 apropos Ezek 36:12).

*Dial* 113f is therefore a perfect counterpart to *1.Apol* 47 and *Dial* 16 (par. *Dial* 108). It is therefore only natural that *Dial* 113f ends with the traditional polemic testimony on Christian baptism versus Jewish lustrations, Jer 2:13 - in a combined version where the focus is on Jerusalem and the Hadrianic decree. The last element, Jer 3:8, reads: «I have given Jerusalem a bill of divorce in your sight.»

To conclude: Taken together, *Dial* 16 par. and *Dial* 113f state a very simple point of view: The «old» circumcision now excludes from Jerusalem/the land, while the new, the «second» circumcision admits to Jerusalem/the land.

This brings us back to the unmistakable characteristic of the tradition in *Dial* 113f when compared with Justin's Christian prececessors: Justin's tradition has *a remarkably concrete conception of the «inheritance».* Jerusalem and the land are at stake; the Hadrianic decree is a theologically important event.

It is hardly necessary to add that as far as the relationship between Church and Israel is concerned, this material represents the «substitution» model.

(β) *Dial* 138.[230]

The obvious point of comparison is 1 Pt 3:19-21. The following points are common:

The deluge is a type on Christian baptism.

Eight souls were saved.

Baptism derives its saving effect from Christ's resurrection.

In some particulars, Justin - or his source? - can be said to make explicit ideas which may be implicit in the text of 1 Pt,[231] or to complete and substantiate the basic ideas:

The eight souls were a type on the eighth day, on

which Christ rose from the dead.

The wood (ξύλον) which saved Noah is a type of the cross.[232]

---

230. On this important passage, cf. esp. P. Lundberg, *Typologie baptismale,* pp. 186f; J. Daniélou, *Sacramentum Futuri,* pp. 74-79; *idem, Gospel Message,* pp. 206f-208. Rich material from Jewish and Christian sources on Noah and the flood generally is collected in J. P. Lewis, *A study of the Interpretation of Noah and the Flood in Jewish and Christian Literature* (Leiden, 1968).

231. Cf. Kelly in his *comm. ad loc.:«*. . . there is probably a deeper significance in his mention of the number *eight*. For Christians this number designated the eighth day, i.e. the day on which Christ rose from the dead and on which the believer entered the Church by baptism, customarily administered early on Easter, the eighth day *par excellence.»* (Pp. 158f, - followed by a reference to *Dial* 138). Cf. further Lundberg, *Typologie baptismale,* pp. 98-116; Daniélou, *Sacramentum Futuri,* pp. 74f.

It is interesting to note that in Jewish texts the ark is likewise called a ξύλον, *Sap.Sal.* 10:4; 14:7.

The point where Justin adds a new dimension to the typology of 1 Pt, is his Noah/Christ typology. «For Christ, the firstborn of every creature (πρωτό-τοκος πάσης κτίσεως), has become again the head of another race (ἀρχὴ ἄλλου γένους), which was begotten anew of him (ἀναγεννηθέντος ὑπ' αὐτοῦ) by water and faith and wood (ξύλον)» (*Dial.* 138:2).

The concept of Noah as the ancestor of the new human race after the flood, «the head of another race», is known to Philo and hinted at in *Sap.Sal.* 14:6.[233] Philo says that Noah was «both the end and beginning (ἀρχή) of mankind.» *Quest. in Gen.* I:96. Noah was destined καὶ τέλος γενέσθαι τῆς κατακρίτου γενεᾶς καὶ ἀρχὴν τῆς ἀνυπαιτίου [γενεᾶς], *De praemiis* 23, cf. also *De Abr.* 46.[234] The rabbis also state that the world was reconstructed from one man, *Lev.Rab.* 5:1, p.61.[235]

This idea is turned into a magnificent typology on Christ in Justin's text. The resultant idea is remarkably close to Col 1:15ff:

| *Dial.* 138:2 | Col 1 |
|---|---|
| ὁ γὰρ Χριστός, | vss. 15f: Christ is... |
| πρωτότοκος πάσης κτίσεως ὤν | πρωτότοκος πάσης κτίσεως |
| | ὅτι ἐν αὐτῷ ἐκτίσθη τὰ πάντα... |
| καὶ ἀρχὴ πάλιν | vs. 18: ... ὅς ἐστιν ἀρχή |
| ἄλλου γένους γέγονε | πρωτότοκος |
| τοῦ ἀναγεννηθέντος ὑπ' αὐτοῦ... | ἐκ τῶν νεκρῶν... |

The Christological hymn in Col 1:15-20 has a two-step structure: Christ is mediator in the first creation (vss. 15-17), and he is head of the second creation brought about by his resurrection from the dead (vss. 18-20). The same structure is nicely preserved in Justin's text. At the same time there are differences: Col 1:18ff focuses on Christ's resurrection, *Dial.* 138:2 on the regeneration brought about in baptism. And the ἀρχή concept in Justin is so intimately linked to the Noah typology, that it hardly derives directly from Col 1:18. I am therefore inclined to believe that the similarities

---

232. On the ark as a ξύλον, type of the cross, cf. esp. G. Q. Reijners, *The Terminology of the Holy Cross in Early Christian Literature as based upon Old Testament Typology* (Graecitas Christianorum Primaeva 2, Nijmegen, 1965), pp. 45f.

233. Cf. also Sir 44:17f.

234. In *Vit. Mos.* II:63-65, Philo describes a complete rejuvenation of everything in nature after the deluge. The first Christian writer to echo this may be the author of *1. Clem.*, cf. *1.Clem.* 9:4:»Noah was found faithful in his service, in foretelling a new beginning to the world (παλιγγενεσίαν κόσμῳ).»

235. The passage is a midrash on Job 34:29 ('It was done to a nation, and to a man as one'):»By 'nation' is meant the generation of the flood, and by 'man' is meant Noah;'As one' means: He had to reconstitute His world from one man.'As one' also indicates that He had to set up his world from one nation.»

between the two passages should not rashly be explained by direct literary dependence. There may be more to it. I suspect we have in *Dial.* 138 a tradition combining Petrine and Pauline motives, and enriching them by motives familiar in Jewish tradition.

There is another indication that the ones responsible for the material in *Dial.* 138 were in close contact with Judaism. Is 54:9 is quoted as a testimony on the flood, in a very deviant text. The rabbis chose the same text (Is 54:9ff) as the *Haftarah* to Gen 6:9ff in the triennial cycle of synagogal readings.[236] Looking at the text, we observe a non-LXX word: ἔσωσα. This term occurs twice within the text 1 Pt 3:20f - it is a main catchword. Probably the one responsible for Justin's deviant text was not only familiar with rabbinic tradition, he also was drawing upon 1 Pt 3:19-21 or a similar tradition.

A last element in the Noah/Christ typology should be noticed. In Gen 5:29 the name of Noah receives the following explanation: οὗτος διαναπαύσει ἡμᾶς ἀπὸ τῶν ἔργων ἡμῶν. Justin never quotes this verse, but compare his saying about Christ in *Dial.* 138:3: For his believers, Christ «has prepared beforehand *a rest* in Jerusalem» (ἀνάπαυσιν προητοίμασεν ἐν ᾽Ιερουσαλήμ). I suspect this also to be a traditional deposit - if Justin had been aware of the typological correspondence to Noah here, he would probably not have missed to point it out.

And the last quoted text brings us back to the Jerusalem theme once more. The salvation brought about in baptism has for its goal *the eschatological rest in Jerusalem*. Therefore Justin opens his whole exposition in *Dial.* 138 be saying that Isaiah (in Is 54:9) spoke «with reference to Jerusalem». I doubt that this remark derives from the context in Isaiah. I believe it derives from the tradition Justin is following in *Dial.* 138 as a whole. The tradition in *Dial.* 138 may thus well be one piece with the tradition behind *Dial.* 113f.

I would like to pause here, and add some general remarks on the soteriological motifs inherent in the material surveyed here. It is also relevant to recall the paschal lamb passages analysed above. Taken together, *Dial.* 40; 111:3f; 113f, and 138 can be seen to place two well-known soteriological motifs - closely related to baptism - within a wider framework concerned with the idea of a new creation.

The paschal lamb typology brings out the idea of remission of sins through Christ's expiatory blood - applied to the believer in baptism. The idea of a new creation breaks through in the concept that the baptizand resembles Adam: On him Gen 2:7 is fulfilled in a new way.

The flood typology enshrines the idea that the believer in his baptism passes through the waters of Sheol. We shall return to this concept more fully below, *ad Dial.* 86. But here again the idea of a new creation provides

---

236. Cf. A. Guilding, *The Fourth Gospel and Jewish Worship* (Oxford, 1960), p. 63. The length of the *haphtarah* varies: Is 54:9-11; 54:9-17; 54:9 - 55:5.

the framework which adds depth to Justin's tradition. Through baptism, believers are made to be members of the new humanity which has for its head (ἀρχή) Christ, the second Noah. Christ is the one who brings about the new creation in baptism, and he also is the one who is going to renew heaven and earth. Baptism is a piece of realized eschatology«, pointing forward to the restoration of the whole world through Christ. Justin has little more than hints at this important motif of the new creation. (It is more clearly brought out in the related material in *Barnabas*). It seems he has not been able to exploit this idea in his polemic with Trypho. But one can reasonably surmise that Justin's tradition had one of its main focuses of interest precisely in this soteriological motif.

In itself, this combination of ideas is nothing peculiar. But it serves to underline that one should not take Justin's »kerygma« tradition to be so poor in soteriological motives as might appear from a surface reading of the *Apology*.

One peculiarity stands out, however, viz. the quite remarkable concreteness of the motifs concerned with the land and Jerusalem. Christ the re-creator of man and the re-creator of heaven and earth, is to shine as an everlasting light in Jerusalem, he is to be the eternal king and priest of Jerusalem. As a second Joshua, he distributes the land to his people.

This characteristic of Justin's inherited tradition will be plain also when we turn to *Dial.* 139.

(γ) *Dial.* 139:1 - 140:1.

As far as the evidence goes, Justin is the first Christian writer to comment on Noah's curse and blessings in Gen 9:25-27.[237] Rabbis contemporary with Justin were occupied with these verses,[238] and had to face the same problem as Justin: Why does Noah not curse Ham, the culprit of the story, but instead Ham's son Canaan, of whom no guilt is recorded? «'And he said: Cursed be Canaan'(Gen 9:25): Ham sinned and Canaan is cursed! R.Judah and R. Nehemiah (both ca 150) disagreed. R.Judah said: Since it is written, 'And God blessed Noah and his sons'(Gen 9:1), while there cannot be a curse where a blessing has been given, consequently, 'He said: Cursed be Canaan'. R.Nehemiah explained: It was Canaan who saw it (Noah's shame) and informed them, therefore the curse is attached to him who did wrong.» (*Gen.Rab.* 36:7, p. 293).

It is interesting to note that R.Nehemiah's haggadah was already known to Philo, *Leg.All* II:62,[239] while Justin on the other hand has the same explanation as R.Judah (b.Elai): «For the spirit of prophecy was not going to

---

237. Except that a »presbyter« in Irenaeus may be his predecessor, cf. below.
238. Cf. the useful survey in Lewis, *op.cit.*, pp. 153 - 155.
239. Shotwell, *Exegesis,* also adduces *Quest. in Gen.* 11:77. He correctly observes: »In this instance, Justin adheres more closely to the rabbinic tradition.« (p. 96).

curse the son (Ham), when he had been blessed along with the others by God, but since the punishment of the sin (Ham's sin) was to be throughout the whole race of the son that laughed at the nakedness of his father, he has made the curse start from the son's son.»(*Dial.* 139:1).This parallel is hardly accidental.[240]

The second point Justin makes in *Dial.* 139 concerns the saying that Japheth is going to dwell in the tents (LXX: «houses») of Shem. There is a textual ambiguity here in Gen 9:27 (MT and LXX): Does the «he shall dwell» refer back to God or Japheth? The rabbis differed on this question.[241] Some, like Justin, took the «he» to refer to Japhet - e.g. Bar Kappara (ca 210):«Let the words of the Torah be uttered in the language of Japheth (sc. Greek) in the tents of Shem.» (*Gen. Rab.* 36:8, p. 294.)[242] Justin's interpretation is that Japheth (i.e. Rome) shall dwell in the houses which Shem inherited from Canaan, i.e. the Holy Land: Noah prophesied the conquest of Palestine by the Romans. But to this Justin adds an idea which seems to be without foundation in the text: When Christ came, he called to himself people from both Japheth, Shem,and Canaan, and they all together shall live with Christ in that land and inherit the eternal and incorruptible goods.[243] It is evident that Justin regards the curse resting on Canaan and making him a slave to Shem and Japhet as something provisional, to be abolished at Christ's coming. This idea is without direct parallel in rabbinic literature, but may have been facilitated by the rabbinic notion that the curse on Canaan was unjust and undeserved.[244]

Justin, however, seeks to bolster his point by bringing in the analogy with Jacob, *Dial.* 140:1: Jacob «married also the two bondmaidens of his two free wives, and of them he had sons, to indicate beforehand that Christ should receive to himself all the posterity even of Canaan that are among the race of Japhet as well as them that are free (i.e. Shem and Japheth, Gen 9:25-27, Canaan being their slave) and should consider them children and co-heirs.» This point is anticipated in Justin's treatment of the Rachel-Leah theme in *Dial.* 134: «For since Noah gave his two sons the seed of the third for bondage to them, Christ has now come to restore again the two free children, and also the bondservants who are among them, deeming all who keep his commandments worthy of the same blessing even as all who were born to Jacob from the free and from the bondmaidens became his sons, and received equal honour.»( *Dial.* 134:4).

---

240. Cf. Lewis, p. 153, n. 9:«Justin knew this Haggadah.»
241. Cf. Lewis, p. 154.
242. A similar interpretation is preserved in the *Targm Ps. Jonathan ad loc.*:«May the Lord beautify the borders of Japhet and may his sons be proselytes and dwell in the school of Shem.» (Transl. according to Lewis, *op. cit*, p. 99).
243. W. Rordorf,'Christus als Logos und Nomos', has tried to exploit *Dial.* 139 as a testimony to the «third race» concept in Justin, pp. 432f. But one has to do violence to Justin's exegesis to read this concept into it.
244. Cf. *Kidd.* 28a, and Str. Bill. III, p. 310.

One cannot escape the impression that all this is somewhat forced. *Dial.* 134:3 and 134:5fin. contain a very simple and straightforward typology: Leah is a type of the Synagogue, Rachel a type of the Church. The introduction of the bondmaiden motif is not called for, and it only blurs the logic of the Leah-Rachel typology. It seems the theme of the bondmaidens has been secondarily introduced in order to bolster the complicated Canaan-Shem-Japheth typology in *Dial.* 139. But perhaps this typology was also more simple in its original form?

Let us bring in a «presbyter» tradition reported by Irenaeus. «With respect to those misdeeds for which the Scriptures themselves blame the patriarchs and prophets, we ought not to inveigh against them, nor become like Ham, who ridiculed the shame of his father, and so fell under a curse; but we should give thanks to God in their behalf, inasmuch as their sins have been forgiven them through the advent of our Lord; for he said that they gave thanks (for us), and glorified in our salvation. With respect to those actions, again, on which the Scriptures pass no censure, ... we ought not to be accusers ..., but we should search for a type.» (*Adv.Haer.* IV:31:1).

There are several interesting features in this passage. The last saying about sinful actions being meant as types, is close to Justin's point of view, *Dial.* 134:1-3;141:4. But the most relevant saying is the one about Ham. First, we notice that the presbyter seems to refer the curse directly to Ham. Next, he says that Ham's sin was forgiven at Christ's coming.

I suspect this presbyter tradition lies behind Irenaeus' own treatment of the Noah curse and blessing in *Dem* 20f. Irenaeus here says that while Noah blessed Shem and Japheth, he cursed Ham. And he quotes a deviant version of Gen 9:25-27 which reads Ham instead of Canaan. Irenaeus then explains: Ham means the Canaanites, Hittites, Jebusites, Gergesites, Sodomites, Arabs, Phoenicians, Egyptians, and Lydians - i.e. the Gentiles of the OT.[245] Shem means Abraham and his descendants, i.e. the Israel of the OT. Japhet means »the Gentiles of the calling«; »so 'enlarge' refers to the calling from the Gentiles, that is to say, the Church, and he 'dwells in the house of Shem', that is to say, in the inheritage of the patriarchs, in Christ Jesus receiving the birthright.« In one respect Irenaeus does not follow the presbyter: He has no note on the forgiveness of Ham's sin. But he agrees with the presbyter - against the MT, LXX and Justin - in attributing the curse to Ham. And his typology is much simpler than Justin's. For Irenaeus Japheth is *the Church,* which takes the place of Shem. In other words: Irenaeus' typology expresses a theology of the «substitution» type. One may speculate that Irenaeus here has preserved a more original version of the tradition behind *Dial.* 139.

Two factors may have brought about the more complicated version in Justin. First, he has turned to the LXX text which is faithfully quoted in *Dial.*

---

245. Irenaeus seems to have in mind the peoples expelled from Canaan during Israel's conquest. Cf. the note in J. P. Smith, *Demonstration,* p. 157.

139:3. This necessitated the introduction of Canaan into the typology, and it seems Justin transformed the idea of forgivenness of Ham's sin to a theory that Canaan's servitude would end with the coming of Christ. Next, Justin wants to bring in the motif of the Roman devastation of Judaea. This makes him identify Japheth with the Romans. The Church must then be sought in Canaan's posterity.

If the above suggestions are not too far from the truth, they may indicate that Justin himself is responsible for the complexities in *Dial.* 139 as well as the secondary bondmaiden motif in *Dial.* 134. It would also seem that Justin himself had knowledge of the rabbinic theory why Canaan was cursed instead of Ham.

To conclude: *Dial.* 139 in its present form contains a rather complex exegesis of Gen 9:25-27, resulting in the idea that Christ has set men free both among Jews, Romans, and bondmen. But behind this chapter there may stand a tradition which - as in Irenaeus - made the Church dwell in the house of Shem, i.e. made the Christians take over the land after the Jews. This would be in a line with the other testimonies and types we have found in Justin, *Dial.* 113f etc.(cf. above). This original idea may shine through in *Dial.* 139:5: All men believing in Christ «will be together with him in that land, and will inherit the eternal, incorruptible goods.»

Conclusion:

Justin's material in *Dial.* 113f and 138f is concerned with two themes: baptism and the land (Jerusalem). Baptism is conceived of as a second circumcision, admitting to the land - while carnal circumcision excludes.

The baptismal motif is related to the baptismal testimonies in *Barn.* 6:8-19 and 11:1-12:1. The land motif is very dominant in this material. At his second coming, Christ is established as the eternal king of Jerusalem, priest forever, distributing the land as an eternal possession (Joshua typology).

Let me add a final note on this idea of Christ's reign in Jerusalem. There is nothing in this tradition which suggests that this reign is conceived of as a transitory state, a Messianic «Zwischenreich», to be replaced by «the world to come». Justin's material seems rather to enshrine the old Jewish conception, according to which the restoration of the Messianic reign in Jerusalem marks the final stage of redemption. Or - to be a little more precise - Justin's material once again seems to be remarkably close to the TP. The TP do not contain the later two-stage eschatology (which is expressed clearly for the first time in 4 Ezra and Rev 20-22). «*Die Testamente vertreten... die nationalen Zukunftsgedanken des jüdischen Volkes; ... die messianische Zeit (wird) die Zeit der absoluten Heilsvollendung sein ... (so) dass also ein neuer höherer Äon nach der Zeit des Messias nicht mehr zu erwarten ist.*»[246]

---

246. Str. Bill. IV, pp. 803f. Billerbeck has a very useful review of the traditional one-stage, nationalistic eschatology contained i.a. in *Jubilees, Sirach, Sap.Sal, Tobit, Baruch, 1 Enoch*

But, like the TP, Justin's material connects this one-stage eschatology with the idea of a *cosmic re-creation*. Cf. esp. *Test.Lev.* 18:10-14: «And he shall open the gates of paradise, and shall remove the threatening sword against Adam. And he shall give to the saints to eat from the tree of life, and the spirit of holiness shall be on them. And Beliar shall be bound by him, and he shall give power to his children to tread upon the evil spirits. . . . Then shall Abraham and Isaac and Jacob exult . . .» See also *Test.Sim.* 6:5-7: «. . . for the Lord God, the Mighty One of Israel, shall appear on earth [as a man], and himself save Adam. Then shall all the spirits of deceit be given to be trodden under foot, and men shall rule over wicked spirits. Then I shall arise in joy . . . because God hath taken a body and eaten with men and saved men .» The Jerusalem motif is not foreign in this context: «And the saints shall rest in Eden, and in the New Jerusalem shall the righteous rejoice . . . And no longer shall Jerusalem endure desolation, nor Israel be led captive; for the Lord shall be in the midst of it [living amongst men].»

One should also compare the Jerusalem-centered, one-stage eschatology of the Jewish *Sibyllina.* To this I shall return below.

It is now time to return to the people of God concept. I shall complete my analysis by treating the theme which Justin no doubt regarded as the final stroke of all he had to say on the topic: The Church is Israel.

(d) The new Israel.[247]

In Paul, the elect status of Christians is expressed first and foremost in the statement that they are the true children of Abraham, Gal 3:6-29; 4:21-31; Rom 4:13-25.

*Barnabas* (*Barn.* 13:7) and Justin carry on this line of thought. We have seen above how Justin in *Dial.* 119:4fin - 121:1 constructs an argument not unlike Gal 3:16. Justin's argument can be summarized like this:

---

etc., *ibid.*, pp. 799-802. The radicalised, but still one-stage eschatology of the TP is treated on pp. 802-804. On the transition to a two-stage eschatology, coupled with the emergence of the «Zwischenreich» idea, cf. *ibid.*, pp. 808ff, and esp. H.-A. Wilcke, *Das Problem eines messianischen Zwischenreichs bei Paulus* (AThANT 51, Zrich-Stuttgart, 1967), pp. 37-45. I believe Wilcke is right to locate the first unambiguous expressions of the «Zwischenreich» idea in *4 Ezra* and Revelation 20. A. L. Feder, *Justins des Märtyrers Lehre von Jesus Christus, dem Messias und dem menschgewordenen Sohne Gottes* (Freiburg im Breisgau, 1906), pp. 23ff, correctly observes that Justin outside *Dial.* 80f speaks as if he was no millennialist. Feder deems *Dial.* 80f a late development of Justin's ideas. Feder has not, however, related this to the question of different traditions and sources behind Justin's writings. Cf. also Goodenough's remark:«There seems to be no way of reconciling the millennium with the clear implication of Justin's other remarks that the new Jerusalem will be an eternal inheritance.» (*Theology*, p. 285). In my article (Norwegian)'Patristiske merknader til begrepet «Guds rike» ('Patristic notes to the concept of the «Kingdom of God'»), *Israel - Kristus-Kirken, Sverre Aalen Jubilee Volume* (Oslo - Bergen - Tromsø, 1970), pp. 163-182, I did not pay sufficient attention to the question of conflicting traditions in Justin, but I still believe I was right to point out that Justin has problems with the distinction between the millennium and the eternal salvation in Jerusalem, pp. 165-168.

247. On this theme in Justin, cf. esp. P. Richardson, *Israel*, pp. 9-14.

(A) Christians are the people of God promised to Abraham (Gen 15:5?)
when God said that Abraham should be the father of many nations
(Gen 17:4). By «many nations» God could not mean the posterity of
Ishmael, Esau etc., i.e. the Arabs, Idumeans etc. - for to be father of
many nations in this «natural» way was no prerogative of Abraham:
others also could boast that, not to speak of Noah, who became the
ancestor of all peoples.[248] The promise to Abraham must therefore
have a more specific meaning. It means that Abraham should
become the spiritual ancestor of all those who - like him -obey God's
calling and believe God's word (Gen 12:1ff).(*Dial.* 119:4fin-6).

(B) This is confirmed when we study the handing down of the promise
of blessing given to Abraham (Gen 12:3). It is not valid for all
Abraham's descendants, but only for Isaac, Gen 26:4:»And all the
nations of the earth (i.e. the nations of which Abraham shall be the
father) shall be blessed in thy seed.« After Isaac, only Jacob received
the promise, Gen 28:14: »And all the tribes of the earth shall be
blessed in thee and thy seed.« Both these texts prove that the seed
spoken of is not the carnal descendants, but only a certain line of
descent. This line is carried down through Judah, Gen 49:10, Pharez,
Jesse, and David. (Besides, this continued selection *within* Israel is a
sign to the Israelites that only some of them will be found to be true
children of Abraham.) (In *Dial* 120:3-6 Justin is side-tracked by his
familiar proof-text Gen 49:10) . When David repeated the promise,
he substituted the ambiguous »in his seed« with the direct »in him«, Ps
72:17, i.e. the »seed« spoken of to the Patriarchs *is Christ*. All nations
have been blessed in him, and thus the promise to Abraham has
been fulfilled.(*Dial.* 120:1-121:1).

Let me begin with pointing out that Justin seems eager to continue the
line of election within Israel *beyond Jacob*. Paul, in his analogous argument
in Rom 9:6-13, stops with Jacob. Why should Justin be concerned with
continuing the line with Judah, Pharez, Jesse etc., and establish a direct link
from David to Christ?

Let us bring in a rabbinic passage. It is *Sifre Deut* to Deut 32:9: »'For the
portion of the Lord is his people . . .' This is to be compared to a king who
had a field and he gave it to tenants. The tenants began stealing it. He (the
king) took it from them and gave it to their sons. They turned out to be

---

248. Shotwell, *Exegesis*, pp. 32f, takes *Dial.* 119:4 as the main example of Hillel's exegetical rule
*kelal upherat* («a more precise statement of the general by the particular and vice versa»):
»Here he defines the general term «nations» by the particular descendants of Abraham.« I hold
this to be a misunderstanding of Justin's reasoning. Justin's meaning is *not* that «many
peoples» are exemplified by Ishmael, Esau and the Ammonites - it is exactly the opposite:
»Many nations« cannot mean Ishmael, Esau etc. - for Christ promises Abraham something
exceptional, and to be father of many nations in the way Abraham became the father of
Ishmael etc., is nothing exceptional.

worse than their predecessors. He took it from their sons and gave it to their grandchildren. They, in turn, were worse than their antecedents. A son was born to him (the king). He said to them ( the tenants), 'Go forth from the midst of that which belongs to me. It is not my wish that you be in its midst. Give me my portion that I may make it known as my own.' Thus when Abraham our father came into the world, worthless offsprings issued from him, Ishmael and the sons of Qeturah; when Isaac our father came into the world, worthless progeny issued from him, Esau and the princes of Edom. They turned out to be worse than their predecessors. When Jacob arrived, no unworthy offspring issued from him, but all his children were born worthy like himself, as it is stated in Scriptures, 'And Jacob was a perfect man, dwelling in the houses of study' (Gen 25:27 as translated by the rabbis).From what point on does God claim his portion? From Jacob, as it is stated in Scriptures, 'For the portion of the Lord is his people, Jacob the lot of his inheritance'(Deut 32:9). And Scriptures also states, 'For the Lord has chosen Jacob for himself, Israel for his treasure'(Ps 135:4).»[249]

E.Mihaly has subjected this passage to a minute analysis.[250] I shall summarize his interpretation in a kind of paraphrase of the rabbinic text:

At what point in history did God elect Israel? *Not* with Abraham, because not all Abraham's descendants were worthy: Ishmael and the sons of Qeturah! *Not* with Isaac - and for the same reason. But *all* of Jacob's sons were worthy - the election thus starts with Jacob: God claimed his people as his portion when Jacob became the lot of his inheritance, Deut 32:9. In this text «his people» is none other than Israel, Ps 135:4.

This is a rebuttal of Christians, who argue from the election of Abraham to the election of Christians (Paul in Rom 4 and Gal 3, cf. also Rom 9:6ff: not all sons of Abraham and Isaac were sons of the promise). The rabbi recognizes the force of the argument that not all carnal descendants of Abraham and Isaac were chosen, but turns this against the Christians and points out that the argument is not valid for Jacob: From him, the election follows all descendants!

I find this interpretation of the meaning and the setting of the rabbinic text convincing in itself, and I think one can adduce an observation not mentioned by Mihaly, which corroborates his point of view. The fact is that one can observe on the Christian side *a gradual shift of emphasis from Abraham to Jacob*[251] when the theme of people of God and election is treated. In Justin, Jacob plays a far greater role in the people of God discussion than Abraham, and it is easy to read Justin's argument in *Dial.* 119:4 - 121:2 as a try to counter-attack the rabbinic argument quoted above; in other words: a try to re-establish the Pauline argument.

---

249. Translation according to E. Mihaly,'Election', pp. 105f.
250. Cf. p.320, n.178
251. We have observed a marked emphasis on Scriptural types related to Jacob in *Barnabas* already, cf. above, p.332.

The first Christian writer to apply OT texts talking about «the house of Israel» and «Israel» and «Jacob» to Christians, is the author of *1.Clem.* Is it purely accidental that the passage quoted with most emphasis is precisely Deut 32:8f?

*1.Clem.* seems to take this reference to Christians in Deut 32:8f for granted, but Justin, repeating the testimony, seems to have looked up the context in Deut 32. He is therefore unable just to take the reference to Christians for granted. His comment on the passage betrays his difficulty: «From these words (Deut 32:8f) you will understand that of old God dispersed all men by their nations and languages; yet out of all the nations he took to himself your nation, a nation unprofitable and disobedient and unbelieving; and he showed that those who were chosen from every nation have obeyed his will through Christ, whom he calls Jacob and names Israel, so these (believers in Christ) must also be both Jacob and Israel, as I said before at some length.« *(Dial* 130:3). Justin seems to give Deut 32:9 a double reference: to the Jews *and* to Christians = the new Israel. But he is not able to *argue* this point from the text itself - the double reference is something he carries with him from previous, independent arguments.

Thus, for Justin the simple procedure of *1.Clem.* was no longer sufficient. He knows that the rabbis could not be refuted on such simple terms. Let us therefore turn to his main argument on the new Israel theme, which comes in *Dial* 121:4 - 125:5. Notice, by the way, the nice sequence here: After the »Abraham argument« has been re-established in *Dial* 119-121, Justin goes on to the Jacob/Israel theme - now the main point of controversy.

The section begins (121:4 - 123:2) with a discussion on some texts in Isaiah which speak about the salvation of Gentiles: Is 49:6; Is 42:16/43:10; Is 42:6f; Is 49:8; Ps 2:7f; Is 14:1.[252]

The three first texts and the last one exhibit some non-LXX readings (we have surmised a testimony source for Is 42:6f above, on textual grounds). The close thematic unity between the texts strengthens the assumption that a testimony source is at play. What do the texts say?

Is 49:6      The servant of the Lord
             (1) restores the tribes of Jacob and brings the
                 dispersion of Israel back, and
             (2) is set as a φῶς ἐθνῶν to their salvation.
Is 42:16/43:10   Blind men (the Gentiles) are brought (to salvation)
                 along ways they did not know. (The idea is very similar
                 to Is 65:1).

---

252. Concerning *Dial* 121-123, there is much useful comment in P. J. Donahue's unpublished dissertation on microfilm, *Jewish-Christian Controversy in the Second Century: A Study in the Dialogue of Justin Martyr* (Yale 1973), pp. 176-189; cf. also the microfilm dissertation of W. S. Kurz, *The Function of Christological Proof from Prophecy for Luke and Justin* (Yale, 1976), pp. 239f.

Is 42:6f   The servant of the Lord is a φῶς ἐθνῶν, he opens their blind eyes.
Is 49:8    The servant of the Lord is a διαθήκη ἐθνῶν.

One observation immediately springs to the eye: The first of these texts is a testimony of the »association« type. The nations (τὰ ἔθνη) are added to the restored tribes of Jacob. This may be a confirmation of my suggestion above that a substratum in Justin's tradition is closer to the association model than Justin is.

Is 49:6 is quoted as a major testimony to the Gentile mission in Acts 13:47 (cf. also Lk 2:32, Acts 26:23). *Barnabas* testifies to the enrichment of this testimony cluster (14:7-9: Is 42:6f; 49:6f; 61:1f). Justin seems to depend on a similar tradition. It seems the tradition Justin is here following had no intention of proving that the Church is Israel. And Justin makes no attempt to do so either -not with these texts. His theme in *Dial.* 121:4 - 123:2 is the question of proselytes. Which proselytes are envisaged by the texts - the proselytes of the Law or the proselytes of Christ? Justin makes us believe that the Jews already had applied these texts to the proselytes, and that they held the φῶς to be the Law. We shall return more fully to this theme below; here I may anticipate the statement that Justin's information very likely is correct. One should note especially *Dial.* 123:1. Justin first quotes Is 14:1 (non-LXX) as a Jewish standard text on (Jewish) proselytes, and then comments: »A proselyte who is circumcised with the object of joining the people is like one who is native-born.« This can be directly confirmed from rabbinic texts: Is 14:1 is an important testimony on proselytism[253] and the rabbis said about the proselyte: »When he comes up after his ablution he is deemed to be an Israelite in all respects.« (*Yeb.* 47b, p. 311).[254]

To conclude: Justin's material in *Dial.* 121:4 - 123:2 represents a Christianized version of a Jewish proselyte tradition.[255] The fact that Christ takes the place of the Law, points to a close connection to the »Law out from Zion« testimonies treated below, and I shall not presently pursue this theme further. But why is this material included in the present stage of the *Dialogue?* It does not prove what Justin is out to prove. It does not prove that Christians are Israel, that Christians are the true descendants of Jacob.

I think we find the answer to this question when we read on to *Dial.* 123:8f. Here another text concerning the servant of the Lord is quoted, Is 42:1-4. Thematically it is very close to the other servant texts treated above, and on textual grounds we have surmised a testimony source at play in *Dial.* 123:8. So this text was probably part of the same source as the texts in *Dial.*

---

253. *Yeb.* 47b (p. 312), cf. allusions in *Yeb.* 109b (p. 762); *Nidd.* 13b (p. 88).
254. Cf. also *Yeb.* 48b (p. 320):»R. Jose said: One who has become a proselyte is like a child newly born.«
255. I think Donahue is right in relating this material to the over-all setting of the *Dialogue:* Justin and Trypho are *competing missionaries*; Jewish proselytism is a main antagonist for Justin. (*Op. cit*, esp. p. 179).

121:4 123:2. And this last text is relevant for Justin's purpose, not because it calls the Gentiles «Israel» - it does not - but because *the servant* is called «Jacob» and «Israel». Christians are Israel because *Christ* is Israel, *Dial.* 123:9. Because of the importance of this proof-text, Justin also included the other texts joined to it in his source, although they did not contribute to his main point.

One can reasonably doubt whether Is 42:1-4 in Justin's source had the function of proving that Christians are Israel - very likely it was just another testimony on the servant of the Lord bringing salvation to the Gentiles.

Perhaps yet another text belonging to this dossier is to be found in *Dial.* 135:1. The whole section *Dial.* 135:1-3 takes up the argument in *Dial.* 123:8f: Is 42:1-4 is repeated, and the new text Is 43:15 is quoted: «I am the Lord God . . . who showed forth Israel your king.» In Justin's source this may have been yet another testimony on the servant, but Justin tries to evaluate the text in his «Israel» discussion: Jacob was never king, so the saying must refer to Jesus. «As therefore he calls Christ Israel and Jacob, so also we, quarried from the bowels of Christ, are the true race of Israel.»

So far, so good. But it seems Justin has not felt that this argument built on Is 42:1ff was entirely satisfactory. It proved that Christians had a right to the name «Israel», but it did not establish a direct connexion to Jacob the Patriarch. It did not answer the rabbi who said that God's election of Jacob meant God's election of *all Jacob's progeny*.

I suppose this was the reason why Justin had to introduce material from another source in *Dial.* 124f (cf. the source analysis above, pp. 187f). The decisive point comes in *Dial.* 125, where Justin connects Jacob and Jesus by means of typology: Jacob was a type of Christ. This is shown from their common name Israel. Israel means «a man overcoming (=*isra*) power (=*el*).» Christ showed himself to be «*Israel*» when he overcame Satan. He lent his name to Jacob when Jacob likewise overcame him who appeared to him.

Now, strictly speaking, Justin has still not proved his point fully. He has proved that Jesus is «Israel» and that Jacob was a type of Jesus borrowing the name Israel from him.

But a strict and direct proof that believing Gentiles are called «Israel» or «the seed of Jacob» in the OT is still missing. It is now time to pay attention to the three texts in *Dial.* 123:5f:

| | |
|---|---|
| Jer 31:27 | I will raise up to Israel and to Judah the seed of man and the seed of beasts. |
| Is 19:24f | In that day shall Israel be third among the Assyrians and Egyptians, blessed in the land which the Lord Sabaoth blessed, saying: Blessed shall my people be which is in Egypt and among the Assyrians, and my inheritance is Israel. |

Ezek 36:12  And I will beget men upon you (viz. you montains of
Israel), namely my people Israel, and they shall inherit
you, and you shall be a possession for them …

It is difficult to say with certainty exactly how Justin will have these texts
understood. Prigent[256] takes the first text to mean that Jacob's progeny will
be divided: Some will become «beasts», i.e. Jews, while some will become
«men», i.e. Christians. I have no better suggestion. If Prigent is right, this text
may be said to prove in a more direct way that Christians are Jacob's seed.

The second text is probably understood by Justin as talking about an
«Israel» other than the Jews, an «Israel» hidden, so to speak, among the
Gentile nations.

It may be relevant here to touch briefly on the idea of Christians as a
«third» people besides Greeks and Jews. This is found in the *Kerygma
Petrou,* fragm.2a fin.:«A new (covenant, referring to Jer 31:31) has he made
with us. For what has reference to the Greeks and Jews is old. But we are
Christians, who as a third race (τρίτῳ γένει) worship him in a new way.»
This is a way of speaking which is not found in Justin. (In the *Kerygma
Petrou* we notice that «Israel» seems reserved for the Jews, fragm. 3). One
could nevertheless speculate whether Is 19:24 was originally picked out by
someone seeking Scriptural support for the «third race» conception. The
text would not be ideal, however (the third people is called Israel and is
contrasted to Assyrians and Egyptians), and I doubt that this surmise is
right.[257]

The third prooftext (Ezek 36:12) strictly speaking proves nothing, since it
presupposes what is to be proved, viz. that the Israel to inherit Jerusalem are
the Christians. But here we shall probably connect this text with Is 65:9 as
treated in *Dial.* 135f. (There are allusions to Jer 31:27 and Ezek 36:12 in
*Dial.* 136:2 immediately after the separate quotation of Is 65:9). Justin
remarks that Is 65:8 implies the rejection of Israel, hence the meaning of Is
65:9 must be that *another «seed of Jacob»* shall inherit the holy mountain:
«And I will lead out the seed that is from Jacob and Judah; and it shall inherit
my holy mountain.» The rejection of the Jews may also have been read out
of Is 65:11f within the same long LXX excerpt (Is 65:9-12).

In his further comment on Is 65:9, Justin makes an interesting distinction
between σπέρμα 'Ιακὼβ (= the Christians) and «those *born* of Jacob», οἱ ἐξ
'Ιακὼβ γεγεννημένοι (= the Jews) *(Dial.* 135:5). «You yourselves perceive
that this seed of Jacob which is here spoken of is of another kind, for none

---

256. *Justin,* p. 296. Prigent refers to Is 1:2-4 (quoted in *1.Apol* 37:1f) as a corroboration.
257. Recently, W. Rordorf has argued that the «third race» concept is really found in Justin, although
the term itself does not occur ('Christus als Logos und Nomos', pp. 432f). He takes Noah's
sons in *Dial.* 139 and Jacob's wives in *Dial.* 134 as proofs of this assertion. But in neither of
these texts does the characteristic triad Jews, Greeks, Christians occur.

of you would suppose it was spoken about your people. For it is not granted that *they who are of the seed of Jacob* can leave a right of entrance to *them that are born of Jacob* . . .» If one grants Justin's exegesis, this is the best answer given to the rabbinic attack in the entire *Dialogue.*

As a whole, I think Justin's argument on the new Israel theme is one of the most intricate and elaborate in the *Dialogue.* He has re-dressed the Pauline argument concerning Abraham in a very able way, and he has exploited two kinds of «Jacob« material: the Servant of the Lord testimonies and a Jacob/Christ typology. But it is only in the four last-mentioned texts that he acheives a direct Scriptural proof that Christians are the seed of Jacob, hence Israel. Were these four texts Justin's own contribution to the material? They are not quoted by any Christian writer before him, nor by any writer after him in the second and third centuries, Origen excepted.[258] They were thus not part of the common, traditional dossier of prooftexts within the Church.

On the other hand, the two texts which belong most closely together, viz. Ezek 36:12 and Is 65:9, are divided from each other by several chapters. We have seen reasons above to believe that the source behind *Dial.* 121-123 is re-used in *Dial.* 135f. This may mean that the four texts studied above also derive from this source. (It should be noted that Jer 31:27 shows two non-LXX readings. In fact, the text is only probative in the non-LXX version [τῷ Ἰσραηλ and τῷ Ἰουδα instead of LXX τὸν].[259] It seems these text were transmitted to Justin in some kind of testimony source, and I suspect we have here one of the most distinctive and original creations of the »school« tradition inherited by Justin.

To conclude: P. Richardson's thesis that Justin is the first to argue that Christians are Israel is substantiated when one makes an internal analysis of Justin's inherited material. There may be a substratum of »association« testimonies related to the tradition of the AJ II; for the most part Justin's material on the people of God is dominated by a sharply emphasized substitution concept. Christians are the new people of God, disinheriting the Jews. But Christians are not called Israel on that account.

What prompted the concept of the Church being Israel, was probably Jewish polemic which seemed to invalidate the traditional «Abraham» argument: God's election of his people started with *Jacob*, not Abraham. This caused a shift in emphasis also on the Christian side. The Christian

---

258. The only occurrence of one of these four texts in Origen is an allusion to Jer 31:27 in *In Joh.* 1:27:190 (GCS 10, p. 35).( I am here relying on the Scriptural indices in the GCS editions of Origen). Origen is reminded of this OT passage in a context where he is speaking of different classes of men saved by Christ the Good Shepherd. The implicit exegesis is different from Justin's. On Is 65:8f it may be relevant to note that the Syrian fathers exploited this text in a peculiar vine/ Christ typology, cf. Murray, *Symbols,* pp. 113-120/284-286.
259. The other non-LXX reading (ἐγερῶ for LXX σπερῶ ) may be due to scribal error, for in his allusion in *Dial.* 136:2 Justin reads σπείρειν with the LXX.

consciousness of election had to be re-stated: Christians are not only Abraham's children, they are also *Jacob's seed.* They are Israel!

Justin's quite laborious exegetical justification of this claim shows that this re-statement was no self-explanatory commonplace in the early Church.[260]

## 5. The new Law going out from Zion.[261]

(a) The light of the Gentiles.

Let me begin this section with some remarks on the most relevant Jewish material.[262]

When a Gentile turns from idol worship to a life in obedience to God and his Law, he is said to turn from darkness to light, from death to life. His eyes were blind, but have been opened. He has been enlightened. And the light is the Law.

I quote some representative passages. «We must rejoice with them (the proselytes), as if, though blind at the first they had recovered their sight and had come from the deepest darkness to behold the most radiant light» (Philo).[263] Praying for the would-be proselyte Asenath, Joseph says: «O Lord God . . . you who make all alive, who calls from darkness to light (καλέσας ἀπὸ τοῦ σκότους εἰς τὸ φῶς) and from error (πλάνη) to truth, and from death to life . . .»[264] Asenath says to Michael: «Blessed be the Lord God, who has sent you to deliver me from darkness and lead me to light.»[265] The Patriarch Levi says to his descendants: «If you fall back to darkness by your ungodliness - what shall the Gentiles do, who walk in blindness? You will bring a curse on your people, to which the light of the law was given, to enlighten every man. You will put this light aside, teaching commandments contrary to God's.»[266] Cf. *Test. Gad.* 5:7: «The true conversion (worked) by God abolishes ignorance and puts darkness to flight, enlightens the eyes and brings knowledge to the soul.» The Jewish Sibyl speaks in the same vein: «Cease, vain mortals, your roaming in dark and obscure black night, and leave the darkness of night, receive the light.»[267]

---

260. Von Harnack's statement that the New Israel concept was an inevitable inference implicit in the self-consciousness of early Christians (quoted above), may not be as evident as Harnack will make us believe.

261. On this theme in Justin, cf. P. G. Verweijs, *Evangelium,* pp. 216-241, esp. pp. 223ff.

262. Cf. the useful collection of Greek Jewish texts in K. Berger,'Jüdisch-hellenistische Missionsliteratur und apokryphe Apostelakten', *Kairos* 17 (1975), pp. 232-48.

263. *De Virtut.* 179. This text is part of the important section Περὶ μετάνοιας in *De Virtut.* 175-186.

264. *Joseph and Asenath* 8:10.Text,Philonenko, pp. 156/58 - my own translation.

265. *Ibid.,* 15:13, Philonenko, p. 184 - my translation.

266. *Test. Lev.* 14:4, MS α. This and the following quotations from the TP are my own translations, adapted to Becker's in *JSHRZ* III:1.

267. *Sib. Fragm.* 1, lines 25-27; translation according to R. M. Grant, *Theophilus of Antioch: Ad Autolycum* (*OEChT,* Oxford, 1970), p. 89.

It is not explicitly stated in all these passages, but no doubt the enlightening power belongs to the Law.[268] In *Test.Lev.* 14:3, the sons of Levi are called οἱ φωστῆρες τοῦ Ἰσραήλ (Greek MS α), no doubt in their capacity as preachers of the Law.[269] Cf. also *Test. Lev.* 18:9: «And in his (the end-time priest's) priesthood the Gentiles shall be multiplied in knowledge upon the earth, and enlightened (φωτισθήσονται) through the grace of the Lord . . . and the lawless shall cease to do evil.» In *Test. Lev.* 19:1 we have the following parallelism: «Choose for yourselves

ἢ τὸ φῶς ἢ τὸ σκότος,

ἢ τὸν νόμον κυρίου ἢ τὰ ἔργα τοῦ βελίαρ.»[270]

The rabbis also talk about the Law as the light of the world: «Just as oil (gives) life to the world, so too do the words of the Torah (give) life to the world. Just as oil gives light to the world, so too do the words of the Torah give light to the world.»[271] Cf. also the rabbi Paul talking about a proselytizing Jew in Rom 2:17-20: . . . σὺ Ἰουδαῖος ἐπονομάζῃ καὶ ἐπαναπαύῃ νόμῳ . . . κατηχούμενος ἐκ τοῦ νόμου, πέποιθάς τε σεαυτὸν ὁδηγὸν εἶναι τυφλῶν, φῶς τῶν ἐν σκότει . . . ἔχοντα τὴν μόρφωσιν τῆς γνώσεως καὶ τῆς ἀληθείας ἐν τῷ νόμῳ.

We return now to *Dial.* 121:4 - 123:2[272]. Some of the testimonies here contain catchwords which make one believe that they already formed the basis for the Greek Jewish texts we have been quoting: «a light for the Gentiles», Is 49:6 and 42:6; «I will bring blind men on a way they have not known . . .», Is 42:16;«. . . to open they eyes of the blind . . .», Is 42:7. Let us also review some passages where Justin relates the Jewish position:

«You . . . suppose that this (i.e. Is 49:6) was said of the stranger (γηόραν) and the proselytes.» (122:1).

---

268. On this idea, see esp. S. Aalen, *Die Begriffe «Licht» und «Finsternis» im Alten Testament, im Spätjudentum und im Rabbinismus* (Skr.N.V. II, 1951, 1, Oslo), pp.183-195.
269. Cf. Aalen, *op. cit.*, p. 188.
270. Cf. also *Test.Reub.* 3:8. On the Law as light, see further Sir 45:17; *4 Ezra* 14:20f; *Syriac Baruch* 17:4; 38:1-4; 46:2ff; 52:9; Philo, *Vit.Mos.* II:27.44.
271. *Deut.Rab.* 7:3 (p. 134) - the passage is a midrash on Song 1:3. Another beautiful midrash on the Law as a light is the following in *Ex.Rab.* 36:3 (pp. 439f):«Another explanation of 'A leafy olive tree'(Jer 11:16). Just see how the words of the Torah give forth light to a man when he studies them; but he who does not occupy himself with the Torah and does not know it, stumbles. It can be compared to one who stands in a dark place; as soon as he starts walking, he stumbles against a stone; he then strikes a gutter, falls into it and knocks his face on the ground - and all because he has no lamp in his hand. It is the same with the ordinary individual who has no Torah in him; he strikes against sin, stumbles, and dies, while the Holy Spirit exclaims:'He shall die for lack of instruction'(Prov 5:23); and 'instruction' means the Torah . . . But those who study the Torah give forth light wherever they may be. It is like one standing in the dark with a lamp in his hand; when he sees a stone, he does not stumble, neither does he fall over a gutter because he has a lamp in his hand, as it says, Thy word is a lamp unto my feet, and a light unto my path'(Ps 119:105) . . . What is the lamp of God? The Torah, as it says, 'For the commandment is a lamp, and the teaching is light'(Prov 6:23).» Cf. also *B.B.* 3b.4a (pp. 10f).
272. Many valuable observations on the formal structure of Justin's argument in this section in Kurz, *op. cit.*, pp. 240-44.

According to the Jews, Is 42:6f is spoken «with reference to the Law and the proselytes.» (122:3).

One of Trypho's companions: Is 42:6f spoken «with reference to the Law and those who have been enlightened (τοὺς φωτιζομένους) by it. Now these are the proselytes.» (122:4).

Jews think «that the eyes of the proselytes have been opened». The proselytes are πεφωτισμένοι (123:2).

It is evident that Justin's report on the Jewish point of view is substantiated by the relevant Jewish literature, except for the explicit reference to Is 42:6f and Is 49:6 - but that may be due to the character of the sources.(The Greek texts quoted above have no explicit OT quotations, except Philo, but he very seldom has quotations outside the Pentateuch).

Justin takes this Jewish material over entirely, his only modification is to substitute the Law with Christ: Is 49:6 was «said of us who have been enlightened through Jesus», 122:1.

Is 42:6f is spoken «with reference to the Christ, and concerning the Gentiles who have been enlightened», 122:3.

We must not refer these texts to «the old Law and its proselytes, but to Christ and his proselytes, us Gentiles, whom he enlightened», 122:5.

This taking over of Jewish terminology concerning the proselytes is not only evident in *Dial* 121-123. One should also compare Justin's language in *1.Apol.* 61:12f: «This washing (i.e. baptism) is called φωτισμός, since those who learn these things (i.e. the baptismal instruction) are enlightened within (φωτιζόμενοι τὴν διάνοιαν). The enlightened (ὁ φωτιζόμενος) is also washed in the name of Jesus Christ . . .»

Justin is not the first Christian writer to apply Jewish proselyte terminology to Christian converts, and a brief review of the relevant material in his Christian precursors may be useful to bring out the peculiar profile of Justin's material. I first just quote the most important passages, then add some relevant comment.

«What partnership have righteousness and iniquity (ἀνομία)? Or what fellowship has light with darkness? What accord has Christ with Belial?»(2 Cor 6:14f - cf. esp. *Test. Lev.* 19:1).

«Once you were darkness, but now you are light in the Lord» (Eph 5:8, cf. also vss. 9-14).

«. . . to share in the inheritance of the saints in the light. He has delivered us from the dominion of darkness . . .» (Col 1:12f, cf. also 2 Cor 4:6; 1 Thess 5:5).

«. . . God . . . who called you out of darkness into his marvellous light» (1 Pt 2:9).

«(I send you (Paul) to the Gentiles) to open their eyes, that they may turn from darkness to light and from the power of Satan to God . . .» (Acts 26:18f).

«It is impossible to restore again to repentance those who have once been enlightened (τοὺς . . . φωτισθέντας) . . .» (Heb 6:4, cf. 10:32).

«. . . Jesus Christ, through whom he called us from darkness to light, from ignorance (ἀγνωσία) to full knowledge (ἐπίγνωσις) of the glory of his name« ( *1.Clem.* 59:2).

»For he gave us the light . . . We were maimed in our understanding, worshipping stone . . . the works of man, and our whole life was nothing else than death. We were covered with darkness, and our eyes were full of mist; but we have received our sight . . .« ( *2.Clem.* 1:4-6).

»Jesus the Lord . . . was prepared for this purpose, that when he appeared he might redeem from darkness our hearts which were already paid over to death, and given over to the iniquity of error (τῆς πλάνης ἀνομίᾳ), and by his word make a covenant with us . . . He should redeem us from darkness and prepare a holy people for himself.«( *Barn.* 14:5f. In 14:7f quotations of Is 42:6f and 49:6f follow).

It is easy to see how the Jewish »wordfield« is taken over almost entire in these texts.[273] The situation of Gentiles before conversion is described with terms like σκοτία, ἀνομία, ἀγνωσία, πλάνη, θάνατος, service to Belial or Satan, worship of idols. The situation of the converts is described by terms such as φῶς, δικαιοσύνη, ἐπίγνωσις, receiving the sight, being enlightened, having one's eyes opened, serving God (or Christ). These wordfields clearly reflect the original orientation towards the Law. But the Law theme itself has disappeared from all these texts. They are in that respect thoroughly Christianized. They do not suggest much even about Christ as the (new) Law. In *Barnabas,* διαθήκη, not Law, is the catchword, and the whole of ch. 14 is centered on one of *Barnabas'* main points: There is only one convenant, not two. The whole context positively excludes much of Justin's material on the Law theme.

But in Justin there is more at stake than the mere taking over of a wordfield. Justin is keenly aware that this tradition in Judaism has to do with the Law. One should note especially the way he contrasts »the old Law and its proselytes« with »Christ and his proselytes« in *Dial.* 122:5.[274]

No doubt a Christology which identifies Christ with the (new) Law in person is at play here. This motif connects this material in Justin with the testimonies we are now going to study.

(b) The Law going out from Zion.[275]

(1) Let us again start with some relevant Jewish material. There are a few rabbinic texts which hint at the idea of a new Torah in the messianic age (or

---

273. Cf. K. Berger's remark: ». . . *man (wird) eine Art halb-technischer Schulsprache annehmen müssen, in der es zur Ausbildung bestimmter Begriffsfelder und relativ fixierter Formeln .. gekommen ist. Diese Schulsprache bildet eine beachtliche Kontinuität zwischen jüdischer und christlicher Mission.*«. ('Missionsliteratur', p. 239).

274. Cf. Kurz, *op. cit.,* pp. 239f, who also stresses Justin's keen awareness of the Jewish background for his own concept.

275. On this theme in Justin, cf. esp: Daniélou, *Theology,* pp. 163-166; E. Luther Copeland, 'Nomos as a Medium of Revelation - Paralleling Logos - in Ante-Nicene Christianity', *StTh* 27 (1973), pp. 51-61; W. Rordorf, 'Logos und Nomos'.

the age to come). Their interpretation is still controversial among the experts.[276] Some texts have been interpreted as if they taught that the Torah will be abolished in the Messianic age, or that the Messiah (or God) will teach a new Torah. But this interpretation is dubious. It seems rather that the meaning of the rabbis is that the Messiah will settle disputed halakic questions and bring Israel to a deeper understanding of the Torah given at Sinai.[277]

There remain, however, some passages which undeniably speak of the annullment of some specific ritual commandments in the Messianic age. Two of them deserve to be quoted in full:

«R. Judan b. R. Simeon (ca 320) said:Behemoth and the Leviathan are to engage in a wild-beast contest before the righteous in the Time to Come, and whoever has not been a spectator at the wildbeast contests of the heathen nations in this world will be accorded the boon of seeing one in the World to Come. How will they be slaughtered? Behemoth will, with its horns, pull Leviathan down and rend it, and Leviathan will, with its fins, pull Behemoth down and pierce it through. The Sages said: And is this a valid method of slaughter? (Follows a reference to *M. Hul* 1:2, which proves the answer to be no).R.Abin b. Kahana (ca 310) said: The Holy One, blessed be he, said:'A new Law shall go forth from me'(Is 51:4),i.e. a renewal of the Law . . .[278] R. Berekiah (ca 340) said in the name of R. Isaac (ca 300): In the Time to Come, the Holy One, blessed be he, will make a banquet for his righteous servants, and whoever has not eaten *nebelah* in this world will have the privilege of enjoying it in the World to Come.» (*Lev.Rab.* 13:3, p. 167). «'The Lord will loose the bonds'(Ps 146:7). What does the verse mean by the words 'loose the bonds'? Some say that of every animal whose flesh it is forbidden to eat in this world, the Holy One, blessed be he, will declare in the time-to-come that the eating of its flesh is permitted. Thus in the verse 'That which hath been is that which shall be, and that which hath been given is that which shall be given (Prov 1:9), the words 'that which hath been given' refer to the animals that were given as food before the time of the sons of Noah, for God said: 'Every moving thing that liveth shall be food for you; as the green herb have I given you all'(Gen 9:3). That is to say, »As I give the green herbs as food to all, so once I gave both beasts and cattle as food to all. But why did God declare the flesh of some animals forbidden?

---

276. Cf. i.a. W. D. Davies, *The Setting of the Sermon on the Mount* (Cambridge, 1966), pp. 156-190/447-450; J. Jervell,'Die offenbarte und die verborgene Tora. Zur Vorstellung über die neue Tora im Rabbinismus', *StTh* 25 (1971), pp. 90-108; P. Schäfer,'Die Torah der messianischen Zeit', *ZNW* 65 (1974), pp. 27-42.

277. This is the interpretation advanced by Schäfer, *art. cit.*, but cf. the somewhat different point of view in Jervell, *art. cit.*, pp. 95ff.

278. J. Israelstam in the Soncino translation has:»'Instruction (Torah) shall go forth from Me'(Is 51:4), i.e. an exceptional temporary ruling will go forth from Me.» This hardly captures the meaning of the Hebrew text:תורה חדשה מאתי תצא חדוש תורה מאתי תצא, cf. Davies, *op. cit.*, p. 166, and Jervell, *art. cit.*, p. 104.

In order to see who would accept his commandments and who would not accept them. In the time-to-come, however, God will again permit the eating of that flesh which he has forbidden.« (*Midr. Ps.* to Ps 146:7, pp. 365f).[279]

Three points in these passages are of special relevance to our purpose. (1) In the last text we find a reflection on why God gave the commandments concerning unclean animals, i.e. we have a reflection on the »grounds for the commandments«. P.Schäfer presumes that this midrash therefore derives from »*Kreisen . . . die sich mit den «Gründen» der Gebote und Verbote beschäftigten, mit den ta'ame ham-miswot.*[280] *Wir haben zahlreiche Belege dafür, dass sowohl im hellenistischen als auch schon im frühen rabbinischen Judentum die Frage nach den Gründen der Gebote häufig gestellt wurde; durch Angriffe der heidnischen Umwelt veranlassst, konzentrierte sich diese Erforschung . . . ganz besonders auf die Reinheits- und Unreinheitsgesetze und auf die Vorschriften für das rituelle Schlachten der Tiere. Genau diese Gebote sind aber in den behandelten Texten als änderungsbedürftig genannt.*«[281] Let us put the point of the Midrash this way: Some ritual commandments were given only to test Israel's obedience - in the world to come (probably — the Messianic age) they will be abolished. (2) The essential permissibility of all animals is argued from Gen 9:3, containing the analogy with the green herbs. (3) The abolition of ritual commandments concerning slaughter is argued from Is 51:4, where the Midrash reads תורה חדשה, for MT תורה.

Turning to Justin, we first notice that in the *Dialogue*, Is 51:4f is the first testimony he quotes on the New Law, *Dial.* 11:3. One next notices that Justin in *Dial.* 20:1-3 shows acquaintance with rabbinical discussions on unclean animals based on Gen 9:3.[282] Trypho is understood to argue that just as all herbs are permitted, but we do not eat all herbs, so we do not eat all meat. Justin argues that this is an invalid analogy: The reason why we do not eat all herbs, is that some of them by their natural properties are unfit for eating, not that they are ritually unclean. This sounds very much like an echo of discussions among the «investigators of the grounds of the commandments» among the rabbis.

The rabbinic conception of the «New Law» is that of a Law purged from precepts only temporary valid in this world. In Justin also the new Law is really the old Law, only purged from temporary accommodations made necessary because of Israel's hardness of heart.

It thus seems evident that Justin's material has evolved in a milieu closely in contact with rabbinic thinking about the Law.

---

279. Further passages which may express similar ideas are quoted by Davies, pp. 167ff.
280. Jervell made the same suggestion, *art. cit.*, p. 105.
281. Schafer, *art. cit.*, p. 41.
282. Cf. Goldfahn, 'Aggada', pp. 57f, who also refers to *Sanh.* 59b. cf. also Ginzberg V, pp. 189f.

Looking at the interrelations within Justin's material, we notice that in *Dial.* 11 the New Law idea is linked to the conception of the light of the Gentiles, and to Gen 49:10. The idea of the Law as a light for the Gentiles occurs within the OT quotation itself «A law shall go forth from me and my judgement εἰς φῶς ἐθνῶν . . .» Christ is this new Law enlightening the Gentiles, he is also the new Covenant promised in Jer 31:31: «He is the new Law and the new Covenant, and the προσδοκία . . . τῶν ἐθνῶν» (*Dial.* 11:4; cf. 11:2; 12:2; 43:1). The designation «expectation of the Gentiles» reminds one of Gen 49:10, and we have seen above that the idea of Christ as the new Law may have prompted the inclusion of Is 51:5 in the combined testimony in *1.Apol.* 32 (Num 24:17/Is 11:1/Is 51:5), parallel to Gen 49:10.[283]

Exactly in what sense is Christ the new Law? In order to answer that question, we shall turn to the remaining material on the new Law theme, first and foremost the main testimony, Is 2:3.

(2) For the rabbis, Is 2:3 meant that normative *Halakah* issued from Jerusalem. «In the words of Sirach (24:10.23), the wisdom of God, in the form of the Torah, had a permanent dwelling on Zion. The Jews' highest doctrinal court, the Great Sanhedrin, held its sessions within the actual Temple area . . . It was from this place that the Torah proceeded to the whole of Israel . . . »[284] «The Great Court . . . was in the Chamber of Hewn Stone (within the Temple ), whence the Law goes forth (cf. Is 2:3) to all Israel, as it is written . . . (Deut 17:10)« (*M. Sanh.* 11:2, p. 399).[285] In a debate on *Halakah* between Babylonian and Palestinian Tannaim ca 150, the following dialogue takes place: *»Es erhob sich R. Nathan und machte den Beschluss: Soll etwa von Babel die Tora ausgehn und das Wort Gottes von Nehar-Peqod? Sie antworteten ihm: 'Denn von Zion wird die Tora ausgehn und Jahves Wort von Jerusalem'«* (p *Ned.* 6:13).[286] We hear the former rabbi Paul speaking when he addresses the same question to the Corinthians who had taken liberties with Christian 'Halakah': ἢ ἀφ' ὑμῶν ὁ λόγος τοῦ θεοῦ ἐξῆλθεν . . . (1 Cor 14:36). The »right« answer to this rhetorical question might well be: No, the word of God issues fom Jerusalem, Is 2:3.[287] How wide an application Paul gave to this concept, is difficult to say.

---

283. As we have seen above, the Targums to Gen 49:11f may allude to Bar Kokhba's reinforcement of the *Halakah*. The Christian rebuttal would then be to point out Christ's universal implementation of the Law.

284. B. Gerhardsson, *Memory and Manuscript. Oral Tradition and Written Transmission in Rabbinic Judaism and Early Christianity* (ASNU 22, Lund-Copenhagen, 1964(2nd ed.)), p. 214.

285. Concerning the Temple as the center of Torah study and teaching, cf. also Sh. Safrai, 'Pilgrimage to Jerusalem at the Time of the Second Temple', Immanuel 5 (1975, pp. 51-62), pp. 52f.

286. Billerbeck's translation, III, p. 469. A parallel occurs in *p Sanh.* 1:3. Cf. also *B.B.* 21a (p. 105): «They . . . made an ordinance that teachers of children should be appointed in Jerusalem. By what verse did they guide themselves? - By the verse, 'For from Zion shall the Torah go forth'.» Cf. further *Ber.* 63b (p. 399).

287. Cf. Gerhardsson, *op. cit.,* p. 275.

As we have seen, for Justin Is 2:3 is fulfilled in the apostles' preaching to the ends of the world. How is this linked to the idea of Christ as the new Law? Let us quote *Dial* 11:4 in its entirety: »If, therefore, God predicted that he would make a new Covenant (Jer 31:31), and this for a light to the nations (Is 51:4), and we see and are convinced that, through the name of the crucified Jesus Christ, men have drawn near to God, leaving behind them idolatry and other sinful practices (ἀδικία), and have kept the faith and have practiced piety even unto death, then everyone can clearly see from these deeds and the accompanying powerful miracles that he indeed is the new Law, the new Covenant, and the expectation (Gen 49:10) of those who, from every nation, have awaited the blessings of God.«

Christ is the new Law quite simply because he accomplishes the most important function of the Law (cf. the next section): *He turns men from idolatry and iniquity to worship of God and a pious life.* The means by which Christ does this is the preached kerygma - the kerygma is his »rod of power« being sent out from Jerusalem, Ps 110:2 (*1.Apol.* 45:5; *Dial.* 83:4). It is his λόγος ἰσχυρός, *1.Apol.* 45:5. The risen and enthroned Christ reigns through his powerful word, carried from Jerusalem to the ends of the world by the twelve apostles. Through Christ's reign, men turn from idols to God. This is, quite succinctly, Justin's idea of Christ as the Law. Christ - through the apostles' kerygma - *fulfils the function of the Law.* One should therefore not construe a too great difference between the passages where Justin speaks of Christ as the new Law in person, and the passages where he speaks of Christ as the (new) Lawgiver, νομοθέτης, *Dial.* 11:2; 12:2; 14:3.

After this juxtaposition of Justin's ideas and the rabbinic material, let me add a brief review of Justin's Christian precursors. Paul once describes his own mission as carried out ἀπὸ 'Ιερουσαλήμ, Rom 15:19. He may well have conceived of his mission in the light of Is 2:3, cf. on 1 Cor 14:36 above. But there is not much explicit evidence in Paul; all one can say is that the idea may be implied in the passages referred to.

One may suggest that Is 2:3 was an important text to Luke,[288] although he nowhere quotes it. The apostolic kerygma is described as a word going out from Jerusalem to the ends of the world. This is not only said in programmatic sayings (Lk 24:47; Acts 1:8); it is deeply embedded in the overall structure of Acts. This »out from Jerusalem« motif is so distinct that it can hardly be unrelated to Is 2:3. But Luke seems not to share Justin's identification of Christ in person with the new Law, and it would probably be foreign to Luke to speak of the Gospel as the Law going out from Zion. That may be the reason why an explicit quotation of Is 2:3 is lacking. In the Isaiah prophecy, Luke could no doubt adopt the phrase λόγος κυρίου ἐξ' Ιερουσαλήμ ἐξελεύσεται, in fact, ὁ λόγος κυρίου (or τοῦ θεοῦ) is one of his

---

288. So E. Franklin, *Christ the Lord,* pp. 121f.

favourite terms for the apostolic kerygma.[289] But it is otherwise with the νόμος, which for Luke always refers to the Law of Moses.[290]

In Hermas, *Sim.* VIII:3 we find an interpretation of the parable of the willow-tree (*Sim.* VIII:1). The willow-tree »is God's law which was given to all the world. And this law is God's Son preached to the ends of the earth« (*Sim.* VIII:3:2). With this text should be compared *Sim* IX:16:5: »... these apostles and teachers who preached the name of the Son of God ...« and *Sim.* IX:25:2:»Apostles and teachers who preached to all of the world, and taught reverently and purely the word of the Lord ...«

It is difficult to know whether Is 2:3 lurks in the background of these passages, since Hermas does not quote the OT at all. It should be noted that the »out from Jerusalem« motif in Paul and Luke is lacking. On the other hand, Hermas has a straightforward identification of Christ with the Law preached to the ends of the world.[291]

The closest parallel to Justin's conception comes in the *Kerygma Petrou.* Clement says three times that Peter in the *Kerygma* calls the Lord λόγος καὶ νόμος (*Strom.* I:29:182; II:15:68; *Ecl. proph.* 58). There is a strong assumption that this is derived from Is 2:3,[292] in fact, Clement connects this verse with the KP in *Ecl. proph.* 58: »The Lord is himself called Law and Word according to Peter in the *Kerygma*, and also according to the prophet who writes: the Law shall go out from Zion and the word of God from Jerusalem.« And there are further parallels to Justin. The *Kerygma Petrou* shares with Justin Jer 31:31 as a main testimony on the new Covenant, and as we have seen already, Justin shows traces of the non-LXX version read by the *Kerygma.* The *Kerygma* also shares with Justin the idea of the twelve apostles as the ones who carry the Gospel to the ends of the world (fragm. 4).

We have noticed repeatedly that Justin in his conception of the apostolic mission is markedly Lukan. It is a pity that so little is preserved of the *Kerygma Petrou*: I suspect that it would have proved a link between Luke and Justin in several respects.

In any case, it is relevant to note that some Lukan features also can be seen to be deeply embedded in Justin's testimony material. Ps 96:10 (interpolated) seems to be closely related to Ps 110:2, [293] and both texts express the organic sequence between the *historia Iesu* and his *present*

---

289. Lk 1:2; Acts 4:4.29.31; 8:25; 10:44; 11:19; 13:46; 14:25; 16:6.32; etc.
290. Acts 13:38; 15:5; 28:32; Lk 24:44. cf. Jervell, *Luke*, pp. 136-138. We may here have the reason why Luke never *quotes* Is 2:3.
291. On this Christological concept in Hermas, see esp. L. Pernveden, *The Concept of the Church in the Shepherd of Hermas* (STL 27, Lund, 1966), pp. 52-57.
292. This is assumed by most commentators, cf. literature listed above, p.231, n.5.
293. Franklin surmises that Ps 110:2 and Ps 2:8 already were important texts for Luke (*Christ The Lord*, p. 136) .

*reign through the kerygma*: Christ reigns from the tree. His passion and resurrection/enthronement result in his rod of power going out from Jerusalem, Ps 110:1 —► Ps 110:2.[294] In the »creed« summary in *1.Apol.* 31, the whole enumeration of points to be proved debouches - not in Christ's return to judgement, but in the apostolic mission.

Compare with this Lk 24:46f:

»Thus it is written,  (1) that Christ should suffer

(2) and on the third day rise from the dead,

(3) and that repentance and forgivenness of sins
should be preached in his name to all nations,
beginning from Jerusalem.«

Here, as in Justin, the apostolic mission is seen in immediate conjunction with the Christological «creed». The saving power of the risen Christ is carried out to all nations in the preaching of the Gospel: The *historia Iesu* is continued in the proclamation of the kerygma.[295] This idea is not only embedded in the very structure of the whole of Luke's twin books, it is directly expressed in other texts,too: «(Paul is) saying nothing but what the prophets and Moses said would come to pass:

that Christ must suffer,

and that, by being the first to rise from the dead,

he would proclaim light both to the people and to the Gentiles» (Acts 26:22f).

This last text is of special relevance also in that it connects the ideas of Christ's reign and the enlightenment of Israel and the Gentiles, cf. also in the same vein Lk 2:32.

It is time to conclude. Following the most distinctive features of Justin's material, it seems we can trace a trajectory from Luke (first hints in Paul), via the *Kerygma Petrou*, to Justin's tradition. The growth and development of this tradition is marked by a continued contact with Jewish theology.

This means that the Lukan features in Justin's theology on this point are not merely due to his reading of Luke/Acts, although a direct literary dependence seems evident, and may have reinforced Lukan peculiarities inherent in Justin's material. The most direct proof that a living, continuous tradition links the two authors, is that Lukan features are deeply embedded in Justin's - mostly non-Lukan - OT testimonies on the apostolic mission, and the Lukan features in the *Kerygma Petrou.*

---

294. Daniélou, *Études,* stresses this sequence of *ascensio, sessio* and *missio* in Justin's material (pp. 46-49), cf. also Beskow, *Rex Gloriae,* p. 102. This is, roughly speaking, a Lukan feature in Justin: While the other synoptics take Ps 110:1 as describing a session which is going to be revealed at the *parousia,* Luke stresses Christ's present reign. Cf. Kurz, *Christological Proof,* pp. 225f.

295. «The first writer, apart from Luke, to assume that the world mission of the Apostles should be told in the same breath as the history of Jesus' death, resurrection, and ascension is Justin Martyr.... The missionary activity of the Apostles 'from Jerusalem' is (for Justin) as much part of the history of salvation as the work of Jesus. - (O'Neill, *Theology of Acts,* p.10).

We shall be able to characterise Justin's tradition further when we pursue the suggestions above that Christians according to Justin keep the Law.

(c) The people keeping the Law.

In his descriptions of Christians, Justin is eager to employ the very terms which in Jewish Greek writings are applied to the pious, Law-obedient Jew. Christians are δίκαιοι, they are characterised by εὐσέβεια, θεοσέβεια,[296] δικαιοπραξία etc.[297] But do they keep the Law? True, the new people do not observe the ritual commandments - but then these commandments are really not part of the Law, not of the eternal Law (see above). They are a temporary accommodation made necessary by the σκληροκαρδία of the Jews, but they have nothing to do with εὐσέβεια, δικαιοπραξία etc. I therefore take it that essentially Justin's answer to the above question is a 'yes' - Christians keep the Law, the essential Law.

When Justin shall describe the εὐσέβεια of Christians, he most regularly concentrates on two features, closely interrelated: Christians turn from idols to the true God, and they prefer martyrdom to idolatrous offerings. Let us review some relevant passages:

«By the name of him who was crucified, Jesus Christ, men part from idols and all other iniquity; and draw near to God, and make confession of him, and worship, enduring unto death.» (*Dial* 11:4).

For Christians, who even endure torture and death, it would be an easy thing to observe the ritual commandments, but it is not necessary, *Dial* 18:2f.

Christians have been made wise by the eternal Law, which is evident from the fact that «we cannot be brought to deny his name even by the threat of death.» Formerly we worshipped idols, now we worship God alone, *Dial* 30:2f.

Solomon practised idolatry, «a thing which they who from among the nations have come by Jesus ... to know God ... do not suffer to be done.

---

296. In Greek Jewish writings of the period, εὐσέβεια, θεοσέβεια and cognates are often used to describe the law-obediant Jew, refusing to deny his Jewish identity in face of persecutions. Cf. W. Foerster, art.' εὐσεβής etc', *ThDNT* VII, pp. 175181; D. Kaufmann-Bühler, art. 'Eusebeia', *RAC* 6, cols. 985-1052, esp. cols. 1020-23; G. Bertram, art.' θεοσεβής etc.', *ThDNT* III, pp. 124-126. The two terms are especially frequent as designations of pious, law-obediant Jews in *4 Macc.*; they also occur in Josephus.

297. A brief review of the evidence in Justin: *Dial* 10:3 (Trypho): You Christians claim to εὐσεβεῖν, but, like the Gentiles, you do not observe the law. *Dial* 11:4: By the name of Jesus Gentiles part from idols and practise εὐσέβεια. *Dial* 12:3 and 14:2: Jews regard observance of ceremonial laws to be εὐσέβεια. *Dial* 45:3: The Law of Moses comprises not only ritual commandments, but also τὰ φύσει καλὰ καὶ εὐσεβῆ καὶ δίκαια. *Dial* 93:2: Jesus said that all δικαιοσύνη καὶ εὐσέβεια was fulfilled through the double commandment of love. In *Dial* 46:7; 47:2; 47:5, εὐσέβεια and δικαιοπραξία are taken as equivalents, in *Dial* 110:3 and 136:2 the synonym is δικαιοσύνη.

θεοσέβεια and cognates: *Dial* 44:2: Only some of the commandments given by Moses are relevant for θεοσέβεια. *Dial* 52:4: By Christ the Gentiles have become θεοσεβεῖς καὶ δίκαιοι. Cf. further *Dial* 53:6; 91:3; 110:2.4; 118:3; 119:6; 131:5.

On the contrary, they suffer every kind of outrage and punishment, even to death itself, that they should neither commit idolatry nor eat things offered to idols.»(*Dial.* 34:8).

With might has Christ's word «persuaded many to forsake the demons whom they were serving, and by him to believe on God . . .» (*Dial.* 83:4).

Men of all nations have by the mystery of the cross «turned to the worship of God from their vain idols and demons.» (*Dial.* 91:3). «We, who have come to know the true worship of God from the Law and the Word that went forth from Jerusalem by the apostles of Jesus, have fled for refuge (κατεφύγομεν - all. to Zech. 2:15) to him who is God of Jacob and God of Israel. And we who were full of war . . . and every kind of evil, have . . . changed our weapons of war . . . and farm piety, righteousness, the love of man, faith and hope . . . Though we are beheaded, and crucified, and exposed to beasts . . . it is plain that we do not forsake the confession of our faith.» (*Dial.* 110:2-4, cf. also *Dial.* 131:2).

Let us compare this with some rabbinic sayings: «The law against idolatry outweighs all other commandments in the Torah. For it is said:'Then shall it be, if it be done in error by the congregation, it being hid from their eyes', etc. (Num 15:24). Scripture here singles out one law, mentioning it separately. And which law is it? It is the law against idolatry» (*Mekh.* Pisha V: 40-43, pp. 36f). «R. Johanan (died 279) said ( apropos Esther 2:5: 'there was a Jew (taken to mean: a descendant of Judah) . . . whose name was Mordecai . . . a Benjaminite') : He did indeed come from Benjamin. Why then was he called 'a Jew'? Because he repudiated idolatry.[298] For anyone who repudiates idolatry is called 'a Jew', as it is written, 'There are certain Jews' etc. (Dan 3:12 - Hananiah, Mishael and Azariah were not of Judah's tribe).» (*Meg.* 13a p.74). «R.Simon b. Pazzi (ca 280) once introduced an exposition of the Book of Chronicles as follows:'All thy words are one (i.e. numerous names in the Book of Chronicles refer to the same person) , and we know how to find their inner meaning. (It is written) ,'And his wife the Jewess bore Jered . . . (1 Chron 4:18). Why was she (the daughter of Pharaoh) called a Jewess? Because she repudiated idolatry, as it is written,'And the daughter of Pharaoh went down to bathe in the river', and R.Johanan (commenting on this) said that she went down to cleanse herself (by means of the ceremonial bath taken by a proselyte) from the idols of her father's house.» (*Meg.* 13a, p. 74). «Whoever acknowledges idolatry disavows the whole Torah, and whoever disavows idolatry acknowledges the whole Torah.« (*Sifre Deut* § 28).[299] In *Kidd.* 40a (p.199) the question is asked whether sins in thought only should be reckoned as sins. The answer is no. «Then what of

---

298. The parallel passage in *Esther Rab.* 6:2 (pp. 73f) brings out the implicit etymology here: «. . . because he proclaimed the unity of God's name, he was called 'Yehudi', as much as to say *yehidi* (=one who proclaims the unity).» (The midrash is quoted in full below, pp. 366f.)

299. Ed. Finkelstein, p. 123 - the quotation is taken from Urbach *The Sages* p. 697 n. 10. Cf. also the parallel in *Sifre Num.* 111, quoted ibid.

the verse, 'that I may take the house of Israel in their own heart'? (Ezek 14:5). - Said R. Aha b. Jacob (ca 325): That refers to idolatry, for a Master said: Idolatry is so heinous that he who rejects it is as though he admits (the truth of) the whole Torah.»

These rabbinic sayings[300] are of course not meant as declarations that circumcision and the ritual commandments can be dispensed with when you want to become a Jew, a member of the chosen people. One could perhaps render the meaning of the rabbis by saying that Gentiles who rejected idolatry were «Jews» *honoris causa*. Although none of the passages quoted are Tannaitic, there are good reasons for thinking that the idea expressed here is older than the quoted authorities,[301] and one has every reason to think that a Jew would grasp Justin's point about Christians observing the Torah by their rejection of idolatry.[302]

One should also note that the idea of martyrdom for Biblical mono-theism was given new urgency during the Bar Kokhba uprising. The wellknown story of Rabbi Akiba's martyrdom during the revolt brings this to the fore:

«When R.Akiba was taken out for execution, it was the hour for the recital of the Shema, and while they combed his flesh with iron combs, he was accepting upon himself the kingship of heaven (i.e. recited the *Shema*).His disciples said to him: Our teacher, even to this point? He said to them: All my days I have been troubled by this verse, 'with all thy soul', which I interpret, 'even if he takes thy soul'. I said: When shall I have the opportu-nity of fulfilling this? Now that I have the opportunity shall I not fulfil it? He prolonged the word *ehad* until he expired while saying it. A *bath kol* went forth and proclaimed:'Happy art thou, Akiba, that thy soul has departed with the word *ehad*,» (*Berak.* 61b, p.386). Justin's stress on Christian martyrdom for Biblical monotheism may have been prompted by a similar emphasis in Jewish circles.

The obedience and faithfulness to the great commandment of the Torah shown by Christians is contrasted to the unfaithfulness of the Jews.[303] The

---

300. Cf. also the material in Str. Bill. III, pp. 96f; Montefiore/Loewe, pp. 252f/570; S. S. Cohon,'The Unity of God. A Study in Hellenistic and Rabbinic Theology', *HUCA* 26 (1955, pp. 425-79), p. 445.

301. Cf. Urbach, *The Sages* I, pp. 22f.

302. Montefiore/Loewe quote a telling passage from *Tanhuma*:«And God says:'It is enough that the proselyte has abandoned his idolatry, and come to thee, therefore I urge thee to love him . . .» (p. 570).

303. Since we have seen parallels between Justin's Christological testimony material and the interpolations in the TP, it may be of relevance to notice that the Christology of the oldest interpolations also is dominated by the Law concept:«*In Dan 6:9 wird der Heiden Heiland als Gesetzeslehrer dargestellt. . . . Die Berechtigung der Heiden zum Heil wird daran aufgezeigt dass sie nach dem Gesetz leben, Dan 6:6.*» (Jervell, 'Interpolator', p. 47). While the Levites neglect the Torah, Christ renews the knowledge and observance of the Torah throughout the world. «At the time of Israel's lawlessness, the Lord will turn from them and to a people doing his will.» (*Test. Dan* 6:6, reading ποιοῦντα with MS β, cf. Becker's translation *ad loc.* (p. 97). The whole sentence is no doubt a Christian interpolation)

Jews, according to Justin, have precisely committed the Gentile sin *kat exochen*: They are idolaters, as especially demonstrated in the Golden Calf episode, *Dial.* 19:5f; 20:4; 22:1.11; 34:8; 46:6; 67:8; 92:4; 93:4; 130:4; 131:2; 132:1, and in their sacrificing their children to demons, *Dial.* 19:6; 27:2; 73:6; 133:1. The «substitution» model for the Jews/Gentiles relation can hardly be more sharply emphasised than when Justin describes how a total inversion has taken place between Jews and Gentiles: «For in the same way that you (Jews) provoked him by committing idolatry, so also has he deemed them (the Gentiles ), though (formerly) idolaters, to know his will, and to inherit the inheritance that is with him» (*Dial.* 130:4).

One can observe that the rabbis were painfully aware of the force of this reference to the Golden Calf episode. «Side by side with candid admissions that the worship of the golden calf had been the sin *par excellence,* from which Israel had never been completely absolved, we meet with a vast apologetic and polemic literature which aims at freeing Israel from this heavy burden of guilt.»[304] Perhaps one can also see a rebuttal of Justin's kind of argument when the rabbis stated that «the craving for idolatry had been uprooted and removed from Israel already at the beginning of the Second Temple period.»[305]

(d) The 'Christians before Christ'.

In Jewish literature, Abraham is sometimes regarded as the model prose-lyte: He abandoned idols, was persecuted, he was even thrown into a fiery furnace.[306] This last legend is clearly formed on the model of Dan 3: Ananiah, Azariah, and Mishael being thrown into the fiery furnace because of their rejection of idolatry. In Dan 3:12 these three are called ἄνδρες Ιουδαίοι (=MT יהודאין גברין ). Abraham is therefore taken toget-her with these three in texts which speak about the model «Jew», Mordecai, he who refused idol worship and confessed the unity of God.

I have already quoted one midrash on Esther 2:5 ('A Jew . . . Mordecai . . . a Benjaminite') which joins Mordecai and the three men (above, 364). In *Esther Rab* 6:2 (pp. 73f) we find an expanded version of the same midrash: «Why was he called 'a Judaean'; surely he was a Benjaminite? Because he declared the unity of God's name in the face of all mankind . . . The fact is that when Ahasuerus ordered that all should bow down to Haman, the latter fixed an idolatrous image on his breast for the purpose of making all bow down to an idol. When Haman saw that Mordecai did not bow down to it, he was filled with wrath. Said Mordecai to him: 'There is a Lord who is exalted above all the exalted; how can I abandon Him and bow down to an idol?' And so because he proclaimed the unity of God's name he was called

---

304. Smolar and Aberbach,'Golden calf', p. 102. Cf. also Bergmann, *Apologetik,* pp. 141f.
305. Urbach, *The Sages* I, p. 22.
306. The material is conveniently summarized in Ginzberg I, pp. 193-203.

'Yehudi', as much as to say *yehidi* (i.e. one who proclaims the unity). Some say that he was equal to Abraham in his generation. Just as our father Abraham allowed himself to be cast into the fiery furnace and converted his fellow-men and made them acknowledge the greatness of the Holy One, blessed be He, as it says,'And the souls which they had gotten (converted) in Haran' (Gen 12:5), so in the days of Mordecai men acknowledged the greatness of the Holy One, blessed be He, as it says,'And many from among the peoples of the land became Jews'(Esther 8:17), and he proclaimed the unity of God's name and sanctified it. Therefore he was called 'Yehudi', as it says, a Judaean man; read not 'Yehudi' but 'yehidi'.»

In *1.Apol.* 46 Justin has an excursus on the responsibility of men who lived before Christ - are they responsible for their idol worship? Justin's answer is yes. Even before Christ it was possible to live according to reason, i.e. to reject idol worship. Among the Greeks, «Socrates and Heraclitus and others like them» rejected idolatry, «among the barbarians, Abraham, Ananiah, Azariah, and Mishael; and Elijah and many others . . .» (*1.Apol.* 46:3). E. Benz[307] in his study of this and related passages in Justin says that it is «*unerfindlich*» why Abraham was included in this list of men who were accused of *asebeia* because of their rejection of idolatry.[308] I think the rabbinic material clarifies the issue, and proves that Justin depends on Jewish tradition: Socrates, Heraclitus and the others who *rejected idolatry* would be «Jews» *honoris causa* according to the rabbinic criterion. They could be seen as counterparts to Abraham and the three men in the fiery furnace.

Some further suggestions: This excursus (*1.Apol.* 46) occurs at the end of the «new Law» section in the *Apology.* The «Law going out from Zion» makes men law-obedient, they prefer martyrdom to idolatry. Was the tradition of Abraham and the three men already part of the New Law tradition in Justin's source?

Justin in other passages connects the motif of pagan martyrs for monotheism with his *logos* and *logos spermatikos* idea.[309] In Philo, *logos* and *nomos* are interchangeable concepts.[310] According to Justin, the activity of the *logos spermatikos* is to disparage idol/demon worship and lead men to the true God and a pious life.[311] In other words: The activity of the *logos* in

---

307. E. Benz,'Christus und Socrates in der alten Kirche. Ein Beitrag zum altkirchlichen Verständnis des Märtyrers und des Martyriums', *ZNW* 43 (1950/51), pp. 195-224.
308. *Art. cit.*, p. 203, n. 20.
309. I may be allowed to refer to the fuller treatment of the issue in my article (Norwegian) 'Åpenbaring utenfor åpenbaringen? Antikk religion, gresk filosofi og kristen tro ifølge Justin Martyr' ('Revelation outside Scripture? Antique Religion, Greek Philosophy and Christian Faith according to Justin Martyr'), *TTK* 49 (1978), pp. 261-282.
310. Cf. Wolfson, *Philo* I, pp. 258f.
311. Compare the two *logos spermatikos* passages (*2.Apol.* 8:2f and 13:3) with the following passages: *1.Apol.* 5:3f; *2.Apol.* 10:2-8. I have analysed these in some detail in my above mentioned article, pp. 264-273, with references to relevant literature.

these passages in Justin is conceived in «Law» terms, and accords with the rabbinic idea of Gentile «Jews».

I am on this background inclined to believe that one shall have to look for a Jewish substratum in Justin's apologetics concerning the «Christians before Christ», and I think this material may already have been part of the «New Law» tradition as it reached Justin.

Excursus II: *Justin's polemic against idolatry.*[312]

Briefly summarized, Justin has this to say about the origin of pagan religion: (1) The «sons of God» who comitted fornication with the daughters of men in Gen 6:1-4 were angels of high rank. Their offspring live on as demons.[313] (2) These demons have enticed men to think that they, the demons, are gods.[314] Scriptural testimony: Ps 96:5. [315]

Element 1 here has parallels in Jewish literature: *Jub.* 4:15.22; 5:1-11; 10; 1-14: *1 Enoch* 6-16; 86; *Test.Reub.* 5:6f: *2 Enoch* 7:5ff. It seems also to be reflected in the LXX translation of Gen 6:2, no matter whether ἄγγελοι or υἱοὶ τοῦ θεοῦ is the original reading.[316] «As far back as we can go in the exegetical tradition on Gen 6:1-4, בְּנֵי אֱלֹהִים are taken as angels».[317] At a later date, the rabbis rejected this exegesis.[318] The first explicitly to deny it was R. Simeon b. Yohai (ca 140):«R. Simeon b. Yohai called them (i.e. בְּנֵי אֱלֹהִים ) the sons of the nobles; R. Simeon b. Yohai cursed all who called them sons of God.» (*Gen.Rab.* 26:5:2, p. 213). This became the standard rabbinic point of view. «The Talmud never speaks of fallen or rebel angels. This is no accident, nor were the rabbis ignorant of the legend. They knew it and suppressed it.»[319] It is evidence of Justin's up-to-date knowledge of Jewish exegesis that he lets Trypho - the contemporary of R. Simeon b. Yohai - express the rabbinic opposition against the older Jewish tradition which Justin himself is following, *Dial.* 79:1.

The second element in Justin's polemic versus idolatry - viz. the identification of the giants/demons of Gen 6:2 with the pagan gods - has no direct counterpart in Jewish literature. «This is something new. It has some precedents in Hellenistic thought, but none whatever in Judaism. The rabbinic teachers did not doubt the existence of evil spirits; but they never identified them with pagan gods.»[320] This statement by Bamberger only needs a slight modification: There may in fact be some anticipations of Justin's idea prior to the rabbinic sources.

Josephus' paraphrase of Gen 6:1-4 runs like this:«For many angels of God now consorted with women and begat sons who were overbearing and disdainful of every virtue, such confidence had they in their strength; in fact the deeds that tradition ascribes to them resemble the audacious exploits told by the Greeks of the giants.» (*Ant.* I:73 ). Josephus is here probably drawing on a non-Biblical tradition about the «Giants» of Gen 6, resembling *1 Enoch* 7f. Here the Giants are pictured as instructors of different (mostly negative) cultural

---

312. A useful survey of Jewish polemic against idolatry is given in S. S. Cohon, 'The Unity of God', pp. 430-438.

313. *1.Apol.* 5:2; *2.Apol.* 5:2-5.

314. *Ibid.*

315. *Dial.* 55:2; 73:2; 79:4; 83:4.

316. Generally on the fall of the angels in Jewish literature, cf. Ginzberg I, pp. 147-151; A. Lods, 'La chute des anges. Origine et portée de cette speculation', *RHPhR* 7 (1927), pp. 295-315; H. B. Kuhn, 'The Angelology of the Non-canonical Jewish Apocalypses', *JBL* 67 (1948), pp. 211-19; R. J. Bamberger, *Fallen Angels* (Philad., 1952); Ph. S. Alexander, 'The Targumim and Early Exegesis of «Sons of God» in Genesis 6', *JJS* 23 (1972), pp. 60-71.

317. Alexander, *art. cit.*, p. 61. On Philo's exegesis of Gen 6:2, cf. Heinisch, *Einfluss Philos,* pp. 180f.

318. Cf. Goldfahn, 'Aggada', pp. 261f.

319. Bamberger, *op. cit.*, p. 90. This corresponds to a throughout rationalistic approach towards the phenomenon of idolatry and idols in rabbinic literature, cf. esp. Urbach, *The Sages* I, pp. 23-25, and A. Marmorstein, 'The Unity of God in Rabbinic Literature', *HUCA* 1 (1924), pp. 467-99, esp. pp. 473-487.

320. Bamberger, *op. cit.*, p. 74.

abilities - a function ascribed to the gods or heroes in Greek religion.[321] Josephus himself shows little interest in the whole incident, and his passage is probably a faint echo of a richer material. He has no identification between Biblical and Greek »Giants«, but the tradition on which he is drawing may have been on its way towards this identification.[322]

The LXX translators seem to have identified demons and pagan gods: πάντες οἱ θεοὶ τῶν ἐθνῶν δαιμόνια Ps 96:5. Δαιμόνια here render MT אֱלִילִים . Cf. also Deut 32:17: ἔθυσαν δαιμονίοις ( שֵׁדִים ) καὶ οὐ θεῷ, θεοῖς ( אֱלֹהִים ) οἷς οὐκ ᾔδεισαν . . . This last passage is echoed in Baruch 4:7: παρωξύνατε γὰρ τὸν ποιήσαντα ὑμᾶς θύσαντες δαιμονίοις καὶ οὐ θεῷ. But the most telling adaption comes in 1.Enoch. 19:1: »Uriel said to me: Here shall the angels stand, who mixed themselves with the women - and their spirits have made mankind unclean . . . and they will seduce them to sacrifice to the demons as if to gods . . .« This is Justin's conception in nuce.[323] It thus seems that Justin's polemic against idolatry is also dependent on a Jewish tradition - a tradition which was abandoned by the rabbis in the years preceeding Justin's days. He therefore has to defend this conception against Trypho. Let me finally remark that this polemic would be ideally adapted to the polemic against sacrifices in Justin's tradition about the sacrificial cult. The emphasis in the Jewish tradition on which Justin depends for his anti-idolatry polemic is on *sacrifices* to idols ( *1 Enoch*, LXX), this accords with the vice contracted by the Israelites during their stay in Egypt (so the AJ II) - God's temporary remedy being the sacrificial cult of the OT. I am thus tempted to think that Justin's polemic against idolatry may well have been part of the »kerygma« tradition studied in the foregoing chapters.

(e) Exhortation to conversion.

«Behold, I have set before you good and evil, choose the good.» With this free version of Deut 30:15/19 Justin's tradition (in this case: the KP?) addresses the would-be converts. These words were spoken by God to Adam, says Justin. Facing the choice of becoming a Christian and accepting baptism, each man has the opportunity of making Adam's choice over again ( *1.Apol.* 44:1-4). .

Very likely this text had its original setting in Jewish proselytizing practice - it is known to Philo.[324]

The direct admonition to baptism comes through Is 1:16-20: Wash and become clean. The Jewish Sibylline oracles may reflect Is 1:16ff in their exhortation to proselyte baptism:[325] «Have done with swords and moanings

---

321. Cf. P. D. Hanson,'Rebellion in Heaven, Azazel and Euhemeristic Heroes in 1 Enoch 6-11', *JBL* 96 (1977), pp. 195-233, esp. pp. 227-231.

322. On the parallels between Josephus and Justin, cf. Heinisch, *Einfluss Philos*, p. 181.

323. So also Ginzberg V, pp. 151-154: Justin's theory goes back to the pseudepigraphic Jewish literature.

324. *Deus Immut.* 50. Philo has a similar combination of Deut 30:15/19 as in Justin and Clement of Alexandria (= the KP?):' Ἰδοὺ δέδωκα πρὸ προσώπου σου τὴν ζωὴν καὶ τὸν θάνατον, τὸ ἀγαθὸν καὶ τὸ κακόν, ἔκλεξαι τὴν ζωήν. It i s relevant to notice that Philo quotes this text as a testimony on the freedom of choice with which man was created, §§45-49. In §48 Gen 2 is not far behind the text!

325. Not necessarily the proselyte baptism of rabbinic, normative Judaism, although *Sib.* IV, 163ff is often quoted as a witness of the »normal« proselyte baptism, e.g. Schürer III, p. 132; Str. Bill. I, p. 106, n. 1; J. Jeremias, *Die Kindertaufe in den ersten Vier Jahrhunderten* (Göttingen, 1958), pp. 29/37/41. But cf. the more careful discussion in W. Brandt, *Baptismen*, pp. 87-90. Brandt believes that the Fourth Sibyl reflects the conversion bath practised among some heretical Jewish sect. J. J. Collins also thinks of a Jewish baptismal sect as the milieu behind *IV Sib.*, cf. his article 'The Place of the Fourth Sibyl in the Development of Jewish Sibyllina', *JJS* 25 (1974), pp. 365-380, esp. pp. 377-380. There is greater unanimity in the view that Is 1:16 is referred to, see e.g. Brandt, *loc.cit.*, and Collins, *art. cit.*, p. 378, n. 72.

and killing of men and deeds of violence, and wash (λούσασθε) your whole bodies in ever-running rivers, and, stretching your hands to heaven, seek forgivenness for your former deeds, and with praises ask pardon for your bitter ungodliness ... But if with evil mind ye obey me not, but delighting in ungodliness ye receive all these words with ill-affected ears, then fire shall come upon the whole world, and a mighty sign with sword and trumpet ....» (IV: 163-174). Note that the quotation of Is 1:20 in Clem.A-lex. (*Protr.* 95:2 - cf. synopsis above, 230) - which we have surmised derives from the KP - reads a non-LXX *fire* in the text: ἐὰν δὲ μὴ ὑπακούσητε μου μηδὲ θελήσητε μάχαιρα ὑμᾶς καὶ πῦρ κατέδεται, and cf. Justin's comment on his LXX text (without fire!) in *1.Apol.* 44:5:«the sword of God *is the fire,* of which those who chose to do what is evil are made the fuel.»[326]

The urgency is brought near to the would-be convert by means of references to the resurrection and judgement impending on all men, Ezek 37:7f; Is 66:24. Each man's responsibility for his own salvation is emphasized by Ezek 14:20/18/Deut 24:16/Ezek 14:14. When *2.Clem.* (6:8; 7:6) rehearses these testimonies (Ezek 14:14/20; Is 66:24), the author is very likely reminding his readers of things they were taught in their very first encounter with the missionary preaching of the Church (cf. the baptismal references immediately attached to both testimonies). Compared with *2.Clem.,* it seems Justin's testimony material once more betrays a closer contact with Judaeo-Christian milieus still addressing their Jewish brethren. Is 1:9 was probably part of Justin's dossier: Israel is now in a state of exile and calamity - so turn to God and his Christ; do not trust your Jewish descent (Ezek 14:20 etc.).

Let us a last time also adduce *Dial.* 24:3:
δεῦτε σὺν ἐμοὶ πάντες οἱ φοβούμενοι τὸν θεόν,
οἱ θέλοντες τὰ ἀγαθὰ Ἰερουσαλὴμ ἰδεῖν.
δεῦτε, πορευθῶμεν τῷ φωτὶ κυρίου ...
δεῦτε, πάντα τὰ ἔθνη, συναχθῶμεν εἰς Ἰερουσαλημ ...
The closest parallel to this kind of missionary exhortation is again to be found in the Jewish Sibyllines:
δεῦτε, πεσόντες ἅπαντες ἐπὶ θονὶ λισσώμεσθα ἀθάνατον
βασιλῆα ...
πέμπωμεν πρὸς ναόν ...
δεῦτε, θεοῦ κατὰ δῆμον ἐπὶ στομάτεσσι πεσοντες ...
(III:716-18.725).
The whole of *Sib.* III:702-795 is a mighty vision of all peoples gathering in Jerusalem, carrying their gifts to the Temple. «*Dans le désastre universel qui*

---

326. This closeness between *1.Apol.* 44 and *Sib.* IV: 163ff is not surprising in view of the similarities observed above between the «baptismal» theology of *Sib.* IV and Justin's tradition, cf.above, p.297, n.126

*menace le monde, le temple de Jérusalem apparaît toujours comme l'asile de salut où se rassembleront les élus.*[327]

The Christian missionary tradition which addresses God-fearing Gentiles in *Dial.* 24:3, inviting them to God's salvation in Jerusalem, is walking in the footsteps of Jewish mission to the same addressees. At the same time, a radical discontinuity with regard to the Jewish people is expressed in precisely the same context:.«. . . for he has dismissed his people, the House of Jacob . . .»

*General conclusions and some suggestions.*

If the above analyses of Justin's material have come somewhere near the truth, it seems we are justified in hearing two distinct voices speaking to us through Justin's tradition.

The first is the voice of Jewish Christians addressing their fellow Jews in the distressing years immediately after the Bar Kokhba revolt. Theirs is a message of repentance and salvation for Israel; a presentation of the true Messiah after the frustrating experience with the failure of Bar Kokhba. If we try to delineate more precisely their theology, it would be something like this: Jesus is the Messiah promised by the Scriptures. In the Scriptures, two comings of the Messiah are predicted: One inglorious in which the Messiah should suffer, die, and be resurrected; and one in glory when he comes to take over the eternal kingdom. Jesus has fulfilled the prophecies about the first coming in lowliness - this guarantees his second coming in glory.

The saving effect of the career of Jesus is concentrated in the remission of sins: Jesus is the perfect paschal lamb, and his propitiary blood is applied to the believer in baptism. Jesus washes his believers in his blood. The sacrificial cult of the OT was instituted as an accomodation to Israel's proneness towards idolatry. Jesus makes an end to sacrifices; remission of sins is now to be obtained in baptism. In baptism a new man is created, begotten by Christ who is the head of a new humanity. He is also the one who once shall renew heaven and earth and shine as an everlasting light in a renewed Jerusalem.

The Jews crucified Jesus. The Jewish Christians here employ the old theme of the killing of the prophets in order to bring their fellow Jews to repentance. Jesus was the Just One, the last in a long line of just men before him. Because of their killing the Just One, Israel is punished with devastation of their land and city, and a prohibition to enter Jerusalem. Salvation comes through repentance and baptism.

---

327. A. Causse,'La propagande juive et l'hellénisme', *RHPhR* 3 (1923, pp. 397-414) p. 406. Cf. also *idem*,'La mythe de la nouvelle Jérusalem du Deutéro-Esaie à la IIIe Sibylle', *RHPhR* 18 (1938, pp. 377-414), pp. 406-414.

The prophets predicted that the Messiah should receive faith among the Gentiles rather than among the Jews. The Gentiles take the place of the unbelieving among the Jews.

This tradition which we reconstruct behind Justin corresponds roughly to the Judaeo-Christian theology contained in the AJ II.[328] It also has close parallels in the Christian interpolations in the TP - especially with regard to Christology and the concern for Israel's salvation.

We have to do with a theology which favoured a mission to the Gentiles and which in its practical consequences probably did not differ much from Paul. But it was un-Pauline, maybe slightly anti-Pauline. It solved the Law problem along other lines than Paul.

If we try to follow the line of tradition further into the Judaism of the first century, it seems we are brought in close contact with the milieu behind the 3rd and 4th Books of the Sibyllina, perhaps especially the Fourth.

The second voice speaking to us from Justin's material is the voice of triumphant Gentile Christianity. It is a Gentile Christianity still in close contact with rabbinic exegesis, still vitally concerned with Jerusalem and the land. It is a Gentile Christianity which absorbs the Judaeo-Christian tradition described above - while deeply modifying the concept of the people of God, circumcision, and the other rites affecting Jewish identity. The Christological testimonies are left untouched by this transformation, while the theological work with the people of God idea ends up with the concept of the (mainly) Gentile Christian Church as the new Israel. And the deuteronomistic preaching of guilt and repentance to the Jews begins to deteriorate to the self-righteous, unconcerned slogan which should foster so much Christian anti-Semitism in the history of the Church.

At the same time, the continued contact with Jewish exegesis, and the continued concern for Jerusalem and the land, are remarkable features of this Gentile Christian tradition. True, a doctrine about salvation in Jerusalem is present in other Christian writers of the late second century -e.g. Irenaeus and Tertullian. But one can hardly escape the impression that in these writers this is a piece of learned theology - precisely a *doctrine*. Not so in Justin's material. Here we meet Christians vitally, personally concerned about the happenings in Jerusalem and the Holy Land. This tradition has a remarkably concrete conception of salvation in Jerusalem and the land: The Hadrianic decree is an event of the most eminent theological signifi-

---

328. As we have seen, the AJ II seems to represent the shared tradition in a more primitive version than the one found in Justin. This corroborates the dating proposed by Strecker (cf. above, p. 252 ): The AJ II is hardly much later than Justin - its author may well have been his contemporary.

cance!³²⁹ God himself has closed the city to the circumcised - the uncircumcised believers are now to take their place. «Come with me, all . . . who wish to see the good things of Jerusalem. Come, let us go in the light of the Lord, for he has dismissed his people, the House of Jacob. Come, all ye nations, let us be gathered together at Jerusalem»(*Dial.* 24:3).

It may be audacious, but let me here at once adduce a passage from a modern historian which almost reads like a background report: «. . . *les Ebionites tombent, en tant que Juifs, parce que circoncis, sous le coup de l'interdiction faite par Hadrien à tout Israël de pénétrer et de vivre dans Jerusalem-Aelia. La ville sainte n'est plus leur ville. La grande Eglise peut alors les y remplacer. C'est au lendemain de la guerre qu'une communauté de chrétiens de la gentilité s'organise à Jérusalem, sous le gouvernement de l'évêque Marcus. Cette installation, en un pareil moment, a valeur de symbole. Elle consacre à la fois la faillite du judéo-christianisme, renié d'un côté comme il l'est de l'autre, et l'opposition irréductible entre le christianisme et Israël: c'est parmi le malheur des Juifs, et comme dans les fourgons de Rome, que les chrétiens venus du paganisme, adoptés à la place du peuple rebelle, font leur entrëe dans Sion.»* - This is Marcel Simon describing the events of AD 135.³³⁰

Is this the setting of Justin's tradition? Is this the reason for the vital concern for Jerusalem, the missionary invitation to Jerusalem? The ones speaking to us in Justin's material - are they Gentile Christians inheriting the traditions of the (Greek-speaking) Judaeo-Christians of Palestine, at the same time disinheriting their Jewish Christian brethren, taking their place in Jerusalem?

I can think of no setting better suited to explain the remarkable fact that in Justin's material there is a marked discontinuity in the people of God concept, while at the same time there is an unbroken concern for Jerusalem. And I can see nothing which excludes the possibility that Justin got his fundamental theological «education» in Palestine. He was born in Samaria -he may well have been converted to Christianity while still in Palestine. The Judaeo-Christian community behind the AJ II should probably be located in or near Pella, and in any case seems to have regarded themselves as the heirs of the Jerusalem community. Their theology is remarkably close to the Judaeo-Christian tradition which Justin's Gentile Christian tradition claims as its own.

---

329. It may be relevant to point out that among Palestinian rabbis contemporary with Justin, there seems to have been vivid eschatological expectations that Jerusalem will be restored from its present (post-Hadrianic) condition. Cf. Klausner, *Messianic Idea*, pp. 504f. I take from Klausner the following saying attributed to R. Jose b. Dormaskith (immediately after 135 AD):«The land of Israel (one MS: Jerusalem) is destined to be enlarged and spread out on all sides like this fig tree, which is small at the bottom.... And the gates of Jerusalem are destined to reach to Damascus .. as it is written:(Is 2:2), and as it is further written, «And many peoples shall go and say:'come ye..(Is 2:3).» (*Sifre Deut.* 1 end, Klausner, *op. cit.*, p. 505).

330. *Verus Israel,* p. 89. Cf. also J. Jocz, *Jewish People and Jesus Christ,* p. 71.

Of course this must remain a mere proposal. The only relevant fact known with certainty is that Justin began his life in Samaria and ended it in Rome, and along this circuit one can imagine other likely geographical locations for the «school» which left its theological imprint upon him. One can think of Antioch. In the seventies of the second century we meet there Theophilus of Antioch, a man deeply impregnated with Jewish and Judaeo-Christian tradition. It deserves notice that Theophilus probably is the first to quote the *Kerygma Petrou*[331] - unless our surmises about Justin are correct. Antioch is also a likely candidate as the place of origin for the *Gospel of Peter*[332] - another writing with which Justin's tradition has some relation.

In any case one has to imagine a milieu in close contact with rabbinic exegesis and Judaeo-Christian tradition. And one should probably not go too far from Palestine.

### 6. *Dial.* 86: Wood and water.[333]

I have singled out this passage for separate treatment, because I am uncertain about which material this passage is most closely related to. It seems to be somewhat isolated in Justin by its contents.

Refining our previous grouping of the material contained in *Dial* 86 (cf. above p. |215|), one can draw up the follwing outline.[334]

Heading: Christ's cross carried τὸ σύμβολον

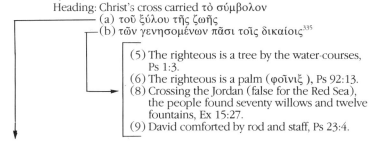

(a) τοῦ ξύλου τῆς ζωῆς
(b) τῶν γενησομένων πᾶσι τοῖς δικαίοις[335]

(5) The righteous is a tree by the water-courses, Ps 1:3.
(6) The righteous is a palm (φοῖνιξ ), Ps 92:13.
(8) Crossing the Jordan (false for the Red Sea), the people found seventy willows and twelve fountains, Ex 15:27.
(9) David comforted by rod and staff, Ps 23:4.

---

331. Cf. G. Quispel and R. M. Grant,'Note on the Petrine Apocrypha', *VC* 6 (1952), pp. 31f: *Ad Autol* I:14 probably alludes to KP Fragm. 3.

332. Cf. *ibid.*; and further Ch. Maurer in his introduction to the Gospel of Peter in *NT Apoc.* I, p. 180 (Syria); a review of proposed localizations in M. G. Mara's «Conclusion» in his SC edition (pp. 215-218).

333. On this chapter, see esp. P. Lundberg, *Typologie baptismale,* pp. 185-187; Daniélou, *Theology,* pp. 276f; Prigent, *Justin,* pp. 194-199; Reijners, *Holy Cross,* pp. 38-44.

334. The numbers in parenthesis indicate the place of each topic within the sequence of *Dial.* 86.

335. The syntax of the first sentence in *Dial.* 86 is extremely difficult. I here presuppose the minute analysis of Reijners, pp. 38-41, which I find convincing. In opposition to almost all existing translations, which make the tree of life a type of the cross, Reijners argues that it is the other way round: The cross is a symbol of the tree of life (the translations ignore the genitive in τοῦ ξύλου τῆς ζωῆς).

( 1) Moses released the people with a rod:
    (α) He divided the sea with his rod.
    (β) He made water spring from the rock with his rod.
    (γ) He made the water at Marah sweet with a tree (ξύλον).
( 2) Jacob's rod:
    (α) By casting rods into the water-troughs, Jacob made the sheep conceive.
    (β) With his rod Jacob crossed the Jordan.
            Excurses:    Jacob's ladder.
                         Jacob's anointing of the stone.
                         On anointing.
( 3) The rod of Aaron pointed him out as priest.
( 4) Christ will come as a rod from the root of Jesse, Is 11:1.
( 7) God appeared to Abraham from a tree, Gen 18:1.
(10) Elisha's rod cast into Jordan made the iron axe float up.
(11) Judah's rod marked him out as the father of Tamar's children.

One first notices that element 4 marks itself out as not being a type, but a prophecy. Besides, it is here Christ himself, not his cross, which is meant by the ῥάβδος. I therefore suspect that this element was not part of the original sequence.

Element 7 also falls outside the sequence on two indications: It intrudes into the types of righteous believers (nrs. 5-9), and it seems to presuppose Justin's argument on the theophanies. Besides, it is not a ῥάβδος testimony.

All the remaining types on Christ's cross (except one) contain the catchword ῥάβδος, and all except two connect rod with water. Chronologically we get the sequence: rod of Jacob, of Judah, of Moses, of Aaron, of Elisha. These rods are given a double reference: backwards to the tree of life, forwards to the cross of Christ.

All of this may seem quite bizarre to the modern reader, but would certainly appeal to contemporary readers versed in Jewish speculations on Aaron's staff. «'And the staff of Aaron'(Num 17:21). Some say that it was the staff which had been in the hands of Judah, in regard to which it says 'And thy staff that is in thy hand' (Gen 38:18). Others say that it was the staff that had been in the hand of Moses . . . That same staff was held in the hand of every king until the Temple was destroyed, and then it was (divinely) hidden away. That same staff is also destined to be held in the hand of the king Messiah . . . as it says,'The staff of thy strength the Lord will send out from Zion: Rule thou in the midst of thine enemies'(Ps 110:2·)» ( *Num. Rab.* 18, pp.743f). A somewhat similar speculation on the staff of Moses is preserved in *Pirqe de Rabbi Eliezer* 40 (22c). According to this, the staff was held in succession by Adam, Enoch, Noah, Shem, Abraham, Isaac, Jacob, Joseph, and Moses.[336]

---

336. Cf. Str. Bill. III, p. 746.

The lateness of the sources in which these traditions are found[337] precludes any idea of their being source material for Justin's speculations, but they prove that Justin's exposition would appeal to Jews. One also notes with interest the junction between staff speculation and Ps 110:2. We surmised above that *Dial.* 86 may have been added as an elaboration *ad vocem* ῥάβδος in *Dial.* 83 (= Ps 110:2).

The next point to be evaluated, is the connexion in Justin between rods and water.

The crossing of the Red Sea, Ex 14, is exploited as a baptismal type already in 1 Cor 10:2. The water from the rock may be referred to in *Barn.* 11:3, also a baptismal passage. One should therefore very likely look for a baptismal typology in Justin's list too. The idea contained in Justin's imagery may be delineated like this: The power of the cross secures a safe passage through the waters of baptism (Ex 14 and Gen 32:10), the cross has made the salvific baptismal water available (Ex 17:1ff: water from the rock), the cross turns the Sheol waters of baptism into sweet, saving water (Ex 15:25: the waters at Marah). By the power of the Cross, the baptismal water becomes a generic water (Jacob's sheep).[338]

It seems that very early in the second century a tradition can be discerned which conceives of the baptismal water as the waters of Sheol, and takes the descent into the baptismal font to be a descent into Sheol. This is coupled with the idea of Christ's descent to Sheol: In his baptism, the believer re-enacts Christ's descent, and he can do it safely, because Christ has conquered Sheol and broken its power.[339] In this context one also encounters the strange idea that Christ's cross participated in his descent (and ascent).[340] Probably the cross is here envisaged as the mighty sign of Christ's victory — precisely his ῥάβδος δυνάμεως — which he brings with him in his harrowing of Sheol.

---

337. *Num.Rab.* 15-23 derives from older Tanhuma-midrashes, but these are hardly earlier than the fifth century, cf. Strack, *Einleitung*, p. 207. *Pirqe de R. Eliezer* is dated by Strack to the beginning of the 9th century, *ibid.*, p. 217. A somewhat parallel tradition in *Gen.Rab.* 85:9 (p. 795) may also have been written down at a late date: »R. Hunia (ca 350) said (commenting on Gen 38:18, Judah's staff): . . . 'and thy staff' alludes to the royal Messiah, as in the verse, 'The staff of thy strength the Lord will send out from Zion' (Ps 110:2).« But also in older sources we find speculations concerning Aaron's staff. In *Pes.* 54a (p. 267) it is enumerated among the things created on the eve of the (first) sabbath. In *Yoma* 52b (p. 245), par. *Mekh.* on Ex 16:33, it said that the staff was hidden away together with the ark - to be revealed in the end-time. J. Daniélou, *Gospel Message*, p. 208, n. 33, refers to Ps.Philo, *Antiquitates Biblicae* (end of 1st century AD) as a witness of early Jewish staff speculation. Here Jacob's rods are associated with Aaron's rod, 17:1-4.

338. I therefore believe Prigent is wrong when he takes the ῥάβδοι types to be types of *Christ*, not the cross, *Justin*, pp. 197f. I would rather endorse Danielou's statement: »What is characteristic here is that these symbols should by preference be associated with the cross, a fact which points to a privileged position of the cross, and so suggests an archaic stage of theology.« (*Theology*, p. 277). Cf. also A. H. Couratin, 'Justin Martyr and Confirmation - A Note', *Theology* 55 (1952, pp. 158-60), p. 160.

339. The classic study of this topic is P. Lundberg's *Théologie baptismale*.

340. E.g. *Gospel of Peter*, 39-42; *Sib.* VI:26-28; *Acts of John*, 97f, cf. also *Barn.* 12:1.

Justin's types may very well derive from a tradition embodying the same concepts. One should note especially the story of Elisha throwing a tree in the Jordan, bringing the iron axehead up.[341] In Hermas, *Sim.* IX:16 we find a very similar idea: Stones are brought up from the (Sheol) waters, these stones symbolize the righteous men of the OT. One is also reminded of Justin's Ps.Jer logion on Christ's descent: He goes down to Hades to save the righteous men of the OT. The iron axehead at the bottom of Jordan may originally also have referred to the OT patriarchs abiding Christ's salvation in Sheol, although Justin has given it a more general application: the axehead stands for all sinners sunk in death. The ξύλον descends to Sheol to bring the patriarchs or, generally, sinners - up to life.[342]

A reference to Christ's descent to Sheol may even be implied in one of Justin's testimonies on the believers, viz. Ps 23:4. Justin only quotes part of the verse, but the context not quoted may be significant: ἐὰν γὰρ καὶ πορευθῶ ἐν μέσῳ σκιᾶς θανάτου... «Il paraît donc que le verset était entendu du Christ (or: the believer?) et que la »vallée d'ombre mortelle« est la descente du Christ aux Enfers.» (Daniélou).[343] Daniélou points to a text in Irenaeus confirming this assumption: «For as the Lord 'went away in the midst of the shadow of death' where the souls of the dead were, yet afterwards arose in the body . . .»(*Adv.Haer.* V:31:2). It is interesting that this passage comes not very long after Irenaeus has quoted the Ps.Jer saying about the descent of the Lord.

A further confirmation that Ps 23:4 was interpreted in this vein even prior to Justin, may be found in *1.Clem.* 26:2. Here Clement quotes as a resurrection testimony Ps 3:6: ἐκοιμήθην καὶ ὕπνωσα, ἐξηγέρθην, ὅτι σὺ μετ' ἐμοῦ εἶ. As has often been observed, ' the italicized ' words do not stem from Ps 3:6, but from Ps 23:4.

Daniélou may be right in suggesting that this conflation is deliberate and based on an exegesis of Ps 23:4 which understood this text as a *descensus* testimony.[344]

Returning to *Dial.* 86, we notice that Justin also has types on Christian believers. Ps 1:3; Ps 92:13, Ex 15:27: The believers are like trees, planted by the water. One suspects that this also refers to baptism: The water of Ps 1:3, the fountains of Ex 15:27 may well be references to the water of baptism. One also notes that Justin sees a type of believers in the tree of life of Paradise, the tree under which (according to the rabbis), the four rivers

---

341. Cf. esp. Lundberg, p. 185.
342. Cf. Ignatius' saying: The Christians are stones of the temple of the Father, »carried up to the heights by the engine of Jesus Christ, that is the cross....« (*Eph.* 9:1). The interpretation in Irenaeus, *Adv.Haer.* V:17:4, that the axe is the word of God, is hardly primitive.
343. *Études*, p. 142.
344. *Ibid.*

came forth. The rabbis also saw a connexion between the tree of life and the tree of Ps 1:3. In a *Baraita* in the *Palestinian Talmud* ( *Ber.* 1:2c) it is said about the tree of life: «. . . *alle Teilung der Schöpfungswasser teilte sich unter ihm. Und was ist der Schriftgrund?* ;*'Er ist wie ein Baum, gepflanzt an den Wasserteilungen'* (Ps 1:3).[345] To be probative, this text presupposes an identification between tree of life and the tree spoken of in Ps 1:3. In *Psal. Sal.* 14:35 and 1QH 8:4ff there are equations of the pious man, the tree of Ps 1:3 and the tree of life in Paradise.

Let us now turn to an important precursor of Justin, *Barnabas.* In *Barn.* 11:1—12:1 we find a fuller development of some of the ideas one can discern behind *Dial.* 86.[346]

The passage in *Barnabas* has a significant introduction:». . . let us enquire if the Lord took pains to foretell the water (of baptism) and the cross.« Here we meet the same close connexion between cross and baptism which is everywhere present in *Dial.* 86. *Barn.* 11 may be summarized in the following analytical paraphrase: [347]

Jer 2:12f:   Israel has rejected the only true baptism.

Is 16:1f:   Israel already declared Sinai to be a desert rock, i.e. they showed disbelief concerning the water from the rock (Ex 17:1-7/Num 20:1-11), the type of baptism. The Lord will punish them.

Is 45:2f:   Christ's victorious descent to Sheol.

Is 33:16-18:   The baptized is placed on the Temple mountain, by the faithful waters.

Ps 1:3-6:   The baptized is like a Paradise tree planted by the water-course. Comment: »Mark how he described the water and the cross together. For he means this: blessed are those who hoped on the cross, and descended into the water . . .«

Ezek 20:6.15:   «And the land of Jacob was praised above every land». Comment: «He means to say that he is glorifying the vessel of his Spirit.»

Ezek 47:1-12:   The baptized are like trees by the Temple river. Comment: «He means to say that we go down into the water full of sins and foulness, and we come up bearing the fruit of fear in our hearts, and having hope on Jesus in the Spirit . . .»

«Similarly, again, he describes the cross in another Prophet, who says, »And when shall all these things be accomplished? saith the Lord. When the tree shall fall and rise, and when blood shall flow from the tree«.

---

345. Str. Bill. IV, p. 1124.
346. Cf. Lundberg, *op. cit.,* p. 185: *-Justin a, lui aussi, connu la tradition testimoniale qui a été reproduite dans l'épître de Barnabé.«*
347. I here presuppose the detailed exegesis put forward in Lundberg, pp. 178-184; cf. also my article 'Tidlig kristen dåpsteologi', pp. 83-93, with references to further literature.

Among the relevant points to note in our context are the following: Although *Barn.* sees the «tree» of Ps 1:3 as a designation of the baptized believer, he also hears a reference to the cross in this text, cf. the comment in *Barn.* 11:8. The same double reference is implied in Justin's treatment of the tree of life in *Dial.* 86:1. In the prophetical *agraphon* in *Barn.* 12:1, it seems that the descent and ascent of the cross (the ξύλον) is seen as a model for the descent and ascent of the believer in baptism (cf. *Barn.* 11:8.11).[348]

I believe we encounter in *Dial.* 86 and *Barn.* 11:1-12:1 independent adaptions of a rich material related to the theology of baptism. It remains to be asked whether *Dial.* 86 has motives which links this chapter to other material in Justin. We have observed already the implicit *descensus* idea in some of the types. This points to the Ps. Jer logion in *Dial.* 72. The motif of baptism may be another link to this chapter of the *Dialogue:* The three first texts in *Dial.* 72 have the motif of the paschal lamb as their common denominator, and we have seen that the whole paschal lamb typology has baptismal connotations. This may also point to the underlying unity between paschal lamb motif and descent motif in *Dial.* 72.

The idea of salvation through the waters of Sheol is also implicit in the Deluge typology of *Dial.* 138; likewise the juxtaposition of water and wood. I take this as an indication that *Dial.* 86 is related to the «kerygma source» - or perhaps directly derives from it.

---

348. Concerning *Barn.* 12:1, see esp. J. Daniélou, 'Un *testimonium* sur la vigne dans *Barn.*, XII', in *idem, Etudes,* pp. 99-107.

## CHAPTER THREE

# THE EXEGETICAL TRADITIONS BEHIND *DIAL.* 48-107.

## 1. *The recapitulation idea (I): Pre-existence and virgin birth.*

As we have seen in Part Two, Justin's treatment of the virgin birth in the *Dialogue* is much more elaborate than in the *Apology*, and his argument is different. We found, besides, two layers in his arguments on pre-existence and virgin birth: (1) An argument based on an interpolated version of Is 7:10ff and an adjacent cluster of testimonies: Ps 72:5/17; Ps 110:3; Is 53:8; Dan 2:34; Ps 45:13; Gen 1:26; Prov 8:22f. (2) An argument starting from texts proving the existence of «another God» in Scripture (*Dial.* 56-60; 75 (par. *Dial.* 126-29)). The main burden of this argument rests on a detailed analysis of some OT theophanies. In accordance with my analysis in Part Two, I am here only concerned with the first unit, while the argument concerning the theopanies is singled out for separate treatment below (pp. 409ff).

Let us begin with a brief review of the rabbinic evidence concerning Justin's virgin birth testimonies.

Is 7:14 and Is 8:4 are referred to Hezekiah by the Jews, says Justin. Two rabbinic passages confirm this.[1] Four men, says R. Abba b. Kahana (ca 310), obtained knowledge of God unaided: Abraham, Job, Hezekiah, the Messiah. «Hezekiah king of Judah also learned to know the Holy One, blessed be he, by his own unaided effort. How do we know? Because it is in fact written of him, 'Curd and honey shall he eat when he knoweth to refuse evil, and choose the Good'(Is 7:15).» (*Num.Rab.* 14:2, p. 568). «Israel and Hezekiah sat that night and recited the Hallel, for it was Passover, yet were in terror lest at any moment Jerusalem might fall at his (Sennacherib's) hand. When they arose early in the morning to recite the 'Shema' and pray, they found their enemies dead corpses; for this reason did God say to Isaiah: Call his name *Maher-shalal-hash-baz* (Is 8:3), and he (Hezekiah) did indeed hasten to plunder their spoil. And call the other *Immanuel,* that is, 'I will be with him', as it says:'With him is an arm of flesh; but with us . . . (2 Chron 32:8).« (*Ex.Rab.* 18:5, p.221). The first of these passages takes Is 7:14ff as a prophecy about Hezekiah, the second passage seems to take Is 7:14 and 8:3 as sayings about the prophet's sons, but refers the import of the names to Hezekiah. One cannot know how old this rabbinic *haggadah* is,

---

1. Cf. Goldfahn,'Aggada', pp. 147f, and Klausner, *Messianic Idea,* pp. 464f.

but there is a possibility that the interpolated version of Is 7:10ff known to Justin, derives from a Christian theologian versed in rabbinic exegesis. We have seen reasons above to think this theologian wrote prior to Marcion.

The Jewish material on Ps 72:5/17 is richer. *I Enoch* 48:3 may contain an allusion to Ps 72:17. There are several rabbinic passages which contain sayings (one of them attributed to the early Tanna Jose the Galilean) which deduce the length of the Messianic age from Ps 72:5.[2] More directly concerned with the Messiah is the idea that Ps 72:17 proves the pre-existence of the Messiah's name.[3] The *Targum on Psalms* has the same idea in its paraphrase of Ps 72:17.[4] It is a disputed question among the experts whether this implies the conception of a pre-existence of the Messiah himself.[5] To our purpose it is not necessary to decide that question - what is evident in any case, is that a Christian familiar with the rabbinic interpretation of Ps 72:17 would easily turn this verse into a testimony on Christ's pre-existence.[6]

Ps 110:3 is not referred to the pre-existence of the Messiah in rabbinic sources, as far as I have been able to ascertain.[7] In a (late) midrash Ps 110:3 is applied to the «orphaned» redeemer, together with Zech 6:12 and Is 53:2.[8] But perhaps the LXX translators of Ps 110 entertained the idea of a pre-existent Messiah.[9] Is 53:8 is not referred to the birth or descent of the Messiah in rabbinic literature. Whether this verse lingers in the background of a passage like *4. Ezra* 13:52, is doubtful.

Dan 2:34 is referred to the Messiah by Resh Laqish (ca 250).[10] The Messianic exegesis of the testimony is probably older, since *4.Ezra* applies Dan 2:34 to the Messianic Son of Man, *4.Ezra* 13:6f.[11] One can conclude

---

2. Cf. the material gathered in Str. Bill. III, pp. 825f.

3. The most important passages are mentioned above, p. 266 with notes.

4. Cf. Levey, *Messiah*, p. 117.

5. Cf. i.a. L Ginzberg,'Die Haggada bei den Kirchenvätern und in der apokryphischen Literatur', *MGWJ* 42 (1898, pp. 537-550), pp. 541-545; Klausner, *Messianic Idea*, pp. 460f ; Urbach, *The Sages* I, pp. 684f; II, pp. 1005f .

6. Cf. Ginzberg, *art. ct.*: «*Wir dürfen . . . ohne Weiteres voraussetzen, dass die Praeexistenzlehre ein viel umstrittener Punkt zwischen Juden und Christen war, denn obwohl . . . die Praeexistenz des jüdischen Messias weit entfernt ist von der christlichen Logoslehre, so ist doch . . . nicht zu leugnen, dass von einem geschickten Apologeten der jüdische praeexistirende Messias leicht in christlichem Sinne gedeutet werden konnte.»* (p. 544).

7. But it occurs in a medieval source. «R. Isaac ben Moses Arama (15th century) quotes the verse in his commentary on Gen 47, stressing the unique and marvelous character of this prophecy of the Messiah's nativity.» (Hay, *Psalm 110* p. 32).

8. Cf. Str. Bill. I, pp. 49f.

9. So Str. Bill. II, p. 334. It is hardly necessary to my purpose to enter a full discussion of Jewish interpretation of Ps 110 as a whole. Cf. i.a. Str. Bill. IV, pp. 452-465; and Hay, *Psalm 110*, pp. 21-33.

10. See the numerous references in Str. Bill. I, p. 69; III, p. 506; IV p. 927.

11. Dan 2:34f is very likely hinted at in Lk 20:18, cf. esp. M. Black, 'The Christological Use of the Old Testament in the New Testament', *NTS* 18 (1971/72, pp. 114) pp. 11-14. But there is no question of the virgin birth here.

from this that Justin's material on several points has contact with Jewish exegesis.

There are few, if any, Christian writers prior to Justin who use these additional testimonies to Is 7:14. In *2.Clem.* 14:1 there is probably an allusion to Ps 72:5/17: The Church is created πρὸ ἡλίου καὶ σελήνης. The Jewish material makes one believe that Justin's Christological reference is primary, compared with this ecclesiological interpretation, and that consequently the Christological application of Ps 72:5/17 is older than *2.Clem.*

We have observed above (200f) that the tendency of Justin's source is to circumvent the textually problematic Is 7:14. The decisive argument for the virgin birth hinges on Is 8:4,[12] matched in the infancy narratives by Mt 2:1-12. The anti-Hezekiah polemic is deeply integrated into this source. This probably means that also the demonological thrust of the argument is pre-Justinian: The one predicted by Is 8:4 should liberate men from the power of demons already as a little baby - a thing never done by Hezekiah. This power over demons is due to the divine nature of the one born by the virgin: He is born before the morning star (Ps 110:3), before sun and moon (Ps 72:5/17), he is the stone cut without hands (Dan 2:34).Three passages bring this connexion out clearly: «Now he was also before Morning Star and

---

12. In an article entitled 'L'étoile de Jacob et la mission chrétienne à Damas' (*VC* 11 (1957), pp. 121-138), J. Daniélou has made some proposals which, if correct, would supply fascinating background material for the employment of Is 8:4 as a Christological testimony. Briefly delineated Daniélou's thesis is this: During their exile in «the land of Damascus», the Qumran Essenes lived in the castle Kochba near Damascus. This explains the popularity of the «Star» testimony Num 24:17 in the Damascus document and the other Qumran writings. During their stay in the land of Damascus the Essenes came into contact with Iranian *magi* and were deeply influenced by them. Some - like Dositheus, the teacher of Simon Magus -developed a heretical, proto-Gnostic mixture of Essenism and Iranian dualism. Dositheus lived at Kochba and applied Num 24:17 to himself. Others condemned this syncretism, and among them are found some of the early Essenic converts to Christianity, e.g. Stephen. As Christians they carried on their fight against the Iranian syncretism associated with Damascus and Samaria (Simon Magus). The earliest Christian texts on the star and the Magi stem from Syria: Mt 2; Ignatius. It is easy to see that this would provide an excellent explanation for the choice of Is 8:4 as a testimony fulfilled in the story of the Magi: Christ is to deliver the «wealth of Damascus and the spoil of Samaria», i.e. the people bound by the Iranian syncretism of the *magi* as it is taught in Damascus and Samaria! But there are many fragile components in Daniélou's impressive construction, first and foremost the whole idea of an Essenic exile by Damascus, which is pivotal in Daniélous theory. F. M. Cross in his authoritative study of the Qumran community *(The Ancient Library of Qumran and Modern Biblical Studies* (Rev. ed., New York, 1961)) has argued - convincingly, it seems - that «the land of Damascus» in the Damascus document is simply a «prophetical code-word» for the surroundings of Qumran. A direct contact between the Qumran people and Iranian dualists is also a disputable hypothesis. All taken together, I believe Daniélou's construction is far to fragile to serve as a basis for a likely hypothesis about Justin's use of Is 8:4. This can be further substantiated by a closer examination of Justin's exegesis of the text. For him, «Damascus» is not directly connected with the Magi; he has to interpolate the idea that Damascus belongs to *Arabia.* The Magi came from Arabia, and Damascus belongs to Arabia, so the Magi are covered by the catchword «Damascus». To conclude: I think one has to dispense with Daniélou's hypothesis, at least as far as the material in Justin is concerned.

Moon, and endured to be made flesh and be born by the Virgin who was of the race of David, in order that by this dispensation of God the serpent who did evil in the beginning and the angels who became like it, might be destroyed, and death be brought into contempt . . .»(*Dial* 45:4). «And again he says in different words:'I give you authority to tread upon serpents . . . and on every form of the enemy's power'. So now we who believe on Jesus our Lord who was crucified under Pontius Pilate exorcise all the demons and evil spirits, and thus hold them subject to us . . . And David proclaimed that he would be born of the womb before sun and moon according to the will of the Father, and declared that he, being Christ, was the Mighty God, and was to be worshipped.»(*Dial* 76:6f).

«And with might has his word persuaded many to forsake the demons, whom they were serving . . . And the phrase 'in the splendour of the saints, of the womb before the morning star did I beget thee,' was spoken to Christ, as we said before.»(*Dial* 83:4).

It is evident from these passages that the pre-existence testimonies adjacent to Is 7:10ff are intimately bound up with the idea of a divine, pre-existent Messiah who is Lord over the devil and the demons.

To characterize this concept further, let us turn to some other, related, passages in the *Dialogue*. «What is really a sign (Is 7:10) . . . namely the first-born of all creatures to become incarnate through a virgin's womb . . . this he (God) anticipated by the spirit of the prophets in various ways, as I have related to you . . .; just as Eve came into being from one rib of Adam, and as all other living creatures were begotten by the word of God in the beginning.»(*Dial* 84:2) Here the virgin birth is seen as an analogy to the first creation of man (Eve) in Gen 2. God - in Jesus - is making a new beginning as radical as when he first created man. This leads us on to the concept of Christ as the second, the new Adam. Just as the devil tempted Adam, so he tempted Jesus after his baptism, «for as he led Adam astray, he thought that he could do some harm to him also.» (*Dial* 103:6). The new Adam conquers where the first Adam was conquered, because the second Adam is God's divine, pre-existent Son. «And finding him written down in the memoirs of the Apostles as Son of God and calling him Son, we have understood that he is so, and also that he came forth before all things that were made of the Father . . . He has become man by the Virgin, in order that by the same way in which disobedience caused by the serpent took its beginning, by this way should it also take its destruction» (*Dial* 100:4). In *Dial* 100:5 an Eve/Mary contrast is introduced to complete the Adam/ Christ typology. *Dial* 100:6 concludes: By Mary «has he been born, about whom we have proved so many Scriptures have been spoken, by means of whom God destroys both the serpent and those angels and men that became like it, but for them that repent of their evil deeds . . . does he work deliverance from death.»

In the analysis of *Dial* 100; 103, and 106 above (221ff), I surmised a common denominator behind these passages: In the temptation story,

Christ as the Son of God, the second Adam, is tested. The temptation follows immediately after the heavenly voice has proclaimed 'Thou art my son . . .' This is especially clear in *Dial.* 103:5f: The devil is addressed as Satanas by Jesus, «signifying that he had obtained a name made up from the action he performed. For *sata* in the language of Jews and Syrians is 'apostate' and *nas* is a name from which the interpretation of 'serpent' is taken. So from both expressions comes the one name *satanas*. Moreover this devil - at the very moment that he ascended from the river Jordan, when the utterance had been spoken to him, 'Thou art my Son, to-day have I begotten thee' - is recorded in the Memoirs of the Apostles as coming up to him and tempting him, even as far as to say to him, 'Worship me', and Christ answered him, 'Get behind me, Satanas; the Lord thy God shalt thou worship, and him alone shalt thou serve'. For as he led Adam astray, he thought that he could do some harm to him also.« The special relevance of this passage is that it proves how deeply the recapitulation idea is integrated in Justin's inherited material. The etymology[13] given for Satanas has a special function: It proves that the 'Satanas' encountered by Jesus in his temptation was the same as the 'serpent' encountered by Adam - Satanas means 'apostate serpent', i.e. the serpent of Gen 3! In other words: Jesus met the same adversary as the first Adam.[14]

As we have seen, in the above version of Jesus' rebuke of Satan, a phrase from Mt. 16 has been incorporated: At Caesarea Philippi Peter recognizes that Jesus is the Son of God, and again Jesus is tested by Peter=Satan.

We here face early Gospel exegesis which interpreted the Son of God concept in »recapitulation« terms: Christ proves himself to be Son of God by conquering where Adam was conquered. The same Adam/Christ relation is expressed in *Dial.* 124f. *Dial.* 124 first brings the testimony on Adam's (and Eve's) fall, Ps 82:6f. (As Justin remarks in *Dial.* 124:3, this is not the purpose to which the testimony is quoted in the present argument of the *Dialogue*. but it is no doubt the purpose to which the text was quoted in Justin's source). In fact, the Son of God concept is central to Justin's use of and comments on the text even in its present setting: »(Men) were made, like God, free from suffering and immortal, if they kept his precepts, and were deemed worthy of being called by him his sons. But they became like Adam and Eve, and prepared death for themselves.« (*Dial.* 124:4).

A combined Adam/Christ and Jacob/Christ typology follows in *Dial.* 125, but only the Jacob/Christ typology is relevant in the present content of the *Dialogue*, and only this is explicitly developed. Christ in his conquering of

---

13. An Aramaic/Hebrew etymology for the *Greek* version of Satan's name!

14. I owe this observation to M. Steiner, *La tentation de Jésus dans l'interprétation patristique de Saint Justin à Origéne* (EB, Paris, 1962), pp. 13f.

the devil is not only the new Adam, he is also the true »Israel«, for Israel means »a man overcoming power«.[15]

It seems to me that we have in these passages the later Irenaean recapitulation theology *in nuce.*[16] Although the very term ἀνακεφαλαίωσις does not occur in any of the quoted texts, there is evidence in Irenaeus himself that Justin knew and used this term. In *Adv.Haer.* IV:6:2 Irenaeus brings the following quotation from Justin (the Greek retroversion of the italicized phrase is A. Rousseau's in the SC edition):

Καὶ καλῶς ὁ᾽ Ἰουστῖνος ἐν τῷ πρὸς Μαρκίωνα συντάγματί φησιν ὅτι αὐτῷ τῷ Κυρίῳ οὐκ ἂν ἐπείσθην ἄλλον Θεὸν καταγγέλλοντι παρὰ τὸν Δημιουργὸν et factorem et nutritorem nostrum; sed quoniam ab uno Deo, qui et hunc mundum fecit et nos plasmavit et omnia continet et administrat, unigenitus Filius venit ad nos, *suum plasma in semetipsum recapitulans* (τὸ ἴδιον πλάσμα εἰς ἑαυτὸν ἀνακεφαλαιωσάμενος), firma est mea ad eum fides et immobilis erga Patrem dilectio, utraque Domino nobis praebente.[17]

Christ - the co-creator of man - by becoming man himself creates humanity anew. He becomes «the head of another race». I think the Adam/Christ passages quoted above eloquently bring out what is here meant by «recapitulation».

Can the tradition embodied in these «recapitulation» passages be traced in earlier Christian writers?

In the NT, Paul and Luke claim our attention. One is led to think of the Pauline Adam/Christ typology in Rom. 5:12-21 and 1 Cor 15: 45-49. There is a basic correspondence of ideas between these Pauline texts and Justin's. At the same time there are differences, first and foremost the emphasis on the demonological framework in Justin. There is a great amount of *Gospel exegesis* embodied in Justin's material, as shown by the prominent position accorded the temptation story. On the other hand, Paul's stress on the fact

---

15. Cf. relevant Jewish material gathered in E. Schweizer,'Die Kirche als Leib Christi in den paulinischen Homologumena', *ThLZ* 86 (1961, cols. 161-174), cols. 167f. »... *Jakob ist deutliche Parallelgestalt zu Adam und Noah.*« (col. 168, with references to Philonic passages).
16. Cf. i.a. Daniélou, *Gospel Message,* p. 205.
17. The Greek part of the quotation is preserved in Eus. *E.H.* IV:18:9. J. A. Robinson ('On a Quotation from Justin in Irenaeus', *JTS* 31(1930), pp. 374-78) has argued that the quotation only comprises Eusebius' Greek excerpt, because several terms in the Latin part are used by Irenaeus himself elsewhere. But this in itself is hardly a sufficient reason to deny that Justin is responsible for the Latin part of the quotation, because one cannot exclude a certain amount of terminological overlapping between the two authors - Iranaeus may simply have been influenced by Justin! Looking at the context in Irenaeus, one observes that Irenaeus has paraphrased the entire quotation in his introduction to it, but whereas Irenaeus writes in »we«-style, the quotation is in »I« style. This doublet is a strong argument that the quotation comprises also the Latin part, and I thus think there is every reason to stick to the traditional delineation of the extent of the quotation - which is also followed in the recent *SC* edition of the text (p. 441).

that Christ's victory for men and his free gift to men are «so much more» compared with Adam's fall, is lacking in Justin.

There is thus no question of simple literary borrowing from Paul. Turning to Luke, we notice that on the level of redaction history, Luke has emphasized the concept of Christ the second Adam, Son of God, precisely in his handling of the temptation story. Between the baptism of Jesus and his temptation by the devil, Luke has inserted the genealogy of Jesus, tracing the line all the way back to «Adam, the son of God» (Lk 3:38). There is thus established a telling prelude to the devil's first address to Jesus: 'If you are the Son of God . . . (Lk 4:3).[18]

We have perhaps an echo of Luke's genealogy in *Dial.* 100:3, where Justin, seemingly *malapropos,* explains the title «Son of Man» as signifying Christ's descent from Adam. Immediately before, Justin has tried to relate the title to Matthew's genealogy, and he represents the two explanations as possible alternatives: «He called himself Son of Man . . . either from his birth by the Virgin, who was . . . of the race of David and Jacob and Isaac and Abraham, or because Adam himself is father even of those who have been enumerated.»

But again, the striking similarities of idea between our two writers cannot be satisfactorily explained by simple literary dependence. In fact, the essential element of the *Satanas* etymology in Justin presupposes Matthew's version of the temptation story, not Luke's: Only in Matthew is the devil addressed as Satan. On the whole, Justin's Gospel material in the recapitulation passages is closer to Matthew than to Luke. To put it a little crudely: Justin's tradition quotes Matthew, but thinks like Luke. This points to a common, living tradition, which cannot be explained on a purely literary level.

It is time to return to some details in Justin's texts, which may throw further light on the profile and setting of his tradition. My first remark concerns the Jacob/Christ typology in *Dial.* 125. Christ conquered the devil - Jacob, as his type, conquered «a power». The logic of this typology requires that the «power» is a hostile, at least an antagonistic power. This is not what Justin himself says, however, because he has introduced his theophany theory at this point, and therefore states that the «power» was Christ. This complicates and confuses the typology considerably. I think this is a secondary complication of an originally simple typology which regarded the «power» as hostile.

This is confirmed by the fact that there exists in Jewish sources a tradition which conceived of Jacob's foe as a hostile rival. In the «Prayer of Joseph» (henceforward = PJ) the patriarch Jacob is portrayed as an incarnation of

---

18. Cf. e.g. Klostermann, *comm. ad loc.,* p. 57; F. Hahn, *Christologische Hoheitstitel. Ihre Geschichte im Christentum* (FRLANT 83, 3rd ed., Göttingen, 1966), p.117; M. Dorner, *Das Heil Gottes. Studien zur Theologie des Lukanischen Doppelwerkes* (BBB 51, Köln-Bonn, 1978), pp. 27f.

the angel Israel, «the first-born (πρωτόγονος) of every creature». (Notice how this concept of Jacob would easily lend itself to Christological exploitation: Jacob, type of Christ, the πρωτότοκος πάσης κτίσεως). The archangel Uriel is seized by envy, and comes to fight with Jacob/Israel.[19] J.Z.Smith has subjected this Jewish *apokryphon* to a minute analysis[20] and come to the conclusion that it reflects «first or second century Jewish mysticism»,[21] and contains «a myth on the mystery of Israel».[22] The etymology of the name «Israel» in the PJ («a man seeing God») is different from Justin's,[23] and I do not want to posit a direct literary dependence between Justin's source and the PJ. All I want to suggest is that the Christian author responsible for the Jacob/Christ typology in *Dial.* 125 very likely had knowledge of a Jewish Jacob/Israel speculation similar to the one found in PJ.[24] (On the general importance of the Jacob/Israel theme in Jewish/ Christian controversy, I refer to the discussion above; pp. 345ff)

My second remark concerns the idea of pre-existence. In the allusion to Ps 72:5/17 in *2.Clem.* 14:1 we read that the spiritual Church was created (ἐκτισμένη) before sun and moon. This recalls Prov 8:22: ἔκτισέν με ἀρχὴν ὁδῶν αὐτοῦ. If a Christological reference of *2.Clem.*'s tradition is more original than the present ecclesiological (cf. above, 382), we may face here a tradition combining Ps 72:5/17 and Prov 8:22: A «Wisdom» Christology stressing Christ's pre-existence.

Let us pursue this suggestion by turning to Irenaeus, *Dem.* 43. Here we find three pre-existence testimonies: (1) a targum on Gen 1:1;[25] (2) a combined quotation of Ps 110:3/Ps 72:17, quoted as «Jeremiah»; (3) a pseudo-Jeremiah quotation:«Blessed is he who existed before he was made man.» The text which especially claims our attention is the targum on Gen 1:1. It seems the text expresses the idea that the Son was «created» before heaven and earth (see discussion above p. 236) This is no doubt read into Gen 1:1 from Prov 8:22, which is interpreted Christologically.

---

19. The fragments of this apocryphon are preserved by Origen, *In Joh.* II:31 (25): 189-190; and in *In Gen.* III:9. I have used the text in A.-M. Denis, *Fragmenta*, pp. 61f. General information about recent research is given in idem, *Introduction*, pp. 125-127.

20. J. Z. Smith, 'The Prayer of Joseph',*Religions in Antiquity. Essays in Memory of E. R. Goodenough* (Suppl. to Numen, 14, Leiden, 1968), pp. 253-294. cf. also E. Schweizer, *art. cit.*, cols. 167f.

21. Smith, *art. cit.*, p. 291.

22. *Ibid.*, p. 287.

23. But the same as in several rabbinic texts ( אִישׁ רָאָה אֵל ) and in Philo. See the survey in Ginzberg V, pp. 307f, n. 253.

24. For rabbinic material relating to the idea of the PJ, cf. Ginzberg V, pp. 305/309f.

25. On this text, cf. literature listed above, p.235, n.16

This combination of Prov 8:22 and Gen 1:1 is commonplace in rabbinic literature[26] and is hinted at in Christian literature prior to Justin.[27] But in these sources the combination is made in a more refined way: The ראשית = Wisdom of Prov 8:22 is identified with the ראשית of Gen 1:1, thus obtaining the idea «by Wisdom God created . . . .»[28] The targum in *Dem.* 43 makes the combination in a more outward manner: It so to speak interpolates Prov 8:22 into Gen 1:1: God first created the Son (Wisdom) - then heaven and earth.

This combination of Wisdom Christology and pre-existence testimonies in Irenaeus - possibly already in *2.Clem.* -encourages the following consideration: Justin's Wisdom Christology in *Dial.* 61f may derive from the same source as the pre-existence and virgin birth testimonies in *Dial.* 63ff.

*Dial.* 61:1 - 62:4 stands out from the context by not being devoted to the theme of theophanies. One notes the solemn introduction in *Dial.* 61:1: «Yet another testimony from the Scriptures will I give to you, my friends, . . . namely that God has begotten as a »Beginning« (ἀρχή) before all his creatures a kind of resonable power from himself (δύναμίν τινα ἐξ ἑαυτοῦ λογικήν), which is also called by the Holy Spirit the Glory of the Lord, and sometimes Son, and sometimes Wisdom, and sometimes angel, and sometimes God, and sometimes Lord and Word . . .» This passage serves to introduce the long quotation of Prov 8:22-36,[29] and one notices how Justin strives to connect two series of Christological predicates: The one derives from the theophany argument (glory, angel, God, Lord); the other from the Wisdom Christology: Son, Wisdom, Word.

---

26. Cf. i.a. Ginzberg,'Haggada ', pp. 539-547; Str. Bill. II, pp. 356f; G. F. Moore, *Judaism* I, pp. 263-269; K. Schubert,'Einige Beobachtungen zum Verständnis des Logosbegriffes im Frührabbinischen Schrifttum-, *Judaica* 9 (1953, pp. 65-80), pp. 76-80; H.-F. Weiss, *Untersuchungen zur Kosmologie des hellenistischen und palästinensischen Judentums* (TU 97, Berlin, 1966), pp. 196-199/292-300; M. Hengel, *Judentum und Hellenismus* (WUNT 10, Tübingen, 1969), pp. 307-318; Urbach, *The Sages* I, pp. 198f.

27. Esp. Col 1:15ff seems to depend on this rabbinic idea, cf. esp. c. F. Burney, 'Christ as the APXH of creation (Prov. VIII 22, Col I 15-18, Rev III 14)', *JTS* 27 (1926), pp. 160-177; and compare to this study Lohse's *comm. ad loc.*

28. This is the reading in Gen 1:1 of the Fragmentary Targum. cf. also *Sanh.* 38a (p. 241):«'Wisdom hath builded her house'(Prov 9:1), - this is the attribute of the Holy One, blessed be He, who created the world by wisdom.»

29. Prigent, *Justin*, pp. 129f, strives to read *Dial.* 61:1 as a paraphrase of Gen 1:1 rather than as an introduction to Prov 8:22ff. He takes ἀρχή and δύναμις λογική to reflect the same double rendering of ראשית as he finds in *Dem.* 43 and *Adv. Prax* 800. 5. I have two problems with this. (1) I question whether the targum in *Dem.* 43 can really be said to give a *double* rendering of ראשית . I believe one should rather call «a Son» an *interpolation* from Prov 8:22 (So also Nautin, 'Genese, 1,1-2-, p. 85). (2) Justin's passage is a perfect introduction to Prov 8:22ff - there is no reason to look for cryptic references to another text. This means that while Justin may have known the source behind *Dem.* 43 (cf. pp. 235f), he has not dared to reproduce its version of Gen 1:1. He may have felt the same uncertainty as Tertullian did concerning this targumizing of the text. Instead, he has brought forward the text he thought unambiguous: Prov 8:22ff.

It goes without saying that Prov 8:22ff expresses Wisdom Christology, but I suspect the same is true with the next testimony, Gen 1:26.[30] Justin's point is that the Father spoke to the Son when he said: 'Let us make'. In Jewish sources we find the idea that God consulted his Wisdom in Gen 1:26 (*Sap.Sal.* 9:1ff; 10:2; *2 Enoch* 30:8).[31] Among Christian writers, it is Theophilus who seems to have preserved the idea in its most original form: «God is found saying 'Let us make man . . .' as if he needed assistance; but he said 'Let us make' to none other than his own *Logos* and his own *Sophia.*»[32] The only Christian element here is the doubleness of *Logos* and *Sophia* (corresponding to Son and Spirit), in other respects the idea is entirely Jewish.

The high age of this Christological topic is attested by *Barn.* 5:5 and 6:12.

It is not only the closeness between *Dial.* 61f (Wisdom Christology) and *Dial.* 63ff (Pre-existence, virgin birt, »recapitulation«) in the present sequence of the *Dialogue* which indicates an original connexion of Wisdom and recapitulation Christology. Apart from the evidence in *2.Clem.* and Irenaeus presented above, which connects Ps 72:17 etc. with the Wisdom motif, there is a distinctive phrase in Justin which always occurs within the recapitulation passages, and which almost certainly derives from Prov 8:22: Christ is πρωτότοκος πάσης κτίσεως: *Dial.* 84:2; 85:2; 100:2; 125:3; 138:2.[33] The characteristic distribution of this term makes one believe that it was already part of Justin's tradition, whether it is directly inspired by Col 1:15 or not.

---

30. So also R. Mc L. Wilson, 'The Early History of the Exegesis of Gen 1.26', *Studia Patristica* 1 (TU 63, Berlin, 1957, pp. 420-437), p. 422:«(Justin) understands the text (Gen 1:26) of Wisdom, with a reference to Prov 8:21ff, which he has quoted in the preceeding section.»

31. On this Jewish concept, cf. esp. J. Jervell, *Imago Dei. Gen 1,26f im Spätjudentum in der Gnosis und in den paulinischen Briefen* (FRLANT 70, Göttingen, 1960), pp. 48-51. Goodenough, *Theology*, pp. 114/145f (following Goldfahn, pp. 145f), finds that Justin knew both Tannaitic and Philonic interpretations of Gen 1:26f. This indeed seems to be true concerning Justin's polemic against Jewish exegesis:

| *Dial.* 61:2f | *Gen.Rab.* 8:3 (pp.56f): |
|---|---|
| Jewish *teachers* say: | «With whom has he taken counsel? |
| (1) God conversed with himself | (b) With his own heart . . . |
| (2) God conversed with the elements: the earth etc. | (a) with the works of heaven and earth . . .» |
| (3) Jewish *heretics* say: | |
| | *Gen. Rab.* 8:4 (p 57): |
| (a) He conversed with the angels | (c) «With the angels . . .» |
| | Philo, *Confus. Ling.* 179: |
| (b) They also say the body of man was made by angels | The bad impulses in man created by the powers . . . |

Friedlander, *Studien*, p. 111, takes the rabbinic suggestions to be provoked by Christian exploitation of the plurals in Gen 1:26. But, like Goodenough, he fails to ask for the Jewish background for Justin's *own* idea.

32. Theophilus, *Ad Autol.* 11:18. cf. the instructive comments in Ginzberg 'Die Haggada bei den Kirchenvätern und in der apokryphischen Litteratur', *MGWJ* 43 (1899- *passim*), pp. 61-63.

33. The single πρωτότοκος occurs as an equivalent of λόγος in some passages in the *1.Apology*: 23:2; 33:6; 46:2; 63:15. On πρωτότοκος as deriving from Prov 8:22, cf. Burney, *art.cit.*

Let me add here a suggestion concerning the »recapitulation« source in Irenaeus. In *Dem.* 39f Irenaeus combines allusions to motifs from Col 1:15ff with the virgin birth concept and a non-LXX version of Is 9:5 (»Wonderful Counsellor and God the Mighty« = MT!). This testimony recurs in the same non-LXX version in *Dem.* 54f:»And he calls Him 'Wonderful Counsellor', even (counsellor) of the Father; whereby it is pointed out that it is with Him that the Father works all things . . . as we have in the first of the Mosaic books . . . (quotation of Gen 1:26). For He is here seen clearly, the Father addressing the Son, as *Wonderful Counsellor of the Father.*« This accords well with the concept I have meant to discern behind *Dial.* 61f: God *consulting* his Wisdom, Christ. It should be noted that *Dem.* 56 proves that Irenaeus read the standard LXX text of Is 9:5 in his Isaiah MS. In other words: Is Irenaeus dependent upon Justin's source - the *Controversy between Jason and Papiscus?* Justin's LXX allusion to Is 9:5 in *Dial.* 76:3 - a »recapitulation« passage - might then be a LXX substitute for the non-LXX text of his source, preserved in Irenaeus.

My third remark concerns the anti-Solomon polemic in *Dial.* 34:7f. In Jewish literature, Solomon is a figure of prime importance.[34] As supreme possessor of Wisdom, he is said not only to excell Abraham, Moses, Joseph, Adam - he even is master over the demons. »Solomon the master of demons« is a theme hinted at in rabbinic literature,[35] but it seems to have flourished mostly among the rank and file Jews of the Diaspora.[36] In Greek magical papyri, Jewish and pagan, Solomon is a main figure.[37] In order, however, to get a more sober and representative testimony, let me quote Josephus: »There was no form of nature with which he was not acquainted or which he passed over without examining, but he studied them all philosophically and revealed the most complete knowledge of their several properties. And God granted him knowledge of the art used against demons for the benefit and healing of men. He composed incantations by which illnesses are relieved, and left behind forms of exorcisms with which those possessed by demons drive them out, never to return. And this kind of cure is of very great power among us to this day, for I have seen a certain Eleazar, a countryman of mine, in the presence of Vespasian, his sons, tribunes and a number of other soldiers, free men possessed by demons, and this was the manner of the cure: he put to the nose of the possessed man a ring which had under its seal one of the roots prescribed by Solomon, and then, as the man smelled it, drew out the demon through his nostrils, and, when the man at once fell down, adjured the demon never to come back into him, speaking Solomon's name and reciting the incantations which he had composed . . . And when this was done, the understanding and wisdom of Solomon were clearly revealed, on account of which we have been induced to speak of these things, in order that all men may

---

34. »He is one of the few (three or ten) monarchs who ruled over the entire world«, Ginzberg VI, p. 289 - cf. Justin in *Dial.* 34:7:» neither did all the kings do him hommage, nor did he reign as far as the ends of the world.«
35. See the material summarized in Ginzberg IV, pp. 149-154, with notes VI, pp. 291-293. '
36. Cf. the popular tale contained in the *Testament of Solomon.*
37. See the rich material in K. Preisendanz, art.'Solomon', P.-W. *Suppl.* 8 (Stuttgart, 1956), cols. 660-704.

know the greatness of his nature and how God favoured him.« (*Ant.* VIII: 44-49).

Compare this with the following passage in Justin: »When exorcised by the name of this very One who is the Son of God and *first-born of every creature* (NB!), and was born by the virgin . . . every demon is overcome and subdued. But if you exorcise by any name of persons born among you, whether kings, or righteous men, or prophets or patriarchs, not one of the demons will be made subject to you.« This is from *Dial.* 85:2f - a commentary on Ps 24:7: Christ, not Solomon, is the Lord of the powers, κύριος τῶν δυνάμεων. True, Solomon who built the temple was a great king, but nevertheless practised idolatry (*Dial.* 34:7) - he was not κύριος τῶν δυνά-μεων, on the contrary, he was the slave of the »powers«.[38]

It is easy to see the organic connexion between this polemic and the Wisdom Christology: Solomon may have partaken of wisdom - but Christ is Wisdom in person, Wisdom incarnated. Hence his supreme power over the devil and all his host. Hence also the connexion between pre-existence/-virgin birth idea and the topic of Christ's power over the demons, analysed above.

This »here is more than Solomon« polemic is initiated in the NT (Mt 12:42 par. Lk 11:31), it is probably implied in the Son of David Christology of the synoptics.[39] Its increased emphasis in Justin is an eloquent testimony to the continued and close contact with Judaism preserved throughout the development of this tradition.

## 2. The recapitulation idea (II): The baptism of Jesus.[40]

I have argued above that the narrative of Jesus' baptism in *Dial.* 88:3.8 derives from the »recapitulation« source. Let us briefly recapitulate the contents of the narrative:

Jesus came to the Jordan, being supposed to be the son of Joseph . . .

(a) When Jesus went down to the water, fire was kindled in the Jordan.

---

38. Goldfahn, 'Aggada' , p. 60, points to *Shab.* 56b as a possible rabbinic reaction to this kind of Christian polemic: He who says that Solomon sinned, errs. Other rabbinic texts admit that after his idolatry, Solomon lost his power over demons, and was seized by great fear of them, *Pes. de R. Kahana,* Piska 5:3 (pp. 95f), cf. more material in Ginzberg IV, pp. 153f; VI, pp. 292f.

39. Cf. i.a. E. Lövestam,'Jésus Fils de David chez les Synoptiques', *StTh* 28 (1974), pp. 97-109; K. Berger,'Die königlichen Messiastraditionen des Neuen Testaments', *NTS* 20 (1974), pp. 1-44; D. C. Duling,'Solomon, Exorcism and the Son of David', *HTR* 68 (1975), pp. 235-252; *idem,* 'Therapeutic Son of David: An Element in Matthew's Christological Apologetic', *NTS* 24(1978), pp. 392-410.

40. Cf. i.a. K. Schlütz, *Isaias 11:2 (die sieben en des Hl. Geistes) in den ersten vier Jahrhunderten* (Alttestamentliche Abhandlungen 11:4, Münster im Westfalen, 1932), pp. 39-46; E. Bammel,-'Die Täufertraditionen bei Justin', *Studia Patristica* 8 (TU 93, Berlin, 1966), pp. 53-61; D. A. Bertrand, *Le baptême de Jesus. Histoire de l'exégèse aux deux premiers siècles* (BGBE 14, Tübingen, 1973), pp. 91-98; H. Braun,'Entscheidende Motive in den Berichten über die Taufe Jesu von Markus bis Justin', *ZThK* 50 (1953), pp. 39-43.

(b) When he was rising up from the water, the Holy Spirit fluttered down upon him as it were a dove.

> Comment: It was on behalf of men who from the time of Adam had fallen under the deceit of the serpent . . .

(c) A voice came at the same time out of the heavens - it had been predicted by David:»Thou art my Son, to-day have I begotten thee».

What is the intention and concern of this narrative? I think one shall have to emphasize the Son of God concept. Men believed that Jesus was the son of *Joseph*, but the heavenly voice proclaimed him as *God's* Son. Perhaps the mention of the fire is related to this idea: It may have been conceived of as a purifying or *testing*fire, cf. *Sib*.VI:1-7: «I sing from the heart the great son and famous of the Immortal, to whom the Most High, his begetter, gave a throne to take ere he was born; for according to the flesh he was raised up the second time, after he had washed in the stream of the river Jordan, which is borne along on silvery foot, drawing its waves. Who first, *escaping from fire,* shall see God coming in sweet spirit, on the white wings of a dove.» The precise meaning of this poetic text is not easy to grasp, but it would seem that this text also works with the Son of God idea, and that Jesus at his baptism was tested as God's Son by the fire, but not *made* God's Son by his baptism. This, I gather, is also the idea embodied in Justin's narrative: Jesus was not *made* or *established* God's Son in his baptism,[41] but he was *proved* to be God's Son - proved by testing, or by conquering the fire (of judgement?).[42]

Justin has not commented on this fire motif in his narrative - probably he no longer knew its meaning.He has pushed the idea of the narrative even further away from adoptionism: For him Jesus is not even proved or tested as God's Son - he is only *proclaimed* as such.

Otherwise, Justin's comments may be perfectly in line with the idea of the narrative. For Justin, Jesus' proclamation as God's Son triggers the whole recapitulation concept. *Dial.* 88:4f is a perfect parallel to the other recapitulation passages (esp. *Dial.* 124f):« . . . it was all on behalf of the race of men, which from the time of Adam had fallen under death and the deceit of the serpent, each man acting ill by his own fault. For God, purposing that they who were born in freedom of choice and with authority over themselves, both angels and men, should do whatever he gave each the power to be able to do, made them such that if they were to choose what was well-pleasing to him, he would keep them immortal and free from punishment, but if they should do evil, he would punish each as he thought best.»

---

41. Concerning the rendering of the heavenly voice according to Ps 2:7, cf. above, p.199, n.53.
42. Cf. esp. Bertrand, *op. cit.,* p. 128. Bammel, *art. cit.,* pp. 55-57, also thinks of a testing fire: «*Durch Wasser und Feuer bewährt erweist sich Jesus als der, über dem die Taufproklamation ausgerufen werden soll.*» (p. 55). On the other hand, one should not exclude the possibility that Justin's narrative enshrines an idea similar to the one in *Rec.* I:48:4f: Jesus in his baptism *puts out* the fire in store for sinners.

*Dial.* 124f is not only an exellent parallel and commentary on this passage; one suspects that in *Dial.* 125:4 we have the sequel to *Dial.* 88:8: In the temptation story, the testing of God's Son is continued, and he proves himself to be «Isra-el», a man overcomming the evil power. In fact, the link between *Dial.* 88:3.8 and *Dial.* 125:4 is found in another «recapitulation» passage, viz. *Dial.* 103:6 (cf above, p. 222f). Here we read:«Moreover this devil *at the very moment that He (Christ) ascended from the river Jordan, when the utterance had been spoken to Him: Thou art my Son* . . . - is recorded in the Memoirs . . . as coming up to Him and tempting Him . . .» It is interesting to notice that the only two Semitic etymologies provided by Justin both refer to the temptation story: «Satanas» and «Israel» (*Dial.* 103:5 and 125:4) - and as we have seen already (p. 223), they presuppose a harmonistic version of the temptation story which is not created *ad hoc* by Justin. The gist of the whole material is succinctly summarized in *Dial.* 103:6: As the devil led Adam astray, he thought he could seduce the second Adam also.

### 3. The recapitulation idea (III): Types on the passion.

Our material for this chapter is found in *Dial.* 90f and 94 with parallels. We find the following topics, closely interconnected (cf. analysis above, pp. 216ff):
(a) The battle against Amalek
(b) The Messiah of Joseph
(c) The brazen serpent
Let us take a closer look at each of them.

(a) The battle against Amalek.
The relevant passage in *Barnabas* runs like this:«And he says again to Moses, when Israel was warred upon by strangers, and in order to remind those who were warred upon that they were delivered unto death by reason of their sins - the Spirit speaks to the heart of Moses to make a representation of the cross, and of him who should suffer, because, he says, unless they put their trust in him, they shall suffer war for ever. Moses therefore placed one shield upon another in the midst of the fight, and standing there raised above them kept stretching out his hands, and so Israel again began to be victorious: then, whenever he let them drop they began to perish. Why? That they may know that they cannot be saved if they do not hope on him.»(*Barn.* 12:2-3, in 12:4 Is 65:2 is quoted).

This text can best be characterized as Christian targumizing of the Exodus text. The following additions to the OT text stand out:
(1) The war served to remind Israel of their sins.
(2) Moses made a type of the cross by placing one shield upon another.
(3) Moses stretching out his hands was a type of Christ on the cross.
(4) Unless Israel put their hope on Christ, they will suffer war forever.

Let us compare this with Justin's rendering of the same passage. Justin's exposition can be summarized thus:

(a) Moses prayed to God with outstreched hands, being supported by Hor and Aaron. This was a type of the cross.
(b) Moses was seated on a stone. The stone signifies Christ.
(c) Moses prayed thus until the evening - Christ remained on the cross until the evening.
(d) Joshua - carrying Jesus' name - defeated Amalek.

The only element in *Barnabas* which has a correspondence in Justin, is element 3, but here Justin has LXX details not found in *Barnabas*. In all other respects, there is a remarkable lack of correspondence between the two authors. Justin is much closer to the Biblical text.

*Barnabas* returns to the Amalek battle in 12:9f: «Moses therefore says to Jesus the son of Naue, after giving him this name, when he sent him to spy out the land, 'Take a book in thy hands and write what the Lord saith, that the Son of God shall in the last day tear up by the roots the whole house of Amalek'. See again Jesus, not as son of man, but as Son of God, but manifested in a type in the flesh.» Now, *Barnabas* seems here not to connect the saying about Amalek - a free, targumizing version of Ex 17:14/16 - with its Biblical context, viz. the battle against Amalek. Instead, he connects it with Joshua's spying of the land. It is difficult to know what interpretation of the Amalek motif is implied in this. In any case Justin has a treatment of the same OT text which is completely independent of *Barnabas*. «The lord is said to 'fight with hidden hand against Amalek' (Ex 17:16 with notable variant readings)[43] and you will not deny that Amalek fell. But if it is said that only in the glorious advent of Christ Amalek will be fought, what kind of fruit will that word of Scripture have which says 'with hidden hand God fights against Amalek'? You can perceive that some hidden power of God belonged to Christ in his crucifixion, at whom even the demons tremble, and, in fact, all powers and authorities of the earth.» This is obviously independent of *Barnabas,* but the non-LXX quotation of Ex 17:16 suggests a source other than the Biblical text. One notices the closeness in idea between this passage and the other recapitulation passages. Is the present text and the whole »Amalek« material derived from the »recapitulation« source? Let us again adduce a rabbinic passage: »R. Eleazar[44] says: When will the name of these people (Amalek) be blotted out? At the time when idolatry will be eradicated together with its worshippers, and God will be recognized throughout the world as the One, and his kingdom will be established for all eternity.«(*Mekh.* Amalek II:155-158, pp. 158f).[45]

---

43. Cf. Smit Sibinga, pp. 43-46.
44. According to Str. Bill. I, p. 179 identical with Eliezer b. Hyrkanos (ca 90 AD). It seems to me, however, that the context points to Eleazar of Modiim (died 135 AD).
45. The rabbinical parallels are numerous, cf. Str. Bill. I, p. 927; III, p.53; IV, pp. 830/898; Ginzberg III, pp. 54-63.

This is remarkably close to Justin's interpretation, which sees as the real Amalek (not defeated by Joshua) the demons, worshipped as gods by the pagans.[46]

Justin has other points of contact with Jewish exegesis, and like the above example, they have no correspondence in *Barnabas*. He says that Moses was praying with outstretched hands. This may be a natural inference from the Biblical narrative, but neither the LXX nor *Barnabas* state this explicitly. It is expressly said in the *Fragmentary Targum* and *Targum Ps. Jonathan,* however.[47] Smit Sibinga also means to detect other parallels between Justin's rendering of Ex 17:9ff and the Targums.[48]

I believe all this points to a source other than *Barnabas,* and the passage in *Dial.* 49:8 is a strong indication that this source is the »recapitulation« source.

(b) The Messiah of Joseph.[49]

As we have seen, some rabbis think that Deut 33:17 ('his firstling bull-ock') points to Joshua and his defeat of Amalek. It is relevant to note that Joshua and the »Messiah anointed for war« (= the Messiah ben Ephraim) are interchangeable in some rabbinic passages: »'Ephraim also is the defence of my head' (Ps 60:9) alludes to the *Messiah anointed for war* who will be descended from Ephraim, as may be inferred from the text, 'His firstling bullock, majesty is his'(Deut 33:17)« (*Num.Rab.* 14:1, p. 558). »'Ephraim also is the defence of my head.' This alludes to *Joshua the Son of Nun*, who came from Ephraim; as it says, 'of the tribe of Ephraim, Hoshea the son of Nun'(Num 13:8)« (*Num.Rab.* 14:1, p. 565).

It would seem that Joshua figures as a type of the Messiah ben Ephraim, and this is confirmed by a third passage: »You find that whoever takes up arms at the command of the Omnipresent, (God) loves him forever. For thus you will observe in the case of Joshua who joined issue with Amalek and dealt with them in accordance with the law and the commandments, as it is said, 'And Joshua comfited Amalek', etc. (Ex 17:13f), and so the Holy One, blessed be he, promised him, 'out of your tribe (Ephraim) will I

---

46. It may be of interest to notice in the passing that in the same *Mekhilta* tractate, Eliezer b. Hyrkanos combines the motif of Amalek's destruction in the days of the Messiah with Ps 72:5 (*Amalek* II:189-192, p. 161, - a parallel passage in *Pes.Rab.* 29a refers the saying to R. Jose the Galilean (ca 110). Str. Bill. III, p. 825, believes that this is the correct reference).

47. Cf. Smit Sibinga, p. 134.

48. *Ibid.*

49. On this enigmatic concept in rabbinic literature, cf. esp. Str. Bill. II, pp. 292-299; J. Klausner, *Messianic Idea*, pp. 483-501; S. Hurwitz, *Die Gestalt des sterbenden Messias. Religionspsycho-logische Aspekte der jüdischen Apokalyptik* (Studien aus dem C. G. Jung-Institut 8, Zürich-Stuttgart, 1958) J. Heinemann, 'The Messiah of Ephraim and the Premature Exodus of the Tribe of Ephraim', *HTR* 68(1975), pp. 1-15.

always raise up one that shall punish Amalek: 'Out of Ephraim shall come they whose root is in Amalek' (Judg 5:14)« (*Num.Rab* 1:12, p.19).[50]

The passages here quoted are anonymous, but it is possible to argue that they contain an early tradition of the Messiah ben Ephraim. J. Heinemann has pointed out a striking feature in the texts which deal with this Messianic figure: Some of the texts speak of a victorious warrior, while others speak of his death in battle. »We must therefore assume that the motif of the Messiah ben Joseph underwent, at some time, a radical transformation; and there can be no doubt that, if we know this legend in two versions, one which tells only of the militant, victorious Messiah, while the other adds his death in battle, the one relating his tragic end must be the later one.«[51] Heinemann further argues that the transformation came about as a reflex of Bar Kokhba's defeat. The victorious Messiah ben Joseph is pre-Bar Kokhba; in the idea of his dying in battle the fate of Bar Kokhba has left its imprint.[52]

This means that the concept of the Messiah ben Joseph must have come very much to the fore in the years during and immediately after the Bar Kokhba uprising. It may therefore also have been in these years that Christians seized the concept and turned it to their advantage. It deserves notice that Justin's »Joseph« (—Christ) in *Dial.* 91:1-3 is a triumphant figure -despite the reference to the cross found in the »horns of the unicorn«. That is: Justin's basis seems to be the pre-Bar Kokhba version of the concept. One should also note that the rabbis seem to have applied Deut 33:17 to the triumphant, not the dying, Messiah ben Joseph/Ephraim.[53] The classic testimony on the dying Messiah ben Joseph is Zech 12:10ff.[54]

Another Christian modification can be seen in the fact that Justin no longer speaks of a Messiah *son of* Joseph. Jesus did not descend from Joseph. Instead, it seems Justin sees Joseph as a type of Jesus, or that he quite simply identifies Jesus with the »Joseph« spoken of in Deut 33:13-17. Justin is not explicit about this, but cf. *Dial.* 126:1 which includes Joseph among the designations under which Moses has spoken about Christ.

---

50. *Targum Ps. Jonathan* to Ex 40:11 also makes the Messiah ben Ephraim descend from Joshua, cf. Levey, *Messiah*, p. 15.
51. Heinemann, *art. cit.*, p. 6.
52. *Ibid*, pp. 8-10. Cf. also Klausner, *Messianic Idea*, p. 496.
53. Some relevant passages: *Gen.Rab.* 99:2 (pp. 974f):»Joseph is opposed to the kingdom of Edom (Rome). The one has horns and the other has horns. The one has horns:'His firstling bullock, majesty is his ... (Deut 13:17). ... By whose hand will the kingdom of Edom fall? By the hand of the anointed for war, who will be descended from Joseph. R. Pinehas said in the name of R. Samuel b. Nahman (ca 260)'We have a tradition that Esau will fall only by the hand of Rachel's descendants ...« (This last passage is also contained in *Gen.Rab.* 75:5, p. 692). *Gen.Rab.* (New Version) 97 (p. 910):»Joseph he opposed to the wicked empire, for there is a tradition that Esau will fall only through the hands of Rachel's descendants ...« Gen.Rab. 75:6 (p. 698):»The Rabbis maintained (ad Gen 32:6): Ox is an allusion to the one anointed for battle, as it says .. (Deut 33:17).«
54. Cf. material gathered in Str. Bill. II, pp. 298f, and cf. above, p.269, n.49.

It remains to be added that Justin in his comment on this topic is entirely in line with his ideas about the Amalek battle. As we saw, the rabbis took Amalek's defeat in the end of days to imply the abolition of idolatry. Justin's idea is similar, and one should compare with this Justin's comment on Deut 33:17: »For being pushed by a horn, that is to say, being made contrite, men of all nations have by means of this mystery turned to the worship of God from their vain idols and demons.« (*Dial.* 91:3).

(c) The cursed serpent.

The NT basis for this typology is John 3:14f: καὶ καθὼς Μωϋσῆς ὕψωσεν τὸν ὄφιν ἐν τῇ ἐρήμῳ, οὕτως ὑψωθῆναι δεῖ τὸν υἱὸν τοῦ ἀνθρώπου, ἵνα πᾶς ὁ πιστεύων ἐν αὐτῷ ἔχῃ ζωὴν αἰώνιον. John interprets the concept of 'looking', Num 21:8f, by the concept of believing. The same is done in the relevant *Mekhilta* passage quoted above, and in the Targums. [55]

This emphasis on faith is carried on in *Barnabas'* treatment of the brazen serpent. *Barn.* 12:5-7. But apart from this, *Barnabas* does not seem to depend on John's characteristic non-LXX terminology. Barnabas is closer to the LXX: He has dropped the term ὑψοῦν, and introduced the LXX term σημεῖον. On the other hand, his own deviations from the LXX are considerable, and can once again best be described as Christian targumizing of the Biblical text. A good example is his rendering of Num 21:8:

| Num 21:8 LXX | *Barn.* 12:7 |
|---|---|
| καὶ εἶπεν κύριος πρὸς Μωυσῆν . . . <br> καὶ ἔσται ἐὰν δάκῃ ὄφις <br> ἄνθρωπον <br> πᾶς ὁ δεδηγμένος | εἶπεν δὲ Μωϋσῆς πρὸς αὐτούς <br> ὅταν, φησίν, δηχθῇ <br> τις ὑμῶν |
| ἰδὼν αὐτὸν | ἐλθέτω ἐπὶ τὸν ὄφιν <br> τὸν ἐπὶ τοῦ ξύλου ἐπικείμενον <br> καὶ ἐλπισάτω πιστεύσας ὅτι αὐτὸς <br> ὢν νεκρὸς δύναται ζωοποιῆσαι |
| ζήσεται | καὶ παραχρῆμα σωθήσεται |

Among the Christian additions, the saying that the serpent is ἐπὶ τοῦ ξύλου ἐπικείμενον is of special interest. We may have here an allusion to Deut 21:22f.[56] This OT text is essential in Justin's treatment of the brazen serpent typology.

---

55. Cf. Brown, *comm.*, p. 133; Str. Bill. II, p. 329.
56. That *Barnabas* knew the Christological application of Deut 21:23, is shown by *Barn.* 7:7.9

There are several points in common between *Barnabas* and Justin:

| *Barn.* 12:5-7 | Justin |
|---|---|
| (1) Moses made a *type* referring to Jesus, viz. the *sign*[57] made when the Israelites were falling. | "... the provision made against the serpents that bit Israel was a *type* and a *sign*." *Dial.* 91:3. |
| (2) The Lord made the serpents bite the Israelites to remind them that the fall took place in Eve through the serpent.[58] | "... the serpent, who caused the transgression to be made by Adam". *Dial.* 94:1. |
| (3) Moses seemingly violated his own prohibition against molten images (Deut 27:15). Reason: "to show a type of Jesus." | God ordered Moses to make the brazen serpent, despite his own prohibition (Ex 20:4). Reason: "by this he proclaimed a mystery." *Dial.* 94:1f; 112:1f. |
| (4) Everyone who puts his hope on the serpent, believing that it, though dead, is able to give life, shall be saved | The serpent was to be for salvation for those who believed that it prefigured Christ. *Dial.* 91:4. |

On closer inspection, this list of parallels conceals some marked differences.[59] The two authors' argument that the serpent prefigures Jesus run along quite different lines. *Barnabas* says: The serpent, though dead, was able to give life. In the same way Jesus - thought to be dead - gives life. Justin says: By "crucifying" the serpent, Moses signified that through the cross (of Christ) death was to come to the serpent. For *Barnabas*, the serpent of Gen 3 is represented in the serpents that bit Israel, for Justin he is

---

57. Probably we have in *Dial.* 72:1 another pre-Justinian testimony to the brazen serpent typology: In the Ps-Ezra quotation Ezra says: "... we are about to humble him on a sign (ἐν σημείῳ), and afterwards hope on him (cf. *Barn.* 12:7) ...." The strange substitution of cross by 'sign' is easily explicable from Num 21:8f.

58. Cf. *Num.Rab.* 19:22 (pp. 770f):-'And the Lord sent fiery serpents among the people' (Num 21:6). What reason did he see for punishing them by means of serpents? Because the serpent, who was the first to speak slander, had been cursed, and they did not learn a lesson from him. The Holy One, blessed be he, therefore, said, 'Let the serpent, who was the first to introduce slander, come and punish those who speak slander.'"

59. One should also compare the paraphrase of Num 21:6-9 in *1.Apol.* 60:2-4. This passage contains i.a. the following non-LXX features: Moses *speaking to the people; faith* necessary; *salvation.* These are common with *Barnabas.* The remaining non-LXX features in *Barnabas* do not recur in *1.Apol.* 60. On the other hand, *1.Apol.* 60 has the following non-LXX features not shared with or derived from *Barnabas*: The people met "poisonous beasts, vipers and asps ...."; Moses made the serpent "by an inspiration and influence that came from God"; Moses placed the serpent ἐπί (over?) the Holy Tent; the snakes *died.* One should note that these features do not recur in the paraphrases in the *Dialogue.* I have surmised above that Justin in *1.Apol.* 59f follows a separate source, a tract on borrowings from Moses in the philosophers. This source seems to have targumized the Numeri text independently of *Barnabas.*

represented by the brazen serpent itself.[60] In this way Justin's version of the typology is brought to express the »recapitulation« idea - in fact some of the racapitulation passages quoted above can be seen to contain references to the brazen serpent typology. Compare the following passages:

By the sign of the brazen serpent, Moses proclaimed a mystery, viz. that God «would destroy the power of the serpent, who caused the transgression to be made by Adam, but bring salvation to them that believe on him who was by this sign, namely the cross, to be put to death, from the bites of the serpent, namely, evil deeds, idolatries, and other iniquities.» (*Dial.* 94:2). Christ was born by the Virgin «in order that by this dispensation of God the serpent who did evil in the beginning . . . might be destroyed and death be brought into contempt . . . (and) completely cease to trouble them that believe on him.» (*Dial.* 45:4). Christ has become man by the Virgin «in order that by the same way in which the disobedience caused by the serpent took its beginning, by this way should it also take its destruction.»(*Dial.* 100:4). Jesus has been born by the Virgin, and by him «God destroys both the serpent and those angels and men that became like it, but for them that repent . . . and belive on him, does he work deliverance from death.»*(Dial.* 100:6).

No doubt we have in all these passages a common idea and a common terminology.

It also seems Is 27:1 was a testimony contained in Justin's source: Christ is the mighty sword of God which shall slay the serpent, *Dial.* 91:4 and 100:4, cf. also 112:2 (i.e. two «brazen serpent» passages, one «recapitulation» passage).

I conclude that Justin's treatment of the brazen serpent typology derives from his «recapitulation» source. Justin *may* also have borrowed some ideas from *Barnabas*, but one cannot know whether these details were already part of the recapitulation source.[61]

Concluding remarks (sections 1-3):

It may help to bring out the peculiar profile of the tradition studied in these sections, when we briefly compare it with the Christological tradition of the *Apology*. There the polemic against Jewish denial of the Messiahship of Jesus was conducted from the two *parousias* scheme. The tradition in the *Apology* thus goes a far way in admitting that Jesus did not fulfil the triumphant aspects of OT Messianism. On the soteriological issues, this tradition concentrates on the ideas of expiatory suffering and remission of

---

60. Hilgenfeld, 'Citate', pp. 396f, made a detailed comparison of *Barnabas* and Justin on this point, and concluded: They have several non-LXX features in common, but Justin is not directly dependent upon *Barnabas*.

61. We have seen repeatedly that Justin seems to depend on a source similar to *Barnabas* rather than directly upon *Barnabas*. There is nothing which excludes the same explanation in this case also.

sins. - There is no dispute with Judaism as to what texts in the OT are Messianic, the main subject of controversy is the two parousias pattern and the inherent anti Bar Kokhba polemic.

In the «recapitulation» material the tone is somewhat different. The Jews are said to apply important Messianic passages to Hezekiah or Solomon. The rebuttal is to show that the Messiah envisaged by those passaqes is a superhuman Messiah, being God's first-begotten Son, Wisdom personified - who as a second Adam, Son of God, conquers Satan and repairs all the disastrous effects of Adam's fall. The dispute with Judaism is here carried to a deeper level: It not so much concerns the simple question whether Jesus fulfilled OT Messianic prophecies or not. It goes on to ask *what kind* of Messiah the Scriptures compel us to await. The task of the Messiah exceeds all human power - and was accomplished by Jesus, God's Son.

There is some overlapping in Christological testimonies between the two traditions, but they keep their distinct profiles even on this level. In the «recapitulation» source we find testimonies on the pre-existence of Christ, while on the other hand the second *parousia* testimonies seem to recede into the background, and Is 53 is substituted by the brazen serpent as a main OT testimony on Christ's passion.

One should not exaggerate the cleavage between the two traditions, however. (If the recapitulation source is identical with Aristo of Pella's *Controversy,* the common link to Pella shared with the AJ II should be noted). As we have seen, they both, in different respects, are anticipated by features of Luke's Christology. Luke has the conception of Jesus as the second Adam, so important to the recapitulation material. The temptation story is rendered in a remarkably Lukan vein.

This tradition rests on a similar amalgam of Matthean and Lukan materials in its handling of the Gospel story as we found in the *Apology.* The handling of the brazen serpent incident seems not directly dependent on John, and also seems to neglect Paul's use of Deut 21:23 in Gal. 3:13. The closeness to Jewish exegesis is evident on several points, and one may hear some echoes of the Bar Kokhba uprising.

I now turn to the eschatological material in *Dial.* 80-83; 118:2. As I have said in Part II, I suspect that this material derives from the same source as the one treated hitherto. But the evidence is not so unambiguous that I have wanted to include it under the «recapitulation» heading.

## 4. The redeemer of Jerusalem[62]

Let us begin by quoting Justin's comment on Ps 110:1 in *Dial.* 83:1. The Jewish teachers have dared to refer this verse to Hezekiah, «as though he was bidden be seated on the right side of the temple, when the king of Assyria sent to him with threats, and it was signified to him by Isaiah that he should not be afraid of him. And indeed Isaiah's words were so fulfilled, and the king of Assyria was turned back that he should not wage war against Jerusalem in the days of Hezekiah, and an angel of the Lord slew the camp of the Assyrians up to a hundred and eighty-five thousand men, as we know and acknowledge.»

No direct confirmation of this can be found in rabbinic sources.[63] Yet Justin's information may be correct. It seems that some Rabbis, as a rebuttal of Christian exploitation of some Messianic prophecies in the OT, tended to give these OT passages a «historical» rather than a Messianic interpretation.[64] «R.Hillel[65] said: There shall be no Messiah for Israel, because they have already enjoyed him in the days of Hezekiah.» (*Sanh.*99a, p. 669).[66]

Justin carries on the anti-Hezekiah polemic in *Dial.* 83:3: Hezekiah was not priest forever. «And who does not know that he is not the redeemer of Jerusalem? And that he himself did not send a rod of power into Jerusalem, and rule in the midst of his enemies, but that it was God who turned his enemies away from him as he wept and wailed.» This polemic may also rest on correct ideas about contemporary Jewish exegesis, applying Ps 110:2 to Jerusalem's salvation in the days of Hezekiah.

---

62. On Justin's millennialism, cf. i.a. von Engelhardt, *Christenthum*, pp. 302-309; A. L. Feder, *Jesus Christus,* pp. 236-247; Goodenough, *Theology* p. 283-287, C. Andresen, *Logos und Nomos,* pp. 324f; L. W. Barnard, 'Justin Martyr's Eschatology' *VC* 19 (1965), pp. 86-98, esp. pp. 92-95. A. O. Wieland's dissertation *(Die Eschatologie Justins des Philosophen und Märtyrers,* Innsbruck, 1969), is surprisingly summary on the issue, pp. 146-148.
63. Cf. Goldfahn, pp. 152f.
64. *Ibid,* cf. also *idem,* p. 106:«*In Folge der Disputationen, in denen die Christen auf solche Stellen besonders Gewicht legten, sah man sich genötigt, der Phantasie Schranken zu setzen und zur nüchternen Exegese zuruck zu kehren. Eine grosse Anzahl messianischer Stellen wurden so dann auf Hiskia bezogen . . .*«
65. The Soncino translator takes him to be the brother of Judah II, ca 250, while Str. Bill. (I, p. 31) identifies him with Hillel b. Shemuel b. Nachman, hence ca 300.
66. In a midrash on Is 9:6 ('Of the increase ( לםרבה ) of his government and peace there shall be no end') it is asked why the *mem* in לםרבה is a closed *men* (i.e. a *mem finalis*). Bar Kappara (ca 210) answers:« The Holy One, blessed be he, wished to appoint Hezekiah as the Messiah, and Sennacherib as Gog and Magog; whereupon the Attribute of Justice said before the Holy One, blessed be he: 'Sovereign of the Universe. If Thou didst not make David the Messiah, who uttered so many hymns and psalms before Thee, wilt Thou appoint Hezekiah as such, who did not hymn Thee in spite of all these miracles which Thou wroughtest for him?' Therefore it was closed.« (*Sanh.* 94a, p. 630).

As we have seen above (p. 86), the peculiar reading of Justin's deviant Ps 110 text in *Dial.* 83 agrees perfectly with his anti-Hezekiah polemic: ῥάβδον δυνάμεως ἐξαποστελεῖ ἐπὶ' Ἰερουσαλήμ. Christ, not Hezekiah, sends a rod of power into Jerusalem. Christ, not Hezekiah, is the redeemer of Jerusalem, ὁ λυτρούμενος τὴν 'Ἰερουσαλήμ. It was suggested above that this idea may be related to the millennarian concept in *Dial.* 80f.[67] It is difficult to state much with certainty here, because we cannot know how much relevant material has been lost in the lacuna, *Dial.* 74:3/4 (cf. above, 213f). In any case, one notes that the millenium is related to *Jerusalem* in a significant way in *Dial.* 80:1; 80:5 and 81:4.[68] Comparing with Revelation 20:4-6 one finds there nothing similar. The Jerusalem motif is only hinted at in Rev 20:9 (ἡ παρεμβολὴ τῶν ἁγίων καὶ ἡ πόλις ἡ ἠγαπημένη) - John has reserved the Jerusalem idea for full development in Rev 21f.

Taking the Jerusalem motif as our clue, we turn to a closer examination of Justin's millennarian ideas. It may be useful to pursue the comparison with Revelation a little further. In Revelation texts like Is 65:17 and Ezek 40-48 are referred to the New Jerusalem, Rev 21f, not the millennium. But in Justin they are referred to the millennium, and the millennium takes place in a new-built Jerusalem, «as the prophets Ezekiel and Isaiah and all the rest acknowledge.»(*Dial.* 80:5). The reference intended by «Isaiah» is no doubt the following quotation Is 65:17-25, and «Ezechiel» may be a reference to the material behind *Dial.* 118:2 (see below).

This means that the millennium has another character in Justin. He has so to speak combined Rev 20:4-6 and Rev 21f to one concept. This means that Justin has problems with defining the difference in content between the millennium and the eternal life following afterwards, and a termination of the millennium as described in Rev 20:7-10 has no parallel in Justin. His only remark on the transition from millennium to eternal life is a direct paraphrase of Revelation, which omits any mention of the Gog/Magog episode terminating the millennium in Revelation, and which on the whole is remarkably summary and vague: «And further, a man among us named John, one of the apostles of Christ, prophesied in a Revelation made to him

---

67. I also suggested that Justin's anti-Hezekiah source may have related Ps 110:1 to «the man of apostasy» concept, Dan 7:25 (*Dial.* 32:3f). On Justin's polemic concerning Dan 7:25, cf. Goldfahn, pp. 58f. Justin's hints are too scanty to allow safe conclusions regarding his place within the trajectory of the Antichrist idea. I have surmised above that his exegesis of Dan 7:25 is the same as in Revelation. For Jewish exegesis, cf. also Klausner, *Messianic Idea*, p. 424.

68. Justin says that the millennium is going to take place in an *enlarged and adorned* Jerusalem. The enlargement of Jerusalem is known also from rabbinic sources, cf. above, p. 373, n. 329. Another passage: Eleazar of Modiin (died 135) said:«It is written 'At that time they shall call Jerusalem the throne of the Lord; and all the nations shall be gathered unto it'(Jer 3:17). Is it possible to say that Jerusalem will be able to hold so many? Never fear - the Holy One, blessed be he, will say to Jerusalem: Extend thyself, enlarge thyself, receive thy hosts ...»(*Pes. Rab.*, Piska 21:8, p. 429).

that they who have believed our Christ will spend a thousand years in Jerusalem, and that afterwards the universal, and, in one word, eternal resurrection of all at once, will take place, and also the judgement. And this too our Lord said: 'They shall neither marry, nor be given marriage, but shall be equal to angels, being children of God of the resurrection'» (*Dial.* 81:4).

After the general resurrection, which marks the transition from millennium to eternal life, men shall be like angels. It is difficult to assess exactly how Justin would have the Jesus logion understood. Does he have a very spiritualized concept of the eternal life? I shall leave this question open. Let me only add that Justin normally describes Christians' gathering in Jerusalem in such a way that the reader must assume that this is the final goal of redemption history, and not a syllable indicates that this is only a transitory state, to be replaced by something totally different, *Dial.* 24:2; 25:1; 26:1; 76:4; 85:7; 113:5; 138:3. As we have surmised above, Justin at least in some of these passages is dependent upon a source which was not millennarian and which located the final redemption in the land and Jerusalem.

It is evident that Justin's conception of the millennium in *Dial.* 80f has its own profile, compared with Revelation. Is Justin drawing upon a millennial tradition independent of Revelation? We begin our further quest by a closer examination of Justin's Scriptural argument on the millennium. Two passages are relevant: *Dial.* 81 and 118:2.

(1) *Dial.* 81. Justin's argument can be summarized like this: In Is 65:22 it is promised that the (Messianic) days of God's people shall be like «the days of the tree». The tree here envisaged is the Paradise tree of knowledge - one of its days amounts to thousand years. Proof: Gen 2:17: Adam was to die on the very day he ate of the fruit of the tree. If this saying shall be regarded as fulfilled, the «day» here spoken of must exceed Adam's life-time, i.e. it must be one of those days spoken of in Ps 90:4: «a day of the Lord is a thousand years.» If so, Adam died on the same day on which he sinned.

If we break down this argument into its separate components, we obtain the following list:

(A) Is 65:17-25 is a prophecy on the millennium.

(B) «The tree» in Is 65:22 is the tree of knowledge in Paradise.

(C) The «day» in Gen 2:17 is one of the Lord's days = 1000 years, Ps 90:4.

Behind each of these components one can trace precedents in Jewish and/or Christian literature.

Before we turn to this, let me remark that in the following section I employ for convenience the term «Messianic age» to refer to the idea of a Messianic *Zwischenreich* of limited durance, while the rabbinic term «age to come» is used to refer to the idea of an unlimited eternal life following after the Messianic age.[69]

---

69. On the rabbinic terminology, cf. Str. Bill. IV, pp. 799ff.

(A) Single verses from Is 65:17-25 are referred to the Messianic age in rabbinical literature.[70] This is of interest, since Revelation clearly refers these verses to the age to come. But Justin is not without Christian precursors. Eusebius quotes from Gaius concerning the heretic Cerinth, who flourished in Trajan's time: «He says that after the resurrection the kingdom of Christ will be set up on earth, and that in Jerusalem the body will again serve as the instrument of desires and pleasures. And since he is an enemy of the divine Scriptures and sets out to deceive, he says that there will be a marriage feast lasting a thousand years.»[71] This passage will be treated in some detail in the excursus below. Here it is sufficient to point out that the idea of «bodily pleasures» might well derive from Is 65:20-23 - literally applied to the millennium. Probably Is 65:17ff is also referred to in the millennial tradition of Papias, as referred by Irenaeus: «. . . when also the creation, having been renovated and set free (cf. Is 65:17), shall bring forth an abundance of all kinds of food from the dew of heaven, and from the fertility of the earth . . . (follows the famous dominical saying about the enormous fertility of the vine etc.(cf. Is 65:21)).[72] All animals feeding only on the produce of the earth, shall in those days live in peaceful harmony . . . (cf. Is 65:25).»(Adv. Haer. V:33:3f) The material here quoted is perhaps sufficient to give some plausibility to J. Daniélou's statement that Is 65:20-25 was «the basic text of Asiatic millenarianism.»[73]

(B) In Is 65:22, the Hebrew text reads: «Like the days of the tree shall the days of my people be.» The LXX renders this: κατὰ γὰρ τὰς ἡμέρας τοῦ ξύλου τῆς ζωῆς ἔσονται αἱ ἡμέραι τοῦ λαοῦ μου. The idea expressed in this translation must be that the eschatological events described in Is 65:17ff represent a return of paradisic life to man. A further development of this idea recurs in rabbinic literature. In a midrashic comment on the *plene* spelling of *toledoth* in Gen 2:4 (the extra *waw* has the numeral value 6), Rabbi Judan says in the name of R. Abun (ca 325?): «The six corresponds to the six things which were taken away from Adam, viz., his lustre, his immortality (lit. life), his height, the fruit of the earth, the fruit of the trees, and the luminaries . . . R. Berekiah said in the name of R. Samuel b. Nahman (ca 260): Though these things were created in their fulness, yet when Adam sinned they were spoiled, and they will not again return in their perfection until the son of Perez[74] (viz. the Messiah) comes . . . These are they: his lustre, his immortality (etc.) . . . Whence do we know it of . . . his immortality? 'For as the days of a tree shall the days of my people be'(Is

70. Cf. the material gathered in Str. Bill. III, pp. 824ff; IV, pp. 851ff.
71. *E.H.* III:28:2, translation according to A. F. J. Klijn and G. J. Reinink, *Patristic Evidence for Jewish-Christian Sects* (Suppl. to NT 36, Leiden, 1973), p. 141.
72. An almost *verbatim* parallel occurs in *Syr. Baruch*, 29:5.
73. *Theology*, p. 387- but cf. my reservations concerning «Asiatic» below.
74. The only other *plene* spelling of *toledoth* occurs in Ruth 4:18:'These are the *toledoth* of Perez'.

65:22).« (*Gen. Rab.* 12:6, pp. 91-93). One MS to *Gen.Rab.* adds here a saying of R. Simeon b. Yohai (ca 150) which is also found in other parallel texts: «'Tree' refers to nought but the Torah, as it is said, 'She is a tree of life to them that lay hold upon her'(Prov 3:18). Hence man will be immortal like the Torah itself.»[75] The premiss of R.Simeon's comment must be the conviction that the »tree« of Is 65:22 is the tree of life (as in the LXX), hence it can further be identified with the Torah by means of Prov. 3:18.

The basic agreement between the Is LXX and these rabbinical comments points to a continuous tradition within Jewish exegesis of Is 65:22 and its context: The prophecy speaks about the restoration of paradisic life to man in the Messianic age; paradisic life connected with the tree of life.

Very likely Justin is in contact with this tradition. At the same time he has a significant modification of the idea: For him the tree of Is 65:22 is not the tree of life, but the tree of knowledge. This modification is necessary to connect this testimony to the idea of a millennial Messianic age, as the following material makes plain.

(C) Again we can begin with a rabbinical passage: »For thus spoke I (God) to him:'For in the day that thou eatest thereof thou shalt surely die'(Gen 2:17). Now ye (i.e. the ministering angels) do not know whether that means one day of mine or one day of yours. But behold. I will grant him one day of mine, which is a thousand years (cf. Ps 90:4), and he will live nine hundred and thirty years«. (*Gen. Rab.* 19:8, p.154). The idea contained in this and parallel passages[76] within the rabbinic literature, is old within Judaism.

This can be proved by the following passage in the *Book of Jubilees.* »Adam died seventy years before attaining a thousand years, for one thousand years are as one day in heaven; and this was because of that which is written concerning the tree of knowledge: On the day that ye eat thereof ye shall die. For this reason he died before completing the years of his day.«(4:30).[77] It is from this tradition that Justin's reference to Gen 2:17 and Ps 90:4[78] derive, and it is this exegesis which necessitates the change of reference for the tree in Is 65:22.

---

75. A parallel occurs in *Num.Rab.* 13:12, p. 524.

76. I.a. *Num.Rab.* 5:4 (p. 148):»and the Holy One, blessed be He, prolonged his day, for though it says:'For in the day that thou eatest thereof thou shalt surely die'(Gen 2:17), he (Adam) lived nine hundred and thirty years, not completing the'day'of the Holy One, blessed be He.« In a similar passage in *Num.Rab.*14:12 (p. 621), the length of the Lord's 'day' is proved from Ps 90:4. See further Ginzberg I, pp. 75f.

77. It also deserves notice that in *Jub.* 23:27f - a passage somewhat parallel to 4:30 - there is in vs. 28 a probable allusion to Is 65:20, and in vs. 17 perhaps an allusion to Is 65:22.

78. Ps 90:4 is taken to prove that the days of the Messiah will last one thousand years in a midrash attributed to R. Eliezer (ca 90 AD), Midr. Ps. (Braude II, p. 97), cf. Klausner, *Messianic Idea,* pp. 420/496.

This combination of elements B and C I have not been able to find in any writer prior to Justin,[79] and it is of interest to note that it does not recur in Irenaeus. But the »testimony« version of Is 65:22 seems to be adapted to Justin's exegesis, and this is an indication that Justin is here following a source.

To conclude: This study of *Dial.* 81 confirms our surmise above, viz. that Justin in his deviations from Revelation is not simply making his own personal modifications of the millennial ideas of Revelation - he is following another tradition besides Revelation. This tradition seems to have developed in very close contact with Jewish exegesis.

After this analysis of the material in *Dial.* 80f, let me add some comments on the idea in *Dial.* 118:2: Christ is to reign in the House of the Lord in Jerusalem as an eternal priest. That Justin did not conceive of this rebuilt temple in purely spiritual categories, is made plain by his added comment in which he spiritualizes the sacrifices, but not the »house« and its altar. [80] But obviously Justin is aware that even the concept of a sacrificial service is not spiritualized by everyone. Against such tendencies he warns.

We have an important testimony that this was no hypothetical danger. According to Dionysius of Alexandria,[81] the heretic Cerinth claimed that the earthly kingdom of Christ would bring i.a. ἑορτάς καὶ θυσίας καὶ ἱερείων σφαγαῖς, i.e. a restoration of the sacrificial cult. We have seen already that Justin exhibits contact with the same tradition as represented by Cerinth in *Dial.* 81. *Dial.* 118:2 would seem to indicate that while the two authors shared a basic stock of prophecies on the millennium, Justin did not share the gross literalism of Cerinth - perhaps the polemic in *Dial.* 118:2 is directed against Cerinth![82]

I have taken this material together with the »recapitulation« passages treated in sections 1-3. A common denominator is the anti-Hezekiah polemic. One can hardly say that Justin emphasizes the recapitulation idea in his treatment of the millennium, but I believe one can recognize it in his material. The millennial exegesis of Is 65:22 is obtained by a combination

---

79. In the rabbinical sources one might see a common link in the idea that Ps 90:4 speaks about the (two) days of the *Torah* (preceeding the creation of the world, Prov 8:30 combined with Ps 90:4), *Cant.Rab.*V:II: §1 (p. 239); *Gen.Rab.* 8:2 (p.56); *Lev.Rab.* 19:1 (p. 234). As we have seen, the tree of Is 65:22 was identified with the Torah by R. Simeon b. Yohai. But the idea here is one of eternal duration.

80. Concerning the idea of a rebuilding of the Temple in early Christian thought prior to Justin, cf. M. Simon,'Retour du Christ et reconstruction du temple dans la pensée chrétienne primitive', in *idem, Recherches d'Histoire Judéo-Chretienne* (Etudes Juives 6, Paris, 1962), pp. 9-19. Simon is probably right in regarding the concept of a rebuilding of Jerusalem and its Temple as a typically Judaeo-Christian idea. Justin's source *may* have conceived of the rebuilt Temple in more concrete terms than he does himself.

81. *Apud* Eus. *E.H.* III:28:4.

82. Perhaps Justin also has the rabbis in mind. »For the Temple will be rebuilt and the sacrifices will be offered therein as in former times.« (*Sifre Num.* 92, quoted from Klausner, *Messianic Idea,* p- 513 - more rabbinic material *ibid,* pp. 513-15.)

of eschatology with the story of Adam's fall in Paradise. In the millennium, *the reversal of Adam's fall* reaches its fulfilment: The people of God enjoys a Paradisic »day«, like Adam's »day«, but receiving life where Adam earned death.[83] (A similar recapitulation idea, but related to Christ's death on the same sixth day on which Adam sinned and died, is beautifully brought out by Irenaeus. *Adv. Haer.* V:23:2).

To conclude: Justin's millennarian material has a theological profile somewhat different from Revelation, and also somewhat different from Irenaeus' tradition. It is usual to think of Asia Minor as the mother soil of early Christian chiliasm. The relative independence of Justin's material compared with Revelation and Irenaeus - one could also add Papias - may indicate that one should not automatically derive Justin's millennarian ideas from a milieu in Asia Minor. The anti-Hezekiah polemic and the implicit recapitulation idea link Justin's material to the rest of the «recapitulation source», and one may again have to do with Aristo of Pella, representing a Palestinian tradition. One notices especially the direct recourse to the Hebrew text in the crucial testimony Is 65:22.

Excursus III: *Was Cerinth a millennialist?*

The earliest evidence on Cerinth is contradictory: Was he a millennialist — as we have presupposed in the foregoing chapter — or was he a Gnostic?[84]

On the one hand we have the reports of Gaius and Dionysius of Alexandria.[85]

Gaius: «But Cerinth also, by means of relevations, said to be written by a great apostle, brings before us miraculous things in a deceitful way, saying that they were revealed to him by angels. And he says that after the resurrection the kingdom of Christ will be set up on earth, and that in Jerusalem the body will again serve as the instrument of desires and pleasures (ἐπιθυμίαι καὶ ἡδοναί). And since he is an enemy of the divine Scriptures and sets out to deceive, he says that there will be a marriage feast lasting a thousand years (ἀριθμὸν χιλιονταετίας ἐν γάμῳ ἑορτῆς).» *(Apud* Eus. *E.H.* III:28:2).

Dionysius of Alexandria: «But Cerinth . . . wanted to give his own fiction a respectable name. For the doctrine which he taught was this: that the kingdom of Christ will be an earthly one. And he dreamt that it would consist in these things he himself was devoted to, because he was a lover of the body and altogether carnal, namely in the delights of the belly and of the sexual passion, that is to say in eating and drinking and marrying, and — because of this he thought he could provide himself with a better reputation — in festivals and sacrifices and the slaying of victims (ἑορταῖς καὶ θυσίαις καὶ ἱερείων σφαγαῖς).» *(ibid.,* 28:4f).[86]

---

83. Prigent also treats *Dial.* 80f under the heading of «recapitulation» *'Justin'* pp. 20ff. Cf. his remark on Is 65:22: «*Le verset 22 annonce la récapitulation (le mot n'y est pas) des jours d'Adam . . .* » (p. 21). Cf. also p. 325, n.2.

84. W. Bauer, art. 'Cerinth', *RGG*[3] I, col. 1632: A pure Gnostic. G. Bardy, in the most extensive and careful discussion to date, 'Cerinthe', *RB* 30 (1921), pp. 344-373, reached the opposite conclusion: Cerinth's millennarian doctrines are authentic - not the Gnostic theories ascribed to him by Irenaeus. Some try to combine the two aspects, like J. Daniélou, *Theology*, p. 68: Cerinth was a gnosticizing Judaeo-Christian!

85. Hippolytus' commentary on Revelation, preserved in a fragment *apud* Dionysius Bar Salibi, is a third witness on the same line, cf. Bardy, *art. cit.*, p. 353.

86. This and the foregoing text are rendered according to the translation in Klijn and Reinink, *Evidence*, pp. 141/143. The same applies to the following quotation of Irenaeus, *ibid.* pp. 103/5.

On the other hand we have the report of Irenaeus: «And a certain Cerinth, then, in Asia taught (1) that the world was not made by the Supreme God but by a certain Power highly separated and far removed from that Principality who transcended the universe and which is ignorant of the one who is above all, God. (2) He suggested that Jesus was not born of a virgin (because that seemed to him impossible), but that he was the son of Joseph and Mary in the same way as all other men, but he was more versed in righteousness, prudence and wisdom than other men. (3) And after his baptism, Christ descended upon him from that Principality that is above all in the form of a dove. And then he proclaimed the unknown Father and performed miracles. But at last Christ flew away again from Jesus; Jesus suffered and rose again while Christ remained impassible, being a spiritual being.» *(Adv. Haer.* I:26:1).

According to Gaius and Dionysius, Cerinth was a crude millennialist, according to Irenaeus he was a typical Gnostic. In modern research, both alternatives have had their advocates. But the most recent and authoritative treatment of the issue, made by A.F.J. Klijn and G.J. Reinink, refuses to accept either version.[87] Irenaeus had no more precise information about Cerinth than the knowledge that he was a heretic, condemned by John. Since for Irenaeus heresy is Gnosticism, he concluded that Cerinth was a Gnostic and attributed to him Gnostic points of view. Gaius, on the other hand, was an anti-millennarian who tried tó discredit the Revelation of John by ascribing it to Cerinth. Hence Cerinth's «millennarianism», developed further by Dionysius who has Gaius as his only source.

Simple and elegant as this theory is, I cannot find it convincing. It is true that Gaius' report on Cerint's millennarian doctrine may be no more than a caricature of Rev 20—22. But one cannot say the same about Dionysius' report. He says that Cerinth envisaged a *re-establishment of the sacrificial cult.* This cannot be derived from Gaius, if Gaius' only source for Cerinth's supposed doctrine was Revelation. And Dionysius has no motive for inventing this idea, because he obviously deems it *more acceptable* than the rest of Cerinth's ideas: Cerinth only added the re-establishment of the sacrificial cult in order to make his other notions seem more respectable. Dionysius' report on this point cannot be derived from Gaius,[88] and does indeed look authentic. Dionysius was a trained and critical philologian, and one should not lightly dismiss his evidence. Besides, if Cerinth was well-known as a - perhaps «crude» - millennarian, it would explain why Gaius made precisely him the author of Revelation.[89] If Gaius had knowledge of the hostility between John and Cerinth - reported by Irenaeus - this would be a most effective way of dissociating John not only from the authorship of Revelation, but also from all kinds of apocalyptic chiliasm.

Concerning Irenaeus, one notices that the Gnostic doctrines ascribed to Cerinth (passages 1 and 3 in the quotation above), are rather commonplace - they would fit many Gnostics. On that point I think Klijn's and Reinink's explanation is correct.[90] Irenaeus was a chiliast himself and would hardly find millennarian doctrine in Cerinth to be very offensive - if he had knowledge of it. But the sharp rejection of Cerinth by John would naturally lead Irenaeus to suspect that Cerinth was a Gnostic. There remain, however, some striking details in Irenaeus' report. These are:

Jesus born of Joseph and Mary in the same way as all other men, i.e. rejection of the Virgin birth.

Jesus more righteous, prudent and wise than other men.

The body of Jesus rose from the dead.

---

87. Klijn and Reinink, *op. cit.*, pp. 3-19.

88. In this I disagree with Bardy, *art. cit.*, p. 361.

89. It is interesting to compare the followino two statements by von Campenhausen in his recent treatment of Gaius:«Es ist keineswegs sicher, dass erst Gaius auf diese Zuschreibung verfallen ist. Gaius erscheint bei aller Schärfe der Polemik doch als ruhig argumentierender Gelehrter, der sich mehr auf sachlich-philologische Gründe als auf tendenziöse Einfälle beruft.» (*Entstehung der christlichen Bibel*, p. 278). «Warum gerade Kerinth von Gaius als Verfasser nahmhaft gemacht wurde, wird sich kaum sicher ausmachen lassen» (*ibid*, n.161). I believe my proposal makes good sense in both respects.

90. Cf. also Bardy, pp. 345-347.

In themselves, these statements are not necessarily Gnostic, they are in fact perfectly compatible with a Judaeo-Christian Christology of «ebionitic» type. Maybe Irenaeus has here preserved genuine traces of Cerinth's doctrine.

With this background, one should probably not too easily dismiss the evidence of Epiphanius,[91] who says that the followers of Cerinth are Jews, proud of their circumcision, arguing for its necessity from Jesus' own circumcision and Mt 10:25:«It suffices for a pupil to become as his master». They also emphasized Jesus' observance of the Law, and they rejected Paul. Taken together, this evidence point to a Judaeo-Christian theologian with an adoptionist Christology, teaching literal fulfilment of OT prophecies in the millennium, and practicing the Law. Is he envisaged in Rev 2:9?

I think the polemic in Justin *Dial.* 118:2 points to the existence of crude chiliasm of the type attributed to Cerinth. The statements in Dionysius and Justin's polemic match perfectly, and Justin's evidence therefore indirectly confirms Dionysius'.[92]

## 5. The theophanies and the second God [93]

I have argued above that the passages treating the theophanies and proving the existence of a 'second God', are perhaps the most original contribution made by Justin to the development of the Scriptural proof. It is now time to examine that contention in some detail. We shall also have to take issue with a theory which has sometimes been put forward with special reference to this part of the *Dialogue,* viz. that here Justin is a pupil of Philo. P. Heinisch and E. R. Goodenough argued this with great conviction.[94] More recently, the tendency has been to deny influence from Philo.[95] This is a main thesis for W. A. Shotwell in his study of Justin's exegesis.[96] However, the case for Philonic influence has been restated most recently by D. C. Trakatellis, and his arguments cannot be overlooked.[97] The entire issue

---

91. *Panarion,* Anakephalaiosis Tom. II:28; 28:5:1 - both passages quoted in Klijn and Reinink, pp. 160-64.

92. In the main this conclusion concurs with Bardy's, *art. cit.* Bardy also accepts the millennarian ideas attributed to Cerinth as authentic, see esp. pp. 356f/372. But Bardy discards the evidence of Epiphanius. He believes Epiphanius describes Judaeo-Christians of his own day, who have nothing to do with Cerinth, pp. 369ff.

93. Select bibliography on the theophanies in Justin: Goodenough, *Theology,* pp. 141-147; J. Lebreton, *Histoire du dogme de la Trinité* II (Paris, 1928), pp. 663-677 ('Note G: L'interpretation des theophanies chez les apologistes....'); J. Barbel, *Christos Angelos* (*Theophaneia* Beitrage zur Religions- und Kirchengeschichte des Altertums 3, Bonn, 1941 (repr. with an Appendix, Bonn, 1964)), pp. 50-63; A. Hanson, 'Theophanies in the Old Testament and the Second Person of the Trinity', *Hermathena* 65 (1945), pp. 67-73; B. Kominiak, *The Theophanies of the Old Testament in the Writings of St. Justin* (The Catholic University of America, Studies in Sacred Theology, 2nd Ser. 14, Washington, 1948); G. Aeby, *Les missions divines de saint Justin à Origène* (Paradosis 12, Freiburg, 1958), pp. 6-15; G. T. Armstrong, *Die Genesis in der Alten Kirche. Die drei Kirchenväter* (RGRH 4, Tübingen, 1962), pp. 42-48; D. C. Trakatellis, *The Pre-Existence of Christ in the Writings of Justin Martyr* (Harvard Dissertations in Religion 6, Missoula, 1976), pp. 53-92.

94. P. Heinisch, *Einfluss Philos,* pp. 195-211; Goodennough, *Theology,* pp. 141-147.

95. Cf. e.g. Lebreton, *op. cit.,* pp. 667-672; R.P.C Hanson, *Allegory and Event* (London, 1959). pp.107f; L. W. Barnard, *Justin Martyr,* pp. 93-96/112f.

96. *Exegesis,* esp. pp. 96ff.

97. Trakatellis, *loc. cit.*

calls for a fresh examination. One should not, however, be so preoccupied with Philo that other possible sources of influence are neglected.

(a) The theophany to Abraham, Gen 18f.[98]

Justin's argument may be summarized like this: One of the three »men« who appeared to Abraham was not an angel but God. This God, however, cannot be identical with the Father. Proof: Gen 19:24: 'The Lord (viz. the lord talking with Abraham) rained upon Sodom brimstone and fire from the Lord out of heaven'(viz. the Lord in heaven, the Father).

Trakatellis traces this argument to influence from Philo.[99] He says that Philo is the only one before Justin to differentiate between the three angels in Gen 18: »Philo departs from the traditional idea of the three visitors as being three angels and introduces instead a sharp differentiation between them.« In support of this contention he refers to *Mut.Nom.* 15; *Sacr.* 59; and *De Abr.* 121.142-45.[100] But a closer examination of these texts shows that Trakatellis' assertion cannot be accepted without major qualifications.

Philo's main passage on Gen 18 is *De Abr.* 107-141. This text clearly falls into two parts: first the literal meaning of the text is expounded in 107-118; then the allegorical interpretation is given in 119-141. In the first section, Philo simply says that the three men were three angels: »I do not know how to express the vast happiness and blessedness of that house where angels did not shrink from halting and receiving hospitality from men . . . angels, those holy and divine beings, the servitors and lieutenants of the primal God whom he employs as ambassadors to announce the predictions which he wills to make to our race«. (*ibid.*,115). One cannot therefore say that Philo does not share the traditional idea[101] of there being three angels. It is on the allegorical level that he differentiates among the three men, but then none of the three are called ἄγγελοι in the technical sense of angels. Abraham's seeing the three men is taken to signify the soul's vision of God:· «The single object presents to it a triple vision, one representing the reality, the other two the shadows reflected from it . . . The central place is held by the Father of the universe, . . . while on either side of him are the senior δυνάμεις, the nearest to him, the creative and the kingly.«(*ibid.*, 119-121). Philo goes on to explain that the creative δύναμις can be called God, and the kingly Lord, and that the vision of a 'trinity' rather than a unity is a lower phase in the ascent of the soul - the perfect soul sees God as a unity (*ibid.*, 122ff).

98. On this theme in Justin, cf. the studies listed in note 93, and besides: A. d'Alès,'La Theophanie de Mambré devant la tradition des Peres', *RSR* 20 (1930) pp. 150-60; L. Thunberg, 'Early Christian interpretations of the Three Angels in Gen 18', *Studia Patristica* 7 (TU 92, Berlin, 1966), pp. 560-70; K. Hruby, 'Exégèse rabbinique et exéqèse patristique', *RSR* 47 (1973, pp. 341-72), pp. 359-369.

99. Trakatellis, *Pre-Existence*, pp. 60-68. So also Heinisch, *Einfluss Philos*, pp. 194f; Goodenough, *Theology*, pp. 114f.

100. *Pre-Existence*, pp. 61f.

101. Cf. Ginzberg I, pp. 240-245; V, pp. 234-236.

In *De Sacr.* 59 Philo alludes briefly to his allegorical exposition in *De Abr.* 119ff, and *Mut.Nom.* 15 he interprets the saying 'The Lord was seen of Abraham' (which is Gen 17:1, not 18:1 as Trakatellis seems to suppose)[102] on an allegorical level. It means that Abraham = the soul, «saw» God's kingly δύναμις.

I think this is sufficient to show that Trakatellis' references do not prove his point - on the contrary, they prove a great distance between our two authors. While for Philo the text has two levels - on the one, three angels; on the other, God the Father and his two powers - for Justin the text has a single meaning: Abraham was visited by Christ and two angels. He emphatically challenges the view of Trypho - and Philo! - that «the three who were in the tent with Abraham were all angels.»(*Dial.* 56:9). And the notion that one of the three men should signify the Father of the Universe is utterly unacceptable to Justin. It is precisely this idea he has to combat in order to establish his own Christological interpretation: The third man was God, but not the Father of the Universe.[103]

The common feature to which Trakatellis points, viz. the differentiation between the one and the two men, is already present in the Biblical text: The two men go on to Sodom, the third abides with Abraham. That this was part of Philo's reason for treating the third man as superior to the two others (on the allegorical level), is indicated in *De Abr.* 142-146. Justin's separate treatment of the third man is also directly dependent on the OT text. There is thus no reason to posit a dependence upon Philo here.[104] A second argument is advanced by Trakatellis in his contention that Justin depends on Philo: Also Philo «made the identification of God who appeared at Mamre and Sodom with Logos in more than one instance.»[105] If this were correct, it would mean that Philo on other occasions advanced an interpretation of Gen 18 contradicting the one presented above. But let us examine the passages adduced by Trakatellis to support his view.

---

102. *Pre-Existence*, p. 61.
103. I believe Aeby and Thunberg in their above mentioned articles are right to stress that later *trinitarian* exegesis of Gen 18 owes more to Philo than the simple Christological exegesis of most ante-Nicene Fathers.
104. Also the rabbis and Josephus distinguished between the one and the two, cf. texts quoted in L. Williams' note *ad Dial.* 56:5 (pp. 111f). How christian adaption of Philo's exegesis turns out, one can study in Origen, *In cant.* II (GCS 33, p. 158): *Trinitatis ibi mysterium prodebatur.* Which means that Origen accepts Philo's identification of one of the three «men» with the highest God, *the Father*. Cf. Thunberg, *art. cit.*, pp. 565-69, who also quotes later patristic material for a trinitarian interpretation.
105. *Pre-Existence*, p. 62. It should be noted that Trakatellis correctly, - in my opinion - has dismissed one of the texts adduced by Goodenough (*Theology*, p. 115; repeated by Shotwell, p. 97), viz. *De Cherub.* 27:«And in the midst between the two (highest *dynameis*) there is a third which unites them, λόγος, for it is through λόγος that God is both ruler and good.» This passage cannot be adduced as an interpretation of the Mamre theophany. Philo is here allegorizing the sword of the cherubim in Gen 3:24.

In *Leg.All.* III:217-219 Philo comments on Sarah's laughing: «. . . and she laughed in her mind and said, Not yet hath happiness befallen me till now, but my Lord (the divine Word) is greater, to whom this must needs belong and whom I must believe when he promises good.« The first thing to notice is that Philo is here not commenting on Gen 18, but on Gen 17:15-17. Secondly: The »divine Word« seems simply to mean the divine oracle of Gen 17:15f, cf. the introduction to the quotation in 217: »the divine word shall testify in these words . . .«[106] This text cannot be said to prove Trakatellis' point

The next text is *De Somn.* I:85. Here Philo says that »sun« can refer to the Word, and quotes Gen 19:23f in support of this. The meaning seems to be that the »sun« = the Logos was the active agent in pouring down brimstone and fire on Sodom and Gomorrah, but there is no identification of the Logos and the third man, and Philo omits in Gen 19:24 the words which are crucial to Justin: παρὰ κυρίου.

The third text adduced by Trakatellis is *Migr.Abr.* 173f. I shall return to this text below, here I anticipate the conclusion: This text does not prove that the third man appearing to Abraham is identified with the Logos.

Last but not least, one notices that Justin never calls Christ Logos in his treatment of the appearance to Abraham, *Dial.* 56f. It thus seems that Philo is of little help in providing a background for Justin's treatment of the Abraham theophany.

I therefore believe one shall have to disregard Philo as a source for Justin's argument on Gen 18f. My analysis in Part II has made me belive that one should rather see *Dial.* 56f as an extensive elaboration of one single traditional testimony: Gen 19:24.[107] As I have argued above, this testimony seems to belong to a cluster of testimonies intended to prove the existence of two Gods, Lords etc. in the OT. In this original setting, the testimony was not embedded in a theory of theophanies being appearances of Christ.

It is now time to bring in supporting evidence for this contention from Jewish sources.

Let me adduce a rabbinic passage:[108] «A *Min* once said to R. Ishmael b.Jose (ca 180): It is written, 'Then the Lord caused to rain upon Sodom and Gomorrah brimstone and fire from the Lord'(Gen 19:24), but 'from him' should have been written! A certain fuller said, Leave him to me, I will answer him. It is written, 'And Lamech said to his wives, Ada and Zillah, Hear my voice, ye wives of Lamech'; but he should have said, 'my wives.' But such

---

106. Perhaps one should translate »to which« and »it« instead of »to whom« and »he« in the quotation above.
107. Kominiak, *op. cit*, in his minute analysis of Justin's argument, clearly demonstrates the crucial role of Gen 19:24: Justin's entire argument concerning Gen 18 is mainly preparatory for his treatment of Gen 19:24 (*op. cit*, pp. 23-47, esp. p. 34. cf. also Trakatellis, *Pre-Existence*, p. 65).
108. M. Friedländer called attention to this passage, *Studien*, pp. 106-l08, cf. also M. Simon, *Verus Israel*, pp. 230f, and K. Hruby, 'Exegese' , p. 360. A parallel is preserved in *Gen.Rab.* 51.

is the Scriptural idiom - so here too, it is the Scriptural idiom.[109] - Whence do you know that? asked he (R.Ishmael). I heard it in a public discourse of R.Meir, (he answered)." (*Sanh.* 38b, p. 246). If this attribution of the argument to R.Meir (ca 150) can be trusted,[110] it means that Gen 19:24 was a disputed text in public controversy between Jews and Christians[111] in Palestine[112] at the same time as Justin was writing his *Dialogue* - or even earlier.

It is relevant to notice that the only subject for controversy in the Talmudic passage is the plurality of Lords in Gen 19:24 - there is no question of the theophanies as such. In the preceding context several passages are enumerated which the *minim* take as proof of more than one God: Gen 1:26; Gen 11:7; Gen 35:7; Deut 4:7; 2 Sam 7:23; Dan 7:9; Ex 24:1. In several of these instances, the argument of the *minim* are based on grammatical plurals in verbs applied to God, i.e. they are based on the Hebrew text and seem to be at home in a Palestinian setting.

If we take it that the duality of Lords in Gen 19:24 was the original argument, Justin's argument concerning the theophany in Gen 18f can be seen as a logical deduction: The one Lord spoken of in Gen 19:24 must be the one talking to Abraham, i.e. one of the three appearing to Abraham in Gen 18.[113]

The Talmudic passage makes one think of Judaeo-Christian origin for the original argument built on Gen 19:24.

(b) The theophanies to Jacob.

Reading through the Jacob narratives in Genesis, one notices the following instances where God appears or speaks to Jacob:
(A) Gen 28:12-22: The dream at Bethel
(B) Gen 31:3: The Lord saying to Jacob: Return to the land of thy Fathers.

---

109. For other rabbinic rebuttals, cf. A. Büchler,'Über die Minim von Sepphoris und Tiberias im zweiten und dritten Jahrhundert', *Judaica, Festschrift zu Herman Cohens siebzigstem Geburtstage* (Berlin, 1912, pp. 271-295), p. 285.

110. It is taken for granted by W. Bacher, *Aggada* II, pp. 7f/36; Büchler, *art. cit.*, pp. 284f, and Hruby, *art. cit.*, p.360. It is, indeed, not unlikely, since R. Meir seems to have been occupied with anti-Christian polemic, cf. *Shab.* 116a (unrecensed text), where he takes εὐαγγέλιον to mean גליון אוֹן, Bacher II, p. 36.

111. I take it that the *Min* was a Christian, and very likely a Judaeo-Christian, since *Min* normally seems to refer to Jews, cf. esp. K. Hruby, *Die Stellung der jüdischen Gesetzeslehrer zur werdenden Kirche* (Schriften zur Judentumskunde 4, Zürich, 1971), pp. 16-19, with brief review of relevant literature and points of view.

112. Cf. Büchler, *art. cit.*, who surmises that the fuller heard R. Meir's exposition in Sepphoris (pp. 284f).

113. Shotwell, *Exegesis*, pp. 34f, takes Justin's argument concerning Gen 19:24 and Ps 110:1 as examples of Hillel's *binyan ab* principle applied within a single verse of Scripture. As one can easily see from the rabbinic example cited by Shotwell, p. 91 (Deut 24:6), this is rather far-fetched. The same must be said about Shotwell's attempt, pp. 35-38, to subsume more of Justin's reasoning in *Dial.* 56-58 under the *binyan ab* principle.

(C) Gen 31:10-13: The dream in Haran. The angel of God saying to Jacob: I am the God that appeared to thee in the Place of God (Bethel).
(D) Gen 32:24-32: The man fighting with Jacob at Pniel.
(E) Gen 35:1.3.7.9-15: God talking to Jacob, and appearing to him at Bethel.

In *Dial.* 58 Justin treats this material in the order CDEA. The decisive argument hinges on the combination of C and A: The God appearing to Jacob in Bethel cannot be the Father, since in Gen 31:11 he is called «the angel of God», i.e. the messenger of God the Father. This argument can also be said to cover element E, but strictly speaking not D.

Trakatellis[114] is certainly right to insist that *Dial.* 58 and the treatment there given of four theophanies to Jacob, should be considered as an appendix to *Dial.* 56f: In his exegesis of Gen 18f Justin has established that the second God is called by Moses θεός, κύριος, ἄγγελος, and ἀνήρ. In *Dial.* 58 he goes on to trace these designations in the Jacob theophanies. Here no trace of an original pivotal testimony stands out. It seems Justin is working on his own with the LXX text, applying the hermeneutical principle derived from his work with Gen 18f.[115]

However, Trakatellis thinks he is able to adduce Philonic background material here, too.[116] We shall breiefly look at the relevant texts. Apropos Gen 28:11 Philo says: «Meet and right then is it that Jacob, having come to sense-perception, meets not God but a word of God, even as did Abraham, the grandfather of his wisdom.» Trakatellis takes this to mean that »the one who appeared to Jacob was the λόγος»,[117] thus leading us to think of the theophany to Jacob in Gen 28:12-15. But this is not what Philo says. He is allegorizing Gen 28:10f: Having come to Haran, Jacob «meets a place» (=Bethel). Haran, explains Philo, means sense-perception, while the «place» refers to the next stage in the spiritual progress of the soul: The contemplation of the divine Logos, which is the next best to contemplating God himself, *De Somn.* I:68-74.

Again, Philo in *De Somn.* I:120-132 expounds the literal (120-126) and allegorical meaning of the stone used by Jacob as a pillow, Gen 28:11. This stone means a divine word on which the soul resets.[118] «The divine word

---

114. *Pre-Existence*, pp. 68f.
115. Trakatellis, p. 69, n. 4, reports that F. Bosse, *Der präexistente Christus des Justinus Martyr. Eine Episode aus der Geschichte des christologischen Dogmas* (Inaug. Dissertation, Greifswald, 1891 (inaccessible to me)), reached a similar conclusion: The whole theophanic section has developed out of the theophany to Abraham.
116. *Pre-Existence*, pp. 68-73, cf. also Heinisch, *Einfluss Philos*, pp. 143-146.
117. *Pre-Existence*, pp. 69f.
118. The same equation of the place Bethel with the divine Logos is expressed in *De Migr. Abr.* 5f, another text quoted by Trakatellis to prove his point, *op. cit.*, p. 70, n. 45. On the meaning of this allegorization of «place» = Logos, cf. Wolfson, *Philo* I, pp. 240-47, esp. p. 245:«The Logos is the place of the intelligible world as well as of the ideas of which the intelligible world consists.» Cf. also H.-F. Weiss, *Kosmologie*, pp. 254/58.

readily listens to and accepts the athlete to be first of all a pupil, then . . . he fastens on the gloves as a trainer does and summons him to the exercises, then closes with him and forces him to wrestle until he has developed in him an irresistible strength, and by the breath of divine inspiration he changes ears into eyes, and gives him when remodelled in a new form the name Israel - he who sees.» (*De Somn.* I:129). Philo here moves on from Jacob's «rest» on the word of God in Gen 28:11 to his spiritual fight with it in Gen 32. The significance of the latter motif will be treated below. It does not imply that the one seen by Jacob in his dream, Gen 28:12ff, was the Logos.[119] On the contrary, coming to the phrase 'and the Lord stood firmly upon it (the ladder)', Philo expressly says that this was «He who is Lord and God of the Universe», the God of Abraham and Isaac, *De Somn* 159. Philo has already so allegorized the other elements in Jacob's dream that he felt no anthropomorhic obstacle in the Lord standing on the top of the ladder. There is thus no indication of ideas anticipating Justin's in Philo's handling of the Bethel theophany.

The only one of the Jacob theophanies which Philo expounds in a manner similar to Justin, is the theophany at Pniel, Gen 32:22-31 (*Dial.* 58:6f).[120] I have already quoted the pertinent passage from *De Somn.* I:129. To this can be added *Mut.Nom.* 87: «Jacob was renamed by an angel, God's minister (ὑπηρέτης), the Word, in aknowledgement that what is below the Existent cannot produce permanence.» In both passages Philo identifies the man wrestling with Jacob as the λόγος = ἄγγελος.

We have seen already that Justin's identification of the man as Christ wrestling with Jacob creates confusion within a simple Jacob/Christ typology. One cannot exclude the possibility that Justin here has introduced a Philonic idea foreign to his Christian source. On the other hand, the characteristic Logos concept of Philo is lacking in Justin's comments on the Pniel theophany, and Justin may again quite simply be applying his general principle that theophanies should be ascribed to Christ.

As far as Justin's exegesis of the theophanies is concerned, the alleged parallels in Philo thus shrink to nearly nothing on closer inspection. But there remains some more general similarities on the level of terminology. Trakatellis is right in pointing out[121] that Philo can call the Logos of God a ὑπηρέτης, very much like Justin when he speaks of the ἄγγελος/θεός of the theophanies.

Justin: ... ὁ ... ὀφθεὶς θεός καὶ ὑπηρέτης ὢν τοῦ ποιητοῦ τῶν ὅλων θεοῦ, *Dial.* 57:3.

οὗτος ὁ ὀφθεὶς τοῖς πατριάρχαις λεγόμενος θεὸς ... ἵνα καὶ ἐκ

---

119. Trakatellis is wrong when he quotes this passage as another testimony that Philo identified *the one seen by Jacob* with the Logos, *op. cit.*, p. 70, n. 45.
120. Cf. the remarks in Lebreton; *op. cit.*, pp. 670f.
121. *Pre-Existence*, pp. 71f.

τούτων ἐπιγνῶτε αὐτὸν ὑπηρετοῦντα τῷ τῶν ὅλων πατρί, *Dial.*
58:3.

Philo: δίδωσι δὲ (ὁ θεὸς) λόγῳ χρώμενος ὑπηρέτῃ δωρεῶν ᾧ καὶ τὸν
κόσμον εἰργάζετο, *Deus Imm.* 57.

τὸν δὲ ᾿Ιακὼβ (μετωνόμασεν), ἄγγελος ὑπηρέτης τοῦ θεοῦ,
λόγος, *Mut. Nom.* 87.

To this can be added a passage where Philo defends the application of
the term θεός to the Logos. His reasoning here is not unlike Justin's: «'I am
the God who appeared to thee in the Place of God'(Gen 31:13) . . . do not
fail to mark the language used, but carefully inquire whether there are two
Gods; for we read 'I am the God who appeared to thee' not 'in my place',
but 'in the place of God', as though it were another's.»(*De Somn.*1:227f).
Philo's point is that the Logos can improperly be called 'god' (without the
article), and the text means that the place was the place of the Logos.
Formally, this is not unlike Justin's reasoning, and the text (Gen 31:13) is
crucial to Justin also, though he inverts the identification: For him, Christ is
speaking, not God as in Philo.

These instances of parallels are hardly sufficient to establish sure proof of
direct dependence on Justin's part, but direct or indirect contact with the
Philonic ideas cannot be excluded.

What is lacking in Philo is the elaborate argument establishing the
identity of the one appearing in the theophanies, based on different
passages in Genesis separated by several chapters. Here Justin is obviously
working directly with the Biblical text.

In two cases, Justin's attention to the Jacob incidents may have been
helped by typological treatments of the same incidents contained in his
sources.

The theophany at Bethel is mentioned in *Dial.* 86:2f. Here Justin brings
out a threefold Christological interpretation:

(1) Christ stationed on the ladder, as previously shown (crossreference
    to *Dial.* 58:11-13). The context suggests a typology ladder/cross.

(2) The anointed stone a type of Christ the Stone.[122]

(3) The anointing of the stone a type of Christ's anointing. Testimony: Ps
    45:8.

We have seen above that the last two elements are quite likely traditional
deposits, and even the ladder/cross typology in 1 might be traditional. It
seems the theophany theory in element 1 is grafted on to earlier, purely
typological material.

---

122. Cf. J. Jeremias: «*(dem Spätjudentum) galt der Bethelstein, auf dem die Jakobsleiter gestanden
hatte, als der heilige Felsen, den Gott vor der Weltschöpfung erschaffen haben und von dem
aus er die Welt ausgebreitet haben sollte.*» ('Die Berufung des Nathanael (Jo 1,45-51)', *Angelos*
3, (1928, pp. 2-5), pp. 4f).

The Pniel theophany is subjected to a typological treatment in *Dial.* 125 (cf.above,386f). Here also there seems to be no theophany theory implied in the original typology, on the contrary, the theophany theory complicates and partly confuses the typology. One further notices that the second repetition of the theophany theory, *Dial.* 126-129, so obviously stands out as a secondary addition or excursus on *Dial.* 125.

We thus arrive at the conclusion that Justin very likely is creative in applying the theophany theory to Jacob material originally having another orientation. A general influence from Philo cannot be excluded, but in his detailed exegetical argument, Justin goes his own ways, often contradicting Philo.

(c) The burning bush.

I have made a rather detailed analysis of Justin's argument concerning this text above, 47-50. In *1. Apol.* 62f Justin bases himself on a non-LXX version of Ex 3:2ff, stating that the Jews take the angel talking to Moses to be the Father - which is obviously absurd. In *Dial.* 59f Justin has turned to the LXX text, and has observed that the Jewish objection would in fact be different: A Jew would not identify the angel appearing with the God speaking, but would say that both an angel and God appeared to Moses. This last interpretation can in fact be confirmed from rabbinic sources, though of a later date.[123] The angel is dentified as Michael by R.Johanan (died 279), or Gabriel by R. Hanina (ca 225).[124] Perhaps an older Tanna held the view ascribed to the Jews in the *Apology*: «*'Und Mose hütete (das Vieh)..., und der Engel des Herrn erschien ihm (in einer Feuerflamme aus dem Dornbusch heraus)' (Ex 3:1f). R. Eliezer (b.Hyrkanos, ca 90) sagte: Warum erschien der Heilige, gepriesen sei Er, vom hohen Himmel herab und sprach mit ihm aus dem Dornbusch?*» (*Mekh. de R. Simon*, I to Ex 3:2.)[125] This may be the idea attributed to the Jews in *1.Apol.* 63:14, but not necessarily. Rabbi Eliezer may tacitly presuppose the principle stated in *Ex.Rab.* 32:9 (anonymously): «Whereever the angel appeared, the Shekinah appeared also, as it says, 'And the angel of the Lord appeared unto him in a flame of fire', and immediately after, it says, 'God called unto him'» (p. 412f).[126]

---

123. Cf. i.a. Goldfahn, pp. 113-115.
124. *Ex.Rab.* 2:5, cf. Str. Bill. II, p. 91. Cf. the valuable comments in A. M. Goldberg, *Untersuchungen über die Vorstellung von der Schekhinah in der frühen rabbinischen Literatur (Studia Judaica.* Forschungen zur Wissenschaft des Judentums 5, Berlin, 1969), pp. 172f, with more rabbinic texts. Büchler, *art. cit.*, believes that this rabbinic conception is conscious anti-Christian exegesis by the rabbis, provoked by Christian writers like Justin, p. 287.
125. Quoted from P. Kuhn, *Gottes Selbsterniedrigung in der Theologie der Rabbinen* (StANT 17, München, 1968), p. 36.
126. The distinction between angel and Shekhinah is emphasized in *Ex.Rab.* 2:5 and parr., cf. Goldberg, *op. cit.*, pp.202/341f. «*Die Schekhinah ist nicht mit dem Engel identisch.*» (*ibid.*, p. 342). But cf. *ibid.*, pp. 339f for material with the opposite tendency.

Trakatellis again thinks Philo offers important clues to Justin's handling of the burning bush theophany.[127] Philo treats this in *De Vitæ Mos.* I:65-70. The crucial passage is this: «In the midst of the flame was a form (μορφή) of the fairest beauty, unlike any visible object, an image (εἰκών) supremely divine in appearance, refulgent with a light brighter than the light of fire. It might be supposed that this was the image of him that IS; but let us rather call it an angel or herald, since, with a silence that spoke more clearly than speech, it employed as it were the miracle of sight to herald future events» (*ibid.,* 66). Trakatellis combines this passage with *Spec. Leg.* 1:81: «the image of God is the Word through whom the whole universe was framed»; *Conf. Ling.* 97: «. . . his image, the most holy Word,» and *De Somn.* I:238f: «. . . some regard the image of God, his angel the Word, as his very self.» Trakatellis concludes: «. . . the agent of the theophany is the Logos.»[128] I think this conclusion is more definite than the evidence allows. It is true that for Philo the image of God is the Logos,[129] but while Philo considers this a possible identification of the μορφη τις visible in the bush, he himself prefers a more vague identification. In *De Vit.Mos.* 67 he goes on to give a symbolic exposition of the burning bush: The bush is a symbol of the afflicted Israel in Egypt, the fire symbolizes the oppressors. «The angel was a symbol of God's providence, which all silently brings relief to the greatest dangers, exceeding every hope.» It deserves notice that Philo does not present the angel as identical with the one speaking with Moses in the theophany. On the contrary, he emphasizes the silence of the angel. The one speaking to Moses is God himself, *De Vit.Mos.* I:71. Philo's exposition is on this point similar to the rabbinic exegesis referred to above, and also identical with Trypho's point of view: «He who was seen in a flame of fire was an angel, and he who conversed with Moses was God, so that both an angel and God, two together, were in that vision.»(*Dial.* 60:1). Philo offers no foundation whatever for the main point in Justin, viz. the identity of the angel and the one addressing Moses.

A final remark can serve as a transition to our treatment of the Joshua theme and the theophany to Joshua. In anonymous rabbinical texts, the angel appearing to Moses in the burning bush is identified with the angel appearing to the patriarchs, the guardian angel leading Israel (Ex 23:20), and the «captain of the host of the Lord» appearing to Joshua (Josh 5:13-15).[130]

---

127. *Pre-Existence,* pp. 73-80.
128. *Op. cit.,* p. 74. The same assertion in Heinisch, *Einfluss Philos,* pp. 217f.
129. Cf. i.a. Jervell, *Imago Dei,* pp. 53-56.
130. *Ex.Rab.* 32:9 (pp. 412f):«The Holy One, blessed be He, said to Moses:'He who guarded the patriarchs will also guard the children', for so you find in the case of Abraham . . . 'The Lord, God of heaven .. He will send His angel before thee'(Gen 24:7). And what did Jacob say to his children? 'The angel who hath redeemed me from all evil'(Gen 48:16). . . . Wherever the angel appeared, the Shechinah appeared also, as it says, 'And the angel of the Lord appeared unto him..'(Ex 3:2) and immediately after, it says,'God called unto him (vs. 4).» Partly parallel material occurs in *Ex.Rab.* 32:3 (p. 408) and *Gen. Rab.* 97:3 (pp. 938f). Cf. comments on

(d) The guardian angel, Ex 23:20f.

As Trakatellis rightly points out,[131] Justin's use of this text is radically different from the use of the same text in the Synoptics. In the synoptic tradition, Ex 23:20 serves as one of the testimonies applied to John the Baptist. Justin applies the same text to *Joshua.* Are there precedents for this?

Trakatellis again points to Philo.[132] In *De Agric.* 51 and *Migr.Abr.* 174, Philo identifies the Logos with the guardian angel of Ex 23:20. Now, the thrust of Justin's argument in *Dial.* 75 is the identification of the angel with *Joshua.* Christ is here - for once - not identified with the angel, but is presented *as the one speaking* in Ex 23:20f. This means that Justin's exegesis is entirely different from Philo's. But perhaps Justin's source was closer to Philo?

Let us try to probe a little behind Justin's exposition. First, there is a typological tradition concerning Joshua. The re-naming of Joshua is seen is a significant event in *Barn.* 12:8-10, quoted above (p.394).[133] *Barnabas* is only working on the typological level: Joshua is a type of Jesus - there is no question of the pre-existent Christ lending his name to Joshua. Justin's rich material concerning the Jushua typology has been treated in some detail above (p. 334ff). In *Dial.* 75 he adds a new dimension to this typology by introducing his theophany theory: The name Joshua receives in Num 13:16 is *the name of the God speaking in Ex 6:3 and Ex 23:20f,* i.e. the God appearing to Abraham, Isaac, etc., i.e. the pre-existent Christ.

By this device, the Joshua typology is transformed to a new level of argument: The name of the pre-existent God lending his name to Joshua is Jesus. But is this the conception originally attached to Ex 23:20f? Let me adduce a rabbinic passage: «Once a *Min* said to R. Idith: It is written, And unto Moses He said, Come up to the Lord' (Ex 24:1). But surely it should have stated,'Come up unto *me.*' - It was Metatron (who said that), he replied, whose name is similar to that of his Master, for it is written,'For my name is in him'(Ex 23:21). But if so, (he retorted), we should worship him! The same passage, however, - replied R. Idith - says:'Be not rebellious ( תמר ) against him,' i.e. exchange ( תמר derived from מור ) Me not for him. But if so, why is it stated:'He will not pardon your transgressions? (i.e. how could he then have authority to forgive sins?)

---

these passages in Goldberg, *Schekhinah*, pp. 341f. The uncertain and possibly late date of these traditions does not allow the conclusion that when Justin made the same combination of motives, he was dependent on rabbinical haggadah. This must remain a possibility, incapable of proof. It nevertheless is interesting to observe the quite similar combinations connected with the »angel« catchword.

131. *Pre-Existence*, p. 82.
132. *Ibid.*
133. Cf. the analysis of *Barn.* 12:8f in Prigent, *Les Testimonia*, pp. 122f, and (somewhat different) in *idem, l'Epître*, p. 172, note. Concerning rabbinical interpretations of the changing of Joshua's name, cf. Str. Bill. I, pp. 64/247. There is no significant parallel to the emphasis on the significance of Joshua's new name in Christian writers.

He answered: By our troth we would not accept him even as messenger (bringing forgivenness), for it is written,'And he said unto him, If Thy (personal) presence go not etc.( Ex 33:15).« (*Sanh.* 38b, pp. 245f).[134] One first notices that this passage in *Sanh.* 38b immediately preceedes the discussion on Gen 19:24 quoted above. The *min* may very well be a Christian,[135] identifying the guardian angel of Ex 23:21 with Christ, and arguing Christ's divinity from this text. I suspect this may be the argument originally attached to Justin's testimony; in other words, the ἄγγελος may originally have referred to Christ, not Joshua as in *Dial.* 75. If so, the argument was originally not concerned with the *name* Jesus, but with the *divinity* (Jahve's Name) conferred to Christ.

However, all this can only be suggested rather tentatively, because the rabbinic evidence is considerably later than Justin,[136] and may reflect a later stage of the debate with Christians. In any case, Justin's idea that the »angel« is Joshua, may have been prompted by another text which probably was part of Justin's argument, viz. Deut 31:2f as quoted in *Dial.* 126:6:» . . . the Lord thy God who goeth before thy face, he shall destroy the nations.« Where Justin's quotation breaks off, the LXX continues: . . . καὶ κατακλη-ρονομήσεις αὐτούς καὶ 'Ιησοῦς ὁ προπορευόμενος πρὸ προσώπου σου . . . Thus Joshua and »the Lord thy God« are said to perform much the same action. We have seen reasons above (p. 214) to think that the present fragment in *Dial.* 74:4 (Deut 31:16-18) is only the last part of a long quotation of Deut 31:2ff, introducing Joshua as the one leading Israel into the promised land. Although this text also operates on the level of typology, the parallelism of the acts performed by Joshua and the »God« spoken of, may have prompted Justin's idea.

---

134. A selection of comments on this important passage: Friedländer, *Studien,* pp. 112f; H. L. Strack, *Jesus, die Häretiker und die Christen nach den ältesten jüdischen Angaben* (Schriften des Institutum Judaicum in Berlin 37, Leipzig, 1910) pp 73*-75*; H. Odeberg, *3 Enoch or The Hebrew Book of Enoch* (Cambridge, 1928 (repr. New York, 1973)), Introd., p. 90; G. Scholem, *Jewish Gnosticism, Merkabah Mysticism, and Talmudic Tradition* (New York, 1960), pp. 46f; H. Bietenhard, *Die himmlische Welt im Urchristentum und Spätjudentum* (WUNT 2, Tübingen 1951), p. 149, S. S. Cohon, 'The Unity of God', pp. 463-465; Urbach, *The Sages* I, p. 139.

135. This is argued by Friedländer, *loc. cit.,* and assumed by Urbach, *loc. cit.*

136. Rabbi Idith - or Idi, the readings of the MSS vary - cannot be identified with certainty (cf. Urbach II, p. 742), but seems to have been an Amora of the 4th century, cf. Strack, *op. cit,* p. 75*:». . . wahrscheinlich Sohn des Ja'akob bar Idi, Tradent der gleichfalls zur dritten Genera-tion gehörigen palästinischen Lehrer Semuel bar Nahman.*« The argument against apotheosis of Metatron is certainly older, however. In *Hag.* 14b/15a it is said that the apostasy of Aher, the famous teacher of R. Meir, was due to a vision in which he saw Metatron *sitting* in God's presence. He took this to mean that Metatron shared in God's divinity. (It would exceed the scope of the present study to embark on a discussion of the figure of Metatron. Cf. esp. Odeberg's Introduction to 3 Enoch; Bietenhard, *op. cit,* pp. 149-160; S. S. Cohon, 'Unity of God', pp. 476-79; G. Scholem, *Kabbalah* (Library of Jewish Knowledge, Jerusalem, 1974(paperb. ed. 1977)), pp. 377-381; Urbach, *loc. cit.*).

(e) The theophany to Joshua.

As we have seen already, in rabbinical sources the guardian angel who appeared to the patriarchs is identified with the man seen by Joshua, Josh 5:13ff. Even without impetus from rabbinical exegesis, Justin would be prompted to make the same identification. It follows from his general principle about theophanies, and, besides, Josh 5:15 is very reminiscent of Ex 3:5, a text which already had been interpreted as a saying of Christ.

The lack of any mention of the Joshua theophany in Philo serves to underline Justin's independence of Philo.

(f) General statements.

Justin can state the result of his argument concerning the theophanies as a general principle: «He who was seen of Abraham and Isaac and Jacob and the other patriarchs» was Christ, *Dial.* 126:5. A direct Scriptural support is found in God's (i.e. Christ's) words to Moses at the burning bush: «I am the God of Abraham, the God of Isaac, the God of Jacob, the God of thy fathers . . .» (Ex 3:6 in the version of *1.Apol.* 63:7). Justin clearly interprets this to mean: I am the God *who appeared to* Abraham, Isaac, Jacob and the other patriarchs, *Dial.* 59:3; 60:2f; 126:5.

In *Dial.* 126:6 and 127:1.3f Justin rather casually adds some more applications of this general principle, but none of them are elaborated:

(1) Christ is the angel conversing with Moses in Num 11:4-23.
(2) Christ is the «Lord thy God» going in front of Israel,
    Deut 31:2f (on this text, see above).
(3) Gen 11:5: Christ is the one «coming down».
(4) Gen 7:16: Christ shuts Noah's ark.
(5) The glory at Sinai was Christ's glory.
(6) The glory in the tabernacle and the Temple was from «God» (= Christ?).

Justin can express his exegetical principle as a philosophical maxim: «No person whatever, even though he be of slight intelligence, will dare to say that the Maker and Father of the universe left all that is above heaven, and appeared on a little section of the earth.» (*Dial.* 60:2).[137] Trakatellis[138] aptly parallels this with Philo's remarks on the Sinai theophany: «What is the meaning of the words 'and the glory of God came down upon Mt Sinai'? (Scripture) clearly puts to shame those who whether through impiety or through foolishness believe that there are movements of place or of change in the Deity.» *(Quest. and answ. on Ex* Nr.45, p. 89; cf also Nr. 37)[139] One

---

137. Cf. also the somewhat fuller statement of the same maxime in *Dial.* 127:2. For comments on this «philosophical» principle, cf. i.a. Kominiak, *op. cit.*, pp. 50-52/61-65; Goodenough, *Theology*, pp. 124-127; Lebreton, *Histoire* II, pp. 426-428; Aeby, *op. cit.*, pp. 8f.
138. *Pre-Existence*, p. 76.
139. To these texts can be added *Conf. Linn.* 136/139.

can also adduce some rabbinic passages, e.g. *Sukkah* 5a: «R.Jose (ca 150) stated, Neither did the Shekinah ever descend to earth, nor did Moses or Elijah ever ascend to heaven, as it is written, 'The heavens are the heavens of the Lord, but the earth hath he given to the sons of men'(Ps 115:16). But did not the Shekinah descend to earth? Is it not in fact written, 'And the Lord came down upon Mount Sinai'? (Ex 19:20) - That was above ten handbreadths (from the summit).» (p. 15).[140]   Justin's philosophical premise would thus hardly be offensive to his Jewish interlocutor.

I have assumed above that Justin in his treatment of the theophanies is footing on testimonies (of Judaeo-Christian provenance), proving the existence of another God and Lord besides the Father, whose name is Jesus. None of these testimonies imply a general theory about all theophanies being Christophanies. I have suggested that this generalization, and the whole emphasis on the theophany idea, may be Justin's own contribution to the development of this tradition, and that it is directed against Marcion.

But can one trace some precedents even to this general theory about the theophanies?

It is time to comment briefly on an important passage in *Dial.* 128:2f.[141] «. . . there are some who wish to anticipate my explanation, and to assert that the power which was from the Father of the universe and appeared to Moses or to Abraham or to Jacob was called Angel when he came forth unto men, since by that power are the messages from the Father carried to men; and Glory, since he appears sometimes in an appearance that cannot be reckoned by space; and was called sometimes a man (ἄνδρα) and a human being (ἄνθρωπον), since he makes his appearance in the fashion of such forms as the Father wills. And they call him Word, since he also bears to men the discourses that come from the Father. But they assert that this power can never be cut off or separated from the Father, in the same way that, as they say, the light of the sun on earth cannot be cut off or separated, though the sun is in heaven. And when the sun sets the light is borne away with it. So the Father, they affirm, makes, when he will, his power to spring forward, and, when he will, he draws it back again into himself. They teach that in this way he also made the angels.»

A disputed question concerning this passage is whether the conception described and attacked by Justin is Jewish or Christian - in the latter case an

140. Cf. the instructive comments on this text, with rabbinic parallels, in Goldberg, *Schekhinah*, pp. 37-40. Urbach parallels R. Jose's dictum with Justin's in *Dial.* 60:2 (*The Sages* I, pp. 49f).
141. On this passage, cf. A. von Harnack, *Dogmengeschichte* I, p. 217, n. 2; Lebreton, *Histoire* II, pp. 674-76; F.J. Dölger, 'Sonne und Sonnenstrahl als Gleichnis in der Logostheologie des christlichen Altertums', in *idem, Antike und Christentum. Kultur- und religionsgeschichtliche Studien* I (Münster im Westfalen, 1929), pp. 271-290; esp. pp. 274f; J. Moffat, 'Two Notes on Ignatius and Justin Martyr', *HTR* 23 (1930), (pp. 153-159), pp- 158f; Trakatellis, *Pre-Existence*, pp. 35-37.

early form of Christological dynamism.[142] However that may be, it seems we are facing a concept ante-dating Justin, which generalizes about the theophanies in much the same way as he does himself. The identification of ἄγγελος with δόξα, ἀνήρ, ἄνθρωπος, λόγος, and δύναμις can roughly be called Philonic.[143] But the emphatic notion of this δύναμις being sent out and then withdrawn into the Father, having no permanent hypostatic existence - this is hardly Philonic. One is rather reminded of the OT description of God's spirit (Ps 104:29f).[144]

There is one Jewish Hellenistic writing which makes a synthesis of the concepts of God's Spirit and God's Wisdom, viz. the *Sapientia Salomonis*.[145] Here the Wisdom=Spirit is likened to a radiance (ἀπαύασμα) of God, the eternal light, and an effluence (ἀπόρροια) of his glory, 7:25f.[146] The relevance of this for Justin is increased when one adds the observation that in *Sap.Sal.* 10f Wisdom is seen as the agent in a whole series of salvific events and theophanies from Adam to Moses.[147]

It is relevant to note a clear echo of *Sap. Sal.* 7:25 in Athenagoras,[148] *Legatio* 10:4: «. . . this . . . holy Spirit, which is active in those who speak prophetically, we regard as an effluence (ἀπόρροια) of God which *flows forth* (ἀπορρέον) *from him and returns like a ray of the sun.*» It is evident that Athenagoras applies to *the Spirit* exactly the concept which Justin refuses to apply to Christ! And it is evident that this concept in Athenagoras is inspired by *Sap.Sal.* 7.

## Conclusion

If there is any influence from Philo on Justin's treatment of the theophanies, it is at best distant, and mainly operative in some general modes of

---

142. Harnack, Lebreton, Moffat and Trakatellis *locc. cit.*, take the text as a report on Jewish views, but Harnack contemplates an inner-Christian polemic against Christological Modalists, so also Archambault in his note *ad loc*,(pp. 258f). Goodenough, strange to say, takes *Dial* 128:3 as expressing Justin's own view (*Theology*, pp. 148f); the same mistake is apparently made by J. M. Ford, 'The Ray, the Root and the River. A Note on the Jewish Origin of Trinitarian Images', *Studia Patristica* 11:2 (TU 108, Berlin, 1972, pp. 158-165), p. 160.

143. Cf. Lebreton II, p. 676. For a general comparison between the Logos theology of Philo and Justin, cf. A. L. Feder, *Lehre*, pp. 137-143. P. Heinisch states that *Dial* 128 describes the doctrine of Philo (*Einfluss Philos*, pp. 139f) — hardly correct.

144. One should also notice that Justin attributes to his opponents a denial of the permanent existence of the angels. This position has its closest parallel in some rabbinic sayings, cf. Goldfahn, pp. 114f.

145. Cf. i.a. H. Ringgren, *Word and Wisdom. Studies in the Hypostatization of Divine Qualities and Functions in the Ancient Near East* (Lund, 1947), p. 115. Further W. Schencke, *Die Chokma (Sophia) in der jüdischen Hypostasenspekulation* (Skr. N.V. II, 1912, 6, Kristiania (Oslo), 1913), pp. 44f; B. L. Mack, *Logos und Sophia* (Göttingen, 1973), p. 64.

146. On this text, see the recent discussion in Mack, pp. 66-72, cf. also Schencke, p. 42; Ringgren, pp. 116-118.

147. Heinisch rightly points out *Sap.* 10f as an important background for Justin's theophany concept (*Einfluss Philos*, p. 145).

148. Cf. A. J. Malherbe, 'The Holy Spirit in Athenagoras', *JTS* New Ser. 20 (1969), pp. 538-542.

argument rather than in concrete exegesis of texts. In the latter respect, Justin exhibits a marked independence of Philo, often directly contradicting or ignoring Philonic exegesis.[149] One is lead to search in other quarters for Justin's precursors, and we have seen reasons to believe that Justin is working (1) with traditional Christian proof-texts - possibly deriving from Judaeo-Christians debating their fellow Jews - proving that the OT knows of two 'Gods', 'Lords' etc (but implying no theory on theophanies); and (2) with typological material. He has developed this material to support a general theory about theophanies being always Christophanies - and a precedent for this generalization may be sought in the Jewish Wisdom concept as found in the *Sapientia Salomonis*.

We have seen reasons to believe that the single occurrence of the theophany argument in the *Apology* (*1. Apol.* 63) reflects a formulation of the argument which is anti-Marcion. But we also noticed that this anti-Marcion version is not directly based on the LXX text. One should therefore allow for a great amount of fresh casting of Justin's material in the *Dialogue*. He may still be writing with an eye to Marcion and his disciples.

---

149. The review in Shotwell, *Exegesis*, pp. 94-99, demonstrates that this conclusion is valid even if one widens the scope to embrace all cases in which Philo and Justin comment on the same Biblical text.

# CONCLUSIONS AND SUGGESTIONS FOR FURTHER RESEARCH

Instead of once more summarizing the results of the different sections of this study, I shall try to present the main conclusions in the form of a comprehensive theory of how the exegetical parts of Justin's writings came to look the way they do.

In the prologue to his *Dialogue*, Justin indicates that he was converted to Christianity by encountering a proclamation of the Christian kerygma in which the argument from prophecy played a dominant role. This way of presenting the Christian Gospel deeply influenced Justin - he adopts it himself.

Maybe Justin received a more thorough instruction concerning the Old Testament prophecies already at this initiory stage. Or perhaps he later became the pupil of some «school» in which exposition of Old Testament prophecies was a main occupation. In any case, Justin is handing on a tradition which is clearly missionary. The OT proof-texts are commended to the Gentile listener (or reader) by means of a modified version of the Aristeas legend about LXX origins. While the legend in its Jewish version had served to emphasize the divinity and sublimity of the Law, it now was adapted to a new purpose: It guaranteed the reliability of the Greek version of the ancient Hebrew prophecies which had predicted Christ.

The prooftexts themselves were presented in a free, targumizing version of the standard LXX text, closely adapted to Christian exegesis and polemic concerns. It is difficult to know exactly in which literary format these proof-texts were transmitted to Justin, but it seems that Bousset's proposal still has much to be said for it: Justin may have become heir to «*Schriftbe-weistraktate*» which were part of a «school» tradition. These tracts probably also comprised brief «fulfilment reports» (the latter are important clues to the theological concerns of this exegetical tradition). In some particulars, this proof-text tradition was closely related to the missionary tradition contained in the *Kerygma Petrou*. In fact, Justin may have included material from the *Kerygma* into his own exposition.

While this tradition appealed to the authority of the LXX translators for its OT texts, it made Christ - through his apostles - the ultimate authority of interpretation. Christ is not only the one who fulfils OT prophecy - he is also the great expounder of the prophecies, τῶν ἀγνοουμένων προφητειῶν ἐξηγητής (*1.Apol.* 32:2). We encounter this tradition of texts and exposition in its purest form in *1.Apol.* 31-53. Here Justin is still almost entirely dependent on the received texts and the adjacent exegesis. Within the series of quotations devoted to Christ's career, only Is 53 and Ps 110:1-3 are quoted directly from LXX MSS - the rest are given exactly as found in Justin's «*Schriftbeweistraktate*», and with the appended fulfilment reports still recognizable. Justin's main modification is a re-arrangement within the series, motivated by Justin's fear that his readers might not recognize some of his proof-texts as real prophecies (e.g. Is 9:5; Ps 22; Is 53). Justin has had to intervene with a hermeneutical excursus on the modes of speech in prophecy, but he has drawn his examples from the same source which furnished him with the Christological testimonies. Apart from more testimonies on the passion ( *1.Apol.* 38), this hermeneutical excursus comprises testimonies which describe the reign of the enthroned Christ (Ps 110:1) through the apostolic kerygma (Ps 110:2; Ps 96:10; Is 2:3 etc.); the disbelief of the Jews and the resulting devastation of Judaea ( *1.Apol.* 47-49); and a couple of anti-cultic testimonies.

These latter themes are treated more fully in the opening and concluding sections of Justin's *Dialogue,* chs. 11-47 and 108-141. The groundwork of testimony material in these chapters is closely related to chs. 37 and 47-49 of the *Apology,* and derives, if not entirely from the same literary source, then at least from the same tradition. But Justin has gained more independence in his handling of the traditional material.

(1) He more often has had direct recourse to the LXX text, and brings long LXX excerpts instead of the condensed, modified text of the transmitted testimonies. This, however, has confronted him with a problem. In some cases the LXX text was less suited to the traditional exegesis. And some of the (apocryphal) testimonies were simply not to be found in the LXX writings from which they purported to be derived. For Justin, the texts of his testimony sources are authenticated by his Christian teachers and the Aristeas legend, and he therefore believes that the reponsibility for the discrepancies must lie with the Jewish scribes producing the LXX MSS. To some extent he is right, viz. in so far as some of the Bible MSS from which he draws his long excerpts, do not represent the standard LXX, but a recensed text - recensed in order to conform more perfectly with the emerging proto-Massoretic Hebrew text. On the other hand, Justin's «testimony» quotations are as a rule based on the unrecensed, «standard» LXX. There is thus an element of truth in Justin's «solution» of the textual problem. But he is of course wrong in claiming his very deviant testimonies to be the the original LXX text.

(2) Justin has amplified and supplemeted the traditional texts and arguments. In *Dial* 11-47 he is on mainly traditional ground in chs. 11-29. But in *Dial.* 30-39 Justin has combined some of the traditional testimonies on Christ's reign with exegetical material from another source - partly relating to the same testimonies. (This new source recurs as the main source behind the Christological section, chs. 48-107; the anti-Hezekiah or «recapitulation» source as I have called it). Justin has found LXX substitutes for the textually disputed Ps 96:10. He has also inserted an excursus on Christian heretics, *Dial.* 35. - He is also very much on his own in the concluding chapters 46f concerning the observance of the Law by Jewish Christians.

In *Dial.* 108ff, Justin is probably covering traditional ground in 108-117. In *Dial.* 118 he inserts eschatological material from the »recapitulation« source; he then goes on to add a re-statement of the Pauline argument concerning Christians as Abraham's seed, *Dial.* 119-121. This re-statement tries to answer rabbinic attacks on the Pauline line of thought. Justin then proceeds with an attempt to show that Christians not only are Abraham's seed, but also the seed of Jacob, and thus entitled to the name »Israel«, 122-125/135f. He has here combined three sources. From the »kerygma« source he reproduces material showing that Christ is the »light of the Gentiles«, and - incidentally - is called »Israel« and »Jacob« (121:4 - 123:3/8). From the »recapitulation« source he adduces a Jacob/Christ typology, *Dial.* 124f, and to this he adds a cluster of testimonies directly speaking about a new Israel (*Dial.* 123:5f and 135f). This third element seems to be an original contribution by Justin or his »school«. In *Dial.* 130 he once more re-states a Pauline argument to suit his own purposes, and in *Dial.* 131-4/138-141 is back on traditional ground deriving mainly from the »kerygma« source. (There are some adjustments of argument necessitated by the LXX text).

The most substantial modifications *vis-a-vis* the *Apology* and the «kerygma» source occur within the Christological section of the *Dialogue.* In *Dial.* 49-54; *Dial.* 84 and *Dial.* 97 one can recognize renewed employment of the «kerygma» source behind *1.Apol.* 32ff, probably also in *Dial.* 72-74. I have also argued that the same source may be at play in *Dial.* 87f. But the main bulk of Justin's exposition derive from another source with a markedly different orientation. I have called this the «recapitulation source». It seems that much exegetical argument in *Dial.* 30-39/43 and 63-107 derives from this source, which perhaps is identical with Aristo of Pella's «Controversy». But again Justin has amplified his source and added new material. The most substantial additions are (1) the section on the theophanies (*Dial.* 56-60/75, with doublet in *Dial.* 126-29); (2) the Pauline argument concerning Deut 21:23 (*Dial.* 95); and (3) the commentary on Ps 22 in *Dial.* 98-106. Within this commentary, material of the «recapitulation» type seems to have been inserted (*Dial.* 100; 103:5f; 106:3f), attached to different Psalm verses in a rather artificial manner. There are some indications that the Psalm commentary may have existed prior to its incorporation into the *Dialogue.*

The section on the theophanies is probably one of Justin's most original exegetical contributions. He is here drawing on older testimony material which proved the existence of a «second God» in the Old Testament. Justin develops this into a general theory about OT theophanies being always appearances of Christ. The target of this theophany argument is probably Marcion.

Such - in rough outline - is the picture of the *genesis* of Justin's exegetical works which emerges from the present study. In order to get a grasp of the theological traditions which have gone into Justin's intricate web of OT exegesis, it may be convenient to analyse his material in a corresponding three-step pattern: (1) the theology of the «kerygma» tradition; (2) the theology of the «recapitulation» source; and (3) the theology of the materials added *ad hoc* by Justin. In all three cases one shall have to pose the question of Justin's relationship to the employed material.

(1) In the «kerygma» source, one can basically discern two strata: We have to do with a Judaeo-Christian tradition which has passed through Gentile Christian hands before it reached Justin. The Judaeo-Christian substratum is discernible in three main elements of the «kerygma» source: (a) the Christological testimonies; (b) the deuteronomistic scheme of sin - exile - future redemption (for Israel!); and (c) the concept of two components within the Law.

(a) The Christological testimonies express a Christology which *focuses on Christ as the one who fulfils OT Messianic prophecies*. This corresponds to the fact that the pre-existence idea associated with the Wisdom concept of the OT plays no role in this Christology, while on the other hand the two *parousias* pattern safeguards Jesus' complete fulfilment of OT Messianism: His fulfilment of the «humility» prophecies in his first coming guarantees his future fulfilment of the «glory» prophecies. The *historia Iesu* runs through the stages of virgin birth, anointing with the Spirit (= baptism by John/«Elijah»); passion as the Just One and as God's perfect paschal lamb; resurrection/ascension and enthronement at God's right hand; present reign through the kerygma, the Law going out from Jerusalem to the ends of the world, proclaimed to all men by the apostles.

The NT writer who comes closest to this Christology is Luke - a later and even closer parallel occurs in the Christian interpolations of the TP. By the two parousias pattern and the dominant position accorded to Gen 49:10 as a Christological testimony, this tradition is also closely related to the AJ II (= *Ps. Clem. Rec.* I:33-71). Two characteristic features substantiate the Judaeo-Christian nature of this tradition. First, there is an inherent polemic against the Messianic claims of Bar Kokhba. Secondly, there is a vital concern for the salvation of the pious men of the OT, and for the conversion and salvation of Israel. Compared with the NT, the dossier of Messianic prooftexts has a markedly Jewish profile - one might even say rabbinic. Most of the added testimonies were important Messianic passages according to the rabbis also.

(b) In a deeply concerned attempt to bring their fellow Jews to repentance (= belief in Jesus), the Judaeo-Christians behind this tradition employ the old deuteronomistic pattern of repentance exhortation: The Jews are guilty of a great sin - the rejection and crucifixion of Jesus, the Just One. Their present calamity results from this; the way to salvation and national restoration consists in repentance and faith in Jesus.

The closest parallels to this pattern of preaching is again to be found in the interpolated passages of the TP and in the AJ II.

(c) The ceremonial law is not part of the eternal Law of God, but only a temporary admission necessitated by Israel's tendency towards idolatry and apostasy. (It seems that this point of view originally envisaged the sacrificial cult.) Christ makes men Law-obedient: He turns men from idolatry to true worship of God. He thereby fulfils the function of the Law, and makes the ceremonial law superfluous. Baptism replaces sacrifices as the means whereby remission of sins is obtained. Law-obedient Gentiles replace the disbelieving Jews, and are thus joined to Israel.

A very close parallel to this conception occurs in the AJ II. Christ making men Law-obedient is also an important motif in the Christology of the Christian interpolations of the TP. Jewish antecedents may he sought in the *Sibyllina*, especially the Fourth Book.

This tradition has been appropriated by Gentile Christians who left the Christological testimonies intact; kept the idea of the apostolic kerygma being the Law going out from Zion; turned the deuteronomistic preaching of Jewish guilt into an anti-Jewish slogan; sharpened the polemic against ritual observances; and deeply modified the people of God concept. The Hadrianic decree which closed Jerusalem to the Jews and made it a city for Gentiles only, is seen as a significant act of God: It is a signal that the Church from the Gentiles is to take the place of the Jews. The Church is the new people, fulfilling the Law, whereas the Jews are always found to be idolators and apostates. Christians are to inherit the city and the land at Christ's return.

Justin himself, or his immediate precursors, - in debate with rabbinic exegesis - develops this to the concept that Christians are Jacob's seed, «Israel». Justin also sharpens another aspect of this tradition: He says that circumcision was given to the Jews with the express purpose of excluding them from Jerusalem and the land in these last days.

It is striking to observe that while this Gentile Christian adaption of the tradition virtually disinherits the Judaeo-Christian predecessors, it keeps in close contact with Jewish exegesis. This is probably to be explained by the phenomenon of missionary competition: The Church addressed the Gentile God-fearers who had already been the adressees of Jewish proselytizing efforts. Another remarkable characteristic of this tradition is the intense concern about the land and the city of Jerusalem. This may point to Palestinian provenance. The «conquest» of Jerusalem by a Gentile Christian community after 135 AD must have had a symbolic sigficance which would match the tendency in Justin's tradition perfectly.

There can be no doubt that Justin has been deeply influenced by this tradition. It may represent the theology of the one(s) who converted him to Christianity; in any case he presents this tradition (in the *First Apology*) as quite simply identical with the apostolic kerygma. There are especially two areas where Justin's own thinking has been decisively shaped by the «kerygma» tradition: his Law theology, and his people of God concept. On the other hand, he seems to have had a certain reserve with regard to the

Christology of this tradition. We have seen reasons to believe that the baptism of Jesus was conceived of as a Messianic anointing with the Spirit by John (= second Elijah), and we have seen how Justin carefully corrects this. He has no ear for the deep concern for Israel's salvation inherent in this tradition, and the soteriological motifs sometimes come through only casually and without emphasis. Justin exploits with most success the two parousias pattern, and the simple correspondence between prediction and fulfillment posited in the «kerygma» source, i.e. its formal proof-from-prophecy aspect, but he does not seem fully turned to the deeper concerns of this Christology.

(2) This may be part of the explanation why Justin in the *Dialogue* introduces a new source of tradition precisely in the Christological section, the «recapitulation» source.

It may perhaps be said that the Christolooy of this tradition had a greater thematic concentration on one concept: Christ is the second Adam. He has conquered the Devil, and is now able to set men free from the dominion of Satan and his host, the demons. The Christological concern of this tradition is not so much to show that Christ in all details has fulfilled (or shall fulfil) OT Messianic prophecies. It is rather occupied with the question of what *kind* of Messiah the OT leads us to expect. It makes much out of the Wisdom concept: Christ has his power over demons precisely because he is the first-born before every creature, God's own Son, mediating at the creation of the world, having a share in God's own divine power. The polemic concern in this tradition is to show that all Jewish candidates for the role of the Messiah fall short of these super-human dimensions. Hezekiah had no divine power to restore Jerusalem - Solomon was not the master of demons, he was their slave.

This was a Christology which Justin could fully endorse. Or perhaps one should put it the other way round: This Christological concept became a fundamental influence upon Justin's own thinking.

The two traditions here delineated constitute the basic groundwork of Justin's exegesis, and account for most of his parallels with writings like *Barnabas, 1.* and *2. Clement,* Hebrews and John - and probably also some of his Matthean and Lukan testimony material. To this Justin adds some testimonies directly borrowed from Matthew or Luke, but they can hardly be called substantial additions.

(3) Turning to the more significant additions made by Justi himself, we must first pay due attention to his quite substantial employment of Pauline testimonies. Not only are Pauline quotations frequently borrowed by Justin; in two crucial passages of the *Dialogue* Justin states Pauline points of view with considerable insight and emphasis. If my analysis of *Dial.* 91-95 is correct, Justin has here sacrificed a main point in the argument of the «recapitulation» source in favour of Paul's argument concerning Deut 21:23. And in *Dial.* 119-121 the Pauline argument concerning Christ and Christians being Abraham's seed is re-stated with considerable skill.

Justin may not have been aware of the tension between Paul's theology and the theology of the «kerygma» tradition, especially in their respective concepts of the Law. His attempt to combine them undeniably has the result that he fails to grasp the deeper implications of Paul's doctrine of justification by faith. But probably Justin was unaware of this. In any case it would seem that Paul for Justin was an authority of some importance, and that he strived to integrate Pauline arguments into his inherited, largely non-Pauline, tradition.

Justin's second major addition is his section on the theophanies. If my analysis above is correct, he has started from testimonies of Judaeo-Christian provenance, proving the existence of two Gods or Lords in some OT verses. Influenced by Jewish conceptions of the divine Wisdom as the agent in theophanies (*Sap.Sal.* 10f), Justin has worked these testimonies into a general theory about all theophanies of the OT being appearances of the pre-existent Christ. In the debate with Judaism not much new argument is gained by this (compared with the testimonies), and I have suggested that the original addressee of this argument may have been Marcion. The point would have been to prove that Christ was intimately involved in OT history - that he was not unknown to the patriarchs, and that even his name was revealed to Moses. However, in its present formulation in the *Dialogue*, Justin tries to exploit the argument also in the anti-Jewish polemic, and scores an extra point against Marcion by having Trypho accept the force of the argument. Of course adoptionist Christians would also be possible addressees of this section the *Dialogue,* cf. *Dial.* 48. But against them the pre-existence concept of the «recapitulation» source would have sufficed.

It remains to be remarked that Justin also has made other additions from sources containing OT material, but these are strictly speaking not parts of the Scriptural proof. In *1.Apol.* 54f and *Dial.* 69f Justin has added material from a source which was occupied with demonic imitations of OT Messianic prophecies, and in *1.Apol.* 59f he has a little tract on philosophic borrowings from Moses. One should not exclude the possibility that these two blocks of material derive from the same source, which might well be an earlier Christian *Apology.* But these texts and these problems have received minor attention in the present study, and I shall refrain from sheer speculation.

What could be the relevance of the theory here presented? Let me make a few suggestions, catching up some questions asked in the Introduction.

(1) The undeniable parallels between Justin and Luke are not a simple product of Justin reading Luke-Acts. In some respects Justin's «kerygma» tradition is closer to Luke than Justin himself. This tradition has a Christology with a profile similar to Luke's. The Lukan ideas about Christ instructing the apostles concerning the meaning of OT prophecy, and Christ reigning through the apostolic kerygma (Is 2:3), were also probably parts of this tradition as it reached Justin (cf. esp. the KP!). There is also a *substratum* in Justin's material concerning the people of God which is close to

Luke. These similarities are probably not to be explained as direct dependence on Luke, because on the level of proof-texts, there is surprisingly
little in common between Luke and Justin's «kerygma» testimonies. This, on
the other hand, indicates that it is too simple to explain all differences
between Justin and Luke as a natural «development» (Overbeck). There are
markedly non-Lukan ideas even in the oldest strand of the «kerygma»
tradition in Justin, and these ideas are not developed out of Lukan conceptions, but betray independent theologians who had ideas of their own. This
is true i.e. of the Law concept, and further the apparent neglect of Paul and
specifically Pauline arguments in the «kerygma» source. (One should notice
the anti-Pauline tendency of the AJ II version of this tradition).

It is hardly necessary to add that Justin's Christology is not derived from
Luke, but mainly from the tradition represented by the «recapitulation»
source. This source - like the «kerygma» tradition - has elements in its
Christology which agrees with important components in Luke's, but on the
whole the «recapitulation« tradition is independent and partly different
from Luke, especially with regard to the importance accorded to the
pre-existence idea and the Wisdom concept.

There remains, however, one aspect which makes it reasonable to speak
about Justin as the «Luke of the second century«. He represents the same
kind of comprehensive synthesis between Pauline and non-Pauline traditions as Luke.

(2) Justin's exegetical material is a sensitive indicator of the considerable
influence exerted by Judaeo-Christians on the «mainstream» theology of the
second century. When talking about Judaeo-Christians, attention is easily
focused exclusively on the sects and splinter groups described by the
Church Fathers. One should not overlook, however, the important group of
Jewish believers who remained part of mainstream Christianity, and decisively influenced its development. Of special importance is the fact that a
solution of the Law problem different from Paul's was chanelled into
mainstream theology through the «kerygma» tradition and Justin. In many
ways this tackling of the Law problem was more convenient and «reasonable» than Paul's radical in-depth treatment of the issue in Galatians and
Romans. But it did not predispose the mainstream theologians of the
second century for a sympathetic and profound understanding of Paul's
doctrine of justification, even though they regarded Paul as a supreme
authority. One should not overlook, however, that this tradition contained
other soteriological motifs which expressed genuine insights concernig
the saving work of Christ. Especially the ideas related to baptism and the
concept of a new creation through Christ were later to find their mature
expression in Irenaeus' recapitulation theology.

There is another tenet within this Gentile Christian appropriation of a
Judaeo-Christian tradition which partly concurs with, partly may be deter-
mined by the non-Pauline solution of the Law problem. Because there is
no profound understanding of Paul's justification doctrine in Rom 1-4,

there is likewise no genuine understanding of Paul's in-depth treatment of the phenomenon of Israel's unbelief in Rom 11. Therefore the hope of salvation for Israel - still contained in the Judaeo-Christian *substratum* of Justin's material - is soon lost sight of, and the deuteronomistic preaching of guilt and repentance deteriorates into a self-righteous declaration that «you Jews» have an intrinsic quality of disbelief, while «we Gentiles» have a greater willingness to belief. Justin falls into exactly that Gentile Christian *hybris* against which Paul so urgently warns in Rom 11:17-22. This *hybris* did Christian theology no good, and is another indication of the loss of important Pauline perspectives. On the other hand, one should not underestimate the valuable Christological insights gained in Justin's development of the «New Israel» theme. Christ is true Israel *in persona,* and Christians through him have a share in the promises to Israel.

(3) The present study has underlined the importance of the missionary setting for the development of Christian theology. To be more exact: One should pay careful attention to the phenomenon of *missionary competition* between Jews and Christians. Much the same people were addressed: Gentile God-fearers. The Jews must have felt that the Church stole their potential converts. This situation of missionary competition is the mould in which Justin's two main traditions of OT exegesis have been cast. This at once explains the double phenomenon of close contact with Jewish exegesis and sharp polemic against Judaism.

The missionary setting of Justin's exegetical material may also indicate a basic unity of provenance for his exegesis and his apologetics. As one can easily observe from the KP, the basic apologetic topics were traditional items in the missionary preacing to Gentiles. One can trace these basic features further backwards through Acts 17:22-31 and Acts 14:15-17, right back to 1 Thess 1:9f. One may suggest that if more source material had been preserved of the early missionary preaching, one would more easily see the considerable continuity between the Apologists and their Christian predecessors.

One may also suggest that within the missionary competition, there was a quite massive take-over of Jewish missionary preaching to Gentiles - that is: Jewish apologetic. The present study has made me believe that Goodenough was basically right: Justin is heir of much of the apologetic tradition of Hellenistic Judaism, except that Goodenough unduly took Hellenistic Judaism to mean Philo. I think there is still work to be done in relating Justin to the whole scope of Jewish apologetic and missionary literature in Greek. This might also bring Justin's originality as an apologist into sharper focus. It might then turn out that his contribution to the missionary and apologetic tradition of the Church not so much is a Hellenistic concept of God - this may already have become part of this tradition through the mediating role of Jewish apologetics - but rather the anti-Platonic argument of the Old Man in *Dial.* 3—7.

What in any case seems clear to me, is that «hellenization» and profound influence from Judaism should not be seen as alternatives. Goodenough is probably right: In Justin's days Jews might well serve as the transmission channel for Hellenistic influence. And this transmission channel could have furnished Christian theological tradition with many of the concepts which now strike us as typically Hellenistic.

With these sparse suggestions I pause. I do not claim that they exhaust the potentialities implicit in the material analysed in this study. In fact, nothing would gratify the present author more than if someone else were able to see connexions and patterns not seen by me. *Non enim vincimur. quando nobis offeruntur meliora, sed instruimur* (Cyprian, *Ep.* 71:3).

# JUSTIN'S QUOTATION MATERIAL IN IRENAEUS AND TERTULLIAN.

The problem raised in this Appendix would require a separate and quite substantial monograph if it were to be discussed in its full scope. The following lines are therefore meant only as a kind of pilot study, concerned mainly with the following question: Do we find indications in Irenaeus' and Tertullian's OT quotations which lead to the conclusion that these writers depend on Justin's sources employed in the *Apology* and/or the *Dialogue*; or do we rather find indications of direct dependence on the present text of these works?

The relevance of this question for the present study is brought out in the analysis of P. Prigent *(Justin, passim)*. He often takes quotation sequences in Irenaeus and Tertullian as clues in his analysis of Justin's source (his own *Syntagma)*, assuming that Irenaeus and Tertullian depend on Justin's source rather than on the text of the *Apology* and the *Dialogue*.

In order to test this, I have compared all non-LXX quotations in Justin with the corresponding quotations in Irenaeus and Tertullian. There are a few cases in which Justin has a perfect LXX text, while the same quotation recurs in a non-LXX text in the later writers. Here I make no claim to completeness, but I have made some pilot studies, and I doubt that there is much relevant material to be found.

My result is briefly summarized this: There are a few cases in which Irenaeus or Tertullian do seem to depend on Justin's source rather than on his present exposition in the *Apology* or the *Dialogue*. There are considerably more cases in which the opposite holds true. In the vast majority of cases, neither alternative can be proved: there is no *need* to go behind Justin's preserved works to find Irenaeus' or Tertullian's sources, nor can a direct recourse to Justin's sources be disproved. But in that case, the «economy of hypothesis» principle opts for restraint in supposing hypothetical sources instead of known ones.

I present the material in the order here indicated. First (A) I comment on those cases which seem to indicate direct recourse to Justin's sources, next (B) I treat those cases in which the later writers can be proved to depend on Justin's present text, not on his sources. In category (C) I comment briefly on the rest of the examined cases.

In several instances I have commented upon the quotation sequences within which the quotations occur. But a full investigation of all relevant material would exceed the scope of this Appendix. I have included one test-case, however, which seemed to me particularly instructive (E).

Regarding Justin's non-LXX quotations, it emerges as a general conclusion that they either disappear totally in Irenaeus and Tertullian, or they re-appear as LXX texts, in excerpts often exceeding Justin's short non-LXX texts. This does not speak for an intensive use of Justin's sources.

On the whole, I am inclined to believe that the literary relations between on the one hand Irenaeus and Tertullian, and on the other hand Justin, Justin's sources and other known or lost writings, is so complex that the available evidence hardly allows a complete and convincing reconstruction. One can make reasonable, even cogent proposals on particular points, but one should be careful not to generalize, and I think one thing may be said with certainty: The theory true to all the facts is bound to be complex.

A final note:

When I speak about Tertullians texts as «septuagintal», I have no intention of deciding the debated question whether Tertullian used an existing Latin translation, or translated the Greek LXX in each case himself. If Tertullian quotes from a Latin Old Testament, it should clearly be regarded as a daughter translation of the LXX. Cf. T. P. O'Malley, *Tertullian and the Bible (Latinitas Christianorum Primaeva* 21, Nijmegen/Utrecht, 1967), with review of previous research pp. 2—8.

## A: *Irenaeus and Tertullian dependent on Justin's source*

(1) Ezek 37:7f etc. ( *1.Apol* 52:5f)

| Ezek 37 LXX | *1. Apol.* 52:5f | Tertullian: *De Res.* 32:1 |
|---|---|---|
| | | Et mandabo piscibùs maris et eructuabunt ossa, quae sunt comesta, et faciam conpaginem ad conpaginem et os ad os |
| vs. 7: <br>... καὶ προσήγαγε τὰ ὀστᾶ ἑκάτερον[a] πρὸς τὴν ἁρμονίαν αὐτοῦ. <br>vs. 8: ... ἐπ᾽ αὐτὰ νεῦρα καὶ σάρκες ἐφύοντο ... | σθναχθήσεται ἁρμονία πρὸς ἁρμονίαν καὶ ὀστέον πρὸς ὀστέον <br><br><br> καὶ σάρκες ἀναφυήσονται | |
| Is 45:23b LXX | | |
| ... ὅτι ἐμοὶ κάμψει πᾶν γόνυ καὶ ἐξομολογήσεται πᾶσα γλῶσσα τῷ θεῷ | καὶ πᾶν γόνυ κάμψει τῷ κυρίῳ καὶ πᾶσα γλῶσσα ἐξομολογήσεται αὐτῷ | |
| a) Lucianic MSS = MT: ὀστέον πρὸς ὀστέον ἔκαστον. | | |

(marginal note in Tertullian column: cf. *1. Enoch* 61:5)

In *1. Apol.* 52:3—8, Justin has a passage on the resurrection of the dead. Two testimonies are quoted: Ezek 37:7f/Is 45:23 as «Ezekiel the prophet» and Is 66:24 anonymously. It is known from Procopius that Justin had written a separate treatise *De Resurrectione*. Prigent has made a good case for the theory that this tract is partly preserved in the extracts in the *Sacra Parallela*.[1] The main thrust of Prigent's argument is the demonstration that both Irenaeus and Tertullian seem to depend on the treatise excerpted in the *Sacra Parallela*. (It is not the other way round, as often claimed).

I think a closer study of Ezek 37:7f in *1.Apol.* 52:5f and Tertullian's *De Resurrectione* 29-32 may confirm this.[2] Chapters 29-31 in Tertullian's tract are concerned with a refutation of non-literal exegesis of Ezek 37:1-14 (quoted in 29:2-15, basically LXX text). In this refutation are included some more OT proof-texts: Mal 3:20f; Is 66:14; Is 26:19; *Is 66:22-24* ( LXX -quoted in the order: vss. 23b; 22; 24 ). So far, one could assume that *1.Apol.* 52:5-8 was a main source behind Tertullian: He looks both of Justin's texts up in the LXX and adds some more testimonies. But this explanation breaks down in *De Res.* 32:1. Here we find another, non-LXX version of Ezek 37:7[3] which is curiously combined with a text reminiscent of *1 Enoch* 61:5 (see synopsis). Here *1.Apol.* 52 cannot be Tertullian's direct source, and a common source behind both passages cannot be ruled out.

Now, as it is probable that Tertullian adapted Justin's treatise on the resurrection in his own book on the same subject, I think one can reasonably surmise that Justin's treatise is Tertullian's source for the combined, non-LXX version of *1 Enoch* 61:5/Ezek 37:7 found in *De Res.* 32:1. *1.Apol.* 52 may excerpt from the same, combined text, which in that case comprised (at least) the elements *1Enoch* 61:5; Ezek 37:7f; Is 45:23.

Justin's text in *1.Apol.* 52 and - by hypothesis - in his *De Res.* is quite likely to derive ultimately from a testimony source prior to Justin.

I have surmised above that this was the Christological part of the «Kerygma source». I cannot find sure indications that Tertullian had direct access to this source.

---

1. Prigent, *Justin* pp. 36-68, up-dating and amplifying Zahn's argument, 'Studien', pp. 1-37.
2. Prigent has not commented on this parallel.
3. Not listed in the BP I.

(2) Hos 10:6 and Ps 22:15 (*Dial.* 103:4-8)

In *Dial.* 103:4 Justin quotes Hos 10:6 as a testimony on Jesus being sent bound to Herod. There is a striking lack of correspondence between text and narrative.

*Narrative:*

ᾧ (viz. Herod) καὶ Πιλάτος χαριζόμενος δεδεμένον τὸν Ἰησοῦν ἔπεηψε

*Text:* καὶ γε αὐτὸν εἰς Ἀσσυρίου ἀπήνεγκαν ξένια τῷ βασιλεῖ.

The *narrative* takes no notice of «to Assyria», and the *text* has no mention of *binding.*

Now, let us compare Justin's text with the LXX of Hos 10:6: καὶ αὐτὸν εἰς Ἀσσυρίους δήσαντες ἀπήνεγκαν ξένια τῷ βασιλεῖ . . . Justin's text translates      as καίγε and omits δήσαντες which has to foundation in the Hebrew text. Barthélemy is probably right in suggesting that Justin's text is copied from his καιγε *Dodekapropheton* MS.[4]

This leaves us with the possibility that Justin in his source found a «testimony» text better adapted to his narrative. It probably contained the LXX reading δήσαντες, and if it also omitted «Assyria», the correspondence would be perfect. Now let us turn to Irenaeus, *Dem.* 77. Here we read: «And they brought him bound as a present to the king» - i.e. exactly the text surmised to linger in the background in *Dial.* 103:4. Turning to Tertullian, we read in *Adv.Marc.* IV:42:3: *et uinctum eum docent xenium regi.* Again the same text, but one cannot exclude the possibility that Tertullian depends upon Irenaeus, because other quotations in the context are common to the two authors.

Returning to Irenaeus, we notice that his quotation of Hos 10:6 is followed by the following citations: Ps Jer; Is 65:2 (LXX); Ps 22:17 (LXX); *Ps 22:15b* (non-LXX); *Ps 22:21/Ps 119:120/Ps 22:17*; Deut 28:66 (LXX); Ps 22:18b.19 (LXX). In this sequence the two italicized non-LXX texts claim our attention. Justin in *Dial.* 103:7f - i.e. shortly after the Hos 10:6 quotation - comments upon Ps 22:15 (LXX) in the following way:

ἐντρόμου τῆς καρδίας δῆλον ὅτι οὔσης

καὶ τῶν ὀστῶν ὁμοίως

καὶ ἐοικυίας τῆς καρδίας κηρῷ τηκομένῳ εἰς τὴν κοιλίαν.

This corresponds exactly to the extract from Ps 22:15 in Irenaeus' non-LXX version: «My heart is become like wax melting in the midst of my bowels; and they have scattered my bones.» Very likely Irenaeus again depends on Justin's source: Justin's comment seems adapted to Irenaeus' text.

The other non-LXX quotation in Irenaeus' sequence is probably taken from *Barnabas.*[5]

| *Barn.* 5:13 | *Dem.* 79 | |
|---|---|---|
| Φεῖσαί μου τῆς ψυχῆς ἀπὸ ῥομφαίας | Deliver my soul from the sword | Ps 22:21 |
| καὶ καθήλωσόν μου τὰς σάρκας | and my body from the nailing | Ps 119:120 |
| ὅτι πονηρευομένων συναγωγὴ ἐπανέστησάν μοι | for the council of the malignant is risen up over me | Ps 22:17 |

The only significant variant between the two texts, viz. «(deliver) my body from the nailing» instead of «nail my body (or: flesh)» is not sufficient to prove that *Barnabas* was not Irenaeus' source.[6] Very probably the variant reading in the *Demonstration* is due to a scribal misunderstanding in the transmission of the Armenian text. A minimal emendation restores an Armenian text exactly corresponding to *Barnabas*, and this is the text required by Irenaeus' own argument in the context.[7] In two other cases Irenaeus borrows composite,

---

4. Barthélemy, *Devanciers*, p. 208.
5. Cf. esp. L-M. Froidevaux, 'Sur trois textes cités par saint Irénée',*RSR* 44 (1956, pp. 408-421), pp. 408-414.
6. Both Prigent, *Les Testimonia*, pp. 166-168, and Kraft, *Epistle*, pp. 142ff, believe that Barnabas and Irenaeus are dependent upon a common source, but I think Froidevaux, *loc. cit.*, has argued convincingly that *Barnabas* was Irenaeus' source.
7. Cf. the detailed argument for this in Froidevaux, pp. 411-413.

non-LXX texts from *Barnabas*,[8] so it is very likely to be the case here also. I find this passage in Irenaeus particularly instructive. It warns against any too simple theory about Irenaeus' sources. Irenaeus seems to combine material from three sources in this short passage: Justin's source behind *Dial.* 103; further *1.Apol.* 35 and *Barnabas.* One should also notice that Irenaeus in his treatment of material from Ps 22 in some respects seems influenced from Justin's *Dialogue.* Justin's testimony source combined Ps 22:19/17 with Ps 3:6. In *Dial.* 97 Ps 3:5f is detached from Ps 22:19/17 and is quoted according to the LXX. The same separate treatment of Ps 3:6LXX recurs in *Dem.* 73. (The Ps Jer quotation in *Dem.* 78 may also be taken from the *Dialogue.*)

To conclude: It seems we shall have to reckon with a multiplicity of sources behind *Dem.* 77-80: *Barnabas, 1.Apology, Dialogue,* and the source behind *Dial.* 103. One can, however, think of one suggestion which to some extent simplifies the picture. We know from Eusebius that Justin wrote a work entitled -*Psaltes*-.[9] Was it a commentary on selected Psalms? Is the present commentary on Ps 22 in *Dial.* 98-106 a second revision of the commentary on Ps 22 contained in that work? Does Irenaeus excerpt his Justinian testimonies (Hos 10:6; Is 65:2; Ps 22:15.17.19) from that work?

All this may be possible surmises, but I doubt that the evidence is sufficient to warrant any conclusions.[10]

*B: Irenaeus or Tertullian dependent on the* Apology *or the* Dialogue

(3) Is 52:5 (*Dial.* 17:2 - cf.above, p. 114)

Prigent[11] has with good reason proposed that in *Dial.* 17:2 Justin's mainly LXX text of Is 52.5 is a substitute for a non-LXX text in his source. Turning to Tertullian, we find four quotations of Is 52:5:

| *Adv.Jud.* 13:26 | *Adv.Marc.* V:13:7 | *Adv.Marc.* III:23:3 | *Adv.Marc.* IV:14:16 |
|---|---|---|---|
| sicut scriptum est: propter vos nomen domini blasphematur in gentibus | propter vos nomen dei blasphematur | sicut scriptum est: propter vos blasphematur nomen meum in nationibus | sicut per Esaiam. . propter vos blasphematur nomen meum in nationibus |

*Adv. Marc.* III:23:3 and IV:14:16 seem to depend on Justin's text in *Dial.* 17:2 (-*per Esaiam*- and omission of διὰ παντός), while *Adv.Jud.* 13:26 and *Adv.Marc.* V:13:7 echo Rom 2:24 directly (*sicut scriptum est* =Rom 2:24 καθὼς γέγραπται; -*nomen dei*-).

If Prigent's surmises about the source behind *Dial.* 17 is correct, Tertullian depends on the present text of *Dial.* 17:2, not Justin's source, in *Adv.Marc.* III:23:3 and *Adv.Marc.* IV:14:16.

---

8. Is 50:8-10 (non-LXX) in *Barn.* 6:1f is copied in *Adv.Haer.* IV:33:13 and *Dem.* 88 (cf. Froidevaux, *art. cit.,* pp. 415-17); Ps 51:19 (non-LXX, expanded) in *Barn.* 2:10 is reproduced in *Adv.Haer.* IV:17:2 (cf. Froidevaux, pp. 417-19); to these parallels analysed by Froidevaux, one can also add Is 66:1 in *Barn.* 16:2 which is copied in *Dem.* 45.

9. *E. H.* IV:18:5.

10. In *Adv.Haer.* IV:33:12f Irenaeus has a long chain of allusions, a part of which may recall the present sequence in *1.Apol.* 38:1-6: Is 65:2; Ps 22:8.19.16; Ps 3:6 (the chain is interrupted by three formal quotations after Ps 22:8.19.16). But most probably Irenaeus is here just drawing on his memory.

11. *Justin,* pp. 133f.

(4) Zech 12:10-12 ( *1.Apol* 52:10-12, cf.above, pp. 76 - 78.

As we have seen, Justin in *1.Apol.* 52:10-12 has a very modified, combined version of Zech 12:10-12. This does not recur in Irenaeus or Tertullian. In the *Dialogue*, his paraphrase of the same text in *Dial.* 32:2 seems to depend on the καιγε version which Justin read in his *Dodekapropheton* MS.[12] Tertullian seems to depend directly on this paraphrase in the *Dialogue*:

| | |
|---|---|
| *Dial.* 32:2 | *Adv.Marc.* III:7:6 |
| ἐπιγνώσεσθε εἰς ὃν ἐξεκεντήσατε | Tunc et cognoscent eum qui compugnerunt |
| καὶ κόψονται... | et caedunt pectora sua |
| φυλὴ πρὸς φυλήν... | tribus ad tribum. |

This agreement with the paraphrase in *Dial.* 32:2 goes against both the LXX text and the quotation in Rev 1:7, as well as Justin's testimony text in *1.Apol.* 52. One especially notices the non-LXX reading *cognoscent* = ἐπιγνώσεσθε transposed to the 3rd person.

In *De Res.* 26:5 Tertullian quotes Zech 12:10 according to the text in John 19:37. In *De Res.* 51:1 he has an allusion to Zech 12:12 which again presupposes the Justinian version in *Dial.* 32:2. *De Res.* 22:10 has a free rendering of Zech 12:10.12 which also agrees with *Dial.* 32:2, except that Tertullian here reads «looking on» with John 19:37. The allusion to Zech 12:10 in *De Carne* 24:4 combines the two readings: «see» and «acknowledge».

There is no trace of the other components of *1.Apol.* 52:10-12 in Tertullian.

(5) Mal 1:10b-12a (*Dial.* 28:5; 41:2; 117:1 - synopsis next page)[13]

Justin's version of the text, in its triple transmission (see synopsis), seems to be neither LXX nor καιγε. Thus Barthélemy's contention is probably right: «Je crois qu'il s'agit encore là d'une citation empruntée à un vieux recueil chretien de Testimonia.»[14] Tertullian quotes Mal 1:10b-11 four times. There are several variants, but apart from minor omissions, it seems they can easily be explained as translation variants. The text being translated is identical with Justin's in *Dial.* 28:5, except that Tertullian has dropped the final phrase: ὑμεῖς δὲ βεβηλοῦτε αὐτό. His purpose in adducing the passage is in each case to extol the spiritual sacrifices offered by Christians. This may explain why he dropped the final, anti-Jewish saying in Justin's text.[15]

Looking for quotation sequences, we find the most relevant in *Adv.Marc.* IV:1:4-8. Tertullian's theme here is the prediction of a new law and a new testament by the OT Creator. After introducing the theme by means of Is 2:3f; Is 51:4 (cf. *Dial.* 11:3); Ps 19:8 (cf. *Dial.* 30); Is 10:23, Tertullian focuses on the idea of *novelty: uetera transierunt, noua oriuntur, ecce facio noua...* (cf. 2 Cor 5:17 and Is 43:19)*; nouate uobis nouamen nouum...* (Jer 4:3f, the same excerpt as in *Dial.* 28:2); *... testamentum nouum...* (Jer 31:31f, the same excerpt as in *Dial.* 11:3); *... testamentum aeternum...* (Is 55:3, cf. *Dial.* 12:1). To this sequence, which is closely related to *Dial.* 11f and 28-30, is added Mal 1:10-11 from *Dial.* 28:5, although this text *does not contain any of the main catchwords*!

This indicates that *Dial.* 28 is among Tertullian's sources here, and that his various versions of Mal. 1:10f derive from the version given in the *Dialogue*. (We shall see below that Tertullian probably has translated Justin's version of Dan 7:13f in *Dial.* 31).

---

12. Cf. Barthélemy, *Devanciers*, p. 211, and above, p.78. Prigent, pp. 80f, seems to have overlooked this, and apparently derives Justin's allusion from the *Syntagma.* Strange to say, he goes on, pp. 316-318, to derive the quite different Zech text of *1.Apol.* 52:10-12 from the same source -the *Syntagma*!

13. To this text, cf. Barthélemy, *Devanciers*, p. 212, and esp. Prigent, *Justin*, pp. 273-277.

14. Barthelemy, *ibid.*

15. I thus find Prigent's argument, p. 277, unnecessary and unconvincing.

~ *A.J.* 5:4

| Mal 1:10—12 LXX | *Dial.* 28:5 = 41:2 | *Adv.Marc.* III:22:6 ~ *Adv.Marc.* IV:1:8 ~ *Adv.Jud.* 5:7 |
|---|---|---|
| vs. 10<br>... οὐκ ἔστι μοι θέλημά^a ἐν ὑμῖν<br>λέγει κύριος παντοκράτωρ<br>καὶ θυσίαν οὐ προσδέξομαι<br>ἐκ τῶν χειρῶν ὑμῶν<br>vs. 11<br>διότι ἀπὸ ἀνατολῶν ἡλίου<br>ἕως δυσμῶν<br>τὸ ὄνομά μου δεδόξασται<br>ἐν τοῖς ἔθνεσι<br>καὶ ἐν παντὶ τόπῳ<br>θυμίαμα προσάγεται^b<br>τῷ ὀνόματί μου<br>καὶ θυσία καθαρά<br><br>διότι μέγα τὸ ὄνομά μου<br>ἐν τοῖς ἔθνεσι<br>λέγει κύριος παντοκράτωρ<br>vs. 12<br>ὑμεῖς δὲ βεβηλοῦτε αὐτό... | *Dial.* 28:5 = *Dial.* 41:2<br>οὐκ ἔστι θέλημά μου ἐν ὑμῖν<br>λέγει κύριος<br>καὶ τὰς θυσίας ὑμῶν οὐ προσδέχομαι^a<br>ἐκ τῶν χειρῶν ὑμῶν<br><br>διότι ἀπὸ ἀνατολῆς ἡλίου<br>ἕως δυσμῶν<br>τὸ ὄνομά μου δεδόξασται<br>ἐν τοῖς ἔθνεσι<br>καὶ ἐν παντὶ τόπῳ<br>θυσία^b προσφέρεται<br>τῷ ὀνόματί μου<br>καὶ θυσία καθαρά       *Dial.* 117:1<br><br>ὅτι τιμᾶται^c τὸ ὄνομά μου<br>ἐν τοῖς ἔθνεσι<br>λέγει κύριος<br><br>ὑμεῖς δὲ βεβηλοῦτε αὐτό | non est^a voluntas mea^b in vobis^c<br>dicit^d dominus<br>^het sacrificia^f vestra non accipiam^gh<br>^de manibus vestris^i<br><br>quoniam ^jab ortu solis^j<br>usque ^kin occasum^k<br>nomen meum glorificatum^l est<br>in nationibus^m<br>et in omni loco ^nsacrificium offertur<br>nomini meo<br>et sacrificium mundum^n |
| a) Bo Syh and others: θέλημά μου<br>b) 544 and some Fathers: προσφέρεται | a) *Dial.* 41:2 = *Dial.* 117:1 προσδέξομαι<br>b) *Dial.* 41:2: θυμίαμα<br>c) *Dial.* 41:2: μέγα<br><br>n-n) *A.J.* 5:7: sacrificia munda offeruntur nomini meo, dicit dominus<br>*A.J.* 5:4: offeruntur sacrificia munda. | a) *A.J.* 5:7 add. nobis<br>b) *A.J.* 5:7 om.<br>c-c) *A.M.* III:22:6 om.<br>d) *A.M.* IV:1:8: inquit<br>e) *A.J.* 5:7 om.<br>f) *A.J.* 5:7 om.<br>g) *A.M.* III:22:6: excipiam<br>h-h) *A.J.* 5:4: non recipiam sacrificium<br>i-i) *A.M.* III:22:6 om.<br>j-j) *A.M.* IV:1:8: a solis ortu; *A.J.* 5:4 = 5:7: ab oriente sole<br>k-k) *A.J.* 5:4: ad occidentem; *A.J.* 5:7: in occidentem; *A.M.* IV:1:8: ad occasum.<br>l) *A.J.* 5:4 = 5:7: clarificatum<br>m) *A.J.* 5:4 = 5:7: omnibus gentibus; *A.J.* 5:4 add. dicit dominus omnipotens; *A.M.* IV:1:8 transp: glorificatum est in nationibus nomen meum. |

(6) Ps 22:17/19/Ps 3:6 ( *1.Apol* 38:4 et al., cf. above, pp. 80 -82)

Tertullian has several allusions to and quotations of Ps 22:17.19:

| | | |
|---|---|---|
| *Adv.Jud.* 13:10: | Is 65:2; | Ps 22:17b.18/Ps 69:22 |
| *Adv.Jud.* 10:4: | | Ps 22:17b;  Ps 69:22;  Ps 22:19 |
| *Adv.Jud.* 10:13<br>par. *Adv.Marc.* III:19:5 | | Ps 22:17b;  Ps 22:22 |
| *Adv.Marc.* IV:42:4: | Ps 22:19; | Ps 22:17b;  Ps 22:17a.18b/8.9a |
| *De Res.* 20:5 (allusions) | Ps 22:17b; | Ps 22:19;  Ps 69:22;  Ps 22:8 |

All the texts are LXX - there is nowhere a trace of the deviant readings of Justin's source, and nowhere a trace of Ps 3:6. On the contrary, there are some indications that Tertullian depends on passages in the present text of *Apology* and *Dialogue*.

(1) *Adv.Jud.* 13:9f looks like a condensation of *1.Apol.* 32-35: allusion to Mic 5:1 (cf. *1.Apol* 34);[16] Gen 49:10 (cf. *1.Apol.* 32); quotations of Is 65:2 (cf. *1.Apol.* 35:3); Ps 22:17f (cf. *1.Apol.* 35:5). Justin opens his comment on Ps 22:17/19 in *1.Apol.* 35:6 by saying: καὶ ὁ μὲν Δαυείδ . . . οὐδὲν τούτων ἔπαθεν.. Tertullian begins his comment on Ps 22:17f and 69:22 with an almost verbatim translation: *haec David passus non est...*

(2) Close to *1.Apol.* 35 is also *Adv.Jud.* 10:11-14 (par. *Adv.Marc.* III:19:5): Ps 96:10b (with interpolation, cf. *1.Apol.* 41:4); Is 9:5a (= *1.Apol.* 35:2, but closer to the LXX); Jer 11:19 (cf. *Dial.* 72:2); Ps 22:17; Ps 22:22 (cf. *Dial.* 105:2f - Tertullian reproduces a shortened version of Justin's exegesis of this text); comment: *quam crucem nec ipse David passus est...*

The addition of material from Justin's commentary on Ps 22 in *Dial.* 105 is of special relevance, because there is every reason to think that the commentary on Ps 22 is Justin's own work.

(3) Tertullians comment on Ps 22:17 etc.[17] in *Adv.Jud.* 10:14 also betrays knowledge of Justin's comment on the same text in *Dial.* 97:4. Tertullian: *quam crucem nec ipse David passus est nec ullus regum Iudaeorum.* Justin:«... no one in your race who was called anointed king ever had his feet and hands dug through . . . and died by this way of mystery, namely crucifixion...» In *Adv.Marc.* IV:13:2 Tertullian quotes Ps 3:5 in a text identical with the LXX text of *Dial.* 97:1. We notice that Tertullian quotes a verse from Ps 3 not included in Justin's testimony source.

To conclude: It seems there are good reasons to think that Tertullian for his texts and exegesis depends on Justin's *Apology* and *Dialogue*.

(7) Ps 24:7f ( *1.Apol.* 51:7, cf. above, pp. 82f)

Justin in *1.Apol.* 51:7 quotes a non-LXX version of Ps 24:7f. In *Dial.* 36 he quotes the LXX text of the Psalm, but in his paraphrase and exegesis of the text partly introduces readings from the non-LXX text of *1.Apol.* 51:7. The result is an amalgam of «testimony» and LXX features.

Irenaeus in *Dem.* 84f seems to depend directly on this *mixed* material in the *Dialogue*. The evidence is best put down in a chart:

---

16. Mic 5:1 may well be Justin's own addition in *1.Apol.* 34, cf. above, p.119.
17. Cf. Prigent's discussion in *Justin*, pp. 204-215, esp. 213.

*Dial.* 36:3-6
(Ps 24 LXX quoted)


... ὁ ἡμέτερος Χριστὸς ὅτε ἐκ
νεκρῶν ἀνέστη καὶ ἀνέβαινεν
εἰς τὸν οὐρανὸν κελεύονται
οἱ ἐν τοῖς οὐρανοῖς ταχθέντες
ὑπὸ τοῦ θεοῦ ἄρχοντες
*ἀνοῖξαι τὰς πύλας τῶν οὐρανῶν*
*ἵνα εἰσέλθῃ* οὗτος ὅς ἐστι
βασιλεὺς τῆς δόξης
καὶ ἀναβὰς
καθίσῃ ἐν δεξιᾷ τοῦ πατρός


ἕως ἂν θῇ τοὺς ἐχθροὺς
ὑποπόδιον τῶν ποδῶν αὐτοῦ ...


... ἐπυνθάνοντο
τίς ἐστιν οὗτος ὁ βασιλεὺς
τῆς δόξης;
καὶ ἀποκρίνεται αὐτοῖς
... κύριος τῶν δυνάμεων
αὐτὸς οὗτος ἐστιν
ὁ βασιλεὺς τῆς δόξης

*Dem.* 84
(Ps 24:7 LXX quoted)
... the «eternal gates» (LXX) are
*the heavens.*
... He was also visible in His
ascension, and when the
principalities[18]saw Him, the angels
underneath called to those who were
on the firmament: 'Take up your gates,
and be lifted up, O ye eternal gates,
*that* the king of glory enter in.'
*Dem.* 85.
And as He is risen and ascended,
He awaits ever at the Father's
right hand ...
when all His enemies are made
subject to Him (Ps 110:1 quot.)
*Dem.* 84
And when these wondered and said:
Who is this?

those ... testify a second time:
The Lord strong and mighty
He is
the king of glory.

As one can easily see, Justin's paraphrasing exposition in *Dial.* 36:5f rests on the LXX text, but some reminiscenses of the «testimony» text in *1.Apol.* 51:7 remain (italicized phrases). Irenaeus also quotes the LXX, but in his exposition he echoes the amalgam of LXX and non-LXX readings found in *Dial.* 36. There is no trace of independent recourse to Justin's source.[19] Another echo of *Dial.* 36:5 (... ἀνοῖξαι τὰς πύλας τῶν οὐρανῶν ...) may be heard in *Adv.Haer* III:16:8: ᾧ ἠνοίχθησαν αἱ πύλαι τοῦ οὐρανοῦ.

In *Adv.Haer.* IV:33:13 an allusion (LXX) to Ps 24:7 is followed by a quotation of Ps 19:7 and Ps 99:1. Cf. *Dial.* 36f: Ps 24:1-10; Ps 47:6-10 and Ps 99:1-9; and further *Dial.* 64:4-8: Ps 99:1-7; Ps 72:1-5.17-19; Ps 19:1-7. (*Dem.* 85 also quotes Ps 19:7).[20]

(8) Ps 72:17 (*Dial.* 121:1f - cf above, pp. 84f)

One passage in Tertullian is of special interest. In *Adv.Marc.* V:9:6-13 we find a treatment of Ps 110:1-4 and several verses of Ps 72. The exposition is so close to *Dial.* 32:6 - 34:8 and *Dial.* 83, that even Prigent comments: «*Assurément c'est bien à Justin que Tertullien emprunte son interprétation du Ps 110 ...*»,[21] and: «*Indiscutablement Tertullien avait sous*

---

18. Cf. J. P. Smith, note *ad loc.* (p. 209, n. 338): «an exegesis of the word «princes» (... ἄρχοντες) ».
19. Cf. Prigent's remark on *Dem.* 84: «*Les modifications du thème ne doivent pas masquer l'identité fondamentale de cette exégèse avec celle de Justin qui est evidemment la source d'Irénée.*» (*Justin*, p. 100). Cf. also Daniélou, *Theology*, pp. 259-262.
20. Tertullian: A casual allusion to Ps 24:7-10 in *De Cor.* 14:4 is too short to allow any inferences as to text-type. More relevant is an allusion in *De Fuga* 12:2: *Subleuatae sunt portae sempiternae, ut introiret rex gloriae, Dominus uirtutum,* ... In the context previous to the allusion there are allusions to i.a. Is 53:7 and Is 53:12. Tertullian may thus depend on *1.Apol.* 50f. But on the textual level, he sticks to the LXX text. *Scorp.* 10:7 quotes the LXX of Ps 24:7-no trace of other Justinian testimonies in the context. The LXX quotation of Ps 24:10 in *Adv.Marc.* V:17:5 seems also to be irrelevant to our quest. The same is true of the casual allusion in *Adv.Prax.* 17:2.
21. *Justin*, p. 84.

*les yeux le texte de Justin.*[22] Tertullian is not drawing on a testimony version of Ps 72:5.17, but on the whole LXX text of the Psalm. His list of quotations from Ps 72 runs like this: vss. 1, 6, 8, 11, 17f, and 9.

Nevertheless, there are two possible echoes of the deviant text of Ps 72:17 in *Dial* 121:1: omission of εὐλογημένον and telescoping of the last two lines ( *Adv.Marc.* V:9:11f ). In other words: Tertullian's text of Ps 72:17 is a mixture of LXX and Justin's «testimony» text in *Dial.* 121:1. The simplest explanation is that both versions were found in Tertullians source, i.e. that his source was Justin's *Dialogue.*[23] One parallel in particular corroborates this:[24]

| *Dial.* 34:7f | | *Adv.Marc.* V:9:9-13 | |
|---|---|---|---|
| Ps 72 is not spoken about Solomon: | | Ps 72 does not apply to Solomon: | |
| οὔτε γὰρ πάντες οἱ βασιλεῖς προσεκύνησαν αὐτῷ | vs.11 | adorabunt illum omnes reges. Quem omnes, nisi Christum? | (2) |
| οὔτε μέχρι τῶν περάτων τῆς οἰκουμένης ἐβασίλευσεν | vs.8 | Dominabitur ... usque ad terminus terrae. Haec soli datum est Christo; ceterum Salomon uni et modicae Iudaeae imperavit. | (1) |
| οὔτε οἱ ἐχθροί αὐτοῦ ἔμπροσθεν αὐτοῦ πεσόντες χοῦν ἔλειξαν | vs.9 | ... itaque cum in medio psalmo ..: Inimici eius pulverem lingent, ... | |
| ἀλλὰ καὶ τολμῶ λέγειν ἃ γέγραπται ἐν ταῖς Βασιλείαις ὑπ' αὐτοῦ πραχθέντα, ὅτι διὰ γυναῖκα ἐν Σιδῶνι εἰδωλολάτρει | | Contra Salomon, *audeo dicere,* etiam quam habuit in deo gloriam amisit *per mulierem* in *idolatriam* usque pertractus. | |

To conclude: Tertullian depends on the passages *Dial.* 32-34; 83, and 121.[25]

(9) Ps 96:10 (cf. above, pp. 35ff)

Tertullian asks in *Adv.Marc.* III:19:1: «Come now, when you read in the words of David, *dominus regnavit a ligno,* I want to know what you understand by it.» The parallel in *Adv.Jud.* 10:11 has instead of «David» «the Psalms». In the context we find the following text sequence (identical in *Adv.Jud.* and *Adv.Marc.*): Deut 33:17; Gen 49:5f; Ex 17:10-13; Num 21:8f; Ps 96:10; Is 9:5; Ps 96:10; Jer 11:19; Ps 22:17.22; Is 57:2 etc. Is 9:5 and Ps 22:17 remind one of *1.Apol.* 35:2.5; Deut 33:17, Ex 17:10-13 and Num 21:8f occur together in *Dial.* 91/94; Ps 96:10 and Jer 11:19 are close to each other in *Dial.* 72f.

As we have seen above, these texts derive from different sources,[26] and Justin may have been the first to combine them in his writings. It would thus seem that Tertullian is here drawing on different passages in the *Apology* and the *Dialogue.*

22. *Ibid.,* p. 89 *ad* Ps 72. Nevertheless, Prigent also in these two cases tries to argue that Tertullian read Justin's exposition not in the *Dialogue,* but in the *Syntagma.*
23. So also Hommes, *Testimoniaboek,* pp. 70f.
24. Cf. *Justin,* p. 89.
25. In *Adv.Marc.* IV:14:4 Tertullian states that Ps 72:4.11.12a.13f are spoken not about David but about Christ. No dependence on Justin or his source is visible. In *Adv.Marc.* III:13:8 = *Adv.Jud.* 9:12 there are quotations of Ps 72;15b.10b apropos the Magi story. No dependence upon Justin.
26. This is one of those instances where I find Prigent's internal analysis of Justin's writings unsatisfactory because he reads the sequences of later writers into Justin's source, *Justin,* pp. 179-194.

(10) Dan 7:13f (*Apol.* 51:9; *Dial.* 31, cf.above, pp.80 - 90)

In three short allusions to Dan 7:13 ( *Adv.Haer.* III:19:2; IV:33:1; 33:11 ), Irenaeus perhaps reflects Justin's deviant reading ἐπάνω τῶν νεφελῶν: *super nubes.*[27] If so, one need look no further than *1.Apol.* 51:9 and Justin's other allusions to find Irenaeus' source.[28]

Tertullian:

In *De Carne* 15:1 he has an allusion which also reads *super nubes,* thus probably recalling *1.Apol.* 51:9 etc.

Three quotations of Dan 7:13f are of special interest:

| *Dial.* 31:3f | *Adv. Jud.* 14:4 = *Adv. Marc.* III:7:4 | |
|---|---|---|
| καὶ ἰδοὺ μετὰ τῶν νεφελῶν | et[a]ecce cum nubibus | ⎤ |
| τοῦ οὐρανοῦ | caeli[b] | |
| ὡς υἱὸς ἀνθρώπου ἐρχόμενος | tamquam filius hominis ueniens[c] | |
| καὶ ἦλθεν ἕως τοῦ παλαιοῦ | uenit usque ad ueterem | ⎦ |
| τῶν ἡμερῶν | dierum | |
| καὶ παρῆν ἐνώπιον αὐτοῦ | et[d] aderat in conspectu eius | |
| καὶ οἱ παρεστηκότες | et qui adsistebant | |
| προσήγαγον αὐτόν | adduxerunt eum[e] | |
| καὶ ἐδόθη αὐτῷ ἐξουσία | et data est illi[f] potestas | |
| καὶ τιμὴ βασιλική | regia[g] | = *Adv.Marc.* |
| καὶ πάντα τὰ ἔθνη τῆς γῆς | et [i]omnis nationes[h] terrae[i] | IV:39:11 |
| κατὰ γένη | secundum genus[j] | |
| καὶ πᾶσα δόξα λατρεύουσα | ct omnis gloria[k] seruiens ei[l] | ⎤ |
| καὶ ἡ ἐξουσία αὐτοῦ | et potestas eius | |
| ἐξουσία αἰώνιος | aeterna[m] | |
| ἥτις οὐ μὴ ἀρθῇ | quae non auferetur | |
| καὶ ἡ βασιλεία αὐτοῦ | et regnum eius | |
| οὐ μὴ φθαρῇ | quod non corrumpetur[n] | ⎦ |

a) Om. *A.M.* IV:39:11
b) *A.M.* IV:39:11: caeli nubibus
c) *A.M.* IV:39:11: adueniens
d) Om. *A.M.* III:7:4
e) *A.M.* III:7:4: illum
f) *A.M.* III:7:4: ei
g) *A.M.* IV:39:11: regia potestas
h) *A.J.* 14:4: Om. nationes
i-i) *A.M.* IV:39:11: uniuersae nationes
j) *A.M.* III:7:4: genera
k) *A.M.* IV:39:11: gloria omnis
l) *A.M.* IV:39:11: seruiens illi;
   *A.M.* III:7:4: famulabunda
m) *A.M.* III:7:4: usque in aeuum
n) *A.M.* III:7:4: uitiabitur

The data in the synopsis call, I think, for a very simple explanation: Tertullian's text is a translation of Justin's in *Dial.* 31:3f, and the variants in Tertullian's rendering are translation variants.

P.Prigent has argued that the deviant reading in *1.Apol.* 51:9 was the reading found in Justin's *Syntagma,* while the text in *Dial.* 31 is copied from Justin's Daniel scroll.[29] If so, it is

---

27. A. Rousseau in his Greek retroversion in the SC ed. writes ἐπί, probably influenced by the LXX text.
28. So also, apparently, Prigent, *Justin,* p. 79, n. 1. In *Adv.Haer.* IV:20:10 Irenaeus has a paraphrase of Dan 7:13f following «Theodotion», and reading *in nubibus.*
29. *Justin,* pp. 78-81.

evident that Tertullian in this case is dependent on the *Dialogue*, not the *Syntagma* - contrary to Prigent's main thesis. Unfortunately, Prigent is silent about this evidence in Tertullian.

The remaining short allusions in Tertullian say little about the problem ( *Adv.Marc.* IV:24:11: *in nubibus; Adv.Marc.* IV:10:12: *cum caeli nubibus; Adv.Marc.* IV:10:9f: irrelevant). In *Adv.Jud.* 6:2 there is a short allusion to Dan 7:14 which seems to accord with the long Justinian text treated above.

I think these cases are sufficient to show that whatever access Irenaeus and Tertullian may have had to Justin's sources, their use of the *Apology* and the *Dialogue* is manifest. They often reflect features of Justin's exegesis which derive directly from Justin's own work with the LXX text - not from his testimony sources. I believe Prigent has fallen prey to a systematic underestimation of Irenaeus' and Tertullian's direct use of Justin's preserved writings.

Let me add some considerations of a more general nature. In such an ambitious work as the *Dialogue* we have every reason to expect that Justin had the intention of making a more complete, comprehensive, and thorough presentation of the Christian argument from prophecy than offered in any of his sources. If so, the *Dialogue* - taken together with the *Apology* -would be the best and most comprehensive mine of exegetical argument from which Irenaeus and Tertullian could draw. This is not to say that they relied solely on these works -we have seen that Irenaeus quotes *Barnabas*, and Tertullian have taken arguments from *Barnabas* - but the *Apology* and the *Dialogue* are always strong candidates when we look for exegetical sources behind the two later writers.

*(C) Remaining cases of non-LXX texts in Justin.*

(11) Gen. 17:14 (*Dial.* 10:3; 23:4).

Irenaeus: No occurrence. Tertullian: Two allusions, *Adv. Jud.* 3:1 (LXX text); *Adv. Jud.* 2:10 (too short to allow conclusions).

(12) Gen 49:10f (cf. above, pp. 25 - 29)

There is good reason to think that Irenaeus in Dem. 57 is dependent directly on 1. *Apol.* 32. His version of the text (see synopsis p. 26) shows striking accordance with 1.*Apol.* 32 (against the LXX), except that Irenaeus in the last two lines of vs. 11 adjusts his text to the LXX. (Smit Sibinga has made a mistake:«In Irenaeus' parallel text all of v. 11 is missing», p. 78). He shares Justin's reference, when he says:«Moses in Genesis speaks as follows . . .» He shares Justin's paraphrase of the ᾧ ἀπόκειται: «for whom lies in store a kingship». And although Irenaeus in the text of Gen 49:11 follows the LXX in having Christ's στολή washed in wine, there is no mention of wine in Irenaeus' exegesis:«His robe', as also 'His garment', are those who believe in Him, and whom He has cleansed, redeeming us with His blood. And His blood was called 'the blood of the grape' because, just as no man makes blood of the grape . . . so too His nature of flesh and His blood were not the work of man, but made by God.» This is all parallel to I.*Apol.* 32:5-11. There is no reason to go behind this text to find Irenaeus' source. Irenaeus returns to Gen 49:10-12 in *Adv.Haer.* IV:I0:2. This time the text is septuagintal throughout, except that the reading ᾧ ἀπόκειται is retained: *cui repositum est.*

Tertullian also seems to follow a septuagintal text in his only formal quotation of Gen 49:11 in *Adv.Marc.* IV:40:6. His exegetical comments seem inspired from Justin, but are adjusted to the LXX text.

(13) Ex 3:2ff (1. *Apol.* 63:7, cf. above, pp. 47 - 50)

Irenaeus and Tertullian: Several LXX quotations and allusions to different verses in Ex 3:2ff, but no echo of Justin's deviant text.

(14) Ex 15:27: Seventy *willows* (ἰτέας), twelve fountains. (*Dial* 86:5).

Irenaeus, *Dem.* 46: Twelve fountains. Tertullian, *Adv.Marc.* IV:24:1: Twelve wells, seventy palm-trees (*arbusta palmarum* = LXX στελέχη φοινίκων).

(15) Ex 32:6 *(Dial.* 20:1, cf. above, pp. 117f)

Irenaeus: No references.
Tertullian quotes Ex 32:6 in a text very close to *Dial.* 20:1 in *De Ieiun.* 6:2f: *manducauit populus et bibit, et surrexerunt ludere.* Then, after some comment, he quotes a LXX text of Deut 32:15, extending one stichos beyond Justin's excerpt in *Dial.* 20:1. Tertullian thus probably copies this text directly from the LXX, as is indicated in his subsequent remark: *Denique in eodem Deuteronomio* . . . There is thus no need to go behind *Dial.* 20 to find Tertullian's source. The casual allusions in *De Cor.* 9:3 and *Adv. Marc.* 11:18:2 also point to the text in *Dial.* 20:1. (Prigent recognizes this, *Justin,* p. 258).

(16) Num 24:17 et al. (cf. above, pp. 50 - 52)

The two Irenaean quotations of Num 24:17 quoted in the text above (p. 51) may well have *Dial.* 106:4 as their source. But Irenaeus also seems to have adapted *1.Apol.* 32f as his source -viz. in *Dem.* 57-59. We find the sequence Gen 49:10f; Is 7:14 (allusion); Num 24:17; Is 11:1-10. It seems that Irenaeus has identified two components of Justin's composite quotation in *1.Apol.* 32:12 - he gives Num 24:17 according to the fuller version in *Dial.* 106:4, and quotes the full LXX text of Is 11:1-10. He seems not to have recognized the third element in Justin's composite quotation (Is 51:5). (Smit Sibinga, p. 49, has another explanation of the relation between Justin and Irenaeus:-Irenaeus, Epideixis 58-59, seems to reflect an earlier stage of Justin's and Irenaeus' common source, in which Num 24:17 and Is 11:1-10, written out in full and without much commentary, were well distinguished.- For several reasons this is unlikely. It leaves Justin's mistake in attributing the whole text to Isaiah unexplained. And it presupposes that the third element in Justin's composite quotation is Is 11:10 - which is hardly correct.) In Tertullian we find no quotation of Num 24:17 or Is 51:5. He has two formal quotations of Is 11:1-3. In *Adv.Marc,* V:8:4 he has the text in a context which is totally different from Justin's. The text is LXX - also where Justin's is not. The same text recurs in *Adv.Jud.* 9:26 (the differences between the two texts look like translation variants) - here also the context is unlike Justin's. Tertullian may have been directed to this text by Justin, but seems to be working directly with the LXX text. His other allusions (*Adv.Marc.* III:17:3; IV:1:8; 36:11;*De Coron.* 13:2; 15:2; *De Carn.* 21:5;22:6) to Is 11:1(f) yield nothing to our purpose, except perhaps *Adv.Marc.* III:17:4, which seems to depend on *Dial.* 87:4f. There is thus neither in Irenaeus nor in Tertullian any trace of direct recourse to Justin's source or sources.

(17) Num 27:18b/11:17 *(Dial.* 49:6)

Irenaeus: Fragm. 19 (Harvey II, p. 488): Num 27:18a LXX - no dependence upon Justin. Tertullian: No references.

(18) Deut 32:4/Ps 92:16 *(Dial.* 92:5).

Irenaeus: *Adv.Haer.* III:18:7: Deut 32:4 LXX. Tertullian: No references.

(19) Deut 32:7b-9 *(Dial.* 131:1, cf. above, pp. 29f)

Irenaeus in *Adv.Haer.* III:12:9 quotes Deut 32:8f according to the LXX text. He may be quoting from a Deut MS, or he may depend on *Dial.* 131:1, or perhaps on *1. Clem.* The context is such that no safe conclusion is possible.
A possible allusion to Deut 32:8 in Tertullian's *Adv.Prax.* 17:3 presupposes Justin's -Jewish- text in *Dial.* 131:1: *filii.* If Tertullian depends on Justin,he depends on the long Deut quotation which Justin has excerpted from his Deut MS - not on Justin's testimony source. But the evidence is scanty.

(20) Deut 32:21 and 32:22 (cf. above, pp. 52f)

Irenaeus in *Dem.* 95 quotes Deut 32:21 (the whole verse) in what may be called a Pauline text: Irenaeus has changed the first part of the verse - not quoted by Paul - from 3rd to 2nd person plural, to make it agree with the Pauline form of the second part of the verse. In the context Irenaeus has other Pauline and NT quotations: Hos 2:23f/1:10 = Rom 9:25f; Mt 3:9; Ezek 36:26f; Jn 1:14; Is 54:1 = Gal 4:27; Deut 28:44 (allusion); Deut 32:21. One gets the impression that Irenaeus is working directly with Rom 9f, adding other relevant NT and OT material. There are some parallels in terminology between *Dem.* 95 and *Dial.* 119, but no echoes of the remaining quotation material in *Dial.*119. (Prigent, *Justin,* pp. 291f, argues that Irenaeus in *Dem.* 92-95 follows a source which can be discerned also behind *Dial.* 119f: *1.Apol.* 48-54, and *Dial.* 23-27. I believe rather that Prigent's table p. 292 shows that Irenaeus was drawing on these chapters in the *Apology* and the *Dialogue* - besides on Paul, as said).

Tertullian quotes Deut 32:20f in a LXX text in *Adv.Marc.* IV:31:6. In the context he is expounding Lk 14:12-24. One of his comments on Deut 32:20f may point to *Dial.* 119 as a source. *Ad* vs. 20a he says:«. . . that is, that others will take possession of their (i.e. the Jews') place.» (Cf. *Dial.* 119:5:«. . . we shall inherit the Holy Land together with Abraham . . .») This is not a very striking parallel, however, and one is hardly entitled to say more than that *Dial.* 119 may linger in the background here.

The quotation of Deut 32:22 in *1.Apol.* 60:9 - and its supposed source - has left no trace in Irenaeus or Tertullian.

(21) Is 1:7/ Jer 50:3b ( *1.Apol.* 47:5, cf. above, pp. 53f)

Irenaeus: No references.
Tertullian: In *Adv.Jud.* 3:4f we find the following sequence of LXX quotations: Is 1:7f; Is 1:2b; Is 1:15; Is 1:4. No doubt Tertullian is here working directly with the LXX of Is 1. ( A good LXX text of Is 1:7 is also given in *Adv.Jud.* 13:4). Turning to *Adv.Jud.* 13:26 = *Adv.Marc.* III:23:3, we find, however, a partly nonLXX text of Is 1:7f, which on one point agrees with Justin's text in *1.Apol.* 47:5: It reads *terra eorum* (and the rest of Is 1:7 in the 3rd person plural) instead of the LXX ἡ γῆ ὑμῶν. I doubt that one can conclude much from this. The changes vis a vis the LXX text smooth the text to fit Tertullian's context, and may very well be his own modifications. There is no trace of Jer 50:3 in Tertullian - a direct recourse to Justin's source is thus far from certain, although it cannot be ruled out in this case.

(22) Is 1:11 - 15/ Is 58:6f ( *1.Apol.* 37:5 - 8, cf. above, pp. 55f)

Irenaeus and Tertullian:
The only echo of Justin's peculiar non-LXX text in *1.Apol.* 37:5-8 I have been able to find is in Tertullian, *Adv.Marc.* IV:12:4 (= *Adv.Jud.* 4:2): *neomenias et sabbata uestra odit anima mea* (the *Adv.Jud.* parallel has only *sabbata vestra.*. ). As one can easily glean from the synopsis, p. 56, this allusive quotation is closer to Justin's deviant text than to the LXX of Is 1:13f.

In *Adv.Jud.* 5:6 Tertullian has an interpolated text of Is 1:11-12 (vs. 13b is interpolated into the middle of vs. 11). However, the interpolation is marked out by redactional formulas which clearly show that the interpolator is Tertullian himself.

(23) Is 3:10 et al. ( *Dial.*136:2, cf. above, pp. 30f)

In Irenaeus, there is no trace of the quotation sequence we have recognized in Justin - Is 57:1f is quoted in *Dem.*72, but in another sequence of texts. Is 3:10 and Is 5:20 are not quoted by him.
Tertullian once quotes Is 57:1 and Is 3:10 together, and has the deviant text in Is 3:10. The terminological link between the two texts is preserved in the Latin: *Viri iusti auferantur -auferamus iustum, Adv. Marc.* III:22:5. One cannot exclude the possibility that Tertullian has his quotations from Justin's source, but there is no trace of Is 5:20, and it is also possible that Tertullian combines readings from *Dial.* 16f and *Dial.* 136f.

(24) Is 5:20 *(1. Apol.* 49:7, cf. above, p. 31)

Irenaeus and Tertullian: No references.

(25) Is 6:10 *(Dial.* 12:2; 33:1; 69:4, cf. above, pp. 120f)

Irenaeus and Tertullian: No trace of the deviant text I have conjectured behind Justin's allusions.

(26) Is 7:10-17 with Is 8:4 interpolated *(Dial.* 43; 66, cf. above, pp. 32 - 34)

Irenaeus seems to have recognized the interpolation in Justin's long quotations, and treats the LXX text of Is 8:3f as a separate Messianic (!) prophecy in *Adv Haer.* III:16:4. His exegesis echoes Justin's in the *Dialogue.* (In *Adv.Haer.* IV:33:11 he has a combined, allusive quotation of Is 8:3/9:6).

Tertullian may in *Adv.Marc.* III:12:1 and *Adv.Jud.* 9:1f depend on Justin's source, but via Marcion, cf. above, pp. 239f.

(27) Is 9:5a *(1. Apol.* 35:2, cf. above, p. 146)

Irenaeus has in *Dem.* 56 a LXX excerpt of Is 9:5-7. But in *Dem.* 40 and 54 he has a non-LXX version (= TM!) of Is 9:5b, which possibly may derive from Justin's source in *Dial.* 76:3 (cf. *Dial.* 126:1). Cf. discussion above, p. 390.

(29) Is 35:6/5/Is 26:19 *(1. Apol.* 48:2, cf. above, pp. 58f)

Irenaeus: It seems that Irenaeus in *Adv.Haer.* IV:33:11 has *1.Apol.* 48:2 as his source (cf. Prigent, *Justin,* pp. 167f), but he has made some modifications. He has eliminated the phrases from Mt 11:5 and instead introduced more material from Is 35 and Is 26:19 (not the same stichos as in Justin), - and to this he has added the Is 53 quotation of Mt 8:17, converting aorist into future in line with the preceeding texts. One can here observe a theologian at work, who has greater familiarity than Justin with as well OT as NT texts. - In the parallel passage *Dem.* 67 Irenaeus has gone further in quoting the texts directly from the LXX. The sequence is: Is 53:3f(=Mt 8:17); Is 29:18; 35:3-6; 26:19. Prigent, *Justin,* tentatively suggests that Irenaeus here also may depend on Justin's source, but I can see no indications for this.

In Tertullian the picture is more confusing (see esp. the detailed discussion in Prigent, *Justin,* pp. 168f). He has a composite quotation in *Adv.Jud.* 9:30 (Is 35:4b/ Is 29:18/Is 35:5b/6b/6a. If he depends on a written source, it was similar to, but hardly the same as Justin's (cf. Prigent, p. 169). The parallel in *Adv.Marc.* III:17:5 quotes only Is 53:4 (=Mt 8:17). Perhaps this is due to influence from Irenaeus, although Prigent denies this (p. 169, n. 2).

(28) Is 14:1 *(Dial.* 123:1)

Irenaeus and Tertullian: No references.

(30) Is 42:1-4 *(Dial* 123:8, cf. above, pp. 60f)

Irenaeus quotes Is 42:1-4 in *Adv.Hear* III:11:6. On closer inspection, his quotation appears to be entirely derived from Mt: The text combines Mt 3:17=17:5 with Mt 12:18-21. There is no trace of Justin's peculiarities in *Dial.* 123 or *Dial.* 135. Justin s main point (the christological designations «Jacob» and «Israel») are absent in Irenaeus' text. Irenaeus can thus be seen to work directly with Matthew, not with Justin or his source. (The casual allusion in *Adv.Hear.* IV:20:10 presupposes the text in *Adv.Haer.* III:11:6).

Tertullian has one quotation of Is 42:1 in *Adv.Prax.* 11:5. It goes with Mt 12:18, except for the LXX reading «bring out» instead of «announce». Is 42:2.3a is quoted four times, two times with readings from Mt and LXX (*Adv.Marc.* III:17:4 and the parallel *Adv.Jud.* 9:28); and two times in a purely Matthean text (*Adv.Marc.* IV:23:8; *De Pat.* 3:4). His four short quotations of Is 42:4b (*Adv Marc.* III:21:2; V:2:5; 4:4; 4:11) go with Mt 12:21, except that the last one reads *credent* for *sperabunt* (i.e. a free quotation). - The oscillation between LXX and Mt is not surprising in a writer so familiar with the Bible as Tertullian, and the single instance in which he agrees with Justin (*Dial.* 123:8) against Mt - within an otherwise Matthean text, *Adv.Prax.* 11:5 - is hardly sufficient to warrant any inferences. He may depend on Justin, or the coincidence may be accidental.

(31) Is 42:6f (*Dial.* 122:3, cf. above, p. 62)

Irenaeus: No reference.
Tertullian quotes Is 42:6b.7 in *Adv.Jud.* 12:2 (parallel *Adv.Marc.* III:20:1) following the LXX. The allusion to Is 42:6 in *Adv.Marc* IV:11:1 is too short to tell anything about the text. The same is true of *Adv.Marc.* V:7:1 The short quotations in *Adv.Marc.* V:2:5 (*posui te in lumen nationum*) and V:6:1 (*posito in lumen nationum*) are probably renderings of Is 49:6, not Is 42:6. (The *BP* I lists the passages under both references).

(32) Is 42:16a/43:10a *(Dial.* 122:1)

Irenaeus: *Adv.Haer.* III:6:2: Is 43:10, LXX text. *Adv.Haer.* IV:5:1: Is 43:10-12 LXX text. Tertullian: No references.

(33) Is 53:12 *(1. Apol.* 50:2, cf. above, pp. 62f)

Irenaeus has no quotation of Is 53:12.
Tertullian has free, allusive quotations in *De Fuga* 12:2; *Adv.Marc.* IV:10:2; 42:4; *De Res.* 20:5; and two formal quotations, *Adv.Jud.*. 10:16 and (parallel) *Adv.Marc.* III:19:9. The latter follows the LXX text, and no trace of Justin's variant text is to be found in the allusions.

(34) Is 55:3-5 *(Dial.* 12, cf. above, pp. 63f)

Irenaeus: No reference.
Tertullian has one quotation (Is 55:3f in *Adv.Marc.* III:20:5) and three allusions (Is 55:3-5 in *Adv.Marc.* III:20:10; Is 55:3 in *Adv.Marc.* III:20:8 and IV:1:7) - all follow the LXX, not the text of *Dial.* 12.

(35) Is 65:1-3 (cf. above, pp. 65 - 67)

Irenaeus quotes Is 65:1 in *Dem.* 92 according to the «standard» LXX text (against Justin's slightly deviant LXX quotations in. *Dial.* 24 and *1.Apol.* 49). The shorter quotation in *Adv.Haer.* III:6:1 (Is 65:1a) and the allusion to Is 65:1a in *Adv.Haer.* III:9:2 presuppose the same text. Is 65:2a is quoted according to the LXX (against Justin's «testimony» version) in *Dem.* 79, and the allusion to the same text in *Adv.Haer.* IV:33:12 again goes with the LXX text against Justin's. The only evidence in Tertullian is a LXX quotation of Is 65:2 in *Adv.Jud* 13:10.

(36) Is 65:22 *(Dial.* 81:3, cf. above, p. 67)

Irenaeus has one LXX quotation: Is 65:18-22 (*Adv. Haer.* IV:34:4) and one LXX allusion (*Adv.Haer.* V:15:1, Is 65:22). He has no echo of Justin's deviant text, and his exegesis is different.

(37) Is 66:1 *(1.Apol.* 37:3; *Dial.* 22:11, cf. above p. 124)

Irenaeus in *Dem.* 45 quotes Is 66:1 in a text exactly corresponding to Barnabas' text in *Barn.* 16:2. To this quotation he adds an allusive quotation of Is 40:12, alluding only to the part of the verse which is quoted in *Barn.* 16:2. I can see no reason to avoid the simplest explanation: Irenaeus depends on *Barn.* 16:2. In *Adv.Haer.* IV:2:5 we find a short quotation of Is 66:1a in a text identical with LXX, *Barn.*, and Acts 7. The allusive quotation in *Adv.Haer.* IV:3:1 seems to refer to the same LXX text. There is thus no trace of Justin's deviant text in Irenaeus. Tertullian has two short allusions to Is 66:1a in *Adv.Marc.* II:25:2 and *Adv.Prax.* 16:6. They are too short to allow for any conclusions.

(38) Is 66:24 *(1. Apol.* 52:8; *Dial.* 140:3, cf. above, pp. 67 - 69)

Irenaeus: No reference.
Tertullian quotes Is 66:22-24 selectively in *De Res.* 31,7-9, according to the LXX text. There

are points of contact with Justin in the context which may indicate recourse to Justin's source in *1.Apol.* 52. Cf. above in this Appendix, nr. 1.

(39) Jer 2:13/Is 16:1/Jer 3:8 *(Dial.* 114:5, cf. above, pp. 69f)

There is no unambiguous echo of this combined text in Irenaeus or Tertullian. Irenaeus alludes to Jer 2:13 in *Adv.Haer.* III:24:1, but the text is too short and free to warrant any conclusions as to text-type. Tertullian quotes Jer 2:10-13 in *Adv.Jud.* 13:13f. The text has some deviations from the LXX, but accords in no case with *Dial.* 114:5 (nor with Barnabas).

(40) Jer 4:3f *(Dial.* 28:2f, cf. above, pp. 70 - 72)

Irenaeus: No reference.
Tertullian quotes Jer 4:3f in *Adv. Jud.* 3:7; *Adv. Marc.* I:20:4, and IV:1:6. The text is LXX - no trace of the other Justinian texts. The same is true of the short phrases from Jer 4:3 in *Adv. Marc.* IV:11:9; V:19:11; *De Pud.* 6:2. Only two quotations of Jer 4:4 are of interest, since they both are combined with Deut 10:16. *Adv.Marc.* V:4:10 reads: *memor dictum per Hieremiam: et circumcidimini praeputia cordis uestri; quia et Moyses: circumcidetis duricordiam uestram.* The other text, *Adv.Marc.* V:13:7, is almost identical. I suspect that Tertullian is here recalling *Dial.* 15f rather than *Barn.* 9:5f, because he has *praeputia* in Jer 4:4 (lacking in Barnabas). Another observation also points in the same direction: In *Adv. Marc.* V:13:7 we have a third quotation, viz. Is 52:5, before Jer 4:4. The same quotation is found in *Dial.* 17:2, i.e. not far from Jer 4:4 and Deut 10:16f. A direct dependence upon *Dial.* 15-17 is thus not unlikely.

(41) Jer 7:21f/Jer 31:32 *(Dial.* 22:6)

Irenaeus: *Adv.Haer.* IV:17:3: a long LXX excerpt of Jer 7:21-24. Tertullian: No references.

(42) Jer 9:25 *(1. Apol.* 53:11, cf. above, pp. 70 - 72)

Irenaeus and Tertullian: No references.

(43) Jer 31:27 *(Dial.* 123:5)

Irenaeus and Tertullian: No references.

(44) Ezek 3:17-19 *(Dial.* 82:3)

Irenaeus and Tertullian: No references.

(45) Joel 3:1-2 *(Dial.* 87:6, cf. above, pp. 122f)

Irenaeus has one formal quotation of Joel 3:1f in *Adv.Haer* III:12:1. The context as well as the text-type of the quotation makes it quite plain that Irenaeus is excerpting directly from Acts 2 (his text agrees with Acts 2 against Justin's in *Dial.* 87:6). His allusion in *Adv. Haer.* III:17:1 may also refer to the Acts text, the remaining allusions are too vague to allow any inference concerning text-type *(Adv.Haer.* III:33:15; V:1:1; *Dem.* 89). Tertullian quotes a shortened version of Acts 2:17f in *Adv.Marc.* V:8:6 - he agrees with the text of Acts against *Dial.* 87. The remaining short quotations and allusions go with Acts 2, or are too vague to allow of any conclusion *(Adv.Marc.* V:4:2; 4:4; 11:4; 17:4; *De Res.* 10:2;63:7). There is thus no echo of Justin's deviant text in these two writers.

(46) Zech 2:15 *(Dial.* 119:3, cf. above, pp. 73f)

Irenaeus and Tertullian: No references.

(47) Zech 9:9 *(1. Apol.* 35:11, cf. above, pp. 74 -76)

Irenaeus quotes Zech 9:9 as «Isaiah» in *Dem.* 65, the text largely following Mt 21:5 (against *1.Apol.* 35:11). In *Adv. Haer.* III:19:2 he has an allusion (*super pullum asinae sedens*) which presupposes a Greek text ἐπὶ πῶλον ὄνου = *Dial.* 53:3 (and my suggested emendation of *1.Apol.*35:11, cf.above, p. 74, n.112). The same allusion recurs in *Adv.Haer.* IV:33:1-12. There seems to be no sure indication that Irenaeus had independent recourse to Justin s hypothetical source in *1.Apol.* 35:11. Tertullian's single allusion in *De coron.* 13:2 is too short to warrant any conclusions as to text-type.

(48) Zech 12:10-12 et.al. *(1. Apol.* 52:10-12, cf. above, pp. 76 - 78)

Irenaeus: Of the additional texts included in Justin's composite quotation, Is 43:5-7 is quoted in a LXX text in *Adv.Haer.* IV:14:1. Immediately following the quotation there is an allusion to Mt 24:28, which indicates that Irenaeus' attention to the Isaiah prophecy may have been called forth by the Matthean passage. Some dependence upon *1. Apol.* 52:10 is also possible, but no trace of Justin's other material is to be found in the context in Irenaeus. He has a short quotation of Zech 12:10 (*videbunt in quem compunxerunt*) in *Adv.Haer.* IV: 33:11, prefixed by an allusion to Dan 7:13. The same sequence is present in *Dial.* 14:8. This passage, as well as Irenaeus, deal with the traditional topic of the two parousias. There need not be any direct dependence on the literary level, cf. the arguments concerning this parallel in N. Brox, 'Zum literarischen Verhaltnis zwischen Justin und Irenaus', *ZNW* 58 (1967, pp. 121-28), pp. 124-28.
On Tertullian, see this Appendix nr. 4.

(49) Ps 19:6 *(1. Apol.* 54:9, cf. above, p. 82)

Irenaeus: No reference.
Tertullian quotes Ps 19:6f in *Adv.Marc.* IV:11:7. The text is LXX - except that Tertullian leaves out vs. 6b, exactly the stichos found in Justin's testimony text. There is thus no reason to suspect dependence upon Justin or his source here.

(50) Ps 82:6f *(Dial.* 124:2, cf. above, pp. 34f)

Irenaeus has two quotations of Ps 82:6f, *Adv.Haer.* III:19:1 and IV:38:4. In both cases the text is LXX, reading *homines.* In his exegesis, Irenaeus seems to echo Justin in *Dial.* 124. There is nothing which excludes that Irenaeus depends directly on *Dial.* 124. Tertullian: no quotation of Ps 82:7.

(51) Job 1:6 *(Dial.* 79:4)

Irenaeus and Tertullian: No references.

(52) Lam 4:20 *(1. Apol.* 55:5, cf. above, p. 162)

Irenaeus: *Dem.* 71 and *Adv.Haer.* III:10:3 quote a LXX text which excludes Justin's exegesis.
Tertullian has two non-LXX quotations in *Adv.Marc.* III:6:7 and *Adv.Prax.* 14:10, but not like Justin's and adapted to an entirely different exegesis. Tertullian is thus probably independent of Justin and Justin's source.

(53) Dan 2:34 (non-LXX and non-«θ», *Dial.* 70:1)

Irenaeus: *Adv.Haer.* V:26:1 quotes Dan 2:33f in a «θ» text. *Adv.Haer.* IV:20:11 has a shorter excerpt from the same text. Tertullian alludes to Dan 2:34f «θ» in *Adv.Jud.* 3:8, his allusions in *Adv.Marc.* III:7:3 = *Adv.Jud.* 14:3 do not allow any judgement on text-type.

(54) 1 Chron 17:13f *(Dial.* 118:2, cf, above, p. 205)

Irenaeus quotes the LXX of 2 Sam 7:12f in *Dem.* 36. Tertullian alludes to the LXX text of 1 Chron 17:11-14 in Adv.Marc. III:20:8f.

(55) The testimonies in *Dial.* 72 (cf. above, pp. 40 - 42)

Justin's Ps. Ezra quotation does not recur in any later writer except Lactantius. His text (see synopsis p. 40) is a rather faithful translation of Justin's, and there is no need to go behind Justin's *Dialogue* to find his source. The context in Lactantius suggests that he may be combining testimonies from different sources, i.a. Cyprian's *Testimonies,* cf. Prigent, *Justin,* pp. 176-78; Harris, *Testimonies* I, pp. 80f. I cannot see on what reasons Daniélou states: «Lactantius gives the same text with variants which prove that he did not take it from Justin» (*Theology,* p. 102).

Jer 11:19 recurs three times in Tertullian (see synopsis. Two of the passages are parallels: *Adv.Jud.* 10:11-16=*Adv.Marc.* III:19). On the level of text-type, the evidence is too scanty to warrant any safe conclusion. But the two parallel passages in Tertullian contain an interesting sequence of quotations, cf.this Appendix nr.9.

The Ps. Jer quotation occurs six times in Irenaeus. Three of these are apparently loose quotations from memory (no attribution), viz.*Adv.Haer.* IV:33:1.12; V:31:1. (In IV:33:1 the context clearly proves that we have to do with a quotation from memory). In the remaining three cases one have to do with formal quotations from a written source - these are included in the synopsis (p. 41). In *Adv.Haer* IV:22:1 and *Dem.* 78 the text is introduced as 'Jeremiah' (as in Justin). In *Adv.Haer.* III:20:4 the text is quoted as 'Isaiah', but A. Rousseau has marshalled good reasons to think that the reading in Irenaeus' original was 'Jeremiah' in this case also, cf. his remarks in the SC edition of *Adv.Haer.* III, vol. I, p. 354. - Was Irenaeus' source *Dial.* 72? Irenaeus' text has a significant variant (*Sanctus Israel* instead of *Dial.* 72:4: ὁ θεὸς ἀπὸ 'Ισραὴλ) and an addition to Justin' text (*uti salvaret eos,* = σῶσαι αὐτοὺς in A. Rousseau's Greek retroversion, SC ed. *ad loc.*). If the Parisinus has preserved Justin's text faithfully in *Dial.* 72:4, one shall have to assume that Irenaeus has had direct access to Justin's source. But of this one cannot be sure. The reading of the *Dialogue* is rather awkward, and many suggest that one should emend ὁ θεὸς ἀπὸ 'Ισραὴλ to ὁ ἅγιος 'Ισραὴλ, or ὁ θεὸς ἅγιος 'Ισραὴλ (the last alternative is printed without comment in Archambault's edition, following Otto. The emendation is accepted by Haeuser, Williams, and Falls in their respective translations, cf. also Prigent, *Justin,* p. 173. As far as I am aware, J. Daniélou is the only one who accepts the reading of the Parisinus without question, *Theology,* pp. 235f). Since casual omissions are not rare in the *Parisinus,* one cannot be sure, either, that Irenaeus' final words in the Ps. Jer text were not present in Justin's text as Irenaeus read it. It thus seems that a simple comparison of the quotations regarding their text is no sufficient basis for definite statements about dependence between the two authors.

(E) *A quotation sequence in Irenaeus:* Dem. 53-65

In *Dem.* 53-65 we find an interesting quotation sequence which has so many parallels in *1. Apol.* 32-35 that some sort of contact must be assumed. The following analytic table summarize the most relevant observations (the parallels with *1.Apol.* 32ff are marked with an asterisk.):

| Dem. 53-65 | Comments |
|---|---|
| *Is 7:14-17 (LXX) | A LXX expansion of Justin's non-LXX text in *1. Apol.* 33. |
| Is 61:1 (LXX) | Probably inspired from Lk 4:18. |
| Is 66:7 (LXX) | Cf. *Dial.* 85:8f: Is 66:5-11 (LXX), and comment below. |
| Is 9:5a (non-LXX, close to MT) ⌐→ Gen 1:26f | Different from Justin's non-LXX text in *1. Apol.* 35:1, and not adapted to Justin's exegesis. Probably derived from a parallel testimony source, cf. J. P. Smith, *Demonstration,* pp. 33f, and comment below. |
| *Is 9:4b-6 (LXX) | «Whose government is set upon his shoulders» (missing in the former non-LXX quotation) interpreted exactly as in *1. Apol.* 35:2. |

| *Gen 49:10f | The text of *1. Apol.* 32, but partly corrected according to the LXX text - cf. this Appendix, nr. 12. Irenaeus' exegesis echoes *1. Apol.* 32. |
|---|---|
| *Num 24:17 (non-LXX) | Dependent upon *1. Apol.* 32 (sequence) and *Dial.* 106:4 (text and exegesis). |
| *Is 11:1-10 (LXX) | A LXX substitute for the combined quotation in *1. Apol.* 32:12, cf. this Appendix, nr. 16. In Irenaeus partly original exegesis of the full LXX text. |
| Am 9:11 (LXX) | Cf. Acts 15:16. Not in Justin. |
| *Mic 5:1 (non-LXX) | No doubt inspired from *1. Apol.* 34, where the Micah quotation is Justin's own addition to his source. But Irenaeus seems to have consulted Matthew also, because his text has the final «my people Israel» of Mt 2:6 which is omitted by Justin. |
| Ps 132:10-12 (LXX) | Not in Justin, but cf. Acts 2:30. |
| *Zech 9:9 (non-LXX) | Very close to the text in Mt 21:5, but rather out-of-place in Irenaeus' context, thus very likely inspired from his source: *1. Apol.* 32-35. |

One first notices that Irenaeus' sequence correspond to Justin's in cases where I have argued that Justin deviates from his source: The *delayed* quotation of Zech 9:9, the addition of Mic 5:1. Further: Most of the added texts in Irenaeus are LXX excerpts, and some of them are well-known OT testimonies of the NT. There is thus every reason to believe that Irenaeus is drawing directly upon *1.Apol.* 32-35, partly modifying, correcting, and expanding Justin's quotation dossier, using the LXX and Matthew as his textual authorities.

Two quotations call for special comment. Irenaeus' non-LXX, hebraizing version of Is 9:5a is combined in an interesting way with Gen 1:26: The child born to us is identical with the one with whom the Father took counsel at the creation of man. This has no correspondence in *1.Apol.* 32-35, but has some relationship with *Dial.* 61f. Irenaeus may depend on the same source here as Justin in *Dial.* 61f . Cf above, p. 390.

Irenaeus' quotation of Is 66:7 is supposed by Bousset to be the primitive testimony nucleus behind Justin's long LXX excerpt in *Dial.* 85:8f (Is 66:5-11), *Schulbetrieb*, pp. 290/306. Bousset believes that Is 66:7 originally - as in Irenaeus - was a testimony on the virgin birth, but that Justin missed this point in his source. This is no doubt an attractive proposal. However, Is 66:7 is very close to Is 54:1, and this could suggest that the ecclesiastical interpretation of Justin is the most primitive one. (Would Justin have missed a virgin birth testimony, if it had been presented to him as such in his source?) Irenaeus may thus secondarily have extracted Is 66:7 as a virgin birth testimony from Justin's long quotation in *Dial.* 85. - I find it difficult to take a stand here, but am on the whole slightly inclined towards the latter alternative. Cf. also the suggestions of Prigent, *Justin*, pp. 101f.

The following tables comprise all formal quotations in Justin and the most obvious allusions (some very vague and uncertain allusions listed in the *Biblia Patristica* I are not included). The quotations are differentiated with respect to text-types. «LXX quotation» means a quotation which exhibits a basically LXX text-type. Listing in this rubrique does therefore not exclude minor variant readings.

In the column to the right I have given page references to the pages of the present study most relevant for the text in question. The conclusion of my discussion is briefly indicated within parenthesis. «Test.» means that the quotation found in Justin has been suggested to him by a testimony source. In such cases non-LXX quotations are likely to derive directly from the testimony source. Some summary comment is added to the tables.

| Genesis | Allusion or paraphrase | Non-LXX quotation | LXX quotation | Comment, pp. |
|---|---|---|---|---|
| 1:1-3 | | | *1. Apol.* 59:2-4 | 52f (tract on |
| 1:1f | | | *1. Apol.* 64:2 | borrowings |
| 1:2 | | | *1. Apol.* 60:6 | from Moses) |
| 1:26-28a | | | *Dial.* 62:1 | 389 (*Barn.* 5:5; |
| 2:7 | *Dial.* 40:1 | | | 6:12) |
| 2:8f | *Dial.* 86:1 | | | |
| 2:17 | *Dial.* | 81:3 | | |
| 2:21f | *Dial.* 84:2 | | | |
| 3:1-6 | *Dial.* 79:4 | | | |
| 3:1 | *Dial.* 103:5 | | | |
| 3:9 | *Dial.* 99:3 | | | |
| 3:14 | *Dial.* 79:4; 91:4; 112:2 | | | |
| 3:15 | *Dial.* 102:3 | | | |
| 3:22 | | | *Dial.* 62:3; 129:2 | |
| 4:4 | *Dial.* 19:3 | | | |
| 4:9 | *Dial.* 99:3 | | | |
| 4:20 | *Dial.* 117:5 | | | |
| 5:24 | *Dial.* 19:3 | | | 127 (Heb 11:5) |
| 6:1-5 | *1. Apol.* 5:2; *2. Apol.* 5:3 | | | 368f (*1 Enoch* 6ff) |
| 7 | *Dial.* 19:4 | | | |
| 7:16 | *Dial.* 127:1 | | | |
| 7:19f | *Dial.* 138:3 | | | |
| 9:3 | *Dial.* 20:2 | | | |
| 9:4f | *Dial.* 20:1 | | | |

| | | | | |
|---|---|---|---|---|
| 9:24-27 | *Dial.* 134:4; 139:1f | | *Dial.* 139:3 | 341-44 (non-LXX source?) |
| 11:5 | *Dial.* 127:1 | | | |
| 11:6 | | | *Dial.* 102:4 | |
| 11:7-9 | *Dial.* 130:3 | | | |
| 12:1 | *Dial.* 119:5 | | | |
| 14:18-20 | *Dial.* 19:4; 33:2 | | | 127 (Heb 7:1ff) |
| 14:18 | *Dial.* 113:5 | | | |
| 15:6 | *Dial.* 23:4; 119:6 | *Dial.* 92:3=Rom 4:3 | | 114f |
| 17:4f | *Dial.* 119:4 | | | |
| 17:5 | *Dial.* 11:5; 113:2 | | | 93 (Rom 4:17) |
| 17:11 | *Dial.* 23:4 | | | |
| 17:12-14 | *Dial.* 41:4 | | | |
| 17:12 | *Dial.* 10:3 | | | |
| 17:14b | | *Dial.* 10:3; 23:4 | | |
| 17:15 | *Dial.* 113:2 | | | |
| 17:22 | | | *Dial.* 127:1 | |
| 18:1-3 . . . 19:27f | | | *Dial.* 56:2 | |
| 18:1f | *Dial.* 56:10; 58:3. 10; 59:1 | | *Dial.* 86:5; 126:4 | |
| 18:6-8 | *Dial.* 57:1 | | | |
| 18:13f | | | *Dial.* 56:17; 126:4 | |
| 18:14 | *Dial.* 56:6 | | | |
| 18:16f | | | *Dial.* 56:17 | |
| 18:16 | | | *Dial.* 126:4 | |
| 18:17 | *Dial.* 126:5 | | | |
| 18:20-23a | | | *Dial.* 56:18 | |
| 18:20f | *Dial.* 129:1 | | | |
| 18:33-19:1 | | | *Dial.* 56:19 | |
| 19:10 | | | *Dial.* 56:19 | |
| 19:16-25a | | | *Dial.* 56:19-21 | |
| 19:23-25 | | | *Dial.* 56:12 | |
| 19:24 | *Dial.* 60:5 | | | 209, n. 62 |
| | *1. Apol.* 53:8; | | *Dial.* 56:23; 127:5; 129:1 | (test. source?) |
| 21:2 | *Dial.* 84:4 | | | |
| 21:9-12 | | | *Dial.* 56:7 | |
| 21:12 | | | *Dial.* 56:8 | |
| 22:17 | *Dial.* 120:2 | | | |
| 26:4 | | | *Dial.* 120:1 | |
| 28:10-19 | | | *Dial.* 58:11-13 | |
| 28:12f | *Dial.* 86:2 | | | |

| | | | | |
|---|---|---|---|---|
| 28:14 | | | *Dial.* 120:1 | |
| 28:18 | *Dial.* 86:2 | | | |
| 29:16-30 | *Dial.* 134:3 | | | |
| 29:17 | *Dial.* 134:5 | | | |
| 30:25-43 | *Dial.* 134:5 | | | |
| 30:37f | *Dial.* 86:2 | | | |
| 31:10-13 | | | *Dial.* 58:4f | |
| 31:11 | *Dial.* 56:10; 58:3; 60:5` | | | |
| 31:13/35:1 | *Dial.* 60:5; 86:2? | | | |
| 31:19-34 | *Dial.* 134:5 | | | |
| 32:11 | *Dial.* 86:2 | | | |
| 32:16 | *Dial.* 112:4 | | | |
| 32:23-31 | | | *Dial.* 58:6f | |
| 32:25 | *Dial.* 58:10; 59:1 | | *Dial.* 126:3 | |
| 32:26 | *Dial.* 125:5 | | | |
| 32:29 | *Dial.* 75:2; 106:3; 125:3 | | | |
| 32:31 | | | *Dial.* 126:3 | |
| 35:6-10 | 35:7: *Dial.* 60:5 | | *Dial.* 58:8 | |
| 36:1 | *Dial.* 119:4 | | | |
| 38:25f | *Dial.* 86:6 | | | |
| 49:8-12 | | | *Dial.* 52:2 | |
| 49:10f | vs. 10: *1. Apol.* 32:2.4; *Dial.* 52:4; 126:1<br><br>vs. 11: *1. Apol.* 32:5; *Dial.* 63:2; 69:2; 76:2 | *1. Apol.* 32:1; 32:4f; 32:7.9; 54:5;<br><br>*Dial.* 120:3f | vs. 10: *Dial.* 120:3<br><br>vs. 11: *Dial.* 53:1; 54:1 | 25 - 29 |

It is evident that Justin had a complete Genesis MS to his disposal and that he was well read in it. This is especially obvious in *Dial.* 56ff. Testimony sources may be discerned in some cases, cf. the remarks in the column to the right. Testimony sources may also be contemplated for the non-LXX versions of Gen 2:17 and 17:14, cf. Smit Sibinga *ad locc.*

| Exodus: | Allusion or paraphrase | Non-LXX quotation | LXX quotation | Comment, pp. |
|---|---|---|---|---|
| 2:23a ... 3:16 | | | *Dial.* 59:2 | 47 - 50 |
| 3:2-6 | *Dial.* 59:1; 60:1; 127:4 | | | |
| 3:2-4a | | | *Dial.* 60:4 | |
| 3:2/14f/ 6/10 | | *1. Apol.* 63:7f; *1. Apol.* 63:11.17 | | 47 - 50 (test. source). |
| 3:5 | | *1. Apol.* 62:3 | | |
| 6:2-4 | | | *Dial.* 126:2 | |
| 6:3 | *Dial.* 56:11; 75:1.4 | | | |

| | | | | |
|---|---|---|---|---|
| 7:12.22 and 8:7 | *Dial.* 69:1; 79:4 | | | |
| 12:1-7 | *Dial.* 40:1; 111:3 | | | |
| 12:9 | *Dial.* 40:3 | | | |
| 12:13 | *Dial.* 111:4 | | | |
| 13:9.16 | *Dial.* 46:5 | | | |
| 13:21 | *Dial.* 131:3 | | | |
| 14 | *Dial.* 131:3 | | | |
| 14:16 | *Dial.* 86:1; 138:2 | | | |
| 14:19 | *Dial.* 131:6 | | | |
| 15:23-25 | *Dial.* 86:1 | | | |
| 15:27 | *Dial.* 86:5 (non-LXX) | | | 445 |
| 16:3 | *Dial.* 126:6 | | | |
| 16:4 | *Dial.* 131:3 | | | |
| 16:7 | *Dial.* 61:1 | | | |
| 16:13-16 | *Dial.* 73:6 | | | |
| 16:13 | *Dial.* 131:6 | | | |
| 17:5f | *Dial.* 86:1; 131:6 | | | |
| 17:9-16 | *Dial.* 90:4; 91:3; . 97:1; 111:1; 112:2; 131:4 | | | 394 (test. source) |
| 17:16 | | *Dial.* 49:8 | | |
| 19:16-18 | *Dial.* 67:9f | | | |
| 20:4 | *Dial.* 94:1; 112:1 | | | |
| 20:18f | *Dial.* 67:9 | | | |
| 20:22a/ 23:20f | | *Dial.* 75:1 | | |
| 23:21 | *Dial.* 75:2 | | | |
| 32:1-6 | *Dial.* 19:5; 73:6 132:1 | | | |
| 32:6/ Deut 32:15 | | *Dial.* 20:1 | | 117f (test. source) |

Justin's paraphrases of Exodus material are concentrated in *Dial.* 40 with doublettes (paschal lamb typology); *Dial.* 86 (baptismal types); *Dial.* 9lff (battle against Amalek) and *Dial.* 131 (miracles during desert wandering). In all these cases we have seen reasons to suspect testimony sources. The same is true of the theophany in the burning bush (Ex 3) and the guardian angel motif (Ex 23:20f etc). It is only in *Dial.* 59f (par. *Dial.* 126) that direct recourse to the Exodus LXX can be posited with certainty.

| Leviticus: | Allusion or paraphrase | Non-LXX quotation | LXX quotation | Comment, pp. |
|---|---|---|---|---|
| 12:3 | *Dial.* 27:5? | | | |
| 14:10 | *Dial.* 41:1 | | | |
| 16:5 | *Dial.* 40:4; 111:1 (non-LXX) | | | 307 - 311 |
| 23:6 | *Dial.* 14:3 | | | |
| 26:40f | | | *Dial.* 16:1 | |

The quotation in *Dial.* 16:1 is probably copied directly from a Leviticus MS, cf. the introduction: καὶ ἐν τῷ Λευιτικῷ. But probably Justin was guided to this text by the testimony collection employed in *Dial.* 15f. In none of the remaining allusions can a direct use of Leviticus be proved. In *Dial.* 40f (par. 111) I have posited testimony material.

| Numeri: | Allusion or paraphrase | Non-LXX quotation | LXX quotation | Comment, pp. |
|---|---|---|---|---|
| 11:4 | *Dial.* 126:6 | | | |
| 11:23 | | | *Dial.* 126:6 | |
| 11:31f | *Dial.* 131:6 | | | |
| 12:7 | *Dial.* 46:3; 56:1; 79:4; 130:1 | | | 126 |
| 13:6 | *Dial.* 113:1? | | | |
| 13:16 | *Dial.* 75:2; 106:3; 113:1 | | | 419f *(Barn.* 12:8-10) |
| 14:6 | *Dial.* 113:1 | | | |
| 15:37-40 | *Dial.* 46:5 | | | |
| 17:20-23 | *Dial.* 86:4 | | | |
| 20:8 | *Dial.* 86:1 | | | |
| 20:11 | *Dial.* 131:6 | | | |
| 21:6-9 | *1. Apol.* 60:2-4 | | | 53 and 398, n. 59 (test. source) |
| | *Dial.* 91:4; 94:1; 112:1; 131:4 | | | 397 - 399 (test. source) |
| 24:17/Is 11:1/51:5 | | *1. Apol.* 32:12 | | 50 - 52 (test.) |
| 24:17 | *Dial.* 126:1 | *Dial.* 106:4 | | 50 - 52 (test.) |
| 27:18 | *Dial.* 49:6 | | | |
| 28:9f | *Dial.* 27:5? | | | |
| 33:9 | *Dial.* 86:5 | | | |

The LXX quotation of Num 11:23 is given at the end of a summary paraphrase of Num 11:1-22; this suggests that Justin has a Num MS before him in this case. In the remaining cases Justin seems to rely heavily on traditional testimony material.

| Deuter-onomy: | Allusion or paraphrase | Non-LXX quotation | LXX quotation | Comment |
|---|---|---|---|---|
| 4:19 | *Dial.* 55:1; 121:2 | | | |
| 4:34 | *Dial.* 131:3 | | | |
| 5:15 | *Dial.* 11:1 | | | |
| 6:8f | *Dial.* 46:5 | | | |
| 6:13f | | *Dial.* 125:4 | | 101 (= Mt 4:10) |
| 8:4 | *Dial.* 131:6 | | | haggadic addition |
| 10:16f | | | *Dial.* 16:1 | 70 - 72 (test. source related to *Barn.* 9:5) |
| 10:17 | *Dial.* 55:1 | | | |
| 11:18 | *Dial.* 46:5 | | | |
| 14:2 | *Dial.* 119:4 ? | | | |
| 16:5f | *Dial.* 40:2 | | | |
| 21:23 | *Dial.* 32:1; 89:2; 90:1; 94:5 | *Dial.* 96:1=Gal 3:13 | | 118f |
| 24:16/ Ezek 14:20 etc. | | *Dial.* 45:3; 140:3 | | 67 - 69 (test.) |
| 25:19 | *Dial.* 131:4 ? | | | |
| 27:26 | | *Dial.* 95:1=Gal 3:13 | | 118f |
| 30:15/19 | | *1. Apol.* 44:1 | | 230f (test.) |
| 31:2f | | | *Dial.* 126:6 | |
| 31:16-18 | | | *Dial.* 74:4 | 214f |
| 32:4/ Ps 92:16 | | *Dial.* 92:5 | | |
| 32:7-9 | | | *Dial.* 131:1 | 29f (test. text is LXX; long quot. has one non-LXX var.) |
| 32:8 | | | *Dial.* 131:1 | |
| Ex 32:6/ Deut 32:15 | | *Dial.* 20:1 | | 117f (test.) |
| 32:16-23 | | | *Dial.* 119:2 | 53 (Rom 10:19) |
| 32:20 | *Dial.* 20:4; 27:4; 119:6; 123:3; 130:3 | | | |
| 32:22 | | *1. Apol.* 60:9 | | 52f (test.) |
| 32:43 | | | *Dial.* 130:1.4 | 117 (Rom 15:10) |
| 33:7 | *Dial.* 100:1 ? | | | |
| 33:13-17 | *Dial.* 100:1 | | *Dial.* 91:1 | |
| 33:17 | *Dial.* 91:2; 126:1 | | *Dial.* 91:3 | |
| 34:9 | *Dial.* 49:6 ? | | | |

The long LXX quotations prove that Justin had access to a Deut MS. At the same time they betray his dependence on the testimony tradition: In all cases one can with good reason suspect a traditional testimony nucleus — even in the case of the «Joseph» testimony Deut 33:17. Justin is thus hardly original in his exploitation of Deuteronomy.

Joshua - 2 Kings:

| Joshua | Allusion or paraphr. | Non-LXX quotation | LXX quotation | Comment |
|---|---|---|---|---|
| 2:18-21 | *Dial.* 111:4 | | | 128 *(1. Clem.* 12:7f ?) |
| 5:2f | *Dial.* 24:2; 113:6; 114:4 | | | |
| 5:6 | *Dial.* 113:3; 115:5 | | | |
| 5:13-6:2 | *Dial.* 61:1 | | *Dial.* 62:5 | |
| 10:12 | *Dial.* 113:4; 132:1 | | | |
| **1 Sam** | | | | |
| 1:20 | *Dial.* 84:4 | | | |
| 5f | *Dial.* 132:2f | | | Haggadic add. or mistake |
| 28:11-15 | *Dial.* 105:4 | | | |
| **2 Sam** | | | | |
| 7:12-16 | *Dial.* 68:5 (non-LXX) | | | |
| 11f | *Dial.* 141:3f | | | |
| **1 Kings** | | | | |
| 6 | *Dial.* 34:7 | | | |
| 8:10f | *Dial.* 127:3 | | | |
| 11:3 | *Dial.* 34:8 | | | |
| 18 | *Dial.* 69:1 | | | |
| 18:21 | *Dial.* 27:4 ? | | | |
| 19:10/ 14/18 | *Dial.* 46:6 | *Dial.* 39:1 = Rom 11:2-4 | | |
| **2 Kings** | | | | |
| 6:1-7 | *Dial.* 86:6 | | | |
| 19:32-37 | *Dial.* 83:1 | | | = Is 37:33-38 |

One notices that there is only one formal quotation which seems copied directly from a Bible MS, viz. Josh 5:13-6:2. For the rest of the material, it is difficult to assess how direct Justin's knowledge of the historical narratives in these books was. I have surmised above that in *Dial.* 111:4 he has had access to the LXX text, while on the other hand his paraphrase of 2 Kings 6:1-7 in *Dial.* 86 may well derive from the source employed for the rest of that chapter.

| Isaiah: | Earlier ref. | Allusion | Non-LXX quot. | LXX quotation | Comment |
|---|---|---|---|---|---|
| 1:3f | | | | *1. Apol.* 37:1; 63:2.12 | 158 |
| 1:7f | | *Dial.* 52:4 | | | 53f (test.) |
| 1:7/ Jer 50:3 | | *Dial.* 16:2 | *1. Apol.* 47:5 | | |
| 1:7 | | *Dial.* 108:3 | | | |

| | | | | | |
|---|---|---|---|---|---|
| 1:9 | Rom 9:29 | *Dial* 32:2; 55:3 | *1. Apol* 53:7; *Dial* 140:3 | | 67 - 69 (test.) |
| 1:11-15/ Is 58:6f | *Barn.* 2:5 (Is 1:11-13) | | *1. Apol* 37:5-8 | | 55f (test.) |
| 1:13 | *Barn.* 15:8 | *Dial* 13:1 | | | |
| 1:15 | | *Dial* 12:3; 27:2 | | | |
| 1:16-20 | *1. Clem.* 8:4 | | | *1. Apol* 44:3-5; 61:7f | 230f (test.) |
| 1:16 | | *Dial* 12:3; 13:1; 14:1; 44:4 | | *Dial* 18:2 | |
| 1:23 | *Did.* 5:2 *Barn.* 20:2 | *Dial* 27:2 | *Dial* 82:4 | | (test.) |
| 2:2-6 et al. | | *Dial* 24:3 | | | 172 (test.) |
| 2:3f | 2:3: KP fragm. 1 | *Dial* 24:1; 34:1; 43:1 | | *1. Apol* 39:1 | 158f (test.) |
| 2:5f | | | | *Dial* 135:6 | |
| 3:9-15 | | | | *Dial* 133:2 | 30 - 32 (test.) |
| 3:9-11 | | | | *Dial* 17:2 | |
| 3:9f | *Barn.* 6:7 | 3:10: *Dial* 17:3 119:3 | *Dial* 136:2; 137:3 | | |
| 3:16 | | *Dial* 27:3 | | | (test.?) |
| 5:18-25 | | | | *Dial* 133:4 | 30 - 32 (test.) |
| 5:18-20 | | | 5:20: *1. Apol* 49:7 | *Dial* 17:2 | |
| 5:21 | *Barn.* 4:11 | *Dial* 39:5 | | | |
| 6:8 | | *Dial* 75:3 | | | |
| 6:10 | | *Dial* 12:2; 33:1; 69:4 | | | 120f (test.) |
| 7:10-17/ Is 8:4 | | | *Dial* 43:5f; 66:2f | | 32 - 34 (two test. sources) |
| 7:14 | Mt 1:23 | *1. Apol* 54:8; *Dial* passim | *1. Apol* 33:1.4; D. 43:8=Mt 1:23. *Dial* 43:8; 67:1 71:3; 84:3 with Aquila's reading | *Dial* 43:5; 66:2; 67:1; 68:6; 71:3; 84:1 | |
| 8:4 | | | | *Dial* 77:2f; 78:9 | |
| 9:5a | | | *1. Apol* 35:2 | | 146 (test.) |
| 9:5b | | *Dial* 76:3; 126:1 | | | 390 (test.?) |
| 11:1-3 | | | | *Dial* 87:2 | |
| 11:1 | | *Dial* 86:4; 100:4; 126:1 | *1. Apol* 32:12 in comb. test. | | |
| 11:2 | | *Dial* 39:2 | | | |
| 14:1 | | | *Dial* 123:1 | | 349 (test.) |

| | | | | | |
|---|---|---|---|---|---|
| 16:1 | *Barn.* 11:2 | | *Dial.* 114:5 in comb. test. | | 69f (test.) |
| 19:24f | | *Dial.* 125:5 | | *Dial.* 123:5 | 350f |
| 26:2f | | *Dial.* 24:2 (non-LXX) | | | 333 (test.) |
| 27:1 | | *Dial.* 91:4; 100:4; 112:2 | | | 399 (test.) |
| 28:16 | Rom 9:33; 10:11; 1 Pet 2:4.6; *Barn.* 6:4 | *Dial.* 114:4; 126:1 | | | 125f (test.?) |
| 29:13f | | | | *Dial.* 78:11 | |
| 29:13 | Mt 15:8f; | *Dial.* 27:4; 39:5; 48:2; 80:4; 140:2 | | | 57f (Mt) |
| 29:14 | 1 Cor 1:19; *2. Clem.* 3:5 | *Dial.* 38:2 | | *Dial.* 32:5; 123:4 | 57f (Paul?) |
| 29:18f | | *Dial.* 12:2 | | | |
| 30:1-5 | | | | *Dial.* 79:3 | |
| 30:9 | | *Dial.* 130:3 | | | |
| 33:13-19 | 33:16-18: *Barn.* 11:5 | | | *Dial.* 70:2f | |
| 33:16 | | *Dial.* 70:1; 78:6 | | | |
| 35:1-7 | | | | *Dial.* 69:5 | 58f (test.) |
| 35:5f | Mt 11:5 | *1. Apol.* 22:6; 54:10 *Dial.* 69:3 | *1. Apol.* 48:2 | | |
| 39:8 - 40:17 | 40:3: Mt 3:3 (par.) | | | *Dial.* 50:3-5 | 101 (Mt/Lk) |
| 42:1-4 | Mt 12:18-21 | | *Dial.* 123:8 | *Dial.* 135:2 | 60f (test.) |
| 42:1 | | *Dial.* 126:1 | | | |
| 42:5-13 | | | | *Dial.* 65:4-6 | |
| 42:6f | *Barn.* 14:7 | | *Dial.* 122:3 | *Dial.* 26:2 | 62 (test.) |
| 42:8 | | | | *Dial.* 65:1 | |
| 42:16/ 43:10 | | | *Dial.* 122:1 | | 348 (test.) |
| 42:19f | | *Dial.* 27:4; 123:2 | | *Dial.* 123:3 | |
| 43:5f | | | *1. Apol.* 52:10 in comb. testimony | | 76 (test.) |
| 43:15 | | | *Dial.* 135:1 | | 350 (test.) |
| Ezek 37:7f /Is 45:23 | Is 45:23: Rom 14:11; Phil 2:11 | | *1. Apol.* 52:6 | | 436 (test.) |
| 49:6 | Lk 2:32; Acts 13:47. Is 49:6f: *Barn.* 14:8 | | | *Dial.* 121:4 | 348f (test.?) |

| | | | | | |
|---|---|---|---|---|---|
| 49:8 | 2 Cor 6:2 | | | *Dial.* 122:5 | 348f (test.?) |
| 50:4 | | | | *Dial.* 102:5 | |
| 50:6-8 | 50:6f: *Barn.* 5:14; 7:8 | 50:6: *Dial.* 89:3 | | *1. Apol.* 38:2f | 129 (test.?) |
| 51:4f | | 51:4: *Dial.* 11:4; 34:1; 43:1 | | *Dial.* 11:3 | 50-52 (test.) |
| 51:5 | | | *1. Apol.* 32:12 in combined test. | | |
| 52:5 | Rom 2:24 *et al.* | *Dial.* 117:3 | *Dial.* 17:2 | | 114 (test.?) |
| 52:10-54:6 | | | | *Dial.* 13:2-9 | |
| 52:13-53:8 | | | | *1. Apol.* 50:3-11 | |
| 53:8-12 | | | | *1. Apol.* 51:1-5 | |
| 52:15-53:1 | 52:15: Rom 15:21 | | | *Dial.* 118:4 | 95 (Paul) |
| 53:1f | Rom 10:16 | | | *Dial.* 42:2 | 116 (Paul) |
| 53:1 | | *Dial.* 42:3 | | *Dial.* 114:2 | |
| 53:2-9 | | *Dial.* 32:2 | | | |
| 53:2f | | *1. Apol.* 52:3; *Dial.* 14:8; 32:1; 36:6; 49:2; 85:1; 88:8; 100:2; 110:2 | | | |
| 53:3 | | *Dial.* 89:3 | | | |
| 53:4 | | *Dial.* 126:1 | | | |
| 53:5 | *Barn.* 5:2 | *Dial.* 17:1; 32:2; 43:3; 63:2; 95:3; 137:1 | | | 124f (test.?) |
| 53:7 | *Barn.* 5:2 | *Dial.* 72:3; 89:3; 90:1; 111:3; 114:2 | | | 124f (test.?) |
| 53:8 | | *Dial.* 89:3 | | *Dial.* 43:3; 63:2; 68:4; 76:2 | 199f (test.?) |
| 53:9 | | *Dial.* 97:2; 102:7 | | | |
| 53:12 | | *Dial.* 89:3 | *1. Apol.* 50:2 | | 62f (test.) |
| 54:1 | Gal 4:27; *2. Clem.* 2:1 | | *1. Apol.* 53:5 | | 119 (test.?) |
| 54:8f | | | *Dial.* 138:1f | | 340 (test.) |
| 55:3-13 | 55:3: Acts 13:34 | 55:3: *Dial.* 11:2; 118:2 | 55:3-5: *Dial.* 12:1 | *Dial.* 14:4-7 | 63f (test.) |
| 57:1-4 | | 57:1: *Dial.* 16:4; 73:6?; 119:3. | | *Dial.* 16:5 | 31 (test.) |
| | | | | Is 57:1f: *1. Apol.* 48:5f | |
| | | 57:2: *Dial.* 97:2; 118:1 | | 57:1: *Dial.* 110:6 | |
| 57:5 | | *Dial.* 46:6? | | | |
| 58:1-11 | | | | *Dial.* 15:1-6 | 55-57 (test.) |

| | | | | | |
|---|---|---|---|---|---|
| 58:2 | | | *1. Apol.* 35:3 in combined test. | | 65 - 67 (test.) |
| 58:6f | *Barn.* 3:3 | *Dial.* 40:4 | *1. Apol.* 37:8 in combined test. | | 55 - 57 (test.) |
| 58:13f | | 58:13: *Dial.* 12:3 | | *Dial.* 27:1 | 173 (test.) |
| 60:1/19f | Rev 21:11.23 | *Dial.* 113:5 | | | |
| 61:1 | | *Dial.* 12:2 | | | |
| 62:10-63:6 | | | | *Dial.* 26:3f | 172 (test.) |
| 62:12 | *Barn.* 14:6 | *Dial.* 119:3 | | | |
| 63:15-64:11 | | | | *Dial.* 25:2-5 | 172 (test.) |
| 63:17 | | | *1. Apol.* 52:12 in comb. test. | | 77 (test.) |
| 63:18 | Lk 21:24 | *Dial.* 25:1.6 | | | |
| 64:9-11 | | | | *1. Apol.* 47:2f | 172 (test.) |
| 64:10 | | | | *1. Apol.* 52:12 | 77 (test.) |
| 65:1-3 | | | | *1. Apol.* 49:2-4; *Dial.* 24:3f | 65 - 67 (tcst.) |
| 65:1 | Rom 10:20f | *Dial.* 119:4 | | | |
| 65:2 | | *Dial.* 130:3 ? | *1. Apol.* 35:3 in comb. test.; *1. Apol.* 38:1; *Dial.* 114:2 | *Dial.* 97:2 | |
| 65:8-9 | | | | *Dial.* 136:1 | 351f (test.?) |
| 65:9-12 | | *Dial.* 136:2 (vs. 12) | | *Dial.* 135:4 | |
| 65:17-25 | | | | *Dial.* 81:1f | |
| 65:17 | 2 Pet 3:13 | *Dial.* 131:6 | | | |
| 65:22 | | | *Dial.* 81:3 | | 67 (test.) |
| 66:1 | Acts 7:49f; *Barn.* 16:2 | | *1. Apol.* 37:3f; *Dial.* 22:11 | | 124 (test?) |
| 66:5-11 | | 66:5: *Dial.* 96:2 | | *Dial.* 85:8f | 452f (test?) |
| 66:23f | | | | *Dial.* 44:3 | 67 - 69 (test.) |
| 66:24 | Mk 9:48; *2. Clem.* 7:6; 17:5 | *Dial.* 130:2 | *1. Apol.* 52:8; *Dial.* 140:3 | | |

It is evident that Justin relies heavily on traditional testimonies in his employment of his LXX Isaiah MS. Very seldom has Justin exploited new texts not pointed out to him in the testimony tradition. His argument concerning Is 42:8 in *Dial.* 65 may be an example of this. But even here the text occurs in conjunction with a traditional testimony: Is 42:6f.

| Jeremiah: | Earlier ref. | Allusion | Non-LXX quot. | LXX quotation | Comment |
|---|---|---|---|---|---|
| 2:13 | *Barn.* 11:2 in comb. test. | *Dial.* 14:1; 140:1f | *Dial.* 19:2; *Dial.* 114:5 in combined test. | | 69f (test. source related to *Barn.*) |
| 3:8 | | | *Dial.* 114:5 in combined test. | | |
| 3:17 | Rev 22:2 | *Dial.* 24:3 | | | |
| 4:3f | *Barn.* 9:5 | *Dial.* 15:7 | | *Dial.* 28:2 | 70 - 72 (test.) |
| 4:22 | | *Dial.* 27:4; 32:5; 36:2; 123:4; 130:3 | | | |
| 6:16 | Mt 11:29; 2. *Clem.* 6:7 | *Dial.* 123:4 | | | |
| 7:18 | Acts 7:42 | *Dial.* 136:3 | | | |
| 7:21f | 7:22f: *Barn.* 2:7 | | *Dial.* 22:6 | | 111 (test.) |
| 9:24f | Acts 7:51; *Barn.* 9:5 | | 9:25: 1. *Apol.* 53:11 | *Dial.* 28:3 | 70 - 72 (test.) |
| 11:19 | | | | *Dial.* 72:2 | 40 - 42 (test.) |
| 17:9-11 | | 1. *Apol.* 43:2? | | | |
| 31:15 | Mt 2:18 | | *Dial.* 78:8 = Mt 2:18 | | 120 |
| 31:27 | | *Dial.* 136:2 | *Dial.* 123:5 | | 352 (test.?) |
| 31:31f | Heb 8:8-12; 10:16f | *Dial.* 24:1; 34:1; 43:1; 67:9; 118:2 | | *Dial.* 11:3 | 72f (test.) |
| 50:3 | | | 1. *Apol.* 47:5 | | 53f (test.) |

In Jeremiah, Justin seems never to have gone outside the dossier of testimonies transmitted to him by tradition.

| Ezekiel: | Earlier ref. | Allusion | Non-LXX quot. | LXX quotation | Comment |
|---|---|---|---|---|---|
| 1:5 | Rev 4:6 | *Dial.* 126:1? | | | |
| 3:7 | | *Dial.* 27:4? | | | |
| 3:17-19 (=33:7-9) | | | *Dial.* 82:3 | | |
| 14:20/18/ 14 etc. | 2. *Clem.* 6:8 | | *Dial.* 44:2; 45:3; 140:3 | | 67 - 69 (test.) |
| 16:3 | | | | *Dial.* 77:4 | |
| 20:19-26 | | 20:12/20: *Dial.* 19:6 | | *Dial.* 21:2 | |
| 33:11 | 1. *Clem.* 8:2 | 1. *Apol.* 15:8? | | | 127f (possibly no ref. to Ezek) |
| 33:12-20 | | *Dial.* 47:5 | | | |
| 36:12 | | *Dial.* 136:2 | | *Dial.* 123:6 | 351 (test.?) |

| 37:7f/<br>Is 45:23 |  |  | 1. Apol. 52:5 |  | 436 (test.) |
|---|---|---|---|---|---|
| 37:12-14 |  | Dial. 80:5 |  |  |  |
| 45:17-25 |  | Dial. 118:2 |  |  | 205f (test.) |

In a single case, Justin gives an extensive LXX excerpt, but he is obviously led to this text by a traditional testimony alluded to in *Dial.* 19:6. His reliance on the testimony tradition seems to be as complete as in Jeremiah.

| Dodeka-<br>propheton: | Earlier ref. | Allusion | Non-LXX quot. | Καιγε quotation | Comment |
|---|---|---|---|---|---|
| Hos 1:9 | 1 Pet 2:10;<br>cf. Rom 9:25f | Dial. 19:5 |  |  | 115 (Paul?) |
| Hos 10:6 |  |  |  | Dial. 103:4 | 437 (test.) |
| Joel 2:12f |  |  | 1. Apol. 52:11 in<br>combined test. |  | 76f (test.) |
| Joel 3:1f | Acts 2:17ff |  | Dial. 87:6 |  | 122f (test.) |
| Am 5:18-<br>6:7 | 5:25-27:<br>Acts 7:42f |  |  | Dial. 22:2-5 | 123f (Acts?) |
| Jon 3:5-10 |  | Dial. 107:2<br>(καιγε) |  |  | |
| Jon 4:6-9 |  | Dial. 107:3 |  |  | 120 |
| Jon 4:10f |  |  |  | Dial. 107:4 | |
| Mic 4:1-7 |  | 4:3f.6:<br>Dial. 110:3-5 |  | Dial. 109:2f | |
| Mic 5:1 | Mt 2:6 |  | 1. Apol. 34:1;<br>Dial. 78:1 |  | 119 (Mt) |
| Zech 2:10 | Mt 24:31;<br>Did. 10:5 |  | 1. Apol. 52:10 in<br>combined test. |  | 76 - 78 (test.) |
| Zech 2:12 |  | Dial. 137:2 |  |  | |
| Zech 2:14-<br>3:2 |  |  |  | Dial. 115:1 | 73f (test.) |
| Zech 2:15 |  |  | Dial. 119:3 |  | |
| Zech 3:1f | Rev 12:9;<br>20:2 | Dial. 103:5 | Dial. 79:4 |  | |
| Zech 3:1-7 |  | Dial. 116:1-3;<br>117:3 |  |  | |
| Zech 3:8 |  | Dial. 126:1 |  |  | |
| Zech 6:12 | Lk 1:78 | Dial. 100:4;<br>126:1 | Dial. 106:4;<br>121:2 |  | Quotations too<br>short to exhibit<br>text-type |
| Zech 9:9 | Mt 21:5;<br>Jn 12:15 |  | 1. Apol. 35:11 | Dial. 53:3 | 74 - 76 (test.) |
| Zech 12:<br>10-12 etc. |  | Dial. 32:2<br>(καιγε?) | 1. Apol. 52:11f,<br>combined test. |  | 74 - 76 (test.) |
| 12:10f |  | Dial. 118:1 |  |  | |

| | | | | | |
|---|---|---|---|---|---|
| 12:10 | Jn 19:37; Rev 1:7; *Barn.* 7:8f | *Dial.* 14:8; 64:7 | | | |
| 12:12 | Mt 24:30 | *Dial.* 121:2; 126:1 | | | |
| Zech 13:7 | Mt 26:31; *Barn.* 5:12 | *Dial.* 53:5 | | *Dial.* 53:6 | 121 (Mt) |
| Mal 1;10-12 | *Did.* 14:3 | 1:11: *Dial* 116:3; 117:4; 1:12: *Dial* 41:3; 120:4 | *Dial.* 28:5; 41:2; 117:1 | | 439f (test.) |
| Mal 3:23 | Mt 17:11 | *Dial.* 8:4?; 49:2f; 118:1 | | | |

The same remark applies as with Jeremiah and Ezekiel, except that Justin's MS in this case with certainty can be ascribed to the *kaige* recension.

| Psalms: | Earlier ref. | Allusion | Non-LXX quot. | LXX quotation | Comment |
|---|---|---|---|---|---|
| 1:1 - 2:12 | | | | *1. Apol.* 40:8-19 | 159f (test.) |
| 1:3 | *Barn.* 11:8 | | | *Dial.* 86:4 | |
| 2:7f | *1. Clem.* 36:4 | | | *Dial.* 122:6 | |
| 2:7 | Lk 3:22 (Western); Acts 13:38; Heb 1:5 | *Dial.* 61:1; 126:1 | | *Dial.* 88:8; 103:6 | 199 (Lk?) |
| 3:5f | | | | *Dial.* 97:1 | |
| 3:6 | *1. Clem.* 26:2 | | *1. Apol.* 38:5 in comb. test. | | 80 - 82 (test.) |
| 8:4 | | | | *Dial.* 114:3 | |
| 14:3 | | | *Dial.* 27:3 in selective quot. of Rom 3:10-18 | | 93 (Paul) |
| 18:44f | 18:45: *Barn.* 9:1 | | | *Dial.* 28:6 | 129 (test.) |
| 18:46 | | *Dial.* 27:4? | | | |
| 19:2-7 | 19:2-4: *1. Clem.* 27:7 | | | *Dial.* 64:8 | 82 (test. Ps 19:6) |
| 19:3-6 | | | | *1. Apol.* 40:1-4 | 116 (Rom 10:18 for Ps 19:5) |
| 19:5 | Rom 10:18 | | | *Dial.* 42:1 | |
| 19:6 | | *Dial.* 69:3; 75:3; 76:7; 125:2 (all non-LXX) | *1. Apol.* 54:9 | | |
| 19:8 | | *Dial.* 30:1-3; 34:1 | | | |
| 19:10 | | *Dial.* 30:1 | | | |
| 19:11 | | *Dial.* 30:2 | | | |
| 19:14f | | *Dial.* 30:2f | | | |

| | | | | | |
|---|---|---|---|---|---|
| 22:2-24 | | | | Dial. 98:2-5 | |
| 22:2f | | | | Dial. 99:2 | |
| 22:2 | Mt 27:46; Mk 15:34 | | | Dial. 99:1 | 122 (Mt/Mk) |
| 22:3 | | | | Dial. 99:3 | |
| 22:4 | | | | Dial. 100:1 | |
| 22:5-7 | | | | Dial. 101:1 | |
| 22:7 | | | | Dial. 101:2 | |
| 22:8f | Mt 27:39/43 | | 1. Apol. 38:6 | Dial. 101:3 | 79f (test.) |
| 22:10-16 | | | | Dial. 102:1 | 437 (vs. 15 test.?) |
| 22:10 | | | | Dial. 102:2 | |
| 22:11f | | | | Dial. 102:6 | |
| 22:12-15 | | | | Dial. 103:1f | |
| 22:13 | | | | Dial. 103:2 | |
| 22:14 | | Dial. 103:5 | | Dial. 103:3 | |
| 22:15 | | | | Dial. 103:7 | |
| 22:16-19 | | | | Dial. 104:1 | 80 - 82 (test. in vss. 17/19) |
| 22:16 | | | | Dial. 102:5; 103:9 | |
| 22:17-19 | | | | Dial. 97:3 | |
| 22:17/19 | Barn. 6:6 | 1. Apol. 35:7f | 1. Apol. 35:5; 38:4 (in comb. testimony) | | |
| 22:20-22 | | Dial. 105:1 | | Dial. 105:1 | |
| 22:23f | Heb 2:12; Barn. 6:16 | | | Dial. 106:2 | 126 (direct use of the LXX?) |
| 23:4 | 1. Clem. 26:2 | Dial. 86:5 | | | 377 (test.) |
| 24:1-10 | | | | Dial. 36:3f | 82f (test. in vss. 7f) |
| 24:6 | | Dial. 100:4 | | | |
| 24:7f | 24:6-9: Apc. Petri 17 | 24:7: Dial. 36:5; 85:4. 24:8: Dial. 125:2 | 1. Apol. 51:7. | Dial. 85:1; 127:5 (vs. 7 only) | |
| 24:10 | | Dial. 36:6 | | Dial. 85:1 | |
| 32:2 | Rom 4:8 | | | Dial. 141:2 | 115 (Paul?) |
| 33:6 | Apc. Petri 1 | Dial. 61:1? | | | |
| 45:2-18 | | | | Dial. 38:3-5 | 126 (test. nucleus in vss. 7f) |
| 45:7-13 | | | | Dial. 63:4 | |
| 45:7f | Heb 1:8f | 45:8: Dial. 86:3; Dial. 126:1 | | Dial. 56:14. Vs. 8: Dial. 85:1 | |
| 45:11 | | Dial. 76:7; 126:1 (vs. 12) | | Dial. 63:5 | |
| 47:6-10 | | | | Dial. 37:1 | 177 (seized upon by Justin?) |

| | | | | | |
|---|---|---|---|---|---|
| 50:1-23 | 50:14f; *1. Clem.* 52:3 | | | *Dial.* 22:7-10 | 109 (1. Clem.?) |
| 68:19 | Eph 4:8 | | *Dial.* 39:4; 87:6 | | 100 (Eph) |
| 72:1-20 | | vs. 1: *Dial.* 34:2 | | *Dial.* 34:3-6 | |
| 72:1-5/ 17-19 | | | | *Dial.* 64:6 | |
| 72:5 | *2. Clem.* 14:1 | *Dial.* 45:4; 76:7 | | | 235f (vss. 5/17 combined in test.) 85 (another test. source for *Dial.* 121:1f) |
| 72:11 | | *Dial.* 76:7? | | | |
| 72:17 | *2. Clem.* 14:1 | *Dial.* 76:7 | *Dial.* 121:1f | | |
| 78:25 | | *Dial.* 57:2 | | | |
| 82:1-8 | | | | *Dial.* 124:2 | |
| 82:7 | | | | *Dial.* 124:3 | 34f (test.) |
| 90:4 | 2 Pet 3:8; *Barn.* 15:4 | | *Dial.* 81:3 | | 112 (test.) |
| 92:13 | | *Dial.* 86:4 | | | 374ff (test.) |
| 92:16 | | | *Dial.* 92:5 in comb. test. | | cf. on Deut 32:4 |
| 96:1-13 | | | | *Dial.* 73:3f | 35 - 42 (test. version in *1. Apol.* 41:1-4 closer to 1 Chron 16:23ff) |
| 96:1-10/ 1 Chron 16 | | | *1. Apol.* 41:1-4 | | |
| 96:1-3 | | | | *Dial.* 74:1 | |
| 96:5 | | *Dial.* 55:2; 73:2 (both non-LXX); 79:4; 83:4 (both LXX) | | | |
| 96:10 | *Barn.* 8:5 | | *Dial.* 73:1 | | |
| 99:1-9 | | | | *Dial.* 37:3f | 176 (Justin's own substitute for Ps 96?) |
| 99:1-7 | | | | *Dial.* 64:4 | |
| 105:39 | | *Dial.* 131:6? | | | |
| 106:37 | 1 Cor 10:20? | *Dial.* 19:6; 27:2; 73:6; 133:1 | | | |
| 110:1-7 | | | | *Dial.* 32:6 | 86 - 88 (possibly two test. versions) |
| 110:1-4 | | vs. 2: *1. Apol.* 45:5 | *Dial.* 83:2 | *1. Apol.* 45:2-4 | |
| 110:1 | *Multi* | *1. Apol.* 40:7; *Dial.* 32:3; 33:2; 36:5 | *Dial.* 56:14; 83:1; 127:5 | | |
| 110:3 | | *Dial.* 45:4; 76:7 | | *Dial.* 83:4 | 235f (test.) |
| 110:3f | | | | *Dial.* 63:3 | |
| 110:4 | Heb 5:6 et al | *Dial.* 19:4; 96:1; 113:5; 118:1 | | *Dial.* 33:1f | |
| 110:7 | | | | *Dial.* 33:2 | |

| | | | | | |
|---|---|---|---|---|---|
| 115:4-8 | | *Dial.* 69:4 | | | |
| 115:8 | | *Dial.* 55:2 ? | | | |
| 118:24 | Rev 19:7 | *Dial.* 100:4 ? | | | |
| 128:3 | | *Dial.* 110:3 | | | |
| 128:4f | | *Dial.* 24:3 | | | |
| 132:11 | Acts 2:30 | *Dial.* 68:5 (in comb. text) | | | |
| 135:15-18 | | *Dial.* 69:4 ? | | | |
| 148:1f | | | | | *Dial.* 85:6 |

Justin seems most independent in his work with Ps 22. His LXX quotations of Pss 47 and 99 may also be his own contributions to the traditional testimony dossier, possibly also his exploitation of Ps 19:8ff. Elsewhere, he is obviously largely dependent upon traditional testimonies.

| Remaining Scriptures: | Earlier ref. | Allusion | Non-LXX quot. | LXX quotation | Comment |
|---|---|---|---|---|---|
| Job 1:6 | | *Dial.* 103:5 | *Dial.* 79:4 (comb with Job 2:1) | | |
| Prov 8:1/12 | | *Dial.* 100:4 ? *Dial.* 126:1 ? | | | |
| Prov 8:21-36 | 8:22: Col 1:15 Rev 3:14 | *Dial.* 126:1 ? | | *Dial.* 61:3-5 | |
| Prov 8:21-25 | | | | *Dial.* 129:3 | |
| Prov 10:1 | | *Dial.* 119:6 | | | |
| Lam 4:20 | | | *1. Apol.* 55:5 | | 162/451 (test?) |
| Dan 2:34 | Lk 20:18 | *Dial.* 76:1; 100:4; 114:4 | *Dial.* 70:1 (not LXX nor »θ») | | |
| Dan 7:9-28 | | | | *Dial.* 31:2-7 (between LXX and »θ» - καιγε?) | 88 - 90 (test. in Dan 7:13) |
| Dan 7:13f | Mt 24:30 etc. | *1. Apol.* 52:3; *Dial.* 14:8; 32:1; 76:1; 79:2; 86:1; 110:2; 120:4; 126:1 | 7:13: *1. Apol.* 51:9 | | |
| Dan 7:25 | | *Dial.* 32:3f (not the text of *Dial.* 31); *Dial.* 110:2 | | | 203f (test.?) |
| Dan 7:26f | | *Dial.* 46:1; 49:2 | | | |
| 1 Chron 16:25-31 | | | *1. Apol.* 41:1-4 | | Cf. on Ps 96 |
| 1 Chron 16:26 | | | | | Cf. on Ps 96:10 |

| 1 Chron 17:13f | | | *Dial.* 118:2 | | 205 (test.) |
|---|---|---|---|---|---|
| 2 Chron 5:14 (=1 Kings 8:10) | | | | | Cf. on 1 Kings 8:10f |

Again, Justin seems to be working with traditional testimonies, sometimes expanding them to long LXX excerpts (in Daniel possibly from a recensed LXX).

# BIBLIOGRAPHY

## A. TEXTS, TRANSLATIONS AND ANTHOLOGIES

### Bible:

The Hebrew Old Testament is quoted according to the 1962 reprint of Kittel's *Biblia Hebraica*. The LXX is quoted according to the Göttingen editions where available (Genesis, Deuteronomium, Psalms, Isaiah, Jeremiah, Twelve Prophets, Daniel). Elsewhere the LXX text is quoted as in Rahlfs. The apparatus of Brooke-McLean has been consulted for some important texts.

The New Testament is quoted according to the UBS edition of 1966 (Aland/Black/Metzger/-Wikgren: *The Greek New Testament*), unless otherwise indicated. In the counting of OT quotations and allusions, I have preferred the judgement of the 25th edition of Nestle-Aland.

The (protestant) canonical books of the Bible and the OT Apocrypha are quoted according to the RSV translation [1952] (Nelson and Sons, London, 1965).

### Justin. Texts:

de Otto, J. C. Th. *Corpus Apologetarum Christianorum Saeculi Secundi* I-III, 3rd ed., Jena 1876—79 [repr. Wiesbaden, 1969—71].

Pautigny, L. *Justin: Apologies. Texte grec, traduction francaise* (Textes et documents pour l'étude historique du christianisme), Paris, 1904.

Archambault, G. *Justin: Dialogue avec Tryphon. Texte grec, traduction francaise*, I & II (Textes et documents pour l'étude historique du christianisme), Paris, 1909.

Goodspeed, E. J. *Die ältesten Apologeten. Texte mit kurzen Einleitungen*, Göttingen 1914 (pp. 24-265).

Fragments:

Holl, K. *Fragmente vornicänischer Kirchenväter aus den Sacra Parallela* (TU 20), Leipzig, 1899 (pp. 32-53).

Zahn, Th. 'Studien zu Justinus Martyr', *ZKG* 8 (1886), pp. 5-7 [Methodius fragment].

Martyrdom:

Musurillo, H. *The Acts of the Christian Martyrs. Introduction, Texts, and Translations* (OEChT), Oxford, 1972 (pp. 42-61).

### Translations:

Roberts, A. and Donaldson, J. *The Ante-Nicene Fathers* (American reprint), Grand Rapids, 1977, Vol. I, pp. 163-306 [including fragments and *Martyrdom*].

Rauschen, G. *Des heiligen Justinus des Philosophen und Märtyrers Zwei Apologien aus dem Griechischen übersetzt* (BK 13), München, 1913.

Haeuser, Ph. *Des heiligen Philosophen und Märtyrers Justinus Dialog mit dem Juden Tryphon aus dem Griechischen übersetzt und mit einer Einleitung versehen* (BK 33), München, 1917.

Williams, A. L. *Justin Martyr: The Dialogue with Trypho. Translation, Introduction, and Notes*, London, 1930.

Falls, Th. B. *Writings of Saint Justin Martyr* (The Fathers of the Church, A New Translation [ed. L. Schopp *et al*] 6), Washington, 1948 [repr. 1965].

Hardy, E. R. 'The First Apology of Justin, the Martyr', *The Library of Christian Classics* I (ed. C. C. Richardson), London, 1953 (pp. 242-289).

[Unless otherwise indicated, the translations quoted in the present study are those of Williams and Hardy.]

### Index:

Goodspeed, E. J. *Index Apologeticus*, Leipzig, 1912 [repr. Leipzig, 1969].

*Other Christian Writings.*
Apocrypha of the New Testament:
Hennecke, E. and Schneemelcher, W. *New Testament Apocrypha* I & II (English translation ed. by
    R. McL. Wilson), 2nd impression, 1973/75.
Separate editions of texts:
Preuschen, E. *Antilegomena,* Giessen, 1901.
Mara, M. G. *Évangile de Pierre* (SC 201), Paris, 1973.
Dobschütz, E. von *Das Kerygma Petri kritisch untersucht* (TU 11:1), Leipzig, 1893 (pp. 18-27).
[The *Kerygma* is quoted as in Dobschütz, the *Gospel of Peter* as in Mara. For the other relevant
    Greek and Latin texts I have used Preuschen.]

Apostolic Fathers:
Lake, K. *The Apostolic Fathers with an English Translation* I & II (The Loeb Classical Library),
    London-Cambridge [Mass.], 1965 reprint.
Funk, F. X. and Bihlmeyer, K. *Die apostolischen Väter* (2nd ed. by W. Schneemelcher), Tübingen,
    1956.
Separate editions:
Fischer, J. A. *Die apostolischen Väter* (Schriften des Urchristentums, erster Teil), 7th ed., Darmstadt,
    1976 [1. Clement, Ignatius, Polycarp, Quadratus].
Prigent, P. and Kraft, R. A. *Épître de Barnabé* (SC 172), Paris, 1971 [= *Épître.*]
[Where available, the Greek texts of the separate editions are quoted, unless otherwise indicated.
Hermas is quoted as in Lake, the remaining writings as in Funk-Bihlmeyer. English translations are
those of Lake.]
Concordance:
Kraft, H. *Clavis Patrum Apostolicorum,* Darmstadt, 1963.

Athenagoras:
Schoedel, W. R. *Athenagoras: Legatio and De Resurrectione, edited and translated* (OEChT),
    Oxford, 1972.

Clement of Alexandria:
Stählin, O. *Protrepticus und Paedagogus* (GCS 12), Leipzig, 1905.
————— . *Stromata* Buch I-VI (GCS 15), 2nd ed., Leipzig, 1939.
————— . *Stromata* Buch VII und VIII, *Excerpta ex Theodoto* etc. (GCS 17), Leipzig, 1909.

Eusebius:
Schwarz, E. Eusebius Werke 2: *Die Kirchengeschichte,* 1. Teil (GCS 91), Leipzig, 1903.

Irenaeus:
Harvey, W. W. *Sancti Irenaei Episcopi Lugdunensis Libros quinque adversus Haereses* I-II,
    Cambridge, 1857.
Rousseau, A. and Doutreleau, L. *Irénée de Lyon: Contre les hérésies,* Livre III, Tomes I & II (SC 210
    & 211), Paris, 1974.
Rousseau, A. *Irénée de Lyon: Contre les hérésies,* Livre IV, Tomes I & II (SC 100 & 101), Paris, 1965.
————— . *Irénée de Lyon: Contre les hérésies,* Livre V, Tomes I & II (SC 152 & 153), Paris, 1969.
[The text of the SC editions has been preferred, where available. English translation: ANF I, pp.
    315-567.]
Robinson, J. A. *St. Irenaeus: The Demonstration of the Apostolic Preaching* (Translations of
    Christian Literature, Ser. IV), London, 1920.
Smith, J. P. *St. Irenaeus: Proof of the Apostolic Preaching, translated and annotated* (Ancient
    Christian Writers — The Works of the Fathers in Translation 16), Westminster Maryland
    — London, 1952.
[Quotations are from Smith.]

Melito of Sardis:
Hall, S. G. *Melito of Sardis: On Pascha and Fragments, Texts and Translations* (OEChT), Oxford,
    1979.
Blank, J. *Meliton von Sardes: Vom Passa. Die älteste christliche Osterpredigt* (Sophia. Quellen
    östlicher Theologie 3), Freiburg im Breisgau, 1963 [valuable Introduction].
[Quotations are from Hall.]

Pseudo-Clementines:
Rehm, B. *Die Pseudoklementinen II: Recognitionen in Rufins Übersetzung* (GCS 51), Berlin, 1965.
[English translation: ANF VIII, pp. 75-211]

Tertullian:
Borleffs, J. G. Ph. *et al. Qvinti Septimi Florentis Tertulliani Opera,* Pars I & II (CCL I & II), Turnhout, 1954.
Separate editions:
Tränkle, H. *Q. S. F. Tertulliani Adversus Iudaeos. Mit Einleitung und kritischem Kommentar,* Wiesbaden, 1964.
Evans, E. *Tertullian: Adversus Marcionem, edited and translated* (OEChT), Oxford, 1972.
[The Latin text is consequently quoted as in the CCL editions. English translations are from ANF III and IV. For *Adv.Marc.,* I have sometimes preferred Evan's translation.]

Theophilus of Antioch:
Grant, R. M. *Theophilus of Antioch: Ad Autolycum. Text and Translation* (OEChT), Oxford, 1970.

### Jewish Literature
(a) Anthologies of translated texts.
Ginzberg, L. *The Legends of the Jews* I-VII, Philadelphia, 1909-1938.
Montefiore, C. G. and Loewe, H. *A Rabbinic Anthology,* New York, 1974.
Riessler, P. *Altjüdisches Schrifttum ausserhalb der Bibel,* 2nd ed., Heidelberg, 1966.
Strack, H. L. and Billerbeck, P. *Kommentar zum Neuen Testament aus Talmud und Midrasch* I-IV, München, 1922-28 [repr. 1974-78].

(b) Rabbinic Literature in translation.
Danby, H. *The Mishnah,* Oxford, 1938 [repr. 1974].
Epstein, I. (ed.) *The Babylonian Talmud* (Soncino), London, 1938-52.
[Quotations of the *Mishnah* are from Danby; the Babylonian *Gemara* is quoted as in the Soncino translation. Quotations from the Palestinian *Gemara* are most often rendered in the German translations in Str. Bill., in a few cases from other available translations in secondary literature.]
Lauterbach, J. Z. *Mekhilta de-Rabbi Ishmael. A Critical edition . . . with an English Translation, Introduction, and Notes* I-III, Philadelphia, 1933 [repr. 1976].
Freedman, H. and Simon, M. *Midrash Rabbah* I-X (Soncino), London, 1939 [3rd imprint 1961].
Braude, W. G. *The Midrash on Psalms. Translated from the Hebrew and Aramaic* I & II (Yale Judaica Series 13), New Haven, 1959.
——————. *Pesikta Rabbati* I & II (Yale Judaica Series 18), New Haven - London, 1968.
——————. and Kapstein, I. J. *Pesikta de-Rab Kahana,* Philadelphia, 1975.
Diez Macho, A. *Neophyti* 1 I-V, Madrid-Barcelona, 1968-1978.
Odeberg, H. *3 Enoch or The Hebrew Book of Enoch* I-IV, Cambridge, 1928 [repr. New York 1973 with a prolegomenon by J. C. Greenfield].
Rabin, Ch. *Maimonides: The Guide of the Perplexed. An abridged ed. with Introduction and Commentary by J. Guttmann* (Philosophia Judaica), London, 1952.

(c) Qumran Writings
Lohse, E. *Die Texte aus Qumran. Hebräisch und Deutsch,* Darmstadt, 2nd ed. 1971.
Maier, J. *Die Texte vom Toten Meer* I-II, München-Basel, 1960.

(d) Other Jewish Writings - Texts and Translations.
Aristeas:
Hadas, M. *Aristeas to Philocrates (Letter of Aristeas), edited and translated* (Jewish Apocryphal Literature, Dropsie College Edition), New York, 1951.

Joseph and Asenath:
Philonenko, M. *Joseph et Aséneth. Introduction, texte critique, traduction et notes,* Leiden, 1968.

Josephus:
Thackeray, H. St. J. *The Jewish War I-VII, with an English Translation* (The Loeb Classical Library, Josephus, Vols. II-III), London-Cambridge (Mass.), 1927-28 [repr. 1967-68].
Thackeray, H. St. J. *et al. Jewish Antiquities I-XX, with an English Translation* (The Loeb Classical Library, Josephus, Vols. IV-IX), London-Cambridge (Mass.), 1930-65 [repr. 1963-69].

Philo:
Colson, F. H. *et al. Philo I-X, with an English translation* (with two supplementary volumes transl. by R. Marcus) (The Loeb Classical Library), London-Cambridge (Mass.), 1929-1962 [repr. 1961-71].

Pseudepigrapha of the Old Testament:
Denis, A.-M. *Fragmenta Pseudepigraphorum quae supersunt graeca una cum Historicorum et Auctorum Judaeorum Hellenistarum Fragmentis (Pseudepigrapha Veteris Testamenti Graece,* ed. A.-M. Denis et M. de Jonge, III, pp. 47-246), Leiden, 1970 [= *Fragmenta*].
Charles, R. H. *The Apocrypha and Pseudepigrapha Of the Old Testament in English II: Pseudepigrapha,* Oxford, 1913 [repr. 1964].
[The Greek text of the *Sibyllina* is quoted as in J. Geffcken, *Die Orakula Sibyllina* (GCS 8), Leipzig, 1902. The Greek text of the *Testaments of the Twelve Patriarchs* is quoted as in R. H. Charles, *The Greek Version of the Testaments of the Twelve Patriarchs,* Oxford, 1908 (repr. Darmstadt, 1960). In questions of textual criticism I have largely followed J. Becker, *Die Testamente der zwölf Patriarchen* (JSHRZ III:1), Gütersloh, 1974.)

### B. WORKS OF REFERENCE

Benoit, A. *et al. Biblia Patristica. Index des citations et allusions bibliques dans la littérature patristique.* I: *Des origines à Clément d'Alexandrie et Tertullien,* Paris, 1975. II: *Le troisième siècle (Origène excepté),* Paris, 1977.
Blass, F. - Debrunner, A. and Rehkopf, F. *Grammatik des neutestamentlichen Griechisb,* 14th ed., Göttingen, 1975 [= Blass-Debrunner-Rehkopf].
Galling, K. (ed.) *Die Religion in Geschichte und Gegenwart,* 3rd ed., Tübingen, 1957-65.
Gesenius, W. *Hebräisches und aramäisches Handwörterbuch,* 17. Aufl. (ed. by F. Buhl), Berlin-Göttingen-Heidelberg, 1915 [repr. 1962].
Hatch, E. and Redpath, H. A. *A Concordance to the Septuagint I-II,* Oxford, 1897 [repr. Graz, 1954].
Kittel, G. and Friedrich, G. (edd.) *Theological Dictionary of the New Testament* (translated by G. W. Bromiley), Grand Rapids, 1964-74 [repr. 1975-77].
Klauser, Th. (ed.) *Reallexikon für Antike und Christentum,* Stuttgart, 1950ff.
Kühner, R. and Gerth, B. *Ausführliche Grammatik der griechischen Sprache,* II. Teil: *Satzlehre,* 3rd ed., Hannover-Leipzig, 1904 [= Kühner-Gerth].
Lampe, G. W. H. *A Patristic Greek Lexicon,* Oxford, 1961-68.

### C. BOOKS

A few titles to which only casual reference has been made are not included, nor NT commentaries.
Aalen, S. *Die Begriffe ›Licht‹ und ›Finsterniss‹ im Alten Testament, im Spätjudentum und im Rabbinismus* (Skr. N.V. II, 1951:1), Oslo, 1951.
Aberbach, M. and Grossfeld, B. *Targum Onqelos on Genesis 49* (SBL Aramaic Studies 1), Missoula, 1976.
Aeby, G. *Les missions divines de Saint Justin à Origène (Paradosis* 12), Freiburg, 1958.
Alon, G. *Jews, Judaism and the Classical World. Studies in Jewish History in the Times of the Second Temple and Talmud,* Jerusalem, 1977.
Andresen, C. *Logos und Nomos. Die Polemik des Kelsos wider das Christentum,* Berlin, 1955.
Armstrong, G. T. *Die Genesis in der Alten Kirche. Die drei Kirchenväter* (Beiträge zur Geschichte der biblischen Hermeneutik 4), Tübingen, 1962.
Bacher, W. *Die Aggada der Tannaiten I: Von Hillel bis Akiba,* Strassburg, 1903 [repr. Berlin, 1965].
Bamberger, B. J. *Fallen Angels,* Philadelphia, 1952.
Barbel, J. *Christos Angelos (Theophaneia.* Beiträge zur Religions- und Kirchengeschichte des Altertums 3), Bonn, 1941 [repr. with an Appendix, Bonn, 1964].
Bardenhewer, O. *Geschichte der altkirchlichen Literatur* I, Freiburg im Breisgau, 1913 [repr. Darmstadt, 1962] [= *Geschichte*].
Barnard, L. W. *Justin Martyr, His Life and Thought,* Cambridge, 1967.
Barthélemy, D. *Les Devanciers d'Aquila. Première publication intégrale du texte des fragments du Dodékaprophéton* (Suppl. VT 10), Leiden, 1963 [= *Les Devanciers*].
Bauer, W. *Das Leben Jesu im Zeitalter der neutestamentlichen Apokryphen,* Tübingen, 1909 [= *Leben Jesu*].
Becker, J. *Untersuchungen zur Entstehungsgeschichte der Testamente der Zwölf Patriarchen* (Arbeiten zur Geschichte des antiken Judentums und des Urchristentums 8), Leiden, 1970 [= *Testamente*].

Bellinzoni, A. J. *The Sayings of Jesus in the Writings of Justin Martyr* (Suppl. NT 17), Leiden, 1967 [= *Sayings*].

Bergmann, J. *Jüdische Apologetik im neutestamentlichen Zeitalter,* Berlin, 1908 [= *Apologetik*].

Bertrand, D. A. *Le baptême de Jesus. Historie de l'exégèse aux deux premiers siècles* (BGBE 14), Tübingen, 1973.

Beskow, P. *Rex Gloriae. The Kingship of Christ in the Early Church,* Stockholm-Göteborg-Uppsala, 1962 [= *Rex Gloriae*].

Bieder, W. *Die Vorstellung von der Höllenfahrt Jesu Christi* (AThANT 19), Zürich, 1949.

Bietenhard, H. *Die himmlische Welt im Urchristentum und Spätjudentum* (WUNT 2), Tübingen, 1951.

Bousset, W. *Die Evangeliencitate Justins des Märtyrers in ihrem Wert für die Evangelienkritik von neuem untersucht,* Göttingen, 1891 [= *Evangeliencitate*].

—————. *Jüdisch-Christlicher Schulbetrieb in Alexandria und Rom. Literarische Untersuchungen zu Philo und Clemens von Alexandria, Justin und Irenäus* (FRLANT, Neue Folge 6), Göttingen, 1915 [= *Schulbetrieb*].

Brandt, W. *Die jüdischen Baptismen* (BZAW 18), Giessen, 1910 [= *Baptismen*].

Brierre-Narbonne, J. *Les Prophéties messianiques de l'Ancient Testament dans la littérature juive en accord avec le Nouveau Testament* (LOPG), Paris, 1933 [= *Prophéties messianiques*].

—————. *Exégèse talmudique des prophéties messianiques* (LOPG), Paris, 1934.

—————. *Exégèse targumique des prophéties messianiques* (LOPG), Paris, 1935.

—————. *Le Messie souffrant dans la litterature rabbinique* (LOPG), Paris, 1940 [= *Le Messie souffrant*].

Brown, R. E. *The Birth of the Messiah. A Commentary on the Infancy Narratives in Matthew and Luke,* Garden City, New York, 1977.

Campenhausen, H. Freiherr von *Die Entstehung der christlichen Bibel* (BHTh 39), Tübingen, 1968.

Chevallier, M.-A. *L' Esprit et le Messie dans le Bas-Judaisme et le Nouveau Testament* (Études d'histoire et de philosophie religieuses publiées sous les auspices de la Faculté de Théologie Protestante de l'Université de Strasbourg 49), Paris, 1958 [= *L' Esprit et le Messie*].

Conzelmann, H. *Die Mitte der Zeit. Studien zur Theologie des Lukas* (BHTh 17), 5th ed., Tübingen, 1964.

Credner, K. A. *Beiträge zur Einleitung in die biblischen Schriften II: Das alttestamentliche Urevangelium,* Halle, 1838 [= *Urevangelium*].

Cross, Jr., F. M. *The Ancient Library of Qumran and Modern Biblical Studies* (The Haskell Lectures 1956-57), rev. ed., New York, 1961.

Daniélou, J. *Sacramentum Futuri: Études sur les origines de la typologie biblique* (Études de Théologie Historique), Paris, 1950.

—————. *The Theology of Jewish Christianity* (The Development of Christian Doctrine before the Council of Nicaea I) (translated and ed. by J. A. Baker), London, 1964 [= *Theology*].

—————. *Études d'exégèse judéo-chrétienne (Les Testimonia)* (Théologie historique 5), Paris, 1966 [= *Études*].

—————. *Gospel Message and Hellenistic Culture* (A History of Early Christian Doctrine before the Council of Nicaea II) (translated and ed. by J. A. Baker), London-Philadelphia, 1973 [= *Gospel Message*].

Davies, W. D. *The Setting of the Sermon on the Mount,* Cambridge, 1966.

le Déaut, R. *La Nuit Pascale (Analecta Biblica* 22), Rome, 1963.

Denis, A.-M. *Introduction aux pseudépigraphes grecs d'Ancient Testament (Studia in Veteris Testamenti Pseudepigrapha* 1), Leiden, 1970 [= *Introduction*].

Dömer, M. *Das Heil Gottes. Studien zur Theologie des lukanischen Doppelwerkes* (BBB 51), Köln-Bonn, 1978.

Dodd, C. H. *According to the Scriptures. The Substructure of New Testament Theology,* London, 1965 (orig. ed. 1952).

Donahue, P. J. *Jewish-Christian Controversy in the Second Century: A Study in the Dialogue of Justin Martyr,* Yale Dissertation on microfilm, 1973 [= *Controversy*].

Engelhardt, M. von *Das Christenthum Justins des Märtyrers. Eine Untersuchung über die Anfänge der katolischen Glaubenslehre,* Erlangen, 1878 [= *Christentum*].

Feder, A. L. *Justin des Märtyrers Lehre von Jesus Christus, dem Messias und dem menschgewordenen Sohne Gottes. Eine dogmengeschichtliche Monographie,* Freiburg im Breisgau, 1906 [= *Lehre*].

Franklin, E. *Christ the Lord. A Study in the Purpose and Theology of Luke-Acts,* London, 1975.

Friedländer, M. *Patristische und talmudische Studien,* Wien, 1878 [Repr. Westmead, 1972] [= *Studien*].

Gerhardsson, B. *Memory and Manuscript. Oral Tradition and Written Transmission in Rabbinic Judaism and Early Christianity* (ASNU 22), Lund-Copenhagen, 2nd. ed. 1964.

Goldberg, A. M. *Untersuchungen über die Vorstellung von der Schekhinah in der frühen rabbinischen Literatur (Studia Judaica.* Forschungen zur Wissenschaft des Judentums 5), Berlin, 1969 [= *Schekhinah*].

Goodenough, E. R. *The Theology of Justin Martyr. An Investigation into the Conceptions of Early Christian Literature and Its Hellenistic and Judaistic Influences,* Jena, 1923 [repr. Amsterdam, 1968] [= *Theology*].

Goppelt, L. *Typos. Die typologische Deutung des Alten Testaments im Neuen* (BFChTh, 2. Reihe 43), Gütersloh, 1939 [repr. Darmstadt, 1969].

————— . *Christentum und Judentum im ersten und zweiten Jahrhundert. Ein Aufriss der Urgeschichte der Kirche* (BFChTh, 2. Reihe 55), Gütersloh, 1954.

Gundry, R. H. *The Use of the Old Testament in St. Matthew's Gospel* (Suppl. NT 18), Leiden, 1967.

Hagner, D. A. *The Use of the Old and New Testament in Clement of Rome* (Suppl. NT 34), Leiden, 1973 [= *O and NT in Clement*].

Hanson, R. P. C. *Allegory and Event. A Study of the Sources and Significance of Origen's Interpretation of Scripture,* London, 1959.

Harnack, A. von *Die Altercatio Simonis Judaei et Theophili Christiani, nebst Untersuchungen über die antijüdische Polemik in der Alten Kirche* (TU 1:3), Leipzig, 1883.

————— . *Geschichte der altchristlichen Literatur bis Eusebius* I:1, 2nd ed., Leipzig, 1958.

————— . *Lehrbuch der Dogmengeschichte I: Die Entstehung des kirchlichen Dogmas,* 5th ed., Tübingen, 1931.

————— . *Judentum und Judenchristentum in Justins Dialog mit Trypho* (TU 39:1 [pp. 47-98]), Leipzig, 1913.

————— . *Die Mission und Ausbreitung des Christentums* I-II, 4th ed., Leipzig, 1924.

————— . *Marcion: Das Evangelium vom fremden Gott* (TU 45), Leipzig, 1921.

Harris, J. R. *Testimonies* I-II, Cambridge, 1916/20.

Hatch, E. *Essays in Biblical Greek,* Oxford, 1889 [= *Essays*].

Hay, D. M. *Glory at the Right Hand: Psalm 110 in Early Christianity* (SBL Mon. Ser. 18), Nashville-New York, 1973 [= *Psalm 110*].

Heinisch, P. *Der Einfluss Philos auf die älteste christliche Exegese* (Alttestamentliche Abhandlungen, Heft 1/2), Münster im Westfalen, 1908 [= *Einfluss Philos*].

Hengel, M. *Judentum und Hellenismus* (WUNT 10), Tübingen, 1969.

Hoffmann, M. *Der Dialog bei den christlichen Schriftstellern der ersten vier Jahrhunderte* (TU 96), Berlin, 1966.

Hofius, O. *Katapausis. Die Vorstellung vom endzeitlichen Ruheort im Hebräerbrief* (WUNT 11), Tübingen, 1970.

Hommes, N. J. *Het Testimoniaboek. Studiën over O.T. citaten in het N.T. en bij de Patres, met critische beschouwingen over de theorieën van J. Rendel Harris en D. Plooy,* Amsterdam, 1935 [= *Testimoniaboek*].

Hruby, K. *Die Stellung der jüdischen Gesetzeslehrer zur werdenden Kirche* (Schriften zur Judentumskunde 4), Zürich, 1971.

Huber, W. *Passa und Ostern. Untersuchungen zur Osterfeier in der alten Kirche* (BZNW 35), Berlin, 1969.

Hubík, K. *Die Apologien des hl. Justinus des Philosophen und Märtyrers. Literarhistorische Untersuchungen* (Theologische Studien der Leo-Gesellschaft 19), Wien, 1912.

Hultgård, A. *Croyances messaniques des Test. XII Patr. Critique textuelle et commentaire des passages messaniques,* Uppsala, 1971 [= *Croyances messaniques*].

Hurwitz, S. *Die Gestalt des sterbenden Messias. Religionspsychologische Aspekte der jüdischen Apokalyptik* (Studien aus dem C. G. Jung-Institut, Zürich 8), Zürich-Stuttgart, 1958.

Hyldahl, N. *Philosophie und Christentum. Eine Interpretation der Einleitung zum Dialog Justins* (Acta theologica danica 9), Copenhagen, 1966.

Jeremias, J. *Die Passahfeier der Samaritaner* (BZAW 59), Giessen, 1932.

————— . *Die Kindertaufe in den ersten Vier Jahrhunderten,* Göttingen, 1958.

Jervell, J. *Die Abendmahlsworte Jesu,* 4th ed., Göttingen, 1967.

————— . *Imago Dei. Gen 1,26f. im Spätjudentum, in der Gnosis und in den paulinischen Briefen* (FRLANT 76), Göttingen, 1960.

Jervell, J. *Luke and the People of God. A new Look at Luke-Acts,* Mineapolis, 1972 [= *Luke*].

Jocz, J. *The Jewish People and Jesus Christ. A Study in the Relationship between the Jewish People and Jesus Christ,* London, 1949.

Joly, R. *Christianisme et Philosophie. Études sur Justin et les Apologistes grecs du deuxième siècle* (Université Libre de Bruxelles, Faculté de Philosophie et Lettres 52), Brussels, 1973.

de Jonge, M. *The Testaments of the Twelve Patriarchs. A Study of their Text, Composition and Origin,* Assen, 1953 [= *Testaments*].

Kähler, E. *Studien zum Te Deum und zur Geschichte des 24. Psalms in der Alten Kirche* (Veröffentlichungen der Evangelischen Gesellschaft für Liturgieforschung 10), Göttingen, 1958.

Klausner, J. *The Messianic Idea in Israel. From Its Beginning to the Completion of the Mishnah* (transl. by W. F. Stinespring), New York, 1955 [= *Messianic Idea*].

Klijn, A. F. J. and Reinink, G. J. *Patristic Evidence for Jewish-Christian Sects* (Suppl. NT 36), Leiden, 1973 [= *Evidence*].

Koester, H. *Septuaginta und synoptischer Erzählungsstoff im Schriftbeweis Justins des Märtyrers* (Habilitationsschrift), Heidelberg, 1956 [= *Schriftbeweis*].

Kominiak, B. *The Theophanies of the Old Testament in the Writings of St. Justin* (The Catholic University of America, Studies in Sacred Theology, 2nd Ser. 14), Washington, 1948.

Kraft, R. A. *The Epistle of Barnabas, Its Quotations and Their Sources* (Diss. on microfilm), Harvard, 1961 [= *Epistle*].

Kuhn, P. *Gottes Selbsterniedrigung in der Theologie der Rabbinen* (StANT 17), München, 1968.

Kurz, W. S. *The Function of Christological Proof from Prophecy for Luke and Justin* (Diss. on microfilm), Yale, 1976 [= *Christological Proof*].

Lebreton, J. *Histoire du dogme de la Trinite* I-II, Paris, 1927/28.

Levey, S. H. *The Messiah: An Aramaic Interpretation. The Messianic exegesis of the Targum* (Monographs of the Hebrev Union College 2), Cincinatti-New York-Los Angeles-Jerusalem, 1974 [= *Messiah*].

Lewis, J. P. *A Study of the Interpretation of Noah and the Flood in Jewish and Christian Literature,* Leiden, 1968.

Lindemann, A. *Paulus im ältesten Christentum. Das Bild des Apostels und die Rezeption der paulinischen Theologie in der frühchristlichen Literatur bis Marcion* (BHTh 58), Tübingen, 1979 [= *Paulus*].

Lohfink, G. *Die Sammlung Israels. Eine Untersuchung zur lukanischen Ekklesiologie* (StANT 39), München, 1975.

Lohse, B. *Das Passafest der Quartadecimaner* (BFChTh, 2. Reihe, 54), Gütersloh, 1953.

Longenecker, R. N. *The Christology of Early Jewish Christianity* (Studies in Biblical Theology, 2nd Ser. 17), London, 1970 [= *Christology*].

Lundberg, P. *La Typologie baptismale dans l'ancienne église.* (ASNU 10), Leipzig-Uppsala, 1942.

Mack, B. L. *Logos und Sophia. Untersuchungen zur Weisheitstheologie im hellenistischen Judentum* (Studien zur Umwelt des Neuen Testament 10), Göttingen, 1973.

Marmorstein, A. *The Old Rabbinic Doctrine of God* I-II, 1927/37 [repr. New York, 1968].

Massaux, É. *Influence de l'Évangile de saint Matthieu sur la littérature chrétienne avant saint Irénée (Universitas catholica Lovaniensis Dissertationes Series* II, *Tomus* 42), Louvain/-Gembloux, 1950 [= *Influence*].

Michel, O. *Paulus und seine Bibel* (BFChTh, 2. Reihe 18), Gütersloh, 1929 [repr. Darmstadt, 1972] [= *Bibel*].

Mitchell, L. L. *Baptismal Anointing* (Alcuin Club Collections 48), London, 1966.

Moore, G. Foot *Judaism in the First Centuries of the Christian Era. The Age of the Tannaim* I-III, 9th ed., Cambridge (Mass.), 1962.

Murray, R. *Symbols of Church and Kingdom. A Study in Early Syriac Tradition,* Cambridge, 1975 [= *Symbols*].

Nussbaumer, A. *Das Ursymbolum nach der Epideixis des hl. Irenäus und dem Dialog Justin des Märtyrers mit Trypho* (Forschungen zur Christlichen Literatur- und Dogmengeschichte 14:2), Paderborn, 1921.

Oesterley, W. O. E. *The Jewish Background of the Christian Liturgy,* Oxford, 1925.

O' Malley, T. P. *Tertullian and the Bible (Latinitas Christianorum Primaeva* 21), Nijmegen-Utrecht, 1967.

O' Neill, J. C. *The Theology of Acts in its historical Setting,* London, 1961 [= *Theology of Acts*].

Osborn, E. F. *Justin Martyr* (BHTh 47), Tübingen, 1973.

Pernveden, L. *The Concept of the Church in the Shepherd of Hermas* (Studia Theologica Lundensia 27), Lund, 1966.

Philonenko, M. *Les Interpolations chrétiennes des Testaments des Douze Patriarchs et les Manuscrits de Qoumrân,* Paris, 1960.

Plooij, D. *Studies in the Testimony Book* (Verhandelingen der koninklijke Akademie van Wetenschappen te Amsterdam. Afdeeling letterkunde Nieuwe Reeks, Deel XXXII No 2), Amsterdam, 1932.

Popkes, W. *Christus Traditus. Eine Untersuchung zum Begriff der Dahingabe im Neuen Testament* (AThANT 49), Zürich-Stuttgart, 1967.

Posnoff, I. *Les Prophètes dans la synthèse chrétienne de saint Justin* (Dissertation on microfiche), Louvain, 1948.

Prigent, P. *Les Testimonia dans le Christianisme Primitif. L'Épître de Barnabé I-XVI et ses sources* (EB), Paris, 1961 [= *Les Testimonia*].

——— . *Justin et l'Ancient Testament* (EB), Paris, 1964 [= *Justin*].

Rahlfs, A. *Der Text des Septuaginta-Psalters* (Septuaginta-Studien 2), Göttingen, 1907 [repr. 1965].

Reicke, B. *The disobedient Spirits and Christian Baptism. A Study of 1 Pet. III:19 and its Context* (ASNU 13), Copenhagen, 1946.

Reijners, G. Q. *The Terminology of the Holy Cross in Early Christian Literature as based upon Old Testament Typology* (Graecitas Christianorum Primaeva 2), Nijmegen, 1965 [= *Holy Cross*].

Resch, A. *Agrapha. Ausserkanonische Schriftfragmente* (TU 30:3/4), 2nd ed., Leipzig, 1906.

Richardson, P. *Israel in the Apostolic Church* (SNTSt Mon. Ser. 10), Cambridge, 1969 [= *Israel*].

Ringgren, H. *Word and Wisdom. Studies in the Hypostatization of Divine Qualities and Functions in the Ancient Near East,* Lund, 1947.

Schäfer, P. *Rivalität zwischen Engeln und Menschen. Untersuchungen zur rabbinischen Engelvorstellung* (Studia Judaica. Forschungen zur Wissenschaft des Judentums 8), Berlin-New York, 1975.

——— . *Der Bar Kokhba-Aufstand* (Texte und Studien zum Antiken Judentum 1) Tübingen, 1981.

Schenke, W. *Die Chokma (Sophia) in der jüdischen Hypostasenspekulation* (Skr. N.V. II, 1912, 6), Kristiania [Oslo], 1913.

Schlütz, K. *Isaias 11:2 (die sieben Gaben des Hl. Geistes) in den ersten vier christlichen Jahrhunderten* (Alttestamentliche Abhandlungen 11:4), Münster im Westfalen, 1932.

Schnackenburg, R. *Das Johannesevangelium* I (HThKNT 4), Freiburg-Basel-Wien, 1965.

Schoeps, H. J. *Theologie und Geschichte des Judenchristentums,* Tübingen, 1949 [= *Judenchristentum*].

Scholem, G. G. *Jewish Gnosticism, Merkabah Mysticism, and Talmudic Tradition,* New York, 1960.

Schürer, E. *Geschichte des jüdischen Volkes im Zeitalter Jesu Christi* I-III, 3rd ed., Leipzig, 1898/1901.

——— . *The History of the Jewish People in the Age of Jesus Christ (175 B.C. - A.D. 135). A New English Version* Revised and Ed. by G. Vermes and F. Millar, I, Edinburgh, 1973 [= *New Schürer*].

Schulz, S. *Die Stunde der Botschaft. Einführung in die Theologie der vier Evangelisten,* Hamburg-Zürich, 1970.

Shotwell, W. A. *The Biblical Exegesis of Justin Martyr,* London, 1965 [= *Exegesis*].

Sibinga, J. Smith *The Old Testament Text of Justin Martyr I: The Pentateuch,* Leiden, 1963.

Siegfried, C. *Philo von Alexandria als Ausleger des Alten Testaments,* Jena, 1875 [repr. Amsterdam, 1970].

Simon, M. *Verus Israel. Étude sur les relations entre chrétiens et juifs dans l'Empire Romain* (135-425), Paris, 1948 [repr. with a Postscript, 1964].

Steck. O. H. *Israel und das gewaltsame Geschick der Propheten. Untersuchungen zur Überlieferung des deuteronomistischen Geschichtsbildes im Alten Testament, Spätjudentum und Urchristentum* (WMANT 23), Neukirchen-Vluyn, 1967.

Steiner, M. *La Tentation de Jésus dans l'interprétation patristique de Saint Justin à Origène* (EB), Paris, 1962.

Stendahl, K. *The School of St. Matthew and its Use of the Old Testament* (ASNU 20), Lund, 2nd ed. 1969.

Strack, H.L. *Jesus, die Häretiker und die Christen nach den ältesten jüdischen Angaben.* (Schriften des *Institutum Judaicum* in Berlin 37), Leipzig, 1910.
————. *Einleitung in Talmud und Midrasch,* 5th ed. 1920 (repr. München, 1961).
Strecker, G. *Das Judenchristentum in den Pseudoklementinen* (TU 70), Berlin, 1958 (=*Pseudoklementinen*).
Stylianopoulos, Th. *Justin Martyr and the Mosaic Law* (SBL Diss. Ser. 20), Missoula, 1975 (=*Mosaic Law*).
Swete, H.B. *An Introduction to the Old Testament in Greek* (rev. by R.R. Ottley), Cambridge, 1914 (= *Introduction*).
Trakatellis, D.C. *The Pre-Existence of Christ in the Writings of Justin Martyr* (Harvard Dissertations in Religion 6), Missoula, 1976 [= *Pre-Existence*].
Trilling, W. *Das wahre Israel. Studien zur Theologie des Matthäus-Evangeliums* (StANT 10), 3rd ed., München, 1964.
Ungern-Sternberg, A. Freiherr von *Der traditionelle alttestamentliche Schriftbeweis « de Christo» und « de Evangelio» in der Alten Kirche bis zur Zeit Eusebs von Caesarea,* Halle a. S., 1913 [= *Schriftbeweis*].
Urbach, E.E. *The Sages. Their Concepts and Beliefs* I-II (Publications of the Perry Foundation in the Hebrew University of Jerusalem), Jerusalem, 1975.
Verweijs, P.G. *Evangelium und neues Gesetz in der ältesten Christenheit bis auf Marcion,* Utrecht, 1960 [= *Evangelium*].
Voss, B.R. *Der Dialog in der frühchristlichen Literatur* (*Studia et Testimonia Antiqua* 9, München, 1970.
Weiss, H.-F. *Untersuchungen zur Kosmologie des hellenistischen und palästinensischen Judentums* (TU 97), Berlin, 1966 [= *Kosmologie*].
Wengst, K. *Tradition und Theologie des Barnabasbriefes* (Arbeiten zur Kirchengeschichte 42), Berlin, 1971.
Wieland, A.O. *Die Eschatologie Justins des Philosophen und Märtyrers* (Diss.), Innsbruck, 1969.
Wilke, H.-A. *Das Problem eines messianischen Zwischenreichs bei Paulus* (AThANT 51), Zürich-Stuttgart, 1967.
Wilson, St.G. *The Gentiles and the Gentile Mission in Luke-Acts* (SNTSt Mon. Ser. 23), Cambridge, 1973 [= *Gentile Mission*].
Winden, J.C.M. van *An Early Christian Philosopher. Justin Martyr's Dialogue with Trypho Chapters One to Nine* (*Philosophia Patrum.* Interpretation of Patristic Texts 1), Leiden, 1971.
Windisch, H, 'Der Barnabasbrief' (*Handbuch zum Neuen Testament,* Ergänzungsband 3 Tübingen, 1920, pp. 299-413).
Wolf, Chr. *Jeremia im Frühjudentum und Urchristentum* (TU 118), Berlin, 1976.
Wolfson, H.A. *Philo: Foundations of Religious Philosophy in Judaism, Christianity and Islam* I-II, 2nd imprint, Cambridge (Mass), 1948.
Woude, A.S. van der *Die messianischen Vorstellungen der Gemeinde von Qumran* (*Studia Semitica Neerlandica* 3), Assen, 1957 [= *Messianische Vorstellungen*].
Zahn, Th. *Geschichte des Neutestamentlichen Kanons* I:1-2, Erlangen-Leipzig, 1888/89.

## D. ARTICLES

(Entries in dictionaries are not listed, nor a few titles only casually referred to in the footnotes).

d'Alès, A. 'La Théophanie de Mambré devant la tradition des Pères', *RSR* 20 (1930), pp. 150-60.
Alexander, Ph. S. 'The Targumim and Early Exegesis of «Sons of God» in Genesis 6', *JJS* 23 (1972), pp. 60-71.
Allegro, J. M. 'Further Messianic References in Qumran Literature, Document IV', *JBL* 75 (1965), pp. 182-187.
————. 'Fragments of a Qumran Scroll of Eschatological Midrasim', *JBL* 77 (1958), pp. 350-54.
Andresen, C. 'Justin und der mittlere Platonismus', *ZNW* 44 (1952/53), pp. 157-95.
Audet, J.-P. 'L'Hypothèse des testimonia: remarques autor d'un livre récent', *RB* 70 (1963), pp. 381-405.
Aune, D. E. 'Justin Martyr's Use of the Old Testament', *Bulletin of the Evangelical Theological Society* 9 (1966), pp. 179-97.
Bammel, E. 'Die Täufertraditionen bei Justin', *Studia Patristica* 8 (TU 93, ed. F. L. Cross), Berlin, 1966, pp. 53-61.
Bardy, G. 'Cérinthe', *RB* 30 (1921), pp. 344-373.

Barnard, L. W. 'A Note on *Barnabas* 6,8-17', *Studia Patristica* 4:2 (TU 79, ed. F. L. Cross), Berlin, 1961, pp. 262-67.

───────── . The Old Testament and Judaism in the Writings of Justin Martyr', *VT* 14 (1964), pp. 395-406.

───────── . 'Justin Martyr's Eschatology', *VC* 19 (1965), pp. 86-98.

Barthélemy, D. 'Redécouverte d'un chaînon manquant de l'histoire de la Septante', *RB* 60 (1953), pp. 18-29 [repr. in *Qumran and the History of the Biblical Text*, ed. by F. M. Cross and Sh. Talmon, Cambridge (Mass.)/London, 1975, pp. 127-139].

Benz, E. 'Christus und Socrates in der alten Kirche. Ein Beitrag zum altkirchlichen Verständnis des Märtyrers und des Martyriums', *ZNW* 43 (1950/51), pp. 195-224.

Berger, K. 'Hartherzigkeit und Gottes Gesetz. Die Vorgeschichte des antijüdischen Vorwurfs in Mc 10,5', *ZNW* 61 (1970), pp. 1-47.

───────── . 'Die königlichen Messiastraditionen des Neuen Testaments', *NTS* 20 (1974), pp. 1-44.

───────── . 'Jüdisch-hellenistische Missionsliteratur und apokryphe Apostelakten', *Kairos* 17 (1975), pp. 232-248 [= 'Missionsliteratur'].

Black, M. 'The Christological Use of the Old Testament in the New Testament', *NTS* 18 (1971/72), pp. 1-14.

Bokser, B. Z. 'Justin Martyr and the Jews', *JQR* New Series 64 (1973/74), pp. 97-122/204-211.

Braun, H. 'Entscheidende Motive in den Berichten über die Taufe Jesu von Markus bis Justin', *ZThK* 50 (1953), pp. 39-43.

Brown, R. E. 'The Messianism of Qumran', *CBQ* 19 (1957), pp. 53-82 [= 'Messianism'].

Brox, N. 'Zum literarischen Verhältnis zwischen Justin und Irenäeus', *ZNW* 58 (1967), pp. 121-28.

Büchler, A. 'Über die Minim von Sepphoris und Tiberias im zweiten und dritten Jahrhundert', *Judaica, Festschrift zu Herman Cohens siebzigstem Geburtstage*, Berlin, 1912, pp. 271-295.

Burkitt, F. C. 'Justin Martyr and Jeremiah XI 19', *JTS* 33 (1932), pp. 371-73.

Burney, C. F. 'Christ as the *APXH* of Creation (Prov VIII 22, Col I 15-18, Rev III 14)', *JTS* 27 (1926), pp. 160-177.

Causse, A. 'La propagande juive et l'hellénisme', *RHPhR* 3 (1923), pp. 397-414.

───────── . 'Le mythe de la nouvelle Jérusalem du Deutéro-Esaie a la IIIᵉ Sibylle', *RHPhR* 18 (1938), pp. 377-414.

Chadwick, H. 'Justin Martyr's Defence of Christianity', *Bulletin of The John Rylands Library* 47 (1965), pp. 275-97.

Christensen, T. 'Til Spørgsmålet om kristendommens hellenisering' ['Concerning the Problem of the Hellenization of Christianity' (Danish)], *Festskrift til N. H. Søe*, København, 1965, pp. 11-32.

───────── . 'Nyere undersøgelser over Justins Dialog med jøden Tryfon cap. 1-9' ['Recent Studies of Justin's *Dialogue with Trypho the Jew*, chaps. 1-9' (Danish)], *DTT* 39 (1976), pp. 153-165.

Cohon, S. S. 'The Unity of God. A Study in Hellenistic and Rabbinic Theology', *HUCA* 26 (1955), pp. 425-79.

Collins, J. J. 'The Place of the Fourth Sibyl in the Development of the Jewish Sibyllina', *JJS* 25 (1974), pp. 365-80.

Copeland, E. L. 'Nomos as a Medium of Revelation - Paralleling Logos - in Ante-Nicene Christianity', *StTh* 27 (1973), pp. 51-61.

Couratin, A. H. 'Justin Martyr and Confirmation - A Note', *Theology* 55 (1952), pp. 158-60.

Cross, F. M. 'The History of the Biblical Text in the Light of the Discoveries in the Judaean Desert', *HTR* 57 (1964), pp. 281-99.

Dahl, N. A. 'Der Name Israel. Zur Auslegung von Gal. 6:16', *Judaica* 6 (1950), pp. 161-170.

───────── . 'La terre où coulent le lait et le miel selon Barnabé 6,8-19', *Aux sources de la tradition chrétienne, Mélanges M. Goguel*, Neuchâtel-Paris, 1950, pp. 62-70.

───────── . 'Bibelutgaver i oldkirken' ['Bible editions in the Old Church' (Norwegian)], *Kirkens arv og kirkens fremtid, Festskrift til J. Smemo*, Oslo, 1968, pp. 133-151.

Daniélou, J. 'L'étoile de Jacob et la mission chrétienne à Damas', *VC* 11 (1957), pp. 121-138.

Daube, D. 'Rabbinic Methods of Interpretation and Hellenistic Rhetoric', *HUCA* 22 (1949), pp. 239-264.

───────── . 'Alexandrian Methods of Interpretation and the Rabbis', *Festschrift für Hans Lewald*, Basel, 1953, pp. 27-44.

Davey, J. M. 'Justin Martyr and the Fourth Gospel', *Scripture* 17 (1965), pp. 117-22.

le Déaut, R, 'Un phénomène spontané de l'herméneutique juive ancienne: le «targumisme»', *Biblica* 52 (1971), pp. 505-25.

———— · 'La tradition juive ancienne et l'exégèse chrétienne primitive', *RHPbR* 51 (1971), pp. 31-50.

Dölger, F. J. 'Sonne und Sonnenstrahl als Gleichnis in der Logostheologie des christlichen Altertums', in *idem, Antike und Christentum. Kultur- und religionsgeschichtliche Studien* I, Münster im Westfalen, 1929, pp. 271-290.

———— · 'Die Glöckchen am Gewande des jüdischen Hohenpriester nach der Ausdeutung jüdischer, heidnischer und frühchristlicher Schriftsteller', in *idem, Antike und Christentum* IV, Münster (i. W.), 1934, pp. 233-242.

Dubois, J.-D. 'La figure d'Elie dans la perspective lucanienne', *RHPbR* 53 (1973), pp. 155-76.

Duling, D. C. 'Solomon, Exorcism and the Son of David', *HTR* 68 (1975), pp. 235-252.

———— · 'The Therapeutic Son of David; An Element in Matthew's Christological Apologetic', *NTS* 24 (1978), pp. 392-410.

Dupont, J. 'Ascension du Christ et don de l'Esprit d'après Actes 2:33', *Christ and the Spirit in the New Testament. In Honour of C. F. D. Moule,* Cambridge, 1973, pp. 219-228.

Ehrhardt, A. 'Justin Martyr's Two Apologies', *JEH* 4 (1953), pp. 1-12.

Every, E. 'Jews and God-Fearers in the New Testament Period', *Immanuel* 5 (1975), pp. 46-50.

Fitzmyer, J. A. 'The Bar Cochba period', in *idem, Essays on the Semitic Background of the New Testament,* London, 1971, pp. 305-354.

Ford, J. M. 'The Ray, the Root and the River. A Note on the Jewish Origin of Trinitarian Images', *Studia Patristica* 11:2 (TU 108, ed. F. L. Cross), Berlin, 1972, pp. 158-65.

Frend, W. H. C. 'The Old Testament in the Age of the Greek Apologists A. D. 130-180', *SJT* 26 (1973), pp. 129-150.

Froidevaux, L.-M. 'Sur trois textes cités par saint Irénée', *RSR* 44 (1956), pp. 408-421.

Gervais, J. 'L'argument apologetique des prophéties messianique selon saint Justin', *Révue de l'Université d'Ottawa* 13 (1943), pp. 129-46/193-208.

Ginzberg, L. 'Die Haggada bei den Kirchenvätern und in der apokryphischen Litteratur', *MGWJ* 42 (1898), pp. 537-550/43 (1899), pp. 17 ... 547 *(passim)*.

Ginzberg, L. 'Allegorical Interpretation of Scripture', in *idem, On Jewish Law and Lore,* Philadelphia, 1955, pp. 127-150.

Goldfahn, A. H. 'Justinus Martyr und die Agada', *MGWJ* 22 (1873), pp. 49 ... 269 *(passim)*.

Grant, R. M. [Review of P. Prigent, *Justin*], *JBL* 84 (1965), pp. 440-43.

Guttmann, A. 'The End of the Jewish Sacrificial Cult', *HUCA* 38 (1967), pp. 137-48.

Hanhart, R. 'Fragen um die Entstehung der LXX', *VT* 12 (1962), pp. 139-63.

Hanson, A. 'Theophanies in the Old Testament and the Second Person of the Trinity. A Piece of Early Christian Speculation', *Hermathena* 65 (1945), pp. 67-73.

Hanson, P. D. 'Rebellion in Heaven, Azazel and Euhemeristic Heroes in 1 Enoch 6-11', *JBL* 96 (1977), pp. 195-233.

Hauschild, W.-D. 'Der Ertrag der neueren auslegungsgeschichtlichen Forschung für die Patristik', *Verkündigung und Forschung* 16 (1971), pp. 5-25.

Heinemann, J. 'The Messiah of Ephraim and the Premature Exodus of the Tribe of Ephraim', *HTR* 68 (1975), pp. 1-15.

Hengel, M. 'Die Ursprünge der christlichen Mission', *NTS* 18 (1971/72), pp. 15-38.

Higgins, A. J. B. 'Jewish messianic belief in Justin Martyr's *Dialogue with Trypho',* Nov. Test. 9 (1967), pp. 298-305.

Hilgenfeld, A. 'Die alttestamentlichen Citate Justin's in ihrer Bedeutung für die Untersuchung über seine Evangelien', *Theologische Jahrbücher* 9 (1850).

Horbury, W. 'The Benediction of the *Minim* and Early Jewish-Christian Controversy', *JTS* (NS) 33 (1982), pp. 19-61.

Howard, G. 'The Septuagint: A Review of Recent Studies', *Restoration Quarterly* 13 (1970), pp. 154-64.

———— · 'Lucianic Readings in a Greek Twelve Prophets Scroll from the Judaean Desert', *JQR* New Series 62 (1971/72), pp. 51-60.

Hrubv, K. 'Exégèse rabbinique et exégèse patristique', *RSR* 47 (1973), pp. 341-72.

———— · 'Der talmudische Messianismus', *Emuna* 9 (1974), pp. 324-332.

Hübner, H. 'Mark. VII. 1-23 und das 'jüdisch-hellenistische' Gesetzesverständnis', *NTS* 22 (1976), pp. 319-345.

Hüntemann, U. 'Zur Kompositionstechnik Justins. Analyse seiner ersten Apologie', *Theologie und Glaube, Zeitschrift f. d. kath. Klerus* 25 (1933), pp. 410-28.

Jellicoe, S. 'Septuagint Studies in the Current Century', *JBL* 88 (1969), pp. 191-99.

———— · 'Prolegomenon', in *idem* (ed.), *Studies in the Septuagint* (Library of Biblical Studies), New York, 1974, pp. XIII-LXI.

Jeremias, J. 'Die Berufung des Nathanael (Jo 1,45-51)', *Angelos* 3 (1928), pp. 2-5.

———— . 'Das Lamm, das aus der Jungfrau hervorging (Test. Jos. 19:8)', *ZNW* 57 (1966), pp. 216-219.

Jervell, J. 'Ein Interpolator interpretiert. Zu der christlichen Bearbeitung der Testamente der zwölf Patriarchen', *Studien zu den Testamenten der Zwölf Patriarchen*, ed. W. Eltester (BZNW 36), Berlin, 1969, pp. 30-61 [= 'Interpolator'].

———— . 'Die offenbarte und die verborgene Tora. Zur Vorstellung über die neue Tora im Rabbinismus', *StTh* 25 (1971), pp. 90-108.

———— . 'The Mighty Minority', *StTh* 34 (1980), pp. 13-38.

de Jonge, M. 'Recent Studies on the Testaments of the Twelve Patriarchs', *SEÅ* 36 (1971), pp. 77-96.

Kahle, P. 'Die im August 1952 entdeckte Lederrolle mit dem griechischen Text der kleinen Propheten und das Problem der Septuaginta', *ThLZ* 79 (1954), cols. 81-94.

———— · 'Problems of the Septuagint', *Studia Patristica* I (TU 63), Berlin, 1957, pp. 328-338.

Katz, P. 'Das Problem des Urtextes des Septuaginta', *ThZ* 5 (1949), pp. 1-24.

———— . Ἐν πυρὶ φλογός, *ZNW* 46 (1955), pp. 133-138.

———— . 'Septuagintal Studies in the Mid-Century. Their Links with the Past and their Present Tendencies', *The Background of the New Testament and its Eschatology. In Honour of C. H. Dodd,* Cambridge, 1956, pp. 176-208.

———— . 'Justin's Old Testament Quotations and the Greek Dodekapropheton Scroll', *Studia Patristica* I (TU 63), Berlin, 1957, pp. 343-53.

Kimelman, R. '*Birkat Ha-Minim* and the Lack of Evidence for an Anti-Christian Jewish Prayer in Late Antiquity', *Jewish and Christian Self-Definition* Vol. II (eds. E. P. Sanders, A.I. Baumgarten, A. Mendelson), London, 1981, pp. 226-44.

Klijn, A. F. J. 'The Study of Jewish Christianity', *NTS* 20 (1974), pp. 419-431.

Koester, H. Νόμος φύσεως. The Concept of Natural Law in Greek Thought', *Religions in Antiquity, Essays in Memory' of E. R. Goodenough* (Suppl. to Numen 14), Leiden, 1968, pp. 521-41.

Kraft. R. A. 'Barnabas' Isaiah Text and the «Testimony Book» Hypothesis', *JBL* 79 (1960), pp. 336-350.

Krauss, S. 'The Jews in the Works of the Church Fathers', *JQR* 5 (1893), pp. 122-57; 6 (1894), pp. 82-99/225-261.

Lake, K. 'Proselytes and God-Fearers' in F. Jackson and K. Lake, *The Beginnings of Christianity* I:5, London, 1933, pp. 74-96.

Leclerq, J. 'L'idée de la royauté du Christ dans l'Oevre de Saint Justin', *L'Année Théologique* 7 (1946), pp. 83-95.

Liver, J. 'The Doctrine of the Two Messiahs in sectarian Literature in the Time of the Second Commonwealth', *HTR* 52 (1959), pp. 149-85 [= 'Two Messiahs'].

Loader, W. R. G. 'Christ at the Right Hand - Ps CX. 1 in the New Testament', *NTS* 24 (1978), pp. 199-217.

Lods, A. 'La chute des anges. Origine et portée de cette spéculation', *RHPhR* 09 7 (1927), pp. 295-315.

Lövestam, E. 'Jésus Fils de David chez les Synoptiques', *StTh* 28 (1974), pp. 97-109.

Loewe, R. 'The Jewish Midrashim and Patristic and Scholastic Exegesis of the Bible', *Studia Patristica* I (TU 63), Berlin, 1957, pp. 492-514.

Malina, B. J. 'Jewish Christianity or Christian Judaism. Toward a hypothetical Definition', *JSJ* 8 (1976), pp. 46-57.

Manson, T. W. 'The Argument from Prophecy', *JTS* 46 (1945), pp. 129-36.

Marmorstein, A. 'L'Épître de Barnabé et la polémique juive', *REJ* 60 (1910), pp. 213-220.

———— . 'Quelques problèmes de l'ancienne apologétique juive', *REJ* 67 (1914), pp. 161-173.

———— . 'The Unity of God in Rabbinic Literature', *HUCA* 1 (1924), pp. 467-99 [= 'Unity of God'].

Martyn, J. L. 'Clementine Recognitions 1,33-71, Jewish Christianity, and the Fourth Gospel', *God's Christ and His People. Studies in Honour of N. A. Dahl,* Oslo-Bergen-Tromsø, 1977, pp. 265-295 [= 'Clementine Recognitions'].

McEleney, N. J. 'Conversion, Circumcision and the Law', *NTS* 20 (1974), pp. 319-341.

Metzger, B. M. 'The Lucianic Recension of the Greek Bible', in *idem, Chapters in the History of the New Testament textual Criticism,* Leiden, 1963, pp. 1-41 [repr. in S. Jellicoe (ed.), *Studies in the Septuagint,* New York, 1974, pp. 270-291].

Mihaly, E. 'A Rabbinic Defense of the Election of Israel. An Analysis of Sifre Deuteronomy 32:9, Pisqa 312', *HUCA* 35 (1964), pp. 103-143 [= 'Election'].

Moffat, J. 'Two Notes on Ignatius and Justin Martyr', *HTR* 23 (1930), pp. 153-59.

Murmelstein, B. 'Das Lamm in Test. Jos. 19,8', *ZNW* 58 (1967), pp. 273-79.

Murray, R. 'Defining Judaeo-Christianity', *The Heythrop Journal* 15 (1974), pp. 303-310.

————. 'The Exhortation to Candidates for Ascetical Vows at Baptism in the Ancient Syriac Church', *NTS* 21 (1975), pp. 59-80.

Nautin, P. [Annual report of studies], *École des Hautes Études, Annuaire 1967/68* (Paris), pp. 162-167 [= *Annuaire*].

————. 'Genèse 1,1-2, de Justin à Origène', *In Principio. Interprétations des premiers versets de la Genèse* (Études Auqustiennes), Paris, 1973, pp. 61-94 [= 'Genèse 1,1-2'].

————. 'Les citations de la Prédication de Pierre' dans Clément d'Alexandrie, *Strom* VI.V. 39-41', *JTS* New Ser. 25 (1974), pp. 98-105.

Nikiprowetzky, V. 'Réflexions sur quelques problèmes du quatrième et du cinquième livre des Oracles Sibyllins', *HUCA* 43 (1972), pp. 29-76.

Nilson, J. 'To whom is Justin's *Dialogue with Trypho* adressed?', *Theological Studies* 38 (1977), pp. 538-46.

Noack, B. 'Are the Essenes referred to in the Sibylline Oracles', *StTh* 17 (1963), pp. 90-102.

Oeyen, C. 'Die Lehre der göttlichen Kräfte bei Justin', *Studia Patristica* 11 (TU 108, Berlin, 1972), pp. 215-221.

Orlinsky, H. M. 'On the Present State of Proto-Septuagint Studies', *Studies in the Septuagint,* ed. S. Jellicoe, New York, 1974, pp. 78-109.

Overbeck, F. 'Ueber das Verhältniss Justins des Märtyrers zur Apostelgeschichte', *ZWTh* 15 (1872), pp. 305-349.

Paulsen, H. 'Das Kerygma Petri und die urchristliche Apologetik', *ZKG* 88 (1977), pp. 1-37 [= 'Kerygma Petri'].

Pietersma, A. 'Proto-Lucian and the Greek Psalter', *VT* 28 (1978), pp. 66-82.

Prigent, P. 'Quelques testimonia messianiques. Leurs histoire littéraire de Qomrân aux Pères de l'église', *ThZ* 15 (1959), pp. 419-30 [= 'Testimonia messianiques'].

Pycke, N. 'Connaissance rationelle et connaissance de grace chez saint Justin', *Eph. Lov.* 37 (1961), pp. 52-85.

Quispel, G. and Grant, R. M. 'Note on the Petrine Apocrypha', *VC* 6 (1952), pp. 31f.

Rahlfs, R. 'Über Theodotion-Lesarten im Neuen Testament und Aquila-Lesarten bei Justin', *ZNW* 20 (1921), pp. 182-199.

Riegel, S. K. 'Jewish Christianity: Definitions and Terminology', *NTS* 24 (1978), pp. 410-15.

Roberts, C. H. 'The Christian Book and the Greek Papyri', *JTS* 50 (1949), pp. 155-68.

————. 'Books in the Graeco-Roman World and in the New Testament', *The Cambridge History of the Bible I; From the Beginnings to Jerome,* ed. by P. R. Ackroyd and C. F. Evans, Cambridge, 1970, pp. 48-66.

Robinson, J. A. 'On a Quotation from Justin in Irenaeus', *JTS* 31 (1930), pp. 374-78.

Rordorf, W. 'Christus als Logos und Nomos. Das Kerygma Petrou in seinem Verhältnis zu Justin', *Kerygma und Logos. Festschrift für Carl Andresen zum 70. Geburtstag,* Göttingen-Zürich, 1979, pp. 424-434 [= 'Logos und Nomos'].

Sagnard, F. M.-M. 'Y a-t-il un plan du »Dialogue avec Tryphon«?' *Mélanges Joseph de Ghellinck I: Antiquité,* Gembloux, 1951, pp. 171-182.

Salomonsen, B. 'Om rabbinsk hermeneutik' ['On rabbinic hermeneutics' (Danish)], *DTT* 36 (1973), pp. 161-173.

Schäfer, P. 'Die Torah der messianischen Zeit', *ZNW* 65 (1974), pp. 27-42.

————. 'Die sogenannte Synode von Jabne. Zur Trennung von Juden und Christen im ersten/zweiten Jh. n. Chr.', in *idem, Studien zur Geschichte und Theologie des rabbinischen Judentums* (Arbeiten zur Geschichte des Antiken Judentums und des Urchristentums XV), Leiden, 1978, pp. 45-64.

Schmid, W. 'Die Textüberlieferung der Apologie des Justin', *ZNW* 40 (1941), pp. 87-137.

Schmid, W. 'Ein rätselhafter Anachronismus bei Justinus Martyr', *Historisches Jahrbuch* 77 (1957/58), pp. 358-61.

Schneider, H. P. 'Some Reflections on the *Dialogue of Justin Martyr with Trypho*', *SJT* 15 (1962), pp. 164-75.

Schrenk, G. 'Was bedeutet «Israel Gottes»?' *Judaica* 5 (1949), pp. 81-94.

————. 'Der Segenswunsch nach der Kampfepistel', *Judaica* 6 (1950), pp. 170-90.

Schubert, K. 'Einige Beobachtungen zum Verständnis des Logosbegriffes im Frührabbinischen Schrifttum', *Judaica* 9 (1953), pp. 65-80.

————. 'Die Messiaslehre in den Texten von Chirbet Qumran', *BZ*, Neue Folge 1 (1957), pp. 177-197.

————. 'Testamentum Juda 24 im Lichte der Texte von Chirbet Qumran', *WZKM* 53 (1957), pp. 227-236.

Schubert, P. 'The Structure and Significance of Luke 24', *Neutestamentliche Studien für R. Bultmann* (BZNW 21), Berlin, 1954, pp. 165-86.

Schwartz, D. R. 'The Messianic Departure from Judah (4Q Patriarchal Blessings)', *ThZ* 37 (1981), pp. 257-266.

Siegert, F. 'Gottesfürchtige und Sympathisanten', *JSJ* 4 (1973), pp. 109-164.

Simon, M. 'Retour du Christ et reconstruction du temple dans la pensée chrétienne primitive', in *idem, Recherces d'Histoire Judéo-Chrétienne* (Études juives 6), Paris, 1962, pp. 9-19.

————. 'La migration à Pella: Légende ou réalité?' *RSR* 60 (1972), pp. 37-54.

————. 'Reflexions sur le judéo-christianisme', *Christianity, Judaism and Other Greco-Roman Cults. Studies for M. Smith at Sixty* (Studies in Judaism in Late Antiquity 12), Part II, Leiden, 1975, pp. 53-76.

Sjöberg, E. 'Justin als Zeuge vom Glauben an den verborgenen und den leidenden Messias im Judentum', *Interpretationes ad Vetus Testamentum pertinentes, Sigmundo Mowinckel septuagenario missae*, Oslo, 1955, pp. 173-83.

Skarsaune, O. 'The Conversion of Justin Martyr', *StTh* 30 (1976), pp. 53-73.

————. 'Trekk fra nyere Justin-forskning' ['Aspects of recent Research on Justin' (Norwegian)], *DTT* 39 (1976), pp. 231-257.

————. 'Tidlig kristen dåpsteologi i Barnabas' brev' ['Early Christian baptismal Theology in the Epistle of Barnabas' (Norwegian)], *TTK* 47 (1976), pp. 81-105.

————. 'Åpenbaring utenfor åpenbaringen? Antikk religion, gresk filosofi og kristen tro ifølge Justin Martyr' ['Revelation outside Scripture? Antique Religion, Greek Philosophy, and Christian Faith according to Justin Martyr' (Norwegian)], *TTK* 49 (1978), pp. 261-282.

————. 'Patristiske merknader til begrepet «Guds rike»' ['Patristic notes to the concept of the «Kingdom of God»' (Norwegian)], *Israel - Kristus - Kirken, Festskrift til S. Aalen*, Oslo-Bergen-Tromsø, 1979, pp. 163-182.

Smith, J. P. 'Hebrew Christian Midrash in Irenaeus, *Epid.* 43', *Biblica* 38 (1957), pp. 24-34.

Smith, J. Z. 'The Prayer of Joseph', *Religions in Antiquity, Essays in Memory of E. R. Goodenough* (Suppl. to Numen 14), Leiden, 1968, pp. 253-294.

Smolar, L. and Aberbach, M. 'The Golden Calf Episode in Postbiblical Literature', *HUCA* 39 (1968), pp. 91-116 [= 'Golden Calf'].

Stegemann, H. [Review of Prigent, *Testimonia*] *ZKG* 73 (1962), pp. 142-153.

Stemberger, G. 'Die sogenannte «Synode von Jabne» und das frühe Christentum', *Kairos* 19 (1977), pp. 14-21.

Thoma, A. 'Justins literarisches Verhältnis zu Paulus und zum Johannisevangelium', *ZWTh* 18 (1875), pp. 383-412/490-565.

Thomas, K. J. 'The Old Testament Citations in Hebrews', *NTS* 11 (1964/65), pp. 303-25.

Thunberg, L. 'Early Christian Interpretations of the Three Angels in Gen 18', *Studia Patristica* VII (TU 92), Berlin, 1966, pp. 560-70.

Tov, E. 'Lucian and Proto-Lucian: toward a new Solution of the Problem', *RB* 79 (1972), pp. 101-13.

van Unnik, C. W. 'Der Fluch der Gekreuzigten. Deuteronomium 21,23 in der Deutung Justins des Märtyrers', *Kerygma und Logos. Festschrift für Carl Andresen zum 70. Geburtstag*, Göttingen-Zürich, 1979, pp. 483-499.

Weis, P. R. 'Some Samaritanisms of Justin Martyr', *JTS* 45 (1944), pp. 199-205.

Wevers, J. W. 'Proto-Septuagint Studies', *The Seed of Wisdom, Essays in Honour of T. J. Meek*, Toronto, 1964, pp. 58-77 [repr. in S. Jellicoe (ed.), *Studies in the Septuagint*, New York, 1974, pp. 138-157].

Wilson, R. McL. 'The Early History of the Exegesis of Gen 1.26', *Studia Patristica* I (TU 63), Berlin, 1957, pp. 420-437.

Zahn, Th. 'Studien zu Justinus Martyr', *ZKG* 8 (1886), pp. 1-84 [= 'Studien'].

———. '' Über die *'Altercatio legis inter Simonem Judaeum et Theophilum Christianum'* des Euagrius und deren ältere Grundlage', in *idem* and J. Hausleiter (eds.), *Forschungen zur Geschichte des neutestamentlichen Kanons und der altkirchlichen Literatur* 4, Erlangen-Leipzig, 1891, pp. 308-324. [= Altercatio.]

# INDEX OF REFERENCES (SELECTIVE)

Some references of minor significance are not included. Italicized page references signify major treatments of the reference in question. In cases where several verses or passages in the same chapter are found on the same page, the reference is sometimes briefly given as «x:1ff». Some references treated in the notes are included. When the same reference is treated or mentioned in the main text as well as in a note on the same page, the note is referred to within a parenthesis.

The index is structured as follows:

## OLD TESTAMENT

| Genesis | | | | | |
|---|---|---|---|---|---|
| | | | *260-64, 269-273, 286,* | 21:6ff | 53, 216ff *397ff* |
| 1:1 | 235, 387f (n.29) | | 359f, 445, 453 | 21:8f | 397 |
| 1:1ff | 52 | 49:11 | 199ff, 359 n. 283 | 24:17 | *50-52,* 84, 143f, 223 |
| 1:26 | 300f, *389,* 452 | | | | n.85, 261, *264f,* 269- |
| 2:4 | 404 | *Exodus* | | | 273, 382 n.12, |
| 2:7 | 299f | 3,2ff | *47-50,* 211f, 417, 445 | | 446, 453 |
| 2:17 | 403f | 3:5 | 162 | 27:18 | 446 |
| 5:24 | *127* | 3:6 | 102, 421 | | |
| 5:29 | 340 | 6:3 | 419 | *Deuteronomy* | |
| 6:1ff | *368f* | 14 | 376 | 9:12ff | 315 |
| 6:9ff | 340 | 15:25 | 376 | 10:16f | *70-72,* 293 |
| 9:3 | 357f | 15:27 | 374, 377f, 445 | 14:2 | 320 |
| 9:25ff | *341-344* | 17:1ff | 376 | 21:22f | 397 |
| 11:5 | 421 | 17:9ff | 216f | 21:23 | 99, *118, 216ff,* 238, |
| 12:1ff | 346 | 17:13ff | 394f | | 309, 397 n. 56 |
| 14:18ff | *127* | 23:20f | 101, 209, *419f* | 24:16 | *68f,* 153, 370 |
| 15:6 | 93, 97, *114* | 24:3ff | 305 | 27:26 | 99, *118* |
| 17:4 | 346 | 28:33f | 311 | 28:66 | 437 |
| 17:5 | 93 | 32:6 | 98, *117f,* 171, 446 | 30:15ff | 160, 180, 229, |
| 17:8 | 334 | 32:9 | 319 | | 369 |
| 17:14 | 174, 445 | 33:1ff | 299f, 336f | 31:2f | 420 |
| 17:15f | 412 | 39f | 311 | 31:2ff | *214,* 420 |
| 18 | 208 | | | 31:16-18 | 420 |
| 18f | *410-413* | *Leviticus* | | 32:4 | 446 |
| 18:1 | 375 | 14 | 304ff | 32:7ff | *29f,* 189,446 |
| 19:24 | 208, 209 n. 62, 410ff | 14:10ff | 179f, *304ff* | 32:8f | 329 n.211, 347f |
| 26:4 | 109, 186, 346 | 16 | 305, *307ff* | 32:9 | 320 |
| 28:10f | 414 | 16:21 | 310 | 32:15 | 30, 98, 117, 446 |
| 28:12ff | 413f | 23:29 | 179 | | |
| 28:14 | 186, 346 | 26:41 | 314 | 32:16ff | 52f |
| 31:10ff | 414 | | | 32:17 | 314, 369 |
| 31:13 | 413, 416 | *Numbers* | | 32:20ff | 52f |
| 32:24ff | 414f | 11:17 | 446 | 32:21 | 94, 116, 446f |
| 35:1ff | 414 | 12:7 | *126* | 32:22 | 446f |
| 49:10f | *25-29,* 84, *140-44,* | 13:16 | 419 | 32:43 | 95, *117,* 188 |
| | 155f, 186, 195f, | 19:1ff | 305f | 33:13ff | 217 |

## OLD TESTAMENT APOCRYPHA

## NEW TESTAMENT

## RABBINIC LITERATURE

## INDEX OF MODERN AUTHORS

HIEBERT LIBRARY

3 6877 00091 6170

DATE DUE

| | | | |
|---|---|---|---|
| 22-3 weeks | | | |
| OC 07 '0 | | | |
| NO 04 '0 | | | |
| | | | |
| | | | |
| | | | |
| | | | |
| | | | |
| | | | |
| | | | |
| | | | |
| | | | |

BR
1720
.J8
S52
1987

29336

Skarsaune, Oskar
    The proof from pro-
    phecy.

HIEBERT LIBRARY
Fresno Pacific College - M. B. Seminary
Fresno, Calif. 93702

DEMCO